JOURNAL FOR THE STUDY OF THE OLD TESTAMENT
SUPPLEMENT SERIES
191

Sheffield Academic Press

On the Way to Canon

Creative Tradition History
in the Old Testament

Magne Sæbø

Journal for the Study of the Old Testament
Supplement Series 191

Copyright © 1998 Sheffield Academic Press

Published by
Sheffield Academic Press Ltd
Mansion House
19 Kingfield Road
Sheffield S11 9AS
England

Typeset by Sheffield Academic Press
and
Printed on acid-free paper in Great Britain
by Bookcraft Ltd
Midsomer Norton, Bath

British Library Cataloguing in Publication Data

A catalogue record for this book is available
from the British Library

ISBN 1-85075-927-8

To
Teol. D. George W. Anderson DD
prominent scholar, colleague, friend

... the reinterpretation (sometimes the radical reinterpretation) of the ancient traditions of Israel gives vivid expression to the living relationship between tradition and the continuing life of the community which inherited and interpreted it. Without this awareness of the interaction between tradition and interpretation the Old Testament cannot be understood.

George W. Anderson

CONTENTS

Preface   11
Acknowledgments   13
Abbreviations   16

Chapter 1
TRADITIO-HISTORICAL PERSPECTIVES IN THE OLD
TESTAMENT: INTRODUCTORY REMARKS   21

Part I
OLD TESTAMENT TEXT HISTORY
AS TRADITION HISTORY

Chapter 2
FROM PLURIFORMITY TO UNIFORMITY: THE EMERGENCE
OF THE MASSORETIC TEXT   36

Chapter 3
OBSERVATIONS ON THE TEXT HISTORY OF LEVITICUS
AND THE VALUE OF SOME CAIRO GENIZAH VARIANTS   47

Part II
TRADITION HISTORY: SOME TEXTS

Chapter 4
DIVINE NAMES AND EPITHETS IN GENESIS 49.24B-25A:
METHODOLOGICAL AND TRADITIO-HISTORICAL REMARKS   58

Chapter 5
GOD'S NAME IN EXODUS 3.13-15: AN EXPRESSION
OF REVELATION OR OF VEILING?   78

Chapter 6
FORM-HISTORICAL PERSPECTIVES ON ISAIAH 7.3-9   93

Chapter 7
TRADITIO-HISTORICAL PERSPECTIVES ON ISAIAH 8.9-10:
AN ATTEMPT TO CLARIFY AN OLD *CRUX INTERPRETUM*   108

Chapter 8
FROM EMPIRE TO WORLD RULE: SOME REMARKS
ON PSALMS 72.8; 89.26; ZECHARIAH 9.10B   122

Chapter 9
WHO IS 'THE MAN' IN LAMENTATIONS 3.1?   131

Part III
TRADITION HISTORY: THEOLOGICAL THEMES

Chapter 10
PRIESTLY THEOLOGY AND PRIESTLY CODE: THE CHARACTER
OF THE PRIESTLY LAYER IN THE PENTATEUCH   144

Chapter 11
REFLECTIONS ON OLD TESTAMENT ETHICS: ITS DUAL
CHARACTER AND ITS MODERN APPLICATION   162

Chapter 12
REVELATION IN HISTORY AND AS HISTORY: OBSERVATIONS
ON A TOPICAL THEME FROM AN OLD TESTAMENT POINT
OF VIEW   182

Chapter 13
ON THE RELATIONSHIP BETWEEN 'MESSIANISM' AND
'ESCHATOLOGY' IN THE OLD TESTAMENT: AN ATTEMPT
AT A TERMINOLOGICAL AND FACTUAL CLARIFICATION   197

Chapter 14
OLD TESTAMENT APOCALYPTIC IN ITS RELATION TO
PROPHECY AND WISDOM: THE VIEW OF
GERHARD VON RAD RECONSIDERED   232

Part IV
FROM PLURIFORM TRADITION HISTORY
TO THEOLOGICAL UNITY

Chapter 15
FROM COLLECTIONS TO BOOK: A NEW APPROACH TO
THE HISTORY OF TRADITION AND REDACTION
OF THE BOOK OF PROVERBS   250

Chapter 16
FROM THE INDIVIDUAL TO THE COLLECTIVE: A PATTERN
OF INNER-BIBLICAL INTERPRETATION   259

Chapter 17
ON THE CANONICITY OF THE SONG OF SONGS   271

Chapter 18
FROM 'UNIFYING REFLECTIONS' TO THE CANON: ASPECTS
OF THE TRADITIO-HISTORICAL FINAL STAGES IN
THE DEVELOPMENT OF THE OLD TESTAMENT   285

Part V
WRITING THE HISTORY OF TRADITIONS:
SCHOLARS OF THREE CENTURIES

Chapter 19
JOHANN PHILIPP GABLER AT THE END OF THE EIGHTEENTH
CENTURY: HISTORY AND THEOLOGY   310

Chapter 20
WILLIAM ROBERTSON SMITH AT THE END OF THE
NINETEENTH CENTURY: THEOLOGY AND HISTORY
AND SOCIOLOGY OF RELIGION   327

Chapter 21
SIGMUND MOWINCKEL IN THE FIRST HALF OF THE
TWENTIETH CENTURY: LITERARY CRITICISM
AND TRADITION HISTORY   336

Bibliography	349
Index of References	385
Index of Modern Authors	394

PREFACE

The present volume comprising some of my *opera minora* is dedicated to an old friend of mine, the Revd Professor Emeritus George W. Anderson of Edinburgh, in recognition of all that he has done in bridging British and Scandinavian Old Testament scholarship—being able to read and speak Scandinavian languages. When G.W. Anderson in 1979 edited a new collection of the esteemed volumes of 'Essays by Members of the Society for Old Testament Study' (*The People and the Book* [1925], *Record and Revelation* [1938] and *The Old Testament and Modern Study* [1951]), calling it *Tradition and Interpretation,* he concluded his Introduction by the words (p. xxi) that I have chosen as a motto for this volume of scholarly essays. His words, as well as the book's title, express the very concern of this book as well: the concept of 'Tradition and Interpretation' runs like a scarlet thread through its various studies.

In addition, the reference point of his words was the traditio-historical and theological work of Gerhard von Rad—who in the years 1949–66 was the influential *maestro* of Old Testament teaching and study in Heidelberg, to where students from all over the world came, and where I was also fortunate to stay from 1957 to 1959. In this way, then, some sort of a triangle is formed between Britain, Germany and Scandinavia in which the *traditions* of ancient Israel make up a focal point of communal interest in Old Testament studies, although differently defined. As for my initial studies, as adequately described by Douglas A. Knight in his *Rediscovering the Traditions of Israel* (pp. 367-82), they were 'influenced strongly from both the Scandinavian and German research traditions' (p. 382)—and I tried to combine them.

An author, I think, will always be hesitant about a republication of his studies, since he would like to reformulate his text in many instances, which, however, is neither possible nor fair, in the perspectives of ongoing research. Nevertheless, most of the studies, first of all those that have been translated for this volume, have to various degrees been revised, especially the chapter on Old Testament ethics translated from Norwegian (Chapter 11). With reference to the concluding Bibliography at the end of the book the notes of all studies have been reworked, sometimes even changed in content (this relates also to the four essays which were reprinted in *Ordene og Ordet: Gammeltestamentlige studier* [Oslo: Universitetsforlaget, 1979], and which now constitute Chapters 2, 6, 7 and 8). Future references to the studies republished here should, therefore, be made to the present edition. With reference to the general Bibliography also, the titles of books and articles cited will normally be abbreviated.

Finally, I wish to express my gratitude to Professor David J.A. Clines for accepting this book for publication and for helping me in 'designing' it; and I am very grateful to Dr John Jarick, Executive Editor, Vicky Acklam, Desk Editor, and to all the staff of Sheffield Academic Press for their excellent cooperation. I should also like to thank the translators of the German essays, Mrs Birgit Mänz-Davies (Chapters 3, 6, 7, 8 and 12) and Mr John Baildam (Chapters 5, 10, 13, 16, 18 and 19) as well as cand. theol. Stephen Reid, who translated the one Norwegian study (Chapter 11). I express my grateful thanks to the Norwegian Research Council for its financial support.

Sandvika (near Oslo)   M.S.
March 1998

ACKNOWLEDGMENTS

When listing the original title and place of publication of the essays included in this volume I should also like to thank the first publishers for their kind permission to reprint these essays.

I. *Old Testament Text History as Tradition History*
  2. 'From Pluriformity to Uniformity: Some Remarks on the Emergence of the Massoretic Text, with Special Reference to its Theological Significance', in S. Hidal, B. Johnson, T.N.D. Mettinger and S. Norin (eds.), *Festschrift Gillis Gerleman* (*ASTI*, 11; Leiden: E.J. Brill, 1978), pp. 127-37 (repr. in *OoO*, pp. 42-52); based on a paper read 9 August 1977 at the VII World Congress of Jewish Studies in Jerusalem (session A).
  3. 'Bemerkungen zur Textgeschichte von Leviticus: Welchen Wert haben die Varianten aus der Kairoer Geniza?', in E. Blum, C. Macholz and E.W. Stegemann (eds.), *Die Hebräische Bibel und ihre zweifache Nachgeschichte: Festschrift für Rolf Rendtorff zum 65. Geburtstag* (Neukirchen–Vluyn: Neukirchener Verlag, 1990), pp. 131-39.

II. *Tradition History: Some Texts*
  4. 'Divine Names and Epithets in Genesis 49:24b-25a: Some Methodological and Traditio-Historical Remarks', in A. Lemaire and B. Otzen (eds.), *History and Traditions of Early Israel: Studies Presented to Eduard Nielsen, May 8th 1993* (VTSup, 50; Leiden: E.J. Brill, 1993), pp. 115-32.
  5. 'Offenbarung oder Verhüllung? Bemerkungen zum Charakter des Gottesnamens in Ex 3,13–15', in J. Jeremias and L. Perlitt (eds.), *Die Botschaft und die Boten: Festschrift für Hans Walter Wolff zum 70. Geburtstag* (Neukirchen–Vluyn: Neukirchener Verlag, 1981), pp. 43-55.
  6. 'Formgeschichtliche Erwägungen zu Jes. 7:3–9', *ST* 14 (1960), pp. 54-69 (repr. in *OoO*, pp. 55-70).

7. 'Zur Traditionsgeschichte von Jesaia 8,9-10', *ZAW* 76 (1964), pp. 132-44 (repr. in *OoO*, pp. 71-82).

8. 'Vom Grossreich zum Weltreich: Erwägungen zu Pss. lxxii 8, lxxxix 26; Sach ix 10b', *VT* 28 (1978), pp. 83-91 (repr. in *OoO*, pp. 84-92); based on a paper read 6 October 1976 in the Old Testament section at the Third European Theology Congress in Vienna.

9. 'Who is "The Man" in Lamentations 3? A Fresh Approach to the Interpretation of the Book of Lamentations', in A.G. Auld (ed.), *Understanding Poets and Prophets: Essays in Honour of George Wishart Anderson* (JSOTSup, 152; Sheffield: JSOT Press, 1993), pp. 294-306.

III. *Tradition History: Theological Themes*

10. 'Priestertheologie und Priesterschrift: Zur Eigenart der priesterlichen Schicht im Pentateuch', in *Congress Volume: Vienna 1980* (VTSup, 32; Leiden: E.J. Brill, 1981), pp. 357-74.

11. 'Fra kong Salomo til kong Harald: Refleksjoner omkring den gammeltestamentlige etikks overføringsverdi', in S.D. Mogstad and L. Østnor (eds.), *Forankring og forandring: Verdier for det nye Europa. Festkrift til Ivar Asheim på 65-årsdagen den 5. august 1992* (Oslo: Universitetsforlaget, 1992), pp. 81-96.

12. 'Offenbarung in der Geschichte und als Geschichte: Bemerkungen zu einem aktuellen Thema aus alttestamentlicher Sicht', *ST* 35 (1981), pp. 55-71; based on a lecture given at the Anglo-Scandinavian Theological Conference in Lincoln, England, in August 1975, and then in German form as guest lecture in October 1980 in Åbo and Helsinki.

13. 'Zum Verhältnis von "Messianismus" und "Eschatologie" im Alten Testament: Ein Versuch terminologischer und sachlicher Klärung', in *Der Messias* (JBTh, 8; Neukirchen–Vluyn: Neukirchener Verlag, 1993), pp. 25-55.

14. 'Old Testament Apocalyptic in its Relation to Prophecy and Wisdom: The View of Gerhard von Rad Reconsidered', in K. Jeppesen, K. Nielsen and B. Rosendal (eds.), *In the Last Days: On Jewish and Christian Apocalyptic and its Period* (Festschrift Benedikt Otzen; Aarhus: Aarhus University Press, 1994), pp. 78-91.

IV. *From Pluriform Tradition History to Theological Unity*

15. 'From Collections to Book: A New Approach to the History of Tradition and Redaction of the Book of Proverbs', in *Proceedings of the Ninth World Congress of Jewish Studies, Jerusalem, August 4–12,*

1985, Div. A: The Period of the Bible (Jerusalem: World Union of Jewish Studies, 1986), pp. 99-106.

16. 'Vom Individuellen zum Kollektiven: Zur Frage einiger innerbiblischer Interpretationen', in R. Albertz, F.W. Golka and J. Kegler (eds.), *Schöpfung und Befreiung: Für Claus Westermann zum 80. Geburtstag* (Stuttgart: Calwer Verlag, 1989), pp. 116-25.

17. 'On the Canonicity of the Song of Songs', in M.V. Fox *et al.* (eds.), *Texts, Temples, and Traditions: A Tribute to Menahem Haran* (Winona Lake, IN: Eisenbrauns, 1996), pp. 267-77.

18. 'Vom "Zusammen-Denken" zum Kanon: Aspekte der traditionsgeschichtlichen Endstadien des Alten Testaments', in *Zum Problem des biblischen Kanons* (JBTh, 3; Neukirchen–Vluyn: Neukirchener Verlag, 1988), pp. 115-33.

V. *Writing the History of Traditions: Scholars of Three Centuries*

19. 'Johann Philipp Gablers Bedeutung für die Biblische Theologie: Zum 200-jährigen Jubiläum seiner Antrittsrede vom 30. März 1787', *ZAW* 99 (1987), pp. 1-16.

20. 'Some Problems of Writing a Research History of Old Testament Studies in the Latter Part of the Nineteenth Century—with Special Regard to the Life and Work of William Robertson Smith', in W. Johnstone (ed.), *William Robertson Smith: Essays in Reassessment* (JSOTSup, 189; Sheffield: Sheffield Academic Press, 1995), pp. 243-51.

21. 'Sigmund Mowinckel in his Relation to the Literary Critical School', *SJOT* 2 (1988), pp. 23-35.

ABBREVIATIONS

AASF.B	Annales academiae scientiarum Fennicae; Series B
AB	Anchor Bible
AcOr	*Acta orientalia*
ADB	*Allgemeine deutsche Biographie*
AfO	*Archiv für Orientforschung*
AHw	Wolfram von Soden, *Akkadisches Handwörterbuch* (Wiesbaden: Harrassowitz, 1959–81)
AJSL	*American Journal of Semitic Languages and Literatures*
ANET	James B. Pritchard (ed.), *Ancient Near Eastern Texts Relating to the Old Testament* (Princeton: Princeton University Press, 1950)
AnOr	Analecta orientalia
ANVAO.HF	Avhandlinger utgitt av Det Norske Videnskaps-Akademi i Oslo, II. Historisk-filosofisk Klasse
ASTI	*Annual of the Swedish Theological Institute*
ATANT	Abhandlungen zur Theologie des Alten und Neuen Testaments
AThD	Acta Theologica Danica
ATD	Das Alte Testament Deutsch
BA	*Biblical Archaeologist*
BASOR	*Bulletin of the American Schools of Oriental Research*
BBB	Bonner biblische Beiträge
BCAT	Biblischer Commentar über das Alte Testament
BETL	Bibliotheca ephemeridum theologicarum Lovaniensium
BEvT	Beiträge zur evangelischen Theologie
BHK	R. Kittel (ed.), *Biblia hebraica* (Stuttgart: Württembergische Bibelanstalt, 1937)
BHS	*Biblia hebraica stuttgartensia*
BHT	Beiträge zur historischen Theologie
Bib	*Biblica*
BibLeb	*Bibel und Leben*
Bibl. Stud.	Biblische Studien
BJRL	*Bulletin of the John Rylands University Library of Manchester*
BK	*Bibel und Kirche*
BKAT	Biblischer Kommentar: Altes Testament
BSac	*Bibliotheca Sacra*
BTSt	Biblisch-Theologische Studien

BWANT	Beiträge zur Wissenschaft vom Alten und Neuen Testament
BZ	*Biblische Zeitschrift*
BZAW	Beihefte zur *ZAW*
CAD	Ignace I. Gelb *et al.* (eds.), *The Assyrian Dictionary of the Oriental Institute of the University of Chicago* (Chicago: Oriental Institute, 1964–)
ConBOT	Coniectanea biblica, Old Testament
CBQ	*Catholic Biblical Quarterly*
CHB	P.R. Ackroyd and C.F. Evans (eds.), *Cambridge History of the Bible* (3 vols.; Cambridge: Cambridge University Press, 1970)
CRB	Cahiers de la Revue biblique
CRINT	Compendia rerum iudaicarum ad Novum Testamentum
CTA	A. Herdner (ed.), *Corpus des tablettes en cunéiformes alphabétiques découvertes à Ras Shamra—Ugarit de 1929 à 1939* (Paris: Imprimerie nationale Geuthner, 1963)
CTM	*Concordia Theological Monthly*
DBSup	*Dictionnaire de la Bible, Supplément*
DJD	Discoveries in the Judaean Desert
DLZ	*Deutsche Literatur Zeitung*
EdF	Erträge der Forschung
EHAT	Exegetisches Handbuch zum Alten Testament
EHS	Europäische Hochschulschriften
ErIs	*Eretz Israel*
EvT	*Evangelische Theologie*
FOTL	The Forms of the Old Testament Literature
FRLANT	Forschungen zur Religion und Literatur des Alten und Neuen Testaments
FSThR	Forschungen zur systematischen Theologie und Religionsphilosophie
GesB	W. Gesenius and F. Buhl, *Hebräisches und Aramäisches Handwörterbuch über das Alte Testament*
Ges.Stud.z.AT	*Gesammelte Studien zum Alten Testament*
GKC	*Gesenius' Hebrew Grammar* (ed. E. Kautzsch, revised and trans. A.E. Cowley; Oxford: Clarendon Press, 1910)
HALAT	Ludwig Koehler *et al.* (eds.), *Hebräisches und aramäisches Lexikon zum Alten Testament* (5 vols.; Leiden: E.J. Brill, 1967–95)
HAT	Handbuch zum Alten Testament
HBT	Horizons in Biblical Theology
HKAT	Handkommentar zum Alten Testament
HSAT	Die Heilige Schrift des Alten Testaments
HSS	Harvard Semitic Series
HThS	Harvard Theological Studies
HTR	*Harvard Theological Review*
HUCA	*Hebrew Union College Annual*
ICC	International Critical Commentary
IEJ	*Israel Exploration Journal*

Int	*Interpretation*
JAAR	*Journal of the American Academy of Religion*
JAOS	*Journal of the American Oriental Society*
JB	Jerusalem Bible
JBTh	Jahrbuch für Biblische Theologie
JBL	*Journal of Biblical Literature*
JBR	*Journal of Bible and Religion*
JJS	*Journal of Jewish Studies*
JNES	*Journal of Near Eastern Studies*
JQR	*Jewish Quarterly Review*
JSJ	*Journal for the Study of Judaism in the Persian, Hellenistic and Roman Period*
JSOT	*Journal for the Study of the Old Testament*
JSOTSup	*Journal for the Study of the Old Testament*, Supplement Series
JSS	*Journal of Semitic Studies*
JTS	*Journal of Theological Studies*
Judaica	*Judaica: Beiträge zum Verständnis des jüdischen Schicksals in Vergangenheit und Gegenwart*
Kairos	Kairos: Zeitschrift für Religionswissenschaft und Theologie
KAT	Kommentar zum Alten Testament
KB	Ludwig Koehler and Walter Baumgartner (eds.), *Lexicon in Veteris Testamenti libros* (Leiden: E.J. Brill, 1953)
KD	*Kerygma und Dogma*
KEHAT	Kunzgesfasstes exegetisches Handbuch zum Alten Testament
KHAT	Kurzer Hand-Kommentar zum Alten Testament
MTS	Marburger theologische Studien
NovT	*Novum Testamentum*
NRT	*La nouvelle revue théologique*
NTT	*Norsk Teologisk Tidsskrift*
NZSTh	*Neue Zeitschrift für systematische Theologie*
OBO	Orbis biblicus et orientalis
OLZ	*Orientalistische Literaturzeitung*
OoO	Magne Sæbø, *Ordene og Ordet: Gammeltestamentlige studier* (Oslo: Universitetsforlaget, 1979)
OTS	*Oudtestamentische Studiën*
PW	August Friedrich von Pauly and Georg Wissowa (eds.), *Real-Encyclopädie der classischen Altertumswissenschaft* (Stuttgart: Metzler, 1894–)
RB	*Revue biblique*
RE	*Realencyklopädie für protestantische Theologie und Kirche*
RevistB	*Revista biblica*
RevQ	*Revue de Qumran*
RGG	*Religion in Geschichte und Gegenwart*
RHPR	*Revue d'histoire et de philosophie religieuses*
RHR	*Revue de l'histoire des religions*
RSPT	*Revue des sciences philosophiques et théologiques*
SBL	Society of Biblical Literature

SBLDS	SBL Dissertation Series
SBLMS	SBL Monograph Series
SBS	Stuttgarter Bibelstudien
SBT	Studies in Biblical Theology
SBU	Svenskt Bibliskt Uppslagsverk
SEÅ	*Svensk exegetisk årsbok*
SJOT	*Scandinavian Journal of the Old Testament*
SJT	*Scottish Journal of Theology*
SMHVL	Scripta Minora. Studier utgivna av Kungl. Humanistiska Vetenskapssamfunnet i Lund
SNVAO.HF	Skrifter utgitt av Det Norske Videnskapps-Akademi i Oslo Hist.-Filos. Klasse
STDJ	Studies on the Text of the Desert of Judah
ST	*Studia theologica*
STK	*Svensk teologisk kvartalskrift*
SVSK.HF	Videnskapsselskapets skrifter [Kristiania = Oslo]. Historiskfilosofisk Klasse
TBl	*Theologische Blätter*
TBü	Theologische Bücherei
THAT	Ernst Jenni and Claus Westermann (eds.), *Theologisches Handwörterbuch zum Alten Testament* (Munich: Chr. Kaiser, 1971–76)
ThExh	Theologische Existenz heute
ThR	Theologische Rundschau
ThSt	Theologische Studien
ThWAT	G.J. Botterweck and H. Ringgren (eds.), *Theologisches Wörterbuch zum Alten Testament* (Stuttgart: W. Kohlhammer, 1970–)
TLZ	*Theologische Literaturzeitung*
TRE	*Theologische Realenzyklopädie*
TRev	*Theologische Revue*
TS	*Theological Studies*
TSK	*Theologische Studien und Kritiken*
TT	*Teologisk Tidsskrift*
TTK	*Tidskrift for Teologi og Kirke*
TWNT	Gerhard Kittel and Gerhard Friedrich (eds.), *Theologisches Wörterbuch zum Neuen Testament* (11 vols.; Stuttgart, W. Kohlhammer, 1932–79)
TZ	*Theologische Zeitschrift*
UUÅ	Uppsala universitets årsskrift
UT	Cyrus H. Gordon, *Ugaritic Textbook* (Analecta orientalia, 38; Rome: Pontifical Biblical Institute Press, 1965)
VT	*Vetus Testamentum*
VTSup	*Vetus Testamentum*, Supplements
VF	*Verkündigung und Forschung*
WdF	Wege der Forschüng
WMANT	Wissenschaftliche Monographien zum Alten und Neuen Testament

WO	*Die Welt des Orients*
WTJ	*Westminster Theological Journal*
ZÄS	*Zeitschrift für ägyptische Sprache und Altertumskunde*
ZAW	*Zeitschrift für die alttestamentliche Wissenschaft*
ZBK.AT	Zürcher Bibelkommentare: Altes Testament
ZDMG	*Zeitschrift der deutschen morgenländischen Gesellschaft*
ZDPV	*Zeitschrift des deutschen Palästina-Vereins*
ZKT	*Zeitschrift für katholische Theologie*
ZTK	*Zeitschrift für Theologie und Kirche*
ZTK.B	Zeitschrift für Theologie und Kirche-Beiheft
ZWT	*Zeitschrift für wissenschaftliche Theologie*

Chapter 1

TRADITIO-HISTORICAL PERSPECTIVES IN THE OLD TESTAMENT:
INTRODUCTORY REMARKS

The book itself remains as at the first unchanged
amid the changing interpretations of it.
Benjamin Jowett

The Hebrew Bible/Old Testament—like the whole Bible to which the Oxford theologian Benjamin Jowett (1817–93) refers in the statement above,[1] used here as an epigraph not only for this first chapter but for the consecutive ones as well—seems to stand in a continual conflict of interests. This situation is not without relation to the double character which the 'book itself' apparently has, in its interpretative position and its ecclesiastical, practical use. In a way, the reception of the book is Janus-faced, which again may correspond to the difference between the book's historical genesis and its first use as Scripture. In all this, there are important methodological implications.

1. *'Diachronic' and 'Synchronic'*

It is a commonplace, although often overlooked, that the Hebrew Bible came into being through a complicated formation process over centuries. It may be useful, however, to juxtapose this diachronic and complex character of its genesis with the succeeding synchronic use of its final form and its canonical position as Holy Writ.

The Hebrew Bible originated in Israel's 'community of faith'—to use a well-known phrase of Brevard S. Childs—and became a basic authority of the Jewish 'community of faith'; in addition, it was taken over by the early Christian 'community of faith' and was ever since, as the 'Old Testament', used as a fundamental part of its authoritative

---

1. B. Jowett, 'On the Interpretation of Scripture', in *Essays and Reviews* (London: Longman, Green, Longman & Roberts, 9th edn, 1861), pp. 330-433 (337).

Scripture, constituted as a double Canon.[2] This did not happen because of the various biblical books—or still less, because of their alleged earlier stages—but it was due to the synthetic character of the Book as an integrated whole. It was not as individual *biblia* but as one comprehensive and 'united' *Biblia* that Scripture made its most variegated *Wirkungsgeschichte*, its great impact on Synagogue and Church through the ages, including even its broader cultural and political influence.[3] Definitely, some of its books have been more popular than others; but mainly the 'book itself' has been read as a whole and *synchronically*. This is the one side of its dual character.

The other side of the modern Janus-faced position of Scripture is represented by the manifold and critical scrutiny of the Hebrew Bible / Old Testament. This approach—be it granted to speak so generally and in the singular—is also to some extent related to the final and canonical form of Scripture, first of all due to the simple fact that it is the final form of the book that has been the basic point of departure and orientation of all biblical scrutiny, including the critical study of the historical dimensions of the biblical books and texts.

Traditionally, however, the critical study of the Hebrew Bible has had its primary focus on the preceding *diachronic* formation process of its separate books, during a long and complex *history* which includes the final form of the book as well. In some way or another, the matter of 'history', not least the long perspectives of the historical background of the texts, has been—and surely will be—an integral and basic part of scholarly studies of the Hebrew Bible. This should also affect the various synchronic readings of the Bible that have become more conventional in 'postmodern' research; in general this reading has a synthetic character and is influenced by the literary approach of the so-called New Criticism that had its heyday around the middle of the century,[4]

2.   See B.S. Childs, *Introduction to the Old Testament as Scripture* (London: SCM Press, 1979). Cf. the discussion with Childs in, i.a., M.G. Brett, *Biblical Criticism in Crisis? The Impact of the Canonical Approach on Old Testament Studies* (Cambridge: Cambridge University Press, 1991); P.R. Noble, *The Canonical Approach: A Critical Reconstruction of the Hermeneutics of Brevard S. Childs* (Biblical Interpretation Series, 16; Leiden: E.J. Brill, 1995); see also the critical remarks in Ch. 18 below.

3.   Cf. L. Diestel, *Geschichte des Alten Testamentes in der christlichen Kirche* (Jena: Mauke's Verlag, 1869; repr. Leipzig, 1981); C. Kannengiesser (ed.), *Bible de tous les temps*, I–VIII (Paris: Beauchesne, 1984–89).

4.   Cf., in general, J. Barton, *Reading the Old Testament: Method in Biblical*

and in parts of current Bible studies it is represented by varying forms of 'structuralistic', 'holistic', 'intertextual' or other equivalent readings of the Scripture 'as literature'.[5] But even here the aspect of historical perspectives can scarcely be of no interest, in particular where there are distinct differences between otherwise similar or closely related texts, or when one focuses not just on individual texts but also on the complex whole of many and mutually incongruous texts. Basically, then, the historical aspects or even the diachronic perspective may not only have their 'natural' place in historico-critical studies of the Bible, but the same may also be the case in synthetic and synchronic readings of biblical texts; these aspects and perspectives can hardly be ignored.

The 'diachronic' and the 'synchronic' approach, therefore, are not to be played off against each other but rather to be regarded as complementary. In spite of all extant differences and tensions between them, at their junction the concept of 'tradition' and the perspectives of 'tradition history' may have some combining function, bridging various individual elements in the many and multiform texts with more or less distinct continuity and a growing unity.

Study (repr.; London: Darton, Longman & Todd, 1989), pp. 140-57; D. Norton, *A History of the Bible as Literature*, I–II (Cambridge: Cambridge University Press, 1993); further R. Alter, *The Art of Biblical Narrative* (London: Allen & Unwin, 1981), and *idem, The Art of Biblical Poetry* (Edinburgh: T. & T. Clark, 1990); N. Frye, *The Great Code: The Bible and Literature* (New York and London, 1982); F. McConnell (ed.), *The Bible and the Narrative Tradition* (Oxford: Oxford University Press, 1986), including essays of, i.a., H. Bloom, H.W. Frei and F. Kermode; P.R. House (ed.), *Beyond Form Criticism: Essays in Old Testament Literary Criticism* (Sources for Biblical and Theological Study, 2; Winona Lake, IN: Eisenbrauns, 1992); J.B. Gabel, C.B. Wheeler and A.D. York, *The Bible as Literature: An Introduction* (Oxford: Oxford University Press, 3rd edn, 1996).

5. Cf. Barton, *Reading the Old Testament*, pp. 104-39, 170-71; J. Cheryl Exum and D.J.A. Clines (eds.), *The New Literary Criticism and the Hebrew Bible* (JSOTSup, 143; Sheffield: Sheffield Academic Press, 1993); also D.J.A. Clines, *Interested Parties: The Ideology of Writers and Readers of the Hebrew Bible* (JSOTSup, 205; Sheffield: Sheffield Academic Press, 1995); Brett, *Biblical Criticism in Crisis?*, pp. 156ff.; further, e.g., R.C. Culley, *Studies in the Structure of Hebrew Narrative* (Philadelphia, 1976); K. Nielsen, 'Intertextuality and Biblical Scholarship', *SJOT* 2 (1990), pp. 89-95; W. Johnstone, 'Solomon's Prayer: Is Intentionalism Such a Fallacy?', *ST* 47 (1993), pp. 119-33.

2. *'Tradition' and 'Tradition History'*

Whereas 'history' and 'tradition' in general may be at stake today, at least in some areas of current Bible studies, the issue of 'tradition history' has in particular been questioned, although it has been held in high esteem for a long time. Since it is not only part of the main subject of 'history' but also has even constituted a significant element of modern historico-critical Bible research, it may to some extent have been lumped together with older and needlessly historistic forms of critical study of the Bible. However this may be, it should not be overlooked, as the history of modern biblical research shows, that recent study of the Bible has become a most multifaceted area of research and has changed much during the last generations, and that it also displays a considerable inner self-correction which has to be recognized properly.[6] It is important, therefore, that 'tradition history' is seen and evaluated in both an actual and historically adequate way.

The use of the concept of 'tradition' has been varying and even puzzling; some remarks of clarification may therefore be required. The notion is used in a wider as well as in a more restricted sense. As for its wider and general sense, which on this occasion will represent some kind of framework, 'tradition' has been characterized by Douglas Knight, in his study on modern traditio-historical research, in the following way: 'Scholarly research of the past century has come to recognize the fundamental role played by *tradition* in the history of mankind. As an ubiquitous element of human culture it constitutes the link between generations, the bond between present and past, a foundational factor of the community, a means for the individual to become integrated in a whole extending beyond himself';[7] and, with reference to H.-G. Gadamer, he adds, 'Tradition occupies furthermore a central position in the structure of knowledge and understanding, and thus one must reckon with it as an integral aspect of the general hermeneutical

---

6. See, e.g., H.H. Rowley (ed.), *The Old Testament and Modern Study: A Generation of Discovery and Research* (Oxford: Clarendon Press, 1951); G.W. Anderson (ed.), *Tradition and Interpretation: Essays by Members of the Society for Old Testament Study* (Oxford: Clarendon Press, 1979).

7. D.A. Knight, *Rediscovering the Traditions of Israel: The Development of the Traditio-Historical Research of the Old Testament, with Special Consideration of Scandinavian Contributions* (SBLDS, 9; Missoula, MT: SBL, 1973; rev. edn, 1976), p. 1.

process'.[8] Against the background of this wider sense and use of the notion, the focus here, however, will be on 'tradition' in its more restricted sense, referring to the study of 'tradition' and especially to the use of the term 'tradition history' in modern Old Testament research, and in particular as it has been carried out, with some variation, in Germany and in Scandinavia.[9]

The modern use of 'tradition' and 'tradition history' in Old Testament and oriental research was, with some roots in earlier studies,[10] distinctively promoted by Hermann Gunkel (1862–1932) at the beginning of this century.[11] In contrast to the extant literary-critical school, dominated by J. Wellhausen (which had laid special emphasis on the literary character of the books and on a transmission in mainly written form), Gunkel, without abandoning the literary-critical analysis and its literary 'sources', focused particularly on the pre-literary stages of the material. In doing so he managed to cause a real 'turning point', that

8.   Knight, *Rediscovering the Traditions of Israel*, p. 1; cf. H.-G. Gadamer, *Wahrheit und Methode* (Tübingen: J.C.B. Mohr, 1960; 5th edn, 1986; ET *Truth and Method* [New York: Crossroad, 1982]), Part 2, pp. 250ff.

9.   In addition to the study of Knight, *Rediscovering the Traditions of Israel*, cf. E. Nielsen, *Oral Tradition: A Modern Problem in Old Testament Introduction* (SBT, 11; London: SCM Press, 1954); K. Koch, *Was ist Formgeschichte?* (Neukirchen–Vluyn: Neukirchener Verlag, 2nd edn, 1967; ET *The Growth of the Biblical Tradition: The Form-Critical Method* (London: A. & C. Black, 1969), esp. pp. 3-90; H.-J. Kraus, 'Zur Geschichte des Überlieferungsbegriffs in der alttestamentlichen Wissenschaft', in *idem, Biblisch-theologische Aufsätze* (Neukirchen–Vluyn: Neukirchener Verlag, 1972), pp. 278-95; H. Ringgren, 'Literarkritik, Formgeschichte, Überlieferungsgeschichte: Erwägungen zur Methodenfrage der alttestamentlichen Exegese', *TLZ* 91 (1966), cols. 641-50; W.E. Rast, *Tradition History and the Old Testament* (Philadelphia: Fortress Press, 1972). On Gunneweg see n. 19 below.

10.   Cf. Knight, *Rediscovering the Traditions of Israel*, pp. 37-72; Nielsen, *Oral Tradition*, p.12; Kraus, 'Zur Geschichte des Überlieferungsbegriffs', pp. 278ff.

11.   Among the works of Gunkel see esp. *Genesis* (HKAT, 1.1; Göttingen: Vandenhoeck & Ruprecht, 8th edn, 1969 [1901]); *Die israelitische Literatur* (1906; repr. Darmstadt: Wissenschaftliche Buchgesellschaft, 1963); *Reden und Aufsätze* (Göttingen: Vandenhoeck & Ruprecht, 1913). On Gunkel see, e.g., W. Klatt, *Hermann Gunkel* (FRLANT, 100; Göttingen: Vandenhoeck & Ruprecht, 1969). Further, cf. Knight, *Rediscovering the Traditions of Israel*, pp. 71-83; Nielsen, *Oral Tradition*, p. 12; Rast, *Tradition History*, pp. 2-9.

may be called a 'shift of paradigm',[12] in the study of the Old Testament, founding or fostering in a tripartite way new procedures in biblical research.[13] First, he paid great attention to the question of form and genre of literature (*Gattung*), including the respective cultural, cultic or social setting (*Sitz im Leben*) of the form units, whereby he gave rise to a methodically new *form-historical* or *form-critical* approach that also included sociological aspects. Second, he drew attention to the ideological content of the texts and forms, notably with regard to specific motifs and distinctive ideas, whereby he contributed decisively to a *traditio-historical* approach. Third, as far as motifs and ideas turned out to have similar or parallel counterparts in neighbouring religions he also included comparative religio-historical viewpoints and thus fostered a *religio-historical* approach. Last, but not least, in his concentration on the pre-literary background of the traditions he gave a stronger prominence to the *oral* form of transmission than had been the case before.[14] In various ways, then, Gunkel decisively changed and influenced the modern scrutiny of the Old Testament.

In all this, with the new weight on an oral and long tradition, the old question of the *author* of the individual biblical books—which in the literary-critical school as regards the Pentateuch (possibly also Joshua) had been 'transferred' to the production of its four main 'sources' (with J, E, D and P as 'authors')—had now become considerably more complicated and, correspondingly, the author more anonymous. As regards the understanding and explication of the formation of the biblical books, there has, to some extent, been a turning of interest from the traditionally person-related issue of author to a more matter-oriented issue of various forms, traditions and compositions, or, recently, of the present text as a whole, as 'independent' literature. As far as the question of authorship is still relevant, it is posed by some scholars more in terms of a collective 'circle' than of one single author. More or less,

12. Cf. T.S. Kuhn, *The Structure of Scientific Revolution* (International Encyclopedia of Unified Science, 2.2; Chicago, 1962), pp. x, 43-51.

13. Cf. S. Mowinckel, *Prophecy and Tradition: The Prophetic Books in the Light of the Study of the Growth and History of the Tradition* (ANVAO.HF, 1946.3; Oslo: Jacob Dybwad, 1946), p. 99: 'Characteristic of Gunkel is not that he builds on the literary source criticism and partly develops it, but all that he gives beyond and independently of source criticism, viz. the whole form- and traditio-historical analysis and interpretation'.

14. Cf. Gunkel, *Genesis*, pp. viiif.

then, there has been a shift from personal to supra-personal aspects; but there are variations.

In the German arena, on the one hand, Martin Noth (1902–68), in his traditio-historical study on the Deuteronomistic History (comprising Joshua to Kings) and the Chronistic History (comprising the Chronicles and Ezra–Nehemiah), has a specific concern in the procedures of transmission of the variegated tradition material and in the different ways of composition of the books. He may combine a literary-critical and a form- and traditio-historical approach when he, as for the Deuteronomistic History, regards the Deuteronomist to be 'not only the "Redactor" but the author of a history work that collected the received and widely different traditions and combined them according to a well reasoned plan'.[15] In a similar way, but with more importance attached to the different bodies of traditions and their contents, Gerhard von Rad (1901–71)—to whose scholarly work the notion of 'Tradition History' probably has been attributed more often than to any other scholar's work—describes in his many minor studies and especially in his *Theologie des Alten Testaments* a real *history* of traditions. Beginning with the local and often cultic connexion of a specific tradition (its *Haftpunkt*), the further history of it, within a 'restless' process of transforming and interpretative transmission, led to some independence but mostly to an integration into and a combination with other traditions or tradition elements so that a growth of tradition came into being (*Traditionsballungen*), and along with this the emergence of literature (*Literaturwerdung*) as well.[16] When von Rad, to a great extent,

15. Martin Noth, *Überlieferungsgeschichtliche Studien* (Tübingen: M. Niemeyer, 1943; Darmstadt: Wissenschaftliche Buchgesellschaft, 2nd edn, 1957; ET *The Deuteronomistic History* [JSOTSup, 15; Sheffield: JSOT Press, 1981]), p. 11, (with spaced type), 'Dtr war nicht nur "Redaktor", sondern der Autor eines Geschichtswerkes, das die überkommenen, überaus verschiedenartigen Überlieferungsstoffe zusammenfasste und nach einem durchdachten Plane aneinanderreihte'. Cf. also his *Überlieferungsgeschichte des Pentateuch* (Stuttgart: W. Kohlhammer, 1948; 3rd edn, 1966). On Noth in this context, see, e.g., Knight, *Rediscovering the Traditions of Israel*, pp. 141-71.

16. Cf. esp. G. von Rad, *Das formgeschichtliche Problem des Hexateuch* (BWANT, 4.26; Stuttgart: W. Kohlhammer, 1938; repr. in *idem, Gesammelte Studien zum Alten Testament* [TBü, 8; Munich: Chr. Kaiser Verlag; 4th edn, 1971]), pp. 9-86; *idem, Theologie des Alten Testaments. I. Die Theologie der geschichtlichen Überlieferungen Israels*; II. *Die Theologie der prophetischen Überlieferungen Israels* (Munich: Chr. Kaiser Verlag, 1957–60; 9th edn, 1987); *idem,*

structured his *Theologie des Alten Testaments* on the basis of his own earlier exegetical and theological studies, he made its structure more isagogical, thereby also attributing to it a greater proximity than usual to what might be called an Old Testament history of literature,[17] and he made the variegated history of the multiple traditions more theological in character.[18]

On the German scene, then, both Noth and von Rad were outstanding representatives of a traditio-historical approach, but each in his own way. Whereas Noth, when speaking of *Überlieferungsgeschichte*, mainly, as it seems, had the varying ways of transmission and composition of the tradition material in view, von Rad, when speaking of the historical and prophetic *Überlieferungen* of Israel, first of all focused upon the theological content and significance of the traditions. For both of them, however, the alternative issue of oral versus written transmission may have been of secondary importance; but it is likely that the written form had the preference. When A.H.J. Gunneweg, inspired by comtemporary Scandinavian studies in the Old Testament, discussed this issue critically he too, in conclusion, favoured the written form of transmission in the prophetic books of the Old Testament, saying, 'The written tradition was the authentic, official one. The oral tradition, however…has only a subordinate significance'.[19]

Gesammelte Studien zum Alten Testament, II (TBü, 48; Munich: Chr. Kaiser Verlag, 1973).

17. Cf. Gunkel, *Die israelitische Literatur*.

18. On G. von Rad see, e.g., J.L. Crenshaw, *Gerhard von Rad* (Waco, TX: Word Books, 1979); esp. on his *Theologie des Alten Testaments* see, e.g., D.G. Spriggs, *Two Old Testament Theologies: A Comparative Evaluation of the Contributions of Eichrodt and von Rad to our Understanding of the Nature of Old Testament Theology* (SBT, 2.30; London: SCM Press, 1974). Here, especially, see Knight, *Rediscovering the Traditions of Israel*, pp. 97-142; and below Chs. 6, 13, 14 and 18.

19. A.H.J. Gunneweg, *Mündliche und schriftliche Tradition der vorexilischen Prophetenbücher als Problem der neueren Prophetenforschung* (FRLANT, 73; Göttingen: Vandenhoeck & Ruprecht, 1959) p. 122: 'Die schriftliche Tradition war die authentische, offizielle. Hingegen kommt der mündlichen Tradition, obwohl sie sonst, d.h. ausserhalb der mit Tempel und Hof verbundenen Kreise, die übliche war, nur untergeordnete Bedeutung zu'; cf. also I. Willi-Plein, 'Spuren der Unterscheidung von mündlichem und schriftlichem Wort im Alten Testament', in G. Sellin and F. Vouga (eds.), *Logos und Buchstabe: Mündlichkeit und Schriftlichkeit im Judentum und Christentum der Antike* (Tübingen: Francke Verlag, 1996), pp. 77-89.

In Scandinavia, on the other hand, the question of oral versus written transmission of the rich Old Testament tradition material became an important issue, and even more so as here—unlike the general tendency among German Old Testament scholars—the main object of the traditio-historical research was not as much the Pentateuch and the historical books as the prophetic literature. The first studies that explicitly focused on this issue were made in 1935 by H.S. Nyberg, of Uppsala, in a well-known study on Hosea,[20] and in 1938 by Harris Birkeland, of Oslo, on all the prophetic books of the Old Testament, though somewhat briefly.[21] Sigmund Mowinckel (1884–1965) did not only support his favourite student Birkeland,[22] but followed up with his own studies, whereby he also could refer to his earlier studies on the composition of the book of Jeremiah (1913)[23] as well as on the disciples of Isaiah (1926),[24] among others; in 1942 he published an article on the emergence of the prophetic literature,[25] which in 1946 he revised and enlarged as his final contribution to the issue: *Prophecy and Tradition*.[26] At the same time, Ivan Engnell (1906–64) followed in the footsteps of his teacher H.S. Nyberg and issued the first volume—the next

20. H.S. Nyberg, *Studien zum Hoseabuche* (UUÅ, 1935.6; Uppsala: A.-B. Lundequistska, 1935), esp. pp. 1-20. On Nyberg and other representatives of 'the Beginnings' of the Scandinavian debate on traditio-historical problems, see, i.a., Knight, *Rediscovering the Traditions of Israel*, pp. 215-59.

21. H. Birkeland, *Zum hebräischen Traditionswesen: Die Komposition der prophetischen Bücher des Alten Testaments* (ANVAO.HF, 1938.1; Oslo: Jacob Dybwad, 1938), esp. the methodological part, pp. 5-25. On Birkeland see Knight, *Rediscovering the Traditions of Israel*, pp. 239-43; Gunneweg, *Mündliche und schriftliche Tradition*, pp. 9f.

22. S. Mowinckel, in a review of Birkeland's study, 'Om tilblivelsen av profetbøkene', *NTT* 39 (1938), pp. 318-20 (320): 'Jeg tror også at man må regne noget mer med den skriftlige overlevering og bearbeidelse enn B. i den første begeistring gjør'.

23. S. Mowinckel, *Zur Komposition des Buches Jeremia* (SVSK.HF, 1913.5; Kristiania [Oslo]: Jacob Dybwad, 1913), esp. pp. 31-45, on the 'source C'.

24. S. Mowinckel, *Jesaja-disiplene: Profetien fra Jesaja til Jeremia* (Oslo: H. Aschehoug, 1926), esp. pp. 10-16.

25. S. Mowinckel, 'Opkomsten av profetlitteraturen', *NTT* 43 (1942), pp. 65-111.

26. See n. 13 above. On Mowinckel see, e.g., Knight, *Rediscovering the Traditions of Israel*, pp. 250-58; Gunneweg, *Mündliche und schriftliche Tradition*, pp. 10-12, 14; further, cf. M. Sæbø, 'Mowinckel, Sigmund (1884–1965)', *TRE*, XXIII, pp. 384-88; and Ch. 21 below.

one never did appear—of what was to be a methodically new traditio-historical introduction to the Old Testament,[27] and which he comple-mented with several articles in the theological dictionary *Svenskt Bibliskt Uppslagsverk*, posthumously; a selection of these articles was brought out in English.[28]

Common to these Scandinavian scholars is the basic view that the Old Testament is the final result of a long and complex process of tra-dition and creative formation where the oral transmission was the pri-mary form of the living tradition, handed down in specific circles of 'traditionists' of various kinds, and that the written form was relatively late. But there were differences among these scholars too, perhaps not as great as one may often get the impression. Engnell, for example, who strongly focused on the oral tradition and emphatically attacked the 'western book-thinking' of the literary-critical approach, also underscored the necessity of critical analysis and that the traditio-histor-ical view 'combines analysis and synthesis'.[29] On the other hand, Mow-inckel, who insistently gave emphasis to the creative function of prophetic and other tradition-circles and to the significance of the oral tradition, also highlighted 'the necessity of literary criticism';[30] and in a preliminary conclusion he states 'that a traditio-historical consideration of the O.T. is obliged to reckon with both written and oral tradition, both with the work of the transmitting process and of consciously working "authors" on the collection, arrangement and shaping of the tradition'.[31] It may be obvious that with these divergent views on the

27. I. Engnell, *Gamla Testamentet: En traditionshistorisk inledning*, I (Stock-holm: Svenska Kyrkans Diakonistyrelses Bokförlag, 1945). Like Gunkel, he deals above all with the 'forms of literature' (pp. 39-108) and the religio-historical, especially Canaanite, aspects (pp. 109-67).

28. I. Engnell, *Critical Essays on the Old Testament: A Rigid Scrutiny* (trans. J.T. Willis, with the collaboration of H. Ringgren; London: SPCK, 1970); cf. also his 'Methodological Aspects of Old Testament Study', in *Congress Volume: Oxford 1959* (VTSup, 7; Leiden: E.J. Brill, 1960), pp. 13-30. On Engnell see, e.g., Nielsen, *Oral Tradition*, pp. 14-17; Gunneweg, *Mündliche und schriftliche Tradi-tion*, pp. 12-19; Knight, *Rediscovering the Traditions of Israel*, pp. 260-91; and on other representatives of the 'Uppsala school', see pp. 292-338, as well as on other near related scholars, see pp. 339-82.

29. Engnell, *Gamla Testamentet*, p. 10; cf. also his 'Profetia och tradition', *SEÅ* 12 (1947; Festschrift J. Lindblom), pp. 94-123.

30. Mowinckel, *Prophecy and Tradition*, pp. 19-36.

31. Mowinckel, *Prophecy and Tradition*, p. 33.

character of the tradition there were also differences of opinion as regards the question of the *ipsissima verba* of the prophets: whereas Engnell considered it impossible to 'get behind the tradition circle' in this respect,[32] Mowinckel regarded this stand to be 'a principle of scientific dogmatism', which he rejected; for him 'tradition history' first of all meant 'a critical presentation of the *history* of tradition'.[33]

Finally, it is in the nature of the case that the discussion of questions of this kind as well as the concrete scrutiny of the Old Testament tradition material always will be connected with an unavoidable uncertainty.[34] Already in the relation between the two sides of the notion of 'tradition' and 'tradition history', that is, between the 'formal' side of *transmission* of the complex material and the 'inner' content related side of the many and variegated *traditions*, there will be a zone of tension and ambivalence; for in their interrelatedness there is to some degree also reciprocity if not an interaction involved.[35] Although the two sides should be kept apart, both in principle and terminologically, as has been done tentatively above, it may prove helpful to take a further step forward by endorsing the distinction that Douglas Knight[36] and recently Michael Fishbane[37] have applied when they distinguish between the *traditio*, in the sense of transmission of the tradition material, and the *traditum* (resp. *tradita*), in the sense of the received

32. Engnell, *Gamla Testamentet*, pp. 30, 41-43; cf. also 'Profetia och tradition', pp. 110-23.

33. Cf. Mowinckel, *Prophecy and Tradition*, pp. 84-88: 'A tradition history which does not want to distinguish between "strata" in the tradition is no tradition history"' (p. 86); '"Behind the tradition" there loom, after all, the powerful figures of the prophets, who have created that very tradition, and in a number of cases their "own words" speak to us so clearly that we cannot take amiss' (p. 88). Cf. the similar position of von Rad, mentioned above.

34. Cf. Knight, *Rediscovering the Traditions of Israel*, pp. 369f., with reference to M. Sæbø, *Sacharja 9–14: Untersuchungen von Text und Form* (WMANT, 34; Neukirchen–Vluyn: Neukirchener Verlag, 1969).

35. Cf. Helmer Ringgren's discussion of the relationship of 'Überlieferungs-geschichte' and 'Traditionsgeschichte'; see n. 9 above.

36. Knight, *Rediscovering the Traditions of Israel*, pp. 5-20. Cf. also, with another terminology, G. Fohrer, 'Tradition und Interpretation', ZAW 73 (1961), pp. 1-30.

37. M. Fishbane, *Biblical Interpretation in Ancient Israel* (Oxford: Clarendon Press, 1985), pp. 6f, and *passim*; cf. also *idem*, 'Inner-Biblical Exegesis', in M. Sæbø (ed.), *Hebrew Bible/Old Testament: The History of its Interpretation*. I.1. *Antiquity* (Göttingen: Vandenhoeck & Ruprecht, 1996), pp. 33-48.

traditions as a 'complex result of a long and varied process of transmission', and which in turn became the object of new actualizations
and re-interpretations, under changed conditions in new situations.[38] In
all this there was always a creative movement forward, a long way
towards the final and most authoritative *traditum* of the canon of the
Hebrew Bible / Old Testament.

3. *Theological Significance of the 'Tradition History'*

When it finally comes to the discipline of Old Testament theology, one
might perhaps assume, at least *prima facie*—harking back to the
opening section of these introductory remarks—that a theological
approach basically would relate more heavily to the 'synchronic' than
to the 'diachronic' aspect, and that 'tradition history' in some way or
another would just represent a problematic factor. The extensive and
relatively hard debate on the way in which Gerhard von Rad had structured his *Theologie des Alten Testaments* may point in this direction.[39]
When von Rad's special theological approach raised so many challenging methodological problems, it may first of all be grounded in his
basic criticism of all earlier 'doctrinal' and 'systematic' structures of
biblical theology, in contrast to his own traditio-historical form of presentation of an Old Testament theology; for like the Old Testament as a
whole as well, its theology was not some timeless 'doctrinal' entity, but
had come into being as a result of a long historical and theological process of tradition; in some way, von Rad seems to have taken the last
consequences of Gabler's basic 'distinction between biblical and dogmatic theology'.[40] At this point, Douglas Knight may have asked the
key question, saying, 'What does it mean if the theological "message"
of the Old Testament was always growing, in flux, adapting to new situations—and not the expression of timeless, absolutistic revelation?',
whereupon, at the crossroads of Old Testament tradition history and

---

38. Fishbane, *Biblical Interpretation in Ancient Israel*, p. 6; here he also adds:
'At each stage in the *traditio*, the *traditum* was adapted, transformed, or reinterpreted... Materials were thus detribalized and nationalized; depolytheized and
monotheized; reorganized and reconceptualized'.

39. See n. 16 above; cf., e.g., W. Zimmerli, review of *Theologie des Alten Testaments*, by G. von Rad, *VT* 13 (1963), pp. 100-11.

40. See further Ch. 19 below.

theology, he discusses the specific problems of divine 'revelation' in relation to the multiple theological tradition process.[41]

Although the debate on von Rad's *Theologie des Alten Testaments* seems to have blown itself out for the time being, there are, however, still many open questions; problems such as the relationship of theological multiplicity and unity, or of an ever changing process in motion and theological continuity, or of the theologically productive circles of ancient Israel.[42] The scholarly debate on these and related issues—not least in the wake of Gerhard von Rad and Brevard Childs—must go on; and most of the following chapters will be understood as contributions to this debate.

41. See D.A. Knight (ed.), *Tradition and Theology in the Old Testament* (Philadelphia: Fortress Press, 1977, with many significant contributions), p. 5; cf. *idem*, 'Revelation through Tradition', in *idem* (ed.), *Tradition and Theology*, pp. 143-80; and cf. Ch. 12 below. Further, cf. G. Gloege, *Offenbarung und Überlieferung: Ein dogmatischer Entwurf* (Theologische Forschung, 6; Hamburg-Volksdorf: Reich, 1954).

42. Cf. M. Sæbø, 'Hvem var Israels teologer [Who were Israel's theologians]? Om struktureringen av "den gammeltestamentlige teologi"', *SEÅ* 41–42 (1976–77; Festschrift H. Ringgren), pp. 189-205; repr. in *OoO*, pp. 25-41; see further Ch. 18 below.

Part I

OLD TESTAMENT TEXT HISTORY AS TRADITION HISTORY

Chapter 2

FROM PLURIFORMITY TO UNIFORMITY:
THE EMERGENCE OF THE MASSORETIC TEXT

1. *Introductory Considerations*

Historical studies and critical work on the text of the Hebrew Bible
have generally been regarded as an area of little theological concern.

As for Protestant theology in general, where basic importance always
has been attached to the Bible as the principal theological authority,
this phenomenon may seem rather surprising. From a historical perspective it is, after all, capable of being explained why representatives
of dogmatics and of textual criticism have not been in conflict, nor
even, generally speaking, in contact.

There are, however, parts of Protestant theology where the fundamental attitude in this field is very different. In strong conservative
circles of a 'fundamentalist' type there is a general scepticism and
opposition to much of the historical work done in biblical studies. The
infallibility of the Sacred Books is stressed heavily by some authors,
because the authority is referred to the present state of the books, or to
the Bible as a book in a strict sense.

One could assume that text criticism here would be regarded as a
severe obstacle to theological work; but that is not a clear-cut matter.
On the contrary, text-critical work is generally not abandoned, especially as the great mass of variant readings cannot be overlooked today:
while the 'higher' literary criticism is mostly rejected in these circles,
the 'lower' textual criticism is admitted, to some extent. There is, however, a tendency to minimize the existence of real variants and to regard
as many variants as possible as 'scribal errors'. Scriptural 'infallibility'
is projected back in time: behind the imperfect transmission of the text
there is assumed to be an *urtext* without the later faults, a perfect
'model-codex'.

R.K. Harrison, who in his *Introduction to the Old Testament* has an extensive chapter on 'textual criticism', ends his discussion by stating that:

> ...the textual critic will not be content with merely producing as perfect a restoration as possible of the one complete, though textually faulty, Hebrew recension that has been handed down by tradition. If the doctrine of inspiration means anything at all for the written Word of God, it surely refers to *the original autographs*, since subsequent copyists, however gifted or diligent, were not themselves inspired. The true objective of the textual critic, therefore, should be the restoration of the Hebrew to the point where it is as near as possible to what the original author is deemed to have written.[1]

The problem, however, is whether the perspective of this view matches with the factual evidence of the early stages of the biblical text, according to the testimony of the Hebrew tradition and the ancient versions alike.

2. *Basic Attitudes in Modern Text-critical Work on the Hebrew Bible*

The theory of 'original autographs' or of one single *urtext* (respectively a 'model-codex'), from which every variant reading is to be explained as a deviation, is not at all new in modern text-critical work on the Hebrew Bible, that is, for the last two centuries.

When B. Kennicott and J.B. de Rossi in the years between 1776 and 1788 had published their immense collections of variant readings found in mediaeval manuscripts of the Hebrew Bible, the first impression was that the bulk of variants did not show any real variants but rather gave a convincing testimony to the immutability of the Massoretic Text.[2] A few years later, in 1797, E.F.K. Rosenmüller stated that the different manuscripts 'all represented *one* recension, all stem from one source...'[3] And in 1863 Paul de Lagarde replaced the earlier 'one

---

1. R.K. Harrison, *Introduction to the Old Testament* (London: Tyndale Press, 1970), p. 259.

2. B. Kennicott (ed.), *Vetus Testamentum Hebraicum, cum variis lectionibus*, I–II (Oxford, 1776–80); J.B. de Rossi, *Variae lectiones Veteris Testamenti...examinatae opera et studio*, I–IV (Parma, 1784–88). Cf. C. Steuernagel, *Lehrbuch der Einleitung in das Alte Testament* (Tübingen; J.C.B. Mohr, 1912), p. 20.

3. E.F.K. Rosenmüller, *Handbuch der biblischen Kritik und Exegese*, I (Göttingen: Vandenhoeck & Ruprecht, 1797), p. 247: '...dass sie [i.e. the codices

recension' theory by advancing his *archetype theory*, according to which all manuscripts of the Hebrew Bible derive from one single exemplar (or 'model-codex').[4] This theory of a Massoretic archetype, dated to about 100 CE, has had a great impact on the text-critical work up to now—regardless of the rather scanty evidence for the argument of de Lagarde as well as his specific view of the Greek version, the 'Egyptian recension', as 'another family' of the common (Massoretic) text, whose '*urform*' could be traced with the help of the restored '*urform*' of the Greek version.[5]

The weakest point in the well-known Lagardean theory was its quite insufficient consideration of the *pre*-history of the Hebrew text. It is, however, just here that later research, especially in our own generation, has proved the history of the text to be a highly complex one, owing to new evidence of a very great variety.

A few decades after de Lagarde's advancing of his theory, Paul Kahle started publishing the first of his many and multiple text studies which turned out to be most effective in opposing the Lagardean unified picture of transmission of the Bible text. Kahle initiated his magnificent career by analysing the Samaritan Targum to the Pentateuch (1898); he focused, however, his extensive studies on the differing Babylonian and Palestinian Massoretic Text forms and then he expanded his work to studies on the varying Greek translations, whose genesis he compared with that of the (Aramaic) Targums. It all revealed both real variants and independent text traditions.[6]

---

collected by Kennicott] sämmtlich im Ganzen *eine* Recension darstellen, aus einer Quelle geflossen sind...'; translation here by S. Talmon, 'The Old Testament Text', *CHB*, I, p. 172; now in F.M. Cross and S. Talmon (eds.), *Qumran and the History of the Biblical Text* (Cambridge, MA: Harvard University Press, 1975), p. 14.

4. P. de Lagarde, *Anmerkungen zur griechischen Übersetzung der Proverbien* (Leipzig, 1863), pp. 1-2.

5. 'über diesen archetypus des masoretischen textes würden wir nur durch conjectur hinausgelangen können, wenn uns nicht die griechische version des alten testaments die möglichkeit verschaffte, wenigstens eine schlechte übersetzung eines einer anderen familie angehörenden manuscripts zu benutzen... wollen wir über den hebräischen text ins klare kommen, so gilt es zunächst die urform der griechischen übersetzung zu finden. ehe diese vorliegt, darf die aegyptische recension nicht zur kontrolle der palästinensischen benutzt werden'; de Lagarde, *Anmerkungen*, p. 2.

6. Among Kahle's numerous text-historical works his *The Cairo Geniza* (Oxford: Basil Blackwell, 2nd edn, 1959) is to be mentioned especially; as for the rest cf. A. Bentzen, *Introduction to the Old Testament*, I (Copenhagen: G.E.C. Gad,

Diverging readings in the rabbinical literature had at the same time been pointed out by V. Aptowitzer as late real variants.[7] The same conclusion, by the way, had been reached by A. Geiger years before him.[8]

The text-critical work by Kahle and others brought about a new, complex picture of the text history which showed a hitherto unknown *pluriformity*, not only with regard to the pre-Massoretic Text tradition, which from now on was paid greater attention, but also as far as the later, 'standard' Massoretic Text was concerned. Kahle conveyed other dimensions to the biblical text study as well: diachronically, a true historical aspect of stages and development; and synchronically, the coexistence of diverse text forms belonging to different groups or communities.

Half a century after the publication of Kahle's first study, the scholarly world was overwhelmed by the findings of the Qumran Scrolls.

Inter alia they were highly—but also differently—esteemed on account of their great *text-critical* value. In the beginning, one first of all noticed their old and consistent testimony to the traditional Massoretic Text.[9] But in the course of time as scrolls and fragments—both in Hebrew and of the ancient versions—multiplied and were scrutinized, the Qumran texts revealed even more a textual situation in flux, just preceding the state of the final fixation of the Massoretic Text. Indeed, quoting M. Greenberg, what is 'exceedingly valuable in these manuscripts and fragments is their evidence for the antiquity and reality of variants whose existence, attested to heretofore only by the versions, has been questionable'.[10] And so, on the whole, these texts, although often fragmentary, 'present in a nutshell... the intricate and variegated problems of the Hebrew text and versions', as S. Talmon puts it.[11]

1961), pp. 52-65, or Talmon, in Cross and Talmon (eds.), *Qumran and the History*, pp. 17-22.

7.   V. Aptowitzer, *Das Schriftwort in der rabbinischen Literatur* (5 vols.; New York: Ktav, repr. 1970).

8.   Ludwig Geiger (ed.), *Abraham Geigers Nachgelassene Schriften*, IV (Berlin, 1876), pp. 28-30.

9.   Cf. among others M. Burrows, *The Dead Sea Scrolls* (New York: Viking Press, 1956), pp. 102-10.

10. M. Greenberg, 'The Stabilization of the Text of the Hebrew Bible, Reviewed in the Light of the Biblical Materials from the Judean Desert', *JAOS* 76 (1956), pp. 157-67 (165).

11. Cross and Talmon (eds.), *Qumran and the History*, p. 27.

In Qumran, then, as through the work of Kahle, we meet a remarkable textual *pluriformity*, a diversity of text traditions which differ in
time (more than 300 years) as well as from book to book. In Qumran
there was evidently—so it would seem—no normative 'standard' text.
But proto-Massoretic texts are also well attested here, along with differing Hebrew forms which coincide with those of the Samaritan Pentateuch and of the Greek versions.

However, later findings in the area, as those from Murabba'ât (see
n. 21), testify that the Massoretic form became prevalent in the time
between the two Revolts, probably even earlier.

Facing this distinct diversity of text traditions, W.F. Albright, by
1955, had already remodelled the older 'one recension' theory to a new
theory of different *local recensions* of a much earlier date than the
Lagardean archetype. So he reckoned first 'that many of the older
books of our Hebrew Bible were edited in approximately their present
form in Babylonia and were then brought back to Palestine by the
returning exiles during the late sixth and the fifth centuries BC'.[12] Secondly, he assumed 'an older Hebrew recension which differed from
MT', behind the Egyptian Greek translations of the later LXX.

In the hands of Frank M. Cross, however, this was expanded to a
theory of *three* local recensions. Besides the two recensions just mentioned, Cross reckons with a specific Palestinian text form which is
assumed to have much in common with that of the Samaritan Pentateuch. Further, he has left Albright's notion of a (redactional)
'recension' and speaks now only of 'local texts', including also to some
extent an aspect of living tradition.[13]

But in spite of this, the 'local texts' theory of Cross is characterized
by very *formal* arguments, especially so when he makes a textual
'short, pristine form' and an 'expansionist, fuller form' a pair of opposite criteria for classifying texts—without asking for contents and

---

12. W.F. Albright, 'New Light on Early Recensions of the Hebrew Bible',
BASOR 140 (1955), pp. 27-33.

13. Cf. F.M. Cross, 'The History of the Biblical Text in the Light of Discoveries in the Judean Desert', *HTR* 57 (1964), pp. 281-99 (also in Cross and Talmon
[eds.], *Qumran and the History*, pp. 177-95 [esp. §4, pp. 193-95]), with his 'The
Contribution of the Qumran Discoveries to the Study of the Biblical Text', *IEJ* 16
(1966), pp. 81-95 (also in Cross and Talmon [eds.], *Qumran and the History*,
pp. 278-92 [esp. p. 282 n. 21]), and most recently his 'The Evolution of a Theory of
Local Texts', in Cross and Talmon (eds.), *Qumran and the History*, pp. 306-20.

motives;[14] and also when he heavily stresses the necessary geographic isolation of specific text forms, if they are to exist over a longer period.[15] But the coexistence of divergent text forms in the community of Qumran is of itself sufficient evidence against this assumption. Altogether, the lack of traditio- and socio-historical, as well as ideological viewpoints, is obvious here.

In his discussion with Frank M. Cross, Shemarjahu Talmon, first of all, has questioned some of these and other weak points in the 'local texts' theory. The criticism of Talmon—aiming not only at details but also at the basic attitude of the theory as well—is based upon and substantiated by extensive historical and exegetical text studies which have exhibited the nearness of the textual transmission to the formative literary process of the texts, elucidated by literary phenomena like conflations and stylistics of different kinds.[16] By all this a very important aspect of the text history has been brought out, clearer than before: namely, the textual transmission as a living creative tradition, related to specific social bodies of groups or communities as the milieus of the tradition; there they have had their functional *Sitz im Leben*.[17] One could have wished, however, that Talmon, whose arguments are also rather formal, would have taken the ideological and specific theological factors of the process of transmission a bit more into consideration.

In the recent discussion of Cross and Talmon we may—to some degree—see the long shadows of the earlier opposite positions of de Lagarde and Kahle.

In view of the very comprehensive textual study of the Hebrew Bible during the last generations it must now be recognized that in this area of scholarly work, especially with the increasing manuscriptal evidence, the problems of the textual history have turned out to be much more complicated than ever before. It has also become unavoidably

14. Cf. Cross and Talmon (eds.), *Qumran and the History*, pp. 282-92, 306ff.

15. Cf. Cross and Talmon (eds.), *Qumran and the History*, pp. 283-84, 309.

16. Besides the paper referred to in n. 3 above, Cross and Talmon (eds.), *Qumran and the History*, pp. 35-41, cf. S. Talmon, 'DSIa as a Witness to Ancient Exegesis of the Book of Isaiah', *ASTI* 1 (1962), pp. 62-72 (also in Cross and Talmon [eds.], *Qumran and the History*, pp. 116-26); and his 'Aspects of the Textual Transmission of the Bible in the Light of Qumran Manuscripts', *Textus* 4 (1964), pp. 95-132 (also in Cross and Talmon [eds.], *Qumran and the History*, pp. 226-63); and most recently his 'The Textual Study of the Bible—A New Outlook', in Cross and Talmon (eds.), *Qumran and the History*, pp. 321-400.

17. Cross and Talmon (eds.), *Qumran and the History*, pp. 39-41, 378-81.

clear that biblical text history and textual criticism cannot be isolated from other parts and methods of biblical research but need to be incorporated into it. Tentatively, this will be somewhat clarified in the next section.

3. Basic Issues in the Contemporary Study of the Massoretic Text

In the textual research of the Hebrew Bible the fact of an exactly fixed Massoretic Text has been the very foundation, but at the same time very differently interpreted.

Facing the subsequent history of the fixed text one has—as has been shown—identified its starting-point with an *archetype*, like a 'riverhead running off into numerous rivulents', as Talmon says.[18] Also, after the textual fixation there are divergent text traditions. H.M. Orlinsky and others have rightly stated that there never existed *the* Massoretic Text.[19] Generally, however, the exceedingly high *unitary* character of the text has been—even rightly—emphasized, among others by such an expert in text history as M. Goshen-Gottstein.[20] But the greatest problems and the most urgent tasks of the text study today lie, after all, not on this later side of fixation but before it; they are related to the emergence of this text form, to its complex *pre-history*.

The history of the emergence of the Massoretic Text has been elucidated considerably by the various documents from the Wilderness of Judaea, especially when those from Qumran are compared with those from Murabb'ât.[21] The textual problems, however, are still enormous and the present state of research is definitely not perspicuous.

Now, some of the confusing perplexity may be rooted in the differing terminology used. First of all, the use of the term 'archetype' is very confusing and it would be better to leave it out of the further discussion, even if it is backdated and used hypothetically of an assumed

18. Cross and Talmon (eds.), *Qumran and the History*, p. 19.

19. H.M. Orlinsky in his Prolegomenon ('The Masoretic Text: A Critical Evaluation') to the new edition of C.D. Ginsburg, *Introduction to the Massoretico-Critical Edition of the Hebrew Bible* (New York: Ktav, 1966), pp. i-xlv, esp. pp. xxixff.

20. M.H. Goshen-Gottstein, 'The Rise of the Tiberian Bible Text', in A. Altmann (ed.), *Biblical and Other Studies* (Cambridge, MA: Harvard University Press, 1963), pp. 82, 121.

21. Cf., i.a., Cross and Talmon (eds.), *Qumran and the History*, pp. 24-27 (Talmon); 183f. (Cross); p. 212 (Skehan), with references to further literature.

urtext. Secondly, one differs in describing the very process of the textual emergence. So one speaks—not seldom with references to rabbinical statements such as that of the three scrolls in the Temple—of the 'promulgation', the 'stabilization', the 'standardization' or the 'fixation' of the text.[22] These terms are evidently not synonymous or equivalent; with the exception of the term 'promulgation', which might be misleading, they can be used with confidence; but one should be aware of their referring to different stages of the whole process, which primarily is to be described by careful analysis of the textual material itself.

With regard to the first stages of the process, which are the most inaccessible, one might refer to an interesting statement made by J. Wellhausen in his well-known study (1871) on the text of the books of Samuel; he says that sometimes 'the border between the text and gloss [is] so fluid that one does not know whether the removal of a verse that interrupts the context, belongs to the task of the textual or to that of the literary criticism'.[23] Thus Wellhausen, through text-critical and exegetical observations, had realized that the two methodologically different and often fully separated operations of the *textual*, so-called 'lower', and the *literary*, so-called 'higher', criticism may coincide on the same point in a given text. This means that the creative formation of a text has not ended when the more 'technical' transmission of the text 'takes over'; rather, they may overlap each other.

The same phenomenon is now to be observed in the scrolls and fragments from Qumran, for example in 1QIs[a], where P.W. Skehan, among others, has detected 'an exegetical process at work within the transmission of the text itself, in Hebrew'.[24] Regarding the Qumran manuscripts much more could be mentioned about this specific topic.[25]

In 1972 Emanuel Tov published an article on the textual difference between the Massoretic and Septuagintal form of the book of Jeremiah, where—as will be known—Hebrew fragments from Qumran support

22. Besides Greenberg, 'The Stabilization of the Text', see, e.g., M.H. Segal, 'The Promulgation of the Authoritative Text of the Hebrew Bible', *JBL* 72 (1953), pp. 35-47; Cross, in Cross and Talmon (eds.), *Qumran and the History*, pp. 183-84, 314.

23. J. Wellhausen, *Der Text der Bücher Samuelis untersucht* (Göttingen: Vandenhoeck & Ruprecht, 1871), p. 25 n. 2.

24. P.W. Skehan, 'The Qumran Manuscripts and Textual Criticism', in *Congress Volume: Strasbourg 1956* (VTSup, 4; Leiden: E.J. Brill, 1957), pp. 148-60 (also in Cross and Talmon [eds.], *Qumran and the History*, pp. 212-25 [215]).

25. See esp. the works of Talmon, referred to in n. 16 above.

the shorter form of the Greek version. From his investigations Tov concludes that in this case there are not only two different text types extant, but one has to characterize the two forms as 'witnesses of two different traditions of redaction'.[26]

In other words, the Qumran material has in these and many similar cases actualized the observation made by Wellhausen more than a century ago. One may, however, also substantiate his observation apart from the new Qumran material, by further detailed work on the Massoretic Text itself, just as he did, in view of its history and of the whole evidence of the ancient versions around the Hebrew text.

For my own part, I had a good opportunity some years ago to make observations on this same subject, whereby my basic position in these matters then developed. In my studies on the text and form of chs. 9–14 of the book of Zechariah, I stated in the Prolegomena the methodological difference and the concrete separation between the text-critical and the literary- and form-critical operations. For the sake of methodological sobriety I also divided my book into two distinct parts (or in German terms: 'Arbeitsgänge').[27] During my detailed investigation of the text, however, I realized in many instances that the text history in a strict sense was mingled with the still living (creative) literary '*Traditionsgeschichte*' of the text. Or, put in other words, *the creative element did continue in the various forms of the transmission of the text, in its Hebrew form as well as in the non-Hebrew versions.* The transmission of the text turned out to be *productive*, not only *re-productive*. My main conclusion was that the text transmission really had to be understood as 'Traditionsgeschichte', as a variegated and at the same time continuous *tradition history*. And as such it had to be integrated in the biblical tradition history in a broader sense.[28]

In his most recent contribution to the above-mentioned discussion with F.M. Cross, Talmon has also dealt with this problem, and in a very illuminating way.[29] Here he has—as has already been pointed out— given important sociological viewpoints which are crucial also for the

---

26. E. Tov, 'L'incidence de la critique textuelle sur la critique littéraire dans le livre de Jérémie', *RB* 79 (1972), pp. 189-99 (191).

27. Sæbø, *Sacharja 9–14*, pp. 13-21, 25-30, 31-42.

28. Sæbø, *Sacharja 9–14*, pp. 127-32.

29. Cf. Cross and Talmon (eds.), *Qumran and the History*, pp. 20, 23-24, 26, 32-33, 325-28, 378-81.

other aspect of the textual history related to the final 'fixation' of the text.

When coming to the question of the final 'fixation' of the text, we may once more quote from Wellhausen's text-critical study of the year 1871. He says: 'The Massorah has forced a text that for a long time has been very fluid, to stop, amid its fluidity.'[30] From this one may presume—as the case often seems to have been—that the process of the final 'fixation' is assumed to be rather momentary. There is, however, evidence that also indicates that the last part of the emergence of the text did not happen overnight but forms *the later stages of a longer process of traditio-historical character.*[31] Here it may be mentioned that Talmon not only has called attention to the socio-historical structure bearing the tradition, as mentioned above (we would say, the traditio-historical milieu), but also has made the interesting observation that the basic attitude to the scriptural or textual tradition was deeply different in the Qumran community and in the 'official' community of 'rabbinic Judaism': while the latter 'innovated new styles and types of literary compositions', because these circles... 'consciously had terminated the writing of "biblical" literature', so the former still lived in the pluriform and creative textual tradition and still thought of itself as a part of the 'biblical Israel'.[32]

This observation opens a new access to the long-realized nearness or parallelism between the final textual 'fixation' and the emergence of a *canon* of holy and normative Scriptures. Indeed, it opens a new understanding of the *canon process* itself.[33] But what is more important in this connexion is the observation that the final 'fixation' of the biblical text was related to a specific social group, where it originated and was developed in correspondence with basic theological attitudes and tenets.

---

30. Wellhausen, *Der Text der Bücher Samuelis untersucht*, p. 16: 'Die Massora hat einen bislang sehr fliessenden Text mitten im Fluss zum Stehen gezwungen.'

31. Cf. esp. B. Albrektson, 'Recension eller tradition? Några synpunkter på den gammaltestamentliga konsonanttextens standardisering', *SEÅ* 40 (1975), pp. 18-35.

32. Talmon, in Cross and Talmon (eds.), *Qumran and the History*, pp. 378-81.

33. Cf. n. 32 and also J.A. Sanders, *Torah and Canon* (Philadelphia: Fortress Press, 1972); A.C. Sundberg, Jr, *The Old Testament and the Early Church* (HThS, 20; Cambridge, MA: Harvard University Press, 1964).

4. *Conclusion—and a Desideratum*

The long lines of the scholarly work on the biblical text are to be kept in mind, because not every new assumption is new. In fact, we are standing today on the shoulders of great scholars like Geiger and Ginsburg, Wellhausen and Kahle; and we have to pursue their work and renew their insights in the face of all new evidence.

In the light of the available evidence today, the phantom of an assumed infallible 'archetype' of the biblical text has no place on the stage any more. What we see is the saga of a long and complicated process, a live tradition, leading from the proclaiming, preaching and teaching of priests, prophets and wise men of Israel *to the texts of their words*, and *from a pluriformity to a uniformity* of the texts, in the end a sacred and normative text, superior to others. The text was never something that *was* (*Gewesenes*) but in total something that *became* (*Gewordenes*) Our text-historical task and aim are to roll the whole process back, in all its complexity, as far back as possible; and that will differ from text to text and from book to book.

Last, but not least, a desideratum which—harking back to my introductory remarks—is meant for my theological colleagues, especially those in Systematic Theology. As I have been pleading for a greater integration of the text-historical work in general Bible studies, including a reciprocal impact of the involved disciplines, I should also like most earnestly to plead for much greater attention to be paid to the matter of text history, including its perspectives of traditions, in the theological reflections on the tenets of the Bible as the Word of God and as a theological authority today.

Chapter 3

OBSERVATIONS ON THE TEXT HISTORY OF LEVITICUS
AND THE VALUE OF SOME CAIRO GENIZAH VARIANTS

Quell's edition of the books of Exodus and Leviticus for the *Biblia hebraica stuttgartensia* (*BHS*) differs from the preceding edition of Kittel's *Biblia hebraica* (*BHK*), among other things in that it relatively often cites variants from the *Cairo Genizah* (CG) and a few from the Qumran findings.

As far as the book of Leviticus is concerned, to which R. Rendtorff, among others, has attributed a substantial part of his research,[1] the apparatus of the *BHS* does not provide less than 110 CG-variants but only one single and rather unimportant one from Qumran[2] and none at all of the *Targum Neophyti I*[3]—this only to mention the more recent

1. See, e.g., R. Rendtorff, *Die Gesetze in der Priesterschrift* (FRLANT, 62; Göttingen: Vandenhoeck & Ruprecht, 1954; 2nd edn, 1963); *Studien zur Geschichte des Opfers im Alten Testament* (WMANT, 24; Neukirchen–Vluyn: Neukirchener Verlag, 1967); and now mainly *Leviticus* (BKAT, 3.1; Neukirchen–Vluyn: Neukirchener Verlag, 1985).

2. Lev. 20.21, which attests a הוא (instead of the MT היא); see DJD, I, p. 52. Many more Qumran-variants could have been mentioned; see DJD, I, pp. 51-53; DJD, III, pp. 56-57, 106; otherwise possibly S.A. Birnbaum, 'The Leviticus Fragments from the Cave', *BASOR* 118 (1950), pp. 20-27; Skehan, 'The Qumran Manuscripts and Textual Criticism', pp. 148-60; J.P.M. van der Ploeg, 'Lev. IX,23–X,2, dans un texte de Qumran', in Siegfried Wagner (ed.), *Bibel und Qumran* (Festschrift H. Bardtke; Berlin: Evangelische Haupt-Bibelgesellschaft, 1968), pp. 153-55; also D.N. Freedman and K.A. Matthews, *The Paleo-Hebrew Leviticus Scroll* (*11QpaleoLev*) (Winona Lake, IN: Eisenbrauns, 1985).

3. See A. Díez Macho, *The Recently Discovered Palestinian Targum: Its Antiquity and Relationship with Other Targums* (VTSup, 7; Leiden: E.J. Brill, 1960), pp. 222-45 (critically on the subject P. Wernberg-Møller, 'An Inquiry into the Validity of the Text-critical Argument for an Early Dating of the Recently Discovered Palestinian Targum', *VT* 12 [1962], pp. 312-30); furthermore, e.g., R. le Deaut, 'Lévitique XXII 26–XXIII 44 dans le Targum palestinien: De l'importance des

textual material. This, though, now poses the critical question of what text-historical and text-critical value the mentioned CG-variants might have. Unfortunately, it can only be followed up very briefly in our context.

The large findings in the Genizah of the Ezra-Synagogue in old Cairo, discovered mainly towards the end of the last century, were generally—and rightly so—thought to be of great importance, as, for example, Paul Kahle stated, 'the importance of the M S fragments brought to our notice from the Cairo Geniza can hardly be exaggerated'.[4] The material from the Genizah, though, is of very different types;[5] in our context we will only be able to discuss briefly the biblical fragments and among them only those regarding Leviticus. The usage and evaluation of the material is furthermore crucially influenced by the fact that it was transported to totally different places very early on and is now being kept in those places; that means they can be found in the USA as well as in Europe (including Leningrad), but mainly in the University Libraries of Cambridge and Oxford;[6] the large Taylor-Schlechter Collections (T-S) in Cambridge being the most important.

If one critically considers the CG-variants to Leviticus of the *BHS*, several observations can be made that should be revealing as far as the

gloses du codex Neofiti 1', *VT* 18 (1968), pp. 458-71; now mainly A. Díez Macho, *Neophyti 1: Targum palestinense MS de la Biblioteca Vaticana.* III. *Levitico* (Madrid and Barcelona: Consejo Superior de Investigaciones Científicas, 1971).

4.   Kahle, *The Cairo Geniza*, p. vii.

5.   Cf. S. Schechter, *Studies in Judaism* (2 vols.; Freeport, NY: Books for Libraries Press, 1976 [1896]), II, pp. 1-30; Kahle, *The Cairo Geniza*, pp. 3-13; in particular S.D. Goitein, *A Mediterranean Society: The Jewish Communities in the Arab World as Portrayed in the Documents of the Cairo Geniza* (3 vols.; Berkeley: University of California Press, 1967-78), esp. I, pp. vii-xi, 1-28.

6.   See Kahle, *The Cairo Geniza*; Goitein, *A Mediterranean Society*. For the Taylor-Schechter Collection see now the provisional overview by S.C. Reif, *A Guide to the Taylor-Schechter Genizah Collection* (Cambridge: Cambridge University Press, 1973), and in the Cambridge University Library Genizah Series (ed. S.C. Reif) in particular Part 2: M.C. Davis, *Hebrew Bible Manuscripts in the Cambridge Genizah Collections.* I. *Taylor-Schechter Old Series and Other Genizah Collections in the Cambridge University Library* (Cambridge: Cambridge University Press, 1978); see likewise Part 3: S. Hopkins, *A Miscellany of Literary Pieces from the Cambridge Genizah Collections: A Catalogue and Selection of Texts in the Taylor-Schechter Collection, Old Series, Box a45* (Cambridge: Cambridge University Press, 1978). Contrary to these, the fragments in the Bodleian Library in Oxford have not found the same attention; see Kahle, *The Cairo Geniza*, p. 8.

evaluation of the text-critical profile of the edition is concerned.

For once, the CG-variants are named with a simple 'C', that is, without any notes to or descriptions of the individual basis of the fragments. This process is even more questionable since, when having a closer look at them, the fragments present themselves very differently in many ways.[7] The fact that some fragments are written on parchment and others on paper can be significant. The distinctiveness of the individual fragments, though, is most important in view of their text-critical value and usage. Some of the fragments also seem to reflect certain school activities which should not be overlooked when evaluating the variants; we will come back to this later.

Quell has obviously assessed 'only' the most important parts of the Taylor-Schechter collections (i.e. the fragments within the numbers T-S A2, 3, 22, 24, 25 and 28, but not A26 [with 211 fragments to Lev.]) as well as some 'MSS Heb.' of the Bodleian collection in Oxford.[8] Even though these collections are quite extensive and important they still do not contain the complete biblical CG-material. From this point of view the *BHS* edition is not only insufficiently precise but also seems to pretend more than it does factually hold.

The CG-variants represent many omissions in relation to the MT, that is to say about 62 of the total 110 citings (or 56.4%). This can apply to the dismissal of some words or complete verses (16.19; 24.4) or larger parts of the text (see 11.4-5; 17.10-12).

There are several valid reasons for the different omissions in the CG-fragments and it is also important to pay attention to the changing character of the individual fragments. Often, though, the omissions seem to be due to little or no care in copying, in particular since they contain no less than 17 homoioteleuta—sometimes of large extent[9]—and a

---

7.   See foremost Reif, *A Guide*; also Davis, *Hebrew Bible Manuscripts*, pp. ix-xiv (Introduction).

8.   According to a letter that was sent to me by my colleague H.P. Rüger in March 1979, Quell most likely based his work only on the collations of the CG-variant which Rueger and M. Dietrich created 'Ende der 50er Jahre in Oxford und Cambridge'. That is all I am aware of; likewise, I do not know when Quell finished the manuscript of his edition. I myself visited Cambridge in August 1979 and April 1986 in order to examine the crucial texts more closely, i.e. as a preliminary study to a commentary on Leviticus for the KAT series which was later abandoned by the publisher for marketing reasons.

9.   1.5; 2.4; 4.25; 5.5; 8.15; 9.7; 11.4-5, 6, 42-43; 14.27; 16.2, 27; 17.4; 25.14-15, 18-19; 26.13 and 27.33; see also 11.15.

significant homoioarcton (17.10-12). From the point of view of textual history the text-critical value of fragments with variants of a kind like this should not be overestimated. This critical judgment will be substantiated by the following point.

It also stands out remarkably that the CG-variants mentioned in the *BHS* in an overwhelming majority are not supported by other ancient textual evidence, that is, in 95 out of 110 cases (or 86.4%). In that sense, then, most of the variants do not fit into the textual history of Leviticus, which may be best understood as tradition history,[10] but stand on their own. The text-critical value of these text-historical 'naked' facts is generally lessened accordingly.

The critical remarks that have been made so far will have put the CG-information of the *BHS* into a rather negative perspective. Although the CG-fragments are not without any text-critical value at all, it seems advisable not to consult the information given by the *BHS* without extremely critical reservations.[11] Yet more remains to be said.

The complete picture of the fragments is by far a richer one and among its noteworthy elements—which unfortunately are not expressed in the *BHS*—one can find a vocalization that often deviates from the MT. As far as the changing vocalization of the fragments is concerned, M.C. Davis created a division of three 'types': he differentiated between 'standard Tiberian'; 'predominantly standard Tiberian'; and 'non-standard vocalization'.[12] The deviations are linguistically and historically interesting for the later Hebrew, but in our context the text-historical perspective is far more crucial. Since we are dealing with a Massoretic and a non-Massoretic type of text the different variants of the CG-vocalization offer a significant opportunity to broaden the non-Massoretic biblical text material which also has grown out of other sources.[13]

If the relation of the CG-variants to the remaining textual history of the book in many ways seems very complex and generally weak,

---

10. For this view of the textual history see Chapter 2 above. Cf. M.H. Goshen-Gottstein, 'The Textual Criticism of the Old Testament: Rise, Decline, Rebirth', *JBL* 102 (1983), pp. 365-99.

11. See below, pp. 52-55.

12. Davis, *Hebrew Bible Manuscripts*, p. xii, as well as pp. 1ff. (*passim*).

13. Including the question of the type 'Ben Naphtali'; see Davis, *Hebrew Bible Manuscripts*, p. xii; see likewise Sæbø, *Sacharja 9–14*, pp. 31-39 (with references to further important texts).

another relation of the CG-fragments comes even stronger to the fore, that is, the relation to its own 'milieu', to which it owes the creation of its own specific character over a longer span of time. In this respect, the book of Leviticus has a special place.

The colourful 'milieu' of old Cairo, in which the rich material of the Genizah originated, has been presented extensively by S.D. Goitein in his work *A Mediterranean Society*. On this occasion, his remarks on education and the professional class are particularly instructive;[14] through this insight important parts of the fragments become easier to explain.

As previously mentioned, the fragments already differ significantly in their external appearance, that is, as far as their format and scribal character is concerned. It becomes obvious that relatively many frag-ments—in particular among the paper fragments of the boxes A25 and A26—are written with so many mistakes and so clumsily that they caused the following remark by M.C. Davis: 'The inexpert character of the script suggests that the fragment is a child's writing exercise'.[15] Exercise-like references to the Hebrew alphabet and individual letters as well as accidental scribbles give further rise to the assumption that several of the fragments may have been products of children.[16] One can also find different types of small 'exercise books' put together from individual pages that likewise fit into a classroom situation.[17]

In view of these and similar circumstances one will hardly go wrong

14. Goitein, *A Mediterranean Society*, II, pp. 171-272, in particular pp. 171-240; see likewise S. Krauss, *Talmudische Archaeologie* (repr.; 3 vols.; New York: Arno Press, 1979 [1910–12]), III, pp. 131-98, 199-239. Furthermore, regarding the question of schools in more ancient, already biblical times, cf., e.g., O. Plöger, *Sprüche Salomos (Proverbia)* (BKAT, 17; Neukirchen–Vluyn: Neukirchener Verlag, 1984), pp. 111f. (with reference to older literature); also A. Lemaire, *Les écoles et la formation de la Bible dans l'ancien Israël* (OBO, 39; Fribourg: Editions universitaires; Göttingen: Vandenhoeck & Ruprecht, 1981); D.W. Jamieson-Drake, *Scribes and Schools in Monarchic Judah: A Socio-Archaeological Approach* (Sheffield: Almond Press, 1991).

15. Davis, *Hebrew Bible Manuscripts*, p. 91; the relevant sections in A25 are 4, 10, 16, 46, 77, 98, 99, 113, 116, 119, 122, 125, 135, 149, 161, 164, 168, 169, 177, 188, 189, 192, and cf. 163, 171, 173, 178, 193, 201; and in A26 sections 11, 18, 21, 22, 23, 26, 49, 52, 78, 89, 111, 122, 137, 142, 144, 160, 173, 181, 191, 203, and cf. 188.

16. See, e.g., A25.10, 106 and also A26.3, 52, 78, 83, 86, 208, 210.

17. See, e.g., A25.24, 77, 185, 186, 188, 192 and A26.34, 44a, 52, 83, 86, 146, 177, 208, 210.

when suggesting that many of the fragments—that is, mainly the paper
ones—stem from some kind of a school situation. The study of the
Bible was elementary in the teaching of pupils[18] and, therefore, for
learning to write. Of particular interest in this context is that the teaching of the Bible began—apart from the book of Genesis—with
Leviticus.[19]

Another matter deserves attention here. Apart from the many omissions and the fragment classified as 'children's writing-exercises'
already mentioned, a further characteristic of the fragments stands out:
with regard to the MT the individual words and phrases are often written erroneously or have been replaced by other words and have then
later been corrected above the line or at the side. The corrections seem
to have been made by another hand—possibly that of the teacher; they
are often done in different ink.

In retrospect to the above-mentioned points two further suspicions
can be held: first, the many fragments with 'writing-mistakes' and corrections cannot simply be identified as those fragments that present
themselves as 'children's writings' and yet there may be fluid transitions between the two groups. Second, there is the considerable possibility that a 'writing-mistake' does not have to be accidental but that it
really belongs to an older, non-Massoretic tradition of text. For that
reason one will have to see the CG-fragments in a double perspective,
that is, that of an actual school situation as well as that of an old and
differing or non-Massoretic tradition. In the latter case a variant will be
of even more particular interest; the *BHS*, however, does not provide
sufficient information on it.

After all these general observations and considerations, which may
be most important where method is concerned, particular attention may
now be given to the individual CG-variants of the apparatus of the

18. See Goitein, *A Mediterranean Society*, II, pp. 173ff., about the instruction of
children; on the instruction of adults (192ff.) he says, among other things: 'The
study of the Hebrew Bible...formed the most important constituent of the general
curriculum of any educated man... Many Fragments of translations into Arabic of
the Bible, commentaries, and treaties give the impression of being notes of students
and teachers rather than finished literary products' (p. 206). See also S. Schechter,
'The Child in Jewish Literature', in *Studies in Judaism*, I, pp. 343-80, esp. 369ff.

19. See Krauss, *Talmudische Archaeologie*, III, p. 235: 'Der Unterricht in der
Bibel wurde von alters her mit dem 3. Buche Mosis, mit Levitikus, dem Priester-
gesetze, begonnen.' According to M.C. Davis, the first instructions seemed to
prefer Genesis and Leviticus.

BHS, but it is only possible—in order to be brief—to refer to a limited selection of the information.

In some cases it is surprising that certain information is given at all or in the present form. That is particularly true for little meaningful omissions where, for example, an important word in the context is missing, be it the name of a deity (1.3: in the expression לפני יהוה), an object (4.6; 17.6) or any other necessary part of a sentence (7.34, 38; 10.10; 11.2; 24.9). Usually these passages have been corrected by filling in the omitted word at a later time; even when the problem was only an obvious writing mistake (4.22; 6.8; 12.8).[20] The information proves to be particularly problematic if the omission or mistake should be caused by a children's writing-exercise.[21] Finally, one may also ask why the rather uninteresting היא for the MT הוא occurs so often.[22]

There are, on the other hand, passages where it would have been of advantage for the *BHS* if it had indicated variants of the CG-fragments, and then as support for other evidence of differing readings within the oldest textual tradition. When in 4.8, for example, the rather remarkable variant את is registered instead of על, with reference to relatively many text witnesses, also the 'mini-book' T-S A24.43 that has the same variant could have been presented.[23] When, further, the *BHS* in 5.11, with reference to Sam., LXX and Syr., exhibits the variant יצק instead of the MT form ישים, also T-S A26.88 could have been indicated.[24] In 11.15 where ancient versions display some textual ambivalence, both as for the form את and for the verse as a whole, the information that this word lacks in T-S A25.34 (but filled in at the margin) would have been of

---

20. So, e.g., 6.8 in A25.16 (see 4.25 in A25.124, not listed in the *BHS*), 7.34 in A25.152 where the missing word has been inserted above the line (as also the missing כ in תאכלהו v. 24), 13.28 in A25.75 and 18.30 in A25.196.

21. So 6.8 in A25.16, see Davis, *Hebrew Bible Manuscripts*, pp. 92f.; or 9.7 (homoioteleuton) in A22.127, where a line has been skipped; Davis, *Hebrew Bible Manuscripts*, p. 75, does not go into enough detail here.

22. So in 2.15; 6.10; 11.39; 16.31; 17.14; 25.10, 11, 12, but not in 5.9 in which the *BHS* uses Sam. and Targ. as references for the variant היא instead of mentioning Oxford MS Heb. c51, fol. 6a. See n. 2 above.

23. Davis, *Hebrew Bible Manuscripts*, p. 84, does not mention the many deviations of the little book that contains six pages and comprises Lev. 1.11–4.35. Cf. also K. Elliger, *Leviticus* (HAT, 1.4; Tübingen: J.C.B. Mohr, 1966), pp. 53, 56.

24. Cf. Davis, *Hebrew Bible Manuscripts*, p. 115; also Elliger, *Leviticus*, pp. 55ff.

some interest. In these and other instances, the CG-variants might have enriched the text-historical picture.

However, quite a number of the CG-variants mentioned in the *BHS* are text-historically significant and worth considering. A selection of the data that can be evaluated positively may exhibit the different character of the variants. So, in 11.21 CG attests the *Qere* reading לו, supported by the ancient versions, instead of the *Ketib* לא, whereby a *Qere* reading is changed into a *Ketib*. When in 11.25 some Hebrew MSS, Syr. and also T-S A25.24 read את נבלתם instead of MT מנבלתם this variant may either represent an assimilation to vv. 28 and 40 respectively, being 'a phenomenon of stylistic synonymity',[25] or also an old double tradition; the last possibility is most probably the case in 11.27 where T-S A25.199 alone has נחון instead of MT כפיו.[26] Another double tradition may be presupposed in 14.40 where T-S A3.25, with diverging vocalization, reads לַמְחֲנֶה instead of the MT form לָעִיר.[27] A double tradition that possibly is more dogmatically determined may, finally, be present in 24.18a when here some Hebrew MSS, LXX and Vulg., supported by one CG-variant, omit the word נַפֶּשׁ, probably, in view of the preceding verse, in order to avoid a too near collocation of man and animal.

Among the textual divergences of the CG-fragments a certain tendency of a smoothing simplification or harmonization seems to be the case, whereby the possibility of a certain effect of old specific traditions cannot be strictly excluded. As a first example of this tendency, 4.25 may be mentioned; here the T-S A24.43 omits the second part of the verse. The *BHS* explains this as a homoioteleuton which seems to be the case at first sight. One may ask, however, whether a detailed definition of dealing with sacrificial blood has been simplified deliberately; furthermore, that the omission of the fragment may represent an older, simpler form of the definition of the blood which contained only the first part and which was extended by the second half of the verse

25. So S. Talmon, 'The Textual Study of the Bible—A New Outlook', in Cross and Talmon (eds.), *Qumran and the History*, pp. 321-400 (350); see also Elliger, *Leviticus*, pp. 14ff.

26. נחון is otherwise only to be found in Gen. 3.14 and Lev. 11.42; see also Davis, *Hebrew Bible Manuscripts*, p. 108; Elliger, *Leviticus*.

27. Davis, *Hebrew Bible Manuscripts*, p. 12, refers here to the *BHK*; neither the *BHK* or *BHS*, however, offer a corresponding suggestion or this reference. See also Elliger, *Leviticus*, p. 333 n. 1.

within the course of tradition, and which then was even further specified by the element כֹל, 'all', as it is documented by four Hebrew MSS and the LXX. In any case, one should not assume an accidental omission here. Further, the variant עָמֹק for MT שָׁפָל in 13.20 should not be a surprise; after all, the word appears seven times in Leviticus 13 (3-4, 25, 30-32, 34) and may in 13.20 simply be a straightforward adjustment without any particular text-critical value.[28] Simplifying omissions are likewise to be found in 16.2, 11 and 21. In 16.27, on the other hand, the noteworthy omission in T-S A25.27 and Oxford MS Heb. d73, fol. 1a, possibly corresponds to an older, shorter text which was then traditio-historically extended by this element. Finally, as for the omissions in 26.13 and 16, they may be simplifications, and likewise in 26.20 where the variant השדה instead of MT הארץ are—despite the old and relatively broad evidence in the *BHS*—could possibly be an adjustment to the text in 26.4-22.

Last, but not least, as regards the discussion of the divine names the question may be asked whether in certain fragments an extending tendency also can be shown in this context. This question, however, is best followed up on a broader basis, that is, by consulting the LXX. Anyhow, it is worth mentioning that in 4.7 Oxford MS Heb. d79, fol. 7a, adds 'YHWH' to 'altar', that in 10.12 T-S A28.40 reads 'Moses' instead of 'YHWH' (which could possibly be an adjustment to 10.8), and that furthermore in 23.19 Oxford MS Heb. b5, fol. 11b, uses ליהוה instead of לחטאת, which has been corrected at the side of the fragment, and that finally T-S A25.41 adds the element אני יהוה after 25.18a.

If, in conclusion, one looks back on the general and the particular observations and considerations one can confidently say that the variants of the fragments from the Cairo Genizah listed in the *BHS* offer an extremely ambiguous result: along with accidental and little valuable information there are at the same time many text-historically interesting and significant variants. It is for that reason that one should approach the information given in the *BHS* particularly carefully. With regard to the widely different fragments of the Cairo Genizah one should be reminded of the old and tested text-critical rule: *manuscripta ponderantur, non numerantur.*

---

28. See *BHK* and *BHS*; also see Díez Macho, *Palestinian Targum*, p. 233.

Part II
TRADITION HISTORY: SOME TEXTS

Chapter 4

DIVINE NAMES AND EPITHETS IN GENESIS 49.24B-25A:
METHODOLOGICAL AND TRADITIO-HISTORICAL REMARKS

In recent studies of the Old Testament there seems to be a growing tendency to focus on the history of the religion of Israel. To a great extent
this has been done within the framework of the early social and cultural
history of Israel. Studies of this kind are not new, but it may be characteristic of the present situation—partly prompted by recently discovered
archaeological evidence—that the focus is now fixed on *the question of
God* in early Israel, and on *early Yahwism*.[1]

Within these perspectives, new attention has also been paid to the
very complex and significant text of Gen. 49.24b-25b, not least because
of its unique repleteness of divine names and epithets of archaic character in vv. 24b-25aαβ. Earlier scholars often studied the composition of

1.   Cf. W.F. Albright, *Yahweh and the Gods of Canaan: A Historical Analysis
of Two Contrasting Faiths* (London: Athlone Press, 1968); F.M. Cross, *Canaanite
Myth and Hebrew Epic: Essays in the History of the Religion of Israel* (Cambridge,
MA: Harvard University Press, 1973); D.N. Freedman, 'Divine Names and Titles
in Early Hebrew Poetry', in F.M. Cross *et al.* (eds.), *Magnalia Dei: The Mighty
Acts of God. Essays on the Bible and Archaeology in Memory of G. Ernest Wright*
(Garden City, NY: Doubleday, 1976), pp. 55-107; J.A. Emerton, 'New Light on
Israelite Religion: The Implications of the Inscriptions from Kuntillet 'Ajrud', *ZAW*
94 (1982), pp. 2-20; K. Koch, 'Die Götter, denen die Väter dienten', in *idem,
Studien zur alttestamentlichen und altorientalischen Religionsgeschichte* (Göt-
tingen: Vandenhoeck & Ruprecht, 1988), pp. 9-31; M. Köckert, *Vätergott und
Väterverheissungen: Eine Auseinandersetzung mit Albrecht Alt und seinen Erben*
(Göttingen: Vandenhoeck & Ruprecht, 1988); J.C. de Moor, *The Rise of Yahwism:
The Roots of Israelite Monotheism* (Leuven: Leuven University Press, 1990); S.M.
Olyan, *Asherah and the Cult of Yahweh in Israel* (SBLMS, 34; Atlanta, GA: Schol-
ars Press, 1988); M.S. Smith, *The Early History of God: Yahweh and the Other
Deities in Ancient Israel* (San Francisco: Harper & Row, 1990); J.H. Tigay, *You
Shall Have No Other Gods: Israelite Religion in the Light of Hebrew Inscriptions*
(HSS, 31; Atlanta, GA: Scholars Press, 1986).

Gen. 49.3-27 with a view to its general historical background,[2] but some scholars have in recent times focused more strongly on different religious aspects of the text. This has been done to a large extent within the broader context of Canaanite religion, especially as it has been revealed by Ugaritic texts of Ras Shamra.[3] However, in historical, religio-historical and other respects there is much divergence in the modern scholarly discussion, not least with respect to vv. 24b-25b. Given this state of affairs, it might prove useful, as well as methodologically sound, to pay close attention to the text in its own literary context. This should include comparison with similar texts, and, first of all, with its 'parallel' in Deut. 33.13.[4] Therefore a fresh look at this complex and multifaceted text may start with some of its text-critical and form-historical problems.

1. *Text-critical Remarks*

The Hebrew text of Gen. 49.24b-25aαβ presents problems of two different kinds. First, there are two well-known *cruces* in this small text cut, namely מִשָּׁם in v. 24bβ and וְאֵת in v. 25aβ. In commentaries and monographs for over a century and more there have been numerous proposals for emending the Massoretic text in vv. 24-25, some of which

2. See H.-J. Kittel, 'Die Stammessprüche Israels: Genesis 49 und Deuteronomium 33 traditionsgeschichtlich untersucht' (Theol. Dissertation, Kirchliche Hochschule, Berlin, 1959); A.H.J. Gunneweg, 'Über den Sitz im Leben der sog. Stammessprüche (Gen 49 Dtn 33 Jdc 5)', *ZAW* 76 (1964), pp. 245-55; H.-J. Zobel, *Stammesspruch und Geschichte* (BZAW, 95; Berlin: Alfred Töpelmann, 1965); F.M. Cross and D.N. Freedman, *Studies in Ancient Yahwistic Poetry* (Missoula, MT: Scholars Press, 1975), esp. pp. 69-122; H. Seebass, 'Die Stämmesprüche Gen 49,3-27', *ZAW* 96 (1984), pp. 333-50; cf. also *idem*, 'Die Stämmeliste von Dtn. XXXIII', *VT* 27 (1977), pp. 158-69; *idem*, 'Erwägungen zum altisraelitischen System der zwölf Stämme', *ZAW* 90 (1978), pp. 196-220; C.H.J. de Geus, *The Tribes of Israel* (Assen: Van Gorcum, 1976), esp. pp. 70-96; for further references cf. C. Westermann, *Genesis*. III. *Genesis 37–50* (BKAT, 1.3; Neukirchen–Vluyn: Neukirchener Verlag, 1982), pp. 243-46.
3. Cf., i.a., J. Coppens, 'La bénédiction de Jacob: Son cadre historique à la lumière des parallèles ougaritiques', in *Congress Volume: Strasbourg 1956* (VTSup, 4; Leiden: E.J. Brill, 1957), pp. 97-115; Freedman, 'Divine Names', pp. 63-66; Smith, *Early History*, pp. 16-24.
4. Cf. J.D. Heck, 'A History of Interpretation of Genesis 49 and Deuteronomy 33', *BSac* 147.585 (1990), pp. 16-31.

are merely witnesses to scholarly arbitrariness.[5]

Second, the form and the syntactical relations of vv. 24b-25aαβ to their immediate context in vv. 24a and 25aγδb(-26), within the framework of the rest of the Blessing of Joseph (vv. 22-26), involves some problems that require due attention. However, as far as the usual handling of textual problems and *cruces* is concerned, a basic methodological problem is involved which may be briefly commented upon here. In cases of this kind modern interpreters have often mixed text-critical arguments with literary and other sorts of arguments, instead of distinguishing carefully between them.[6] One may indeed dispute whether such a procedure actually contributes to the accurate understanding of the text, all the more so since the text-critical discussion should in the first instance be based on text-historical evidence, as the ancient textual history has proven to be a tradition history in its own right.[7] Therefore, special heed will be given to this side of the textual problems.

Turning to the evidence for the ancient textual history of Gen. 49.24b-25aαβ, it may be said in general that the versions present a very variegated and somewhat perplexing picture of the text.

The Septuagint (LXX), to begin with, differs very much from the MT of Gen. 49.22-26, and hence also in vv. 24-25. It is hard to form any clear opinion as to what the Hebrew basis, *Vorlage*, may have been like, but it might have been rather different from the present MT. Also, the LXX may, as usual, include elements of interpretation. The LXX text of vv. 24-25 (with vv. 24b-25aαβ italicized) runs as follows:

24   καὶ συνετρίβη μετὰ κράτους τὰ τόξα αὐτῶν,
        καὶ ἐξελύθη τὰ νεῦρα βραχιόνων χειρῶν αὐτῶν
        διὰ χεῖρα δυνάστου Ἰακώβ,
        ἐκεῖθεν ὁ κατισχύσας Ἰσραήλ.
25   *παρὰ θεοῦ τοῦ πατρός σου,*
        καὶ ἐβοήθησέν σοι ὁ θεὸς ὁ ἐμός,

---

5. As an *exemplum instar omnium* note the radical emendation of M. Dahood, 'Is 'Eben Yiśrā'ēl a Divine Title? (Gen. 49,24)', *Bib* 40 (1959), pp. 1002-1007. The extensive emending procedure was heavily criticized by Nyberg, *Studien zum Hoseabuche*, p. 12 and *passim*.

6. Cf., i.a., V. Maag, 'Der Hirte Israels', in *idem, Kultur, Kulturkontakt und Religion* (Göttingen: Vandenhoeck & Ruprecht, 1980), pp. 111-44 (121 n. 19). Westermann exemplifies a host of modern commentators when he makes literary remarks within the context of his text-critical section, cf. *Genesis 37–50*, p. 249.

7. Cf. Sæbø, *Sacharja 9–14*, pp. 25-28; for the theoretical discussion see above, Chapter 2.

καὶ εὐλόγησέν σε εὐλογίαν οὐρανοῦ ἄνωθεν
καὶ εὐλογίαν τῆς ἐχούσης πάντα·
ἕνεκεν εὐλογίας μαστῶν καὶ μήτρας...[8]

With the use of the verbs συνετρίβη and ἐξελύθη, the LXX has strengthened the martial tone of v. 24a, as compared with the MT. By connecting these verbs tighter than in the MT with 'the hand of the Mighty One of Jacob' in v. 24bα the LXX has linked God more immediately with the victory in Joseph's battle than is the case in the MT. Further, by rendering v. 24ba *literatim,* the LXX confirms the MT מִידֵי אֲבִיר יַעֲקֹב. It also confirms the form מִשָּׁם in v. 24bβ. However, it is uncertain what was read and rendered in the case of the two words in the MT רֹעֶה and אֶבֶן since they have no direct rendering.[9] If, by employing the form ὁκατισχύσας the LXX intended to draw a parallel with the verb in v. 25aα (וִיעֶזְרֶךָּ), this would entail combining v. 24bβ with v. 25aα, which would in turn imply a weakening of the transition from indirect to direct address of Joseph in v. 25aα. While it confirms the MT in v. 25aα, the LXX completely deviates from the MT in v. 25aβ, not only with regard to וְאֵת, where it may have read וְאֵל, as we see reflected in ὁ θεὸς ὁ ἐμός, but also with regard to the divine name שַׁדַּי, which is not rendered at all.[10]

In short, some interesting characteristics of the LXX version may be noted: (1) By and large, the LXX seems to reflect the same text form as

8.   J.W. Wevers, *Genesis* (Septuaginta, 1; Göttingen: Vandenhoeck & Ruprecht, 1974), ad loc.

9.   On the probably erroneous listing in E. Hatch, H.A. Redpath *et al.*, *A Concordance to the Septuagint and the Other Greek Versions of the Old Testament* (3 vols.; Oxford: Clarendon Press, 1987; repr. Grand Rapids: Baker Book House, 1983), III, p. 751b, E. Tov (*The Text-Critical Use of the Septuagint in Biblical Research* [Jerusalem, 1981], p. 151) remarks that it 'records κατισχύειν as the equivalent of אבן, even though from a formal point of view the Greek verb reflects both רעה and אבן'; cf. also S. Olofsson, *God Is my Rock: A Study of Translation Technique and Theological Exegesis in the Septuagint* (ConBOT, 31; Stockholm: Almqvist & Wiksell, 1990), pp. 94f.

10.   The LXX has at least six renderings of *šadday*, among which especially παντοκράτωρ and κύριος παντοκράτωρ are known; but one also finds ἐπουράνιος, ὁ Θεός τοῦ οὐρανοῦ, ἱκανος and ὁ τα; πάντα ποιήσας and once (*qol*) *'el šadday* is only partly translated, as (φωνὴ) θεοῦ Σαδδαι (Ezek. 10.5); cf. Hatch, Redpath *et al.*, *Concordance*, III, p. 267a, with references, although the listing of Gen. 49.25 on p. 631b (cf. p. 630a) is disputable. See also M. Weippert, '‏שַׁדַּי‎ *Šaddaj* (Gottesname)', *THAT*, II, cols. 873-81 (874); Olofsson, *God Is my Rock*, pp. 111-16.

the MT, although there are some deviations; obviously, the Hebrew text of vv. 24-25 presented some substantial difficulties to the LXX translators. (2) It is most interesting that *some of the difficulties seem to relate specifically to the divine names and epithets in vv. 24b-25aαβ*. For, on the one hand, the LXX has applied divine names of a commonly known character, those which contain the element θεός in θεός τοῦ πατρός σου and in ὁ θεός ὁ ἐμός, while, on the other hand, such apparently specific names or epithets as Hebrew רעה, 'shepherd', אבן, 'stone', and especially שׁדי, which is otherwise translated in a variety of ways in the Greek Old Testament, have no equivalents here. Only the rare אביר יעקב has been 'preserved' as δυνάστης Ἰακώβ, and may be in a mediating position.[11] The question may be raised as to what the reason for this might be. (3) Last, but not least, this significant state of affairs may be taken to indicate that the procedure of transmitting and translating an ancient text was largely one of an interpretative nature.

The phenomenon of tradition may be demonstrated, briefly, by the other ancient versions.

If we ought above all to pay due attention to the interpretative element in the translating process, this element is, as expected, particularly prevalent in the various *Targumic* traditions. It takes a relatively modest form in *Targum Onqelos* in connexion with the entire pericope, and with respect to vv. 22(-23) specifically it is excessive in the Palestinian Targums, as represented by *Neophyti* (N) *I*.[12] In Targum Neoph. N1, 'Joseph, my son', depicted as a pious and invincible person, is the principal character also in vv. 24-25. In the first part of v. 24 we read that: 'he placed his confidence in the Strong One' (בתקיפה רוחצניה ואשרי). 'He stretched out his hand and his arms to beseech mercy from [למבעיה רחמין מן] the Strong One of his father Jacob [תקיפא דאבוי יעקב]...' It is most interesting in this connexion that here the divine name אביר יעקב is used twice, once in a full and idiomatic translation and once in a freely abridged form as well. On the other hand, the difficult v. 24bβ of the MT is wholly missing except for the word '[the

---

11. The rendering here is singular; otherwise the divine name is mostly translated as θεός (Isa. 60.16; Ps. 132.2, 5) and ἰσχύς (Isa. 49.26), whereas Isa. 1.24 is dubious; cf. Hatch, Redpath *et al.*, *Concordance*, III, p. 219b (with references). Cf. Olofsson, *God Is my Rock*, pp. 87-94.

12. Cf. A. Sperber, *The Bible in Aramaic* (5 vols.; Leiden: E.J. Brill, 1959–73), I; *ad loc.*; Díez Macho, *Neophyti 1*, pp. 334-37, 637-38.

tribes of] Israel'.[13] In v. 25a N1 has preserved the first divine name when it says in its characteristic fashion 'May the Word of the God of your Father be at your aid'. Of even greater interest than this is its rendering of אל (sic!) שׁדי: 'and may the God of the heavens [יאלה שמיא] bless you', as this form is identical with one of the LXX translations (Ps. 90.1/91.1; cf. ἐπουράνιος Ps. 67.14/68.15).[14] *Targum Onqelos* likewise spiritualizes, but does so without focusing on the person of Joseph as in N1, and in the process confirms the divine names in vv. 24bα and 25aα. Like N1, it has no reference to משׁם רעה אבן in v. 24bβ, but only to '[the descendants of] Israel'. However, unlike N1, it confirms literatim the ואת of the MT in v. 25aβ, in the form of the *nota accusativi* (וית שׁדי).

A stronger tendency to confirm the MT is shown by the Peshitta (P) in vv. 24-25, which includes direct translations of the divine names in v. 24bα and in v. 25aα, and even for a substantial part in v. 24bβ. As far as both *cruces* are concerned, P departs from the MT, as it reads שֵׁם, 'name', for שָׁם 'there', and אֵל, 'God', for אֵת. P also omits the preposition *min* at the beginning of v. 25.[15] Whether and, in the event, how P may have been influenced by the LXX or the Targums cannot be discussed here.[16]

The LXX exercised more influence in the Western tradition with respect to the Old Latin (L), the translation style of which, with minor variants, approaches that of the LXX.[17] The influence of the LXX may ultimately also be traceable in the Vulgate (V), even though V is the version that comes closest to the stabilized MT: (24) *sedit in forti arcus eius et dissoluta sunt vincula brachiorum et manium illius per manus potentis Iacob inde pastor egressus est lapis Israhel* (25a) *Deus patris*

13. One may wonder, however, whether there is not an allusion in *Targ. Neophyti* to v. 25aα in the last part of v. 24: 'with the strength of whose arm all the tribes of Israel are sustained'.

14. See n. 10 above.

15. *The Old Testament in Syriac According to the Peshitta Version*, I.1 (Leiden: E.J. Brill, 1977), *ad loc*.

16. Cf. M.D. Koster, 'Which Came First: The Chicken or the Egg? The Development of the Text of the Peshitta of Genesis and Exodus in the Light of Recent Studies', in P.B. Dirksen and M.J. Mulder, *The Peshitta: Its Early Text and History* (Leiden: E.J. Brill, 1988), pp. 99-126, esp. pp. 119-25.

17. In the transition from v. 24bβ to v. 25aα L reads: *inde convalescens / qui praevaluit Israhel* (25) *a deo patris tui et adiuvit te deus meus et benedixit te…* cf. *Vetus Latina*. II. *Genesis* (Freiburg, 1954), p. 514.

tui erit adiutor tuus et Omnipotens benedicet tibi benedictionibus…[18]
As we see, vv. 24b-25a follow the MT rather closely, as they literally
confirm שָׁם in v. 24bβ, as well as the words 'shepherd' and 'stone'.
However, in v. 25aα V, like P, omits the preposition *min*, and in
v. 25aβ it might have read 'God', or at least it seems to have avoided
אֵת by letting the divine name *Omnipotens* alone be the *subject* of the
following verb.

We are thus entitled to conclude that, in the course of the textual
history of Gen. 49.24b-25a the divine names and epithets seem to have
been stumbling-blocks in the process of transmission and translation of
the text.

As far as the conjectural Hebrew *archetype* of vv. 24b-25a is concerned, it might have been fairly close to the present MT. This may
apply to the crucial form שָׁם in v. 24bβ, all the more so as it is wit-
nessed by the LXX, which is the earliest version and which otherwise
deviates here. Apart from this there are no inner-Hebrew variants at this
point. On the other hand, the original text could well have read וְאֵל שַׁדַּי,
since this form is not only attested by such major versions as G, P, Targum Neophyti (and V), but also by Sam. and important Hebrew manuscripts like Ken 150.[19] All these witnesses may represent a significant
non-Massoretic reading. In this instance, the existence of a dual inner-
Hebrew tradition may have had other reasons than purely transmis-
sional ones. As for the rest of v. 24bβ (רֹעֶה אֶבֶן יִשְׂרָאֵל), it is, first of all,
this part that has been regarded as problematic by the LXX and other
witnesses, and which has been dealt with so differently. It may be held
that v. 24bβ is the *lectio difficilior*.

2. *Literary and Form-critical Remarks*

The literary and formal character of Gen. 49.24b-25 seem to be every
bit as complex as the text has turned out to be in text-historical terms,
as is evident from modern critical research. In the scrutiny of this
passage, much attention has been paid to the analysis of the literary

18. R. Weber (ed.), *Biblia Sacra iuxta Vulgatam Versionem*, I (Stuttgart:
Württembergische Bibelanstalt, 1969), *ad loc*.

19. Kennicott (ed.), *Vetus Testamentum Hebraicum*, p. 102 (MSS 84 and 150);
cf. also de Rossi, *Variae lectiones Veteris Testamenti*, I, p. 46b; and C.D. Ginsburg,
The Old Testament. I. *The Pentateuch* (London: British and Foreign Bible Society,
1926 [1911]), *ad loc*.

composition as well as to the definition of the form and genre of Gen. 49.3-27. Within this larger framework of undertakings, an analysis of the literary and formal character of Gen. 49.24b-25a will also have to be carried out,[20] although here only in brief.

The transition from the rather obscure v. 24a to v. 24b represents a shift in style; and the last half-verse seems to begin a new section. While vv. 23-24a are narrative in style and comprise five verbal tense-forms, vv. 24b-25aα contain a structural sequence of *nominal* character, including three nominal constructions, all of which are introduced by the preposition *min*. Further, this sequence is followed by another one, also consisting of three nominal constructions, v. 25aγδb in which the repeated *nomen regens* is the noun בִּרְכֹת, 'blessings' (but v. 26a has different constructions).

As for the *cruces* within this context, the adverb שָׁם in v. 24bβ deviates from the other words introduced by *min* (מִידֵי, v. 24bα, and מֵאֵל, v. 25aα) in being related, not by person (viz. 'hands' resp. 'God'), but by locale ('there'). It is hard to discern exactly the relation of the adverb to the rest of v. 24bβ, even though it is probably not unintelligible. As for וְאֵת in v. 25aβ, this lexeme seems to be ambiguous. It may, as in *Targum Onqelos*, be a *nota accusativi,* but what would the transitive verb then be? Or it might be the preposition אֵת '(together) with'; but such prepositional usage would break off the possible link to the three preceding *min*. In either case, the lexeme in question is difficult to understand.[21] The syntactical position of these two *cruces* seems to be as difficult as their text-historical one, even though they have quite different contexts.

The small unit comprising vv. 24b-25aαβ seems to have a mediatory position between vv. 23-24a, which is of a somewhat martial character, and to which v. 24b may be related, and the section of 'blessings' in vv. 25aγδb-26a, to which v. 25aβ seems to be a link. Additionally,

---

20. Cf. n. 2 above. By recapitulation of earlier research and by his own scrutiny Westermann, *Genesis 37–50*, pp. 246-78, has in a masterly way analysed the form and traditio-historical problems of the chapter. As for vv. 24b-25a, however, he seems to be in a quandary, and in his diagram on p. 276, v. 24b is lacking.

21. See, however, the discussion of J. Blau, 'Zum angeblichen Gebrauch von אֵת vor dem Nominativ',*VT* 4 (1954), pp. 7-19; N. Walker, 'Concerning the Function of '*ēth*', *VT* 5 (1955), pp. 314-15; and, finally, J. Blau, 'Gibt is ein emphatisches '*et* im Bibelhebraeisch?', *VT* 6 (1956), pp. 211-12. Cf. also H.P. Müller, in *ZDPV* 94 (1978), p. 66 n. 64; *HALAT*, pp. 1320a and 1321a.

vv. 24b-25aαβ are of divergent character as well. They point in opposite directions, v. 24b to the preceding and v. 25aαβ to the following. There is also a corresponding formal gap between v. 24b and v. 25aαβ, since v. 24b, together with vv. 22-24a, seems to speak in the third person, whereas v. 25aαβ addresses Joseph in the second person, in company with v. 26a. Targum Neophyti I, which preserves the formal shift here, has direct address in the first half of v. 22 as well, and seems to have smoothed out this formal opposition in the transmitted text. Finally, the listing style of v. 24b differs from that of v. 25aαβ, where a similar enumeration of divine names (אָבִיךָ אֵל and ([אֵל]שַׁדַּי) is expanded by brief verbal clauses, namely וְיַעְזְרֶךָ in v. 25aα and וִיבָרְכֶךָ in v. 25αβ.

These observations may argue for the probability of what is at least in part a new explanation of the literary composition and growth of the verses in question. First, the Blessing of Joseph seems to have been composed of small units, consisting of vv. 22, 23-24a, 24b, 25aαβ, 25aγδb, 26a and 26b, respectively, all differing in many respects. The composition will have been completed (long) before the later text history attested by the LXX onward. Second, the combination of the separate units may have been primarily made by an *additive and associative procedure of linking*, which is to say, between the words יָדָיו v. 24aβ and יְדֵי ('hands') in v. 24βα; further, between the sequence of preposition *min* in v. 24b and, across the formal gap, *min* in v. 25aα, and, finally, between the lexemes for 'bless/blessing' in v. 25aβ and v. 25aγ, that is, between ויברכך and ברכת. In the third place, the existence of small units that are combined in this way corresponds at least partly to what Westermann has defined formally as *Stammessprüche*, consisting of brief 'sayings', like proverbs, about individual tribes.[22]

As has often been observed in modern research, the individual 'tribal sayings' of Gen. 49.3-27 are very heterogeneous, as they vary considerably both in length and formal character. The longest 'sayings' are those dealing with Judah (vv. 8-12) and Joseph (vv. 22-26). Their length may be regarded as an indication of their special significance. When comparing the composition of Genesis 49 with its 'parallel' in Deuteronomy 33, some of their literary and form-historical problems, as well as their respective *traditio-historical* profiles, appear in stronger relief.[23] In the first place, it is significant that in Deuteronomy 33 the

22. Westermann, *Genesis 37–50*, p. 250.
23. Cf. n. 2 above.

inner relationship between Judah and Joseph has changed noticeably to Judah's disadvantage (as is shown by v. 7 compared with vv. 13-17), and that the 'saying' about Levi in Genesis 49 (vv. 5-7) has been totally transformed in a positive sense and expanded in Deuteronomy 33 (vv. 8-11). On this occasion, however, it might be more interesting to compare Gen. 49.24b-25a with Deut. 33.13, and in this connexion a synoptic arrangement will prove useful:

Gen. 49.24b-25:	Deut. 33.13:
מידי אביר יעקב	(וליוסף אמר)
משם רעה אבן ישראל	
מאל אביך ויעזרך	
ואת שדי ויברכך	מברכת יהוה ארצו
ברכת שמים מעל	ממגד שמים מטל
ברכת תהום רבצת תחת	ומתהום רבצת תחת
ברכת שדים ורחם	

The differences between the two texts are apparent. First of all, the various divine names and epithets in Gen. 49.24-25 have 'disappeared' in the Joseph 'saying' of Deut. 33.13-17; in their place, Deuteronomy has 'Yahweh' alone (v. 13). This is not unexpected, as Deuteronomy 33 is as a whole a more markedly theological composition than Genesis 49, and it clearly concentrates on Yahweh. By contrast, Genesis 49 has the name of Yahweh in but a single place, and it does so in a way that breaks with the rest of the context (v. 18), Deuteronomy 33 not only has Yahweh in individual 'sayings' (vv. 7, 13, 21, 23), but also in its framework (vv. 2-5 and 26-29), where Yahweh is first described in theophanic terms (v. 2; cf. Hab. 3.3ff.) and then (vv. 26-27) is also given special epithets like 'God of Jeshurun', 'rider of heavens ... and clouds' (רכב שמים/שחקים),[24] probably also 'eternal God' (אלהי קדם).[25] Finally, Yahweh is in v. 29 even metaphorically described as 'the shield (מגן) of your help, and the sword (חרב) of your trumph' (NRSV). However, when such divine names, epithets and metaphors are used in

---

24. See Ps. 68.5; cf. A. Cooper and M.H. Pope, 'Divine Names and Epithets in the Ugaritic Texts', in *Ras Shamra Parallels*, III (Rome: Pontificium Institutum biblicum, 1981), no. 40, p. 458.

25. So traditionally RSV. The text, however, is somewhat ambiguous. Now the NEB and RNEB have 'who humbled the *gods of old*'. Likewise, the NRSV has 'he subdues the ancient gods'.

the framework of Deuteronomy 33 one may well ask as to why the divine names and epithets of Gen. 49.24b-25a are totally lacking in v. 13.

Westermann may be perfectly justified in defining the original 'tribal sayings' as being brief, like proverbs. When he further maintains that the 'sayings' of Genesis 49 are 'profane', except for those aspects of them which have been further 'elaborated' or 'developed', this, too, may be right for the most part, but not wholly so. For it is at least disputable with respect to vv. 24b-25a. More than that, in view of the variegated composition of Genesis 49, what do the words 'profane' and 'elaborated' or 'developed' really mean? Would sharp distinctions like these be at all appropriate here? Even though Genesis 49 does not use the name of Yahweh, with the exception of the late addition of v. 18, this hardly implies that the composition is 'profane'. The 'sayings', or most of them, may well have been of this character; but the final result is not without theology. On the contrary, the divine names and epithets in vv. 24b-25aαβ constitute an essential part of the theological character of the composition. Moreover, it is *the very accumulation or 'clustering' of names and epithets which represents a real challenge to the study of this chapter*—and this fact requires a better explanation than it has up to now received.

Hermann Gunkel posed this problem in his commentary on Genesis, in terming the phenomenon here a 'solemn accumulation of divine names' and comparing it to a similar form in Gen. 48.15.[26] However, the problem might be more precisely defined as determining the *formal and theological function of these divine names and epithets* in the context of the Joseph 'saying' and of the composition as a whole.

3. The Individual Names and Epithets

The names and epithets of Gen. 49.24b-25aαβ are, as is generally recognized, of various kinds. They have often been analysed,[27] so that

---

26. Gunkel, *Genesis*, p. 486; and to Gen. 48.15 he says, p. 473: '*Häufung der Gottesnamen* bei feierlicher Anrufung vgl. als Parallelen etwa Ps. 80^2 50^1. In solchem Fall nennt der Polytheist alle die Götter, die er verehrt, der antike Monotheist alle die Namen Gottes, die er kennt'. Like Gunkel, Westermann speaks of 'die Häufung der Gottesnamen, die an 48,15-16 erinnert', but he calls it 'eine ebenfalls späte Bildung', *Genesis 37–50*, p. 272.

27. For bibliographical references see Westermann, *Genesis 37–50*, p. 273

brief remarks on each of them will suffice here. The most problematic features are the epithets in v. 24bβ, and somewhat more attention shall be paid to them.

a. אֲבִיר יַעֲקֹב, *'ᵃbîr ya 'ᵃqob*

The first name is rare and, in its other contexts, only late (Ps. 132.2,5; Isa. 49.26; 60.16, and, with 'Israel', also Isa. 1.24). However, since Albrecht Alt's epoch-making study on the subject in 1929,[28] it has commonly been held that the name is very old and belongs to a specific type.[29] This may still be maintained, in spite of recent criticism in favour of a younger date.[30] In addition, there has been some discussion about the exact meaning of אֲבִיר, related to two alternate readings: either אָבִיר*, used solely as part (אֲבִיר) of a divine name in the Old Testament, 'the Mighty One' (6 times, as listed above); or אַבִּיר, meaning mainly 'strong' (17 times), but sometimes (3 or 4) 'bull'.[31] Even though the latter sense is rather restricted, some scholars also relate it to Gen. 49.24b, in part with reference to 1 Kgs 12.25-33.[32] In the present context, as well as in the context of the other instances of אֲבִיר, this

(*Exkurs*), and *idem*, *Genesis. II. Genesis 12–36* (BKAT, 1.2; Neukirchen–Vluyn: Neukirchener Verlag, 1981), pp. 133-35; cf. also W.H. Schmidt, *Exodus* (BKAT, 2.1; Neukirchen–Vluyn: Neukirchener Verlag, 1988), pp. 147-52 (with references).

28. A. Alt, 'Der Gott der Väter', in *idem*, *Kleine Schriften zur Geschichte des Volkes Israel*, I (Munich: Chr. Kaiser Verlag, 1953), pp. 1-78, esp. pp. 24-29; cf. his response to early criticism, 'Zum "Gott der Väter"', *Palästinajahrbuch* 36 (1940), pp. 53-104. Cf. H. Weidmann, *Die Patriarchen und ihre Religion* (Göttingen: Vandenhoeck & Ruprecht, 1968), pp. 126-67; and n. 30 below.

29. Cf., i.a., Zobel, *Stammesspruch*, pp. 22f.; R. de Vaux, *The Early History of Israel* (2 vols.; London: Darton, Longman & Todd, 1978), I, p. 272; Seebass, 'Die Stämmesprüche', pp. 337-39; Koch, 'Die Götter', p. 13.

30. See, i.a., J. Hoftijzer, *Die Verheissungen an die drei Erzväter* (Leiden: E.J. Brill, 1956), pp. 95f.; J. Van Seters, 'The Religion of the Patriarchs in Genesis', *Bib* 61 (1980), pp. 220-33; Köckert, *Vätergott*, pp. 63-67, 147-61; cf. also H. Vorländer, *Mein Gott* (Neukirchen–Vluyn: Neukirchener Verlag, 1975), pp. 203-14; R. Albertz, *Persönliche Frömmigkeit und offizielle Religion* (Stuttgart: Calwer Verlag, 1978), pp. 77-96.

31. Cf. H.H. Schmid, 'אַבִּיר *'abbīr stark'*, *THAT*, I, cols. 25-27; and esp. A.S. Kapelrud, 'אָבִיר אַבִּיר', *ThWAT*, I, cc. 43-46 (with references).

32. Cf. Coppens, 'La bénédiction de Jacob', pp. 101-102; F. Dumermuth, 'Zur deuteronomischen Kulttheologie und ihren Voraussetzungen', *ZAW* 70 (1958), pp. 59-98; M. Weippert, in *ZDPV* 77 (1961), p. 105; Vorländer, *Mein Gott*, p. 186; Smith, *Early History*, pp. 16-17.

sense is definitely unlikely; nor has it any support in the ancient textual history. The theologically motivated distinction expressed by these two words need not be late at all.[33]

b. רעה, *ro'eh*

The word is generally taken to be a noun, 'shepherd',[34] all the more so as the title was an ancient epithet of gods and kings outside of Israel as well.[35] However, it is noteworthy that in the closely related text Gen. 48.15bβ the same form is used verbally as a *participle*, equipped with the *nota acc*. Moreover, it is the predicate in a relative clause that has no relative pronoun, whereas the parallel relative clause in v. 15bα has the relative pronoun:

האלהים אשר התהלכו אבתי
האלהים הרעה אתי מעודי

It is furthermore remarkable that the LXX has a participle (ὁ κατισχύσας) in Gen. 49.24bβ, while at the other end of the textual development, the V has a noun (*pastor*).[36] It might be worth considering, then, that in its original setting רֹעֶה in v. 24bβ may not have been a noun, but a verbal form like the similar form in 48.15b, even though it will have been as a nominal form, namely a *participle*, that became understood as a noun at an early date.[37] If this was the case, then v. 24bβ may furthermore be regarded as a sentence in its own right, in which the next two words represent the subject, and רעה the predicate. As for the relationship to the crucial form משם, finally, the sentence

33. See esp. Kapelrud, 'אָבִיר אֲבִיר', *ThWAT*, I, col. 45; Olofsson, *God Is my Rock*, p. 90.

34. Cf. Maag, 'Der Hirte Israels'; P. de Robert, *Le berger d'Israël* (Neuchâtel, 1968), esp. pp. 41-44; Vorländer, *Mein Gott*, pp. 196f.; J.A. Soggin, 'רעה r'b weiden', *THAT*, II, col. 793; G. Wallis, 'רָעָה rā'āh', *ThWAT*, VII, cols. 566-76, esp. 572-74; also Olofsson, *God Is my Rock*, pp. 94-95.

35. For the Old Testament see n. 34; for Israel's environment see D. Müller, 'Der gute Hirte', *ZÄS* 86 (1961), pp. 126-44; I. Seibert, *Hirt, Herde, König: Zur Herausbildung des Königtums in Mesopotamien* (Berlin: Akademie Verlag, 1969).

36. A similar development may be observed as for נושע, Zech. 9.9; cf. Sæbø, *Sacharja 9–14*, pp. 51-52.

37. Wallis, 'רָעָה rā'āh', *ThWAT*, VII, col. 573, indicates that as far as the kings are concerned the verbal aspects prevail: 'Eher als das nominalisierte Ptz. "Hirte" hat das verbum finitum "weiden" in übertragenem Sinne Eingang gefunden'. This may even be seriously considered in connexion with God as well; see Ps. 23.1 and esp. Ps. 80.2, where there are interesting references both to 'Israel' and to 'Joseph'.

may, in analogy with the construction in 48.15bβ, be held to constitute an asyndetic relative clause, that is, without the relative pronoun.[38] Some such syntactical understanding of v. 24bβ as this would solve a number of problems: there would be no inner opposition between two unrelated nouns (רעה versus אבן) which would then have to be explained away as either a double tradition or a conflation which was later understood as being in apposition; the relation to מֹשֶׁם, or, originally, perhaps to שֵׁם alone, would be easier to explain; and, last but not least, an early shift from verb to noun would also render the text-historical problems both more intelligible and more explicable. On the other hand, an absolute use of a transitive verb is surely a serious problem; but also as a noun רעה is unrelated here.

c. אבן ישראל, *'eben yiśrā'ēl*

The use of אבן, 'stone', in this construction is unique in the Old Testament. It has been questioned, all the more so since צוּר is otherwise used, both rather often and especially in the Psalms, as the specific divine epithet designating God as the 'Rock'.[39] However, as is indicated by a Ugaritic parallel, this is not unique in a broader context,[40] and there is in any case a usage of אבן in Isa. 8.14 that is similar, though not identical, to the use here. There might very well have been religious reasons for the striking 'disproportion' between אבן and צור as divine epithets. On the one hand, אבן ישראל may be connected with specific Bethel traditions.[41] But, on the other hand, there also existed broad,

38. Cf. C. Brockelmann, *Hebräische Syntax* (Neukirchen Kreis Moers: Neukirchener Verlag, 1956), §146.

39. Cf. M.P. Knowles, '"The Rock, his work is perfect": Unusual Imagery for God in Deut. xxxii', *VT* 39 (1989), pp. 307-22; Olofsson, *God Is my Rock*, pp. 94-95; otherwise A.S. Kapelrud, 'אֶבֶן', *ThWAT*, I, cols. 50-53; H.-J. Fabry, 'עוּר', *ThWAT*, VI, cols. 968-83 (with further references); also J. Gamberoni, 'מעבה', *ThWAT*, IV, cols. 1064-74. Without any text-historical support Freedman, 'Divine Names', p. 65, contends that 'The word *'bn* may be understood as by-form of *bn*, "son"', and that 'it should be read as plural', whereby he renders v. 24bβ 'Shepherd of the sons of Israel', as does A.S. van der Woude ('צוּר *ṣūr* Fels', *THAT*, II, cols. 538-43), col. 542; for yet another radical emendation by Dahood—which denies that אבן in this context is a divine epithet—see n. 5 above.

40. Cf. Cooper and Pope, 'Divine Names and Epithets', pp. 336-37; B. Vawter, 'The Canaanite Background of Genesis 49', *CBQ* 17 (1955), pp. 1-18, esp. pp. 7-16.

41. See Gen. 28.11, 17-19; 35.14-15; cf. esp. Kapelrud, 'אֶבֶן', *ThWAT*, I, col. 53.

mostly prophetical polemics against the worship of sacred stones as well as of gods of stone,[42] and that might have had a negative effect on the use of a divine epithet of this kind. Nevertheless, אבן ישׂראל, when used as a divine epithet, represented a highly metaphorical use and conception; at the same time, however, it might have been on the fringe of what was considered theologically tolerable in Israel. In any case, all this is testimony to the early age of the epithet in question.

d. אל אביך, 'ēl 'ābîkā

The character of this divine name is nearly compatible with the first name אביר יעקב. Both of them belong to the ambit of Patriarchal religion and represent one of its most specific characteristics, which indicates the intimate, almost familial, relationship of the faith expressed.[43] There is a religio-historical problem as to the exact understanding of אל as part of this name, and in similar cases like Gen. 46.3, namely, whether it is to be understood generically, as in the usual, anonymous rendering 'God of your father', or as the specific divine name El, hence 'El your father'.[44] This may not actually be relevant to the matter at hand, even though in this context the former example may be the more appropriate.[45] The problem is, however, made more delicate by the next name.

e. שׁדי (אל), ('ēl) šadday

The name שׁדי is generally (40 times out of a total of 48, mostly in Job) used alone;[46] and a discussion of its use in Gen. 49.25aβ, which is

---

42. See Lev. 26.1; Deut. 4.28; 16.22; Isa. 37.19; Jer. 2.27; 3.9; Ezek. 20.32; cf. Kapelrud, 'אֶבֶן', *ThWAT*, I, col. 53; Olofsson, *God Is my Rock*, p. 95.

43. Cf. Alt, 'Der Gott der Väter', pp. 13-24, esp. p. 19; de Vaux, *Early History*, p. 272: 'This religion of the god of the father is the earliest form of patriarchal religion of which we can have any knowledge'; further, i.a., K.T. Andersen, 'Der Gott meines Vaters', *ST* 16 (1962), pp. 170-88; Vorländer, *Mein Gott*, pp. 184-214; E. Jenni, 'אָב 'āb Vater', *THAT*, I, cols. 9-11; W.H. Schmidt, 'אֵל 'ēl Gott', *THAT*, I, cols. 142-49; H. Ringgren, 'אב', *ThWAT*, I, cols. 2-19; F.M. Cross, 'אֵל', *ThWAT*, I, col. 273.

44. Cf. N. Wyatt, 'The Problem of the "God of the Fathers"', *ZAW* 90 (1978), pp. 101-104, and the rebuttal by Seebass, 'Die Stämmesprüche', p. 337 n. 19.

45. Cf., i.a., Schmidt, 'אֵל 'ēl Gott', *THAT*, I, col. 146; also R. de Vaux, 'El et Baal, le Dieu des pères et Yahweh', in *Ugaritica*, VI (Paris, 1969), pp. 501-17; de Moor, *The Rise of Yahwism*, pp. 229-34.

46. Among many studies see E. Burrows, 'The Meaning of El Šaddai', *JTS* 41

presumably the oldest instance,[47] would not seem to be dependent on solving the crucial problem of וְאֵת versus the variant וְאֵל which can claim considerable text-historical support. Yet it is noteworthy that שַׁדַּי never occurs alone in Genesis, but only 'in the full construct form' אֵל שַׁדַּי.[48] Therefore the question may be raised as to whether the *crux* in v. 25aβ might somehow be grounded in the parallelization of the anonymous name אֵל אָבִיךָ with the proper name שַׁדַּי (אֵל). Whatever the case may be, שַׁדַּי is rather often connected with other divine names.[49] Moreover, it is likely that it was linked with Bethel, among other sacred places,[50] and that it was related to the giving of 'blessing', in particular the 'blessing' of fertility.[51] In the first place, then, the name of שַׁדַּי in Gen. 49.25 may be more closely related to the following section than to what precedes, a fact which only serves to intensify the literary problems.

4. *On the Wider Context of the Names and Epithets*

The *divine names and epithets of Gen. 49.24b-25a* seem to have been very significant, especially seen in a religio-historical perspective, as

(1940), pp. 152-61; Cross, *Canaanite Myth and Hebrew Epic*; and esp. K. Koch, 'Šaddaj', in *idem, Studien zur alttestamentlichen*, pp. 118-52 (= *VT* 26 [1976], pp. 299-332); and Weippert, 'שַׁדַּי *Šaddaj* (Gottesname)', *THAT*, II, cols. 873-81; Olofsson, *God Is my Rock*, pp. 111-16; *HALAT*, pp. 1319b-21a (with references).

47. See Burrows, 'The Meaning of El Šaddai', p. 159; Koch, 'Šaddaj', p. 151; cf. also Weippert, 'שַׁדַּי *Šaddaj* (Gottesname)', *THAT*, II, col. 880.

48. Cf. M. Haran, 'The Religion of the Patriarchs: An Attempt at a Synthesis', *ASTI* 4 (1965), pp. 30-55, and see esp. p. 47 n. 10; Weippert, 'שַׁדַּי *Šaddaj* (Gottes-name)', *THAT*, II, cols. 873-74, distinguishes between 'Kurzform' (*šadday*) and 'Langform' (*'el Šadday*). When Koch, 'Die Götter', p. 26, says that 'die direkte Zusammenstellung von El und Schaddai nur in P auftaucht', he also includes in P (Gen. 17.1; 28.3; 35.11; 48.3; Exod. 6.3) the 'full form' in Gen. 43.14 which is otherwise assigned to J (*HALAT*, p. 1319b) or E (cf. O. Eissfeldt, *Hexateuch-Syn-opse: Die Erzählung der fünf Bücher Mose und des Buches Josua mit dem Anfange des Richterbuches* [Darmstadt: Wissenschaftliche Buchgesellschaft, 2nd edn, 1962 (1922)], p. 89), cf. p. 124; and in Gen. 49.25a he prefers the MT reading. Both are disputable.

49. See the listing in Koch, 'Šaddaj', pp. 125-26, 129; cf. Weippert, 'שַׁדַּי *Šaddaj* (Gottesname)', *THAT*, II, col. 880.

50. See Gen. 28.18-19, esp. 35.11-15 and 48.3; cf. Koch, 'Šaddaj', pp. 146-47.

51. See the *birkot*-sequence of vv. 25b-26a, and cf. Koch, 'Šaddaj', pp. 142-46, 151.

each of them has a history of its own. After the preceding brief remarks
on the individual epithets and names, the discussion that was inaugu-
rated in section 2 as to the key question of *what function the specific
accumulation of these names and epithets might have in their context*
must now be pursued. This may be done in a tripartite way, beginning
with the literary composition.

a. *Syntactical*

Syntactically, the specific position of the individual epithet or name
may contribute to a better understanding of the growth of the composition. In particular, it may prove possible to differentiate somewhat further the phenomenon of additive and associative linking of smaller
units which was noted above. The structural sequence of three *min*-
units in vv. 24b-25a varies to a greater extent than is immediately
apparent: the sequence not only bridges the formal gap between vv. 24
and 25, but also includes, on the one hand, a unit (v. 24bβ) which is
possibly not a nominal unit, but a self-contained sentence in its own
right, the original form of which might have been שם רעה אבן ישראל
The insertion of an introductory *min* into this sentence seems to have
transformed it into an asyndetic relative clause. On the other hand, it
includes, v. 25aαβ, two parallel divine epithets or names that have been
expanded by the addition of parallelized sentences promising protection
and blessing, the last of which has been extended through a sequence of
'blessing' descriptions (vv. 25aγδb-26a).

In this complex composition, the formal combining element is represented by the sequence of three *min* which here unifies some fairly dis-
parate material. The different divine epithets and names constitute the
unifying element with respect to the content. In all their diversity, and
in a unique way, the names and epithets hold the variegated materials
together. A tentative translation of vv. 24-25, which also indicates their
structure, may now be given:

> But his bow remained steady,
>> and flexible were his strong arms
>
> from (by/because of) the hands of *the Mighty One of Jacob*,
> from where *the Stone of Israel* is guarding (/protecting),
> from *the God of your father*,
>> who will help you,
>> and *God Almighty*,
>>> who will bless you:

blessings of the heavens above,
blessings of the deep that crouches below,
blessings of the breasts and the womb.[52]

b. *Religio-historical*

The religio-historical study of the divine epithets and names in Gen. 49.24b-25aαβ has concentrated more on them in isolation from one another than in their present combination in the context. In his study on *Šadday*, however, Klaus Koch has commented on the various connexions of this divine name with other divine names and epithets as representing '*Ketten von Gottesbezeichnungen*',[53] but in his interesting study he has given the priority to the possible relationship and identity of the deities in question than to the form-historical and religio-historical problem of what Gunkel, referring to Gen. 48.15, called the 'the solemn accumulation of divine names' (*feierliche Häufung der Gottesnamen*), as mentioned above. The question is whether we find anywhere else a similar phenomenon that may be able to shed some light on this unique structure.

In the Akkadian creation epic, *Enūma eliš*, there is a form which seems to be analogous, but which, as far as I am aware, has not been included in any discussion of Genesis 49, namely the listing of the *fifty names of Marduk* which were recited with due solemnity on the fourth day of the New Year's festival (tablets vi.122–vii.144).[54] With its hymnic style and unique abundance of divine names this 'proclamation' has as one of its goals the broad glorification of the victorious god, as is also announced in the framework of the list (vi.121-23 and especially vii.143-44). The multiplicity of names are intended as an expression of Marduk's supreme position and of his great honour—although the inner relationship of the names involves many problems of 'identification'.[55]

---

52. Cf. the different translation of Cross and Freedman, *Yahwistic Poetry*, pp. 75-76, 89-92.

53. Koch, 'Šaddaj', p. 125.

54. See *ANET* (3rd edn, 1969), pp. 60, 69-72; cf. esp. F.M.T. de Liagre Böhl, 'Die fünfzig Namen des Marduk', *AfO* 11 (1936), pp. 191-218, repr. in *idem*, *Opera Minora* (Groningen/Djakarta, 1953), pp. 282-312, 504-508; also K. Tallqvist, *Akkadische Götterepitheta* (Helsingfors: Finska orientsällskapet, 1938), esp. pp. 362-72.

55. Note also another important aspect observed by Böhl, *Opera Minora*, p. 284: 'Die Zahl gehört zum Kosmos, im Gegensatz zum Chaos. Wenn Marduk als die Summe seiner Funktionen fünfzig Namen hat oder erhält, so bedeutet das, dass

In a similar way, we find that a broad and 'solemn' expression of divine assistance and protection, as well as the blessing of a tribe like Joseph's, is made by a special 'listing' of ancient divine names and epithets in Gen. 49.24b-25aαβ. The prime *raison d'être* for this 'listing' and accumulation, unique in the Old Testament, may be not so much the narrative and assurance of divine help and gifts in itself, which are often and quite variously expressed in the Old Testament, as it is the unparalleled way in which it has been done in this instance. The 'proclamation' of ancient divine names and epithets here may therefore be understood as an *exclusive expression of the power and steadfast reliability of the patriarchal God.* It may not be just an incidental circumstance that this takes place within the framework of the 'saying' of the tribe of Joseph, but it is more likely that this 'saying' of this dominant tribe was regarded as the most strategic point for the proclamation of the dominating position of the ancient God of Israel.

c. *Traditio-historical and Theological*
In traditio-historical and theological perspectives the accumulation of different divine epithets and names in Genesis 49 may involve a deep tension between their mutual diversity and respective history, on the one hand, and the fact of their being 'united' in a composition of this kind, on the other. In spite of their individual history and character, however, the very combination of divine names and epithets may even be understood as a witness to the 'unity' of the patriarchal God, or the other way round, some notion of divine 'unity' may have been a kind of *conditio sine qua non* for the possibility of the special composition of Gen. 49.24b-25aαβ.

This supposition may be additionally substantiated by a triangular comparison of Genesis 49 with Deuteronomy 33 and Exod. 6.2b-3, which represent different traditio-historical strata.[56] When one notes, as

er den Kosmos regiert und umfasst'. See, further, W.G. Lambert, 'The Historical Development of the Mesopotamian Pantheon: A Study in Sophisticated Polytheism', in H. Goedicke and J.J.M. Roberts (eds.), *Unity and Diversity: Essays in the History, Literature, and Religion of the Ancient Near East* (Baltimore: Johns Hopkins University Press, 1975), pp. 191-200; W.G. Lambert, 'Babylonien und Israel', *TRE*, V, pp. 67-79, esp. '7. Babylonischer Monotheismus', pp. 77-78.

56. When Van Seters, 'Religion of the Patriarchs', p. 226, evaluates Gen. 49.25-26 as having 'been borrowed, with a few changes, from the Blessing of Moses', i.e. from Deut. 33.13-16, he is not doing justice to the ancient character of Gen. 49.25. In contrast, Smith, *Early History*, p. 17, finds that the 'phrase *šadayim*

mentioned above, that Deut. 33.13 has 'replaced' the divine names and epithets of Genesis 49 by the one name, *Yahweh*, this may be seen as not only a contrast with the earlier names and epithets—*Yahweh* being now the exclusive name for the God of Israel—but even to some extent as a continuation of the ancient tendency towards what might be termed a 'pluralistic' way of expressing the 'unity' of God. Both in Exodus 3 and, above all, in the P-context of Exod. 6.2b-3, it is just this that has become a programmatic theological stand and 'dogma'.[57] Seen in this perspective, the 'proclamation' of names and epithets in Gen. 49.24b-25a may, in its specific way, represent an early contribution to the monotheistic trend and tendency in Israel's faith and theology.

5. Conclusion

In conclusion it may be stated in all brevity that the accumulative concentration of divine names and epithets in Gen. 49.24b-25a may be regarded as an old and important stepping-stone in the long traditio-historical process of indigenous theological apprehension of God in ancient Israel.

wārahām in v. 25e echoes Ugaritic titles of the goddesses Asherah and Anat', and concludes, p. 22, that 'Genesis 49:25-26 possibly points to an early stage when Israel knew three deities, El, Asherah, and Yahweh'. However, such a linkage of the materials breaks with the whole trend and tendency demonstrated above, and is not likely.

57. See n. 1 above; and N. Lohfink, 'Die priesterschriftliche Abwertung der Tradition von der Offenbarung des Jahwenamens an Mose', *Bib* 49 (1968), pp. 1-18; *idem*, 'Zur Geschichte der Diskussion über den Monotheismus im Alten Israel', in E. Haag (ed.), *Gott, der einzige: Zur Entstehung des Monotheismus in Israel* (Freiburg: Herder, 1985), pp. 9-25.

Chapter 5

GOD'S NAME IN EXODUS 3.13-15:
AN EXPRESSION OF REVELATION OR OF VEILING?

Linguistically and exegetically, historically and theologically, Exod. 3.14 has occupied a key position in Old Testament scholarship and beyond, because it appears to be the only instance in the Old Testament which seems to offer an explanation of the specific Israelite name of God יהוה. The comments and contributions to this central issue are almost countless.[1]

1.   As for the very extensive literature on the question (excluding Old Testament theologies, commentaries and general reference works) special attention may be paid to: R. Abba, 'The Divine Name of Yahweh', *JBL* 80 (1961), pp. 320-28; W.F. Albright, 'The Name Yahweh', *JBL* 43 (1924), pp. 370-78; B. Albrektson, 'The Syntax of אהיה אשר אהיה in Exodus 3:14', in *Words and Meaning: Festschrift D.W. Thomas* (London: Cambridge University Press, 1968), pp. 15-28; B. Alfrink, 'La prononciation "Jehova" du Tétragramme', *OTS* 5 (1948), pp. 43-63; A. Alt, 'Ein ägyptisches Gegenstück zu Ex 3^{14}', *ZAW* 58 (1940), pp. 159-60; W.R. Arnold, 'The Divine Name in Exodus iii.14', *JBL* 24 (1905), pp. 107-65; R.A. Bowman, 'Yahweh the Speaker', *JNES* 3 (1944), pp. 1-8; S.S. Cohon, 'The Name of God', *HUCA* 23 (1951), pp. 579-604; F.M. Cross, 'Yahweh and the God of the Patriarchs', *HTR* 55 (1962), pp. 225-59; L. Delekat, '*Yáho-Yahwáe* und die alttestamentlichen Gottesnamenkorrekturen', in *Tradition und Glaube: Festschrift K.G. Kuhn* (Göttingen: Vandenhoeck & Ruprecht, 1971), pp. 23-75; G.R. Driver, 'The Original Form of the Name "Yahweh": Evidence and Conclusions', *ZAW* 46 (1928), pp. 7-25; *idem*, 'The Interpretation of *Yhwh* as a Participial Form', *JBL* 73 (1954), pp. 125-31; A.-M. Dubarle, 'La signification du nom de Iahweh', *RSPT* 35 (1951), pp. 3-21; B.D. Eerdmans, 'The Name Jahu', *OTS* 5 (1948), pp. 1-29; O. Eissfeldt, 'Neue Zeugnisse für die Aussprache des Tetragramms als Jahwe', *ZAW* 53 (1935), pp. 59-76 (repr. in *idem*, *Kleine Schriften* [Tübingen: J.C.B. Mohr (Paul Siebeck), 1962–79], II, pp. 81-96); K. Elliger, 'Zur Frage nach dem Alter des Jahweglaubens bei den Israeliten', *TBl* 9 (1930), cols. 97-103; D.N. Freedman, 'The Name of the God of Moses', *JBL* 79 (1960), pp. 151-56; J. Gray, 'The God *YW* in the Religion of Canaan', *JNES* 12 (1953), pp. 278-83; S. Herrmann, 'Der

At first sight, one may easily have the impression that in the main question of God's name a certain consensus has been reached, namely that the long form יהוה given above is older than the short form יה/יה (or יהו), and that most probably it may be regarded as the imperfect verb form of the basic root of היה/הוה. On closer examination of the question, however, general agreement in fact counts for little. Rather, most of the questions on this point appear to be still open. The somewhat confusing multifaceted nature of the relevant research, both older and more recent, which acts like an impressive and colourful armada of the most diverse ideas, points of view and interpretations, may be a result partly of the complex nature of the biblical—and subsequently of the extra-biblical—material and of the inadequacy of our actual knowledge, and partly because one does not distinguish sufficiently cleanly or

alttestamentliche Gottesname', *EvT* 26 (1966), pp. 281-93; J.P. Hyatt, 'Yahweh as the "God of My Father"', *VT* 5 (1955), pp. 130-36; J.G. Janzen, 'What's in a Name? "Yahweh" in Exodus 3 and the Wider Biblical Context', *Int* 33 (1979), pp. 227-39; J. Kinyongo, *Origine et signification du nom divin Yahvé à la lumière de récents travaux et de traditions sémitico-bibliques (Ex 3,13-15 et 6,2-8)* (BBB, 35; Bonn: Peter Hanstein, 1970); K.G. Kuhn, 'יו, יהו, יהוה: Über die Entstehung des Namens Jahwe', in *Orientalistische Studien: Festschrift E. Littmann* (Leiden: E.J. Brill, 1935), pp. 25-42; G. Lambert, 'Que signifie le nom divin YHWH?', *NRT* 74 (1952), pp. 897-915; R. Mayer, 'Der Gottesname Jahwe im Lichte der neuesten Forschung', *BZ* NF 2 (1958), pp. 26-53; E.C.B. MacLaurin, 'YHWH: The Origin of the Tetragrammaton', *VT* 12 (1962), pp. 439-63; D.J. McCarthy, 'Exod 3:14: History, Philology and Theology', *CBQ* 40 (1978), pp. 311-22; A.R. Millard, 'YW and YHW Names', *VT* 30 (1980), pp. 208-12; S. Mowinckel, 'The Name of the God of Moses', *HUCA* 32 (1961), pp. 121-33; A. Murtonen, *A Philological and Literary Treatise on the Old Testament Divine Names* (StudOr, 18.1; Helsinki, 1952); S. Norin, 'Jô-Namen und Jehô-Namen', *VT* 29 (1979), pp. 87-97; J. Obermann, 'The Divine Name Yhwh in the Light of Recent Discoveries', *JBL* 68 (1949), pp. 301-23; G.H. Parke-Taylor, *YAHWEH: The Divine Name in the Bible* (Waterloo/Ontario, 1975); M. Rose, *Jahwe: Zum Streit um den alttestamentlichen Gottesnamen* (ThSt, 122; Zürich: Theologischer Verlag, 1978); W.H. Schmidt, 'Der Jahwename und Ex 3,14', in *Textgemäss: Festschrift E. Würthwein* (Göttingen: Vandenhoeck & Ruprecht, 1979), pp. 123-38; M.H. Segal, 'El, Elohim and YHWH in the Bible', *JQR* 46 (1955), pp. 89-115; W. von Soden, 'Jahwe "Er ist, Er erweist sich"', *WO* 3 (1966), pp. 177-87; G.J. Thierry, 'The Pronunciation of the Tetragrammaton', *OTS* 5 (1948), pp. 30-42; R. de Vaux, 'The Revelation of the Divine Name YHWH', in *Proclamation and Presence: Festschrift G.H. Davies* (London, 1970), pp. 48-75; T.C. Vriezen, ''ehje 'ašer 'ehje', in *Festschrift Alfred Bertholet zum 80. Geburtstag* (Tübingen: J.C.B. Mohr, 1950), pp. 498-512; B.N. Wambacq, ''eheyeh 'ašer 'eheyeh', *Bib* 59 (1978), pp. 317-38.

separate clearly enough the various references and connexions which intersect at this point and on which theological assessment and evaluation depend.[2]

In the present chapter there can only be made a few short observations on the ongoing debate about a very extensive and difficult topic, concentrating on three areas, namely the literary nature of Exod. 3.13-15, the linguistic question of God's name, and the theological aspects of both.[3]

1. *Literary Questions*

Considering the literary questions first of all, it may be appropriate to start by referring to the inaugural lecture of Hans Walter Wolff in Heidelberg. At this occasion in his notable reflections in 'Zur Thematik der elohistischen Fragmente im Pentateuch' he attacked 'the bureaucratic murderer of the Elohist' and presented with the aid of several texts positively important characteristics of an 'originally independent source document' E, which among other things consist of linking together traditional material 'by means of stylistic points which demonstrate a highly reflected art of composition' as well as emphasizing the fear of God and obedience in the drafts of a syncretistic era.[4] It is noteworthy, however, that Wolff did not make full use of Exodus 3 for the elohistic subject matter, given that Exod. 3.13-15 could have made an important contribution.

Exod. 3.13-15 belongs admittedly to the elohistic parts of the chapter which can readily give the impression of a homogeneous narrative, which on the other hand fits in to the larger narrative context of Exodus 1–14.[5] Yet the juxtaposition of 3.7-8 and 3.9-12, as well as several

2. Cautiously interpretative summaries are to be found particularly in the contributions of Mayer, 'Der Gottesname Jahwe', and de Vaux, 'Revelation, pp. 48-75, as well as W.H. Schmidt, both in his commentary (*Exodus*) and in the article listed above; cf. n. 44 below.

3. A critical opinion will also be given about methodology in particular, but in order to be brief it will not be possible to undergird much in the way that could be wanted.

4. H.W. Wolff, 'Zur Thematik der elohistischen Fragmente im Pentateuch', *EvT* 29 (1969), pp. 59-72 (also in his *Gesammelte Studien zum AT* [TBü, 22; [Munich: Chr. Kaiser Verlag, rev. edn, 1973], pp. 402-17).

5. Cf. G. Fohrer, *Überlieferung und Geschichte des Exodus: Eine Analyse von Ex 1-15* (BZAW, 91; Berlin: W. de Gruyter, 1964). See also M. Greenberg, 'The

doublings, tensions and repetitions, makes the acceptance of two narrative threads probable;[6] traditionally and even today with relatively great
unanimity they are apportioned to J (3.1abα*, 2-4a, 5, 7-8*, 16-17*)
and to E (3.1bβ*, 4b*, 6, 9-15*).[7] W.H. Schmidt assesses the analysis
of these two interlinked passages, which is continued in his detailed
commentary in a remarkable fashion, as 'a model of literary criticism'.[8]

Here, however, too rigid a literary method of consideration is hardly
adequate. Even textually the position of הָאֱלֹהִים in 1bβ and אֱלֹהִים in 4b
is not certain, as can be noted from *BHK* and *BHS*; otherwise, there is
an interchange between אֱלֹהִים (4b, 14, 15) and הָאֱלֹהִים (1bβ, 6b, 11-
13). Even more obvious are several inequalities in the section 9-12. As
this section—like 13-15 too—is in the form of a speech from God with
a dialogue inserted, the form וְהוֹצֵא in v. 10b (with the somewhat over-
ornate object אֶת־עַמִּי בְנֵי־יִשְׂרָאֵל; cf. 12b, which reads differently) may
appear strange, as does the speaking about God in the third person in
v. 12b. A well-known *crux*—both syntactically and as regards sense—
is produced, moreover, by the word 'token' in v. 12a, to which Childs
dedicates a detailed discussion in his commentary.[9] According to Noth,
v. 12 'has obviously been handed down in a fragmentary fashion'.[10] Be
that as it may, the separation of a particular elohistic level in Exodus 3
is hardly adequate when this 'level' is understood in a too one-dimen-
sional literary way as an isolated source document, or, when differentiating between older and newer material, the older is regarded as
'genuine' and the newer as 'not genuine', in other words as a 'gloss' or
'interpolation'. Rather, accepting the existence of an E-level here, it
would be appropriate to understand (regard) the section as the final

Thematic Unity of Exodus III–XI', in *idem*, *Fourth World Congress of Jewish
Studies: Papers*, I (Jerusalem, 1967), pp. 151-54; G. von Rad, 'Beobachtungen an
der Moseerzählung Exodus 1–14', *EvT* 31 (1971), pp. 579-88 (also in his
Gesammelte Studien zum Alten Testament, II, pp. 189-98). For scholars who deny
the section to E, cf. de Vaux, 'Revelation', p. 48 n. 2.

6.   Cf. W. Richter, *Die sogenannten vorprophetischen Berufungsberichte*
(FRLANT, 101; Göttingen: Vandenhoeck & Ruprecht, 1970), pp. 58-72.

7.   Cf. Schmidt, *Exodus, ad loc.*

8.   Schmidt, *Exodus*, p. 107.

9.   B.S. Childs, *Exodus: A Commentary* (OTL; London: SCM Press, 1974),
pp. 56-60.

10.   M. Noth, *Das zweite Buch Mose: Exodus* (ATD, 5; Göttingen: Vandenhoeck & Ruprecht, 1959), p. 29.

result of a restless tradition process which has passed through several stages.

This traditio-historical view attracts special interest when it comes to considering the much-debated question of the inner relationship of vv. 13-15, especially as it appears to be of considerable importance for the theological assessment.

Verses 13-15 contain a question asked of Moses to God (13) as well as God's answers (14 and 15); it is above all the answers which are problematical. The clumsiness of the triple ויאמר in vv. 14-15a has often been noted, whereby the question has been raised as to which of the answers is the 'correct one' to the question in v. 13, or, to express the matter differently, whether v. 14 or v. 15 is an 'addition'.

W.H. Schmidt has recently dealt with the question in detail in his commentary. First, he mentions a few scholars who regard v. 14 as an 'addition', and even more could be named.[11] He himself sides with the interpretation of Holzinger, who regards v. 15 as a later, editorial 'parenthesis between E and J'. Yet his reasons for this appear to be hardly valid, for first of all he has attached too much importance to the adverb עוד ('moreover') in v. 15a. With a close sequence of three identical verb forms it is in fact only natural that a facilitating adverb should be added to the final verb. Thus the 'moreover' presupposes the triple use of 'said', yet says nothing about the possible 'originality' of the respective single verb forms. Otherwise the stylistic awkwardness affects v. 14 more than v. 15a. And second, it does not really hold true that God is 'the God who reveals his name in v. 14' (Schmidt, *Exodus*, p. 132), for in v. 14 God does not directly tell his name but rather he paraphrases it in an interpretative, explanatory way. This too is actually admitted twice by Schmidt, once in his commentary (p. 134), where he says that v. 14 gives 'only an indirect answer to the question posed in v. 13', whereby he considers also the old textual revision by Wellhausen and others who in v. 14b propose the reading יהוה instead of אהיה, and then in his article on the name Yahweh and Exod. 3.14, where he designates God's reply in this verse as 'interpretation', 'explanation' and 'elucidating commentary'.[12] It is unnecessary, in fact, to consider further details of his argument, for the very breadth and

    11. Schmidt, *Exodus*, p. 131; in addition, could be mentioned de Vaux, 'Revelation', pp. 64f.; Delekat, '*Yáho-Yahwáe*', p. 60 n. 58; McCarthy, 'Exod 3:14', p. 316.
    12. Schmidt, 'Der Jahwename', esp. pp. 125ff.

fussiness of his argument only serve to lay bare the weaknesses and difficulties in his position rather than to justify or consolidate his views.

Accordingly, for good reasons, we should reconsider Noth's straightforward considerations on the passage in his commentary, namely that, when differentiating between material in vv. 14-15, 'the simpler declaration should be regarded as the original one', which means that 'v. 15 should not be seen as a supplementary explanation of v. 14, but rather that the simple mention of names in v. 15 should be regarded as the original answer to the question at the end of v. 13'. For the answer in v. 15a is not 'a combination' of elements in v. 14ab,[13] but it has its counterpart in the question in v. 13, and indeed in almost all points: (לבני ישׂראל); (but in 14b: אל) (אל) בני ישׂראל (each twice); אמר אל אלהי אבתיכם in Only the .מה שמו/זה שמי ;שלחני אליכם;אלהי אב(ו)תיכם 15 has been specified in a similar way as in v. 6a.[14] As far as the conclusion in v. 15bβ is concerned, however, the very similar—though not completely identical—text in Ps. 135.13b has been referred to with the opinion that this conclusion is a later extension, influenced by religious views. This may indeed well be the case, especially as Ps. 135.13a also corresponds to Exod. 3.15bα.

Just as v. 15 appears to be expanded at the end, v. 14 too on the other side of the verse gives the impression of being an extension of it, with the result that v. 15abα is surrounded by further revisions. When Elliger attempted to explain v. 14 as an 'interpolation of the Elohist', who thereby wanted to offer 'an interpretation of the name Yahweh', he found in it 'a revival of style: the Hebrew spirit loves the ingenious, the pun; and it places v. 14 before v. 15 because that is the only possible position if the attraction and the suspense are not to be removed from the play on words'.[15] In a somewhat similar fashion von Rad once spoke in a lecture of 'the psychology of the interpolator', as if the interpolator were unable to wait until after the connecting link in the text, but had to give his opinion in advance. On this matter, however, it seems more informative to consider the material from a form-historical or rather from a redactio-historical point of view.

In the Old Testament in many cases one can observe both in smaller sections as well as in larger portions an editorial process which consists

13. Schmidt, *Exodus*, p. 132.
14. Cf. Arnold, 'The Divine Name in Exodus iii.14', pp. 130-31.
15. Elliger, 'Zur Frage nach dem Alter des Jahweglaubens', p. 100.

of placing a newer piece of tradition material *before* an older one, so
that the older section may be heard and read in the light of the newer,
preceding passage, using it as a kind of hermeneutic key to interpretation. In this regard one might refer to the position of the newer creation
story in Gen. 1.1–2.4a before the older one in Gen. 2.4bff., or the position of the newer part of Proverbs 1–9 before the older sections in
Proverbs 10ff. The same is true as well of Psalm 1 as the gateway to the
Psalter and for the book of Deuteronomy as the beginning of the whole
deuteronomistic work of history. As far as a shorter passage is concerned, one may think, for example, of a remark made by Noth on the
compositional transition of Leviticus 1–7 to 8–9, where he sees the
connexion with the narrative which follows established not only in the
concluding remark in 7.37, 38, but 'just as much in the preceding secondarily interpolated observation in 7.35, 36'.[16] If now the relationship
of vv. 13-15 in Exodus 3 may be evaluated in the light of such a process, it is easily possible to see with Wolff even here 'a highly reflected
art of composition'; it consists of explaining in more detail by means of
the verb היה ('to be/become') the name of God as made manifest in
v. 15, which at the same time is identified with the God of the Fathers,
namely through a personal statement by God (v. 14a), and which further (v. 14b) forms a link with his promise in v. 12a. By means of this
interpretation in v. 14 the link between the new name for God יהוה and
the verb 'to be/become' is expressed directly and thereby guaranteed.
Thus we have already reached our next point.

2. *Linguistic Problems*

The linguistic problems of the name יהוה have been treated frequently,
often with the inclusion of very different, extra-biblical material, some
of which are theophorous names from Ebla (names such as *mi-ka-ya* or
en-na-ni-ya, which appear to verify *Ya* as a divine name).[17] Not only
has this often fragile material, for obvious reasons, been variously

---

16. Noth, *Überlieferungsgeschichte des Pentateuch*, p. 7 n. 10.

17. Cf. G. Pettinato, 'The Royal Archives of Tell-Mardikh-Ebla', *BA* 39 (1976),
p. 50; McCarthy, 'Exod 3:14', pp. 314f. For further extra-biblical material, cf., e.g.,
Kinyongo, *Origine et signification du nom divin Yahvé*; von Soden, 'Jahwe "Er ist,
Er erweist sich"'; Mayer, 'Der Gottesname Jahweh'; and de Vaux, 'Revelation', as
well as D.N. Freedman and P. O'Connor, 'יהוה JHWH', *ThWAT*, III, cols. 533-54,
esp. 535-37.

interpreted, but so has also the frequently debated relationship between the long form יהוה and the short forms יה and יהו; and the issue is then whether the long form is an extension of the short forms (the extension theory), or whether the long form has been abbreviated itself to the various short forms (the abbreviation theory).[18] It is, in other words, a question of respective 'originality'; and from the (etymological and/or historical) question of provenance to that of the meaning of the name, the path often seems very short. In this regard it is expedient, however, to proceed from a methodical point of view in an even more critical and cautious manner than is often the case. For in these matters, in particular it may be regarded as necessary to make or to pay attention to certain distinctions between linguistic explanation and theological interpretation, as well as between statements about a name for God and (direct) statements about God, especially since these are so closely linked. Moreover, we may also consider certain distinctions between (theophorous) personal names and names for God, although they may have something in common, and between the nominal and verbal form of the name, because here there may be some disparity.

On this point it may be appropriate to warn of two different tendencies, particularly the increasing tendency to attach greater importance—thanks to archaeology—to inscriptions, which now are being more frequently discovered, than to the Old Testament tradition material itself (and here we may suggest a comparison with the more general problem of the relationship between biblical archaeology and exegesis).[19] Further, one should warn of the tendency which some have to answer the problems of provenance and meaning of the name of God by means of a (larger or smaller) part and not of the whole material. To this belong the cases where Exod. 3.14 is isolated from its context as *the* main instance. Or it may be referred to the very instructive study of von Soden which, however, is concerned just with the long form יהוה, comparing it with 'old names of the type *Yahwi-ilum*', but overlooking the short forms.[20] On the other hand one may mention Rose's in many

18. Delekat, '*Yáho-Yahwáe*', p. 23 n. 1, where a number of supporters of both theories are mentioned.

19. See n. 16 above, and also Delekat, '*Yáho-Yahwáe*', and Rose, *Yahwe*. The Old Testament tradition material itself, however, should not come off badly, for despite all transforming *traditio* it still contains much (very) old *traditum*.

20. Von Soden, 'Jahwe "Er ist, Er erweist sich"', p. 185; for him Exod. 3.14 also appears to be the point of orientation for the Old Testament.

ways speculative book which sees the original form in the short form
יהו YHW that appears as an element in theophorous names, but which
does not exist independently in the biblical material, and yet dates the
long form from the time of Josiah and almost completely neglects the
short form יה YH which appears as an independent name.[21] For a linguistic or linguistically historical evaluation, however, it is necessary
for the various elements of the whole, multifaceted material to be considered, as is the case, for example, in the works of Kuhn (1935) and of
Delekat in the Kuhn Festschrift (1971). On this occasion, where there is
no possibility to go into great detail, one may above all be referred to
the study by Delekat that is so rich in substance.

In the present situation in which most Old Testament scholars insist
on the long form of the Tetragrammaton יהוה, the attention may be
drawn to some facts, particularly in the biblical material, that are problematic for an opinion of this kind. First, the commonly accepted vocalization of the long form, *yahweh*, which always appears with all four
consonants of יהוה and is never extant in theophorous personal names,
is in fact unknown to us, but yet the form is generally assumed, partly
because of the interpretation by means of the verb היה ('to be/become')
in Exod. 3.14, and partly because of some post-biblical patristic tran-
scriptions; with this vocalization, then, the original form of the divine
name is presupposed to be the verb form *yahweh*, mainly understood
as an imperfect of the basic root *qal* of היה. Since, in this case, the
prefix also has the original form *ya-*, whereas the /w/ is derived from
הוה, the Aramaic equivalent of the Hebrew היה, the assumed form
yahweh is regarded as an archaic one.[22] Second, however, the fourth
consonant of the Tetragrammaton causes here a problem. Given the
accepted form is regarded as an archaic one, the fourth consonant,
which the long form always has preserved and which in this case hardly
can be considered as anything other than a *he mater lectionis*, must
appear strange; for the orthographic phenomenon of the *mater lectionis*,
whose age is admittedly uncertain, will after all be regarded as relatively late. Furthermore, it is rather surprising that God's name does not
form a noun, but—as in so many personal names—a verbal sentence.

21. For criticism of Rose, see also Schmidt, in 'Der Jahwename', p. 126 n. 11.
22. See the larger lexica and grammars; see also, e.g., G. Fohrer, *Geschichte der
israelitischen Religion* (Berlin: W. de Gruyter, 1969), pp. 63ff.; Kuhn, 'Über die
Erstenung', p. 33; Kinyongo, *Origine et signification du nom divin Yahvé*, pp. 47ff.;
cf. Mayer, 'Der Gottesname Jahwe' and de Vaux, 'Revelation'.

The question may then easily be raised as to who the subject may be of the verbal statement of **yahweh* or even as to what the name may be of this unknown 'he'. Von Soden has clearly recognized this problem and admits that the thankful exclamation 'he shows himself' ('Er erweist sich', as he interprets the divine name יהוה) does not represent 'a name at all in the strict sense of the word, admittedly, but rather a statement about God'.[23] He suggests a solution; and for an explanation of the same problem de Vaux refers to a few linguistic analogies that are worth considering.[24] Yet, the assumed verbal sentence, which to be sure has later been substantivized, remains at least striking. All things considered, there emerges great doubt about the verification of the hypothesis of **yahweh* as the (verbal) original form.

This doubt about the most widely recognized thesis is merely strengthened, however, when third, the long form יהוה is linked with the short forms י״ה and יהו, as generally occurs either in one form or the other. Inasmuch as the long form is regarded as the original form, the short forms are explained as abbreviations of it, a point which can be substantiated from linguistically historical grounds.[25] Two things should be borne in mind here. On the one hand the supposed 'intermediate form' יהו (**yahw*; cf. *KB* and *HALAT*) is never attested as an independent name for God in biblical writing, but is found—with varying realization of the consonants and vocalization—only as a theophorous element in personal names. It is used, though, in extra-biblical documents and inscriptions.[26] On the other hand יה/ה״ appears both as an independent name for God (including the common form הללו־יה) as well as as a theophorous element in personal names; moreover it can be compared with early non-Israelite names such as those mentioned above from Ebla.[27] The instances of יה/ה״, as an independent name for God in the Old Testament deserve special consideration, in Delekat's view,[28] and even more so as it occurs particularly in older poetic texts and appears to be interchangeable with יהוה.[29] Moreover, it is especially

23. Von Soden, 'Jahwe "Er ist, Er erweist sich" ', pp. 184-85.

24. De Vaux, 'Revelation', pp. 60f.; cf. also L. Köhler, 'Jod als hebräisches Nominalpräfix, *WO* 1.5 (1950), pp. 25-42 (also in *KB*).

25. Cf., for example, *KB*, p. 369, or *HALAT*, pp. 377-78; see also n. 21 above.

26. Cf. Delekat, '*Yáho-Yahwáe*'; Rose, *Jahwe*.

27. Cf., for example, *HALAT*, p. 376; see also n. 29 below.

28. Delekat, '*Yáho-Yahwáe*', pp. 27-28.

29. The number of examples is difficult to ascertain, since the text is unclear at

noteworthy that it is always a noun and that its second consonant (*he*) always maintains its consonantal value, which is later secured by means of the *he mappicatum* of the Massoretes.

In order to advance a step further, two points must be noted. First, a view of Kuhn which has mostly been overlooked needs to be reconsidered. As did Delekat after him,[30] Kuhn started with the premise of a short form of God's name, namely a hypothetical (non-Israelite[31]) **Yau*, which he regarded 'as the stem *Ya* plus the nominative ending *u*', and which is expanded in Hebrew by means of an *h* to form the double-rooted word *Yáhū*, like the 'double-rooted related nouns אב "father", אח "brother" and חם "father-in-law" in their original forms **'ábū, *'áḥū, *ḥámū*'. From this expanded original form *Yáhū* he derived both *Yah* and *Yahweh*. The latter form is explained as a plural form, which is hardly convincing.[32] Unnecessary is also the detour to consider an original form expanded with *he*, for the name *Yah* (יה/יהּ), like the related nouns, can be explained satisfactorily as a double-rooted noun, whose original form—with the short final vowel of that particular case—was once **yahu*. Generally the final vowels of the three cases disappeared very early on, but Birkeland gives examples showing that 'final vowels were in fact added again *after* they had disappeared'.[33] In this way the other short form יהו could perhaps be explained. However, it may also have been the case that in addition to the name יה there was another old form יו (cf. the Ugaritic form *yw*[34]), with the result that we need to differentiate between two originally different short forms of God's name. To a certain extent this would help to explain the various uses of יה and יהו in the Old Testament and of יהו and the long form in the writings of Elephantine and in the early Christian era, since the long form is documented by the exegetes of the Church at large, as is the pronunciation

certain points. However, the *Yah* in Exod. 15.2 is not as easy to remove as is the case in Delekat, 'Yáho-Yahwáe', p. 27, and Rose, *Jahwe*, p. 42, for it could be the result of haplography.

30. Delekat, 'Yáho-Yahwáe', pp. 56ff.

31. Kuhn, 'Über die Enstehung', p. 34 n. 2; cf. also n. 33 below.

32. Kuhn, 'Über die Enstehung', pp. 34-35. Kuhn mentions other double-rooted names for God, namely the Babylonian God *Nabu* and the word *'ilu* ('god').

33. H. Birkeland, *Akzent und Vokalismus im Althebräischen* (SNVAO.HF, 1940–43; Oslo: Jacob Dybwad, 1941), p. 14; cf. pp. 12-17 (as well as pp. 18-26).

34. Cf. *UT*, Glossary No. 1084, as well as Freedman and O'Connor 'YHWH', pp. 542-43.

Ἰαώ in gnostic-syncretistic circles.[35] The matter cannot be pursued further at this point, but must rest here with these remarks.

Second, it may be referred to that most interesting passage Isa. 38.11, which exhibits a doubled use of יה. There is an important equivalent in manuscripts of the Syrohexapla, where 'the Syriac *yhyh* (= *yāhyâh* and *yahyáh*) ...often appears as a marginal reading of "the Lord" (*māryâ*), where it is a reproduction of *Yahweh (Yhwh)* in the Massoretic Text'; thus Delekat, who alters Isa. 38.11 with the reading *Yihyeh* and adds that 'this is a Hebrew "translation" of the Aramaic *Yahweh*, "he is"'.[36] Yet the reading *Yihyeh* is just as unique as the double reading in Isa. 38.11, and moreover a different construction. The doubled יה יה should not be rejected immediately, since the doubling of a substantive can have a superlative function. The doubled use of God's name can represent an intensifying of the word.[37]

In this way, through the reduplication of the short form, a new possibility opens for explaining the old problem of the relationship between the long form יהוה and the short form יה of the Iraelite name for God. The starting point, however, must then be the oldest form of the short form, which began with *w*, namely **wăhu*, where '*w* in the initial sound of the word became *y* in old Canaanite'[38] and **wăhu* developed into **yăh(u)* and *yah*. Yet, by the doubling of the word, the original *w* has been preserved, in the second instance, because it is now in the middle of the word, thus giving rise to the following *basic form* of the Tetragrammaton: *Yahwah*. This name for God represented an intensification of the old name *Yah*. This surpassing of the old form might be termed a 'revelation' inasmuch as it can be linked with the declaration of the name in Exod. 3.15. This leads on to the issue of the next section.

3. *Theological Problems*

The findings of both analyses given above ought to have placed in a new light the relationship between Exod. 3.14 and 3.15 as well as the

---

35. Rose, *Jahwe*, p. 13; cf. also Alfrink, 'La prononciation "Jehova" ', pp. 43-63.

36. Delekat, '*Yáho-Yahwáe*', pp. 58-59.

37. Cf., e.g., GKC §133k.1, as well as E. König, *Historisch-kritisches Lehrgebäude der hebräischen Sprache*. II.2. *Historisch-comparative Syntax der hebräischen Sprache* (Leipzig, 1897), §88.

38. Cf. R. Meyer, *Hebrew Grammar* (London: SPCK, 1973), §22.4a, p. 97.

relationship between the long and short forms of the Israelite name for God. In this light the very extensive theological problems on the subject should be sharpened towards a current topic which in recent literature has been expressed in a variety of ways, namely the central question: Does there actually exist in Exod. 3.13-15 a *revelation* of the Israelite name יהוה, or is it perhaps more to the point to speak of a conscious *veiling* of God?

The latter position is represented by not a few Old Testament exegetes and other theologians. The main burden of their argument is borne by Exod. 3.14, and above all by the artificially constructed and, in substance, highly reflected declaration אהיה אשר אהיה, whose most peculiar and complicated syntax in the framework of a word from God cannot be discussed more fully here.[39] Dubarle thinks that 'the declaration tends towards an uncertainty which is suitable for a God who is revealing himself and who thus wishes to protect his independence vis-à-vis his creatures'.[40] In a similar way von Rad also finds in the relative clause 'undoubtedly a moment of the uncertain and indeed of the secretive... with the result that the promise of Yahweh's active presence remains at the same time in a certain suspended and intangible state; it is Yahweh's freedom which cannot be pinned down in detail'.[41] Zimmerli also stresses here the freedom of Yahweh which cannot be 'enclosed in the cage of a definition'.[42]

But on the other hand W.H. Schmidt, for example, who in a noteworthy way regards v. 14 as 'genuine' and v. 15 as 'an addition', is able to say with regard to the same declaration in v. 14: 'With this answer God scarcely wants to preserve his independence behind the unmentionable, the indefinable and the unfathomable, or even to deny

39. Cf. Vriezen, '*'ehje 'ašer ehje*', pp. 498-512 and also E. Schild, 'On Exodus iii 14—"I am that I am" ', *VT* 4 (1954), pp. 296-302; cf. the critical notes in Albrektson, 'The Syntax of אהיה אשר אהיה', pp. 15-28.

40. Dubarle, 'La signification du nom de Iahweh', pp. 3-21; here translated from the German translation by Mayer, 'Der Gottesname Jahwe', p. 43.

41. Von Rad, *Theologie des Alten Testaments*, I, p. 194.

42. W. Zimmerli, *Grundriss der alttestamentlichen Theologie* (Theologische Wissenschaft, 3; Stuttgart: W. Kohlhammer, 1972), p. 15; cf. also C. Vriezens, *Theologie des Alten Testaments in Grundzügen* (Neukirchen–Vluyn: Neukirchener Verlag, 1956), p. 201: 'In this name Yahwe makes himself known only in a formal sense by speaking of his presence. This is not yet an actual character definition, for Yahweh does not mention his name.' It is almost as if one could sense the Calvinist *finitum non capax infiniti* in the background.

his name, but he wishes rather to reveal it in a declaratory manner.'[43]

In this regard the denial of the name in Gen. 32.30 or Judg. 13.17f. has occasionally been referred to. But in spite of a certain similarity in the form of question and answer those specific contexts are not comparable with that of Exodus 3. In Exodus 3 rather God is approaching humanity and revealing himself, first, in his appearance in the burning bush scene, then in the name declaration in the elohistic speech in 3.9-15 (with God's promise in vv. 9-10 as a continuation of the preceding section in v. 6 and vv. 7-8, with the question and refusal of Moses in v. 11, the comforting response and promise of God in v. 12, Moses' question in v. 13, and God's response in v. 15, which has been doubly expanded in vv. 14 and 15bβ). There must be no doubt: here God approaches a human being with a view to revealing rather than concealing himself. Thus we may trust the tradition of the Old Testament when it links the manifestation of the special name יהוה—in this way or another (cf. Exod. 6.2)—with Moses.

Just as between יה and יהוה—as has plausibly been shown above—there was a relationship of simultaneously preserving continuity and creative discontinuity, so also in Exod. 3.15 (cf. v. 6 and 6.2) between יהוה and the God of the fathers of the older traditions. It was not an unknown God who was heard in the new name יהוה, and yet one was confronted with a God who revealed himself in a new way.

This same relationship between simultaneous continuity and discontinuity can be seen also in vv. 14 and 15. For it is possible that the proximity of the new name *Yahwah* to the verb הוה/היה may have been sensed at an early stage, perhaps right from the beginning. Whether this is in fact the case or not, the statement in v. 14 has in any event resulted in such a link. This statement about God based on the new name is therefore not just an 'explanation' or 'interpretation' of the name, but rather a *reinterpretation* of the name in v. 15, with the result that the relationship between vv. 14 and 15 may be regarded as *a relationship of revelation and revealing reinterpretation*, or on the other hand, as already pointed out, as a relationship of preserving continuity, particularly of the consonants of the tetragrammaton יהוה, and of reinterpretative discontinuity, particularly of an assumed change of vowels from *Yahwah* to *Yahweh*, which to all appearances became and was the

43. W.H. Schmidt, *Alttestamentlicher Glaube und seine Umwelt* (Neukirchen–Vluyn: Neukirchener Verlag, 4th rev. edn, 1982 [1968]), p. 61; cf. Mayer, 'Der Gottesname Jahwe'; Schild, 'On Exodus iii 14'; and de Vaux, 'Revelation'.

traditional pronunciation until it was shunned for religious reasons.

The revealing of the name יהוה has had a far-reaching theological effect, particularly in the form of early interpretative statements about God (cf., e.g., Exod. 34.6, 14 and Hos. 1.9) and, above all, of a gradually increasing theology of the name of God.[44]

44. Cf. von Rad, *Theologie des Alten Testaments*, I, pp. 193-200, as well as W. Zimmerli, 'Ich bin Jahwe', in *idem, Gottes Offenbarung: Gesammelte Aufsätze* (TBü, 19; Munich: Chr. Kaiser Verlag, 1969), pp. 11-40. Name theology existed in a number of theological circles in Israel, but esp. in the deuteronomistic circle.

Chapter 6

FORM-HISTORICAL PERSPECTIVES ON ISAIAH 7.3-9

The textual state of the so-called Isaiah 'Memorandum'[1] not only presents us with difficult semantic, grammatical and stylistic questions but
also gives us at the same time the impression of a long and complex
development of the material at the hands of its authors. Isa. 7.3-9 offers
a clear indication of the way in which the 'Memorandum' is generally
perceived. The syntactic arrangement of v. 5 is particularly controversial.

Many modern commentators[2] see Isa. 7.5(-6) as giving the subsidiary

1.   The form 'Denkschrift'/'Memorandum' has been widely used for Isa. 6.1–
9.6; cf. especially K. Budde, *Jesaja's Erleben: Eine gemeinverständliche Auslegung der Denkschrift des Propheten* (Gotha, 1928). For recent criticism see
H. Graf Reventlow, 'Das Ende der sog. "Denkschrift" Jesajas', *BN* 38/39 (1987),
pp. 62-67; also various contributions in J. Vermeylen (ed.), *The Book of Isaiah*
(BETL, 81; Leuven: Leuven University Press, 1989).
2.   See, e.g., the commentaries of F. Delitzsch, *Commentar über das Buch
Jesaia* (BCAT, 3.1; Leipzig, 4th edn, 1889); A. Dillmann, *Der Prophet Jesaia*
(KEHAT, 5; Leipzig, 1890); K. Marti, *Das Buch Jesaja* (KHAT, 10; Tübingen:
J.C.B. Mohr, 1900); G.B. Gray, *The Book of Isaiah*. I. *1–27* (ICC; Edinburgh: T. &
T. Clark, 1912); B. Duhm, *Das Buch Jesaia: Übersetzt und erklärt* (HKAT, 3.1;
Göttingen: Vandenhoeck & Ruprecht, 5th edn, 1968 [1892]); F. Feldmann, *Das
Buch Isaias* (EHAT, 14.1; Münster, 1925); O. Procksch, *Jesaja*, I (KAT, 9;
Leipzig: A. Deichert, 1930); E.J. Kissane, *The Book of Isaiah*, I (Dublin, 1941);
A. Bentzen, *Jesaja*, I (Copenhagen: G.E.C. Gad, 1944); J.A. Bewer, *The Book of
Isaiah*, I (Harper's Annotated Bible Series; New York: Harper & Row, 1950);
H. Wildberger, *Jesaja*. I. *Jesaja 1–12* (BKAT, 10.1; Neukirchen–Vluyn: Neu-
kirchener Verlag, 2nd edn, 1980 [1972]). See also H. Gressmann, *Der Messias*
(FRLANT, 43; Göttingen: Vandenhoeck & Ruprecht, 1929), p. 236; E. Jenni, *Die
politischen Voraussagen der Propheten* (ATANT, 29; Zürich: Zwingli-Verlag,
1956), pp. 73ff.; H.W. Wolff, *Immanuel: Das Zeichen, dem widersprochen wird*
(Bibl. Stud., 23; Neukirchen Kreis Moers: Neukirchener Verlag, 1956), pp. 5, 17;
and J. Lindblom, *A Study on the Immanuel Section in Isaiah, Isa. vii,1–ix,6*

clause (basis) and 7.7(-9) as giving the main clause (apodosis):

> (5) Because Aram—with Ephraim and the son of Remaliah—has plotted evil against you, saying, (6) 'Let us go up against Judah and terrify it and conquer it for ourselves and make the son of Tabeel king in it'; (7) therefore thus says the Lord Yahweh: 'It shall not stand, and it shall not come to pass. For the head…'[3]

The superficial motivation of this translation is obviously exegetical; according to that exegesis the following seems to be the only possible solution: the content of God's saying in v. 7 refers to Aram's evil plan (v. 5). The assumed factual content, however, has a syntactical implication, and the syntax is slightly stilted. The translation therefore presents a clear meaning, but leaves open the question whether it is the right one. In respect of the Hebrew, this particular interpretation seems to open up more questions than it is able to answer.

Some scholars have nevertheless understood v. 5 syntactically in a different way, namely as a reason for the statement preceding it.[4] In this case the translation might be as follows:

(SMHVL, 4; Lund: C.W.K. Gleerup, 1958), pp. 11-12. Also, mention should be made of a few grammatically impossible presentations: V. Herntrich, *Der Prophet Jesaja: Kapitel 1–12* (ATD, 17; Göttingen: Vandenhoeck & Ruprecht, 2nd edn, 1954); N.H. Tur-Sinai, *Die heilige Schrift*, III (Jerusalem, 1954); where the difficult text is forced into a *non sequitur*: after the preceding causal sentence ('because…') there comes a full stop. Finally, one may also compare the KJV, RSV and the Zürich Bible.

3.   Wolff, *Immanuel*, pp. 5-6, translates along these lines, though with explanatory footnotes which are not included here.

4.   Cf. König, *Historisch-comparative Syntax*, §389 d and i, as well as his *Das Buch Jesaja* (Gütersloh, 1926), *ad loc.*; Budde, *Jesaja's Erleben*, p. 39; L. Rignell, 'Das Immanuelzeichen: Einige Gesichtspunkte zu Jes. 7', *ST* 11 (1957), pp. 99-119. Cf. J. Koenig, 'Le livre d'Isaïe', in E. Dhorme (ed.), *La Bible: L'Ancien Testament*, II (Paris: Bibliothèque de la Pleiade, 1959), p. 24; also J. Fischer, *Das Buch Isaias* (HSAT, 7.1.1; Bonn, 1937), *ad loc.*, who finds a factual but not a formal link between vv. 5-6 and 7; so also G. von Rad, *Der heilige Krieg im Alten Israel* (Göttingen: Vandenhoeck & Ruprecht, 3rd edn, 1958), p. 56; E. Würthwein, 'Jesaja 7,1-9. Ein Beitrag zu dem Thema: Prophetie und Politik', in *Theologie als Glaubenswagnis* (Festschrift K. Heim; Hamburg: Furche Verlag, 1954), pp. 47-63; repr. in *idem, Wort und Existenz: Studien zum Alten Testament* (Göttingen: Vandenhoeck & Ruprecht, 1970), pp. 127-43; W. Vischer, *Die Immanuel-Botschaft im Rahmen des königlichen Zionsfestes* (ThSt, 45; Zürich: Theologischer Verlag, 1955). Cf. the Vulgate, Luther's Bible and the JB.

(4) And say to him: 'Take heed...and do not let your heart be faint because of these two smouldering stumps of firebrands... (5) because Aram...has plotted evil against you, saying, (6) "Let us go up...and make the son of Tabeel king in it."' [5]

Those who understand v. 5 in this way express themselves more cautiously and less absolutely than those of the former group; often is therefore only a translation proposed and also kept as close as possible to the text of the MT. Though Budde makes a first step to a formal reason, it is not really asserted as an actual reason until Rignell, who wants to take 7.7 as the beginning of a new paragraph. He too, however, holds that the main thrust of the reason lies in an exegetical consideration: in his opinion the common understanding of 7.5-7 would conclude that strictly speaking Isaiah denied that Aram and Ephraim would succeed. Yet this would contradict the facts reported about Aram and Ephraim in 2 Kings and 2 Chronicles.[6] The argument that he derives from these passages is rather thin, however, since 2 Kgs 15.37 has no real bearing on Isa. 7.1ff. and as for 2 Chron. 28.5ff., the relationship between this late passage and the Isaiah pericope is too dubious for anything to be derived for an exegesis of the latter text.

Be that as it may, it is already clear from what has been said that the old controversy—whether v. 5 should be associated with the preceding or with the subsequent material—is being debated on exegetical principles. Hence the following question arises: Is it not possible to solve this problem, which is a formal one, by using pre-exegetical criteria? Could one not reach, on the basis of text- and form-analysis, a valid conclusion to serve as a 'guideline' for the traditional 'verbal' exegesis?

The first step would be a comparison with some of the old translations, in particular the LXX. It appears quickly that the text of the LXX differs widely from that of the MT; this is especially true for the end of v. 4, where the LXX offers a completely different text (ὅταν γὰρ ὀργὴ τοῦ θυροῦ μου γένηται, πάλιν ἰάσομαι), and in v. 7, where the brief divine address is directly reported (τάδε λέγει κύριος σαβαωθ Οὐ μὴ ἐμμείνη ἡ βουλὴ αὕτη οὐδὲ ἔσται). The כִּי of v. 8 is replaced by ἀλλ', and v. 8a is left out. Also in v. 5 there are dislocations and clarifications.[7]

---

5. Budde, *Jesaja's Erleben*, p. 39.
6. Rignell, 'Das Immanuelzeichen', p. 103.
7. According to A. Rahlf, *Septuaginta* (Stuttgart: Priv. Württ Bibelanstalt, 3rd

If the LXX text of this passage differs so much from the MT, it would surely be methodologically wrong to refer only in individual cases to the LXX when working text-critically on the MT.[8] One should rather take into account the Jewish-Alexandrian theology that lies behind the LXX.[9] The scepticism that Engnell expressed towards the LXX, based on Isaiah 6,[10] can thus be endorsed and applied likewise to 7.1ff.[11] Indeed, the Targum to Isa. 7.1ff. comments in the same manner as the LXX.[12]

Hence these translations, which have to be classified as later interpreters and commentators, are of little help for the texual and form-critical work on the MT. If one examines 7.3-9 with regard to its form, however, a few observations can be made (referring for convenience to vv. 3-6 as A and vv. 7-9 as B):

1.	A takes the form of divine speech and closes with a quotation (v. 6); B is prophetic speech and is introduced by the quotation of divine speech in v. 7.[13]

2.	A contains the commission of the prophet by Yahweh; B contains the delivered message of the prophet rooted in a special message of Yahweh.

3.	It is significant that B is introduced by the messenger formula כה אמר יהוה. Are there any other examples where the apodosis following a long subsidiary clause is also introduced by the messenger formula?

edn, 1949). See also the work of J. Ziegler, *Isaias* (Septuaginta Vetus Testamentum Graecum, 14; Göttingen: Vandenhoeck & Ruprecht, 1939).

8.	Engnell warned of this in his *Gamla Testamentet*, p. 31.

9.	Cf. I.L. Seeligmann, *The Septuagint Version of Isaiah: A Discussion of its Problems* (Mededelingen en Verhandelingen, 9; Leiden: E.J. Brill, 1948); see esp. Ch. 4, 'The Translation as a Document of Jewish-Alexandrian Theology' (pp. 95ff.).

10.	I. Engnell, *The Call of Isaiah: An Exegetical and Comparative Study* (UUÅ, 1949.4; Uppsala: Lundeqvistska Bokhandeln, 1949), pp. 10, 12ff.

11.	'Ziegler in his important investigations in the LXX of Isa. has demonstrated such great differences, reinterpretations, and misunderstandings on the side of the translator (or: translators) that, in my opinion, the conclusion seems inevitable that the LXX (here too) at least in parts, goes back to another and much worse recension than that of our MT' (Engnell, *The Call of Isaiah*, p. 12).

12.	J.F. Stenning, *The Targum of Isaiah* (Oxford, 1949).

13.	Cf. H.W. Wolff, *Das Zitat im Prophetenspruch: Eine Studie zur prophetischen Verkündigungsweise* (BEvT, 4; Munich: Chr. Kaiser Verlag, 1939), pp. 9-10.

4. A contains an address in the singular (the 'thou' of the prophet); B uses the plural for its address (but who are those addressed here?).
5. A is narrated in prose; B seems to be written in poetry.
6. Finally, one may point out that the Jewish tradition has inserted a *setumah* between A and B, creating a caesura.

Formally speaking, a good deal seems to support the thesis that vv. 3-6 and vv. 7-9 are to be understood as two different entities. The syntactical controversy of the pericope may be settled in a form-historical way: v. 5, being a causal clause, can only be connected to the preceding clause (v. 4).

Let us now look at the first unit, vv. 3-6, and its controversial conjunction. The conjunction יַעַן כִּי, from יַעַן ('cause for') and the causative particle כִּי, is rare.[14] In some cases that happen to be divine speech, כִּי introduces the substantiating subsidiary clause,[15] a fact that could be seen as supporting the general understanding of Isa. 7.5-7.

If one divides the passage as suggested above one will find that Num. 11.19-20—a conversation between Yahweh and Moses as intercessor— provides an analogy to Isa. 7.4-5: in the context of a divine speech יַעַן כִּי expresses the following causal clause which is concluded by a quotation. The quotation gives a more precise explanation and characterization of the cause (cf. יַעַן).

Since the conjunction יַעַן כִּי can be used as well in the preceding as in the following causal clause, the passages in Numbers and Isaiah seem to be very similar, even analogous, and hence it seems that Num. 11.19-20 can elucidate the Isaiah passage syntactically. This again should support the earlier assumption, though one should not overstate this case.

The skeleton of the structure of Isa. 7.3-6 is very simple. If one takes away the overly ornate style of its sometimes enlightening details, what remains are the two supporting pillars of the divine speech: צֵא ('go forth') and וְאָמַרְתָּ ('and say'). The content can be paraphrased as follows: at the beginning of the hostilities Isaiah received Yahweh's command to take his symbolically named son and go to see Ahaz, to

---

14. KB, p. 389 b; cf. p. 432b, point 17; cf. D.E. Gowan, 'The Use of *ya'an* in Biblical Hebrew', *VT* 21 (1971), pp. 168-85.
15. 1 Kgs 13.21; 21.29; Isa. 3.16; cf. 8.6-7.

relieve him of the anxiety and fear[16] caused by the deployment of the kings Rezon[17] and Pekah. If read and understood in this way, this self-contained unit makes perfect sense, and when Rignell assumes that v. 5 'refers in a way to Ahaz's own understanding of the danger of Aram and Ephraim',[18] one can only agree with him.

It has already been stressed that this unit contains only Yahweh's command, but one should not forget that its fulfilment by the prophet is already included in the Hebrew style of narrative.[19] However, it has often been possible to recognize among the interpretations a tendency of contrasting vv. 3-6 or 3-9 as a scene over against the unit 7.10ff.: what is narrated last does not take place 'at the end of the watercourse of the upper pool' but rather in, for example, the king's palace.[20] The locality, however, does play a certain role in v. 3; the mention of this particular locality seems to make a special statement about the religious attitude of the king and thus conveys a theological meaning. To explore the question of locality any further will be to exhaust the text of 7.1-17 quickly and to do the tenor of its contents hardly any justice. The prophetic tradition is seemingly little interested in tying scenes between important persons to certain localities, but rather to capture vividly the destiny-determining word of Yahweh in its significant moment.

In this case there is no real need, when looking at the transition of A (vv. 3-6) to B (vv. 7-9), to ask about the relation of this unit to the remaining 'scenes'. Just as in the commission in A, so in B the performance of the prophetic duty is described; what we have in front of us is a fragment of prophetic announcement within the same situation of announcement. Our first task should be to shed light on the form of this small unit in the hope of deriving a better understanding of its factual content.

However, it proves difficult to elucidate the form of vv. 7-9. While characterizing vv. 4-6 as an 'admonition' (*Mahnwort*), von Rad calls

---

16. The 'anxiety' and 'fear' are to be understood not in the usual psychological sense but as religious timidity, here equivalent to lack of faith.

17. Cf. Bentzen, *Jesaja*, I, p. 54, and Wolff, *Das Zitat im Prophetenspruch*, p. 5.

18. Rignell, 'Das Immanuelzeichen', p. 103.

19. Cf. W. Baumgarten, 'Ein Kapitel vom hebräischen Erzählungstil', in *Eucharisterion für H. Gunkel* (FRLANT, NF, 19; Göttingen: Vandenhoeck & Ruprecht, 1923), pp. 145-57.

20. Cf. Lindblom, *A Study on the Immanuel Section*, p. 15 Also, ויוסף דבר in 7.10 does not justify the question at issue.

vv. 7-9 a 'promise' (*Verheissung*).[21] Both Würthwein[22] and Wolff[23] follow him. Rignell, on the other hand, classifies v. 7b as a 'judgment-oracle' (*Gerichtsorakel*).[24] How does the matter stand?

One has to examine first the divine speech in v. 7b on its own. Where does the phraseology of this enigmatic statement of Yahweh come from? The particular message is as follows:

לא תקום ולא תהיה

What does the תקום refer to?

According to the usual exegesis, the תקום refers to the 'evil plan', יעץ...רעה in v. 5, and should be translated as '(not) come to pass'.[25] One can, however, look at this from a broader, semantic perspective. First, passages that seem to support the usual exegesis should be pointed out: Isa. 14.24; 40.8; 46.10; Jer. 44.28-29; 51.29; Prov. 19.21. Each of these passsages deals with Yahweh's 'word', 'counsel' or 'plan' (עצה), or 'thoughts' (מחשבות), which stand fast or will endure or will be realized or are supposed to take place.[26] Despite inchoative or durative nuances within the meaning, the fact remains one and the same: the eternal and overwhelming nature of Yahweh's word and actions are emphasized; the contrast is to be found on the human side in general, or among Israel's enemies.[27] They are challenged by the prophet:

> Take counsel together,
>> but it shall be brought to naught;
> speak a word,
>> but it will not stand (Isa. 8.10).[28]

Is the same meaning intended in Isa. 7.7b? Obviously, such an interpretation suggests itself to the commentator, supported by the direction of the Targum as well as of the LXX. Indeed, the LXX renders thus, *expressis verbis*. Yet there exists another group of passages containing

21. Von Rad, *Der heilige Krieg*, p. 56.

22. Würthwein, 'Jesaja 7,1-9', p. 51.

23. Wolff, *Das Zitat im Prophetenspruch*, pp. 15ff.

24. Rignell, 'Das Immanuelzeichen', p. 104.

25. KB, p. 832a.

26. KB, p. 832a. Under 'Bestand haben' ('stand fast') or 'zu Stand kommen' ('take place') only Isa. 40.8 and Jer. 44.28 appear.

27. Cf. Jer. 44.28-29; 51.29-30; Prov. 19.21.

28. Cf. Luther's Bible; S. Mowinckel and N. Messel, *Det gamle testamente. III. De senere profeter* (Oslo: H. Aschehoug, 1944), p. 102.

the root קוּם and which KB[29] and *HALAT* render as '*Bertand haben*/last' and which also could be translated as 'be established, will continue': 1 Sam. 13.14; 24.21; Amos 7.2; and Nah. 1.6. 1 Samuel 13 tells of Saul's military campaigns against the Philistines as well as his impatience and disobedience towards a prophetic and divine word. Saul, the מְשִׁיחַ־יְהוה, the anointed of Yahweh, has acted against a מִצְוַת יְהוה אֱלֹהֶיךָ, 'the commandment of Yahweh your god' (v. 13),[30] and therefore foolishly. The prophet and judge Samuel, who had once anointed him, now condemns him: Yahweh does not wish his kingdom to be established any longer (הֵכִין), so 'now your kingdom shall not continue (לֹא־תָקוּם, v. 14)'.[31] Yahweh will rather search for a man 'after his own heart' and he shall be ruler over Yahweh's people. The narrative of 'David's rise' (1 Sam. 16ff.) seems to intrude here; but the hints of Deuteronomistic tradition at this point cannot be pursued,[32] since the main purpose of the present study is to uncover a certain phraseology.

Furthermore, one may consider 1 Sam. 24.21 in this context. That episode takes place in the desert, in the cave at Engedi, where David has just spared Saul's life. Now Saul speaks: 'Now I know that you shall surely be king, and that the kingdom of Israel shall be established in your hand (וְקָמָה בְּיָדְךָ)'.[33] The first anointed one moves towards his downfall, while the second anointed is promised royal status. In the background lies the particular 'messianic' theology, whose nucleus of crystallization seems to have been the so-called 'Promise of Nathan'.[34] 2 Samuel 7 is especially noteworthy in terms of this examination of phraseology: 'I shall raise up (וַהֲקִימֹתִי) your offspring after you...and I shall establish (וַהֲכִינֹתִי) his kingdom' (v. 12); 'I shall establish (וְכֹנַנְתִּי) the throne of his kingdom for all time' (v. 13); 'your house and your kingdom shall be established (נֶאֱמָן) for ever ...your throne will endure

---

29. KB, p. 832a.

30. Cf. Isa. 7.11; both places have 'Yahweh your God'.

31. Cf. H.W. Hertzberg, *I and II Samuel: A Commentary* (OTL; London: SCM Press, 1964), *ad loc*.

32. Cf. Hertzberg's final paragraphs of his commentary, *I and II Samuel*; also J.A. Soggin, *Das Königtum in Israel* (BZAW, 104; Berlin: Alfred Töpelmann, 1967) pp. 54-57.

33. According to Hertzberg, *I and II Samuel, ad loc*.

34. A. Alt, 'Das Königtum in den Reichen Israel und Juda', in *idem, Kleine Schriften*, II, pp. 116-34, esp. p. 134; von Rad, *Theologie des Alten Testaments*, I, p. 309. See further, Chapter 14 below.

(נכון) for all time' (v. 16).[35] The text here refers to kingships and king-doms by using three different terms which complement each other as well as distinguish themselves from each other: קוּם *hiphil* , כוּן *hiphil* and *polel*, נכון and נאמן. All the passages referred to are concerned with the establishment or decline of a kingdom, a kingdom which shall be strengthened, or not, by Yahweh. The contrasts are: 'establish' (הכין), and 'shall not stand, shall not come to pass' (לא־תקום).

The same is true for Amos 7.2. Amos, in his prophetic capacity, intercedes before Yahweh for the Northern kingdom: 'How can Jacob stand (מי יקום יעקב)? He is so small!' In Nah. 1.6 the statement is not quite as obvious,[36] but in view of the context it is probably right to say that the thrust of the statements of the Song of praise in 1.2-10 is directed towards Nineveh and that the passage describes the downfall of the capital.

In turning from this unanimous result to look again at the passages of the first group, a few comments should be added to what has been said above. In fact, one should read Isa. 14.24 only within the context of the unit 14.24-27. If Yahweh Sebaoth has sworn, 'As I have designed, so shall it be; and as I have planned, so shall it stand (היא תקום)', then, as the direct continuation runs, 'I will break the Assyrian in my land' (i.e. Assyria will be slain). Similar circumstances apply to some of the remaining passages; thus Isa. 46.10, including v. 11, and likewise Jer. 44.28-29; 51.29 (cf. Ps. 2). Yahweh is the navigator of history; his word, counsel and plan has historical power. The existence of Yah-weh's word is exclusive and where the words and plans of humans who are his tools rise up against Yahweh's word and plan only Yahweh's plan becomes reality—to the downfall and annihilation of the adver-sary. Against the background of these phraseological considerations, the interpretation of the message in Isa. 7.7 as a proclamation referring to the annihilation of some kingdom or some capital seems the most appropriate one.

Whose kingdom, though, is meant here? The answer is given in the prophetic speech introduced by כי. The conjunction כי in this particular place has caused rather great problems. Wolff opts for a causative meaning and comments that 'the statement of v. 7b finds an enigmatic

---

35. Cf. Hertzberg, *I and II Samuel, ad loc.*

36. Cf. T.H. Robinson and F. Horst, *Die zwölf kleinen Propheten* (HAT, 1.14; Tübingen: J.C.B. Mohr, 2nd edn, 1954), *ad loc.*

substantiation in vv. 8-9',[37] creating an enigma which he has to solve
with the help of an ellipse. Vriezen understands the conjunction in a
concessive sense and so he does not have to assume an elliptical
meaning for vv. 8-9.[38] Finally, the Jerusalem Bible dismisses the conjunction completely.[39]

The best interpretation so far has been offered by Rignell, because he
has managed to deal with the form as presented; he states: 'The fact
that the oracle is introduced rather abruptly into the context and also
remains an enigma by itself calls—as is so often the case in prophetic
oracles—for an interpretation or comment.' Thus vv. 8-9, 'which is
introduced with the explicative כי, provides such a comment on the
oracle'.[40] His observation supports the solution derived from the above
comments regarding phraseology.

The syntactical relationship between the oracle and its interpretation
is significant. Verses 8a and 9a are nominal clauses which are inserted
as subjects for the finite verb forms of v. 7b by means of the connective
כי. 'If a sentence is supposed to become the subject of another one it
will be introduced by the deictic particle כי.'[41] The oracle and its
prophetic interpretation therefore became a unit:

> Thus says the Lord Yahweh:
> 'It shall not stand,
>   and it shall not come to pass'—
> that the head of Syria is Damascus
>   and the head of Damascus is Rezin,[42]
> and the head of Ephraim is Samaria
>   and the head of Samaria is the son of Remaliah—

If understood and translated this way, each part of the individual sentences gains a clear meaning and a particular and necessary function,
while in the case of a syntactical connexion of vv. 5 and 7 one is driven

37. Wolff, *Das Zitat im Prophetenspruch*, p. 17.

38. T.C. Vriezen, 'Einige Notizen zur Übersetzung des Bindewortes *ki*', in
J. Hempel and L. Rost (eds.), *Von Ugarit bis Qumran* (Festschift O. Eissfeldt;
BZAW, 77; Berlin: Alfred Töpelmann, 1958), pp. 266-75 (269).

39. *La Sainte Bible* (Paris: Editions du Cerf, 1959), p. 996; note b interprets
elliptically: 'Les deux vers sont ironiques: Damas et Samarie n'ont pour chefs que
des hommes, Jérusalem a pour vrai roi Yahvé.'

40. Rignell, 'Das Immanuelzeichen', p. 104.

41. Brockelmann, *Hebräische Syntax*, §159a; cf. §31b; also H.S. Nyberg, *Hebreisk grammatik* (Uppsala: Almqvist & Wiksell, 1952), §97i.

42. As far as Isa. 7.8b is concerned, see the commentaries.

to a rather unconvincing interpretation of vv. 8a and 9a, if not to a disfigurement of the text altogether.[43]

The prophetic interpretation of the oracle leads to a message in the form of a direct address which can be paraphrased as follows:

> In the event that you do not believe,
> you will then certainly not stand![44]

These proverbially brief prophetic words, constructed with paronomasia, are not presented to an individual but to a group of people. Given the context of the announcement of Isa. 7.1ff., one may assume that the addressed group is the Davidic dynasty and especially king Ahaz as its representative. It is conspicuous that the demand of quintessential faith in this particular situation is put to a Davidide.

Among the above considerations regarding the existence of the kingdom, reference has been made to 'the Nathan promise' in 2 Samuel 7, not only promising the eternal existence of the throne of David, but telling of a covenant between Yahweh and King David,[45] which has led recent research to use the term 'Davidic covenant'.[46] This covenant of necessity comprises its own conditions—or rather, its realization lies in the conditions imposed by Yahweh, the Lord of the covenant: 'I will be a father to him [i.e. the Davidide], and he shall be a son to me, so that if he walks astray I will chasten him with a human rod and human strokes' (2 Sam. 7.14);[47] the establishment of the throne will not be threatened for the Davidides, even in the case of disobedience, but will be guaranteed 'as through fire'.[48] Psalm 132.12 stresses this 'condition' even more than the quoted condition: 'If your sons keep my covenant and my testimonies which I shall teach them, their sons shall also sit upon your throne for ever.'[49]

---

43. See Vriezen, 'Einige Notizen', p. 269; and Rignell, 'Das Immanuelzeichen', p. 105.

44. Although this translation is already an exegesis, one may still look for the reason in the following.

45. Cf. 2 Sam. 23.5.

46. Von Rad, *Theologie des Alten Testaments*, I, pp. 306ff. (ref. to further literature).

47. Cf. Hertzberg, *I and II Samuel, ad loc.*

48. Cf. 1 Cor. 3.15.

49. Cf. H.-J. Kraus, *Psalmen*, II (BKAT, 15.2; Neukirchen–Vluyn: Neukirchener Verlag, 5th edn, 1978 [1960]), pp. 777-94, esp. 790-92.

From Ps. 89.31-34[50] to 1 Chronicles 22, however, a different route is taken; regarding the Davidic picture within the history of the 'messianic' theology, it may be said that a path from a *theologia crucis* to a later *theologia gloriae* is followed.[51]

1 Chron. 17.13 contains the parallel verses to 2 Sam. 7.14, but the word of punishment is here missing completely while the promise of Yahweh's compassion is enhanced. Another parallel is 1 Chron. 22.10, which promises an eternal covenant of their throne instead of punishment. 1 Chron. 22.11-13 likewise offers a bright picture: wisdom and understanding will be given to David's son, 'so that you may keep (ולשמור) the law of Yahweh, your God (את־תורת יהוה אלהיך)'.[52] Significant are the concluding words which can be compared to Isa. 7.4: 'Be strong and of good courage; do not be afraid or dismayed.'[53]

The nomistic adaptation of 'the Nathan promise', which is flourishing here, also appears in Ps. 89.31ff. The intention of these verses should nevertheless be understood in the context of the whole Psalm, including the lament of vv. 39-52.[54] The condemnation of the Davidic kingdom is mourned; the 'punishment' has been actually experienced, yet the fault is not Yahweh's but that of the Davidides (v. 33), who have ignored the law of God (vv. 31-32). These verses seem merely to prepare for the lament of the condemnation, and yet the one who is lamenting prays to Yahweh on the grounds of the old, basic promise; for Yahweh alone can provide restitution.

If the history of interpretation of 'the Nathan promise', in different disguises, has led to the glorification of David, the picture in Isaiah 7 definitely represents an older layer of this story and shows a typical Isaianic shift in phraseology. If the prophetic words addressed to the house of David are

50. Cf. von Rad, *Theologie des Alten Testaments*, I, p. 309 n. 5.

51. Cf. von Rad, *Theologie des Alten Testaments*, I, pp. 347-48; also his *Das Geschichtsbild des chronistischen Werkes* (BWANT, 55; Stuttgart: W. Kohlhammer, 1930), pp. 119-32.

52. Cf. again Isa. 7.11.

53. Cf. 1 Chr. 28.4-10, in particular v. 6; v. 10 likewise closes with 'Be of good courage and do it!'

54. Kraus, *Psalmen*, II, *ad loc.*; also E. Rohland, 'Die Bedeutung der Erwählungstraditionen Israels für die Eschatologie der alttestamentlichen Propheten' (PhD Dissertation, University of Heidelberg, 1956), pp. 216-19.

אם לא תאמינו
כי לא תאמנו

then according to what has been said above, the second part of the verse with the *niphal* of אמן will have to correspond to the 'will stand' of those addressed. What 2 Sam. 7.16 had said about the dynasty—'your house and your kingdom will be established [נאמן] for ever'—is now described as being questionable and uncertain by using the same root. The conclusion of the unit contains, therefore, a serious threat against the ruling king of the house of David.

However, not everything has yet been said. The threat to the basic promise to the Davidides is really expressed in the 'condition' given in 2 Sam. 7.14. By alluding to the loyalty of the Davidides to the covenant, a loophole is left for him; the prophet expects the possibility of repentance, a תשובה. For this reason the word of the prophet should not be understood simply as a threat or 'oracle of judgment', but rather as an admonition to the king in which the element of threat is nevertheless apparent. The legitimation of the prophetic admonition is, as far as the tradition is concerned, the divine promise of 'the Nathan promise'. The typical features of Isaiah show in the fact that the 'condition' is formulated as a *condition of faith* by the use of the *hiphil* of אמן. Whence does Isaiah derive this term that so dominates his theology?[55]

As is well known, von Rad recognized with particular emphasis that there exists a significant parallelism[56] between 'faith' in Isaiah[57] and the religious attitude of the Israelites in their holy wars during the premonarchic period. This is especially true for Isaiah 7 as well as the story in Exodus 14, in both of which the 'faith' is directed towards a pure miracle of Yahweh.[58] The divine miracle that demands and at the

---

55. Cf. O. Procksch, *Theologie des Alten Testaments* (Gütersloh: C. Bertelsmann, 1950), pp. 180-82; 600ff.

56. Von Rad, *Der heilige Krieg*, pp. 46ff., 56ff.

57. Here, as well as in 28.16, האמין ב; 30.15, 'be quiet and trust'; 22.11, 'look to Yahweh'. Cf. R. Smend, 'Zur Geschichte von האמין', in *Hebräische Wortforschung* (Festschrift W. Baumgartnen; VTSup, 16; Leiden: E.J. Brill, 1967), pp. 284-90; repr. in *idem, Die Mitte des Alten Testaments: Gesammelte Studien*, I (BEvT, 99; Munich: Chr. Kaiser Verlag, 1986).

58. Von Rad, *Der heilige Krieg*, p. 58: 'On the other hand the difference is obvious: there a narrator who enlightens in an edifying way; here a prophet who wants to prepare the way for the miracle via a call to faith in a context of real distress.'

same time promotes faith[59] is the powerful intervention of Israel's God
that takes place completely independently of Israel's military strength.
It is Yahweh's intervening action that delivers the enemies 'into the
hand' of the Israelites. This 'delivering into the hand' is also an element
of the genre of the (divine) 'word of proof' (*Erweiswort*) which Zimmerli has identified[60] and which is not very different from the saying in
Isa. 7.7-9, except for emphasis on the crucial third element of
recognition.

However, Soggin has recently tried to show with the help of a few
prophetic passages that Yahweh's intervention against Israel by means
of foreign nations is another possibility.[61] His conclusion is that 'it is
part of the prophetic attempt to restore the ideology of a holy war, that
it is not only seen as God's acting towards the nations via Israel, but
rather as a "dialectic" relationship in which the sword is just as easily
turned the other way'.[62] If the word 'faith' in Isa. 7.9b, then, awakened
the old institution of a holy war, and if the negative reference to the
Davidic covenant was meant to be a warning to the fearful and nearly
lost Davidide, it would seem as if King Ahaz is being warned of a holy
war conducted by Yahweh. Yet, after all, the prophet uses the enigmatic message to refer to the imminent non-existence of the two king-
doms of Syria and Ephraim that were once—and will be again
sometime—a part of the Davidic empire.[63] This does not only betray a
Zionistic hope of restoration but first of all it provides a promise to the
king whose faith and 'Davidic' loyalty to the covenant now have to be
consolidated. The entire future of Jerusalem, indeed of 'all Israel',
depends on his loyalty to the covenant and his religious attitude
towards Yahweh, the Holy One of Israel.[64] For this reason the king's

59. Cf. Exod. 14.13-14 and v. 31!

60. W. Zimmerli, 'Das Wort des göttlichen Selbsterweises (Erweiswort), eine
prophetische Gattung', in *Mélanges bibliques: Rédigés en l'honneur de André
Robert* (Travaux de l'Inst. Cath. de Paris, 4; Paris: Bloud & Gay, 1957), pp. 154-
64; repr. in *idem, Gottes Offenbarung*, pp. 120-32.

61. J.A. Soggin, 'Der prophetische Gedanke über den heiligen Krieg, als
Gericht gegen Israel', *VT* 10 (1960), pp. 79-83.

62. Soggin, 'Der prophetische Gedanke über den heiligen Krieg', p. 83.

63. A. Alt, 'Das Grossreich Davids', in *idem, Kleine Schriften*, II, pp. 74-75,
222ff.

64. Würthwein, 'Jesaja 7,1-9', pp. 56ff., raised objections against von Rad, who
assumed 'divine or human action' here; he wants to put the emphasis on the Assyrian question, which hardly seems justified. Although the 'covenant with Assyria' is

faithful attitude has to be won and secured at all costs, and in order to reach this the prophet Isaiah spoke this *verbum concretissimum*,[65] and for no other reason than this the climax of his statement lies neither in the announcement of judgment upon the attacking kings nor in the promise or warning to Ahaz; the statements made in the unit 7.7-9 seen as a whole are rather a *prophetic admonition to the king* in the hour of decision and crisis.

Yet Isa. 7.3-6 is likewise to be seen as a word of prophetic admonition. The same presuppositions of prophetic speech that have been uncovered in B exist in A: the phraseology of the 'spiritual idea of a holy war'[66] as well as of 'the Nathan promise';[67] vv. 4 and 9 both contain elements of the ancient Israelite war language.[68] Yet it would be premature to conclude that therefore A and B constitute a unit, that is to say are a prophetic address of war.[69] One should rather conclude that vv. 3-6 and 7-9 are two Isaianic units that originate out of the same context of announcement and show the same theme; because of this connexion they belong together and are allowed to be heard together. They consititute two words of prophetic admonition that demonstrate to us that the prophet circled around the same topic in different ways, 'to strengthen the king's hand in God'.[70]

part of the situation and power relations of the time, the war with the Syrians is still the concrete occasion for the prophetic speech, and the prophet will hardly be interested in the 'how' of the defence; he does not appear as the counsellor of the king but as messenger of Yahweh.

65. Cf. H.-J. Kraus, *Prophetie und Politik* (ThExh, NF, 36; Munich: Chr. Kaiser Verlag, 1952), pp. 71ff.

66. Von Rad, *Der heilige Krieg*, p. 67.

67. Von Rad, *Der heilige Krieg*, p. 66 n. 2.

68. Cf., e.g., Deut. 20.(1-)3.

69. So Wolff, *Das Zitat im Prophetenspruch*, pp. 15ff.

70. Cf. 1 Sam. 23.16.

Chapter 7

TRADITIO-HISTORICAL PERSPECTIVES ON ISAIAH 8.9-10:
AN ATTEMPT TO CLARIFY AN OLD *CRUX INTERPRETUM*

The following comments refer primarily to the word רֹעוּ that introduces
Isa. 8.9. This seemingly simple verb form has caused considerable perplexity, as translations and interpretations make clear. The fact that the
commentaries also differ regarding the contextual arrangement and
authenticity of 8.9-10[1] is due to different understandings of this oracle,
and it is the opening word that has played an important role in interpretation. It seems advisable, then, to focus first of all on the verb.

1. *The Introductory Verb Form*

The verb has been understood differently. G.B. Gray classified the
various scholarly interpretations into four groups:

> Explanations that have been offered are that it is the impr. of (1) רעע,
> and means *be wicked*; or (2) of רעע, the Aramaic eqivalent of רצץ, and
> means *break*, or more doubtfully still, *be broken*; or (3) of רוע, whence
> comes תרועה, *war-cry,* and means *make an uproar*; but it is the Hiph. of
> this vb. that is used elsewhere; or (4) of רעה (whence רֵעַ), and means
> *associate yourselves* (RV 2nd marg.); but this would require a reflexive
> conjugation.[2]

Gray himself follows the LXX which reads a different verb—together
with several scholars of recent centuries, among whom one should

---

1. Cf. W. Eichrodt, *Der Heilige in Israel: Jesaja 1–12* (Die Botschaft des
Alten Testaments, 17.1; Stuttgart: Calwer Verlag, 1960), pp. 100-101; O. Kaiser,
Das Buch des Propheten Jesaja: Kap. 1–12 (ATD, 17; Göttingen: Vandenhoeck &
Ruprecht, 5th edn, 1981), pp. 182f.; Wildberger, *Jesaja,* I, pp. 329-33. See also G.
Fohrer, 'Zehn Jahre Literatur zur alttestamentlichen Prophetie (1951–1960)', *TRev*
28 (1962), pp. 1-75, 235-97, 301-74.
2. Gray, *The Book of Isaiah,* I, p. 150.

mention chiefly F. Buhl,[3] O. Procksch,[4] A. Bentzen,[5] S. Mowinckel,[6] E.J. Kissane,[7] and recently G. Fohrer[8] and O. Kaiser.[9] Other exegetes such as B. Duhm,[10] E. König,[11] F. Feldmann,[12] L.G. Rignell[13] and W. Eichrodt,[14] on the other hand, have tried to manage with the verb presented in the MT.[15]

Among the old translations, it appears, one has attached special importance to the LXX. And yet, by quoting v. 9 in a paraphrasing manner, the LXX differs considerably from the MT:

γνῶτε ἔθνη καὶ ἡττᾶσθε, ἐπακούσατε ἕως ἐσχάτου τῆς γῆς, ἰσχυκότες ἡττᾶσθε· ἐὰν γὰρ πάλιν ἰσχύσητε, πάλιν ἡττηθήσεσθε.[16]

The LXX reads a form of the verb ידע, and has therefore either not understood the form of the MT or mistaken ר for ד. It has changed the Hebrew 'repetitive style' and made other alterations as well. An attempt to reconstitute its Hebrew source seems useless in this case and its value for text-critical work on the MT therefore remains rather questionable.[17]

3.   F. Buhl, *Jesaja* (Copenhagen: Gyldendalske Boghandel, 2nd edn, 1912), *ad loc.*

4.   Procksch, *Jesaja*, I, *ad loc.*

5.   Bentzen, *Jesaja*, I, *ad loc.*

6.   Mowinckel and Messel, *De senere profeter*, pp. 101f., 785.

7.   Kissane, *The Book of Isaiah*, I, *ad loc.*

8.   See G. Fohrer, *Das Buch Jesaja*, I (Zürcher Bibelkommentare; Zürich: Zwingli-Verlag, 1960).

9.   Kaiser, *Jesaja*, *ad loc.*

10.   רעוּ (the LXX incorrectly: דְעוּ) rhymes with חֹתּוּ'; Duhm, *Das Buch Jesaja*, p. 58. He translates: 'rage…'.

11.   'Shake…'; König, *Das Buch Jesaja*, p. 124. However, in his *Hebräisches und aramäisches Wörterbuch zum AT* (Wiesbaden: M. Sändig, 1910), p. 449, he gives 'rage' (s.v. I רעע).

12.   'Rage…'; Feldmann, *Das Buch Isaias*, pp. 101, 104.

13.   'Act wickedly…'; L. Rignell, 'Das Orakel "Maher-salal Has-bas" Jesaja 8', *ST* 10 (1956), pp. 40-52 (44).

14.   'Rage…'; Eichrodt, *Der Heilige in Israel: Jesaja 1–12*, *ad loc.*

15.   J. Reider, 'Etymological Studies: ידע or ירע and רעע', *JBL* 66 (1947), pp. 315-17, does not discuss Isa. 8.9-10, but instead Judg. 8.16; Ezek. 19.7; Ps. 138.6; Prov. 10.9; Job 21.19.

16.   According to Ziegler, *Isaias*. See the variants in the apparatus.

17.   I. Engnell remarked critically on several occasions on the text-critical value of the LXX, 'Methodological Aspects of Old Testament Study', p. 20 n. 2 (with references to further literature).

The later translations of Aquila, Symmachus and Theodotion, as well as the Targum and the Vulgate read a form of the verb רעה II in translating 'gather'.[18] This particular meaning of the verb is attested only once, in the *hithpael* (Prov. 22.24)[19] and the meaning it carries there does not easily fit in with the notion of people. The form as a imperfect plural is, furthermore, impossible to derive from a *lamed he*-verb. The interpreters of this group of translations may have had a source that represents a tradition differing from the MT. The Syriac translation reads זועו, which means 'tremble'.[20]

It seems as if the difficulties of modern interpreters are in fact just a continuation of the helplessness of the first translators. The problem has always been mainly the verb stem from which to derive this form, which is a *hapax legomenon*.[21] Since, then, the form רעו appears completely isolated and lexically without any reference, as well as without support in the old translations, we can now explain it only in the context of the proverb. This requires the assumption that the proverb can be confined to the passage 8.9-10 as a relatively self-contained unit.

Many interpreters have chosen to explain this via the context, but to me this procedure seems to have been rather too random and inadequate to do justice to the material. There have, for example, been attempts to justify the translation 'recognize' adopted from the LXX on the grounds that this is the best parallel to והאזינו.[22] That does no justice to the first function of the form וחתו.[23] Furthermore, one should not take it for granted that the 'people' who are addressed and 'all the ends of the earth' are simply identical. The hemistichs 9a, c and d as well as 10a and b are constructed analogously, with one pair of verbs each. We are therefore permitted to begin with the imperatives of these hemistichs, excluding for the moment 9b.

It is a feature of the Qumran biblical mansucript 1QIs[a24] that 8.9 and

18. See, e.g. Wildberger, *Jesaja*, I, p. 329.

19. According to *BHK* and KB, also Isa. 11.7 (conjecturally; cf. *HALAT*, 1177a).

20. See S.P. Brock (ed.), *The Old Testament in Syriac*, III.1 (Leiden: E.J. Brill, 1987), *ad loc.*

21. According to S. Mandelkern, *Veteris Testamenti Concordantiae* (Hierosolymis/Tel Aviv, 6th edn, 1964), p. 1104.

22. See, e.g., Bentzen, *Jesaja*, I.

23. See Budde, *Jesaja's Erleben*, p. 81, who changes *waḥottû* to *yaḥdaw*, which means 'at the same time'.

24. M. Burrows (ed.), *The Dead Sea Scrolls of St Mark's Monastery*, I (New

8.10 introduce one line each, so that the similarity of the forms רעו and עצו is clearly stressed:

9   רעו עמים וחתו...

10   עצו עצה ותפר...

Like רְעוּ also, עֻצוּ is a rare form (instead of the common עֻצוּ), which otherwise appears only in Judg. 19.30 and is not derived from the common verb יעץ but from its variant עוץ. The form רעו, which also seems so strange to us, may be influenced by the special form עצו or vice-versa; the form וחתו may have contributed significantly to this special vocalization.[25] The phonetic adjustment of these imperatives, which seems to have been particularly noticed by the Qumran scribes,[26] may thus be the result of a deliberate stylization of the saying.

These observations may have contributed to an understanding of this peculiar form, but nothing has yet been said regarding the connotation of the introductory word, nor the range of meanings it might have here. This can, to some extent, be derived from the meanings of the remaining imperatives—on the assumption that both verses present a relatively unified complex of ideas.

First, the form וחתו, which can be derived from the verb חתת, 'break', 'be full of fear' (KB/*HALAT*). The verb occurs in *qal* 17 times, as in our passage, and 29 (28) times in the *niphal*, twice in the *piel* and five times in the *hiphil*. The occurrences are distributed over 18 (17) passages outside the prophetic literature and 35 within it. Most of the non-prophetic references have the *niphal*: Deut. 1.21; 31.8; Jos. 1.9; 8.1; 10.25; 1 Sam. 2.10(Q); 17.11; 1 Chron. 22.13; 28.20; 2 Chron. 20.15, 17; 32.7.

In most of these cases a second verb, expressing fear, is added to this verb. Together the two verbs seem to have established a set formula, that is, a negatively formulated encouraging word of admonition: אל־תירא ואל־תחת. The positive counterpart appears three times in Jos. 1.2-9 and 10.25: 'Be strong and of good courage!' If we ignore later passages such as 1 Chron. 22.13, 28.20, the context of the admonition word seems to be one of war and battle. References such as Deut. 1.21, Jos. 8.1, 10.25 as well as 2 Chron. 20.15-17, 32.7 are war speeches

Haven: The American Schools of Oriental Research, 1950).

25. See Duhm, *Das Buch Jesaja*, *ad loc*.

26. See S. Holm-Nielsen, *Hodayot: Psalms from Qumran* (AThD, 2; Aarhus: Universitetsforlaget, 1960), pp. 30ff., especially p. 352.

given before the battle and encouraging fearlessness, since fear and
timidity disqualify one from battle (Judg. 7.3ff.). It was even more fatal
when Saul and the whole of Israel 'despaired and were very afraid',
ויחתו ויראו מאד, 1 Sam. 17.11. How much in ancient times the moment
of trembling, paralysis, desperation—in short, debilitating fear—dominated both warfare and the way in which it was described becomes very
clear, and in a baroque way, in the Song of the Sea, Exodus 15:

> 14 When the *peoples* heard, they *trembled*;
>   *pangs seized* the inhabitants of Philistia.
> 15 Then were the chiefs of Edom *dismayed*;
>   the leaders of Moab, *trembling seized them*;
>   all inhabitants of Canaan *were panic-stricken*.
> 16 *Terror* and *dread* fell upon them;
>   because of the greatness of your arm,
>   they *became still as a stone*,
>   while your people, Yahweh, passed by,
> while the people whom you have purchased, passed by.[27]

Although the verb מחת does not occur in Exod. 15.14-16, several terms
allude to the circle of ideas to which it belongs. All of these verbs refer
to military failure and defeat. The language, certainly old and to some
extent stereotyped—partly hymnically, partly deuteronomistically,
partly Chronistically framed—belongs without any doubt with the ideology and institution of the ancient Israelite holy war as especially
shown in the work of G. von Rad.[28]

In other places we are presented with the address of an individual;
although the context of the war disappears into the background it still
dictates the terminology, as in Jos. 1.9 and Deut. 31.7-8 where before
the taking of the land Joshua is appointed as the commander of the
army and the people. It is an appointment that proves itself especially in
warfare. Most interesting is the way, finally, in which this phraseology
takes effect among the prophets.[29]

27. Cf. Noth, *Das zweite Buch Mose: Exodus*.

28. Von Rad, *Der heilige Krieg*. Also, R. de Vaux, *Ancient Israel: Its Life and
Institutions* (trans. J. McHugh; London: Darton, Longman & Todd, 1961),
pp. 213ff.

29. So particularly in the call speech to Jeremiah, Jer. 1.17-19, which is rather
close to Josh. 1.29. Ezek. 2.6 and 3.9 again seem to be dependent on Jeremiah; see
W. Zimmerli, *Ezechiel*, I (BKAT, 13.1; Neukirchen–Vluyn: Neukirchener Verlag,
2nd edn, 1979 [1969]), pp. 16-18, 74ff. Like a military commander, the prophet
will fight against his various enemies without any fear as the appointed one of
Yahweh.

Second, the form הִתְאַזְּרוּ, from √אזר, 'put on' or 'gird oneself' (KB) or 'arm oneself' (GesB). This verb, which occurs 14 (15) times is twice used in reference to God's act of creation and kingship, Ps. 67.7; 93.1; otherwise it refers to humans. It can describe the loincloth of a man, 2 Kgs 1.8, Job 38.3; 40.7; 30.18, or in a methaphorical sense indicate joy, Ps. 30.12; in a few cases it has a military connotation. In Ps. 18.33, 40 (certainly old) and 2 Sam. 22.40 it expresses gratitude towards God:

> For you girded me with strength for the battle
> you made my assailants sink under me.[30]

In Hannah's song of praise the contrast is also to be understood in a military sense:

> The bows of the mighty are broken,
> but the feeble gird on strength.[31]

Finally, the speech installing Cyrus, Isa. 45.1ff., is important in revealing the semantic profile of the verb. According to this verse the loins of the kings will be *ungirded* while the nations will be defeated by Cyrus, who is *girded* by Yahweh (v. 5). Both are due to Yahweh's free will; as master of military and political events, he will grant the power.

Third, the form עֻצוּ, 8.10, from עוץ, 'make a plan' (KB), which is thought to be a variant of יעץ, 'advise', 'plan' (KB). In this particular case one does not need to go through all the references for the more common form יעץ in order to classify the term, but can focus instead on the combination of the phrase עוּץ עֵצָה with its parallel דִּבֶּר דָּבָר.

The noun עצה occurs relatively frequently in the book of Isaiah.[32] It belongs, as H. Wildberger has demonstrated,[33] to those terms which constitute the Isaianic understanding of history. As has often been stressed, politics plays an important role in Isaiah's understanding of

---

30. Cf. Kraus, *Psalmen*, I–II.

31. Cf. Hertzberg, *I and II Samuel*, ad loc.

32. See G. Lisowsky, *Konkordanz zum hebräischen Alten Testament* (Stuttgart: Privileg. Württ. Bibelanstalt, 1958).

33. In his paper 'Jesajas Geschichtsverständnis', in *Congress Volume: Bonn 1962* (VTSup, 9; Leiden: E.J. Brill, 1963), pp. 83-117, especially pp. 87ff. See also J. Fichtner, 'Jahves Plan in der Botschaft des Jesaja', *ZAW* 63 (1951), pp. 16-33; P.A.H. de Boer, 'The Counsellor', in *Wisdom in Israel and in the Ancient Near East* (Festschrift H.H. Rowley; VTSup, 3; Leiden: E.J. Brill, 1955), pp. 42-71.

history.[34] Over against human agreements and plans stands God's plan and counsel, partly difficult to understand or mysterious, partly in sheer opposition to the acts and dealings of men, 5.19; 28.29; 30.1; it is here above all that the dynamics of history are based. The last passage has the parallel terms 'hatch plans' and 'make an alliance',[35] and the continuation, 30.2ff., shows how strong the military and political focus is. These expressions correspond with the word pair in 8.10.

The second term in Isa. 8.10, דַּבְּרוּ דָבָר, also occurs in Hos. 10.4, as a parallel to כרת ברית, 'arrange a meeting' (KB) or 'to enter into a contract'.[36] One should probably think mainly of a 'contract between king and people' and only secondly, between vv. 3 and 4b of 'foreign political agreements'.[37] Be that as it may, the meaning will have to be sought within a political or military-political context. In Isaiah, foreign politics are of particular significance. This becomes clear if one looks at the sentence יעץ עלך ארם רעה in 7.5, stemming from the time of the Syrian–Ephraimite war, and likewise in Isa. 30.1. Terminologically as well as in content, 8.10 therefore seems to be close to 7.3-6 or at least to 7.1ff.[38] In view of the political issue involved, we can assume a far more concrete reference than is actually expressed—at least if we point with Bentzen[39] to Psalm 2, or with Kaiser[40] to the Songs of Zion, Psalms 46, 48 and 76. Although these assumptions are on the mark, they do not quite grasp the special topic of our verses. Their approach has made it possible to take seriously[41] a special cultic tradition of

34. Cf. Procksch, *Jesaja*, I; Kraus, *Prophetie und Politik*.

35. Cf. G. Fohrer, *Das Buch Jesaja*, II (Zürcher Bibelkommentare; Zürich: Zwingli-Verlag, 1962).

36. So H.W. Wolff, *Dodekapropheton. I. Hosea* (BKAT, 14.1; Neukirchen–Vluyn: Neukirchener Verlag, 4th edn, 1990 [1961]), p. 221.

37. So Wolff, *Hosea*, p. 227, following G. Fohrer, 'Der Vertrag zwischen König und Volk in Israel', *ZAW* 71 (1959), pp. 1-22 (17).

38. See Chapter 6 above.

39. Bentzen, *Jesaja*, I, p. 70. Bentzen draws attention to the connexion with the thoughts in 7.4-9; so also Duhm, *Das Buch Jesaja*, p. 58.

40. Kaiser, *Jesaja*, pp. 182f.

41. Cf. Kaiser, *Jesaja*, p. 182. On the fundamental significance of a distinct Zion tradition see esp. Rohland, 'Die Bedeutung', pp. 119ff.; cf. G. von Rad, *Old Testament Theology* (2 vols.; London: SCM Press, 1975), I, pp. 39ff.; II, pp. 155, 292ff.; Kraus, *Psalmen*, I, pp. 94-108 (on the specific Jerusalem-Zion traditions; with further lit.).

Jerusalem, that is, 'the ultimate invulnerability of the city of God';[42] this is a significant factor since it constitutes the stable basis of our passage, as the concluding statement כי עמו אל makes probable.[43] But what is special and exegetically significant in Isa. 8.9-10 is the military phraseology and its political reference—as the semantic sketch above has sought to prove, as well as the particular *address* to (certain) nations, which deserves to be considered as a formal peculiarity.

2. *Form-historical Remarks*

The unit can be understood as prophetic speech.[44] As Duhm has already observed,[45] the specific form of the unit corresponds to Isa. 29.9-10:

9   Stare—and be frozen!
          Look around—and be blind!
        Be drunk—but not with wine,
          stagger—but not with strong drink!
10   For Yahweh has poured out upon you
        a spirit of deep sleep...[46]

Both passages present us with the same powerful transformation between an intended positive whose possibility is then negated, or at least a call which is followed by a reason which then reveals a different factual situation from what the call implies. Following the first verb, the passage should be read as follows:

9— you peoples—and yet be afraid!
      Listen (to it), all the ends of the earth!
      Gird yourselves—and yet be afraid!
      Arm yourselves—and yet be afraid!
10   Make a plan—and yet it will collapse!
      Come to an agreement—and it will not come to pass!
      For 'God is with us'.

42. Kaiser, *Jesaja*, pp. 182.

43. This reason for the preceding was wrongly removed by Duhm (*Das Buch Jesaja, ad loc.*) as an 'addition' that was 'trivial in the mouth of the prophet'. On the other side, Budde (*Jesaja's Erleben*, p. 90) regarded these words as the crystallization of the preceding discourse.

44. See Budde, *Jesaja's Erleben.*

45. Duhm, *Das Buch Jesaja*, p. 58.

46. Cf. Fohrer, *Das Buch Jesaja*, II, pp. 73-76.

Instead of the second part in vv. 9a and 10b one could easily insert 'in vain'. Since the text operates with contrary meanings, what is intended is the opposite to what the prophet initially calls for. With words referring to military and political activity the prophet invites military-political passivity or to the giving up of military operations as well as of political alliances. How is this to be understood? What is really the significance of this invitation?

The answer to this question has been made considerably easier by the work of R. Bach.[47] Investigating the oracles against the nations in the book of Jeremiah and shorter oracles among other prophets[48] he has described two so far unnoticed genres of request/invitation, one of which, the 'invitation to battle', is relevant to our text.[49] He has analysed the particular phraseology and attempted to prove that the genre had its roots in the ancient holy wars of Israel,[50] and that later the prophet partly took on the role of charismatic war-leader.[51]

The invitation to battle, which can be expressed in divine as well as prophetic speech 'is issued in the form of imperatives, almost without any exception in the masculine plural'; the statements refer to (a) the summoning and the advance of troops; (b) the preparation of the weapons or armour; (c) the military action itself. 'The vocabulary is extensive' but without distracting from the theme.[52] In view of the 'circle of people addressed it is noteworthy that names of nations hardly ever occur at all'.[53] The invitation is usually followed by a reason in form of an oracle of doom, less commonly in the form of an oracle of salvation.[54]

According to its form and topic, Isa. 8.9-10 fits into the picture which Bach describes as 'genre of invitation to battle'; but this means only that the background of this particular genre offers the best explanation

---

47. R. Bach, *Die Aufforderungen zur Flucht und zum Kampf im alttestamentlichen Prophetenspruch* (WMANT, 9; Neukirchen Kreis Moers: Neukirchener Verlag, 1962).

48. Bach has not, however examined Isa. 8.9-10.

49. Bach, *Aufforderungen*, pp. 51ff.

50. Bach, *Aufforderungen*, pp. 92ff.

51. 'The "military" function of the charismatic has passed over to the king, while the "charismatic" function of the charismatic seems to have been transferred first to the lot oracle, and then to prophecy' (Bach, *Aufforderungen*, p. 111).

52. Bach, *Aufforderungen*, p. 62f.

53. Bach, *Aufforderungen*, pp. 65, 83.

54. Bach, *Aufforderungen*, pp. 66ff.

for it and that it is not an independent genre itself, but *a prophetic imitation of an older genre*. This shows in the fact mainly that the actual military terminology is attested only in 8.9, while in 8.10 the prophet bends the traditional military content towards the political by using terms of his favoured covenant politics; and this was made all the easier for him because the military and political issues overlap.

Now, Bach expects that the genre, originally a 'short instruction', finally could have come to be fixed as a 'rhetorical form'.[55] But this can hardly apply to the case of Isa. 8.9-10. The particular problem of this oracle lies in the previously mentioned address to the foreign nations. When he discusses oracles that are analogous in this respect, Bach sees the literary use of the genre 'in the prophetic saying as a report of the orders given out by Yahweh to the nations and heard by the prophet';[56] a divine speech is therefore the only possibility that can be considered, and passages such as Jer. 46.3-6 and 46.9-10 as well as Joel 4.9 ff. are also cited in this regard.[57] Alternatively, Bach sees in them 'in the prophetic saying as a quotation of future demands and orders of the attackers',[58] as in Jer. 6.4ff.; the one who utters the demand is therefore the attacking enemy.[59] Since Isa. 8.9f. is dealing with a prophetic oracle to the 'nations' in Bach's explanation seems insufficient and one could only wish he had discussed his view on a broader basis. He certainly suspects, quite correctly, that the request was originally addressed to Israel;[60] this, however, makes it even more important for the understanding the history of the genre to follow up the variety of ways in which it is used by the prophets and in particular to discuss the adaptation of the address to the nations. Let us look at one point that in my opinion is relevant to Isa. 8.9-10.

Bach does not really take seriously that the calls to battle addressed to Israel's enemies are of an *ironic* character when coming from the mouth of the prophet. He mentions the possibility twice, in respect of Joel 4.9ff. and Jer. 46.3-6 and 9f., but only to deny it immediately.[61] In respect of the few passages that Bach considers one probably has to

55. Bach, *Aufforderungen*, pp. 70-71, 73, 81, 85.
56. Bach, *Aufforderungen*, p. 85.
57. Bach, *Aufforderungen*, pp. 71-2, 79-80.
58. Bach, *Aufforderungen*, p. 85.
59. Bach, *Aufforderungen*, p. 69f., 83f., 85f.
60. Bach, *Aufforderungen*, pp. 82-84.
61. Bach, *Aufforderungen*, p. 71f.

agree with him. But the material is actually much more extensive.

The power and effect of mocking oracles and songs was known in Israel from ancient times,[62] and thus they were used as a 'fearful political weapon' that 'conveyed protection and trust for one's own nation while exposing the enemy to contempt and destruction'.[63] Even though the later threats of the prophets replaced these mocking-songs, O. Eissfeldt maintained that there remains a relationship between the two genres, since 'these threats against the nations quite often exhibit motifs of the mocking-song (Isa. 37.22-29; 47)'.[64] The ironic use of the funeral lament was also much favoured,[65] a particular example being Isa. 14.4-21. In the first part of Isaiah (chs. 1–12) one should also expect to find ironic elements, at least as far as Asshur is concerned (10.5ff.).[66] If the attackers in the Syro–Ephraimite war are characterized as these 'two smouldering stumps of firebrands' (7.4),[67] this is likewise scorn and mockery; but also typical is a low estimate of the power and ability of the attacking nations. The prophet possibly borrows this manner of speaking from the old tradition 'since the mocking-song loves the gaudy effect reached by comparing earlier glory and present shame, the arrogance before the fall and the pitiful end'.[68] This phenomenon is as easy to detect in Isa. 8.9-10; as already earlier, the proximity of 7.1ff. and 8.9-10 is obvious also in this respect;[69] for despite the fact that those addressed here are only called 'peoples nations', עמים, the historical occasion for this unit may be as concrete as for 7.1ff. The fact that the addressees are not mentioned by name in this genre is determined by the history of the genre itself.[70]

Rather than calling Isa. 8.9-10 a 'short triumph song' or a 'fragment

62. O. Eissfeldt, *The Old Testament: An Introduction* (Oxford: Oxford University Press, 1965), pp. 75ff., 105ff.

63. Eissfeldt, *The Old Testament: An Introduction*, p. 107.

64. Eissfeldt, *The Old Testament: An Introduction*, p. 108.

65. Eissfeldt, *The Old Testament: An Introduction*, p. 109ff.

66. The mocking can be heard here, though it is not the main emphasis.

67. The irony of the prophet is especially impressive if read against the background of the editorial introduction (7.1-2).

68. Eissfeldt, *The Old Testament: An Introduction*, p. 108.

69. So also Eichrodt, *Der Heilige in Israel*, p. 101.

70. Bach, *Aufforderungen*, pp. 82-84. Thus it is not necessary to understand 'nations' universalistically, i.e. as the equivalent of 'all nations', as often happens; cf. among others, W. Dietrich, *Jesaja und die Politik* (BEvT, 74; Munich: Chr. Kaiser Verlag, 1976), p. 134.

of a Psalm',[71] form-critical considerations lead one to understand the unit as a genuine prophetic oracle in which the prophet imitated the old genre of 'call to the battle', actualized it politically and used it to scorn and mock hostile nations. The certainty of victory that the oracle conveys is not founded in the military strength of Judah/Jerusalem but religiously motivated: God, who has chosen Zion as his dwelling[72] and who is exalted above all armed and aggressive nations, will provide security for his city! Neither psychologically nor politically is it impossible that Isaiah maintained this 'Zion theme' along with his oracles of judgment; in a similar way he often depended on the special Zion tradition elsewhere.[73]

Hence it is reasonable to suppose that, given the links in form and content to 7.1ff., Isa. 8.9-10 belongs to those oracles that have been handed down from their original setting in preaching about the Syro–Ephraimite war.[74] The question about the compositional classification of the unit, which has interested so many exegetes, is secondary:[75] it is possible that the passage found its present position in 8.8b and 8.10 because of an association with the words עמנו אל.[76]

3. *Conclusion*

The context has now been analysed and interpreted in different ways, and it is this context that allows us to understand the problematic opening word רעו. We can thus return to the problems discussed at the outset.

Phraseologically as well as form-historically, Isa. 8.9 appears to be completely orientated towards warfare. Considering this background, it is rather suprising that many modern exegetes have adopted the

71. Cf. Kaiser, *Jesaja*, p. 84.

72. Cf. Isa. 8.18 and the other Isaiah texts, which Rohland, 'Die Bedeutung', pp. 145ff. has discussed in detail.

73. Against Rohland, 'Die Bedeutung', pp. 145ff.; von Rad, *Old Testament Theology*, II, pp. 158ff.

74. So Rohland, 'Die Bedeutung', pp. 169ff., and Lindblom, *A Study on the Immanuel Section*, pp. 31-33.

75. It will not be possible to review here the thesis of an 'Isaianic *Denkschrift*' (6.1–9.6), cf. Budde, *Jesaja's Erleben*, pp. 1ff.; but see recently Reventlow, 'Das Ende der sog. "Denkschrift" Jesajas'.

76. So J. Lindblom in his major study, *Prophecy in Ancient Israel* (Oxford: Basil Blackwell, 1962), p. 248.

translation 'recognize' of the Septuagint. What makes such a translation particularly strange in this context is its *absolute* use. Had it really been used in this sense one would require both a subject and an object of the word 'recognize'.[77] The impression can hardly be avoided that recent exegesis has dealt very uncritically with this point. Not only is the translation 'act ungodlessly' generally an exegetical problem, it does not fit either into the established formal context even though it is appropriate to the preaching of Isaiah.[78] The translation 'rage' derived from the root רעע II verb, 'break' might be acceptable because of its closeness to Psalm 2; but it must be rejected, for such a translation is lexically rather weak and too general for the kind of language used in this passage. It seems to come the closest, yet does not quite fit.

In view of the context the root רוע seems the only possible one for the imperative רעוּ. The imperative furnishes the only instance of a *qal* of this verb, but the meaning will be the same as that of the more common *hiphil*: 'raise a war cry'.[79] The introductory word corresponds then to a ritual of holy war[80] and belongs to the genre of the 'call to battle'.[81]

By attributing this meaning to the first part of this verse a different light is shed on to 8.9b, which has so far been excluded from our examination. On the basis of the war cries of the nations, the 'give ear'

77. Marti, Procksch and Kaiser have clearly experienced a difficulty at this point, because they take 'it' as the object of recognition. But what could 'it' be in this case? However, Dietrich, *Jesaja und die Politik*, p. 134, parallelizing with *ha'ăzînû* 'listen', presupposes, without textual grounds, a verb form *šim'û* and translates 'hear'.

78. Cf. Rignell, 'Das Orakel', p. 44.

79. So already H. Schmidt, 'Jesaja 8, 9 und 10', in G. Bertram (ed.), *Stromata* (Giessen, 1930), pp. 3-10; cf. J. Hempel, *Hebräisches Wörterbuch zu Jesaja* (1936), p. 50: this imperative form belongs to a *double 'ayin* verb. But the *'ayin waw* verb also frequently displays variations, assuming forms identical to the *double 'ayin* verb, and vice versa. See Nyberg, *Hebreisk grammatik*, §52x and y, under Kal imperative (ō instead of ū); and H. Bauer and P. Leander, *Historische Grammatik der hebräischen Sprache*, I (Halle: M. Niemeyer, 1922), §56, especially points (h), (p) and (u); see also (more briefly) GKC 72dd, §110f and g.

80. See the lexica under רוע *hiphil*; cf. P. Humbert, *La 'Terou'a': Analyse d'un rite biblique* (Recueil de travaux publié par la Faculté des Lettres, Université de Neuchâtel, 23; Neuchâtel, 1946), pp. 29f.; von Rad, *Der heilige Krieg*, p. 11; F. Stolz, *Jahwes und Israels Kriege* (ATANT, 60; Zürich: Zwingli-Verlag, 1972), p. 48.

81. Bach, *Aufforderungen*, p. 64.

addressed to 'all far countries'[82] can probably be interpreted not only as listening to God's message delivered by the prophet but also—and possibly even more so—as hearing war cries. The 'far countries' are called as witnesses.[83] Before the tribunal of the whole world the prophet invites the hostile nations to a forlorn battle against the city of God:

> Raise the war cry, you nations—and be dismayed!
> Give ear, all you far countries!

82. On the connexion between the 'nations' and the 'far countries of the earth', cf. the opinion of Duhm, *Das Buch Jesaja*, 58f.; cf. also Procksch, *Theologie des Alten Testaments*, p. 201: 'Isaiah is clearly fond of the concept of the "far" (*merḥāq*: 8,9; 10,3; 17,13; 30.27)'.

83. Cf. H. Graf Reventlow, 'Die Völker als Jahwes Zeugen bei Ezechiel', *ZAW* 71 (1959), pp. 33-43, especially p. 43.

Chapter 8

FROM EMPIRE TO WORLD RULE: SOME REMARKS
ON PSALMS 72.8; 89.26; ZECHARIAH 9.10b

Psalm 72.8 describes the expansion of the dominion of the Davidic king in Jerusalem with the following words: 'May he rule from sea to sea, from the river to the ends of the earth' (וירד מים עד־ים ומנהר עד־אפסי־ארץ). This statement is made in the form of an optative sentence. Apart from the introductory verb form—likewise in the form of an optative—the precise words appear again in Zech. 9.10b.

A similar statement set in the context of a divine promise to David or at least to the Davidic king is also to be found in Ps. 89.26: 'I will set his hand on the sea and his right hand on the rivers' (ושמתי בים ידו ובנהרות ימינו).[1] Missing from this latter passage is the formula מן...עד as an expression of the geographical expansion. The parallel pair of words 'sea/river', on the other hand, occurs in all three passages.

As far as the text is concerned, the passages do not show any significant variations, which makes an examination easier and might be taken as a hint that we are dealing here with a standard formula or with formulaic language. This suspicion can be further substantiated in another way.

The 'expansion' formulae of these passages are in general understood universalistically—often without any further consideration regarding the origin or background of the formulaic language. It is therefore understandable that these passages go unnoticed in geographical handbooks such as those of Simons, Abel or Aharoni.[2] Nor does

---

1. For the translation, cf. Kraus, *Psalmen*, I–II, and A. Weiser, *Die Psalmen*, II (ATD, 15; Göttingen: Vandenhoeck & Ruprecht, 10th edn, 1987 [1963]), where they deal with this passage. See also L.R. Fisher (ed.), *Ras Shamra Parallels*, I (AnOr, 49; Rome: Pontificium Institutum Biblicum, 1972), pp. 195f., esp. p. 218 n. 2.

2. J. Simons, *The Geographical and Topographical Texts of the Old Testament*

my own related study to the subject[3] refer to these texts when the מִן...עַד formula is discussed. On a closer look, however, the question emerges whether the generally assumed universalistic account of ruler-ship of these passages and the 'concrete' use of the formula of expansion מִן...עַד in other local-geographical places should be kept com-pletely apart, as is commonly done. Following Kraus, Soggin has pointed to a more complex matter. Examining Ps. 72.8, he states that 'in this piece we are confronted by a peculiar mixture of local-geo-graphical ("from the river . . .", that is, from the Euphrates) and cosmic terms ("from sea to sea . . . until the ends of the earth")'.[4] In order to understand and appreciate the meaning of the statements from a better perspective, it is advisable to look once again briefly at their stereo-typed phraseology.

The first characteristics that meet the eye are that we are dealing with two Royal Psalms and that all three passages refer to the Davidic King or the Davidic Messiah. Another look at other Royal Psalms for an explanation therefore suggests itself, and has been undertaken quite often. The worldwide persective of Psalms 2 and 110, which speak of the peoples and nations of the world (see also Ps. 18.44-45),[5] has been pointed out as the main characteristic. Although this is not inappropri-ate, the peculiarity of the passages we are looking at here is rather the geographically determined expansion of the dominion of the king or Messiah; in Psalms 2 and 110 (or 18) this issue does not appear in the same way, and is in fact hardly noticeable. The reference to the king has been evaluated differently.

In his book *The Legacy of Canaan*, J. Gray tried to understand the phrase 'from the river to the ends of the earth' in Ps. 72.8b in the light of a statement about El which describes the dwelling of the Canaanite high God:

(Leiden: E.J. Brill, 1959); F.M. Abel, *Géographie de la Palestine*, I–II (Paris: J. Gabalda, 1967); Y. Aharoni, *The Land of the Bible* (London: Burns & Oates, 1968).

3. M. Sæbø, '*Grenzbeschreibung* und Landideal in Alten Testament: Mit besonderer Berücksichtigung der *min-'ad*-Formel', *ZDPV* 90 (1974), pp. 14-37.

4. J.A. Soggin, 'Zum zweiten Psalm', in H.F. Stoebe (ed.), *Wort–Gebot–Glaube: Festschrift für W. Eichrodt* (ATANT, 59; Zürich: Zwingli-Verlag, 1970), pp. 191-207; the quotation is from p. 202.

5. See, e.g., Kraus, *Psalmen*, II, on this passage, especially pp. 147f., on the 'world domination the Judaean King'. See also A. Bentzen, *Fortolkning til de gammeltestamentlige Salmer* (Copenhagen: G.E.C. Gad, 1939), pp. 415-16.

...El at the springs of the two streams (*il.mbk.nhrm*) [in the midst of the depths] of both oceans ([*qrb.apq*].*thmtm*).[6]

Gray states: 'The imagery of the throne of God from which waters flow (Psalm 46.5; cf. Ezekiel 47 and Joel 4.18...), which is localized in Jerusalem, reflects the survival of the tradition of the Canaanite El there, which in turn is reflected in the conception of the Davidic King reigning "from the river to the ends of the earth"...'[7] What speaks against this—apart from the lack of the word נהר in Ezek. 47.1ff. and Joel 4.18—is that v. 8b in Psalm 72 certainly makes no statement about the *centre* of the presence/sphere of power of the Davidic King or about Zion, but speaks of an *expansion* of dominion as it occurs in the parallel phrase 'from sea to sea' (v. 8a, not mentioned by Gray), and its direct continuation in vv. 9-11; the subjects are rather the enemies of the king and foreign kings, indeed all kings and nations that have to honour him. The issue is a dominion as widely spread as possible and its further expansion.

Ahlström takes the same position where Ps. 89.26 is concerned as Gray does regarding Ps. 72.8; both are using the same Ugaritic statements about El.[8] Following Johnson,[9] Ahlström assumes that the words 'sea' (ים) and 'rivers' (נהרות) in Ps. 89.26 do not refer to the 'geographical borders of David's kingdom' and that the verse on the whole does not intend to convey 'geographical facts, but rather a certain ideology and world-view'. The words in question refer to the 'foundations of the world'.[10] By pointing to Pss. 24.2 and 93.3, Ahlström links Ps. 89.26 with the creation of the world and the world rule of Yahweh, and declares: 'If Yahweh now says of the king that he puts his hand in the sea and in the rivers [that is the direction in which he translates the verse], that is in line with the parallelism which exists ideologically between God and the king... In the cultic-ideological context the true

6. J. Gray, *The Legacy of Canaan* (VTSup, 5; Leiden: E.J. Brill, 1965), pp. 113-14, quotes the text Gordon 2 Aqht VI.46ff., which, according to A. Jirku, *Kanaanäische Mythen und Epen aus Ras Shamra-Ugarit* (Gütersloh, 1962), p. 123, corresponds to the text IIB 4.46ff. = CTA vi.46ff.

7. Gray, *The Legacy of Canaan*, p. 114.

8. G.W. Ahlström, *Psalm 89: Eine Liturgie aus dem Ritual des leidenden Königs* (Lund: C.W.K. Gleerup, 1959), pp. 108-10.

9. A.R. Johnson, *Sacral Kingship in Ancient Israel* (Cardiff: University of Wales Press, 1955), p. 24.

10. Ahlström, *Psalm 89*, p. 108.

borders of the kingdom are in principle meaningless.'[11] There is no opportunity here to discuss Ahlström's cult-ideological interpretation as such, but only to point out that his interpretation does not do justice to the historical relationships of the Psalm; this is particularly obvious in the descriptive part beginning with v. 20 as well as in the lament introduced by v. 39. The point here is not so much the 'inner' relationship of God and king but rather the divine promise and deeds regarding the protection of the kingdom and dominion of the king and his dynasty. If there is some sort of 'ideology' involved here at all, then it is probably rather that of the Davidic-Solomonic empire, since behind both the rehearsal of the auspicious promise of God to David via Nathan (2 Sam. 7) and the bitter lament about the present situation, after the downfall of the 'eternal kingdom', lies that illustrious epoch of the former empire as both an ideal and an objective which cannot be generalized or revoked. The context as well as the traditio-historical background lead therefore most probably to a historical and concrete local-geographical understanding of the contents of v. 26; their brevity, and a certain ambiguity mainly with regard to the plural form 'rivers', should not constitute any real hindrance to such an interpretation.

The local-geographical and 'concrete' interpretation of the three passages dealt with here is probably how it was generally understood. Yet it has been applied in different ways. Here we have formulaic phraseology drawn from the stock of the surrounding environment, that is mainly an Assyrian-Babylonian expansion account which, based on an older tradition, has been in use since the eleventh century BCE. The formulaic information being referred to in various contexts is as follows: *ultu tâmti(m) e-li-ti adi tâmti(m) šaplīti*, 'from the Upper sea to the Lower sea'.[12] The 'Upper sea' stands for the sea in the west, the Mediterranean, while at the other end of the west-east line the 'Lower sea' stands for the Persian Gulf. To this local-geographical expansion formula corresponds 'concrete' information in other accounts, such as the description of the scope of the campaign of conquest of the Assyrian king Adadnirari III which states (excluding the names of countries): 'From the banks of the Euphrates I subjugated... to the large sea in the

---

11. Ahlström, *Psalm 89*, p. 109.

12. Several references in *CAD*, E, p. 113b; cf. *AHw*, I, p. 206a. See also B. Meissner, *Babylonien und Assyrien*, II (Heidelberg: Carl Winter, 1925), pp. 372-73.

West under my feet.'[13] Gressmann notes of this report that this was as strange an expression in Assyria, which was situated at the Tigris, as it was in Jerusalem.[14] Moreover, he finds it noteworthy that such pictures travelled all the way from Babylonia via Assyria to Palestine and 'even more astonishing with what endurance they survived up to late centuries', pointing to the postexilic passage Zech. 9.10.[15] But the question that remains for him is whether these formulae themselves travelled, with their specific local-geographical accounts, or whether we are only dealing with a certain form of expansion account which could have been made to fit in or which already existed elsewhere as well. In his commentary on the Psalms, Buhl, for instance, attempted an explanation in this latter manner in the case of Ps. 72.8; he applies the two 'seas' to the Mediterranean and the Gulf of Aqaba, and furthermore connects the אפסי־ארץ with the southern border of the country, namely the Egyptian Wadi. At the same time, though, Buhl admits that the last expression (אפסי־ארץ)—as it has been used in Zech. 9.10—is more likely a hint that 'the originally historically intended determinations of borders have become a formula of unlimited power including the entire world of nations'.[16] The question raised by Buhl nevertheless remains unanswered and undecided by him. In his early book on the royal psalms, Mowinckel, on the contrary, wants to rediscover 'the same borders that were known at the time of Sennacherib', and explains that 'the whole is style, which nobody takes really seriously'.[17] Gressmann, finally, observes: 'did it not suggest itself to us immediately to replace the Euphrates by the Jordan...?'[18] Looking at the traditions of the Old Testament regarding the descriptions of borders, this does not seem quite so obvious.

The descriptions of the borders of the land within the Old Testament are of two different kinds as far as their form is concerned. The most complete form is the one which states the borders of all cardinal points

13. See H. Gressmann, *Altorientalische Texte zum Alten Testament* (Berlin, 1926), pp. 344-45.

14. See Gressmann, *Der Messias*, pp. 19, 199; also his *Der Ursprung der israelitisch-jüdischen Eschatologie* (FRLANT, 6; Göttingen: Vandenhoeck & Ruprecht, 1905), p. 254.

15. Gressmann, *Der Messias*, p. 19.

16. F. Buhl, *Psalmerne, oversatte og fortolkede* (Copenhagen, 1900), p. 469.

17. S. Mowinckel, *Kongesalmerne i det gamle testamente* (Kristiania [Oslo]: H. Aschehoug, 1916), p. 40.

18. Gressmann, *Der Messias*, p. 19.

coherently according to certain fixed border points. This form, for which there are mainly references in Num. 34.3-12 and Ezek. 47.15-20 (see also Josh. 15.2-4 and Ezek. 48.1-2) is, however, of less interest in our context. The other form is that of the מ...עד formula, which determines a territory by means of its outposts ('from...to') and so states the extent of the territory. It usually does so in a north–south and/or east–west direction, which means that one is dealing with simple information corresponding to one direction as well as two sets of data reflecting two crossing directions. The Deuteronomistic history names the extent of the Israelite settlement seven times by the well-known formula 'from Dan to Beerseba'. More often, though, the change in the use of the מ...עד formula indicates a larger ideal state of existence, that is, an empire spreading from the Euphrates in the north to the Egyptian border in the south (determined either by the 'stream of Egypt' or the 'river of Egypt') as well as from the watershed of the Jordan and the Gulf of Aqaba in the east to the Mediterranean in the west.[19] This larger model of the land, which agrees with one of the connected border descriptions of Numbers 34 and Ezekiel 47, corresponds to the expansion of the Davidic-Solomonic Empire, except that in the border descriptions in the historical books, following ancient tradition, Jordan–Dead-Sea–Gulf-of-Aqaba always represents the eastern borderline; the Transjordan area is consequently excluded.[20]

The 'system' of border descriptions of the land according to the large model of the Israelite kingdom, here only briefly described, is most likely the first and most important basis for a correct understanding of the information in the three passages under discussion (Pss. 72.8; 89.26; Zech. 9.10b). Hence these passages will be carefully evaluated in the light of this 'border system'. It seems appropriate to start with Ps. 89.26 and yet first and foremost Ps. 80.12 must be set up for comparison. With the help of the metaphor of the grapevine, Ps. 80.9ff. tells about the rootedness and the expansion of the people in the land in the following way:

19. For all details and references one may refer to my essay mentioned in n. 3 above. (Attention should be drawn to a typographical error, namely the dislocation of the second and third line in the last paragraph of p. 21.)

20. See Sæbø, 'Grenzbeschreibung', pp. 18 and 32; otherwise Alt, 'Das Grossreich Davids', pp. 66-75; recently also Z. Kallai, *Historical Geography of the Bible: The Tribal Territories of Israel* (Jerusalem: Magnes Press; Leiden: E.J. Brill, 1986), especially pp. 99ff.

it sent out its branches to the sea [עד־ים],
and its shoots to the River [אל־נהר].

The people have, as said in v. 10, 'filled the land', and so the 'filled' land reaches from the Mediterranean to the Euphrates; it is—as far as the western and northern parts are concerned—identical to the large model of the land, connected with the Davidic Empire.[21] Since what follows after the lament (which is characteristic for this particular psalm as well as for Psalm 89) is a prayer for the restoration of control over the land, the reference must be to that very territorial extent, namely the former empire.

In the foreground of Psalm 89 is not the people but rather the historical reference to the founder of the empire, King David himself, more obvious and direct than in the previous psalm; the territorial expansion of the power is nevertheless the same in both cases—which is the crucial factor here. Judged by the complete מן...עד formula, the information of Pss. 80.12 and 89.26 is only half complete, since they contain the עד element but lack the מן element indicating the starting point; however, this stresses the expansion in the direction of the Sea and the Euphrates River in the historical sense even more impressively.[22]

Now, turning to the duplicate information of Ps. 72.8 and Zech. 9.10b, it is noticeable that the first part, 'from sea to sea', does not indicate any more precise description of the locality—by names or the definite article—as is usually the case where the formula is used in the historical books; what one finds here is simply מים עד־ים. The reason for this may lie in the poetic style of these passages, since the indeterminate form exists likewise in Ps. 80.12. However, the expression is the more difficult to interpret for its brevity. The individual contexts of the passages and the historical border descriptions seem to exclude the assumption that we are dealing with the aforementioned Assyrian expanse from the Mediterranean to the Persian Gulf. The second 'sea' most likely refers either to the Gulf of Aqaba (see ים־סוף in Exod. 23.31 and 1 Kgs 9.26) or the Dead Sea (see Num. 34.3; Ezek. 47.18; Joel 2.20).[23] The intention was to express the west–east extent of the

21. See Kraus, *Psalmen*, II, pp. 720-22.
22. The plural-form נהרות is difficult to interpret; see however M. Dahood, *Psalms. II. 50–100* (AB; Garden City, NY: Doubleday, 1968), p. 317; also Sæbø, 'Grenzbeschreibung', p. 30.
23. See Sæbø, 'Grenzbeschreibung', p. 29. For Joel 2.20, see W. Rudolph, *Joel–Amos–Obadja–Jona* (KAT, 13.2; Gütersloh: Gütersloher Verlagshaus, 1971),

dominion. The question remains, however, whether this covers every-thing; in particular, in view of the obviously indeterminate form which ignores any concrete terms, one should perhaps consider whether we are possibly presented with a piece of Akkadian cosmology, as shows through in other places in the Old Testament, namely the metaphor of the earth completely surrounded by water—by 'seas'.[24] And yet the statement remains one about the earth rather than about the 'original sea', which is surely not the centre of interest in this particular context, but merely marks the outer demarcation lines. The short stereotyped expression may—almost proverbially—have become a name for the earth according to its most outward demarcation lines, in other words, a name for the earth as a whole (see Amos 8.12). The somewhat ambiva-lent formula 'from sea to sea', which seems to derive its historical ori-gin and its present starting point from the 'system' of the old native border descriptions of the empire, refers to the world in its whole wide extent.[25]

This fact seems to be even more obvious for the second part of the expansion formula of both passages ('from the River to the ends of the earth'). In the traditional way, it takes the river—which has to be the Euphrates in this context—as a starting point; the expansion neverthe-less does not, as is usually the case, end in another watershed,[26] but is stretched to the (farthest) ends of the earth. The intention of the second part of the formula seems to be clearly to embrace the whole world.

From a form-historical point of view this means a crucial change in the whole formula. In most cases the 'sea' determines the end points of an east–west extent and the 'river' that of a north–south one, so that the intersecting lines of the double formula embrace all four points of the compass; in this stereotyped way the wholeness of the territory is expressed. If here, then, the two parts of the double formula describe the entirety of the world, a poetic parallelism is created out of the old territorial double formula.

Seen as a whole, the old expressions of the expansion of the domin-ion of the Davidic King are broken and stretched to the utmost possible,

pp. 64-65, contra A.S. Kapelrud, *Joel Studies* (UUÅ, 1984.4; Uppsala: A.-B. Lundeqvistka Bokhandeln, 1948), pp. 109ff.

24. See Meissner, *Babylonien und Assyrien*, II, pp. 110-12.

25. See Kraus, *Psalmen*, II, pp. 147f.; Alt, 'Das Grossreich Davids', p. 75; Bentzen, *Fortolkning*, p. 415.

26. Sæbø, 'Grenzbeschreibung', pp. 18-19 (§2.2.2).

to the universal, yet without having completely lost their connexion
with the historical and local-geographical basis. The way in which the
expansion of an empire was described has now become a means to
describe the expansion of a world empire. The motive for this universal
extension is, however, not founded in the territorial as such, but in concepts of other—also theological—kinds, views that, among others, took
hold of territorial descriptions and changed them according to their
needs.

Chapter 9

WHO IS 'THE MAN' IN LAMENTATIONS 3.1?

In the perspectives of 'Biblical Interpretation' the book of Lamentations has a most specific position among the Old Testament books.
Unlike the Hebrew canon of the Holy Writ the Alexandrian canon
attached the book to one of the 'great prophets', to the book of
Jeremiah. This well-known placement of the book of Lamentations in
the Septuagint was not only an expression of the traditional Jewish
claim of a Jeremian authorship of the book (*B. Bat.* 14b/15a), even
though the book in the Hebrew canon had an 'independent' position,
but it also became indicative for the main Christian understanding of
the book, as may be seen in the Vulgate and later Christian Bible
translations. Through centuries the book of Lamentations lived its life
in the shadow of the book of Jeremiah; and the traditional assumption
of its Jeremian authorship was virtually unanimous. When, however,
the book's assumed dependence on Jeremiah had become basically
weakened in modern biblical scholarship a host of differing opinions of
the book arose, as to its time and authorship, style and structure, content and theology. In modern research the book seems to represent an
unsolved riddle.[1]

1. *The Character of the Book of Lamentations*

As may be indicated by the issues just mentioned, there are different
aspects of the enigmatic character of the book. Most noteworthy, in the
first instance, is its specific stylistic character since all five chapters of
the book in one way or another have a form related to the Hebrew

---

1. Cf. R. Brandscheidt, *Gotteszorn und Menschenleid: Die Gerichtsklage des
leidenden Gerechten in Klgl 3* (Trierer Theol. Studien, 41; Trier: Paulinus Verlag,
1983), pp. 1-19; C. Westermann, *Die Klagelieder: Forschungsgeschichte und
Auslegung* (Neukirchen–Vluyn: Neukirchener Verlag, 1990), pp. 15-81.

alphabet with its 22 letters. Four of five chapters have a firm *acrostic* structure, following the Hebrew alphabet; ch. 5 has 22 verses but not an acrostic form. This stylistic phenomenon provides the book with a literary unity that is unique in the Old Testament; together with the assumption of Jeremian authorship of the book this unitary character may have contributed to the unanimity of the traditional view of the book.

But there are formal differences as well, not only between Lamentations 1–4 and 5, as already mentioned, but also between chs. 1–2 and 4, on the one hand, and ch. 3, on the other. In the first two chapters a stanza has three lines/bicola (except for 1.7 and 2.19 that have four) and in ch. 4 two lines; and in these three chapters, of which the first two seem to constitute the most coherent formal unity, only the first line of each stanza begins with a letter according to the sequence of the Hebrew alphabet; and each chapter has 22 verses. In Lamentations 3, however, each stanza has three lines and every line of the stanza starts with the same Hebrew letter. Here one has counted lines; therefore Lamentations 3 has 66 verses. In other words, the acrostic style seems to be most fully elaborated, being on the highest level of artistry, in Lamentations 3: the middle chapter of the whole. Perhaps this has been done to present the chapter not only as the middle part of the book but even as its central and most important one. Also, Lamentations 3 starts differently from the other chapters: it begins with an emphatic אֲנִי ('I'), whereas Lamentations 1–2 and 4 start with אֵיכָה ('how!'), which is a standard opening word for a 'dirge' (Isa. 1.21; for קִינָה ['dirge'], that does not occur in Lamentations, cf. Amos 5.1; 8.10; Jer. 9.9; 2 Chron. 35.25). In this way there may be some correspondence between the opening words—being like 'titles'—of these chapters and their acrostic differences.

Second, modern form criticism has traced the formal differences within the book much further; and the unitary impression that the book may leave at first sight is shown to be only a part of the whole picture. With a starting point in the observation that 'political dirge' seems to be the main *genre* of the book,[2] one has differentiated in detail between the various forms included, first of all 'communal lament', in Lamentations 1–2 and 4 and mainly in Lamentations 5, and 'individual lament',

2.　H. Jahnow, *Das hebräische Leichenlied im Rahmen der Völkerdichtung* (BZAW, 36; Giessen: W. de Gruyter, 1923), pp. 168-91.

especially in Lamentations 3.[3] The outcome of this shows that the acrostic units may be covering different and also 'mixed' forms.[4] However, Kraus has strongly questioned the term 'political dirge', maintaining that it is a 'misleading' *genre* determination. He has put forward a new cultic and liturgical explanation, and with reference to some Akkadian texts he has defined the particular genre of the book to be a 'Lament over the Ruined Sanctuary'; thereby he has also tried to explain the difficult question of the book's *Sitz im Leben* as a cultic and liturgical one.[5] But Kraus, who might be right in some details but not in total, has received little support for his theory.[6] As for Lamentations 5, finally, in order to mention but a few samples of recent scholarly views, Westermann will not simply characterize the concluding chapter of the book as a 'communal lament', but he has carefully differentiated between framing prayers (5.1, 21) and a 'we-lament' (5.2-18) as well as other forms.[7] This procedure of detailed differentiation, here and elsewhere in the book, has been characteristic for much recent study on the Lamentations and has contributed to a better understanding of it.

Third, the possibility of different 'voices' in different parts of the book of Lamentations may be regarded as 'a stylistic concern', on a literary level only.[8] However, the question of authorship may easily be raised as well, as it also has been done in different ways, and the more so since the questions of structural unity and of authorship are closely related to each other. Although many scholars go for a unity of authorship of the book,[9] in current research these questions are more complex

3.   H. Gunkel and J. Begrich, *Einleitung in die Psalmen: Die Gattungen der religiösen Lyrik Israels* (HKAT, Ergänzungsband; Göttingen: Vandenhoeck & Ruprecht, 1933), pp. 117, 136; see further section 2 below.

4.   Gunkel and Begrich, *Einleitung in die Psalmen*, pp. 258, 400-401; cf. pp. 407-15.

5.   H.-J. Kraus, *Klagelieder (Threni)* (BKAT, 20; Neukirchen–Vluyn: Neukirchener Verlag, 2nd rev. edn, 1960 [4th edn, 1983]), pp. 8-13.

6.   Cf. criticism by scholars like: W. Rudolph, *Das Buch Ruth–Das hohe Lied–Die Klagelieder* (KAT, 17.1–3; Gütersloh: Gütersloher Verlagshaus, rev. edn, 1962 [1939]), pp. 9-10; Childs, *Introduction to the Old Testament*, p. 592; and Westermann, *Die Klagelieder*, pp. 22-31.

7.   Westermann, *Die Klagelieder*, pp. 60, 172-80.

8.   W.F. Lanahan, 'The Speaking Voice in the Book of Lamentations', *JBL* 93 (1974), pp. 41-49 (41).

9.   Recently, e.g., O. Plöger, *Die Klagelieder* (HAT, 1.18; Tübingen: J.C.B. Mohr, 2nd edn, 1969), pp. 129, 163-64; Brandscheit, *Gotteszorn und Menschenleid*,

and debatable than ever before, and particularly with reference to
Lamentations 3 (see next section). Closely related to this issue is,
moreover, the question of historical situation and the 'time' of authorship, whereby an exilic dating is found to be most likely by the majority of scholars;[10] but for some parts much later datings have been
argued for as well.[11] The very differing views in this matter may represent a substantial challenge to future studies in Lamentations.

Lastly, questions of the content and theology of the book of Lamentations have also been broadly discussed recently, especially with
regard to the problem of what might have been the nearest theological
and traditio-historical context for the book. Of special interest in this
respect—apart from a still held relation to the book of Jeremiah[12]—is
the question of a possible Deuteronomistic influence, and if so, the
extent of it. This aspect has been discussed by some scholars, notably
by Gottwald and Albrektson. Gottwald maintains he has found 'the sit-
uational key to the theology of Lamentations in the tension between
Deuteronomic faith and historical adversity', particularly so in a time
after the Deuteronomic reform, and, more specifically, in the 'terms of
the schema of tragic reversal', to which also the 'theme' of Zion
belonged.[13] Albrektson, in a stimulating discussion with Gottwald,[14]
has more strongly related the theology of Lamentations to the Zion tradition as 'a specific Jerusalem tradition'.[15] For him the theological
'key' is to be found 'in the tension between specific religious conceptions and historical realities: between the confident belief of the Zion

pp. 202-203; B. Johnson, 'Form and Message in Lamentations', *ZAW* 97 (1985),
pp. 58-73 (72).

10. Cf., e.g., N.K. Gottwald, *Studies in the Book of Lamentations* (SBT, 1.14;
London: SCM Press, 1954), p. 21; Childs, *Introduction to the Old Testament*,
p. 593; D.R. Hillers, *Lamentations* (AB, 7A; Garden City, NY: Doubleday, 1984
[1972]), pp. xviii-xix; Johnson, 'Form and Message', pp. 72-73.

11. Cf. currently O. Kaiser, *Einleitung in das Alte Testament* (Gütersloh:
Gütersloher Verlagshaus, 5th rev. edn, 1984), p. 356; and *idem*, *Klagelieder* (ATD,
16.2; Göttingen: Vandenhoeck & Ruprecht, 4th edn, 1992), pp. 105-106.

12. Cf. H. Wiesmann, 'Der Verfasser des Büchleins der Klagelieder—Ein
Augenzeuge der behandelten Ereignisse?', *Bib* 17 (1936); differently Kaiser, *Einleitung*, p. 359.

13   Gottwald, *Studies in the Book of Lamentations*, pp. 52-62.

14. B. Albrektson, *Studies in the Text and Theology of the Book of Lamentations* (Studia Theol. Lundensia, 21; Lund: C.W.K. Gleerup, 1963), pp. 214-30.

15. Albrektson, *Studies in the Text*, p. 219.

traditions in the inviolability of the temple and city, and the actual brutal facts'.[16] Thereafter, Albrektson also discussed the influence of 'Deuteronomic faith', especially related to Deuteronomy 28. In this way he was able to show that the 'opinions encountered in this book have from a traditio-historical point of view roots in at least two directions', i.e. in the two tradition entities just referred to; the 'link' between them is the 'concentration on the temple of Jerusalem'.[17]

The interpretation of Albrektson may prove to be most fruitful for future scrutiny in the book of Lamentations. Concentrating on Zion, however, Albrektson has first of all brought Lamentations 1–2 and 4–5 into focus; Lamentations 3 is not made a subject for similar or corresponding attention in his *Studies,* nor has the lament as form and phenomenon—*mirabile dictu*—received any proper treatment. Therefore, in the present situation a new concentration on the specific character of Lamentations 3 may be essential and appropriate.

2. *The Centrality of Chapter 3*

There seems to be a growing recognition of the central position and significance of ch. 3 in the book of Lamentations. Not only did this chapter constitute the main topic of the monograph of Renate Brandscheidt in 1983, but the discussion of problems in Lamentations 3 runs like a scarlet thread also through the most recent research history of Lamentations by Westermann.[18] The chapter is not only regarded as 'central' but is also said to be 'the most controversial chapter in the book'.[19] Especially in view of Lamentations 3 the opinions of scholars have been differing considerably. To take just one example: an impressive bouquet of widely diverging datings of the chapter, reaching from the time soon after 587 BCE to the third century BCE, has been put together nicely by Kaiser.[20]

There are certainly various reasons for the remarkable plurality of learned views regarding Lamentations 3. To be sure, the varying opinions of scholars may have been dependent on—apart from scholarly

16. Albrektson, *Studies in the Text,* p. 230.
17. Albrektson, *Studies in the Text,* p. 238.
18. Westermann, *Die Klagelieder,* pp. 32-81, esp. 65-71; cf. 137-60, 187-88.
19. Childs, *Introduction to the Old Testament,* p. 592.
20. Kaiser, *Klagelieder,* p. 104.

subjectivity[21]—changing 'attitudes' in biblical studies and may there-fore be regarded as a barometer of altering trends in method. However, the major or really substantial reason is doubtless to be found in the text itself, and then in a double way: the differing views may partly be caused by the very complex structure of the chapter, and partly by the intricate and somewhat confusing question of the identity of 'the man' who presents himself at the opening of the chapter: הגבר אני ('I am the man...').

Much scholarly energy has been used in the identification of this 'man'. As long as the traditional view of the authorship of Lamenta-tions was predominant, it was natural to see the prophet Jeremiah in 'the man',[22] and the more so as Jeremiah was a man of suffering who in his Confessions made many personal complaints (e.g. Jer. 11.18-23; 12.1-5; 15.10-12; 20.7-18). With special reference to the word of 2 Chron. 35.25 a relationship between Jeremiah and King Josiah is established: 'Jeremiah also made a lament for Josiah'; from this late notice an identification of 'the man' with King Josiah has been made, although the description in Lamentations 3 is scarcely comparable to his tragic death. Rudolph has shown that neither of these assumptions may be regarded as plausible.[23] But, on the other hand, Rudolph has renewed an identification with Jeremiah, not directly, but in some 'ideal' form, assuming that Jeremiah has become a 'paradigm' (*Vor-bild*) of suffering, and in 3.1 he is the 'spokesman' of the author, who is the same in all five chapters of Lamentations.[24] In this way, Rudolph may also have intended to include to some extent—without accept-ing—the older view of a 'collective I', representing the 'congregation' (*Gemeinde*) of the people of Israel, as scholars like R. Smend and M. Löhr maintained around 1890.[25] Differently, and yet similarly, Kraus has interpreted ch. 3 as a 'paradigmatic demonstration' of suf-fering (*die Verkündigung des urbildlichen Leidens*);[26] and 'the man' is anonymous.[27] Kaiser, again, will not exclude the possibility that the author of Lamentations 3, from the fourth century, has seen Jeremiah in

---

21. Plöger, *Die Klagelieder*, p. 163.
22. Cf. H. Wiesmann, 'Das 3. Kap. der Klagelieder', *ZKT* 50 (1926), p. 147.
23. Rudolph, *Das Buch Ruth*, pp. 196-99.
24. Rudolph, *Das Buch Ruth*, pp. 227-45.
25. Cf. Westermann, *Die Klagelieder*, pp. 33-34.
26. Kraus, *Klagelieder*, pp. 51-70.
27. Kraus, *Klagelieder*, pp. 54-55.

'the man', as 'the suffering paradigmatic prayer' (*als den im Leiden vorbildlichen Beter*).[28] Most elaborate in this respect, however, is the study of Brandscheidt; she relates Lamentations 3 to 'the suffering experiences of the prophet Jeremiah on the level of universal validity (*Allgemeingültigkeit*)' for the people that is still under the wrath of God; and 'the man' is no historical figure but the 'pious one' in general (*der Fromme*), whose faith, after the catastrophe of his people, has deep scruples.[29] And, very similar, 'the man' is for Hillers 'not a specific historic figure, but rather the typical sufferer. He is an "Everyman", a figure who represents what any man may feel when it seems that God is against him'.[30] More on the 'collective' line is the understanding of Lam. 3.1 by Gordis, who, referring to 'corporate personality', the well-known term of H. Wheeler Robinson, as well as to studies of 'primitive psychology', has characterized 'the man' as a 'fluid personality'.[31] 'By and large', says Childs finally, summing up, 'the majority opinion favours seeing the figure in ch. 3 as a representative figure without a connexion with Jeremiah.'[32]

Many scholars in recent research of Lamentations, then, have favoured interpretations of 'the man' in Lam. 3.1 that either see in him a 'representative figure', an *Urbild* or *Vorbild*, or regard him, in a more general way, as a pious and just 'Everyman'. But one may be reserved with regard to these explanations, because there seem to be adequate grounds for critical questions, as to what sense these notions and terms really might have: whether they are too abstract for the context in Lamentations 3, and whether they are inaccurately neutralizing or suspending the concrete historical aspect of the text. Whatever the sense of these concepts might be, I am inclined to see them as hardly adequate terms for the very concrete descriptions in Lamentations 3. It may, even further, be contended that the special grandeur of the book of Lamentations, in ch. 3 also, is its unique combination of vivid concreteness, extended use of elements from variegated traditions, and of an artistic composition, including the firm form of an acrostic scheme. A proper

28. Kaiser, *Einleitung*, p. 359; cf. Kaiser, *Klagelieder*, p. 158.
29. Brandscheidt, *Gotteszorn und Menschenleid*, p. 350.
30. Hillers, *Lamentations*, p. 64.
31. R. Gordis, *The Song of Songs and Lamentations: A Study, Modern Translation and Commentary* (New York: Ktav, rev. and augmented edn, 1974), pp. 172-74.
32. Childs, *Introduction to the Old Testament*, p. 593.

discussion of the key question, who 'the man' of Lam. 3.1 might be, has to take all three components into balanced consideration.

The very complex composition or structure of Lamentations 3 has been thoroughly analyzed by some scholars; and much scrutiny has been applied to a detailed differentiation of the formal elements of the text; and, again, these efforts have provided rather different results. A prudent and mainly convincing analysis has been presented by Kaiser;[33] and significant monographic contributions have been given, among others, by Brandscheidt, who has focused on the wisdom influence, among many other elements, in this chapter,[34] and by Westermann, who in particular, here as earlier, has paid special attention to the form and content of the lament.[35] It should be unnecessary to rehearse the formal details on this occasion. But, without any possibility of lengthy arguments in this connexion, it may be appropriate to reconsider briefly some of the main issues, where it will be crucial to keep the proper balance of elements involved:

a. The complexity of Lamentations 3 is partly grounded in a hermeneutically significant relation of the main form of the book and this chapter, constituted by a strict and advanced acrostic pattern, on the one hand, and the many and variegated tradition fragments used, on the other. That implies that any literary or phraseological differentiation and comparison between individual elements within the chapter itself or between Lamentations 3 and its context[36] has only limited relevance; for in view of the overarching acrostic form the author has worked rather 'freely' with a rich tradition material.[37]

b. In Lamentations 3 there are units of both an 'I' and a 'we' (in 3.40-47), and they should remain as they are, not being explained, for any reason, by each other, as has been done in some 'collective' theories regarding the 'I'. There is, further, also a difference between the 'I' and his 'people' (cf. 3.14), that may be kept too, although in early Jewish interpretation or *Wirkungsgeschichte* of the text there seems to be a tendency to weaken this aspect, as may be shown by early textual variants

33. Kaiser, *Klagelieder*, pp. 154-60.
34. Brandscheidt, *Gotteszorn und Menschenleid*, pp. 222-23; cf. pp. 29-50.
35. Westermann, *Die Klagelieder*, pp. 66-81, 143-60.
36. Cf., e.g., Brandscheidt, *Gotteszorn und Menschenleid*, p. 220.
37. Cf. Kaiser, *Klagelieder*, p. 154.

to עמי in v. 14.[38] A proper definition of the relationship of 'I' and 'we' in this chapter is difficult but challenging.

c. There are clearly relations in Lamentations 3 between various elements of personal experiences, especially in the beginning of the chapter, apparently connected with the historical situation after 587 BCE, and elements of a more 'timeless' or instructive and wisdom character (as in v. 27 and some other parts of 3.21-39). Although this relationship also is hard to define properly it is hardly adequate to see a wisdom trait in every personal aspect of description, as Brandscheidt seems to do, at least partly.[39]

d. With some connexion to the last point a final comment may be made on the relationship of Lamentations 3 to its immediate context. With good reason it is maintained by many that Lamentations 3 is most likely related to the same historical context of early exile as the chapters around. But, more than that, one may even contend that the sequence of chapters in Lamentations seems to be defined not as much on chronological or redaction-historical grounds as for ideological or theological reasons. The relation of Lamentations 3 to chs. 2 and 4, in particular, may be explained anew in a perspective like this, as will be done tentatively in the next section.

3. *Identifying 'The Man'*

When, finally, we turn to a positive examination of the puzzling question of an identification of 'the man' in Lamentations 3, a fresh approach to the problem will have to take the very complex state of research into due consideration. Even though the number of attempts is most impressive, new insights might still be possible.

Dominantly in the foreground of the book of Lamentations, especially in its first two chapters as well as in the two last ones, stands the figure of Zion, being metaphorically and vividly portrayed as a mourning widow. The historical situation described is the catastrophic fall of Jerusalem in 587 BCE, followed by miserable conditions for the people who had remained in the ruined city.

38. *BHS*; cf. Albrektson, *Studies in the Text*, pp. 137-38; Brandscheidt, *Gotteszorn und Menschenleid*, p. 22.

39. Brandscheidt, *Gotteszorn und Menschenleid*, pp. 222-23.

The theme of Zion has, as already mentioned, been brought into focus first of all by Albrektson. When introducing the 'new ideas' of the specific 'Jerusalem tradition' he says rightly: 'The leading themes here are the election of David and of his house, and the idea of Zion and its temple as the abode of God.'[40] In the succeeding discussion, however, the latter 'idea' is the only issue, not the theme of 'the election of David and of his house'; and that may be regarded as a serious disadvantage not only for the outstanding *Studies* of Albrektson but for the studies of Lamentations in general, and for the interpretation of Lamentations 3 in particular. For the use of the twin themes of Zion and the Davidic king may be regarded as the 'key' to a new solution of the riddle of Lamentations 3, and so also of the book as a whole, especially in view of the sequence of Lamentations 2–3–4.

As for 'the man' in Lam. 3.1, royal identifications have also been brought forward: among many others, first of all an identification with King Josiah; but the inadequacy of this identification has already been pointed out by Rudolph, as mentioned above. Further, Porteous has proposed King Jehoiachin to be 'the man',[41] but without being followed by others; and there is really no special evidence for this assumption in the text,[42] and even less so since Rudolph's dating of Lamentations 1 to 597 has also proved to be less probable.[43] Even though these identifications may rightly be falsified, the matter of a royal identification as such is by no means disproved.

It may be considered as rather curious that scholars so far—and as far as I know—have not seen what might be the nearest identification and the simplest solution of the problem of Lam. 3.1, namely, an identification of 'the man' with the last king of Jerusalem, King Zedekiah, whose fall with the temple and the royal city was most dramatic, as it is realistically narrated in 2 Kgs 25.1-21, especially in the vv. 1-7 (REB):

> In the ninth year of [the] reign [of Zedekiah]... King Nebuchadnezzar of Babylon advanced with his whole army against Jerusalem... the siege lasted till the eleventh year of King Zedekiah. In the fourth month of that

40. Albrektson, *Studies in the Text*, p. 219.
41. N.W. Porteous, 'Jerusalem—Zion: The Growth of a Symbol', in *Verbannung und Heimkehr: Festschrift W. Rudolph* (Tübingen: J.C.B. Mohr, 1961), pp. 235-52; see esp. pp. 244-45.
42. Hillers, *Lamentations*, p. 63.
43. Kaiser, *Klagelieder*, p. 104.

year, on the ninth day of the month, when famine was severe in the city
and there was no food for the people, the city capitulated. When king
Zedekiah of Judah saw this, he and all his armed escort left the city,
fleeing by night... The Chaldaean army pursued the king and overtook
him in the lowlands of Jericho. His men all forsook him and scattered,
and the king was captured and, having been brought before the king of
Babylon at Riblah, he was put on trial and sentenced. Zedekiah's sons
were slain before his eyes; then his eyes were put out, and he was
brought to Babylon bound in bronze fetters.

The text of 2 Kgs 25.1-7, with its parallel in Jer. 52.4-11, seems nearly
to have been overlooked by modern scholars, if compared with 2 Kgs
25.27-30 on the release of King Jehoiachin. But it will be adequately
related to Lamentations 3, since there are some linking features in
2 Kings 25 and Lamentations 3 that may help to elucidate the identification of 'the man' in Lam. 3.1.

When, first of all, both 2 Kgs 25.7b and Lam. 3.7b are speaking of
'bronze fetters', there is clearly some conformity between the texts. The
chains are, at the same time, signs of being a prisoner, as it is directly
stated in the interesting addition in Jer. 52.11b ('put in prison till the
day of his death') and is similarly indicated in the description in Lam.
3.7-9, possibly also in vv. 5-6 and 52-54; and he is treated as a captive
(cf. Lam. 3.15-16). Further, there is a remarkable resemblance, if not
direct connexion, between Lam. 3.2, where 'the man' complains that
'He has driven me away and made me walk in darkness rather than
light' [NIV], and the narrative of 2 Kgs 25.7b saying, 'his eyes were put
out, and he was brought to Babylon...'. Even though the picture of the
deep misery of 'the man' also includes other traditional elements of
individual lament (cf. Lam. 3.10-15), yet it may have been influenced
by the tragic experiences of King Zedekiah in 2 Kings 25, and this
point of reference may have constituted some sort of a 'kernel' for the
extended and more elaborated lament composition of Lamentations 3.
Also, it is scarcely accidental that there are references to the king of
Judah just in the two chapters adjoining Lamentations 3, namely in
Lam. 2.6b ('king and priest alike he spurned') and 2.9b ('Her king and
rulers are exiled among the Gentiles') and, notably, in 4.20, which, says
(REB),

> The Lord's anointed [משיח יהוה], the breath of life to us,
> was caught in their traps;
> although we had thought to live among nations
> safe under his protection.

This may contribute to the impression that the chs. 2–3–4 represent a specific literary sequence in the book of Lamentations. Without a further discussion here, even the relationship of the individual and the collective elements of its lament may be more easily explained through a royal-'messianic' interpretation of Lamentations 3, since the king in a unique way is the primary representative of the people.

The assumption of an identification of 'the man' with the last Davidic king in Jerusalem may, finally, be further substantiated if one refers the picture of 'the man' to the specific Davidic-'messianic' traditions that seem to be rooted in 2 Samuel 7 and are 'developed' in manifold ways in royal Psalms and by some Jerusalem prophets.[44] Remarkably, therefore, the expression of Lam. 3.1b, 'the rod [שבט] of his wrath', may be related to 2 Sam. 7.14b, on the one hand, and to Ps. 89.31-33, on the other; and the complaints of Lam. 3.17-18 (cf. also vv. 14-15 and 59-61) are similar to the lament of Ps. 89.39-46, 51-52, as are also Lam. 3.31-33 in relation to Ps. 89.34. The closeness of Lamentations 3 to Psalm 89 is conspicuous; in general, however, attention has barely been paid to it. Also, the well-known reference to the king of Judah in his unique position in Lam. 4.20, cited above, comes close to the longer description in Ps. 89.19-38. And, in the end, returning to the book of Jeremiah, it can hardly be overlooked that in the composition of Jer. 22–23.8, after the prophet's complaint about and rebuke of the last kings of Judah, ending with King Jehoiachin, there is a messianic saying in 23.5-6, ending with a most noteworthy name: 'Yahweh our Righteousness [צדקנו]', that in some way might be a 'wordplay' with the name of King Zedekiah.

In conclusion, it may briefly be stated that the specific form and composition, theology and message of the book of Lamentations, in particular the sequence of Lamentations 2–4 and the interpretation of the complex Lamentations 3, may find an appropriate 'key' in the special Jerusalem traditions of Zion and David; it is there that it has its primary traditio-historical context. And the enigmatic 'man' of Lam. 3.1 might be the last king of the House of David in Jerusalem, King Zedekiah.

---

44. See Chapter 14 below.

Part III

TRADITION HISTORY: THEOLOGICAL THEMES

Chapter 10

PRIESTLY THEOLOGY AND PRIESTLY CODE: THE CHARACTER
OF THE PRIESTLY LAYER IN THE PENTATEUCH

1. *Some Aspects of Modern Pentateuchal Research*

In the beginnings of the 1980s, Julius Wellhausen's epoch-making
work *Prolegomena zur Geschichte Israels*, which appeared in 1878
under the title *Geschichte Israels*, I, celebrated its centenary.[1] This was
no ordinary anniversary, for the long shadow of this scholar, who—in
the words of Rudolf Smend—is the 'greatest German Old Testament
scholar in history',[2] and the enduring effect of his great work *Prolegomena*, extend right up to our own time. Yet to be sure, between him
and us there are many renowned scholars, who each in their own way,
have advanced Old Testament research in leaps and bounds. As far as
work on the Pentateuch is concerned, mention must be made of other
German Old Testament scholars such as Hermann Gunkel, Hugo
Gressman, Gerhard von Rad and Martin Noth. However, it should not
be superfluous or improper to reach back beyond these and others to

1. The title was changed to *Prolegomena*, etc., with the 2nd edn (Berlin,
1883). Cf. Wellhausen's survey *Geschichte Israels*, which appeared in 1880 as a
private publication, and which was published by Rudolf Smend in Julius Wellhausen, *Grundrisse zum Alten Testament* (TBü, 27; Munich: Chr. Kaiser Verlag,
1965), pp. 13-64.
2. Wellhausen, *Grundrisse*, p. 5. For an appreciation of Wellhausen cf. also
O. Eissfeldt, 'Julius Wellhausen', in *idem, Kleine Schriften* (6 vols.; Tübingen:
J.C.B. Mohr, 1962–79), I, pp. 56-71; R. Smend, 'Julius Wellhausen', in *idem,
Deutsche Alttestamentler in drei Jahrhunderten* (Göttingen: Vandenhoeck &
Ruprecht, 1989), pp. 99-113; H.-J. Kraus, *Geschichte der historisch-kritischen
Erforschung des Alten Testaments* (Neukirchen–Vluyn: Neukirchener Verlag, 3rd
rev. edn, 1982 [1956]), pp. 255-74; as well as L. Perlitt, *Vatke und Wellhausen:
Geschichtsphilosophie Voraussetzungen und historiographische Motive für die
Darstellung der Religion und Geschichte Israels durch Wilhelm Vatke und Julius
Wellhausen* (BZAW, 94; Berlin: Alfred Töpelmann, 1965).

Wellhausen. For he stands there with them all. Moreover, Wellhausen's work may well be considered as the most important point of contact for Jewish and Christian Bible scholars, for both older Jewish exegetes such as David Hoffmann, Benno Jacob, Umberto Cassuto and Yehezkel Kaufmann, as well as current colleagues such as Menaham Haran and Moshe Weinfeld have concerned themselves with his work.[3] However, for a renewed preoccupation with Wellhausen—perhaps we should now read his works again to an even greater degree?—the material argument is the most important. And the present situation invites us to consider just that.

In Pentateuch research today, when so much is in a state of flux, with the result that 'the new wine' is threatening to tear to shreds the old methodological 'wine skins', aim has been taken particularly at the Jahwists. As far as the Elohist is concerned, it was in any case often an uncertain matter.[4] The Deuteronomist has now reached the point of autonomy and has arrived at a position of dominance which, of course, was still completely unthinkable just a short time ago.[5] For the remaining Tetrateuch of Genesis–Numbers (and perhaps parts of Joshua), the Jahwist appears to have become the 'mighty fortress' in whose shadow the so-called priestly writings have moreover stood still. In the context

---

3. Cf. M. Haran, *Biblical Research in Hebrew: A Discussion of its Character and Trends* (Jerusalem: Magnes Press, 1970), and *idem*, *Temples and Temple-Service in Ancient Israel: An Inquiry into the Character of Cult Phenomena and the Historical Setting of the Priestly School* (Oxford: Clarendon Press, 1978); M. Weinfeld, *Deuteronomy and the Deuteronomic School* (Oxford: Clarendon Press, 1972), and *idem*, *Getting at the Roots of Wellhausen's Understanding of the Law of Israel: On the 100th Anniversary of the Prolegomena* (Jerusalem: The Institute for Advanced Studies, The Hebrew University of Jerusalem, Report No. 14/79, 1979). See also K.-J. Illman, 'Modern judisk bibelforskning', *Nordisk Judaistik/Scandinavian Jewish Studies* 1 (1975), pp. 3-14.

4. Cf., e.g., P. Volz and W. Rudolph, *Der Elohist als Erzähler: Ein Irrweg der Pentateuchkritik?* (BZAW, 63; Giessen: Alfred Töpelmann, 1933), esp. pp. 135-42; S. Mowinckel, *Erwägungen zur Pentateuchquellenfrage* (Oslo: Universitetsforlaget, 1964 [sep. edn of *NTT* 65 (1964), pp. 1-138]), pp. 59-118.

5. The number of studies on the deuteronomic work of history and especially of deuteronomic theology has become almost incalculable; many follow the results of von Rad's research. As *exempla instar omnium* one could mention L. Perlitt, *Bundestheologie im Alten Testament* (WMANT, 36; Neukirchen–Vluyn: Neukirchener Verlag, 1969), as well as the work of F. Crüsemann *et al.*, in H.W. Wolff (ed.), *Probleme biblischer Theologie* (Festschrift Gerhard von Rad; Munich: Chr. Kaiser Verlag, 1971).

of the heavy attacks which Hans Heinrich Schmid and especially Rolf Rendtorff have levelled recently against the Jahwist, one seems apart from that to be of the opinion that if the Jahwist is to decline as the 'main source', then the total documentary hypothesis would also decline.[6] In this regard Rendtorff has particularly taken issue with von Rad and Noth on account of very noteworthy arguments against the 'newer' or 'classical' and (until recently) widely accepted document hypothesis ('four-source theory'). He especially reproached them for clinging to the documentary hypothesis despite their traditio-historical methods. However, Rendtorff did not join battle directly with Wellhausen, the 'father' of the classical documentary hypothesis, and that may not be necessarily coincidental. As far as Wellhausen is concerned it was a question of far more than simply the literary-critical method of working, which moreover Rendtorff too did not wish to relinquish.[7] Wellhausen's treatise on and usage of the documentary hypothesis, whereby he showed himself—as other great theologians including those of the Old Testament—to be a collector and interpreter,[8] was

---

6.   R. Rendtorff, 'Der "Jahwist" als Theologe? Zum Dilemma der Pentateuchkritik', in *Congress Volume: Edinburgh 1974* (VTSup, 28; Leiden: E.J. Brill, 1975), pp. 158-66; also see his *Das überlieferungsgeschichtliche Problem des Pentateuch* (BZAW, 147; Berlin: W. de Gruyter, 1977); H.H. Schmid, *Der sogenannte Jahwist: Beobachtungen und Fragen zur Pentateuchforschung* (Zürich: Theologischer Verlag, 1976). In reaction to these works, mention must be made of the following, among others: E. Otto, 'Stehen wir vor einem Umbruch in der Pentateuchkritik?', *VF* 22 (1977), pp. 82-97; W. McKane, review of *Das überlieferungsgeschichtliche Problem des Pentateuch* (BZAW, 147; Berlin: W. de Gruyter, 1977), by R. Rendtorff, in *VT* 28 (1978), pp. 371-82; debating and reviewing articles on the books of Rendtorff and Schmid by R.N. Whybray ('Response to Professor Rendtorff', pp. 11-14), J. Van Seters ('The Yahwist as Theologian? A Response', pp. 15-17), N.E. Wagner ('A Response to Professor Rolf Rendtorff', pp. 20-27), G.E. Coats ('The Yahwist as Theologian? A Critical Reflection', pp. 28-32), R.E. Clements (*'Das überlierfungsgeschichtliche Problem des Pentateuch*, by R. Rendtorff', pp. 45-56), and G.F. Wenham (*'Der sogennante Jahwist* by H.H. Schmid', pp. 57-60), in *JSOT* 3 (1977); as well as H.H. Schmid, 'In Search of New Approaches in Pentateuchal Research', *JSOT* 3 (1977), pp. 33-42, and R. Rendtorff, 'Pentateuchal Studies on the Move', *JSOT* 3 (1977), pp. 43-45; cf. also L. Schmidt, 'Überlegungen zum Jahwisten', *EvT* 37 (1977), pp. 230-47.

7.   *Das überlieferungsgeschichtliche Problem des Pentateuch*, pp. 148-49.

8.   Cf., e.g., Kraus, *Geschichte der historisch-kritischen Erforschung*, p. 260: 'One cannot say that Wellhausen was the genial discoverer of new question formulations, methods and historical aspects... The genial act of Wellhausen, however,

firmly classified within the overall historical interpretation of the Old Testament, both of its religion and its history. 'Wellhausen was a historian', says Otto Eissfeldt pertinently, and he continues:

> He had an eye for detail, for 'antiquities'. The individual periods of the course of history stood before his eyes with the most vivid distinctness... But the aim of his research was always to glimpse the broad lines of development and the main forces of growth... The conception and portrayal of the inner play of forces throughout a course of history is what he always strove for and always achieved. For him history is not the juxtaposition and succession of events and people, but history is rather for him a collaboration and opposition of forces and ideas (*Kleine Schriften*, I, p. 69).

Now, Wellhausen has regularly—and not without reason—been appraised in regard to the philosophical suppositions of his portrayal of the historical-religious development in Israel. However, he was an exegete and historian to an even greater extent than he was a philosopher.[9] Even if philosophical elements of different kinds indeed exist, the thrust of his conception lies in his interpretation of the Old Testament texts themselves. Moreover, if he ended in his interpretation of the texts (whose basic problem lay for him in the dominating pre-eminence of the Law in the Pentateuch) with a blunt contrast of the older Israel and the younger Judaism, and with a devaluation of Judaism and of the Law which was victorious in it, then it is absolutely understandable that this was taken as a radical challenge, especially among Jewish readers and scholars. The fundamental question in all of this will be whether, or to what extent, his view of the texts can really be verified. Explaining the negative judgment of the law in the *Prologemena*, Weinfeld has referred to statements in Wellhausen's earlier book on *Die Pharisäer und die Sadducäer* (Greifswald, 1874).[10] Here there are certainly contexts which must be considered, although they are inadequate if one wishes to establish Wellhausen's understanding of the Law. Wellhausen bases his views in the *Prologemena* not on later phenomena; rather—and we repeat—they are rooted in his interpretation of Old Testament texts, and in fact such texts as are found in the so-called priestly writings, or which are closely linked with them. These will be discussed in due

was the masterly combining of the most varied preliminary work into a sharp and united whole.'

9. Cf. Perlitt, *Vatke und Wellhausen*, especially pp. 153ff.
10. Weinfeld, *Getting at the Roots*, pp. 3ff.

course. For, as he himself says in his summary of the *Prolegomena*:
'We are dealing here with the priestly code and its historical position'[11]
Now, if one wants to make headway with these—somewhat neglected—questions on the priestly code, the way appears first to lead
backwards into the past, in order to begin with Wellhausen's *Prolegomena*. Thus the occasion of the *Prolegomena* celebration may give
an opportunity to examine critically a few important positions within
modern research into the priestly writings, with particular reference to
the older research undertaken by Wellhausen.

2. *Main Characteristics of the Priestly Code*

For the so-called Priestly Code in modern research there has actually
been just one turning point, and that is in Wellhausen's *Prolegomena*. It
emanated from the older thesis of an Elohist 'original text' which has
its origins in 'Leviticus as well as the related parts of the adjoining
books, Exodus 25–40 except for chs. 32–34 and Numbers 1–10, 15–19
and 25–36 with few exceptions', and which therefore—as he says
later—'in accord with its content and origin deserves to be called the
Priestly Code' (pp. 7 and 9). As far as Wellhausen's redating of the
Priestly Code to the postexilic period is concerned, that is, his sub-
scription to the thesis of the *lex post prophetas*, mention is usually
made of his forerunners Eduard Reuss and Karl Heinrich Graf, named
also by Wellhausen himself (p. 4); yet his additional reference to his
predecessors has largely remained disregarded, especially his mention
of Wilhelm Martin Leberecht de Wette and his two-volume *Beiträge
zur Einleitung in das Alte Testament*.[12] If the *Prolegomena* is to be
evaluated properly, it should be placed side by side with de Wette's

11. J. Wellhausen, *Prolegomena zur Geschichte Israels* (Berlin: W. de Gruyter,
rev. edn, 1981 [3rd edn, 1886]), p. v.
12. Vol. 1 of the *Beiträge zur Einleitung in das Alte Testament* (2 vols.; Halle:
M. Niemeyer, 1806–1807) includes first a 'Historical-critical examination of the
books of the Chronicles', pp. 1-132; thereupon follow the 'Results for the history of
the Mosaic books and legislature', pp. 133-299; and vol. 2, *Kritik der israelitischen
Geschichte* (Halle: M. Niemeyer, 1807), identical with its *Erster Theil: Kritik der
mosaischen Geschichte*, includes first 'Maxims' (referring to his hermeneutic and
historiography, pp. 1-18), and then the main section 'Criticism of the books of
Moses as source of history' (pp. 19-408), which is an unbroken survey of the whole
of the Pentateuch, closing with 'Results and Remarks' (pp. 396-408). A reprinted
edition of both volumes was published in 1970 (Darmstadt). Otherwise, cf.
Prolegomena, p. 4.

Beiträge. Thereby the Chronicles chapter of the *Prolegomena* takes on a key status for Wellhausen's critical interpretation and delineation of the history of Israel as is to be inferred from the 'Mosaic history' which was dominated by the Law. For how de Wette was led to his 'criticism of the books of Moses as source of history'—as the main section of the second volume of his *Beiträge* is entitled—by means of a critical examination of Chronicles and its particular historiography (in the first volume of the *Beiträge*), Wellhausen appears to have taken the same path, especially since in 1870 he began his academic career with a dissertation on the genealogy of Judah in 1 Chronicles 2 and 4.[13] For in the case of both scholars 'Chronicles forms the gateway to a historical criticism of the history of Israel', as Thomas Willi correctly puts it in his notable book on Chronicles, referring also to Wellhausen's remark concerning his dependence on de Wette, namely: 'What I have done in the Old Testament has already been done by him.'[14] Yet, differing from his great example, Wellhausen strove for acceptance of the late dating of the Priestly Code (ever since usually abbreviated as P)—and won.

What clearly results for these scholars, then, from the proximity of the Priestly Code to Chronicles—or rather the other way around—is particularly the late historical construction in both works. 'We cannot therefore speak of a tradition from pre-exilic times in Chronicles', says Wellhausen, for example, 'neither in I.1-9 nor in I.10–II.36', and therefore not in the whole of Chronicles (*Prolegomena*, p. 229). 'In the overall picture which the book paints is reflected its own present rather than antiquity' (p. 217). This general statement of Wellhausen became almost a dogma in the literary-critical school as far as the historicity of Chronicles was concerned.[15] For on the foundation of the Law, Chronicles recasts the facts of the past 'and envisions the ancient Hebrew nation exactly according to the pattern of the later Jewish community' (p. 195). And 'the difference in the spirit of the times is due to the

13. J. Wellhausen, 'De gentibus et familiis Judaeis quae I Chr. 2.4. enumerantur' (Theological Dissertation, Göttingen, University of Göttingen, 1870). Cf. *Prolegomena*, p. 223.

14. J. Wellhausen, *Die Chronik als Auslegung: Untersuchungen zur literarischen Gestaltung der historischen Überlieferung Israels* (FRLANT, 106; Göttingen: Vandenhoeck & Ruprecht, 1972), p. 44. Cf. pp. 33ff.

15. Cf. M. Sæbø, 'Chronistische Theologie/Chronistisches Geschichtswerk', *TRE*, VIII, pp. 74-87; W. Johnstone, 'Reactivating the Chronicles Analogy in Pentateuchal Studies, with Special Reference to the Sinai Pericope in Exodus', *ZAW* 99 (1987), pp. 16-37.

influence of the Priestly Code which in the meantime had come into being' (p. 176, cf. also p. 378). Thus, just as the Priestly Code developed, so also did Chronicles. Wellhausen, however, had made the methodological choice of beginning with the later work, namely, Chronicles, in order thus—rolling back the development—to be able through Chronicles to locate the place of the Priestly Code historically.

In this regard also something has been said already on the inner relationship between the historical and narrative parts and the directly legislative elements in the Priestly Code itself. This is an even more important question since Wellhausen attributes the final editing of the Hexateuch to the Priestly Code (pp. 393ff.). Within the already shown perspective, however, the possibility of true historical narrative certainly does not appear to be very great here. 'If apart from Deuteronomy one eliminates also this basic text [i.e. the Priestly Code]', says Wellhausen, 'the Jehovistic history book still remains, which in contrast to both of them essentially is of a narrative kind and divides the tradition material with ease'. Legislative elements exist there only in one place, namely in Exodus 20–23 and in 34 (p. 7). The Priestly Code, on the other hand, 'stifles the narrative by means of the weight of the legislative material' (p. 357), which is the dominant element in it. '*Only the form is historical, it acts either as a framework for the legal material in order to arrange it, or as a mask, in order to disguise it. Generally the thread throughout the narrative is very thin*' (p. 7). 'It is as if P is the red thread upon which the pearls of JE are strung' (p. 345). Thus the Priestly Code includes both a thin narrative thread which nevertheless is significant as a linking element for JE and the whole of the Hexateuch, as well as on the other hand a large accumulation of legislative material in the middle of the Pentateuch, or—as Wellhausen and others have it—of the Hexateuch. In one of his later delineations Wellhausen also formulates the situation thus: 'The Priestly Code in its present form and size does not exhibit the methodical structure and rigid construction which distinguish Q [= *quattuor*, as an abbreviation for the narrative 'Four Covenant Book'], but rather it is a conglomerate in which other layers have attached themselves to an original nucleus (= Q) in a similar kind of crystallization.'[16]

In the last section Wellhausen appears to accept a supplementary

---

16. J. Wellhausen, *Die Composition des Hexateuchs und der historischen Bücher des Alten Testaments* (Berlin: W. de Gruyter, 4th edn, 1963 [2nd edn, 1889], p. 137; cf. p. 3.

process of growth. But even so it is clear that he is very anxious to be able to establish yet another narrative thread after all in the sheer overwhelming dominance of the legislative material in the Priestly Code. Thus it seems as if this special source can be properly classified next to the remaining sources only in this way—that is, as a *historical* source. Yet Wellhausen—who otherwise often wrote caustically—expresses himself on this point remarkably carefully, a fact which might be construed as an acknowledgment of the great difficulty of this problem. Since Theodor Nöldeke's *Untersuchungen*[17] of 1869, by and large commentators have been united about the separation of the texts, that is, about the wider scale of the Priestly Code. The actual—and critical—problem, however, is that of the separation and the more detailed specifics of the material inside the Priestly Code; or expressed differently, it is a question—the actual core question of the material—of what in fact the 'Priestly Code' or 'Priestly Document' (*Priestenschrift*), as it is now called, actually is or is supposed to be.

If, then, with regard to this key question of Wellhausen one looks beyond many other literary critics to more recent scholars in the area of Pentateuch or Hexateuch, one will be able to discern both the extensive effects of the relevant points in Wellhausen as well as more recent and highly notable changes of stress and a certain new direction. Thereby, moreover, one can utter a terminological aside, namely, that already the change from the designation 'Priestly Code' (which, as has already been mentioned, Wellhausen proposed with regard to the legislative foundation material) to the more neutral designation 'Priestly Document' may—perhaps somewhat surprisingly—be an expression of this new direction. Now, while as far as Wellhausen was concerned, there still existed between the narrative and the legislative elements in the Priestly Code a certain equilibrium, *the new direction is above all recognizable in that the weight is now more or less placed predominantly on the narrative/historical part*; and in these circumstances the old designation 'Priestly Code' would not fit well.[18]

If one now turns to Otto Eissfeldt's *Hexateuch-Synopse* (1922), one finds that he concentrated only on the narrative threads of the sources,

17. Theodor Nöldeke, *Untersuchungen zur Kritik des Alten Testaments* (Kiel, 1869); Part 1: 'Die sogenannte Grundschrift des Pentateuchs', pp. 1-144; here especially pp. 143f.

18. Cf. Noth, *Überlieferungsgeschichte des Pentateuch*, p. 9: 'One should supply it (i.e. the "P-narrative") with a kind of neutral designation.'

while all sections of legislative content have been omitted.[19] That could of course, be for pragmatic reasons of space. However, the situation is quite different in the important works of Martin Noth in 1943 and 1948[20] and in Karl Elliger's well-known study 'Sinn und Ursprung der priesterlichen Geschichtserzählung' (1952), as well as in his very notable commentary on Leviticus of 1966.[21] Above all, Noth was indicating the direction here, but so too was Elliger in a different way.

In the appendix to his *Überlieferungsgeschichtliche Studien* (1943) Noth limited the sphere of the P-narrative, which otherwise forms the literary foundation of the Pentateuch, to Genesis–Numbers (together with Deut. 34.1, 7-9) and thus removed from it a sequel narrative of the taking of the land in Joshua (pp. 180-211—different, for example, from Mowinckel[22]). Afterwards he attempted to demonstrate in his *Überlieferungsgeschichte des Pentateuch* (1948) that 'P is a *narrative work* in its whole disposition', and that this is to be interpreted 'even more exclusively than has generally been accepted heretofore' (p. 7; Noth's italics). For the legislative parts, 'which share with the P-narrative the decidedly cultic-ritualistic interest and therefore also a certain language and terminology which had become embedded in priestly circles in Jerusalem', *originally have nothing to do with this narrative work from a literary point of view* (*Überlieferungsgeschichte*; my italics). When Noth then concludes that P turns out to be 'thereby more decidedly and unequivocally a *narrative*' (p. 9; Noth's italics), Rendtorff characterizes this final conclusion—and rightly so—as 'an amazing circumlocution' (*Das überlieferungsgeschichtliche Problem*, p. 112).

To be sure, Noth appears to have experienced certain difficulties, particularly when it comes to a more precise definition of the theology of the P-narrative, but he enforces his view consistently. Despite its designation, the 'Priestly Document' forms no 'decidedly priestly work'; if its author should be a priest, then 'the spirit of his work is not particularly priestly' (*Überlieferungsgeschichte*, p. 260). The theology

---

19. Eissfeldt, *Hexateuch-Synopse*, p. xi.

20. Noth, *Überlieferungsgeschichtliche Studien*. See also n. 17 above.

21. K. Elliger, 'Sinn und Ursprung der priesterlichen Geschichtserzählung', *ZTK* 49 (1952), pp. 121-43, now in his *Kleine Schriften zum Alten Testament* (TBü, 32; Munich: Chr. Kaiser Verlag, 1966), pp. 174-98. See also his *Leviticus*.

22. S. Mowinckel, *Tetrateuch–Pentateuch–Hexateuch: Die Berichte über die Landnahme in den drei altisraelitischen Geschichtswerken* (BZAW, 90; Berlin: Alfred Töpelmann, 1964); cf. also n. 4 above.

of P finds its focal point in the Sinai-*narrative* which gives an account of the inauguration of the lawful cult and 'thus the constitution of the twelve Israelite tribes as a cult community'. However, in this regard it is indubitable 'that herein is expressed the general, and not simply priestly, notion of the correct form of worship in the late period from which the P-narrative comes' (pp. 262-63). After all, it is very surprising how Noth with this theological interpretation of the P-narrative circumvents in a wide arc all that is cultic and priestly. Maybe at this point the heir of Wellhausen's *Prolegomena* takes effect? For, towards the end of his statements, Wellhausen denotes the cult as 'the heathen element in Israelite religion... If it is made to be the most important issue in the Priestly Code, then it appears to represent a systematic relapse into paganism' (p. 442). Certainly no more modern scholar would judge the cult so sharply and pejoratively, since the work of Sigmund Mowinckel and others has exercised a huge reaction—yet the *vestigia terrent*. Basically, it is presumably a question of the power of the system of the documentary hypothesis, as a result of which the priestly writings fundamentally find their claim to existence in being able to show themselves to be both narrative and work of history alongside the other ancient works of history or narrative threads.

Elliger's study 'Sinn und Ursprung der priesterlichen Geschichtserzählung', mentioned above, has actually only served to intensify this aspect in that he has aimed more sharply at the historical situation of the author, the priestly narrator of history. On the whole Elliger also agrees with Noth in the demarcation of the priestly basic text, the so-called Pg, by excluding the narrative in Joshua concerning the taking of the land (*Kleine Schriften*, pp. 174-75). Yet Elliger draws quite different conclusions. He sees the theme of the taking of the land in Canaan against the background of the exile situation of the priestly author and of his addressees as being *clearly present* in his historical narrative (pp. 184-89). 'Our witness is still in exile. Thus we can explain his restraint in cultic matters', says Elliger, while otherwise he repeatedly emphasizes the impact of 'promise' and 'fulfilment' in the priestly historical narrative. Thus, to some extent, Elliger brings the priestly writings close to the narrative technique of J or JE and of the later prophets. On the definitive characteristics of the priestly historical narrative Elliger says:

> It originated in Babylonian exile as a comforting and warning testimony
> to the all-powerfully superior and wonderfully benevolent God of

> promise, the Lord of world history and in particular of the history of
> Israel, the goal of which remains firmly fixed: a great nation, liberated
> for eternal possession of the land of Canaan, and God, the God of this
> nation (p. 198).

In fact, the following simple remark could be made: Is this supposed to
be especially priestly? It appears rather to be the voice of a prophet.

Nevertheless, Elliger has enjoyed no little resonance. People have
spoken, for example, of the 'hope for home-coming in the priestly
writings'.[23] Particularly Walter Brueggemann in an attempt to determine more closely the kerygma of the priestly author, has wanted to
understand Gen. 1.28 against its background of the exile situation,[24]
whereas Sean E. McEvenue has examined its special narrative style.[25]
Most worthy of note is a paper by Norbert Lohfink in which he has
carefully investigated the concept of 'history' in relation to the priestly
writings.[26]

Nevertheless, in all of this a deep doubt gradually emerges. And he
who has ears already hears with renowned champions of the priestly
work of history utterances which might bear witness to a bad con-
science. There are some things which do not quite make sense. Noth's
difficulty in determining the theology of the P-narrative has already
been mentioned. With Elliger, one is somewhat surprised by the
amount of discussion about 'transparency' and 'background' of the
priestly historical narrative, and finally he says plainly and simply:
'Here we are not faced in any way with an actual portrayal of history...
Above all it is clear that basically the interest of the narrator is not in
the historical processes as such, but rather in the truths of faith which
he reads out of them' (p. 195). In his excellent introduction to *Die Entstehung des Alten Testaments*, Rudolf Smend, clearly striving for a
certain balance of the elements discussed, says last of all: '*Despite
everything* P is a *narrative work* which *in whatever way* has as its

23. R. Kilian, 'Die Hoffnung auf Heimkehr in der Priesterschrift', *BibLeb* 7
(1966), pp. 39-51.

24. W. Brueggemann, 'The Kerygma of the Priestly Writers', *ZAW* 84 (1972),
pp. 397-414.

25. S.E. McEvenue, *The Narrative Style of the Priestly Writer* (AnBib, 50;
Rome: Biblical Institute Press, 1971).

26. N. Lohfink, 'Die Priesterschrift und die Geschichte', in *Congress Volume:
Göttingen 1977* (VTSup, 29; Leiden: E.J. Brill, 1978), pp. 189-225.

subject a long succession of events and people.'[27] The section which begins with these words finishes with the following sentence: 'The work as a work of narrative threatens to become disjointed' (p. 51). At the same time Smend warns—and rightly so—of 'a clumsy alternative': 'Here is narrative, and there is law', and he continues thus: 'Unquestionably P wants to offer both. For him both are intertwined in a tight-knit and indispensible way, both also influence each other strongly' (p. 51). Here one can certainly agree with Smend. The far more difficult question is, however, which of the two parts is the original and typical 'priestly' element, whether P then is 'fundamentally' a work of history into which the legal and cultic elements have been inserted secondarily, or whether, on the other hand, the cultic and legal elements—even here one must differentiate more precisely between them—are what is particularly 'priestly', and which gradually by means of tradition have been supplemented and expanded, and thus historically ordered and defined. Both are without doubt relevant. Yet here it is a question of *priority. By means of the documentary hypothesis, literary critics have responded to this basic question very much to the benefit of the historical elements.* Its solution has generally been recognized up to the present day and has enjoyed almost axiomatic value. The question now, however, emerges as to whether the documentary hypothesis—emanating from the older works of history—might not have forced upon the cultic priestly tradition something that was foreign to it, a kind of straitjacket, as it were.

In this context the treatment of the Priestly Document in Gerhard von Rad's *Theologie des Alten Testaments*[28] is even more worthy of note than it may appear to be at first sight. First, as the first point in just three pages, he treats 'the Priestly Document as a work of history'. He clings to his theory, but emphasizes the difference from both D and JE. The 'genuine theological nature of the story' in P is, however, 'of a very different kind from that of historical Jehovistic delineation. The subject of the delineation is not...the secret guidance of humankind...but rather the historical sprouting of particular cultic institutions... We are dealing here with specifically priestly literature whose

27. R. Smend, *Die Entstehung des Alten Testaments* (Theol. Wissenschaft, 1; Stuttgart: W. Kohlhammer, 1978), pp. 49-50 (the central italics are by the author himself).

28. Von Rad, *Theologie des Alten Testaments*, I, pp. 245-93; cf. also his *Die Priesterschrift im Hexateuch* (BWANT, 65; Stuttgart: W. Kohlhammer, 1934).

laws of growth we are even less acquainted with' (p. 246). There then follows a wide-ranging delineation, spread over almost 50 pages, of the *theology* of the Priestly Document which begins with the point about 'tent, ark and glory of God' and which ends with 'sin and atonement' as well as 'clean and unclean, sickness and death' (pp. 247-93).

Moreover, in this delineation one senses the same proportions and the same essential concentration as in the middle part of the Pentateuch itself. The emphasis is on *priestly cult theology*. There then actually exists, however, the possibility of a completely different way of thinking, of a different methodological approach to the material from that of Wellhausen's documentary hypothesis; for one does not need to think so very linearly in a historical and developmental way and to emphasize the accepted end-point as strongly as was the case with Wellhausen, but *from a mid-point* one can get to grips with the material and develop it from the point of view of priestly cult theology whose innermost nucleus appears to be *the presence of the—blessing and atoning—holy God*. The material is exceedingly diverse and has gone through a multilayered history which should be investigated in its striation and stages of development. After all, to this belong also the links with salvatio-historical traditions. How that has operated can be shown at this opportunity, for example, by the festival calendars.

3. *The Festival Calendars: A Sample of Priestly Tradition*

Turning to the so-called festival calendars in Exod. 23.14-17; 34.18, 22-23; Deut. 16.1-17; Lev. 23.4-44 and Numbers 28–29, to which also Ezek. 45.18-25 may be added, one comes upon an area of themes to which Wellhausen paid great attention in his *Prolegomena* (pp. 84-121); yet, against the background of more recent form- and traditio-historical research these calendars ought to have been examined anew. For they have not been discussed as a particular formal and traditio-historical whole, that is to say, as a specific genus in their own right, but almost only in their temporal context as well as in connexion with single festivals.[29] An examination in monograph form would fill a lamentable gap. In the present article, however, only a few short remarks will be made.

29. Important additions can be found in de Vaux, *Ancient Israel*, pp. 484-506; H.-J. Kraus, *Gottesdienst in Israel* (Munich, 2nd edn, 1962), pp. 40-50; cf. also G.B. Gray, *Sacrifice in the Old Testament: Its Theory and Practice* (New York: Ktav, 2nd edn, 1971 [1925]), pp. 271-84.

The calendars have been enumerated in the way in which they are traditionally attributed to the sources or tradition layers, that is, the first and shortest in Exodus 23 to the Book of the Covenant—or as some have it, to E, then Exodus 34 to J, Deuteronomy 16 to D, Leviticus 23 to H and Numbers 28–29 to P. In this way, however, they are isolated and that which they have in common, namely, their continuity, is lost. On the other hand, if one regards them in a *synoptic* delineation as a specific whole, both common elements as well as differences clearly emerge, and a really short and simple base form appears to be at their root. One comes closest to this basic form in Exod. 23.14-17:

14 Three times a year you are to celebrate a festival (*tāḥōg*) to me:

15 (Celebrate) the Feast of Unleavened Bread (the Maṣṣot Festival, *ḥag hamaṣṣôt*); for seven days eat bread made without yeast, as I commanded you, at the appointed time in the month of Abib, for in that month you came out of Egypt.
  None shall appear before me empty-handed.

16 Then (celebrate) the Feast of Harvest with the first-fruits of the crops you sow in your field;
  and (celebrate) the Feast of Ingathering at the end of the year, when you gather in your crops from the field.

17 Three times a year all the men are to appear before Yahweh the Lord.[30]

This calendar—like the rest—is laden with problems at almost every turn. In this context, from a formal point of view it is first of interest in that the statements in vv. 14 and 17 have a framework of a positive-apodictic address, then in that the statements about the festivals are enumerated in the form of a *list*, from which it is clear that the naming of the second festival in v. 16a after mention of the various elements in 15aβb simply begins with *wᵉḥag*. Similarly with the third festival in v. 16bα. Factually interesting is the salvatio-historical argumentation in v. 15b, and furthermore the lack of mention of the Passover festival is noteworthy. In spite of the many interpolations in Exod. 34.19-21, the form observed in Exodus 23 is clearly evident in the next calendar too. In this there are a few more terminological changes (like, for example, the designation *ḥag šābū'ōt* for the second festival in v. 22, but the enumerating form is maintained by means of the word *wᵉḥag*). In contrast to both of these, the third calendar in Deuteronomy 16 is very wordy and bears the typically admonishing style of Deuteronomy. Particularly noticeable here is the fact that the Passover Festival stands

---

30. Textual and literary problems cannot be considered at this point.

dominantly to the fore, and yet, nevertheless, the calendar concludes in vv. 16-17, expanded by typically Deuteronomic material, with the framework-formula 'three times a year', and in so doing, it fails to mention the Passover Festival. The fourth calendar in Leviticus 23 and especially the fifth in Numbers 28–29 are even more verbose, though now, on account of many quite precise sacrifice designations, together with calendar designations which are as precise as possible. Otherwise, the form of God's address to Moses is predominant here. By means of several introductions as well as conclusions in Leviticus 23 a gradual growth in the calendar can be observed. And far more could still be mentioned.

Now, then, a few fundamental considerations may be made with regard to the material which has been dealt with briefly above. In his *Prolegomena* Wellhausen rightly saw a development in the material. However, if he has firmly arranged the material in a quite definite line of development within the framework of a number of documentary writings, the question arises as to what extent this process is appropriate to the material. For example, it may be asked whether the cultic statements in Exodus 23 or even in Deuteronomy 16 are not just as 'priestly' as those in Leviticus and Numbers. Are we not far more likely to be faced here with an absolutely *priestly* tradition material, which on the other hand at different times and in different circumstances—even in a prophetic context like Ezekiel 45—could also take on different forms? A developed system of sacrifice does not have to have a late date given to it, for certainly there was such a system in the service of the temple in the time of the kings. In this regard, the different calendars may have served different purposes. The shorter calendars in Exodus as well as the sermonic ones in Deuteronomy appear to be more devoted to the people, to the laity, whereas the longer and more elaborated ones in Leviticus, and especially in Numbers, bear witness, to a greater extent, to the particular priestly profession. They are, so to speak, 'more learned'.[31] But to wish for this reason alone to attribute these to a specific 'Priestly Document' is not immediately obvious.

A few, then, have expressed themselves also opposed to the view of the many quoted literary critics. In this regard, one may lend an ear to the words of a renowned representative of critical Old Testament

31. Cf. also Rendtorff, *Die Gesetze in der Priesterschrifte*, e.g. p. 77, as well as K. Koch, *Die Priesterschrift von Exodus 25 bis Leviticus 16* (FRLANT, 71; Göttingen: Vandenhoeck & Ruprecht, 1959).

scholarship such as Johannes Hempel, who says in his Pauly-Wissowa article on the 'Priestly Code':

> In P we are not dealing with a written narrative work which itself may have been produced from intermingling source strata and expanded by means of secondary insertions. P is rather to be understood in several layers from the oral instructions of the laity or even of the novices by means of a clergy which has as its aim the correct 'understanding' of Yahweh and of his will and develops in single 'lessons'.[32]

In the past Johannes Pedersen[33] and Ivan Engnell[34] expressed themselves in more or less the same way, as later did Artur Weiser[35] and more recently Haran and Weinfeld, Rolf Rendtorff and also Ronald E. Clements;[36] here the antiquity of the material or the existence of a longer, specific priestly tradition or priestly school are stressed.

Without necessarily having to dispute directly the existence of a Priestly Code or a Priestly Document, a few points may be made—and many more could be mentioned—which speak for a shifting of stress in the opposite direction to that which has been normal until recently, namely *a shifting of stress away from the favoured emphasis on the narrative and historical elements in the priestly tradition, after which the so-called Priestly Document is understood fundamentally as a work of history, to the cultic-ritualistic and legal elements of the priestly traditions as its proprium.* That now leads on to the particular *priestly theology* as its mid-point which supports everything else. Now, in conclusion a discussion of this may be a way of expanding the subject and rounding it off at the same time.

32. PW, XXII, cc. 1943-67; the quotation is col. 1965.

33. J. Pedersen, 'Die Auffassung vom Alten Testament', *ZAW* 49 (1931), pp. 161-81; see also his 'Passahfest und Passahlegende', *ZAW* 52 (1934), pp. 161-75.

34. Engnell, *Gamla Testamentet*, pp. 168-259. See also his *Critical Essays on the Old Testament*, especially pp. 3-11 and 50-67, as well as the article in Svenskt Bibliskt Uppslagsverk (especially the 2nd edn, 1962–63).

35. A. Weiser, *Einleitung in das Alte Testament* (Göttingen: Vandenhoeck & Ruprecht, 5th edn, 1963), pp. 124-30.

36. On Haran and Weinfeld see n. 3 above, and on Rendtorff see n. 6. Otherwise see R.E. Clements, 'Pentateuchal Problems', in Anderson (ed.), *Tradition and Interpretation*, pp. 96-124.

4. *The Theological Context*

For a long time there has existed a lively debate about the basis and form, meaning and aim of an Old Testament theology. In this debate too, 'history' or historical points of view have played a considerable role. I have touched on this elsewhere and in so doing I have attempted to introduce new points of view as well, namely, milieu-historical ones, by asking about the relationship between the most important main types of Old Testament theology to corresponding circles of theologians in ancient Israel. However, it is not possible to expand on this here.[37] Suffice it to say that primarily we may differentiate between three main types of Old Testament theology, namely, between a *salvation theology with a historical emphasis* (and which especially had as its theme the unique deeds of God), and then a *theology of order* (or creation theology) of the wise, and finally a *cult theology* (or salvation theology with a cult emphasis) of the priests, which is of particular interest in this connexion.[38]

Further discussion of the particular cult theology of the priests, which also stretches across historical books—one may think of the Psalms, for example—cannot be undertaken on this occasion. Nevertheless, the main thrust or proprium of the priestly cult theology can be established. Its main thrust—where its pulse beats most quickly—is *the present, the here and now, of divine glory in whatever form it occurs, the salvation-bringing light of the holy and merciful, blessing God in the holy place where the holy rites of the cult are carried out*.[39] From the midst of this priestly cult theology the current literary-critical positions to a certain extent become relative as far as the Priestly Code or the Priestly

37. Sæbø, 'Hvem var Israels teologer?'.

38. On the latter cf., e.g., Haran; see n. 3 above.

39. On this occasion it is not impossible to present a more detailed argument. Priestly theology has been described elsewhere in very different terms; cf., e.g., C. Westermann, 'Die Herrlichkeit Gottes in der Priesterschrift', in *Wort–Gebot–Glaube: Beiträge zur Theologie des Alten Testaments* (Festschrift W. Eichrodt; ATANT, 59; Zürich: Zwingli-Verlag, 1971), pp. 227-49; now in Westermann, *Forschung am Alten Testament: Gesammelte Studien*, II (TBü, 55; Munich: Chr. Vaiser Verlag, 1974), pp. 115-37; W. Zimmerli, 'Sinaibund und Abrahambund: Ein Beitrag zum Verständnis der Priesterschrift', *EvT* 16 (1960), pp. 268-80, repr. in Zimmerli, *Gottes Offenbarung*, pp. 205-16; and E. Cortese, 'La teologia del Documento Sacerdotale', *RevistB* 26 (1978), pp. 113-37, where he treats the theology of Pg and of Ps separately.

Document is concerned. Also, one might say that whoever is unable to see the wood of the religious background in the cult for the many trees of the diverse cultic statements and laws has neither rightly understood nor assessed the Israelite cult, nor Old Testament theology and religion—as was to some extent the case in Julius Wellhausen's *Prolegomena*. As already mentioned, in his view the cultic/ritualistic elements brought the 'true religion' of the Old Testament, as he understood it, into decline (p. 442).

Finally, the centenary of Wellhausen's *Prolegomena zur Geschichte Israels*, with which this essay began, may also bring us to the end. Above the huge effect of this work was discussed. Let us recall the concluding words of Eissfeldt's article on Wellhausen written in 1920, where he says: 'Wellhausen does not belong to the past. He functions in the present and he has much to offer too to the coming generation'.[40]

And yet, a question may be added: Is it not time now to move on from this hundred-year-old work? It would certainly be a high honour for Wellhausen, the old searcher for truth, if we were to search further and in new forms for the truth of the biblical texts.

---

40. See Eissfeldt, *Kleine Schriften*, I, p. 71.

Chapter 11

REFLECTIONS ON OLD TESTAMENT ETHICS:
ITS DUAL CHARACTER AND ITS MODERN APPLICATION

1. *Introductory Remarks*

Do the Old Testament in general and Old Testament ethics in particular still have any normative significance? The question may be rather difficult to answer within the context of the Church, and becomes even more difficult when the question, in more general terms, is asked within the context of modern society. Bearing in mind the three millennia that separate ancient Israelite society from those of modern times, the distance of time may just underscore the distance in matter. In particular, critical questions may be raised in view of a possible transference or application of Old Testament ethics—or at least crucial elements of it—today; one may ask what value such ethics would have in the present context, and to what degree.[1]

With this approach, then, the main questions to be raised will be questions of a fundamental ethical character, though they will be complemented by themes from material ethics; they belong, in other words, to the fundamental problems of ethics, where philosophical and Christian ethics also meet. When these fundamental questions seem to be of more interest today than in the long term, it will, not least in a situation of this kind, remain relevant also to keep the historical dimension and the historical perspectives of the questions in focus. On this occasion, however, the space for discussing these problems is restricted.

At the outset, it may be taken for granted that Christian ethics—now seen apart from the general ethics of philosophy—has an essential need to incorporate Old Testament ethics in its reflection and its 'system'.

---

1. Cf. A. Soete, *Ethos der Rettung—Ethos der Gerechtigkeit: Studien zur Struktur von Normbegründung und Urteilsfindung im Alten Testament und ihrer Relevanz für die ethische Diskussion der Gegenwart* (Würzburg: Echter, 1987).

That would be even more true for systematic Christian theology, especially in its Lutheran form, as it has a clearly defined state of dependence on Scripture as *norma normans,* and thereby also upon the Old Testament. However, the case is not quite as obvious or easy as it initially might seem to be.

First, concerning the usage of biblical material in relation to ethics, there has been a widespread tendency exclusively or mainly to use the New Testament, whereas the Old Testament has barely had any independent function. This complies with a larger context of older and especially modern history of theology where the Old Testament in some influential circles has only been ascribed a very restricted status as canonical Scripture—and subsequently, as a theologically normative instance, as a true *norma normans.*

Second, there has been another pronounced tendency from the interwar years, and especially during the aftermath of the First World War, to strengthen the status of the Old Testament in theology and in Church. This tendency, however, seems to have been most perceptible in exegetics and theology as well as in the preaching of the Church; only to a much lesser degree has there been any usage of Old Testament material in specific ethical reflection.[2] During the 1960s, this situation became somewhat changed by the social-ethical use of the Old Testament, being at best a special case of reading the Old Testament. The usage of biblical texts could, in this instance, be very selective as it concentrated mainly on the socio-critical parts of Amos as well as on the radical preaching of doom by other prophets, or on selected social

---

2.   As for biblical theological works the general low esteem of Old Testament ethics can be seen in most of the larger 'Old Testament theologies' of this century. However, W. Eichrodt, who more than anyone renewed the discipline of Old Testament theology with his *Theologie des Alten Testaments* I–III (Göttingen: Vandenhoeck & Ruprecht, 1933–39; ET *Theology of the Old Testament,* I–II [London: SCM Press, 1961–67]) has an extensive discussion of the impact of Old Testament ethics (vol. 3), emphasizing the place of ethics in a wider theological context; in his tripartite treatment he discusses respectively the 'norms', the 'benefits' and the 'motives' of moral conduct. At the same time, an important monograph was published by J. Hempel, *Das Ethos des Alten Testaments* (BZAW, 67; Berlin: Alfred Töpelmann, 2nd edn, 1964 [1938]); his approach was more orientated towards history of religion and sociology. Among the numerous Old Testament theologies during the post-war era, cf. T.C. Vriezen, *An Outline of Old Testament Theology* (Oxford: Basil Blackwell, 2nd edn, 1970).

concepts like 'right', 'righteousness' and 'peace'.[3] From a general Old
Testament point of view—and also as regards a prophet like Amos—
this kind of ethical use of Old Testament material could, on the one
hand, easily give an impression of being somewhat arbitrary. On the
other hand, it is to be taken positively that the Old Testament creation
theology came more to the fore.

On the whole, the Old Testament scholars themselves were partly to
be blamed for the negative state of affairs, since for a long time the
main tendency among them was to give Old Testament ethics only a
little substantial attention, or not to make the ethical issues a theme as
such. From the perspective of the history of Old Testament research,
this fact is in a way rather surprising, in particular if one reflects on the
great role that ethical aspects played in the conception and influential
literary work of Julius Wellhausen; as is well known, he considered the
prophets to be the creators of what he called the 'ethical monotheism'
in Israel. For the situation during most of the post-war era it may be
symptomatic that the only monographic account of 'Old Testament
ethics', at least on the continental scene, was written by a systematic
theologian from the Netherlands.[4] In recent years, however, Old Testament scholars have done considerably more in this area. Among them
Eckart Otto should be especially mentioned, since over some time he
has fostered the growth of the current interest in Old Testament ethics
and lately has published a major monograph on the subject.[5]

3.　Among many others cf. G. Wanke, 'Zu Grundlagen und Absicht prophet-
ischer Sozialkritik', *KD* 18 (1972), pp. 2-17; C.J.H. Wright, *The Use of the Bible in
Social Ethics* (Bramcote: Grove Books, 1983); recently W.H. Schmidt (with
H. Delkurt and A. Graussner), *Die zehn Gebote im Rahmen alttestamentlicher Ethik*
(EdF, 281; Darmstadt: Wissenschaftliche Buchgesellschaft, 1993).

4.　H. van Oyen, *Ethik des Alten Testaments* (Gütersloh: Gütersloher Verlagshaus, 1967). The book is part of the series *Geschichte der Ethik*; it does not
emphasize the material ethics, but rather gives an account of 'the foundation of
ethical awareness in the European culture', as is stated in the Preface; van Oyen
adds: 'to this both the Old and the New Testament have given substantial contributions'.

5.　In his 'Forschungsgeschichte der Entwürfe einer Ethik im Alten Testament',
VF 36 (1991), pp. 3-37, E. Otto gave an account of the research on Old Testament
ethics, updated in 1990, and in 1994 he published his own presentation, *Theolo-
gische Ethik des Alten Testaments* (Theologische Wissenschaft, 3.2; Stuttgart:
W. Kohlhammer). See also, among many of his contributions, 'Kultus und Ethos in
Jerusalemer Theologie: Ein Beitrag zur theologischen Begründung der Ethik im
Alten Testament', *ZAW* 98 (1986), pp. 161-79; 'Die Geburt des moralischen

In asking which parts of the Old Testament material ethics mainly has used, the answer in most cases will be the commandments of the law codes and, above all, the Decalogue. This fact is neither surprising nor does it miss the point. One has, however, to trace how these references have been done or on what grounds the usage rests—even if that kind of critical evaluation cannot be pursued on this occasion. The critical approach may also be relevant as regards the frequent use of the Old Testament wisdom literature, with its maxims and exhortations, not forgetting its theology of creation[6] as well as the socio-critical references in the preaching of the prophets. In all this, among much else, there is a broad and manifold tangent surface between 'Old Testament ethics' and the specific 'Old Testament theology'; and a further clarifying of their mutual relationship remains a challenge.

2. *Two Points of Departures and Two Movements*

As has been briefly demonstrated, 'the ethics of the Old Testament' cannot be said to be a theme given any priority among Old Testament scholars, but there have been some significant attempts, first of all in recent years.

In comparing the two older presentations referred to above (Eichrodt in his *Theologie des Alten Testaments* and Hempel in his monograph *Das Ethos des Alten Testaments*), one will find, first, that both of them expound the material *diversity* of Old Testament ethics. At the same time, however, they try to establish some kind of unity in this most variegated diversity, by giving a systematic arrangement or 'structural analysis' of the matter—Eichrodt in a theologizing manner and Hempel in a historicizing way. Second, they both draw a line of development from the more or less primitive ethos of people (*Volkssitte*) to the more 'elevated' level of piety and morality. It is beyond doubt that in ancient

Bewusstseins', in E. Otto and S. Uhlig, *Bibel und Christentum im Orient* (Glückstadt: J.J. Agustin, 1991), pp. 63-97. See also J.L. Crenshaw and J.T. Willis (eds.), *Essays in Old Testament Ethics: J. Philip Hyatt in Memoriam* (New York: Ktav, 1974); J. Barton, 'Understanding Old Testament Ethics', *JSOT* 9 (1978), pp. 44-64; R.E. Clements, *Loving One's Neighbour: OT Ethics in Context* (London, 1992); further H.D. Preuss, *Theologie des Alten Testaments*, II (Stuttgart: W. Kohlhammer, 1992; ET *Old Testament Theology*, II [Edinburgh: T. & T. Clark, 1995]), §12.

6.   In this respect, the new treatment of Otto, in his *Theologische Ethik*, represents a considerable step forward.

Israel there was a development of ethics, but the question may be raised whether it is adequately described here, and whether this point should be emphasized when dealing with the peculiar and genuine aspects of the Old Testament *ethos*. In his *An Outline of Old Testament Theology,* Vriezen stressed two 'motives' which he saw as being essential for ethical conduct, namely the concepts of 'awareness of community (*Gemeinschaftsbewusstsein*)' and 'individual responsibility (*individuelle Verantwortlichkeit*)'.[7] It is beyond doubt that the ethics in Israel had both a collective and an individual aspect, and that these aspects were in development. But again, the critical question may be raised whether it is within the difference—and tension—between the collective and the individual 'motives' that one is to make the most adequate differentiation in the ethical material; supposedly not.

At this stage, a glimpse into 'the theology of the Old Testament' may be of some use. In this discipline, during the last generation, the greatest attention has been attracted by the protest of Gerhard von Rad against the systematic approach that for so long had been the standard, found also in different 'Theologies' like those of Eichrodt and Vriezen. An important matter of concern for von Rad was that the treatment of the Old Testament theology should not be directed by an alien, doctrinal 'system' that is enforced on the biblical texts from without, but by a procedure of letting the Old Testament 'speak for itself', in its own way. One gets the impression that von Rad, in his *Theologie des Alten Testaments* (following Johann Gabler who, in 1787, advocated a methodological, clear distinction between biblical and dogmatic theology[8]), now wished to eradicate the last bit of 'dogmatic leaven' and give an account of the Old Testament theology in a radically new way.[9] Without commenting here on von Rad's new solution of the old problem of structuring an 'Old Testament theology', it may be asked,

7.   Vriezen, *An Outline*, Ch. 10, §2.
8.   See Chapter 19 below.
9.   In vols. 1 and 2 of his *Theologie des Alten Testaments*, von Rad focused on the 'historical traditions' and the 'prophetic traditions' respectively; that he missed essential areas by using this approach is apparent. In particular, his methodical procedure generated a broad debate on the need of a 'central point' in describing Old Testament theology, cf. J.H. Hayes and F.C. Prussner, *Old Testament Theology: Its History and Development* (London: SCM Press, 1985), pp. 233-76, esp. pp. 257-60. For a discussion on von Rad's *Theologie des Alten Testaments* see further, among many others, W.H. Schmidt, '"Theologie des Alten Testaments" vor und nach G. von Rad', *VF* 17 (1972), pp. 1-25; Spriggs, *Two Old Testament Theologies*.

however, whether his specific methodological approach represented any obstacle to him in view of dealing with the 'Old Testament ethics' as a separate subject.

When Rudolf Smend, some years ago, in another setting and way, maintained that 'the concept of an "Old Testament ethics" is even more problematic than the concept of an "Old Testament theology"',[10] his dictum clearly underscored the complexity of an enterprise of this kind. But the fact that Smend himself, despite his negative judgment, has written an account on the topic and is going to publish a book on 'Ethics of the Old Testament' may indicate that it should be both possible and necessary to give the subject of 'Old Testament ethics' as a whole some thematic treatment. Recently, Eckart Otto has managed to present both the diversity and the unity of the Old Testament ethics in a relatively coherent way, which in this respect is a considerable achievement.[11] On the other hand, his methodological procedure, focusing on the aspect of 'sanction' in relation to ethics and to ethos, and on the development of the 'motivation (*Begründung*)' of Old Testament ethics in reference to the Book of the Covenant and other related law traditions, to the 'creation order (*Schöpfungsordnung*)' of the wisdom literature and to the 'revelation of God in the history' as different 'sources', has been questioned.[12] Also, the monumental work by Frank Crüsemann on the Torah, presenting a broad overview of the legal history of ancient Israel, is to a great extent on 'Old Testament ethics'.[13]

10. R. Smend, 'Ethik, III: Altes Testament', *TRE*, X, pp. 423-35 (423).

11. Cf. n. 5 above. Further, already in his 'Forschungsgeschichte der Entwürfe', p. 11, Otto had pointed out that an 'important area of discussion in Old Testament scholarship is the question of the structure, systematic and central point of an Old Testament theology. In the field of Old Testament ethics this discussion is completely lacking'; and against Barton, 'Understanding Old Testament Ethics', pp. 44-64, who renounced a unifying account of the ethics of the Old Testament, he claimed that 'one cannot renounce a general description of an Old Testament theology, so neither a general presentation of its ethics. The increasing recognition of its complexity requires an even more intensive reflection on Old Testament ethics as a whole'.

12. See also the critical review of Otto's *Theologische Ethik* by A. Schenker, *Bib* 77 (1996), pp. 560-62.

13. F. Crüsemann, *Die Tora: Theologie und Sozialgeschichte des alttestamentlichen Gesetzes* (Munich: Chr. Kaiser Verlag, 1992; ET *The Torah: Theology and Social History of Old Testament Law* [Edinburgh: T. & T. Clark, 1996]). Cf. the critical review of this work by E. Otto, *TLZ* 118 (1993), cols. 903-10.

The rather complex situation of the discipline of 'Old Testament ethics', as depicted most briefly above, is still open. The discussion of its unsolved problems may be pursued, and it may be appropriate to present some new reflections on the basic question of the characteristics of Old Testament ethics. If, then, another attempt to raise fundamental questions of the Old Testament *ethos* is to be made now, it should be performed on the basis of the Old Testament itself, on its own terms. However, whereas the Old Testament, first of all, presents a rich variety of ethical material, there will also be, at the same time, when perceiving and describing this diversity, a need for disclosing main trends of some unifying character in the same material. An apt point of departure, therefore, may be found at the crossroad of the given diversity of the ethical material and the quest for some unity in it.

Taking, then, the point of departure in the tension of diversity and unity, the material itself appears to reveal different basic ways of reasoning and founding, or 'motivating', of its ethical attitude and conduct. It may be adequate grounds, furthermore, to presume that the Old Testament ethics seems to have 'two moral sources' (to play on the well-known phrase by Henri Bergson, the Jewish thinker who managed to mediate much of the heritage of the Old Testament in his philosophy).[14] It will scarcely be appropriate to take over his distinction between *morale close* and *morale ouverte*, but to a certain extent, his term 'closed morality', referring to a single people's (closed) community with its specific rules, may correspond to the distinctive laws and commandments of the Israelite society; and when using the term 'open morality', designating all of humanity, the general and common, then also a universal feature of this kind is pronounced in several ethical texts of the Old Testament.

At this point one may take a step further, for there appear also to be some crossing or adverse lines in the Old Testament ethical material, running contrary to each other: some from the special to the common and others from the common to the special; and it will be most significant to examine the interdependence of these two different 'movements'. Related to this and perhaps of even greater principal significance is, however, the above mentioned distinction between two different 'sources' for the founding of the morality. In other words, there seems to exist a fundamental difference in ethical motivation or

14. Henri Bergson, *Les deux sources de la morale et de la religion* (Paris: Librairie Felix Alcan, 1932).

legitimization, and a double 'development'. In all, this gives two basically different starting points and ways of stating the reason for the norms of human coexistence, the one being the specific divine legitimization or revelation of laws and commandments, the other being the common, human experience, generating an empirical and rational way of reasoning. *These two basically different ways correspond to the two different 'sources' of the Old Testament ethos.* Moreover, these two different ways or 'movements' from different sources do also meet and influence each other. In addition, there was always a substantial influence from without on the ethos of Israel, as Israel did not constitute any ethical enclave in its times, though having its own distinctive and genuine character. In taking all of these elements into consideration, one can hardly draw a simple line of ethical 'development'; that would surely do no justice to the very complex material which the ethics of Old Testament actually constitutes, and which one has to comprise and comprehend in its redundant extent.

In this fundamental perspective, a few characteristic examples from the ethical material itself may clarify and substantiate the indicated main lines.

3. *Divine Legitimization/Revelation: From the Special to the Common*

Israelite society was a community that experienced great upheavals—sociologically and politically, culturally and religiously as well as ethically. Without facing the very complex problems of the early history of Israel,[15] or, more specifically, the diachrone questions of the development of the ancient Israelite laws and practice of justice[16]—questions which in no way are immaterial for the understanding of the Old

---

15. See, for instance, S. Kreuzer, *Die Frühgeschichte Israels in Bekenntnis und Verkündigung des Alten Testaments* (Berlin: W. de Gruyter, 1989); or N.P. Lemche, *Early Israel: Anthropological and Historical Studies on the Israelite Society before the Monarchy* (Leiden: E.J. Brill, 1985); on this approach cf. W. Thiel, 'Vom revolutionären zum evolutionären Israel? Zu einem neuen Modell der Entstehung Israels', *TLZ* 113 (1988), cols. 401-10.

16. See the works of E. Otto and F. Crüsemann (see nn. 5 and 13 above). As for the legal history of ancient Israel, E. Otto has a number of detailed works in this field, for instance *Wandeln der Rechtsbegründungen in der Gesellschaftsgeschichte des antiken Israel* (Leiden: E.J. Brill, 1988); 'Israels Wurzeln in Kanaan: Auf dem Wege zu einer neuen Kultur- und Sozialgeschichte des antiken Israels', *TRev* 85 (1989), pp. 3-10.

Testament ethics—the attention will on this occasion be focused on that
which is probably the most conspicuous common feature of the Israelite laws and commandments as the basis for human coexistence,
namely that they are characterized by being *given or spoken in the
name of God*. The point is here not a genetic one—how all this came
about—but the simple fact that much of the Old Testament ethical texts
has this special character, in spite of different forms and different set-
tings of the texts, as well as changing eras.

Concerning social authority, there was in early Israel over a period of
time a 'transfer of legitimacy'[17], as in the pre-monarchic era the
authority of the old heads of the kins was weakened in proportion to the
authority given to legal congregations of free citizens 'in the gate',
where court-meetings were held and sentences were passed (cf. Exod.
23.6; Ruth 4.1; Isa. 29.21).[18] The ultimate legitimacy of justice, however, was of a religious character, a certain theologizing in the texts
considered. This basic feature spans the traditional gap between the so-
called 'casuistic laws', above all found in the Book of the Covenant
(Exod. 20.22–23.19), and the 'apodictic laws', for instance found in the
Decalogue (Exod. 20.2-17 par. Deut. 5.7-21); the different forms of
these laws and codes of laws have been much discussed in recent
research.[19] As for the Decalogue, it is presented as a speech of God,
transmitted to the people by Moses; it starts with a preamble where
God, presenting himself, refers to his action of salvation for the people
(20.1), before the proclamation of the laws, the announcement of the
commandments, takes place (20.2-17). Also the Book of the Covenant
is introduced as a speech of God, with an assignment to Moses to
preach the instructions of God; first some religious and cultic laws are
stated (Exod. 20.22-26), then the 'ordinances' (*mishpatim*) 'that you
[i.e. Moses] shall set before them', the Israelites (21.1). This applies, on
a broader scale, to later bodies of Israelite laws as well, first of all 'the

17. On the terminology cf. R. Bendix, *Nation-Building and Citizenship* (New
York: Anchor Books, 1969).
18. Cf. Otto, *Theologische Ethik*, pp. 64-67, who here states 'two sources' of
Israelite justice (*Recht*).
19. The study of A. Alt, 'Die Ursprünge des israelitischen Rechts', now in
idem, *Kleine Schriften*, I, pp. 278-332, was influential here and is still fundamental,
despite further investigations and various criticisms. See further G. Liedke, *Gestalt
und Bezeichnung alttestamentlicher Rechtssätze* (WMANT, 39; Neukirchen–Vluyn:
Neukirchener Verlag, 1971); and, recently, the works of E. Otto and F. Crüsemann
(see nn. 5 and 13, and the Bibliography).

Deuteronomic law' in Deuteronomy 12–26 and the so-called 'Holiness Code' in Leviticus 17–26.[20]

First, this means that the codes of laws in the Old Testament were theologically framed; the laws had, primarily, their religious setting in the revelation of Yahweh at Sinai as he entered his covenant with the people. That gave the justice and the legal practice both its fundamental legitimacy and its motivation.[21] Second, in ancient Israel the justice was not a 'self-contained' institution of its own, but the preaching of the laws was looked after by certain persons of specific authority, like Moses and the 'judges' of various kinds; they preached the laws and passed on the tradition of justice.[22] One can also state this in a more modern way: Israel did not only have fundamental ethical 'values', formulated in concrete laws and commandments, but also had 'carriers' of ethical values—'judges', priests and prophets. As for the pre-monarchic time—before the King and his men changed so much—it could be said of Samuel (1 Sam. 7.15-17):

> Samuel judged Israel as long as he lived. Year by year he went on circuit to Bethel, Gilgal, and Mizpah; he judged Israel at all these places. Then he went back to Ramah; for there was his home, and there he judged Israel; and there he built an altar to Yahweh.

In this way, then, there was not only the existence of a 'democratic' court 'in the gate', there was also a separate 'office' of justice and legal practice. But also with this split of legal authority, God was the foundation and guarantee of justice. This testimony of the texts is at the same time—though in a variety of changing forms—the main religious context of Old Testament ethics. The justice and the concrete laws were 'incorporated' in the revelation and covenant of Yahweh, the God of Israel, and therefore also closely connected with the 'history of salvation' of the people. In a perspective of this kind, the *ethos* and ethics of

---

20. As for studies on the complex diachronic aspects of the legal history see nn. 5, 13 and 16 above.

21. Cf. Childs, *Exodus*, pp. 385-496; and, especially, Crüsemann, *The Torah*, pp. 27-57.

22. Cf. Alt, 'Die Urspünge', esp. pp. 322ff.; also M. Noth, 'Die Gesetze im Pentateuch', now in *idem, Gesammelte Studien zum AT* (TBü, 6; Munich: Chr. Kaiser Verlag, 3rd edn, 1966), pp. 9-141. H.-J. Kraus, *Die prophetische Verkündigung des Rechts in Israel* (ThSt, 51; Zollikon: Evangelischer Verlag, 1957), pp. 6-20, speaks in this respect of a charismatic 'Mosaic office' (*mosaisches Amt*); cf. the recent treatment, and criticism, by Crüsemann, *The Torah*, pp. 59-107.

the Old Testament were given their specific religious motivation and basic theological reason.

Some ethical texts can, however, display a 'movement' beyond this 'closed' morality of Israel. In the first place, one can observe a certain *generalizing tendency*. That occurs, for instance, in the accusations of unjust affairs among the people announced by Isaiah in a number of woes (5.8-24; 10.1-4), as in 5.20:

> Woe to those who call evil good and good evil,
> who make darkness light and light darkness,
> who make bitter sweet and sweet bitter!

In this—perhaps wisdom influenced—*logion* of the prophet, his concern is a general attitude of speaking and living which in a substantial and fundamental way turns ethical 'values' around and will even forward a disintegration of morality itself. However, the passage does not only apply to ethical attitudes and actions as such, the phrasing also has a religious aspect, in particular as regards the connotations of 'good' and 'evil'.[23] The same may be said for other passages of a similar kind, some of which E. Otto, in a critical examination of H.-P. Mathys's treatment of the 'commandment of love' in Lev. 19.18, has denoted as ethical 'fundamental statements (*Grundsatzformulierungen*)', that is, Mic. 6.6-8; Zech. 7.9-10 and Ps. 15.1.[24] As for the use of 'neighbour' in Lev. 19.18, moreover, or as regards the phrasing of Psalm 15, which Otto on several occasions has treated together with Ps. 24.3-6,[25] one may hardly consider these instances to represent simply a universal perspective, not even in the context of the Old Testament theology of creation; for, despite their obvious generalizations, these passages do definitely remain within the 'closed' frame of the people of the covenant, with its faith and theology.

Other passages show, on the other hand, that legal and national *boundaries could be passed*. In certain situations, or when it came to certain ethical borderline cases where individuals had got into difficult social positions or had come into an exposed legal position, the limits

23. Cf. Wildberger, *Jesaja*, I, pp. 195f.

24. Otto, 'Forschungsgeschichte der Entwürfe', pp. 35f.; cf. H.-P. Mathys, *Liebe deinen Nächsten wie dich selbst: Untersuchungen zum alttestamentlichen Gebot der Nächstenliebe* (OBO, 71; Freiburg: Universitätsverlag; Göttingen: Vandenhoeck & Ruprecht, 1987).

25. Cf. Otto, 'Kultus und Ethos', pp. 164-79; 'Die Geburt', p. 78; *Theologische Ethik*, pp. 94-99, 106f.; also Crüsemann, *The Torah*, pp. 325-27.

for the usual legal context could be exceeded. Thus, one may observe in the Book of the Covenant and in 'the Deuteronomic law' that in certain situations it was necessary to show an 'enemy' or 'adversary' some helping 'solidarity' (Exod. 23.4-5; Deut. 10.18-19).[26] Further, a special legal protection for groups of *personae miserabiles* was raised, be it for various reasons, to protect socially impoverished persons, or be it to care for the traditional 'trefoil' of widows, orphans and aliens (or 'immigrant') who all could have a very weak legal position and protection (see, e.g., Exod. 22.21-22; Deut. 10.18-19; Pss. 68.6; 146.9 or Exod. 21.2-11 on the obligations and rights of the slaves). Not least in relation to those who were 'aliens', the boundaries between the 'others' and the 'own people' were crossed to a certain degree: 'You shall not wrong or oppress an alien'; it is backed up with a somewhat general statement: 'for aliens were you yourselves in the land of Egypt' (Exod. 22.20); in Deut. 10.19—with the same argument—the commandment is sharpened: 'You shall *love* the alien'.

In the context of these legal traditions, the prophets often grounded their accusations and their radical judgment of the people in a religious-ethical way. Their preaching was legitimized as divine speech of revelation; but at the same time they advanced and actualized the legal traditions in concrete applications.[27] In addition, the prophets even presented—again in a legal and ethical perspective—different elements of a boundary-breaking or universalistic preaching.

In this connection, it is first close at hand to direct the attention towards the distinctive composition of Amos 1.3–2.3(-16), which initiates the book of Amos in a most specific way, and which has given rise to a variety of explanations.[28] The issue, however, that will invoke the greatest interest at this point is not so much the fact that an Israelite prophet turned against alien nations (that was not unique; see Isa. 13–23; Jer. 46–51; Ezek. 25–32; Zeph. 2.4-15; Zech. 9.1-8), but the highly surprising fact that a prophet in Israel charged and condemned a misdeed which one neighbouring nation (the Moabites) had done towards

26. Cf. Otto, 'Die Geburt', pp. 72ff.

27. See W. Zimmerli, *Das Gesetz und die Propheten: Zum Verständnis des Alten Testaments* (Göttingen: Vandenhoeck & Ruprecht, 1963).

28. See A.S. Kapelrud, *Central Ideas in Amos* (Oslo: Universitetsforlaget, 2nd edn, 1971), pp. 17-33; 59-68; H.W. Wolff, *Dodekapropheten. II. Joel und Amos* (BKAT, 14.2; Neukirchen–Vluyn: Neukirchener Verlag, 1969), pp. 158ff., esp. pp. 164-85.

another neighbouring nation (the Edomites), Amos 2.1-3. The issue here is consequently not only a matter between Israel and its neighbours, as was common, but also a matter of injustice between two non-Israelite peoples; this was an 'inter-national' relationship indeed, and it were as if the prophet had spoken in terms of some 'international law'. But on what legal or ethical grounds did the prophet operate? Would it be on the basis of a creation theology? May the existence of some influence of a more general wisdom teaching be assumed?[29] These questions that are not easy to answer adequately, are worth pondering, and even more so as the prophet in his preaching, when speaking about Yahweh's actions in history, exceeds the national boundaries and even the special election of Israel, for which Amos 9.7 is the most radical example.[30] Here, in a way, the prophet Amos seems to have opened a path from the special to the general and common, or from the 'enclosed' to the 'open' moral—to use again the distinction of Bergson.

Furthermore, yet another form of universal prophetic preaching may be of interest in this context; it is found in the so-called 'Songs of Yahweh's Suffering Servant' in Isaiah 42–53. Among many statements on the Servant's ministry it is for instance said (42.4):

> He will not falter or be crushed,
> until he has established justice (*mishpat*) on earth,
> and for his teaching (*torah*) the far coasts wait.

Or, God says about the mission of the Servant (49.6b): 'I will make you a light to the nations, so that my salvation may reach to the end of the earth'; and, finally, at 53.11-12, in a similar 'boundary-breaking' manner, it is said that 'many' will benefit from his deeds: 'The righteous one, my servant, will make many righteous' (v. 11b). In other respects, it may be observed that Deutero-Isaiah, in a reasoning and 'counter-point' way, supplements his preaching by various motives from the theology of creation.[31]

---

29. This problem was not taken up by H.W. Wolff, *Amos' geistige Heimat* (WMANT, 18; Neukirchen–Vluyn: Neukirchener Verlag, 1964), who otherwise focused upon wisdom influences in the book of Amos, in particular from the 'ancestral wisdom' (*Sippenweisheit*) in Israel, see esp. pp. 37f.

30. See also Amos 9.9; 3.1ff.; cf. R. Smend, 'Das Nein des Amos', in *idem, Die Mitte des Alten Testaments*, pp. 85-103; esp. H. Gese, 'Das Problem von Amos 9,7', in *idem, Alttestamentliche Studien* (Tübingen: J.C.B. Mohr, 1991), pp. 116-21.

31. See Rendtorff, 'Die theologische Stellung des Schöpfungsglaubens bei Deuterojesaja', pp. 209-19.

In the perspectives from Amos, then, these elements are of great significance for the understanding of not only the special character of the prophetic preaching, but also in more general terms for the relation between justice and religion, and between theology and ethics in the Old Testament, not least as regards, within this context, the movement from the special towards the common.

4. *The Human Experience: From the Common to the Special*

The Old Testament *ethos* was, as has been briefly demonstrated, closely related to the special Israelite law traditions as well as to their different reflections and 'offshoots' into the prophetic preaching. At the same time, however, *ethos* and ethics were more than just proclaimed laws and commandments, prescriptions and prohibitions.

Here, as elsewhere, laws could not regulate every detail in human life; neither greed, avarice and covetousness nor friendliness and considerateness, nor reverence and deference can be 'codified'—though it all, negatively or positively, represents an essential part of people's social coexistence. Their gatherings in everyday life as well as at festive occasions were also dependent on a substantial network of 'unwritten laws', many of them belonging to the rich treasure of ancestral wisdom, gained through the varying experiences of the generations. This empirical wisdom was mainly expressed in brief and condensed sentences and sayings, but also in imperative instructions, focused upon the upbringing of the young people. It embodied great ethical resources and helped the young ones to choose the essential 'values' for their ethical attitude and practice, and thus gain and preserve the good consequences in a prosperous life. The variegated *wisdom teaching* was primarily gathered in the special books of wisdom, first of all in the Proverbs of Solomon, containing various collections, then the books of Ecclesiastes and Job, but was also contained in other scriptures of the Old Testament as well as in later books like, above all, Sirach and the Wisdom of Solomon.[32]

---

32. See in particular G. von Rad on Sirach, *Wisdom in Israel* (London: SCM Press, 1972), pp. 240-62; further, W. McKane, *Proverbs: A New Approach* (London: SCM Press, 1970); R.B.Y. Scott, *The Way of Wisdom in the Old Testament* (New York: Macmillan, 1971); J. Day, R.P. Gordon and H.G.M. Williamson (eds.), *Wisdom in Ancient Israel: Essays in Honour of J.A. Emerton* (Cambridge: Cambridge University Press, 1995); and, in a specific ethical context, Otto,

The wisdom teaching was not irreligious, as was sometimes assumed, but did, nevertheless, divert from the remaining theology of ancient Israel. It had primarily a different point of departure; it was not preoccupied with the history of Israel, nor of its election and covenant, nor of the ceremonies and theology of the divine service. It was mainly not directed to the Israelites as such, but was addressed to the individuals as human beings. The wise men did not refer to a 'thus says Yahweh', like the prophets (see, e.g., Amos 1); they did not ground their sayings on divine revelation, but rather on general observations and experiences, and they argued accordingly and persuaded by empirically founded 'counsels' (cf. Jer. 18.18). As the wise men were especially preoccupied with the everyday experiences and the circumstances of human beings, their activity and teaching has been called an early 'humanism' in Israel.[33]

By all this, it was characteristic for the wise men that they, in their reflections on the basis of an extensive accumulation of experiences, sought and gained a deeper insight into certain regularities of human life; they acknowledged 'laws' that revealed a *fundamental order of the world*. The fundamental and steadfast order in the being of things applies both to the creation surrounding the humans and, first and foremost, to the society in which they live. The empirical wisdom teaching, then, did not only observe a variety of situations and experiences, but transformed them into an understanding of the principles of all that happens. *The sayings and teachings of the wise men expressed the human experience of the world in an artistic, concentrated and 'crystallized' form.* Their reflections and teaching, however, did not only embrace the 'laws' and trivialities of normal life within the world of man but acknowledged also that the world is a created world which is capable of bearing witness about God as its creator (Job 12.7-10; Pss. 8, 19 and 104); the fundamental world order has, in other words, its basis in God the Creator.[34] In this setting, the teaching of wisdom may be seen as an Old Testament theology of world order, which is a close

---

Theologische Ethik, pp. 117-74. See also Chapter 15 below.

33. So von Rad, at several occasions, e.g. in *Wisdom*, pp. 57-65; 308f.; 313f.

34. Cf. von Rad, *Wisdom*, pp. 144-66; see, further, H. Gese, *Lehre und Wirklichkeit in der alten Weisheit* (Tübingen: J.C.B. Mohr, 1968); H.H. Schmid, *Gerechtigkeit als Weltordnung* (BHT, 40; Tübingen: J.C.B. Mohr, 1968).

associate to its theology of creation. In addition, it is heavily influenced and marked by ethical and social reflection and various admonitions, which is of special interest here.[35]

In this context, therefore, social and ethical concepts like 'justice' (*mishpat*) and 'righteousness' (*ṣedaqah*) play such an eminent role in the wisdom teaching. It is of basic significance for every human being to find its right place in the divine order and to be God's co-worker for righteousness and justice. This, however, is not easy for any person to accomplish; therefore, wise guidance and discipline need to be received in order to gain insight and understanding, 'for training in discernment of what is right and proper and equitable' (Prov. 1.3).[36] If one succeeds to take one's correct place and to reach a high level of ethical conduct one is 'wise' or 'just'—two expressions that are used synonymously. On the other hand, those who do not find their ethically proper place, but violate law and order in their rebellion, are called 'evil' and 'unjust', 'impudent' and 'stupid'—not as much in regard to their intellectual ability as to their ethical attitude and practice. They will have to face and will be condemned by their own words and deeds; for there is also a 'law' for the necessary binding of human deeds—good or bad—to their respective consequences, for 'as you sow you shall reap'.[37]

The point of departure for the wisdom teaching and its theology of a fundamental world order was *the common, human experience* in its variegated and broad diversity. It reasoned and argued for its counsels and exhortations in a common and rational way; but all this was not done in opposition to the faith and fear of God, though the language was very different from the rest of Old Testament theology. There was, however, also a more obvious development of 'theologizing' in the teaching of wisdom; it moved towards what one somewhat imprecisely might call an Israelite 'natural' or 'normal' theology.

This ethical-theological movement may now, with good reason, be

35. Cf. von Rad, *Wisdom*, pp. 74-96; Otto, *Theologische Ethik*, pp. 152ff.

36. So R.B.Y. Scott, *Proverbs: Ecclesiastes* (AB, 18; Garden City, NY: Doubleday, 1965), p. 33; cf. further H. Delkurt, *Ethische Einsichten in der alttestamentlichen Spruchweisheit* (BTSt, 21; Neukirchen–Vluyn: Neukirchener Verlag, 1993); A.B. Ernst, *Weisheitliche Kurtkritik: Zu Theologie und Ethik des Sprüchebuchs und der Propetie des Jahrhunderts* (BTSt, 23; Neukirchen–Vluyn: Neukirchener Verlag, 1994).

37. Cf. especially K. Koch, *Spuren des hebräischen Denkens: Beiträge zur alttestamentlichen Theologie* (Gesammelte Aufsätze, 1; Neukirchen–Vluyn: Neukirchener Verlag, 1991), pp. 106-66.

called *a movement from the common to the special,* that is, the distinctively Israelite. This surmise may be further substantiated by three brief
text examples. First, at the beginning of the first and dominating
Solomonic Collection (Prov. 10–22.16), there seems to be a theologically framed 'mini-collection' in Prov. 10.2-7 (8-9). Around the kernel
of two sayings that express a common experience about how one gets
poor or rich, namely by one's own work, vv. 4-5, there is a frame of
ethical and religious concepts in vv. 2-3 and 6-7 (and further extended
in vv. 8-9) which render a hermeneutical clue to the nucleus of vv. 4-
5—whereby the meaning of these core proverbs later in the chapter
becomes almost directly opposed by the theological statement of v. 22:

> It is the Lord's blessing that makes a man rich,
>   And painful toil can add no more.[38]

Second, the theologically dominated wisdom teaching is above all
prominent in the first main section of the book of Proverbs (Prov. 1–9),
which also may present the hermeneutical horizon for the succeeding
collections (Prov. 10–31). Most conspicious of the theological language
of the first part is the personification of Wisdom (*chokmah*) in 1.20-33
and, combined with creation theology, in 8.22-31. But essential to the
theological wisdom teaching is also the notion of 'the fear of Yahweh',
and in particular, that this pious attitude is said to be the 'beginning of
knowledge' or the 'beginning of wisdom', as it is stated in the first and
the last chapter of this first collection (Prov. 1.7; 9.10):

> The fear of Yahweh is the beginning of knowledge.
> The beginning of wisdom is the fear of Yahweh,
>   and knowledge of the Holy One is understanding.

Nearly related to this is, third, the focus on 'the law (*torah*)', both in its
broader and its more specific sense (cf., e.g., Prov. 1.8; 6.23; 13.14;
28.4, 7, 9; Pss. 1; 19 [both parts]; 119; also Isa. 5.24); later, there is an
amalgamation of 'wisdom' and 'law' (see especially Sir. 24; Wis.
4.1).[39]

---

38. So Scott, *Proverbs*, p. 82. See also Chapters 15 and 18 below.
39. Cf. von Rad, *Wisdom*, pp. 49; 245-47; J. Blenkinsopp, *Wisdom and Law in the Old Testament: The Ordering of Life in Israel and Early Judaism* (Oxford: Oxford University Press, 1983); Crüsemann, *The Torah*, pp. 329ff.; Otto, *Theologische Ethik*, pp. 256-63.

In the whole context of the wisdom teaching, not only in its most pronounced theological part, man's religious faith and reason are not antagonistic, rather, they cooperate. That what later has fallen apart, was held together by the wise men in Israel—in an enriching dialectic tension. In this perspective, the problem of the rationality of ethics may also be profitably seen and assessed.

5. *In the Converging Centrepoint: Yahweh, the God of Israel*

In the multifaceted plurality of the Old Testament *ethos* and ethics there is a real possibility to lose sight of the overall picture; the discussion above, however, has exhibited some unifying trends which may turn out to be helpful for a better understanding of the subject. Essential is the recognition that the *ethos* of the Old Testament seems to have two different sources, and that furthermore it displays an unrestrained mobility in two contrary and crossing directions. On the one hand, there has been a focus upon the considerable differences in the ethical material, but, on the other, attention has also been given to a simplification and unification of the diversity. This becomes even more clear as one observes that the crossing point of the two movements, referred to above, lies in the 'theological centre' which is the faith in Yahweh, the God of Israel; that is their *converging centrepoint*. At this point, ethics gains a proper foundation that is superior to the individual human beings; at the religious basis there was raised an ethical standard, as it is stated also in a priestly context like Lev. 19.1: 'You shall be holy, for I Yahweh, your God, am holy', where the succeeding preaching of the laws gives a repeated reason: 'I am Yahweh, your God'.[40]

There have, however, been some difficulties in preserving the above mentioned double character of the material; instead there has often been given one-sided interpretations both ways. On the one hand, the usual procedure—as in the treatment of van Oyen—has been to give priority to the distinctive Israelite understanding of the history of revelation and salvation, whereby it became complicated to fit in properly the theology of wisdom and creation. On the other hand, Anette Soete, for example, has recently placed the main focus on the teaching of wisdom and has

40. Cf. Crüsemann, *The Torah*, pp. 277-327; Otto, *Theologische Ethik*, pp. 219-56; also Blenkinsopp, *Wisdom and Law*, pp. 110-13.

correspondingly de-emphasized whatever is reminiscent of any so-called 'revelatory positivism'.[41] However, the aim should rather be to keep together the great span and riches of Old Testament ethics, that is, the very marked combination of religiously motivated norms for human coexistence and a rational processing of common human experience, and also, the combination of a collective community and authoritative individuals.

Finally, one may ask whether the described double basis and character of the Old Testament ethics—which has been put into focus here since it thus far has mostly been overshadowed by the many questions of the material ethics—even has certain points of similarity with the Lutheran notion of the 'two regiments'. That might, in this case, give rise to further ethical reflection in both the fundamental and the material ethics.

Epilogue: And Today?

Harking back to the starting point one may ask: what relevance and value—in this perspective—has the ethics of the Old Testament for us today? The question should not only concern the Church, but also the modern society which in so many ways is marked by sectorization, pluralization, and relativization, especially in view of the normative basis for people's moral attitudes and actions.[42]

First, there needs to be drawn a line in saying that there definitely are limits for an application of the ethics of the Old Testament today: some of it 'was said to those of ancient times', and needs not be passed on. It is then basically important to know where to draw the line—just jumping directly from our context to the specific questions of the material ethics of the Old Testament may pose a number of problems. One cannot bypass the larger context of the whole Bible, including the New Testament, which functions as a 'theological filter', nor can one ignore an ongoing and necessary hermeneutical reflection. The concrete limits are mainly related to the historical, national and social context of the ancient Israel. It materializes, for instance, in matters like slavery, polygamy or in relation to enemies, where the 'categorical imperative'

---

41. See n. 1 above.

42. Cf. also Crüsemann, *The Torah*, pp. 1-5; 365-67; Otto, *Theologische Ethik*, pp. 264-70.

of Jesus, 'Love your enemies and pray for your persecutors' (Mt. 5.44 par.), marks something radically new.

Second, however, given the limits of how much one may apply of Old Testament ethics today, especially in dealing with specific matters of material ethics, this fact should not overshadow those obvious characteristics of positive values that may be applicable also to us; some of this has been shown in the discussion above, and much more might have been mentioned. It was, not least, important to focus upon aspects of the Old Testament theology of creation, especially in the framework of wisdom teaching, where also, to some extent, the possibility of a biblically founded 'humanism' became apparent; the aim in this case would not be some modern dream of 'neutral values', but, on the contrary, the realistic necessity of a religious rooting was displayed. In addition, one may proceed further into the law material and thereby see various ways of how a basic *protection of life* is divinely ordained. Or, in view of the double form of the Decalogue, one may realize the duplicity of basic divine commands and concrete applications of them in context (cf. Exod. 20 par. Deut. 5; Lev. 19.3-4, 11-13; Ps. 15).

Thirdly, the most important aspect in this perspective, however, is that one can benefit from the richness of Old Testament *ethos* and anthropology, with its basically twofold pattern. In the modern, pluralistic society, not least, there may be a need for a comprehensive ethical view and attitude of this kind, by which one can combine a solid religious foundation, including responsibility towards God, the Creator and Lord of life, with a broad human wisdom gained from an empirical and rational understanding of the circumstances of existence for a true human life in a created world of order—as demonstrated in the Old Testament.

Chapter 12

REVELATION IN HISTORY AND AS HISTORY:
OBSERVATIONS ON A TOPICAL THEME FROM
AN OLD TESTAMENT POINT OF VIEW

It is a striking feature of recent Old Testament scholarship that special attention has been paid to the theological aspects of its material. In the process, not only has the relationship of historical tradition and theology been taken up as a topical question,[1] but also the further problem of *revelation and history* which has continually given rise to new considerations and attempts at solution, and which also reaches far beyond Old Testament research.[2] But in all this there is often no sufficiently precise terminology and it may, therefore, be advisable to start with a few short remarks on terminology.

1. Some Remarks on the Terminology

At the beginning of his textbook *The History of Israel*, H. Wheeler Robinson made the following statement:

> History might be called the sacrament of the religion of Israel; through the history of Israel, she saw the face of God and endured as seeing Him who is invisible. But the details of that history with which we shall be concerned—the words and deeds, the thoughts and above all the persistent purposes of the Israelites—these were the bread and wine of the sacrament, which the touch of God transformed into both the symbol and the instrument of His grace for all time. We cannot properly understand the religion without knowing the history, and knowing it, so far as is now possible to us, in its original and actual form.[3]

1. Cf., e.g., Knight (ed.), *Tradition and Theology*.
2. The present essay deliberately offers only some marginal notes from an Old Testament exegete on the theme and does not claim to be a more systematic theological treatment.
3. H. Wheeler Robinson, *The History of Israel* (London, 1957 [1938]), p. 12.

With these impressive—almost solemn—words one of the most eminent representatives of British Old Testament scholarship in the 1930s enters the discussion of the relationship of God's revelation to human history and, in doing so, tackles the contentious terminological question of this relationship. It is noticeable that Wheeler Robinson does not begin with a qualification or some definition of 'history', but instead begins with metaphorical language: history is a 'sacrament'; and so far as the historical details are concerned he does not refer to the historical events but to the 'words and deeds, the thoughts and emotions'. The way he expresses himself is not unique but it may serve as an example of a certain tendency among theologians to speak of 'history' mainly from a theological point of view—in a very indefinite and general way. So, then, in the last chapter of his textbook, Wheeler Robinson attempts to outline Israel's contribution to a philosophy of history—although strictly... 'Israel had no philosophy of history'—including the following as specifically Israelite traits: 'the interaction of faith and event', 'the value of the time-series', 'the unity of history' and 'the relation of transcendence and immanence'.[4] Seen as a whole, Wheeler Robinson seems to be trying to combine differing aspects and factors in the realm of 'history', not to say, bring them into balance where possible.

The American Old Testament scholar Robert H. Pfeiffer, somewhat later, took an opposing position. In a 1951 discussion of 'Facts and Faith in Biblical History' he is of the opinion that the 'unhappy marriage of history and mythology...was never a true union and only divorce will result in the fruitful development of each of the two disciplines'.[5] So he makes an 'appeal for keeping facts and faith, history and revelation, historical research and theological speculation, separate and distinct for their mutual benefit'.[6] Pfeiffer wants to avoid all links between historical research and faith for the sake of the purity of both.

These very different positions of two older scholars constitute the basic positions of the recent debate, provoked mainly by the publication of Gerhard von Rad's *Old Testament Theology*, I–II (1957 and 1960). Gradually the positions have been elaborated—significantly and in

---

4. Wheeler Robinson, *History of Israel*, pp. 220-35; cf. also his definition in *The Old Testament: Its Making and Meaning* (repr.; London, 1961 [1937]), p. 67: 'History is the interpretation of events seen in their proper sequence and relation.'

5. R.H. Pfeiffer, 'Facts and Faith in Biblical History', *JBL* 70 (1951), pp. 1-14; esp. p. 14.

6. Pfeiffer, 'Facts and Faith', p. 13.

different ways—particularly since a study group in Heidelberg, which at first seemed to be influenced by von Rad's theology but which quickly became associated with the name of Wolfhart Pannenberg,[7] broadened the debate into a theologically wider context.[8] A debate has also developed between American and European theologians.[9]

Terminologically it is fair to ask how much the debate has really helped to clarify the concepts: this might have helped somewhat. People still speak generally, without any real precision, on the one hand, of 'revelation' or 'self-revelation of God', and on the other, of 'history', even of 'universal history'. Obviously this question is more than just terminological; but that is exactly why qualification and differentiation are desirable.

Now, so far as the concept 'revelation' goes, theologians like Paul Althaus and Wolfhart Pannenberg, Kornelis H. Miskotte and Edmond Jacob have talked about an 'inflation' of this word,[10] which certainly urges caution and circumspection. Theologically, it is of major importance for 'revelation' to be a biblical concept—or rather a biblical 'issue' for this 'issue' appears not as a noun or concept but only represented in various verbs and formulae.[11]

As for the concept 'history', this is not biblical in the same way as 'revelation', for the OT does not seem to have a word or term for 'history',[12] except in the late expression דברי הימים.[13] On the other

---

7.   W. Pannenberg *et al.* (eds.), *Offenbarung als Geschichte* (Göttingen: Vandenhoeck & Ruprecht, 1963 [1961]); cf. also W. Pannenberg, 'Kerygma und Geschichte', in R. Rendtorff and K. Koch (eds.), *Studien zur Theologie der alttestamentlichen Überlieferungen* (Festschrift G. von Rad; Neukirchen–Vluyn: Neukirchener Verlag, 1961), pp. 129-40.

8.   See nn. 29, 34 and 38 below and also the survey by E. Osswald, 'Geschehene und geglaubte Geschichte in der alttestamentlichen Theologie', *Wissenschaftliche Zeitschrift der Universität Jena* 14 (1965), pp. 705-15.

9.   J.M. Robinson and J.B. Cobb (eds.), *Theology as History* (New Frontiers in Theology, 3; New York: Harper & Row, 1967).

10.   Cf. Pannenberg *et al.* (eds.), *Offenbarung als Geschichte*, p. 7, with reference to P. Althaus; and E. Jacob, *Grundfragen alttestamentlicher Theologie* (Franz Delitzsch–Vorlesung, 1965; Stuttgart: W. Kohlhammer, 1970), p. 25, with reference to Miskotte.

11.   See n. 36 below.

12.   Cf. J. Barr, 'Revelation through History in the Old Testament and in Modern Theology', *Int* 17 (1963), pp. 193-205.

13.   Cf. Sæbø, 'Chronistische Theologie/Chronistisches Geschichtswerk', *TRE*,

hand the Old Testament contains a great deal of historiography of various sorts. Pfeiffer has said that 'the Old Testament contains about every type of history, from the most secular to the most theological'.[14] To make a proper evaluation on the basis of this finding, it is important to recognize clearly the fundamental difference between 'history' and 'historiography' as literary entities, and the very different kinds of historical materials.

Literary-critical and historical-critical work on the Old Testament has clearly underlined that over and above the individual 'historical books' there is the existence of smaller, bigger and even more extensive 'historical works' to take into account, works like that of the so-called 'Yahwist' which are built up out of innumerable small, partly geographically based traditions; or the even more comprehensive historical work of the Deuteronomist, which covers the whole history of the people in the land up until the exile, and is compiled from smaller traditional materials and even from historical works such as the so-called 'History of the Rise of David' or the 'Succession Narrative'.[15] In postexilic times the whole history of Israel was retold in a new way by the Chronicler, and finally by the slightly later—but closely related—work of Ezra—Nehemiah.[16] Furthermore, Israel presented its history many times in the so-called 'historical psalms'.[17] And finally, one should not forget that the prophets expressed an attitude on the historical traditions in many ways, often very critical.[18]

So, clearly, Israel was intensely preoccupied with its 'history' in many diverse forms. The varied sorts of historiography testify how

VIII, pp. 74-87, esp. p. 80; idem, 'יוֹם *jôm*', *ThWAT*, III, cols. 559-61, 566-86, esp. col. 575.

14. Pfeiffer, 'Facts and Faith', p. 5.

15. The relevant literature has become very comprehensive in recent years. Noth, *Überlieferungsgeschichtliche Studien* is still a basic work; cf. J.H. Hayes and J. Maxwell Miller (eds.), *Israelite and Judaean History* (London: SCM Press, 1957), pp. 332ff.; H.W. Wolff, 'Das Kerygma des deuteronomistischen Geschichtswerks', in *idem, Gesammelte Studien zum AT*, pp. 308-24; *idem*, 'Das Kerygma des Jahwisten', in *idem, Gesammelte Studien*, pp. 345-73; Jörg Jeremias, 'Gott und Geschichte im Alten Testament: Überlegungen zum Geschichtsverständnis im Nord- und Südreich Israels', *EvT* 40 (1980), pp. 381-96.

16. See my article in *TRE,* cited above in n. 13.

17. Psalms like 78, 105, 106, 135, also 89 and 132.

18. Cf. W. Zimmerli, 'Prophetic Proclamation and Reinterpretation', in Knight (ed.), *Tradition and Theology*, pp. 69-100.

Israel's 'historical self understanding' was different at different times and in different circles. But this evidence is not so multivoiced to make it impossible or illegitimate, in reference to Israel's 'self-understanding' and theology, to speak also in general terms about 'history'. But one must realize that it is a big and important step from the multifaceted narrating in the concrete historical works to talking about 'history' in the abstract.[19] It might seem banal, but it is necessary to point this out.

A further big step is needed to link the abstract 'history' with the abstract 'revelation' or to relate them to each other. That is why defining their relationship is so problematic, since I am not only talking about phraseology but about deep differences of opinion regarding the substance.

2. On 'Revelation' and 'History'

To familiarize oneself briefly with the basic positions and main characteristics of the recent, almost confusingly multifaceted debate over 'revelation' and 'history', one can hardly avoid considering its roots, its prehistory, which still have an effect, and without which the debate is difficult to understand.

James Barr, with some justification, stated that the current theological interest in 'revelation in history' is to be seen mainly as 'our response to the tremendous and shocking apologetic strains of the nineteenth century imposed primarily by the rise of historical method and historical criticism'.[20] His (maybe one-sided) position echoes a strong condemnation from the nineteenth century itself, originating with J.T. Beck and which Karl Gerhard Steck chose for the epigraph of his book *Die Idee der Heilsgeschichte*:

---

19. On the difficulty in defining the concept of 'history' see Patrick Gardiner (ed.), *Theories of History* (London: Macmillan, 1959); Henri-Irénée Marron, *Über die historische Erkenntnis* (Munich, 1973); V.A. Harvey, *The Historian and the Believer* (London, 1967); further, R.H. Bainton *et al.*, *The Idea of History in the Ancient Near East* (New Haven; London, 1966); C.R. North, *The Old Testament Interpretation of History* (London, 1946); J. MacIntyre, *The Christian Doctrine of History* (Grand Rapids: Eerdmans, 1957); R. Smend, *Elemente alttestamentlichen Geschichtsdenkens* (ThSt, 95; Zürich: EVZ-Verlag, 1968); repr. in *idem*, *Die Mitte des Alten Testaments*, pp. 160-85.

20. So Barr, 'Revelation through History', p. 195.

O, how we now idolize history! Just as reason was idolized in the eight-
eenth century and then, at the beginning of our century, especially in
Schleiermacher's time, feelings, so nowadays people call out as once to
Diana at Ephesus: 'Great is history!'

    History is nowadays the god after which everyone runs, and history
itself is vanity.[21]

Is this only about a theologically suspect 'idolization of history'?

One has to go back beyond the nineteenth century to the eighteenth
century and the period of the Enlightenment to discover how 'history'
in theology became independent. With the fundamental demand of
Johann Philipp Gabler in 1787 to differentiate rightly between biblical
and dogmatic theology, a crucial turning point was reached. Despite
previous failed attempts, Gabler managed not only to prove the independence of exegesis but also to establish it as a historical discipline in
directing attention to differences within the biblical material 'e genere
historico'.[22] He brought a historicizing dynamic into biblical scholarship which has had various consequences.

Old Testament theology, which soon separated itself from the New
Testament theology, gradually concentrated on the phenomenon of
Israel's religion. The different ways of looking at a historical
'development' of the religious phenomena, from a given or assumed
'origin' throughout various epochs, became more and more characteristic of nineteenth- and early twentieth-century biblical scholarship. It
was considerably strengthened by the interest of the Literary-critical
School in the political and cultural (including cultic) history of Israel,
and broadened by the immense volume of newly discovered religio-historical material. The problems of similarity and analogy and of causality between the religion of Israel and the neighbouring religions, the
problem of the relationship of Old Testament theology and the history
of the religion of Israel quickly imposed themselves.[23]

---

21. K.G. Steck, *Die Idee der Heilsgeschichte* (ThSt, 56; Zollikon: Evangelische
Verlag, 1959), p. 3.

22. Cf. R. Smend, 'Johann Philipp Gablers Begründung der Biblischen Theologie', *EvT* 22 (1962), pp. 345-57; repr. in *idem*, *Epochen der Bibelkritik* (BEvT, 109;
Munich: Chr. Kaiser Verlag, 1991), pp. 104-16; see also Chapter 19 below.

23. Cf. O. Eissfeldt, 'Israelitisch–jüdische Religionsgeschichte und alttestamentliche Theologie', in *idem*, *Kleine Schriften*, I, pp 105-14; also H.-J. Kraus, *Die
biblische Theologie* (Neukirchen–Vluyn: Neukirchener Verlag, 1970), pp. 262ff.;
and W. Müller-Lauter, 'Konsequenzen des Historismus in der Philosophie der
Gegenwart', *ZTK* 59 (1962), pp. 226ff.

The relationship between 'revelation' and 'history' was hardly a real theological problem until modern theology—especially Old Testament scholarship—for various reasons concentrated on 'history', and especially since 'history', with its principles of immanent analogy and causality, also became authoritative for the understanding of reality. Thus very little space remained for divine revelation. The deep radicality of the new situation can be demonstrated by putting the word 'revelation' in place of 'God', the subject of the revelation, and noticing that the historical-critical way of working is done *etsi deus non daretur*, 'as if God does exist'. One might think that an insurmountable contradiction exists here: it seems as though 'history' has become the judge before whom everything in theology has to justify itself. This could only mean a far-reaching crisis for the relationship between 'history' and 'revelation', disastrous for the issue of divine revelation. At best, one could, therefore, like Otto Eissfeldt and Pfeiffer, suggest a total separation between the two.[24]

Nevertheless, and perhaps surprisingly, history has been in many ways highly valued theologically by, for example, G. Ernest Wright, who, in his book *God Who Acts: Biblical Theology as Recital*, emphasizes that 'history is the chief medium of revelation'. At the same time, he emphasizes the element of 'interpretation' and further finds 'the chief clues to the theological understanding of the whole Bible', first in its *'peculiar attention to history and to historical traditions as the primary sphere in which God reveals himself'*; second, in 'the immediate nature of God's action in history: that is his election of a special people through whom he would accomplish his purposes'; and third, in the confirmation of the election 'in the event of the covenant ceremony at Sinai'.[25] Surprisingly enough, Wright can then claim that these three elements, which according to him constitute the core of Israelite faith, 'have little abstract or propositional theology within them. They are based on historical events and the influences drawn from them'.[26] A remarkable distinction between 'event' and 'theology' is being made here: in the end, the really decisive element between them is the historical 'event'.

Yet Sigmund Mowinckel had probably been more radical a few years

24. See nn. 5 and the preceding 23.

25. G. Ernest Wright, *God Who Acts: Biblical Theology as Recital* (repr.; SBT, 8; London: SCM Press, 1956 [1952]), pp. 13, 54-56.

26. Wright, *God Who Acts*, p. 56.

earlier. In his *Det gamle testament som Guds ord*, the priority of *general* historical events was more sharply pronounced. 'God's revelation' according to him, is not a 'statement about God', but is rather his 'self-revelation' in the context and in the form of general history, which is actually only a development of God's creative activity; and it is 'just as much in the cosmic as in the earthly sense the big drama', 'in which God reveals himself'. Therefore, history as such is revelatory history and is 'the contemporary historico-political event—the appearance of the Arameans, Asyrians, Babylonians Scythians and Persians onto the stage of history—which in the first place, are the 'word' of God to his people'.[27] So, in fact, Mowinckel thought of 'history' as 'revelation'. His colleague in Oslo, Ivar P. Seierstad, took issue with this immediately. He disagreed primarily with Mowinckel's identification of the divine word with historical events and with his general determining of the history of all people, which implies abolishing the difference between God's 'general' and his 'specific' revelation.[28] The debate between Mowinckel and Seierstad in the 1930s is relatively analogical to the discussion between Rolf Rendtorff and Walther Zimmerli in the 1960s, which will be referred to below.

If such well-known scholars as Mowinckel and Wright so strongly emphasize the revelatory character of 'real history', that is, the meaning of history as the 'revelation of God', that surely is meant to be a positive theological evaluation of biblical 'revelation'; their motive is probably the protection of reality, the reality of 'revelation'. But one tends to think that their strongly historicizing approach is rather a sign of the victory of historicism and that this guarantee of the reality of the biblical 'revelation' and this explanation of its relationship to 'history' is inadequate; rather, it is a false trail.

As already mentioned, the publication of von Rad's *Old Testament Theology* aroused the sharpest debate on this issue. In 1952, when von Rad formulated the almost programmatic sentence, 'the Old Testament is a history book'—and repeated it in 1960 in the second volume—it was perhaps to be expected that he, like Mowinckel and Wright, would

27. S. Mowinckel, *Det gamle testament som Guds ord* (Oslo: Gyldendal Norsk Forlag, 1938; ET *The Old Testament as Word of God* [Oxford, 1960]), pp. 31-37; 109-13.

28. I.P. Seierstad, 'Det gamle testament som Guds ord', *TTK* 10 (1939), pp. 95-116, 154-64; also in his *Budskapet: Et utvalg av gammeltestamentlige artikler* (Oslo: Universitetsforlaget, 1971), pp. 163-95.

have emphasized 'real history'; but the opposite was the case. A special characteristic of von Rad as a scholar was that he continued with and made use of his earlier exegetical work in his account of Old Testament theology—especially on the Hexateuch and Deuteronomy. The traditio-historical method that he had so fruitfully tested in his minor studies was also used in the depiction of Old Testament theology. Thus he invented a totally new kind of Old Testament theology which, on the one hand, departed from the presentations shaped by doctrinal concepts, and on the other, approached and used essentially the modern exegetical security of the Old Testament; and so it came closer to the genre of Introduction to the Old Testament. Despite all its one-sidedness and weaknesses, the structure of von Rad's theology traces a direct line to the basic research of Gabler in his distinction between dogmatic and biblical theology. The difficult question of the relationship between 'revelation' and 'history' could now be seen in a new light.[29]

In his varied work on the Old Testament von Rad treated its 'history' as real history in a theological sense, which means that this history, as all history, carries changes within itself, even in the theologically central issues. 'History' cannot be transferred to a static sphere of unchanging ideas; it is more than a series of 'fluctuating historical destinies' which wraps itself like a cloak round the religion of the Old Testament as a 'self-enclosed basic entity with a persistent basic tendency and unchanging basic character', as Eichrodt put it in the introduction to his important *Theology of the Old Testament*.

Despite his usual efforts to acknowledge historical lines of development, Eichrodt here found himself impelled, in his opposition to the 'high tide of historicism', to bring the genuine religious aspect into the safe sphere of an 'unchanging basic character'.[30] If so, one can perceive in his main theological concerns the heritage of both traditional ecclesiastical theology and also of the philosophical and theological idealism of the nineteenth century.

By contrast, von Rad, in the introduction to his *Old Testament*

---

29. G. von Rad, 'Das Alte Testament ist ein Geschichtsbuch', *EvT* 12 (1952/53), pp. 17-33, in C. Westermann (ed.), *Probleme alttestamentlicher Hermeneutik* (TBü, 11; Munich: Chr. Kaiser Verlag, 1960), pp. 11-17; *idem, Theologie des Alten Testaments*, II, p. 370; on the debate about von Rad's theology of the Old Testament, cf. Schmidt, ' "Theologie des Alten Testaments" ', pp. 1-25, where additional references can be found.

30. Eichrodt, *Theologie des Alten Testaments*, I, pp. v, 5.

Theology focused his attention on Israel's *own* theological work, with its history interpreted as real history. The tradition-history of the historical material had 'taught to see the most varied forms in which the history of God with Israel was depicted in its layers and had made clear how Israel all the time was preoccupied at all times with understanding its history from the point of view of God's specific intervention and how God's deeds and decisions were made differently at different times'.[31] In considering the theological character of the historical traditions of Israel in this way, von Rad had not turned against the 'critically protected' picture of the 'real history' of Israel made by modern historiography; the critical account of Israel's history just seemed to him to be a rather uncertain and inadequate basis on which to build a description of the theology of Israel.

Von Rad criticized the opinions of earlier scholars who believed that behind the depiction of the selected source documents also 'the actual historical sequence—at least in its basic characteristics—could be seen'. Rather, he saw that behind the historical description in the Hexateuch the real historical sequence of events was far from being found but rather specific perceptions and ideas of older traditions... So, from the depiction of the source documents to the historical event the step has become much longer.[32] This longer step is a 'long history of interpretation', in which 'everything is shaped by faith'. 'Even the linking of events by a great path of salvation is not simply a historical reportage but is already a confession of God's leadership.'[33]

By his recognizing of the theological importance of 'faith' and 'confession'—which may count as correlative concepts to God's 'revelation'—for Israel's historical reflection and perception, von Rad not only had brought the concepts 'revelation' and 'history' closer together in a new way but he also had broadened them both. A truly historical aspect has entered into the idea of 'revelation'; and within the broadened notion of 'history', 'event' and 'interpretation' have dovetailed; and this has crystallized in the course of a longer transmission. It is just here that the arguments against von Rad intensified. Franz Hesse, for example, was mostly occupied with a polarity between the two depictions of the history of Israel: in the Old Testament 'salvation history' versus the historico-critical research respectively. Like Wright he

31. Von Rad, *Theologie des Alten Testaments*, I, p. 7.
32. Von Rad, *Theologie des Alten Testaments*, I, p. 18.
33. Von Rad, *Theologie des Alten Testaments*, I, p. 19.

emphasized the basic meaning of historical facticity for theology, and like Mowinckel, he wanted to emphasize the unity of 'salvation history' (as far as one can talk about this) and the 'real history' of Israel; in his own words: 'A separation of the history of Israel from Old Testament salvation history is not possible'. Moreover, 'the salvation history is hidden in, with and under Israel's history'.[34] Hesse's rather one-sided emphasis on the real history and the historico-critical picture of it has been criticized by Gerhard Hasel: 'He actually falls prey to historical positivism. He apparently does not recognize that the historico-critical version of Israel's history is already interpreted history, namely, interpreted on the basis of historico-philosophical premises.'[35]

Even the 'Heidelberg group' round W. Pannenberg, mentioned above, developed, perhaps rather surprisingly, in a similar direction. An anthology edited by Pannenberg contained a study by Rendtorff, 'Ideas of Revelation in Ancient Israel', in which he stressed, like Mowinckel did earlier, that God's 'revelation' was a 'self-revelation' that is a 'self-proof of Yahweh' and 'that Yahweh in his handling of history proved himself to be God'. Furthermore, said Rendtorff, it 'does not need a third person to interpret it', such as a prophet with a specific 'word of Yahweh', 'for the happening itself could and should be recognized as knowledge of God so long as the person who sees it recognizes it as God's doing'.[36]

It is not surprising that a scholar like W. Zimmerli should oppose this. In a sharp retort, which cannot be further elaborated here, Zimmerli explained Rendtorff's description of the relationship of 'revelation' and 'history' thus: 'History stands here curiously absolutized, as something autonomous, in need of no more clarification through the prophetic word as the actual revelation of God'.[37]

34. F. Hesse, 'Die Erforschung der Geschichte Israels als theologische Aufgabe', *KD* 4 (1958), pp. 1-19, esp. p. 13; cf. his 'Kerygma oder geschichtliche Wirklichkeit?', *ZTK* 57 (1960), pp. 17-26; and 'Bewährt sich eine "Theologie der Heilstatsachen" am AT? Zum Verhältnis von Faktum und Deutung', *ZTK* 81 (1969), pp. 1-17; and his *Abschied von der Heilsgeschichte* (ThSt, 108; Zürich: Theologischer Verlag, 1971).

35. G.F. Hasel, *Old Testament Theology: Basic Issues in the Current Debate* (Grand Rapids: Eerdmans, rev. edn, 1975), p. 61.

36. R. Rendtorff, 'Die Offenbarungsvorstellungen im Alten Israel', in Pannenberg *et al.* (eds.), *Offenbarung als Geschichte*, pp. 21-41 (40-41).

37. W. Zimmerli, '"Offenbarung" im Alten Testament', *EvT* 22 (1962), pp. 15-31 (24).

Rendtorff's contribution is best understood in the context of the programme of the 'Heidelberg group', as given in the title of the volume, *Offenbarung als Geschichte*, which reflects Pannenberg's own systematic and philosophical position. But even Pannenberg seems to have changed his emphasis: in an article of 1959 he had stressed the fundamental significance of the idea of God in Israel's historical consciousness and for 'Israel's understanding of reality as a linear history hastening towards its goal'.[38] In 1961, however, from *Offenbarung als Geschichte* onwards, his system gives a more normative role to the notion of 'universal history'. While in 1959 he was more in tune with von Rad, he later moves closer to the position of Mowinckel, although he places more emphasis than Mowinckel on the basic and central meaning of the Christ-event for a 'universal history' which he regards as eschatological. It is hard to see how in the end he can avoid historical positivism, and how, from his perspective, the revelation of God can be appropriately recognized and described.

3. *The Question of 'History'—and the Question of God*

As a final acknowledgment of this recent debate—here merely sketched out—it may be stated first that the most questionable—and difficult—element in this whole problematic area is the word 'history'. Even if 'history'—or more theologically precise definitions such as *Heilsgeschichte*, 'transhistory' or 'universal history'—has played a fairly dominant role in recent theology, it ought not to form the starting point or the point of reference for discussion. The same is true for the term 'revelation'.

Second, on the contrary, although it might seem obvious, the starting point or point of reference should lie only in the biblical texts: it is in the texts that the various positions have to prove themselves. In these texts both 'revelation' and 'history' are related, although differently in various texts and contexts. *Only such definitions of 'revelation' and 'history' may be valid which correspond to the totality of the texts in their complexity and not just to a selection of texts.*

38. W. Pannenberg, 'Heilsgeschehen und Geschichte', *KD* 5 (1959), pp. 218-37; also in C. Westermann (ed.), *Probleme alttestamentlichen Hermeneutik* (TBü, 11; Munich: Chr. Kaiser Verlag, 1960; ET *Essays on Old Testament Interpretation* [London: SCM Press, 1963]), pp. 295-318; esp. p. 298. For a criticism of Pannenberg, see E. Mühlenberg, 'Gott in der Geschichte: Erwägung zur Geschichtstheologie von W. Pannenberg', *KD* 24 (1978), pp. 244-61.

For it has often been the case that only a selection of texts has been taken into account. James Barr has rightly pointed this out; large sections of the Old Testament do not, as he says, 'conform to the idea that revelation through history is the centre of Hebrew thought'. He cites mainly the wisdom literature, the primaeval history and the Psalms, though more could be mentioned. 'All these, then, are examples of literary genres or areas which do not seem readily to fit an entirely history-centred theology of the Old Testament'.[39] Even Wright had to admit that 'in any attempt to outline a discussion of biblical faith it is the wisdom literature which offers the chief difficulty *because it does not fit into the type of faith exhibited in the historical and prophetical literature*'.[40] And then, typically, he launches into a criticism of wisdom teaching from the standpoint of his scheme of 'revelation in history'. One might assert that even von Rad did not succeed in finding a way to 'marry' Old Testament historical theology and wisdom theology. *Hermeneutically as well as theologically one should have a method open to all the differing witnesses of the Old Testament.*

Even the claim that Old Testament 'revelation in history' is unique or at least especially characteristic of Old Testament theology has shown itself to be far too simplistic. With Hartmut Gese[41] and James Barr,[42] Bertil Albrektson explained that similar statements to those made about Yahweh's historical activities can also be found in the neighbouring religions and cultures of Israel.[43] But in important respects Israel's religion is different from the religions from its environment: what Albrektson found typical of Israel's God was 'the word of revelation, which may be about history but cannot simply be deduced from history'. He also emphasized the 'interplay of word and event' which is often very complicated, and he concludes that 'It remains true that events alone are not capable of expressing those ideas of Hebrew religion which are truly distinctive; the Old Testament view of the divine deed is not

39. J. Barr, *Old and New in Interpretation* (London: SCM Press, 1966), pp. 72, 76.

40. Wright, *God Who Acts*, p. 103.

41. H. Gese, 'Geschichtliches Denken im Alten Orient und im Alten Testament', *ZTK* 55 (1958), pp. 127-45; now in his *Von Sinai zum Zion* (BEvT, 64; Munich: Chr. Kaiser Verlag, 1974), pp. 81-98.

42. See nn. 12 and 39 above.

43. B. Albrektson, *History and the Gods: An Essay on the Idea of Historical Events as Divine Manifestations in the Ancient Near East and in Israel* (ConBOT, 1; Lund: C.W.K. Gleerup, 1967).

possible without the divine word'.[44] The fact that wisdom teaching has been mentioned is not accidental. For it does not seem to be amenable to the concepts of either 'revelation' or 'history'. Nevertheless, one should not dismiss out of hand a connexion between 'wisdom' and 'history'. True, one does not find much 'history' in wisdom teaching, that is, history in the sense of unique activities and events; but it is born of a rich and diverse human *experience*, which also belongs to 'historical facts'. The cumulative empirical character of wisdom allows us to speak of 'concentrated' or 'condensed' history which is just as 'real' as 'event history', although it is of a different order. So then, as far as the idea of 'revelation' is concerned, there is good reason to ask whether one should speak rather of a 'natural revelation' derived from a creation-related 'theology of order' in Israelite wisdom (Job 12.7-10). In any case, wisdom seems capable of broadening or differentiating to some extent the concepts of 'revelation' and 'history'.[45]

Third, we have still not reached the heart of the problem, which lies in the *question of God*. If Albrektson found what was typical of Israel to be in 'the *word* of revelation', we might have expected his comparison of the religious differences between Israel and her neighbours to focus on Israel's idea of God in the narrow sense: in Yahwism.

Briefly touching on the new debate about a 'centre' of the Old Testament theology: Georg Fohrer, for instance, has located it in the 'kingdom of God' and the 'community of God',[46] and for Werner H. Schmidt the first commandment is the key to Old Testament theology.[47] The problem here is, first of all, that this and similar issues do not allow themselves to be expressed easily in acts of God or historical events, especially if these are understood as in contradiction to the word of God. Against these and other definitions of 'centre', only such a definition which can be accommodated to the Old Testament *idea of God* carries enough weight and which has the necessary openness to the

44. Albrektson, *History and the Gods*, pp. 118, 122.

45. There will doubtless be much more research on this subject, for example, on the question of the relationship between 'history' and 'wisdom' in the Joseph story, or in the later stages of the Old Testament in the apocalypses, where the relationship between 'history' and 'wisdom' is depicted in an entirely new way; cf. Chapter 15 below.

46. G. Fohrer, *Theologische Grundstrukturen des Alten Testaments* (Berlin: W. de Gruyter, 1972), pp. 95ff.

47. W.H. Schmidt, *Das erste Gebot: Seine Bedeutung für das Alte Testament* (ThExh, 165; Munich: Chr. Kaiser Verlag, 1970).

whole and complex Old Testament material will be adequate and satis-
factory.

In this connexion, as in the more comprehensive debate on
'revelation' and 'history', the *question of God as the actual main question in Old Testament theology* is all too often moved from the centre of
the discussion. For only God, or the idea of God, is able to combine
'event' and 'word', 'revelation' and 'history' in a meaningful way.
Only God is the common denominator of the various theologies of the
OT which talk of him so confusingly and varyingly, and yet which at
the same time mean the One who gives the Old Testament its unity in
an unmistakeable way. If the question of God is ignored theologically
or historically, considerable distortions occur at many points.

Finally, if one thinks that the 'guarantee' of the 'revelation of God'
in the 'reality of history' can also secure the existence of God and the
reality of his actions and words, and be a sort of proof of God, then all
that remains to be said is that one must avoid not only a 'historical positivism' but also a 'revelation positivism'.

On the narrow path between the positive attitudes or tendencies of
both sides we may have to satisfy ourselves with the modest conclusion
that what we actually have are *texts* which often recount 'history' and
which also attest to other sorts or parts of 'reality' that are shaped and
sustained by the faith experiences and confessions of God who has
revealed himself in particular words and deeds. Only these texts allow
themselves to be researched, not the beliefs which sustain them; only
the message of God can be represented, not God himself, *deus per se*.
But we can research the texts, in contrast to modern critical historiography, following the messengers and theologians of Israel and—should
the situation arise—also preach them anew—*etsi deus daretur*.

Chapter 13

ON THE RELATIONSHIP BETWEEN 'MESSIANISM' AND
'ESCHATOLOGY' IN THE OLD TESTAMENT: AN ATTEMPT
AT A TERMINOLOGICAL AND FACTUAL CLARIFICATION

As far as the expressions 'messianism' and 'eschatology' are concerned, one is dealing with two popular terms which have gained currency in Christian theology, as well as two 'problem children' of modern biblical research. If we think that generally too much esteem has been given to these terms in the area of theology and traditionally too much of a burden has been thrust upon them, then that must be true not just for ecclesiastical theology, and for older theology in particular, but also to a great extent for more recent critical research which has been stamped with a religio-historical approach. Indeed, it appears to be characteristic of the changing usage of both terms that there so often remains much to be desired as regards their terminological sharpness, as well as clarification of their factual relationship. And so it might be useful to risk another attempt at producing, if possible, a greater terminological sharpness for the two expressions than has usually been the case, as well as explaining better the factual relationship between them.

1. *Three Samples of Modern Research*

Modern literature on the subject of 'messianism' and 'eschatology' is almost boundless and of a very diverse nature. It extends from all kinds of short studies to a whole range of comprehensive monographs. However, more important than quantity and breadth of approach is the colourful multiplicity of views which can give rise to deep aporia.[1] In a

1. Cf. H. Cazelles, *Le Messie de la Bible* (Paris: Desclée, 1978), pp. 217-24, which in 26 points briefly introduces various 'definitions' of messianism, mainly from more recent research.

recent appraisal, particularly the multiplicity of views is briefly expressed, though an attempt is also made to call attention to common points of view.[2] This is the route which one should continue to follow. Since only selected aspects can be discussed within the constrictions of an article, it is even more important to point out what the most typical aspects are. Thus, three fundamentally different monographs from the first quarter of the twentieth century will be selected as examples and briefly considered, namely those of the conservative Eduard König (1846–1936) as representative of a traditional interpretation, Hugo Gressmann (1877–1927) as representative of the 'religio-historical school' and finally Sigmund Mowinckel (1884–1965), the famous innovator of modern cult research in the area of Old Testament studies.

Although in the process also points which are well known—at least to some—will be touched on, it may nevertheless be of benefit to begin with these writers, for what arose later on in research on 'messianism' and 'eschatology' had to a great extent its origins in their work. If in so doing we lay bare overlapping facts and connecting links which may build bridges to more recent statements on the subject, then that may certainly be useful for an attempt to clarify the current situation.

(a) The time of traditional delineations of 'messianic prophecies', as published, for example, by Franz Delitzsch in 1890 or by Eduard König in 1922,[3] would appear to be definitely past. At any rate, they are no longer published in this form. Their end may be grounded particularly in the methodology, for the procedure of treating selected passages in the sequence of the Old Testament books appears to be adequate neither historically nor theologically as regards the peculiarity of the texts.

This is evident from the work of Eduard König. His presentation of the messianic prophecies consists of two main sections. The first part

2.   Cf. H. Strauss, 'Messias/Messianische Bewegungen, I. Altes Testament', *TRE*, XXII, pp. 617-21. See also *idem*, *Messianisch ohne Messias* (EHS, 23.232; Frankfurt am Main: Peter Lang, 1984), pp. 9-16; G. Stemberger, 'Messias/ Messianische Bewegungen, II (Judentum)', *TRE*, XXII, pp. 622-30; R. Smend, 'Eschatologie, II (AT)', *TRE*, X, pp. 256-64, esp. 256-59; B. Uffenheimer, 'Eschatologie, III. Judentum', *TRE*, X, pp. 264-70.

3.   Cf. F. Delitzsch, *Messianische Weissagungen in geschichtlicher Folge* (Leipzig: A. Edelmann, 2nd edn, 1899 [1890]); E. König, *Die messianischen Weissagungen des Alten Testaments vergleichend, geschichtlich und exegetisch behandelt* (Stuttgart, 2nd and 3rd edn, 1925 [1922]); cf. from the Catholic point of view, e.g., P. Heinisch, *Christus, der Erlöser im Alten Testament* (Graz: Verlag Styria, 1955).

(pp. 1-77) which as 'Introduction' leads into the second part 'Exegesis' (pp. 78-352), serves above all to make use of the 'comparative' and 'historical' side of his approach. This occurs primarily in that the concept of 'prophecy' as well as a larger extra-Israelite material, including 'questionable analogies on messianic prophecies among Indo-Germanic peoples', are considered critically. Thence König examines the historical-critical context of the messianic prophecies with the presented analogies, whereby he takes issue in particular with Gressmann and his book about the origin of eschatology, which will be discussed next (see section [b] below). From this distant religio-historical horizon he arrives at his 'interpretation of the messianic prophecies' which takes place relatively traditionally, and—as Delitzsch did a little earlier and as Heinisch did later—it begins with the so-called 'proto-gospel' in Gen. 3.15;[4] thereafter further messianic and eschatological passages are treated and 'ordered according to...the changes in salvation history which followed one upon the other'.[5]

With his scheme, which in comparison with ecclesiastical tradition was partially novel in approach, König thus attempted to counter critically the radical challenge of Gressmann. But his efforts were hardly up to the task. Moreover, it remains unclear how the 'historico-comparative' in the first part and the 'exegetico–theological' in the second part actually relate to each other, especially since the two main sections are not sufficiently integrated but rather threaten to disintegrate materially. His 'historico-comparative' treatment would appear to be too 'superficial' to cope with the theological profundity of the historical nature of the messianic material in the Old Testament.

The theological interest of König's presentation, as indeed of ecclesiastical tradition in general, which is aimed at the relationship with the New Testament, is certainly a very important biblico-theological interest which is of the utmost significance for the whole of Christian theology. However, the direction of vision remains decisive. Generally the matter has been judged retrospectively, for traditionally New Testament Christology has in fact been the authoritative point of departure. From

---

4.   Cf. Heinisch, *Christus*, pp. 47-60; other sections of Genesis which are treated by him—as in König—are Gen. 9.24-27; 12.1-3; 49.8-12 (pp. 60-78). On Gen. 3.15 cf., e.g., C. Westermann, *Genesis*. I. *Genesis 1–11* (BKAT, 1.1; Neukirchen–Vluyn: Neukirchener Verlag, 3rd edn, 1983 [1974]), pp. 351-56.

5.   It is conspicuous, however, that Isa. 7.14 is mentioned only once, namely in the Introduction (p. 61).

this point of orientation scholars have looked backwards for appropriate 'connecting links' in the Old Testament. Yet as far as the Old Testament texts themselves are concerned, the direction of vision and the corresponding methodical *modus procedendi* should actually be reversed so that one starts with the older and oldest texts in a historico-theological manner, for the phenomena of 'eschatology' and 'messianism', like Old Testament theology in general, do not amount to a 'doctrine' which is somehow or another identifiably external, but rather unambiguously something *historical* which has slowly come into being. Thus the received traditional methodology which was very atomistic and essentially ahistorical, even in König's somewhat looser guise, was only barely suitable for explaining in an appropriate manner the questions which particularly Gressmann raised concerning the origin and development of eschatology and messianism; nor did it manage, or even to grasp and explain positively within their contextual perspective the particular form and the historically and theologically limited content of the relevant Old Testament passages. His methodology may indeed be understood as a legacy of the older dogmatic *loci method* which, after Gabler, has been brought fundamentally and frequently into question, especially within the area of biblical theology.[6]

Thereby the interest of biblical theology as such is not affected, but just the manner in which it is realized, insofar as it turns out to be wrong or inappropriate. In this regard the biblical questions of 'messianism' and 'eschatology' appear again and again to have played a key role, especially in conjunction with the twin terms 'prophecy and fulfilment', which was also discussed and revived by König at the end of his presentation (pp. 353-69). One can certainly query the extent to which that may have occurred correctly or not, and that will be considered later on.

When as for this question Georg Fohrer once criticized the traditionally conservative position exceptionally harshly, for example, by portraying the Messiah as 'a rather insignificant marginal figure' in the Old Testament and the 'general treatment of the Messiah question' to be 'equally wrong as unprofitable',[7] then he shot wide of the mark; yet

---

6. Cf. Smend, 'Johann Philipp Gablers Begründung der biblischen Theologie', pp. 345-57; see further Chapter 19 below.

7. G. Fohrer, *Messiasfrage und Bibelverständnis* (Tübingen: J.C.B. Mohr, 1957), pp. 23 and 8; there also the following statement: 'In the final analysis the Messiah issue forms no more than a heavy burden for Christian faith.' Cf. *idem*,

his over-critical position, which represented a kind of theological nadir in the Messiah question, might be understood as a reaction to the venerable ecclesiastical and theological zenith of the same question. Moreover, Fohrer likewise rejected Gressmann's 'ancient Near-Eastern mythico-cultic interpretation' (p. 9) and the 'religio-historical school'.

(b) Hugo Gressmann's monograph *Der Messias* was not published until 1929, and then posthumously and slightly edited by Hans Schmidt. But as has been mentioned, König referred to Gressmann on many occasions, as did Mowinckel even more so in 1922. This span of years is simply explained, since Gressmann's book on the Messiah is in fact an extensive reworking of his older book *Der Ursprung der israelitisch-jüdischen Eschatologie* (1905), which has 'become a completely new book'.[8] It would now seem appropriate to refer to both of Gressmann's books.

As *Der Ursprung* shows, the topic of eschatology was Gressmann's point of departure around the turn of the century. Given the situation at that time, it was important for him not to interpret eschatology as a late, literary phenomenon in the Old Testament, as did the literary-critical school, but rather on the contrary to portray it as a primitive group of ideas of mythical provenance which was peculiar to the prophets of Israel and which originated in the ancient Near East, particularly in Babylonian religion. These ideas are, on the one hand, said to have included notions of a world catastrophe and the end of the world, and on the other hand, to have included the concept of a world renewal, a golden age and eternal peace. Allegedly they also embraced 'salvation eschatology' and an 'eschatology of catastrophe'. The eschatology thus accepted is no longer extant in its entirety, but is rather 'a large, detailed canvas... which is now lost'.[9] In the Old Testament as we know it, there exist only partial, single fragments of the ancient mythical traditions.

Also the Messiah question of the Old Testament is to be included in the wider sphere of this ancient Near Eastern 'eschatology', as part of a

'Das Alte Testament und das Thema "Christologie"', *EvT* 30 (1970), pp. 281-98.

8.   Cf. Gressmann, *Der Ursprung*, and his *Der Messias*, p. 16*. The work is divided into seven 'books'. See H. Schmidt's foreword which explains the problems of the edition (pp. 3*-7*). Cf. Smend, *Deutsche Alttestamentler*, pp. 173-81, and 315-16, esp. p. 178.

9.   Cf. Gressmann, *Der Ursprung*, p. 191; see also pp. 8-192 (eschatology of catastrophe) and pp. 193-365 (salvation eschatology).

mythical 'salvation eschatology'. For as an eschatological figure the 'Messiah' may originate in ancient Near Eastern concepts of a king of paradise. In this way, Gressmann pushed not only the first human being into the foreground, but particularly the king, since in his opinion the ancient Near Eastern idea of kingship is supposed to have been influenced by even older 'messianic' conceptions.[10] Furthermore, in the oriental 'courtly style' he discovered the religio-historical bridge leading from this even older background to the Old Testament.[11]

Thus does he treat 'the courtly style of the Israelites' in his later work *Der Messias* too, though this time at the beginning of his presentation. This occurs chiefly with the Royal Psalms, especially Psalms 2, 72 and 110, where he transfers his attention more pointedly to the deification of the king.[12] After Gressmann had considered 'prophetic notions' and 'the golden age' in the second and third 'books' of *Der Messias*, and primarily eschatological themes in the Old Testament, he returns to the king in the fourth 'book' entitled 'The Political Messiah' (pp. 195-283), whereby he considers in detail the usual 'Messiah passages' of the prophets—including ancient Near Eastern material—under the concept of the 'returning David'.[13] Later, in the fifth 'book', he considers (in greater depth than in *Der Ursprung*)—the *Ebed-Yahweh* as 'the prophetic Messiah' (pp. 287-339), then, in a number of places in the sixth 'book', 'the Son of man' (pp. 343-414), and, in the seventh 'book', 'the Egyptian messianic hope' (pp. 417-45).[14]

More strongly than in *Der Ursprung*[15] Gressmann later stressed the idea of the Messiah as the unifying figure of eschatology (p. 280):

> Around the Messiah as the named or assumed centre are grouped *the messianic hopes in the broader sense* of the word, the promises of a golden age at the end of time. The Messiah is merely the monarchal peak of eschatology. If he is expunged from the proclamations of the later

10. Cf. Gressmann, *Der Ursprung*, pp. 286-94.

11. Cf. Gressmann, *Der Ursprung*, pp. 250-59.

12. Cf. *Der Messias*, pp. 1-63 (first 'book'), esp. 25-44 ('The King as God').

13. Cf. also Hans Schmidt, *Der Mythos vom wiederkehrenden König im Alten Testament* (Giessen: Alfred Töpelmann, 2nd edn, 1933 [1925]).

14. In a 'supplement' (pp. 447-78) he finally examines, from Jewish sources, 'The Unknown Messiah' and 'Virgil's Fourth Eclogue'.

15. The following quotation differs somewhat from what we find in *Der Ursprung*, p. 7, when Gressmann there warns of the 'great error . . . as if the whole of Israelite–Jewish eschatology revolved essentially around the Messiah, as if without him it were unthinkable'.

prophets, then the inevitable result is the total elimination from their writings of any expectations of salvation.

Thus in both of Gressmann's books, 'eschatology' and 'Messiah' are interwoven in the closest possible sense, although they are treated rather differently. However, if in his considerable revision of his earlier position (*Der Ursprung*) the older Gressmann has shifted his emphasis to some extent more strongly from the ancient eschatological 'group of ideas' in its ancient Near Eastern context to the Messiah-figures of the Old Testament, especially the royal one, as occurs in *Der Messias*, then that may have been forced by, amongst other things, the thorough criticism of his position by Ernst Sellin[16] and Sigmund Mowinckel.[17] For both have claimed as unsubstantiated the acceptance of an eschatology which stemmed from the ancient Near East outside of Israel. Other scholars followed them on this point.[18] As far as Gressmann's solution to the 'origin question' is concerned, Mowinckel claimed (p. 221): 'What this book [i.e. *Der Ursprung*] actually gives us is especially the more or less probable origin of the individual notions which have come together on the eschatological canvas... The final synthesis is suggested in somewhat unclear terms'.[19]

(c) Despite all criticism, however, Sigmund Mowinckel presents a certain parallel argument and proximity to Gressmann, especially in the external aspects. For in his book of 1951 on the Messiah, *Han som kommer* and his English edition *He That Cometh* (1956), Mowinckel too was able to continue one of his earlier studies, namely, the *Psalmenstudien*, II, of 1922, already referred to above, in which creatively and successfully he had laid the foundation for a new solution to the question of the origin of eschatology.[20]

16. Cf. E. Sellin, 'Wesen und Ursprung der alttestamentlichen Eschatologie', in *idem*, *Der alttestamentliche Prophetismus* (Leipzig: A. Deichert, 1912), pp. 102-93. See also L. Dürr, *Ursprung und Ausbau der israelitisch-jüdischen Heilands-erwartung* (Berlin, 1925).

17. Cf. S. Mowinckel, *Psalmenstudien. II. Das Thronbesteigungsfest Jahwäs und der Ursprung der Eschatologie* (Kristiania [Oslo]: Jacob Dybwad, 1922), Part Two, pp. 211-324. In his discussion of the problem he takes issue primarily with Gressmann, Gunkel and Sellin (pp. 220-26).

18. Mowinckel, *Psalmenstudien*, II, pp. 221-22.

19. Cf. also the detailed and critical discussion of *Der Messias* by G. Hölscher, *DLZ*, 3rd ser. 1.37 (1930), pp. 1729-44.

20. See S. Mowinckel, *Han som kommer: Messiasforventningen i det gamle testament og på Jesu tid* (Copenhagen: G.E.C. Gad, 1951). The English translation

As far as the problem itself is concerned Mowinckel, like Gressmann, worked form-historically as well as religio-historically, since a few years earlier he had been with Hermann Gunkel, Gressmann's old friend, in Giessen—although he never considered himself a representative of the religio-historical school.[21] Just as Gressmann had done, Mowinckel too turned from the more extensive questions of eschatology (1922) to the particular question of the Old Testament Messiah (1951). The more radical change of position which in 1922 had led him away from the position and interpretation of Gressmann, was essentially not of a Copernican nature, for also Mowinckel was very mindful of the multifarious links between the Old Testament material and extant ancient Near Eastern ideas. Indeed, even if Gressmann's definition of the 'unity idea of Israelite eschatology' in the form of an ancient Near Eastern eschatological 'group of ideas' was utterly rejected by Mowinckel, the latter nevertheless—like Sellin before him—found an alternative and better 'unity idea' just in Gressmann's book of 1905, namely in his discussion of 'the enthronement of Yahweh' (§27; pp. 294-301). Characteristically, Mowinckel felt able to comment: 'In my opinion, Sellin has quite correctly evaluated the unity idea of Israelite eschatology. It is the idea which Gressmann had hidden in a distant corner of his study, namely, of "the enthronement of Yahweh", and of his future coming to establish his royal dominion over the world'.[22]

However, one might react to this by asking: What did Mowinckel himself, as opposed to Gressmann, make of the 'Sleeping Beauty' which he had now awakened? For she has become the 'Queen' of Old Testament eschatology!

In 1922, however, Mowinckel's great success did not lie so much in his 'discovery' of the theme of 'the enthronement of Yahweh'—this had, of course, already been described by other scholars—but rather in his consistently and broadly executed *cultic* explanation of Yahweh's accession to the throne, namely in the form of a special *festival of the enthronement of Yahweh*, which he, first of all, inferred from those

by G.W. Anderson, *He That Cometh* (Oxford: Basil Blackwell, 1956), represented a partial revision of the text ('from a partly revised Norwegian text', p. ix). See also his 14 'Additional Notes' (pp. 451-68). See n. 17 above on Mowinckel's *Psalmenstudien*, II.

    21. Cf. Sæbø, 'Mowinckel, Sigmund (1884–1965)', *TRE*, XXIII, pp. 315-20.

    22. Mowinckel, *Psalmenstudien*, II, p. 223; cf. p. xi (in his very personal Foreword [pp. xi-xvi]).

Psalms which celebrate the kingship of Yahweh.[23]

Thus, even if Mowinckel did not use as his point of departure an eschatological 'group of ideas' which originated in the ancient Near East, but instead argued vehemently for a *cultic* location of the sovereignty of God, this still has the greatest consequences for the 'question of provenance' of eschatology. For in his view, Israelite-Jewish eschatology had grown in specific circumstances out of the cultic phenomenon or—as he liked to describe it—from the *creative drama* of Yahweh's enthronement festival. And thus, the eschatology became, so to speak, its 'by-product'.

When, however, the religious expectation which had grown out of the cultic experience paled in the light of day, it was changed gradually into an eschatological hope. 'Expectation and faith remained the same. The object of the expectation which it can no longer have in the present is projected into the future.' And so, he boldly adds, 'the origin of eschatology must be explained psychologically, otherwise it cannot be explained at all'.[24] Thus Mowinckel had presented an essentially a cultic-psychological explanation of the origin of Old Testament eschatology. However, when he came to describe the substance of eschatology, he proceeded by and large both religio-historically and mythologically, as had Gressmann. The whole is treated in 14 points under the main heading יוֹם יהוה,[25] of which 'The Messiah' is the last.[26]

However, when Mowinckel considers the figure of the Messiah, he is forced to admit to an aporium. For what is really with the 'Messiah' if as 'eschatological king' he has his origin not only 'indirectly in the concept of the enthronement festival', but also 'from the beginning is

---

23. Mowinckel, *Psalmenstudien*, II, pp. 1-209 (first part).

24. Mowinckel, *Psalmenstudien*, II, p. 324: If 'under the disappointing pressure of a new, strong and unaccustomed experience of the surrounding world...the old experiences could no longer be experienced in full authenticity', then eschatology came into being 'as an escape into the future'; cf. pp. 311-14, and 315-25.

25. Cf. Gressmann, *Der Ursprung*, pp. 8-70, and pp. 141-92; also S. Mowinckel, 'Jahwes dag', *NTT* 59 (1958), pp. 1-56, and pp. 209-29. See further Sæbø, 'יוֹם *jôm*', *ThWAT*, III, cols. 559-86 (with additional literature also on יהוה יוֹם); here, in addition, W. von Soden deals with the Akkadian aspects and J. Bergman with the Egyptian aspects (pp. 561-66).

26. Cf. Mowinckel, *Psalmenstudien*, II, pp. 229-314; esp. 297-311 ('14. The Messiah'). In the summary (pp. 311-14) he is able to conclude 'that all the more important notions of eschatology can be explained by the enthronement myths and the ideas linked with the festival' (p. 311).

additional to Yahweh the king and accordingly a double, a kind of "*doppelgänger*" of Yahweh'? 'Where, then, does the Messiah come from?'[27] In order to solve this problem which is so difficult for his theory, Mowinckel, on the one hand, looks for the 'origin' of the Messiah 'in the ancient Israelite human-divine king' (p. 305), who functions as 'the Great I of the society' (p. 300) and as a 'point of unity' between God and nation (p. 301),[28] and on the other hand, he looks for his 'origin' in the fact that 'the ideal type of the divine Davidic king has been projected into the portrayal of the future' (p. 306). And so we are dealing here 'in contradictory terms', as he says, 'with a compromise between the eschatological myth and the self-evident demands of everyday—although idealized—life' (p. 310).

The academic world, furthermore, would appear to have been almost bewitched by Mowinckel's festival theory and his presentation of it. However, there has been no lack of critical voices.[29] His statements must be considered as particularly questionable, because he fails to explain with sufficient differentiation either the relationship between prevailing ancient Near Eastern concepts and what was indigenous to the Israelites in general, or specifically the relationship between Jahwe and 'his Messiah', who above all is seen in the light of the 'divinity of the king'. Moreover, his special festival theory, which after all is supposed to bear the weight of the whole, appears to hang by a thread which becomes increasingly thinner.[30] Now, to be fair, Mowinckel

27. Mowinckel, *Psalmenstudien*, II, pp. 297-98. Cf. also H.W. Wolff, 'Herrschaft Jahwes und Messiasgestalt im Alten Testament', *ZAW* 54 (1936), pp. 168-202.

28. Cf. Mowinckel, *Psalmenstudien*, II, p. 301: 'The correlation to this concept of the king as incorporation of national community is the idea of the king as incarnation of the national God.'

29. Cf. O. Eissfeldt, 'Jahwe als König', *ZAW* 46 (1928), pp. 81-105; repr. in *idem*, *Kleine Schriften*, I, pp. 172-93.

30. Cf. D. Michel, 'Studien zu den sogenannten Thronbesteigungspsalmen', *VT* 6 (1956), pp. 40-68, and Fohrer, *Messiasfrage*, p. 9: 'However, an enthronement festival, or something similar, in Israel is extremely controversial; and in Babylon, the land of the classical New Year's festival with the enthronement of Marduk and of the king, no eschatology or expectation of Messiah came into existence, although the everyday disappointments were in no way less.' Cf. the partly self-critical unpaginated preface of Mowinckel in the new edition of his *Psalmenstudien*, I–VI (2 vols.; Amsterdam: P. Schippers, 1961), I, where he also defined aspects of his festival theory to which he still adhered.

himself has not exactly hidden the aporia of his position, which stands in his favour. But it would be more desirable if we had a somewhat more convincing and solid solution to the delicate questions of the origin and development of Old Testament 'Messianism' within the framework of its eschatology, and not least of all with regard to the hermeneutic circle of the whole and of its parts. For Mowinckel's 'last synthesis'—to use his own words about Gressmann—remains simply 'even more obscurely hinted at'.[31]

To be sure, Mowinckel soon changed his views here on one important point. Whereas in 1922 he still spoke of 'eschatology' in Amos,[32] in 1926—perhaps influenced by his friend Gustav Hölscher[33]—he changed his mind and adopted a much later origin of 'eschatology', which by this time he regarded as a later Jewish phenomenon, close to apocalyptic;[34] thereby, to some extent, he moved closer to the older literary-critical interpretation, although he did so in his own way.[35] As far as the delineation of the Messiah question is concerned, Mowinckel may likewise have considered this change of mind as convenient, for in *Han som kommer* not only did he cling to the late dating, but he developed his views here even more widely.[36]

Thus Mowinckel differentiated acutely between 'Messiah' as 'an eschatological concept', which does not feature at all in the Old Testament,[37] and 'Messiah' as an 'originally political concept', which was embodied primarily by the present king in Israel (*Han som kommer*, pp. 13-17, or *He That Cometh*, pp. 3-9). However, at the same time there existed 'a historical link' between both interpretations. The problem—and the challenge—of his delineation consisted not least in the attempt to render this link as both obvious and probable.

31. Mowinckel, *Psalmenstudien*, II, p. 221.

32. Cf. Mowinckel, *Psalmenstudien*, II, pp. 264-67.

33. Cf. G. Hölscher, *Die Ursprünge der jüdischen Eschatologie* (Giessen, 1925), p. 3.

34. Cf. Mowinckel, *Jesaja-disiplene*, p. 93, esp. n. 2.

35. As for Mowinckel's relation to the literary critical school see Chapter 21 below.

36. Cf. Mowinckel, *Han som kommer*, p. 89, and *He That Cometh*, pp. 125-26.

37. Mowinckel, *He That Cometh*, pp. 3-4 (cf. *Han som kommer*, pp. 13-14): 'The word "Messiah" by itself, as a title and a name, originated in later Judaism as the designation of an eschatological figure ... "Messiah", "the Anointed One", as a title or technical term for the king of the final age, does not even occur in the Old Testament.'

Just as 'the eschatological Messiah obtained his name from the ancient Israelite sacral title of kings' (pp. 16 or 7), the first chapter of any length (Chapter 3; pp. 24-69 or 21-95) is dedicated to 'the ideal of kingship in ancient Israel'. 'The ancient Near Eastern royal ideology', and thereafter the greatly modified 'Israelite ideal of kingship' are examined in detail. After the Israelite 'future hope' (Chapter 4; pp. 69-88 or 96-124) and especially Isaiah 7; 9.1-6, and 'the early Jewish hope for the future' (Chapter 5; pp. 88-107 or 125-54) as well as 'the place of the king in the future hope: the Messiah' (Chapter 6; pp. 107-29 or 155-86), have been dealt with, there follows as a last chapter in the first part a thorough discussion about the 'Servant of Jahwe' (Chapter 7; pp. 129-73 or 187-257). The second, eschatological part (pp. 174-293 or 262-450), where the subject matter is 'the Messiah in later Judaism', is divided into three parts. After a general outline of 'later Judaic eschatology' (Chapter 8; pp. 174-84 or 261-79) there follow two longer chapters, one about 'the national Messiah' (Chapter 9; pp. 185-226 or 280-345) and the other about 'the son of man' (Chapter 10; pp. 226-93 or 346-450).

Through his impressive and balanced presentation Mowinckel may have been at pains to do justice not only to the abundant and contradictory material both in the ancient Near East as well as in the Old Testament in particular—which naturally was most pertinent for him—but perhaps also to give a—better—response to Gressmann's book on the Messiah, since the course of his presentation corresponds partly with that of Gressmann's *Der Messias*. Even here Mowinckel would be Gressmann's most significant interlocutor.

Mowinckel, moreover, conducted his conversation with Gressmann indirectly, of course, by taking issue in *Han som kommer* with the representatives of the so-called Myth and Ritual School or Anglo-Scandinavian School. This he did both often and in a variety of ways, as well as more acutely than with any other colleagues. For to some extent one would be correct in claiming that these scholars who knew thoroughly Mowinckel's cult-historical method of working nevertheless 'returned' to some degree to Gressmann and the 'religio-historical school'. For when they were speaking not only of the 'ritual pattern' in the ancient Near East (including Israel), with the 'ancient Near Eastern' *sacral* or even *divine kingly ideology* standing dominant at its centre,[38] but also of

---

38. Cf. S.H. Hooke (ed.), *Myth and Ritual* (Oxford, 1933); I. Engnell, 'Studies in Divine Kingship in Ancient Near East' (Dissertation, Uppsala, 1943).

the fact that the 'pattern' by this time had 'disintegrated', or was 'broken up', we recall that Gressmann of course had long spoken not only of the 'group of ideas' but also of the comprehensive 'pattern', which now existed only in 'fragments', especially in the Old Testament.[39] And 'messianic' was to be used by Ivan Engnell fully in the sense of the 'royal ideology'.[40] Mowinckel, however, turned decisively against this, and more polemically than ever.[41]

In conclusion, one might say that despite his closeness to Gressmann, Mowinckel was able to effect a return of Old Testament eschatology from its 'Babylonian captivity' by distancing himself from him. As he had begun it in 1922, so was he able to continue it even more clearly in 1951. Yet, his radical shift in terminology in 1926 remained the actual Achilles heel of his solution and delineation.

2. *On the Problematic Terminology of 'Eschatology'*

The essential problem of the two concepts 'messianism' and 'eschatology' is also a problem of their *terminology*, and in fact probably to a greater extent than is normally seen to be the case. Thus their 'problem history' has ultimately not become so complex and confusing, because the terminological questions have not been sufficiently clearly named and defined; above all, this concerns the terminology of 'eschatology'. 'For the sake of clarity, however, the academic world needs unequivocal terms.'[42] The significance of such an exact terminology should be found especially in its ability to express the intellectual complexity of factual contexts in precise formulations.

As is clear from the outline of the historical research above, 'messianism' and 'eschatology' have often been interpreted as two *closely interwoven* terms. The rationale for this may change, but the end result has remained relatively the same.

Occasionally, however, attempts have been made to subordinate the one concept to the other. Thus, for example, Gressmann and

39. Cf. Gressmann, *Der Ursprung*, pp. 152, 191.

40. Cf. Engnell, 'Studies in Divine Kingship', 43, 176; also *idem*, *Gamla Testamentet*, pp. 141-47, esp. 145-46.

41. Thus on a number of occasions; cf., among others, Mowinckel, *Han som kommer*, p. 294 n. 2, and p. 304 n. 177; or his *He That Cometh*, pp. 451-52 n. 1, and 453-59 nn. 4-8.

42. Gressmann, *Der Messias*, p. 1; cf. pp. 13*–17*.

Mowinckel, in their older books of 1905 and 1922 respectively, have eliminated the Messiah in favour of a 'general' eschatology, while they more or less transposed the relationship in their later works of 1929 and 1951 respectively. Among Jewish scholars like Joseph Klausner, for example, 'the Messianic idea' is more often understood and presented in the sense of the *eschatological* expectation of the Jewish nation.[43] On the other hand, some scholars have argued for as clear a differentiation of the terms 'messianism' and 'eschatology' as possible, so that they may neatly be kept apart, as was the case with T.C. Vriezen, for example.[44] Right as this view may be, in one way or another one has to relate the two concepts to each other.

The problem of their relationship appears not to be so much the 'that' as rather the 'how' of their mutual relationship, since they leave a really multifaceted impression. There is, of course, an 'eschatology' without 'Messiah' and one with 'Messiah', just as there is an 'uneschatological' and an 'eschatological Messiah'.[45] Moreover, both concepts are multiform in their own right and have a complex history. The terminological problem remains therefore first a problem of the most possible appropriate—and to a certain extent flexible—definition of the relationship between two very complex concepts.

The problem of terminology is, moreover, a problem of the right *point of departure*, for the final result depends very much on where the starting point lies which determines the way ahead.

In the traditional view, within the framework of dogmatic eschatology, New Testament Christology—as has already been pointed out above, pp. 198-201—forms the point of departure which signals the way ahead.[46] But in *Der Ursprung* even Gressmann began with the

43. J. Klausner, *The Messianic Idea in Israel: From its Beginning to the Completion of the Mishnah* (trans. W.F. Stinespring; New York, 1955 [1927/1949]), p. 9, differentiates between 'the vague *Messianic expectation*' in the sense of 'eschatology', about which he writes mostly, and 'the more explicit *belief in the Messiah*'. Cf. also 'Appendix: The Jewish and the Christian Messiah' (pp. 519-31). See further G. Scholem, *The Messianic Idea in Judaism* (London: Schocken Books, 1971); J. Neusner *et al.* (eds.), *Judaisms and their Messiahs at the Turn of the Christian Era* (Cambridge: Cambridge University Press, 1987).

44. Cf. Vriezen, *Theologie des Alten Testaments in Grundzügen*, p. 303.

45. The relatively new title of Strauss, *Messianisch ohne Messias* may be typical but is notionally ambiguous and thus unclear.

46. Cf. Fohrer, *Messiasfrage*, p. 3: 'The question of form and meaning of the Messiah was conveyed to the Old Testament first from the New Testament'.

traditional definition of 'eschatology': 'Eschatology is the science of the last things (אַחֲרִית, τὰ ἔσχατα, *de novissimis*). Under this name one used to group together all those views which concerned the end, whether of the individual or of the whole world.' Thereafter he eliminates 'the final destinies of the individual' as well as 'every consideration of dogmatics' and keeps only the reference to the world when he says: 'Recently the word eschatology has been used mostly in a definite sense and has been limited to the group of ideas which is connected with the end of the world and the renewal of the world, and we should consider it only in this narrower interpretation.'[47]

Thereby Gressmann did not actually distance himself from the traditional definition of 'eschatology'. However, as for its content he limited it according to his 'pattern', and in addition he put it in a framework of a history of ideas. When Mowinckel in 1926 chose—as he put it—a 'clearer and sharper use of language', instead of his more open definition of 'eschatology' in the *Psalmenstudien*, II, he only returned to the traditional terminology and turned eschatology back to a history of ideas, referring it to the 'last things' to come.[48] He still maintained this view in 1951/56.[49] What this definition meant for his evaluation of the proclamation of the pre-exilic prophets is clearly expressed, for example, in the following statement: 'In a message of this kind there is no room for eschatology... In their time there was no conception or doctrine of any end of the world or last things.'[50]

Many scholars however, have turned against opinions of this nature, especially since 1950. Among them Horst Dietrich Preuss was able to gather a really colourful bouquet of very different views and attempts, the trend of which is in this way or that to make the word and the concept 'eschatology' applicable again to the Old Testament in general and

47. Gressmann, *Der Ursprung*, p. 1. Cf. also H. Gunkel, *Schöpfung und Chaos in Urzeit und Endzeit* (Göttingen: Vandenhoeck & Ruprecht, 2nd edn, 1921 [1895]).

48. See pp. 207-208 above, esp. nn. 33-34.

49. Cf. Mowinckel, *He That Cometh*, p. 125: 'Eschatology is a doctrine or a complex of ideas about the last things, which is more or less organically coherent and developed. Every eschatology includes in some form or another a dualistic conception of the course of history, and implies that the present state of things and the present world order will suddenly come to an end and be superseded by another of an essentially different kind.'

50. Mowinckel, *He That Cometh*, p. 131, refering to the earlier prophets like Amos or Isaiah; cf. pp. 126-33.

to the prophets in particular.[51] Somewhat later Ursula Struppe edited a corresponding volume of various attitudes towards the Messiah question as revealed in more recent research.[52]

Of special interest—and of course typical for the situation—is Johannes Lindblom's attempt at a rehabilitation of a prophetic 'eschatology'.[53] On the one hand, Lindblom proceeds quite pragmatically and believes that the 'term has gained such currency that it is no longer expedient to limit its parameters so vigorously', that is, to relate 'eschatology' only 'to the end in a more absolute sense'. Then, as far as prophetic literature is concerned, he attempts to 'cleanse' thoroughly the usual use of the term of several 'aberrations' and misuses before he discusses a number of single passages.[54] However, it is astonishing when, on the other hand, Lindblom tries to establish the positive use of 'eschatology', believing that *'the thinking of the two ages'* offers 'the best point of departure'. To be sure, as he says, we are not faced with 'the difference between 'the present age' and 'the future age' until after the Old Testament, 'but the matter itself is already present in the prophets of the Old Testament'.[55] His corresponding conclusion is 'to use the term eschatology where we speak of a new age with radically altered circumstances when compared with the present'.[56]

In a circumspect and helpful way Lindblom certainly contributed considerably to a necessary clarification of the academic use of

51. Cf. H.D. Preuss (ed.), *Eschatologie im Alten Testament* (WdF, 480; Darmstadt: Wissenschaftliche Buchgesellschaft, 1978), especially its informative introduction (pp. 1-19) and the detailed bibliography (pp. 481-95), as well as the overview of research by W. Köhler, 'Prophetie und Eschatologie in der neueren alttestamentichen Forschung', *BibLeb* 9 (1968), pp. 57-81; repr. in Preuss (ed.), *Eschatologie*, pp. 259-92.

52. Cf. U. Struppe (ed.), *Studien zum Messiasbild im Alten Testament* (SBA, 6; Stuttgart: W. Kohlhammer, 1989); cf. also its introduction (pp. 7-21).

53. Cf. J. Lindblom, 'Gibt es eine Eschatologie bei den alttestamentlichen Propheten?', *ST* 6 (1952), pp. 79-114, now in Preuss (ed.), *Eschatologie*, pp. 31-72. Cf. also the similar attempt by T.C. Vriezen, 'Prophetie und Eschatologie', in *Congress Volume: Copenhagen 1953* (VTSup, 1; Leiden: E.J. Brill, 1953), pp. 199-229, now in Preuss (ed.), *Eschatologie*, pp. 88-128.

54. Cf. Preuss (ed.), *Eschatologie*, pp. 36-42, 42-70.

55. Preuss (ed.), *Eschatologie*, p. 33.

56. Preuss (ed.), *Eschatologie*, p. 70; see also 34; cf. p. 71: 'Eschatology must not be confused with apocalyptic... *Apocalyptic is revealed secret instruction with an eschatological content.*'

language on this point, even if his concrete opinions on the individual passages ran their course relatively briefly and to a certain extent atomistically. Most questionable as far as methodology is concerned must be the fact that there is a wide gulf between his very late 'point of departure' and his practical presentations. For the question arises as to whether, and if so, how and when 'one can really speak of a new state of things, of something "quite different"', when we are particularly concerned with pre-exilic prophetic utterances.[57] The fundamental problem which forces itself upon us here should primarily consist of how a bridge can be built between prophetic proclamation (especially in pre-exilic times) and later, dualistic utterances of the absolute end. This is a problem which Lindblom hardly overcame. Moreover, it is complicated considerably by his taking his point of departure to be in the late phase of a long and complex 'development' rather than in its beginnings. Thereby the danger could even arise of the late phase or the 'end result' producing the *measure* against which the earlier phases or even the origin of a phenomenon are to be measured.

This problem occurs too in Joachim Becker's book on the Messiah.[58] His 'point of departure' is in the 'beliefs of the New Testament and the Church' (p. 7). After a historical and critical survey of the usual Messiah passages, he finally arrives again at the 'point of departure' and then makes the following rather enigmatic statement: 'The expectation of the Messiah was dealt with only from a historical point of view. However, that is not the expectation of the Messiah of the Old Testament as such' (p. 88). What, then, is the expectation of the Messiah of the Old Testament 'as such'? It seems here as if two entities have disintegrated; on the one hand, the entity of the ecclesiastical belief, of which in the Old Testament a visionary 'forecast' was usually a part, and on the other hand, the entity of a strictly historical estimation of the traditional, Old Testament Messiah pronouncements, which at best appears to permit the utterance of a 'restorative expectation of a king'. However, here one misses an integrated description of the whole 'way', and again a point of departure—the traditional point of departure—in the late phase may have taken effect negatively.

The problem of terminology is ultimately the problem of an influential *doctrinal* or *idea-historical* structure of the relevant concepts. For

57. Preuss (ed.), *Eschatologie*, p. 34.
58. Cf. J. Becker, *Messiaserwartung im Alten Testament* (SBS, 83; Stuttgart: KBW, 1977).

a system of some kind seems to have been common to most of the descriptions of these concepts.

Quite obviously this was the case in the traditional description which was influenced more or less dogmatically and yet which had a wide effect. As has been mentioned, Gressmann too started to define 'eschatology' as a term, but otherwise he spoke of a 'group of ideas' and a 'pattern'. Religion-historically it was more common to talk of an ancient oriental 'royal *ideology*' when referring to the 'messianic'. Moreover, in this area one spoke very often of 'notions' and 'opinions', as well as 'motives' or even 'structures' of ideas, as did also Fohrer, for example.[59] When Fohrer, referring at the beginning of his book on the Messiah[60] to the 'points of departure', speaks of 'two basic points of view' by differentiating between 'a fundamental New Testament-Christological point of view and an ancient Near Eastern mythico-cultic' one (pp. 3-4), one could raise the critical question as to whether these 'two basic points of view' cannot similarly be regarded as two sides of the same coin, having a doctrinal character, and referring to a history of ideas.

However, one might well ask at this point whether there should be any possibility of being an *alternative* way of approaching the question of 'eschatology'. In this regard, some time ago I undertook an attempt to establish a *new elucidation of the eschatological terminology*.[61]

In my opinion a new angle of incidence on the subject can be found in consideration of the modern, two-winged expression 'eschato-logia'. This could occur by not stressing the second part of the word, 'logia' (i.e. a modern, doctrinal reconstruction of the object as has generally been the case), but by directing one's attention primarily at the first

---

59. Cf. G. Fohrer, 'Die Struktur der alttestamentlichen Eschatologie', *TLZ* 85 (1960), pp. 401-20, also in his *Studien zur alttestamentlichen Prophetie* (BZAW, 99; Berlin: Alfred Töpelmann, 1967), pp. 32-58, now in Preuss (ed.), *Eschatologie*, pp. 147-80. Cf. also C. Steuernagel, 'Die Strukturlinien der Entwicklung der jüdischen Eschatologie', in *Festschrift A. Bertholet* (Tübingen: J.C.B. Mohr, 1950), pp. 479-87.

60. Cf. Fohrer, *Messiasfrage*, pp. 3-11.

61. Cf. M. Sæbø, 'Eschaton und Eschatologia im Alten Testament—in traditionsgeschichtlicher Sicht', in J. Hausmann and H.-J. Zobel (eds.), *Alttestamentlicher Glaube und biblische Theologie* (Festschrift H.D. Preuss; Stuttgart: W. Kohlhammer, 1992), pp. 321-30. Cf. also *idem*, 'Messianism in Chronicles? Some Remarks to the Old Testament Background of the New Testament Christology', *HBT* 2 (1980), pp. 85-109.

part, simply by examining what the Old Testament itself may have to tell about an *eschaton*. In so doing one should attempt to answer such a question neither rashly by means of a reference to the 'end' in the absolute sense of the word,[62] nor etymologically in the 'conventional' sense, but rather more directly semantically with reference to the biblical *linguistic usage*.

One acceptable way appears to lead back to the Hebrew Bible by way of the LXX. By enquiring as to the Hebrew equivalents of the usage particularly of τὸ/τὰ ἔσχατον/τα 'the last' as well as of τὸ πέρας 'limit, conclusion, end' and τὸ τέλος 'end', one is led to the Hebrew nouns אַחֲרִית and קֵץ.[63] If we trace these two nouns from Amos 8 through to the book of Daniel, perhaps more than expected becomes obvious, and it may be informative for the much debated and very controversial question of an Old Testament 'eschatology'.

Here just the following points may be mentioned briefly.[64]

(a) אַחֲרִית and קֵץ are not synonyms, yet they occur almost like twinned words and complement each other as far as the meaning is concerned: אַחֲרִית—like the adverb אַחַר 'afterwards'—refers primarily to a period of time which follows 'afterwards', that is, to the 'future', yet it can also mean 'end', whereas קֵץ, derived from the verb קָצַץ 'to cut (off)', more often and more directly expresses the concept of an abrupt 'end' (of things or people).[65]

(b) The two nouns are chiefly exemplified in the prophetic literature, which may mean a certain revision of Mowinckel's concentration on the Psalms and, beyond them, on the cult and its festivals.

(c) The oldest example of אַחֲרִית is in Amos 8.10, and the oldest example of קֵץ is in Amos 8.2, and here both mean 'end'. The formulation in 8.2 is particularly conspicuous, for within the context of the fourth vision of Amos קֵץ forms an original word-play with קָיִץ

---

62. As has often happened; cf. Lindblom, in Preuss (ed.), *Eschatologie*, pp. 32-33.

63. On the Greek terms cf., e.g., *TWNT*, II, pp. 694-95; IX, p. 306; VIII, pp. 52-54, otherwise Hatch, Redpath *et al.*, *Concordance*; on the Hebrew term see n. 65 below; also see KB, GesB and GMD.

64. For further argument see the articles listed in n. 61, especially Sæbø, 'Eschaton', pp. 325-30.

65. On אַחֲרִית cf. E. Jenni, ''אחר 'ḥr danach', *THAT*, I, cols. 110-18; H. Seebass, 'אַמְרִית', *ThWAT*, I, cols. 224-28; on קֵץ cf. M. Wagner, 'קֵץ qēṣ Ende', *THAT*, II, cols. 659-63; S. Talmon, 'קֵץ qeṣ', *ThWAT*, VII, cols. 84-92, esp. 88-89.

'summer fruit/autumn fruit',[66] when it is said: 'The end (קֵץ) has come for my people Israel'. Indeed, the conclusion or end aspect[67] of this word of judgment is intensified even more by the parallel לֹא עוֹד 'not any longer' ('I will spare them no longer'). The use of אַחֲרִית and קֵץ in Amos 8, however, is not isolated in his proclamation, but is character-istic of the radical No of Amos,[68] to which there belongs a whole addi-tional series of other texts—like 5.18-20, that usually has been regarded as the eschatological *locus classicus*, or 3.1-2 and 4.1-3.[69]

(d) Thus the oldest example of a prophetically proclaimed *eschaton* is no proof of a fixed or even of a 'doctrinal' term, but rather it may be understood as a new way of speaking which has been created in an *ad hoc* manner and which expresses a *kerygmatically* proclaimed, radical *expectation* of a near judgment of God. Thus prophetic 'eschatology' unequivocally began as a 'judgment eschatology' for the near future of the nation.[70] Compared with the unbroken *futurism* of the nation's sal-vation traditions (see, e.g., Ps. 117), this judgment eschatology signified a radical break, even a repeal of the salvatio-historical importance of the old election traditions, as particularly Gerhard von Rad has pointed out; in this connection he has also spoken of an 'eschatologizing of his-torical thinking through the prophets'.[71]

(e) Amos was the first, but he did not remain alone. His particular manner of speaking formed a precedent.[72] This becomes especially clear in Ezekiel 7, where 'the end' has become a fixed or formulaic eschatological term along with other words such as 'calamity', 'the

66. Cf. J. Hausmann, 'קַיִץ *qajiṣ*', *ThWAT*, VII, pp. 26-29, esp. 28-29.

67. Cf. J.H. Grønbaek, 'Zur Frage der Eschatologie in der Verkündigung der Gerichtspropheten', *SEÅ* 24 (1959), pp. 5-21, now in Preuss (ed.), *Eschatologie*, pp. 129-46, esp. 135.

68. Cf. R. Smend, 'Das Nein des Amos', *EvT* 23 (1963), pp. 404-23, now in *idem*, *Die Mitte des Alten Testamentes*, pp. 85-103, esp. 95-96.

69. Cf. also Wolff, *Joel und Amos*, pp. 121-29 (Introduction, §4: *Die Botschaft*).

70. Cf. Grønbaek, 'Zur Frage', p. 141; also pp. 143-44 (against Mowinckel): 'Therefore, as for the question of the real origin of eschatology in Israelite history of religion the discussion is irrelevant as to when the cult lost its actual value among the people.'

71. Von Rad, *Theologie des Alten Testaments*, II, esp. pp. 121-29. Cf. also Rohland, 'Die Bedeutung'. There has been some criticism against von Rad's concept of history; see the next chapter.

72. Thus Rudolph, *Joel–Amos–Obadja–Jona*, p. 239 n. 6.

time', and 'the day' (cf. also Ezek. 21, 30, 34; 33.5).[73] After the catastrophe of the exile, the judgment-eschatological formulaic nature of
'the end' is confirmed impressively in the Book of Lamentations (4.18).

(f) Alongside the judgment-eschatological proclamation of 'the end',
however, there appeared a salvatio-eschatological proclamation of the
prophets, by means of which the older futurism of the salvation traditions was renewed against the background of judgment and punishment
and developed as a *new salvation of God*. This occurred not only by
ensuring that 'the end' (קֵץ) referred to one's enemies, thus signifying
salvation for Israel (Jer. 51.13 and Hab. 2.1-5), but especially by means
of the word אַחֲרִית which refers here to the new 'future' which will
bring salvation (Jer. 29.11 and 31.17, and Deutero-Isaiah (41.22 and
46.10), and also in that the negative 'no longer' (לֹא עוֹד) in Amos 8.2 is
turned in Zechariah after the exile into the positive 'once more/again'
(עוֹד) (1.17). In this way, therefore, there arose a *kerygmatic salvation
eschatology* as well, especially as early in the prophetic proclamation
the notion of a 'two-phased procedure'[74] of divine judgment and salvation appears to have sprung up. In any event, in the course of time it
was developed more and more.

(g) As the way from Amos to Ezekiel has already shown, gradually
an eschatologico-terminological *formulaic convention* was formed, and
simultaneously kerygmatic eschatology was changed increasingly into
a scholarly or 'doctrinal' *eschatology* with specific scholarly contents.
Particularly קֵץ 'end' became linked with several words for 'time' and,
with the meaning of 'time span' or 'period of history',[75] it became the
important foundation of a prophetically eschatological theology of history, where the 'two-phased procedure' contributed to the further periodization of history as is expressed, for example, in Ezekiel 38–39 or in
Zechariah 12–14.[76] This scholarly or didactic-eschatological meaning of
history, resulted in the great eschatological *final drama* of *apocalyptic*
which partially retained the nature of a *secret wisdom* where history
actually 'stands still', as Martin Buber once put it, particularly in the
book of Daniel where both קֵץ and אַחֲרִית occur frequently (8.17; 9.26;

---

73. Cf. Zimmerli, *Ezechiel*, I, pp. 158-86, esp. 169-73.
74. Thus Wolff, *Hosea*, p. 78.
75. Cf. especially Talmon, 'קֵץ *qeṣ*', *ThWAT*, VII, pp. 84-92, esp. 89-90.
76. Cf., e.g., Sæbø, *Sacharja 9–14*, esp. pp. 252-309.

11.27, 35, 40; 12.4, 9, 13, as well as 2.28 and 10.14).[77]

In sum, it may be maintained that Old Testament eschatology is most appropriately interpreted and explained *in a traditio-historical way*. It arose as an original expression of earlier judgment prophecy and thence has experienced a complex development which is characterized particularly by means of the transition from kerygma to doctrine and by means of the dialectic of divine judgment and salvation as well as its changing relationship to the history of the people of Israel, and to the history of nations in general.

3. A Look at the State of the 'Messianic' Text

In referring back to the preceding survey of eschatological queries, now may be posited the following thesis, although a detailed proof is not possible at this stage: The question of the Messiah in the Old Testament has its own character, yet it may be understood in an analogous way to the question of eschatology, and partially it may be combined with it.

As with 'eschatology', methodically it is the best way to begin here too not with the difficult questions, such as those concerning the 'kingdom' or even the 'royal ideology', for example, or even the late phase of messianism,[78] but rather with the more modest—although not unproblematic—question of the relevant Hebrew terminology.

The main term is the verbal adjective מָשִׁיחַ 'anointed one' (derived from the Hebrew verb מָשַׁח 'anoint'), which—like the closely connected verbal adjective/noun נָגִיד 'prince'—is, of course, in the passive form, but which functions as a noun expressing both a special status as well as a specific activity.[79]

---

77. See n. 56 above.

78. Recently E.-J. Waschke has warned of the danger of simply asking 'retrospectively from the point of view of the New Testament', whereby one can 'overlook the proprium of Messianic traditions in the Old Testament', in 'Die Frage nach dem Messias im Alten Testament als Problem alttestamentlicher Theologie und biblischer Hermeneutik', *TLZ* 113 (1988), pp. 321-32, 330.

79. On the word family, see particularly E. Kutsch, *Salbung als Rechtsakt im Alten Testament und im Alten Orient* (BZAW, 87; Berlin: Alfred Töpelmann, 1963); also see K. Seybold, 'מָשַׁח I *māšaḥ*', *ThWAT*, V, pp. 46-59; F. Hesse, 'III. מָשִׁיחַ im Alten Testament', *TWNT*, IX, pp. 491-500; J.A. Soggin, 'מֶלֶךְ *maleek* könig', *THAT*, I, cols. 908-20 (913-14); cf. also T.N.D. Mettinger, *King and Messiah: The Civil and Sacral Legitimation of the Israelite Kings* (ConBOT, 8; Lund: C.W.K. Gleerup, 1976), esp. pp. 185-232.

As far as the semantic profile of the noun מָשִׁיחַ 'anointed one' is concerned, the *dispersion* of the word may in the first instance be informative. It almost fails to occur where one would expect it to—for example, from our reading of the New Testament—that is, in the prophetic texts,[80] but rather, its focal point is in the Deuteronomistic History and in the Psalms. And in these instances it refers almost solely to the king.[81] Second, it is characteristic of the word, when used in reference to the king, that it is never used alone or absolutely, but always *syntagmatically with Yahweh*; thus it is never said '*the* anointed one', but always of מְשִׁיחַ יהוה 'the anointed one *of Yahweh*' (apart from in 2 Sam. 23.1 that has the variant: 'the anointed one of the God of Jacob'), or else a suffix is added to read 'my/your/his anointed one'. This may serve, of course, as a warning against any rash abstraction as far as 'the Messiah' is concerned, especially in regard to the oldest phase. On this point, restraint is even more in order, as the picture immediately becomes much different when the use of verb is taken into consideration. For since the verb מָשַׁח 'anoint', when referring to Yahweh or his representatives such as Samuel, a prophet or priest[82] again and again has a plural subject,[83] whereby the nation or its highest representatives have undertaken the 'anointing' of the king, the question has been much debated as to how the relationship between this 'political' and the theologically more intensely profiled 'sacral' anointing can be more closely determined.[84] The two sides should not be

80. Only in Hab. 3.13, a psalm, and in the special reference to Cyrus in Isa. 45.1.

81. Of a total of 39 examples, there are 18 examples in 1 and 2 Samuel, whereby the textually difficult passage in 2 Sam. 1.21 should be excluded and the late passage in 2 Chron. 6.42 be added; and there are 10 examples in the Psalms, where one can omit the passage which refers to the fathers in Ps. 105.15 (see 1 Chron. 16.22), but can include Hab. 3.13 and Lam. 4.20. Otherwise, Lev. 4.3, 5, 16 and 6.15 refer to the priest, so probably well also in the ambiguous text of Dan. 9.25-26.

82. Sacral anointing by Yahweh: 1 Sam. 10.1; 15.17; 2 Sam. 12.7; 2 Kgs 9.3, 6, 12; 2 Chron. 22.7; also Ps. 89.21; by Samuel: 1 Sam. 9.16; 10.1; 16.3, 12, 13; cf. 11.15 LXX; by a prophet: 1 Kgs 1.34, 45; 19.15, 16; 2 Kgs 9.3, 12 (anointing of Jehu); by a priest: 1 Kgs 1.34, 39, 45; cf. 2 Kgs 11.12; otherwise 2 Chron. 23.11.

83. Thus Judg. 9.8, 15; 2 Sam. 2.4, 7; 5.3, ,17; 1 Kgs 5.15; 2 Kgs 11.12; 23.30; cf. also 1 Chron. 11.3; 19.22; 2 Chron. 23.11. Moreover, the use of verbs exhibits a whole series of different forms and constructions; cf. Seybold, *ThWAT*, V, pp. 48-52.

84. Cf. esp. Kutsch, *Salbung als Rechtsakt, passim*; L. Schmidt, *Menschlicher*

contrasted too heavily, however, since they belong to an interweaving of history and theology which may no longer be possible to unravel. Even in the historical material it can be observed that the expression 'Yahweh's anointed one' 'has become detached from the concrete act of anointing'.[85] The continuation of this tendency in the Psalms emerges also in such a way that the use of the verb מָשַׁח 'anoint' does not occur at all, apart from in Ps. 89.21. A comparison with the verb usage should make it clearer that in a special way the expression 'Yahweh's anointed one' was fundamental for the slowly developing messianic theologoumenon in the Old Testament.

Third, it is also of semantic interest that despite all theologization of the expression 'Yahweh's anointed one', the historical basis of the anointing of the king remains important as the *point of departure* of the theological development of the 'messianic', so that the methodical *modus procedendi* might lead from the historical material to that of the Psalms and not *vice versa*.

With the expression מְשִׁיחַ יהוה 'Yahweh's anointed one', therefore, there is a fundamental definition of the relationship between king and God, namely, that of a clear *subordination* of the king to God. This definition has proved to be very effective, for around it revolves most of what the Old Testament has declared with reference to the 'messianic'. It has its roots in the situation of the introduction of the kingdom to Israel and in the theological explication of it, yet refers also to the preceding period of the 'judges'.

This God–King relationship is reflected to a certain extent in the traditions of the historical material, and then not only in the much debated juxtaposition of passages which are 'opposed' to the king and passages which are 'sympathetic towards the king' in 1 Samuel 8–12,[86] but also

---

Erfolg und Jahwes Initiative (WMANT, 38; Neukirchen–Vluyn: Neukirchener Verlag, 1970), esp. 172-88; Mettinger, *King and Messiah*, pp. 191-208; Seybold, *ThWAT*, V, pp. 48-52.

85. Thus Schmidt, *Menschlicher Erfolg*, p. 188.

86. Cf. H.J. Boecker, *Die Beurteilung der Anfänge des Königtums in den deuteronomistischen Abschnitten des I. Samuelbuches* (WMANT, 31; Neukirchen–Vluyn: Neukirchener Verlag, 1969); W.H. Schmidt, 'Kritik am Königtum', in Wolff (ed.), *Probleme biblischer Theologie*, pp. 440-61; F. Crüsemann, *Der Widerstand gegen das Königtum* (WMANT, 49; Neukirchen–Vluyn: Neukirchener Verlag, 1978); R.E. Clements, 'The Deuteronomistic Interpretation of the Founding of the Monarchy in I. Sam. VIII', *VT* 24 (1974), pp. 398-410; S. Talmon, 'Königtum und Staatsidee im biblischen Israel', in *idem*, *Gesellschaft und Literatur in der*

in the more comprehensive and far more complex presentation of subsequent historical events: from the saviour figures of the 'judges'[87] through Saul[88] to David, whereby not least *the charismatic endowment and mandate* of the 'judges' of the people by means of the Spirit of Yahweh represent a considerable unifying element (cf., e.g., Judg. 6.34; 1 Sam. 10.6, 10; and 16.13-14).[89] By means of the manifold historico-theological 'introduction' of the institution of kingship which was new for Israel, the election of the 'saviour' through Yahweh has been expressed clearly, as has his subordination to him.

The extent to which a reference to the 'judges' here can also be inferred from the use of נָגִיד 'prince/elevated one' cannot be ascertained with certainty.[90] Be that as it may, the word, that was used by Saul (1 Sam. 9.16 and 10.1) and especially by David (1 Sam. 13.14; 25.30; and 2 Sam. 5.2; 6.21 and 7.8), appears to express a *title of sovereignty*, of which 'a special concept of majesty and honour are characteristic' and with which 'the religio–sacral element stands in the foreground'.[91]

hebräischen Bibel: Gesammelte Aufsätze, I (Information Judentum, 8; Neukirchen–Vluyn: Neukirchener Verlag, 1988), pp. 11-43.

87. Cf., e.g., von Rad, *Theologie des Alten Testaments*, I, pp. 340-46; W. Richter, *Traditionsgeschichtliche Untersuchungen zum Richterbuch* (BBB, 18; Bonn: Peter Hanstein, 1966), esp. pp. 319-343; Schmidt, *Menschlicher Erfolg*, pp. 22-53, 189-208; S. Talmon, ' "In jenen Tagen gab es keinen מלך in Israel" (Ri. 18–21)', in *idem, Gesellschaft und Literatur*, pp. 44-55.

88. Cf., e.g., von Rad, *Theologie des Alten Testaments*, I, pp. 336-40; W. Beyerlin, 'Das Königscharisma bei Saul', *ZAW* 73 (1961), pp. 186-201; J.A. Soggin, 'Charisma und Institution im Königtum Sauls', *ZAW* 75 (1963), pp. 53-65; V. Fritz, 'Die Deutungen des Königtums Sauls in den Überlieferungen von seiner Entstehung I Sam 9–11', *ZAW* 88 (1976), pp. 346-62.

89. See, e.g., Mettinger, *King and Messiah*, pp. 233-53.

90. This has been recently problematized. Cf. G.F. Hasel, 'נָגִיד *nāḡîḏ*', *ThWAT*, V, pp. 203-19; also W. Richter, 'Die *nagid*-Formel', *BZ* 9 (1965), pp. 71-84; Schmidt, *Menschlicher Erfolg*, pp. 141-71. Otherwise cf. T. Veijola, *Die ewige Dynastie: David und die Entstehung seiner Dynastie nach der deuteronomistischen Darstellung* (AASF.B, 193; Helsinki: Suomalainen Tiedeakatemia, 1975), pp. 129-30; and his *Das Königtum in der Beurteilung der deuteronomistischen Historiographie: Eine redaktionsgeschichtliche Untersuchung* (AASF.B, 198; Helsinki: Suomalainen Tiedeakatemia, 1977), p. 118; Mettinger, *King and Messiah*, pp. 64-79, 151-84.

91. Thus Hasel, *ThWAT*, V, p. 209.

Thus the word נָגִיד may well serve to complete the expression מְשִׁיחַ יהוה as the main term in a theologically effective way, since this 'title' too was used both for Saul (1 Sam. 24.7, 11; 26.9, 11, 16, 23; 2 Sam. 1.14, 16; and 1 Sam. 12.3, 5) and for David (2 Sam. 19.22; 23.1; cf. also 1 Sam. 16.6 and 2 Sam. 22.51).

It is very conspicuous that most of the examples of מְשִׁיחַ יהוה which refer to Saul occur[92] in the 'Story of David's rise to power' (1 Sam. 16.14–2 Sam. 5[93]) which considers primarily the victorious David; here the narratives of 1 Samuel 24 and 26 have a special significance, bridging the messianic and the theological, where two 'anointed ones of Jahwe' fight against each other. Saul, as 'Yahweh's anointed one', has here been portrayed, on the one hand, as the failing, obscure antitype of David, yet on the other hand, the presentation gives expression to the unique majesty and honour of 'one anointed by Yahweh', namely, by means of his election and in particular by means of his *invulnerability* or *immunity* under the special protection of Yahweh (1 Sam. 24.7; 26.9, 23; and 2 Sam. 1.14). In all of this the *theocratic* 'ideal' is preserved here, just as it is elsewhere in the Deuteronomistic History (see esp. 1 Sam. 12.12-15; cf. also 8.10-18 and the 'law of kingship' in Deut. 17.14-20).[94]

Whereas מְשִׁיחַ יהוה is also used for David in the 'Story of the succession to David'[95] (2 Sam. 19.22), the term does not occur in the important and variously reworked text of 2 Sam. 7.1-17 which is basic for the Davidic dynasty.[96] Rather, נָגִיד is used here (7.8b: 'Prince over

92. Cf. von Rad, *Theologie des Alten Testaments*, I, p. 337: 'The narratives of Saul and David are…David's narratives.' See pp. 336-40 for the full account.

93. J.H. Grønbaek, *Die Geschichte vom Aufstieg Davids (1. Sam. 15–2. Sam. 5): Tradition und Komposition* (AThD, 10; Copenhagen: Munksgaard, 1971) has the historical work begin somewhat earlier.

94. Cf., e.g., Veijola, *Das Königtum*, pp. 49-50, 68-72, 116-18.

95. See, e.g., Crüsemann, *Der Widerstand*, pp. 180-93.

96. Among the many works on 2 Sam. 7, see, e.g., M. Noth, 'David und Israel in 2. Samuel 7', in *idem*, *Gesammelte Studien zum AT* (TBü, 6; Munich: Chr. Kaiser Verlag, 3rd edn, 1966), pp. 334-45; E. Kutsch, 'Die Dynastie von Gottes Gnaden: Probleme der Nathanweissagung in 2. Sam. 7', *ZTK* 58 (1961), pp. 137-53, now in Struppe (ed.), *Messiasbild*, pp. 107-26; H. Gese, 'Der Davidsbund und die Zionserwählung', in *idem*, *Vom Sinai zum Zion*, pp. 113-29, esp. 123-29; Veijola, *Die ewige Dynastie*, pp. 68-79; Mettinger, *King and Messiah*, pp. 48-63; cf. also G.H. Jones, *The Nathan Narratives* (JSOTSup, 80; Sheffield: JSOT Press, 1990).

my people Israel').[97] Important for the fleshing out of the picture of the Messiah in this composition are, on the one hand, the promise of an 'eternal dynasty' (vv. 13-16) as well as the promise of a father–son relationship between Yahweh and David (v. 14a) as an expression of the special *closeness* of the king to God, and on the other hand, a radical emphasis of the subordination of David to God by means of the threat of possible chastisement and punishment (v. 14b). Thus the promised stability of the Davidic kingship is *theocratically* determined. Yet the transition from the elected kingship to the dynastic principle of hereditary kingship may have had a multifarious effect.[98]

The poem of 2 Sam. 23.27[99] which is partially wisdom poetry, and in addition has the divergent form 'the one anointed by the God of Jacob' in the introduction (v. 1), points in two directions, first in the direction of a further theological 'classification' of the 'anointed one' through the venerable name of the 'God of Jacob', and second in the direction of the cult lyrics of the royal psalms; also the element of the charismatic (v. 2) points to a traditio-historical perspective which refers to the past, whereas mention of the 'everlasting covenant' which his 'house' has with God serves as a link, for example, with Ps. 89.4-5, 35 as well as with Ps. 132.10. Thus the picture of the Messiah in the poem reveals both reciprocal continuity with received traditions as well as elements of a continuing tradition.

Psalms 89 and 132, which contain the 'title' מְשִׁיחַ יהוה (Pss. 89.39-52 and 132.10-17), appear in a variety of ways to be closely linked with the messianic-historical traditions and particularly 2 Samuel 7.[100] Even if the historical questions about more exact dating, especially within the Deuteronomistic History, may be really complex and controversial, one may be faced here with an old core tradition which had as its content

---

97. Cf. Schmidt, *Menschlicher Erfolg*, pp. 146-51.

98. Cf. A. Alt, 'Die Staatenbildung der Israeliten in Palästina', in *idem, Kleine Schriften*, II, pp. 1-65, esp. 33-65; see also his 'Das Königtum in den Reichen Israel und Juda', pp. 116-34; and Crüsemann, *Der Widerstand*, pp. 194-222.

99. Cf. Mettinger, *King and Messiah*, pp. 257-58, 279-81; and his 'The Last Words of David: A Study of Structure and Meaning in II Samuel 23.1-7', *SEÅ* 41.42 (1976–77), pp. 147-56.

100. Cf. T. Veijola, *Verheissung in der Krise: Studien zur Literatur und Theologie der Exilszeit anhand des 89. Psalms* (AASF.B, 220; Helsinki: Suomalainen Tiedeakatemia, 1982), esp. pp. 60-75.

David's exceptional position as 'Yahweh's anointed one';[101] the core tradition has developed a unique *election tradition of David,* which moreover appears to be linked closely with a corresponding tradition as regards Zion/Jerusalem.[102] The picture of the Messiah which is based in the historical traditions was gradually expanded into a *messianic David-ology of an unbroken futuristic nature*—into a kind of *theologia gloriae davidica*—in which King David as יהוה מְשִׁיחַ became the messianic *prototype.* He gave a unique lustre to the royal throne in Jerusalem; with him one could even argue in prayer and lamentation, as occurs, for example, in Psalms 89 and 132: 'For the sake of David your servant, do not reject your anointed one' (Ps. 132.10; cf. vv. 1-5 as well as Ps. 89.50-52). The father–son relationship could also be extended broadly: 'Yes, I appoint him as my firstborn, as the most exalted of the kings upon earth' (Ps. 89.28; cf. vv. 27-30).[103] In these and other psalms which can be described as messianic royal psalms—in particular psalms like Psalms 2 and 110 or 45 and 72—there occurred a certain *typification* of מְשִׁיחַ יהוה, whereby particularly his majesty and honour were expanded, even in a cultic–ritualistic way as, for example, would seem to be the case in Psalms 2 and 110, as well as in the Songs of Zion.

The court and the cult of Jerusalem will also have been the special place where many elements of the locally varying 'royal ideology' of the neighbouring nations were introduced, and exercised their influence upon the indigenous traditions of kingship, as has been shown on num-erous occasions in more recent biblical scholarship by scholars like Gressmann, Mowinckel and many others. Indeed, for this reason there is no need to debate this point again.[104] However, as regards the much-

101. Cf. Alt, 'Das Grossreich Davids', pp. 66-75; see also n. 98 above. Cf. von Rad, *Theologie des Alten Testaments,* I, pp. 320-31; S. Herrmann, *Die prophetischen Heilserwartungen im Alten Testament* (BWANT, 85; Stuttgart: W. Kohlhammer, 1965), pp. 92-103.

102. Cf. von Rad, *Theologie des Alten Testaments,* I, p. 320; Rohland, 'Die Bedeutung', esp. pp. 119-208, 209-65; and J. Jeremias, 'Lade und Zion: Zur Entstehung der Ziontradition', in Wolff (ed.), *Probleme biblischer Theologie,* pp. 183-98.

103. Thus with Kraus, *Psalmen,* II, pp. 1054 and 779.

104. See pp. 197-209 above. On the works mentioned there, cf. also H. Ringgren, *The Messiah in the Old Testament* (SBT, 18; London: SCM Press, 1956); and K.-H. Bernhardt, *Das Problem der altorientalischen Königsideologie im Alten Testament* (VTSup, 8; Leiden: E.J. Brill, 1961).

debated question of the ultimate origin of the picture of Messiah, we may not be faced primarily with an ancient oriental origin, but rather with roots in indigenous Israelite traditions. Yet the exterior influences should not be underestimated.

Above all, the alleged *subordination of the Davidic kingship to the kingship of Yahweh* remains of specific importance. When Mowinckel only wants to see in this respect 'inconsistency' and 'compromise' and the Messiah purely as 'a kind of *doppelgänger* of Yahweh',[105] his statements may presumably be based on a misunderstanding of the particular Israelite basis of tradition. It was peculiar to it, for example, that saviour, leader and king were dependent on the Spirit and mandate of God; and if the king were to be close to his God (Ps. 2.2b) or were to sit at his right hand (Ps. 110.1), nevertheless in this unique position of honour he remained for ever only a 'satrap of Yahweh' in *his* kingship.[106] Furthermore, if he were to be granted sovereignty over the earth (Pss. 2.8-10; 72.8-11; 89.26, and 110.1-2, 6), then this would be only for the reason that in so doing he would be permitted to share in the sovereignty of Yahweh over the earth.[107] In the much later work of history in Chronicles this trend increases considerably when it is said there of King David that he should sit 'upon the throne of the kingdom of Yahweh over Israel' (1 Chron. 28.5 and 29.23, and 2 Chron. 9.8).

If, therefore, the tradition of יהוה מְשִׁיחַ 'Jahwe's anointed one' has turned out particularly to be a special *Davidic tradition* in Jerusalem, which in the course of time was expanded considerably, theologically one has adhered throughout to the fact that King David was only what he was or was allowed to be in relationship to Yahweh. His lustre was to a certain extent a reflection of the splendour of Yahweh.[108]

The particular Davidic traditions which yield a futuristic but not eschatological picture of Messiah have now been treated in some detail. That appears to be necessary, first, because these traditions, as the alleged basis of tradition, may have served as a *conditio sine qua non* for the prophetic-messianic proclamation which may be designated as eschatological, and because second, the transition from the non-eschatological to the eschatological picture of Messiah may be regarded as the crucial, and at the same time critical, point.

105. See pp. 202-209 above and nn. 27-28.
106. Cf. Kraus, *Psalmen*, II, pp. 931-32.
107. See Chapter 8 above.
108. Cf., e.g., von Rad, *Theologie des Alten Testaments*, I, pp. 331-36.

For not only did Mowinckel, for example, have great difficulties here, as already mentioned, but more recently so did J. Becker.[109] He speaks only of a 'supposed Messianism in the time of the monarchy' (p. 32) just as he speaks, commencing with Jer. 23.5-6, of a 'restorative royal expectation in the books of the prophets' (p. 53). Finally, he accepts a 'messianological vacuum', presumably because he sees in the 'Messiah' nothing more than a later salvation figure. 'To messianism there belongs essentially a salvation figure, and a royal one at that, stemming from the house of David. This figure is sought in vain right into the second century BC' (p. 74). On the way he has also, for example, 'set aside Isaiah's Sign of Immanuel (7.10-16)' (p. 41). H. Wildberger too appears in his commentary on this passage[110] to have postulated a similar definition of 'Messiah'. For, as opposed to R. Kittel[111] and O. Procksch,[112] he sees in Isa. 7.14 not 'the origin of the notion of Messiah', because he tends to understand 'by Messiah the eschatological bringer of salvation', which, however, means that 'in a messianic prophecy... only salvation can be proclaimed' (pp. 299-300). But just this may be questioned.

It is surely conspicuous that in the actual prophetic proclamation the title of sovereignty יהוה מְשִׁיחַ does not appear to be used in a Davidic way, but is rather avoided; with H. Strauss it may be called 'messianic without Messiah'.[113] On the other hand, however, one should not draw conclusions from the lack of a traditional terminology in the same way as did Mowinckel or Becker. The relevant prophetic texts allow rather for a different interpretation; and here Isa. 7.1-17 is specifically important.

In the view of many scholars, the complex passage in Isa. 7.1-17 and particularly 'the most controversial Bible passage' in 7.14,[114] seems to have been of primary significance for the prophets' picture of the Messiah. Nevertheless, the opinions of scholars differ greatly as to the 'how' of its significance.[115] But even this text may be understood

109. Cf. Becker, *Messiaserwartung*.
110. Cf. Wildberger, *Jesaja*, I, pp. 262-300.
111. Cf. R. Kittel, *Geschichte des Volkes Israel*, II (Stuttgart, 1925), p. 480.
112. Cf. Procksch, *Theologie des Alten Testaments*, pp. 185-87, 583-85.
113. See n. 2 above.
114. M. Buber, *Der Glaube der Propheten* (Zürich, 1950), p. 201.
115. The literature is almost boundless. Apart from Wildberger, *Jesaja*, I,

similarly to Amos 8.2 as a current-kerygmatic word of prophecy originating in a specific situation, and subsequently extending its meaning.
When Isaiah first takes issue with Ahaz as the current representative
of the Davidic kingship, he also takes issue with the traditional messianic 'Davidology'. And when, after words of admonition to the house
of David (7.3-6–7.9),[116] he turns to words of accusation and words of
judgement against it (7.10–14.15-17), he basically relieves the king of
the special messianic promise. For the intrinsically positive 'sign' of
the *birth of a child*—especially as his name will be the confessional
symbolic name עִמָּנוּ אֵל, 'With us (is) God'—can be taken by the king
as a serious threat, since now the new 'one to come', as 'antitype' of
Ahaz, will realize the traditional 'With us (is) God' and thereby will
rightly assume the old messianic inheritance. Just as in his fourth vision
Amos created by means of a play on words a new term 'end', thereby
giving expression to a judgment-eschatological near expectation (8.2),
Isaiah in his confrontation with King Ahaz in the Davidic environment
of Jerusalem similarly undertook a radical *judgment-directed eschato-
logization of the transmitted picture of Messiah* which signified a break
with the old salvation tradition. This declaration of Isaiah presupposes
too that the expected 'revolutionary change' is close at hand.[117]

Second, by means of his utterance about the birth of a child, Isaiah
created a totally new terminology or, rather, a *new metaphoric* which

pp. 262-64, see, e.g., J.J. Stamm, 'Neuere Arbeiten zum Immanuel-Problem', *ZAW*
68 (1956), pp. 46-53; H. Junker, *Ursprung und Grundzüge des Messiasbildes bei
Isajas* (VTSup, 4; Leiden: E.J. Brill, 1957), pp. 181-96; M. Rehm, *Der königliche
Messias im Licht der Immanuel-Weissagungen des Buches Jesaja* (Kevelaer: But-
zon & Bercker, 1968); R. Kilian, *Die Verheissung Immanuels Jes. 7,14* (SBS, 35;
Stuttgart: KWB, 1968) and *idem, Jesaja 1–39* (EdF, 200; Darmstadt: Wissen-
schaftliche Buchgesellschaft, 1983); Dietrich, *Jesaja und die Politik*, pp. 60-99;
H. Barth, 'Jes. 8, 23b–9,6', in Struppe (ed.), *Messiasbild*, pp. 199-229; H. Irsigler,
'Zeichen und Bezeichnetes in Jes. 7, 1-17', in Struppe (ed.), *Messiasbild*, pp. 155-
97; O. Kaiser, 'Jesaja/Jesajabuch', *TRE*, XVI, pp. 636-58, *idem, Jesaja*; A. Laato,
*Who is Immanuel? The Rise and the Foundering of Isaiah's Messianic Expecta-
tions* (Åbo: Åbo Academy Press, 1988).

116. See Ch. 6 above.

117. Cf. O. Kaiser, 'Geschichtliche Erfahrung und eschatologische Erwartung:
Ein Beitrag zur Geschichte der alttestamentlichen Eschatologie im Jesajabuch',
NZSTh 15 (1973), pp. 272-85, now in Preuss (ed.), *Eschatologie*, pp. 444-61; e.g.
p. 445: 'Thus one could call him [i.e. Isaiah] the father of Old Testament eschatol-
ogy.' See also K. Seybold, *Das davidische Königtum im Zeugnis der Propheten*
(FRLANT, 107; Göttingen: Vandenhoeck & Ruprecht, 1972).

signified a completely *new beginning*, and which was to turn out in many ways to be effective. This occurs particularly in clearly expanded form in Isa. 9.1-6, especially in vv. 5-6, where not only do we read of the birth of a child, but where names are given to him as 'new' titles of sovereignty and where eternal duration is promised to the throne and to the kingship of David.[118] In Isa. 9.1-6 we are not dealing simply with the birth of a new house of David, but above all with *new acts of salvation on the part of God* who renews and restores the old. The skilful composition concludes with an allusion to the energetic 'zeal of the Lord of hosts'. If in this conclusion we were to assume a link with the introductory vision of the *king* Yahweh of hosts on the 'high and exalted throne' in Isa. 6.1-5, we might understand Isa. 6.1–9.6 as a special tradition unit in which the current judgment-eschatological declaration of 7.10-14 might be regarded as a principal peculiarity of the new messianic-eschatological near expectation and where both in this fundamental point and within its framework the old *subordination* of King David to the kingship of Yahweh remains intact. Moreover, in the passage Isa. 11.1-5, which appears linked in a contrasting way with 10.33-34, yet another form of the new messianic-eschatological metaphoric extant, namely, a *tree metaphor*.[119] Even the special images of the 'shoot from the stump of Jesse' and of the 'branch from its roots' in v. 2 stress primarily the radical *new beginning*. Yet at the same time the following verses refer back to old traditions, and especially to the important tradition element of the charismatic endowment of the 'saviours' discussed above.[120]

Third, Isaiah too—like Amos—found followers on account of his new proclamation, perhaps first by means of a special 'Isaiah School' (cf. Isa. 8.16-18), which can possibly be inferred to a certain extent from the passages already mentioned in Isa. 9.1-6 and 11.1-5.

---

118. Cf., e.g., Rohland, 'Die Bedeutung', pp. 234-42; H.W. Wolff, *Frieden ohne Ende: Eine Auslegung von Jesaja 7, 1-17 and 9, 1-6* (Bibl. Stud., 35; Neukirchen–Vluyn: Neukirchener Verlag, 1962); J. Vollmer, 'Zur Sprache von Jesaja 9, 1-6', *ZAW* 80 (1968), pp. 343-50; Kaiser, 'Geschichtliche Erfahrung', p. 446; Wildberger, *Jesaja*, I, pp. 362-89; and H. Seebass, *Herrscherverheissungen im Alten Testament* (BTSt, 19; Neukirchen–Vluyn: Neukirchener Verlag, 1992), pp. 5-17.

119. Cf., e.g., K. Nielsen, *There is Hope for a Tree: The Tree as Metaphor in Isaiah* (JSOTSup, 65; Sheffield: JSOT Press, 1989), pp. 123-44; Seebass, *Herrscherverheissungen*, pp. 18-39; and also Wildberger, *Jesaja*, I, pp. 436-62.

120. Cf., e.g., Rohland, 'Die Bedeutung', pp. 239-42.

Moreover, the complex passage in Mic. 5.1-5[121] might be understood in the light of Isaiah's new proclamation, since its theme is similar to that of Isa. 11.1. The extent to which Jeremiah was dependent on Isaiah is certainly debatable, but it seems obvious that after his caustic accusations and declarations of judgment against the last kings on the throne of David in Jerusalem (21.11–23.4) Jeremiah spoke contrastingly of a 'righteous branch' whom Yahweh will 'raise up for David' and to whom the very striking—and likewise confessional—name יהוה צִדְקֵנוּ, 'YHWH (is) our righteousness' is given, a name which may be directed against the last King Zedekiah and in which judgment and salvation have been united (23.5-6).[122] Furthermore, we must note that in Jer. 23.2-3.4 greater weight is given to the new act of salvation of *Yahweh*, who is introduced here as the *shepherd* of his people. This element further serves as a link with the salvation proclamation of *Ezekiel*, particularly in ch. 34, the 'shepherd chapter', where God himself is a shepherd, but where he will appoint his 'servant David'—which presumably may be regarded as a new title of sovereignty—over his people as 'the only shepherd' (v. 23; cf. Ezek. 37.15-28).[123] On the other hand, in Ezek. 17.22-24 the *tree metaphor* has been used once more in the proclamation of an eschatological near expectation.[124]

It is worth pointing out in this instance, that *in the monarchal time after Isaiah* a more or less clearly profiled messianic-eschatological proclamation was delivered by a number of prophets. In one way it was aimed in an accusatory and judgmental manner against the Davidic kings—as a sort of *theologia crucis davidica*—and in one way it became linked in a salvatio-eschatological manner—although in various forms—with the special Davidic traditions.

In the *period without kings*, during and after the exile, this proclamation changed repeatedly, particularly so inasmuch as it was now unequivocally delivered in a *salvatio-eschatological* way. The fact that

121. Cf. Rohland, 'Die Bedeutung', pp. 243-48; A.S. van der Woude, *Micha* (De Prediking van het OT; Nijkerk: G.F. Callenbach, 1985), pp. 163-73; and Seebass, *Herrscherverheissungen*, pp. 40-52.

122. Cf. W. Rudolph, *Jeremia* (HAT, 1.12; Tübingen: J.C.B. Mohr, 2nd edn, 1958), and Rohland, 'Die Bedeutung', pp. 249-53; see further Ch. 9 above.

123. Cf. W. Zimmerli, *Ezechiel*, II (BKAT, 13.2; Neukirchen–Vluyn: Neukirchener Verlag, 2nd edn, 1979), pp. 825-49, and Rohland, 'Die Bedeutung', pp. 256-62.

124. Cf. Zimmerli, *Ezechiel*, I, pp. 372-90, and Rohland, 'Die Bedeutung', pp. 254-56.

in Isa. 45.1 Yahweh refers uniquely to Cyrus, king of Persia, as 'his anointed one' does not need to be of great significance in this context, for the word presumably became a designation of honour, just like 'my shepherd' in 44.28 (likewise referring to Cyrus) or 'David' in Ezek. 34.23.[125] Moreover, *Deutero-Isaiah* was remarkably cautious in regard to the Davidic-messianic.[126] Yet it is more significant that from now on two different trends run parallel to each other. On the one hand, in a retroactive way the fulfilment of high Davidic-messianic expectation is proclaimed, especially by the prophets *Haggai* and *Zechariah* in the early postexilic period, whereby particular interest was shown in Zerubbabel (Hag. 2.20-23; Zech. 3.8; 4.6-10; and 6.11-13).[127] This 'messianic movement' appears, however, to have petered out, without its significance being forgotten, as is expressed not only in Zechariah 9–14, but also of course in the book of Chronicles (cf. 2 Chron. 6.42).[128] On the other hand, as already has been pointed out above, even in this late work of history the *kingship of Yahweh* was pushed into the foreground to the cost of the Davidic kingship. If the well-known passage in Zech. 9.9 is compared with the similar passage in Zech. 2.14, which refers to Yahweh, one can see clearly the extent to which the royal Messiah is *subordinate to* Yahweh the king. Of course, this is nothing new, but it emerges even more clearly at this time. To the honour of Yahweh, one may now rightly speak of the 'weakness of the Messiah'.[129] 'Actually the throne never stood empty, for Yahweh was king over Israel. The state of affairs was incomplete only inasmuch as God at that time had not placed the kingship into the hands of the

125. Cf., e.g., E. Jenni, 'Die Rolle des Kyros bei Deuter.jesaja', *TZ* 10 (1954), pp. 241-56.

126. Cf. Rohland, 'Die Bedeutung', pp. 263-65.

127. Cf., e.g., A. Bentzen, 'Quelques remarques sur le mouvement messianique parmi les juifs aux environs de l'an 520 avant J.-C.', *RHPR* 10 (1930), pp. 493-503; W.A.M. Beuken, *Haggai-Sacharja 1–8: Studien zur Überlieferungsgeschichte der frühnachexilischen Prophetie* (Studia Semitica Neerlandica, 10; Assen: Van Gorcum, 1967); and M. Sæbø, 'The Relation of Sheshbazzar and Zerubbabel Reconsidered', *SEÅ* 54 (1989), pp. 168-77.

128. See n. 61 above. Cf. also Sæbø, *Sacharja 9–14*; *idem*, 'Chronistische Theologie/Chronistisches Geschichtswerk', *TRE*, VIII, pp. 74-87. Further, Seebass, *Herrscherverheissungen*, pp. 53-68, 69-89.

129. Thus with W.H. Schmidt, 'Die Ohnmacht des Messias: Zur Überlieferungsgeschichte der messianischen Weissagungen im Alten Testament', *KD* 15 (1969), pp. 18-34, now in Struppe (ed.), *Messiasbild*, pp. 67-88.

family upon which his special love had fallen for ever.'[130]

To summarize, one may maintain that within the framework of a prophetic eschatology in Isaiah, in connexion with a special Davidic election tradition in Jerusalem, there also arose a messianic-eschatological proclamation which was later expanded and revised in many different ways. In this proclamation, just as in its alleged Davidic tradition, the Davidic-messianic kingship was always unequivocally subordinate to the kingship of Yahweh.[131]

In conclusion, returning to the first section above, one could now briefly broach again the old problem of *prophecy-fulfilment*. For there it was explained why the customary use of these two linked concepts, so rich in tradition, today is hardly used any more. On the other hand, its significance has not thereby disappeared. For the old assurances to the king, their prophetic proclamation and realization, even of a cultic nature, have always included *promise*; and the expectation of its *fulfilment*—resting in faith—has only increased in the course of time.

Instead of a method that defines it as originating in a late period, one may therefore in a traditio-historical way point out a linking together of words of solemn address and interpretation, expectation and current new interpretation.

'But when the time had fully come...' (Gal. 4.4), one is faced again with 'continuity in change'. In connexion with the birth of a child 'from the house and line of David' (Lk. 2.4) and with the 'messianic self-understanding' of Jesus of Nazareth, a completely new reception and interpretation of the Old Testament image of the Messiah was now acquired in the faith and in the radical Christological new interpretation in early Christianity. 'The eschaton had become history', as Talmon has stressed. 'Therein lies the decisive difference between the Christian conception and the other three messianic ideologies of the Samaritans, of the Pharisees and of the Community of the new covenant which had remained at the stage of unfulfilled hope.'[132]

---

130. Thus Beuken, *Haggai-Sacharja 1-8*, pp. 315-16.

131. For reasons of space, only the *royal* Messiah has been discussed here. The very complex questions regarding the 'Servant of Yahweh' in Deutero-Isaiah or regarding the 'Son of man' in Dan. 7 had to be omitted; but see Ch. 16 below.

132. S. Talmon, 'Typen der Messiaserwartung um die Zeitenwende', in Wolff (ed.), *Probleme biblischer Theologie*, pp. 571-88 (587), repr. in *idem*, *Gesellschaft und Literatur*, pp. 209-24, here 224. Cf. also Waschke, 'Die Frage', p. 329: 'Without promise, Christology would remain a purely religion-historical phenomenon and without history it would be a religious idea'.

Chapter 14

OLD TESTAMENT APOCALYPTIC IN ITS RELATION TO PROPHECY
AND WISDOM: THE VIEW OF GERHARD VON RAD RECONSIDERED

1. *General Remarks*

In his paper for the Old Testament Congress in Edinburgh, 1974, on
'Apocalyptic and Dualistic Thinking', Benedikt Otzen—like Hans-
Peter Müller in Uppsala, 1971—started by presenting Gerhard von
Rad's well-known view on the roots of Old Testament Apocalyptic,
'that the idea of Apocalyptic ought first and foremost to be regarded as
a descendant of Wisdom thinking'.[1]

Commenting on the theory of von Rad, Otzen focused particularly on
the 'dualistic thinking in late Judaism'. In this connexion, he also
extended the horizon of the subject matter by incorporating Qumran
and other extra-biblical material and by differentiating between three
types, or 'aspects', of apocalyptic dualism: In addition to 'an *eschatological dualism* (the present world, under the rule of Beliar, will be
succeeded by a new world under the dominion of God)', which, as he
says, 'is next to the apocalyptic idea on which von Rad concentrated',
Otzen distinguished between 'a *psychological–ethical dualism* (the
nature of man is constituted of two opposite powers or "spirits")' and 'a
cosmo–ethical dualism (man and the world divided into two groups led
respectively by the "prince of light" and the "angel of darkness")'
(p. 147).

It might have been of interest to pursue the important lines of Otzen;
but a procedure of this kind would also have to enclose a broader

1. 'Old Testament Wisdom Literature and Dualistic Thinking in Late Judaism', in *Congress Volume: Edinburgh 1974* (VTSup, 28; Leiden: E.J. Brill, 1975),
pp. 146-57 (146). On various other occasions as well, Otzen has commented on the
phenomenon of Apocalyptic. As for H.-P. Müller, cf. his paper 'Mantische
Weisheit und Apokalyptik', in *Congress Volume: Uppsala 1971* (VTSup, 22; Leiden: E.J. Brill, 1972), pp. 268-93. On G. von Rad see nn. 7-8 below.

religio-historical and ideological context, including not only Qumran[2] and gnostic material but Accadian, Egyptian and other texts as well.[3] Although these broader perspectives remain highly relevant for a proper understanding of the phenomenon of Apocalyptic in general and of individual Apocalypses in particular[4]—and even more so as the scholarly literature on the Apocalyptic has grown vast and variegated in recent years,[5] the strong limits set for the present essay indicate a far more restricted issue. An issue of this kind, however, may be found in Gerhard von Rad's view itself; after all, his specific position was the starting point for many critical comments, not only by Müller and Otzen, as mentioned, but also by other scholars.[6]

2. Cf., i.a., F.G. Martínez, *Qumran and Apocalyptic* (STDJ, 9; Leiden: E.J. Brill, 1992).

3. Cf., i.a., H.S. Kvanvig, *Roots of Apocalyptic: The Mesopotamian Background of the Enoch Figure and of the Son of Man* (WMANT, 61; Neukirchen–Vluyn: Neukirchener Verlag, 1988); and J.C.H. Lebram, 'Apokalyptik/Apokalypsen, II. Altes Testament', *TRE*, III, pp. 192-202, who especially stresses the Egyptian background.

4. Cf. J.J. Collins (ed.), *Apocalypse: The Morphology of a Genre* (Semeia, 14; Missoula, MT: Scholars Press, 1979).

5. Besides standard works like D.S. Russell, *The Method and Message of Jewish Apocalyptic* (London: SCM Press, 1971 [1964]); J.M. Schmidt, *Die jüdische Apokalyptik* (Neukirchen–Vluyn: Neukirchener Verlag, 1969), cf., i.a., W. Baumgarten, 'Ein Vierteljahrhundert Danielforschung', *ThR* NF 11 (1939), pp. 59-83, 125-44, 201-28; O. Plöger, *Theokratie und Eschatologie* (WMANT, 2; Neukirchen–Vluyn: Neukirchener Verlag, 2nd edn, 1963 [1959]; P.D. Hanson, *The Dawn of Apocalyptic: The Historical and Sociological Roots of Jewish Apocalyptic Eschatology* (Philadelphia: Fortress Press, rev. edn, 1979); J.M. Schmidt, 'Forschung zur jüdischen Apokalyptik', *VF* 14 (1969), pp. 44-69; K. Koch, *Ratlos vor der Apokalyptik: Eine Streitschrift über ein vernachlässigtes Gebiet der Bibelwissenschaft* (Gütersloh: Gütersloher Verlagshaus, 1970); K. Koch and J.M. Schmidt (eds.), *Apokalyptik* (WdF, 365; Darmstadt: Wissenschaftliche Buchgesellschaft, 1982); R. North, 'Prophecy to Apocalyptic via Zechariah', in *Congress Volume: Uppsala 1971* (VTSup, 22; Leiden: E.J. Brill, 1972), pp. 47-71; H. Gese, 'Anfang und Ende der Apokalyptik, dargestellt am Sacharjabuch', *ZTK* 70 (1973), pp. 20-49, now in *idem, Vom Sinai zum Zion*, pp. 202-30; J. Barr, 'Jewish Apocalyptic in Recent Scholarly Study', *BJRL* 58 (1975), pp. 9-35; U. Luck, 'Das Weltverständnis in der jüdischen Apokalyptik dargestellt am äthiopischen Henoch und am 4. Esra', *ZTK* 73 (1976), pp. 283-305; I. Willi-Plein, 'Das Geheimnis der Apokalyptik', *VT* 27 (1977), pp. 62-81; also M. Hengel, *Judaism and Hellenism* (London, 1974), esp. pp. 175-218.

6. See, i.a., P. von der Osten-Sacken, *Die Apokalyptik in ihrem Verhältnis zu*

Despite the fact that the view of von Rad has been assessed critically in various ways already, yet there may be still more to be said on this point. And what may be said on this occasion will, for practical reasons, be held within the same framework as that of von Rad, which primarily was the context of the Old Testament (its prophetical and wisdom books besides the book of Daniel) including, however, also the book of Sirach and others of the Old Testament's so-called Apocrypha and Pseudepigrapha. It would be fair first to present briefly the view of von Rad.

2. *The Position of Gerhard von Rad*

Having presented a new explanation of the background and emergence of the Apocalyptic and of the book of Daniel in the second volume of his *Theologie des Alten Testaments* in 1960, Gerhard von Rad revised the chapter on Apocalyptic and reinforced his arguments in its fourth edition (1965).[7] Five years later he expanded and specified his argumentation in a monograph on the Wisdom in the Old Testament.[8]

Discussing the position of von Rad one usually starts directly with the chapter on Apocalyptic in his *Theologie des Alten Testaments*, II (pp. 315ff.). It seems, however, to be more appropriate to start with the

---

Prophetie und Weisheit (ThExh, 157; Munich: Chr. Kaiser Verlag, 1969), who mentions some other critics; cf. also North, 'Prophecy to Apocalyptic', pp. 58-62; further H.D. Betz, 'Das Verständnis der Apokalyptik in der Theologie der Pannenberg-Gruppe', *ZTK* 65 (1968), pp. 257-70, who is mainly discussing with D. Rössler, *Gesetz und Geschichte* (WMANT, 3; Neukirchen–Vluyn: Neukirchener Verlag, 2nd edn, 1962 [1960]); cf. also A. Nissen, 'Tora und Geschichte im Spätjudentum', *NovT* 9 (1967), pp. 241-77.

7.   Von Rad, *Theologie des Alten Testaments*, II, pp. 315-37; cf. the Preface (p. 9): 'Das Kapitel über die "Apokalyptik" habe ich neu geschrieben und seine Hauptthese auf breiterer Basis zu begründen gesucht'; see also n. 10 below. Obviously, von Rad was challenged by early criticism of his controversial position, perhaps not least by that of one of 'his own', cf. R. Rendtorff, 'Geschichte und Überlieferung', in R. Rendtorff and K. Koch (eds.), *Studien zur Theologie der alttestamentlichen Überlieferungen* (Festschrift G. von Rad; Neukirchen Kreis Moers: Neukirchener Verlag, 1961), pp. 81-94, esp. p. 93 n. 36.

8.   G. von Rad, *Weisheit in Israel* (Neukirchen–Vluyn: Neukirchener Verlag, 1970; ET *Wisdom in Israel* [London: SCM Press, 1972]), pp. 337-63, where he discusses *Die Determination der Zeiten*, and especially 'the great change in understanding the history' that Apocalyptic brought about, pp. 347-62.

preceding Epilogue (*Nachwort*, pp. 308-14) where he looks back on the main topic of the volume: the phenomenon and characteristics, traditions and books of Old Testament *Prophecy*.

In this postscript to his study of the Prophecy von Rad first pays attention to the enigmatic fact that relatively early in postexilic time the prophets became silent, and he tries to explain the problem. Among various circumstances that are considered by him von Rad points in particular—with reference to Plöger's *Theokratie und Eschatologie*—to 'the inner religious structure of the postexilic community' (p. 308). He claims, thereby, a deep 'separation' between 'the leading priestly aristocracy of Jerusalem', on the one hand, and 'the prophetic-eschatological expectation', on the other; and his surmise is: 'it is possible that the prophetic-eschatological expectation at this time has for ever emigrated from the theocracy' (p. 308). In this connexion, one might think that whereas the theocracy ended in the Law,[9] von Rad would give his consent to the traditional view that the prophetic-eschatological hope was to end in the Apocalyptic of late postexilic time, or, the other way round, that Apocalyptic was, as has been said, a 'child' of the earlier prophetical eschatology. But that was not at all the case; on the contrary, as will be seen.

Somewhat surprisingly, but perhaps in preparation for the subsequent chapter on the Apocalyptic, von Rad, in the Epilogue, then turns to another and quite different issue, harking back to his initial question of what 'the New' (*das Neue*) of the prophetical movement might have been when it first appeared in old Israel (pp. 15, 309). As for this question that is not only related to the radical novelty of Prophecy but also to its specific character, von Rad argues against the ethical and personalistic way of thinking, typical of the nineteenth century and the literary-critical school's understanding of Prophecy; and he defines positively its unique novelty by relating it to the prophets' dependence on *history*, especially on historical traditions of God's election and salvation (*Heilsgeschichte*) of the people of Israel. Thus, enclosed by a beginning of radical novelty and an end of surprising silence the Prophecy of Israel was first of all—as viewed by von Rad—destined by its varying relation to *history*, especially the people's *Heilsgeschichte*; and that, in particular, became obvious in times of crisis and important turning points in the history of the people. Here was 'its prime

---

9. 'Die letztere [i.e. die Theokratie] mündete dann aus in dem Dienst eines heilsgeschichtslosen, zur absoluten Größe gewordenen Gesetzes' (p. 308).

characteristic' (*ihr wichtigstes Spezifikum*, p. 310).

In this way, then, von Rad had both given a brief summary of the essence of Prophecy—and, probably, also prepared his discussion of the Apocalyptic. For when approaching the *Apocalyptic* as a new phenomenon, in the next chapter, he rather sharply stresses its discontinuity to the earlier Prophecy in Israel; and, instead, he relates it to quite another area of the Old Testament, namely the Wisdom literature, as already indicated. When evaluating this position that has surprised many of his colleagues and provoked much criticism, it may not only be assessed in general terms but one should just as much *analyse von Rad's way of arguing* for his stand.[10]

Gerhard von Rad starts his discussion of the Apocalyptic with a reference to the prophetical end in silence, thus linking back to the preceding Epilogue and underscoring the distance of the Apocalyptic from the former Prophecy. But he adds, immediately, that Israel had not yet ceased from eschatological hope and expectations, or from, as he puts it, 'looking, full of expectation, into the future, and speaking of the still outstanding eschatological fulfilments'. However, this expectation was 'another form of eschatology', its motives being fewer (he mentions as examples the new Jerusalem in Tobit 13–14 and the Messiah in *Psalms of Solomon* 17), its hope being 'standardized' and 'monotone'; it was far off from the earlier 'abundance and movability of the prophetical vision of future'; first of all, whereas the older prophets focused on 'a radical crisis between Yahweh and Israel', this later hope 'opens its friendly gate into a time where Israel lives in obedience to the commandments'; thus, the eschatology 'had now been taken into the conceptions of a conservative Law piety'.[11] But 'surprisingly, the religious hope of Israel' expressed itself 'once again'; that happened in the Apocalyptic, and then 'under quite different conditions and in conceptions of a universal breadth, so far not yet reached'.[12]

10. The chapter on '*Daniel und die Apokalyptik*' (pp. 315-37) has a threefold structure in the fourth edition: (1) Apocalyptic and Wisdom (pp. 315-22), that was now rewritten, (2) Traditio-historical problems of the Apocalyptic (pp. 322-30), that was added at the same time, and (3) Daniel (pp. 322-37). See also n. 7 above.

11. 'Die Gegenstände einer eschatologischen Hoffnung, die sich von der Verkündigung der Propheten noch erhalten haben, sind nunmehr in den Vorstellungskreis einer konservativen Gesetzesfrömmigkeit einbezogen worden' (p. 315).

12. So p. 315: 'unter ganz anderen Voraussetzungen und in Konzeptionen von einer bisher noch nicht erreichten universalen Weite'.

In order to explain these new 'conditions' and 'conceptions' von Rad made an interesting detour. Facing the great difficulties that scholars have for a long time had in defining 'Apocalyptic' adequately, he expresses his dissatisfaction with a 'limiting' definition of it as a mere literary phenomenon[13] as well as with an understanding of it as a name of a specific theological mode of thinking or a spiritual current. Instead of the usual description of it by an enumeration of its general characteristics he exhibits an alternative way, asking for the milieu—*die Träger*—behind this specific thinking and current and its various literary products (p. 316), their *Sitz im Leben*, so to speak. In order to do this, he first calls attention to apocalyptic *titles* like 'wise men' (cf. Dan. 1.3-5, 17; 2.48) and 'scribes' (Enoch and Ezra) that were used of men of specific knowledge related to old books; and then he refers in particular to the Parables (or Similitudes) of Enoch (*1 Enoch* 37–71); according to him, the Parables should more correctly be called 'Wisdom Speeches' (*Weisheitsreden* or rather *Lehrreden*), having the style of the sapiential 'saying', משל.[14] He concludes that 'the roots of the Apocalyptic in the first instance seem to be in the traditions of Wisdom' (p. 317).

When von Rad began the positive part of his discussion by bringing in the titles just mentioned he also made a rather remarkable assertion, claiming that these titles 'offer a first help to the designation of place and essence of the Apocalyptic', or, in his own words: 'eine erste Hilfe zur Orts- und Wesensbestimmung der Apokalyptik bietet sich an...' (p. 316). His combination of the words *Ort* and *Wesen* in this way, however, may be regarded as most questionable; but it may have given him a 'point rod' for the shift from a main prophetical to a main sapiential explanation of the Apocalyptic's background.

After this 'first move' he presents other important elements; first of all, he focuses on insight and knowledge (*Erkenntnis*). On the one hand, this is operative in the realm of universal history (referring to *Ass. Mos.* 12.4-5 as an example) as well as in the divine determination; on the other hand, it is effective in the nature and social order surrounding men (p. 317). The most significant here is apparently the notion of

---

13. So p. 316; see also his critical comment, p. 330, n. 28; cf. n. 4 above, and Barr, 'Jewish Apocalyptic', pp. 14-19.

14. So p. 317; see, i.a., Russell, *Method and Message*, pp. 51-52 and *passim*; cf. also E. Hammershaimb, 'Om lignelser og billedtaler i de gammeltestamentlige Pseudepigrafer', *SEÅ* 40 (1975), pp. 36-65.

universal history, and it may be just this notion that has had the greatest methodical consequences for his theory, including the question of eschatology.[15]

For, regarding the Apocalyptic's intense interest in the *eschata,* which remain a key point in the matter, von Rad denies any connexion between the *eschata* of the prophets and the *eschata* of the Apocalyptic; a linkage of this kind is to him simply 'not possible', as he most unreservedly says: 'Aber das ist nicht möglich' (p. 319). The main reason for his surprisingly negative assertion seems to lie in the question of *history*, since, in his opinion, there did not exist any connectedness between the apocalyptic understanding of history as universal history and 'the specific salvatio-historical anchoring of the message of the prophets' (p. 320); and even more so since 'the salvatio-historical rudiment of the older concept of history was abandoned (*preisgegeben*) in Apocalyptic' (p. 321). Here, one may be at the very core of the position of von Rad.

When he further, in the fourth edition of his *Theologie des Alten Testaments,* II, added a section on 'traditio-historical problems of the Apocalyptic' (pp. 322-30) he did not trace possible lines back to the prophetical eschatology of some kind, but the object of his interest and discussion was the tradition background of some *Wisdom* themes and characteristics only.

In this connexion, von Rad focuses, more generally, on the highly learned character of the Apocalyptic, on its *Gelehrsamkeit,* which is lightly observable.[16] Then, in particular, he deals with basic theological elements like the periodizing of history and theodicy, as well as with literary elements like exhortative and catechetical style (pp. 324-26), and he ends up with the fundamental question of what the 'specific apocalyptic' might be. As for this key question, he first asks for a revision of what may be regarded as the most characteristic of Apocalyptic; and, after having ruled out some traditional and well-known aspects as

15. G. von Rad makes another remarkable—and questionable—combination of words (italicized here) when he in this connexion says (p. 318): 'So rundet sich also in der Apokalyptik durch *die Einbeziehung der Universalgeschichte und des eschatologischen Aspektes* das enzyklopädische Bemühen der Weisheit zu einer geradezu hybrid anmutenden universalen Gnosis.'

16. Cf., i.a., G. Hölscher, 'Die Entstehung des Buches Daniel', *TSK* 92 (1919), pp. 136ff.; and von der Osten-Sacken, *Apokalyptik*, p. 9.

being the most specific of Apocalyptic,[17] he positively defines 'the question of the final actualizing of older traditions and methods' (*die Frage der letzten Aktualisierung der älterer Stoffe und Methoden*) to be most characteristic; and he adds: 'Here, first of all, would the Apocalyptic be conceivable' (p. 327).

In this way 'the specific eschatological aspects' are coming up again. Now von Rad is, on the one hand, referring to the well-known fact that traditional Wisdom 'has not been occupied with eschatological matters'.[18] On the other hand, facing this quandary for his theory he relates the eschatological aspects once more to the question of *history*. Uniting the different areas of history and eschatology, then, von Rad asks—as he did in respect of Prophecy—for the specific *New* of Apocalyptic; and he finds it in 'the apocalyptic concept of history' as related to 'the end of history', or, to use his own concluding words: 'But with its vision of the end of history, of a judgment of the world and of a redemption the Apocalyptic, after all, brings something new'.[19] The consequences of this are rather far-reaching, for von Rad contends that this has brought about not only 'the notion of the unity of history' but also an 'eschatologizing of the Wisdom' (p. 329)—a formulation that may be regarded disputable.

Whereas von Rad, in the first two sections of the chapter on the Apocalyptic, had outlined both general and specific characteristics of the apocalyptic phenomenon, in the third section, finally, he applied his main viewpoints to the special form and message of the book of Daniel (pp. 330-37).[20] Contrasting also Daniel to the older prophetical books

17. His list here (p. 327) is most noteworthy: 'Spezifisch apokalyptisch ist weder das Esoterische, noch die Periodisierung der Geschichte, noch die Vorstellung von der Transzendenz der Heilsgüter, noch die Auslegung kanonischer Schriften, noch die Pseudonymität, noch die Auslegung von Traumgesichten, noch die Berichte von Himmelsreisen, noch der Geschichtsbericht im Weissagungsstil.'

18. Cf. von der Osten-Sacken, *Apokalyptik*, p. 9, also (n. 3) with reference to P. Vielhauer in Hennecke and Schneemelcher, *Neutestamentliche Apokryphen*, II, p. 420.

19. So p. 328. This is further discussed in his *Weisheit in Israel*, pp. 347-62; see n. 8 above.

20. On the extensive literature to the book of Daniel, see commentaries like those by O. Plöger, *Das Buch Daniel* (KAT, 18; Gütersloh: Gütersloher Verlagshaus, 1965); N.W. Porteous, *Daniel* (OTL; London: SCM Press, 2nd edn, 1979); L.F. Hartman and A.A. Di Lella, *Daniel* (AB; New York: Doubleday, 1978); M. Delcor, *Le livre de Daniel* (Paris, 1971), and cf. esp. J.C.H. Lebram,

(pp. 330-31), he focused again on the question of *history*, especially on the 'end' or 'fulfilment' of history, *die Geschichtsvollendung* (p. 333). By all this, however, he seems to be moderating, to some extent, his general position worked out in the view of later Apocalypses.[21] On this two remarks may be made.

First, von Rad concedes that 'the real issue of the later Apocalypses, the end of history, is only preluded in the Daniel narratives'; their horizon is still of an 'inner historical' and not yet of any 'transcendental' character.[22] In other words, the distance of the apocalyptic traditions of the book of Daniel to the eschatological parts of some earlier prophetical books may not be as great and deep as von Rad otherwise has maintained.

Second, von Rad points to another specific trait of apocalyptic style in the book of Daniel, that may have the same effect as the feature just mentioned, namely, elements of creative reinterpretation of older prophetic traditions which are apparent in some instances of the book. He refers in particular to the interpretation of '70 years' in Jer. 25.11-12 and 29.10 as '70 weeks of years' (Dan. 9.24, 25-26; also 12.7), whereby he finds a new type of scriptural exegesis.[23] As for Daniel 11 he even considers describing this chapter as an 'Isaiah pesher'.[24] Again, one gets the impression that the apocalyptic linkage to older prophetic traditions obviously seems to have been stronger than von Rad

'Perspektiven der gegenwärtigen Danielforschung', *JSJ* 5 (1975), pp. 1-33; *idem*, 'Daniel/Danielbuch und Zusätze', *TRE*, VIII, pp. 325-49; see, further, n. 5 above.

21. Cf. the references in the two preceding sections; see also his *Weisheit in Israel*, p. 348 n. 14.

22. So p. 333: 'Das eigentliche Thema der späteren Apokalypsen, die Geschichtsvollendung, wird von den Danielerzählungen nur präludiert', and he goes on to say: 'Das Problem der Weltreiche, ihrer übergroßen Macht, ihres Verschwindens und das Auftauchen neuer Reiche, die an ihrer Stelle treten, klingt schon deutlich an; aber der Horizont ist doch noch ein innergeschichtlicher. Erst in den Traumvisionen von Dan. 2 und 7 führt uns der Apokalyptiker an den äußersten Rand, wo sich die Geschichte mit der Transzendenz berührt.'

23. So p. 335, where i.a., he says: 'Im Zuge dieser Interpretation altangesehener Texte hat sich diesen Apokalyptikern in hermeneutischer Hinsicht eine ganz neue Möglichkeit des Verstehens eröffnet, nämlich die eines zweiten Schriftsinnes... Das ist wohl der erste Beleg jener Schriftexegese, die für das Judentum wie das junge Christentum von so großer Bedeutung werden sollte.'

24. So p. 336 n. 39, with reference to I.L. Seeligmann, 'Voraussetzungen der Midraschexegese', in *Congress Volume: Copenhagen 1953* (VTSup, 1; Leiden: E.J. Brill, 1953), pp. 150-81, esp. 171.

generally was ready to admit. Nevertheless, his exegetical honesty caused him to focus also on elements that *per se* would weaken his particular theory.

3. *In the Background of Old Testament Apocalyptic*: *The Traditio-historical Convergence of Prophecy and Wisdom*

In respect of Gerhard von Rad's view on biblical—and early post-biblical—Apocalyptic many questions have been raised, as was partly also the case by the preceding presentation of it. A further assessment of his position may be both positive and critical.

First of all, it has to be said positively indeed that Gerhard von Rad has shown a great exegetical sensibility in his discussing of the Apocalyptic. In different ways and most effectively he managed to highlight significant aspects of it, primarily aspects that are related to its learned character, its *Gelehrsamkeit*. In all probability, there were significant relations between the realm of Wisdom thinking and teaching, on the one hand, and the literary and theological phenomenon of Apocalyptic as well as of concrete Apocalypses, on the other. It will remain positive that von Rad has definitely put this question on the agenda of modern scholarship. But, at the same time, it will remain a matter of discussion whether parts of his arguing as well as his final conclusion and main standpoint are really capable of standing their ground.

Critically, it has already been indicated in some preceding remarks that there are problematic points and even tensions in the arguing of Gerhard von Rad. Without going into details the critical focus may now be put on three questionable issues of his position. Thereby, von Rad may even be set against von Rad—as when Sigmund Mowinckel, methodically, wanted 'to play off Gunkel against Gunkel'.

First, in the triangle of Apocalyptic, Prophecy and Wisdom, where definition and description are controversial regarding each of them as well as regarding their mutual relations, von Rad made some sharp *contrasts* along the axis of Apocalyptic and Prophecy, whereas regarding Apocalyptic and Wisdom he brought into positive focus many possible links. Likewise, he also contrasted the *eschata* of Prophecy and Apocalyptic respectively, while, on the other hand, he even spoke of an 'eschatologizing of the Wisdom', as referred to above. Similarly, he made contrasts in respect of the notion of 'history' in Prophecy and in Apocalyptic. However, with regard to this tendency of contrasting or 'separation' between Prophecy and Apocalyptic—apart from an obvious lack of proper balance of Prophecy and Wisdom—one may ask: with what positive rights has it been pursued?

The key question will in any case be: Given the fact that Apocalyptic created new concepts of eschatology and history—and much is in favour of that—against what background or on what terms did it do it? What was in this respect the *matrix* of Apocalyptic? Was it—to present but this alternative—that of Prophecy or that of Wisdom? Keeping in mind that Prophecy and Wisdom really were like two incommensurable entities, it will not be passed over, on the one hand, that there was in Old Testament Wisdom neither any sense of prophetic eschatology—as also admitted by von Rad—nor any specific relation to history as it was so typical of Prophecy,[25] and, on the other hand, that there were both connexions and deep differences between prophetic and apocalyptic concepts of history and eschatology. Therefore, the essential question, both methodically and substantially, may be raised whether it would be likely or proper to explain the existing differences—not to speak of points of resemblance—on the axis of Prophecy: Apocalyptic by means of the most distant and different current, namely, the Wisdom tradition.

Second, connected with von Rad's tendency of contrasting Prophecy and Apocalyptic is his focus on the *end of Israelite Prophecy*, as has been demonstrated above. However, its value as evidence for the contrast—if not more—between Prophecy and Apocalyptic is rather restricted. For, there is a considerable difference between Prophecy as a literary phenomenon—which indeed ended in silence in relatively early postexilic time—and Prophecy as a spiritual current, that did not come to an end, as also von Rad admitted, but proceeded as a live and productive traditio-historical mainstream.

The last aspect presents as great a problem as the first one; and it is just this aspect that is of greatest interest in this connexion. However, although Otto Plöger, Odil Hannes Steck and other scholars have made meritorious efforts at exploring the spiritual currents of later postexilic times,[26] this part of Israel's theological history is still, to a great extent,

25. Cf., i.a., von Rad, *Theologie des Alten Testaments*, I, pp. 466-67; H.H. Schmid, *Wesen und Geschichte der Weisheit* (BZAW, 101; Berlin: Alfred Töpelmann, 1966); somewhat differently, H.-P. Müller, *Ursprünge und Strukturen alttestamentlicher Weisheit* (BZAW, 109; Berlin: Alfred Töpelmann, 1969), esp. pp. 69-128.

26. Cf. Plöger, *Theokratie*; O.H. Steck, 'Das Problem theologischer

veiled by oblivion; and because of this it also represents a standing challenge for the study of the Old Testament. Therefore, it remains really enigmatic that von Rad, the master of biblical traditio-historical study, did not focus more strongly on an exploration of a possible traditio-historical integration instead of segregation of Prophecy and Apocalyptic. It might, however, be dependent on the next basic point of his theory.

Third, the most significant part of von Rad's view on the Apocalyptic may be found in his understanding and use of the notion of *history*. That is in fact not unexpected. For his concept of the history of Israel, as told and interpreted in the Old Testament and closely connected with its creative tradition history, was the structuring basis of his *Theologie des Alten Testaments* as a whole. The foundation of his historical conception was laid in its first volume where the sacral—salvatio-historical—traditions of the people are discussed. In the second volume of his *Theologie des Alten Testaments* von Rad, most remarkably, was able to integrate also the radical message of the prophets in his historical conception—but not the Apocalyptic; that was 'not possible'.

In this connexion too, a critical question may be raised. For the prophets' varying dependence on Israel's sacral-historical traditions was not at all simple but rather a very complicated matter. As von Rad has convincingly demonstrated, the prophets were not only dependent on various sacral traditions of the people but they also displayed their great independence of them, and even more so as they reinterpreted them twice, and each time differently. First, they opposed them radically; then, they renewed them just as radically, in view of the future. By the radical message of the prophets from Amos to Ezekiel the sacral traditions of Israel were in many ways reshaped; and no one has demonstrated that more clearly than von Rad. In this complex way the prophetic eschatology was 'born'. Would then, one may ask, another new radical *metamorphosis* be so 'impossible' in the 'melting-pot' of late postexilic Apocalyptic?

Strömungen in nachexilischer Zeit', *EvT* 28 (1968), pp. 445-58; *idem*, 'Strömungen theologischer Tradition im Alten Israel', in *idem*, *Wahrnehmungen Gottes im Alten Testament: Gesammelte Studien* (TBü, 70; Munich: Chr. Kaiser Verlag, 1982), pp. 291-317; *idem*, *Der Abschluss der Prophetie im Alten Testament: Ein Versuch zur Frage der Vorgeschichte des Kanons* (BTSt, 17; Neukirchen–Vluyn: Neukirchener Verlag, 1991); see also E. Janssen, *Das Gottesvolk und seine Geschichte* (Neukirchen–Vluyn: Neukirchener Verlag, 1971).

Finally, it may be asserted that an alternative way of this kind in fact
can be found; and, thereby, one may use just the methodological
approach that Gerhard von Rad as exegete so masterly practised: the
traditio-historical. It seems indeed 'possible' to build a traditio-historical bridge over the gulf that has been dug between earlier Prophecy and
later Apocalyptic—and the way, or bridge, may lead via the long and
complex traditio-historical process of *convergence of the eschatology of
Prophecy and the learnedness of Wisdom.*

In some studies I have tried to make a 'development' of this kind
probable.[27] Without rehearsing all the details on this occasion, however,
some main lines that have special regard to the complex tradition process of prophetic eschatology may be drawn in rough outline.

First, as for the specific *phraseology,* it may be observed that in
Daniel 8–12 there is a frequent and formulaic use of the words קֵץ and
אַחֲרִית in the sense of 'end'/'end time', used not only alone, but also in
combinations like עֵת קֵץ 'time of [the] end' (8.17; 11.35, 40; 12.4, 9)
and קֵץ הַיָּמִים 'end of the days/time' (12.13) or בְּאַחֲרִית הַיָּמִים 'at the
end of the days/time' (2.28; 10.14).[28] The words are essential in the
framework of Danielic and (early) apocalyptic understanding of time
and history, especially as they regard the history's character of
'endtime'. But these and similar terms are scarcely characterized adequately as 'standardized' or 'monotone';[29] a traditio-historical perspective evaluation may be more appropriate to the subject.

In his criticism of von Rad's theory Peter von der Osten-Sacken has
started the traditio-historical a long way before the book of Daniel to
the preceding prophetic tradition by referring, in general, the phraseology of these words in Daniel 8–12 to the technical term יוֹם יהוה, 'the
day of Yahweh', which usually has been regarded as the most significant term of prophetic eschatology,[30] and, in particular, to Ezekiel 7
(p. 42). But in this he might have moved further backwards, for already
Ezekiel 7 represents a later stage of a prophetic tradition that began in a
most special manner in Amos 8.2. Here, as part of the Amosian 'vision

---

27. See above Ch. 13, 'On the Relationship between "Messianism" and "Eschatology"'.

28. See Sæbø, 'Eschaton und Eschatologia', p. 330.

29. Cf. von Rad, *Theologie des Alten Testaments*, II, p. 315, above p. 231.

30. Von der Osten-Sacken, *Apokalyptik*, pp. 39-43 and 35-38; cf. Preuss (ed.),
Eschatologie; Sæbø, 'יוֹם *jôm*', *ThWAT*, III, cols. 583-85; see also above Ch. 13.

cycle', the radical doom message of Amos was given in the form of a unique pun or 'a sound-play on the keywords "summer fruit" (קָיִץ) and "end" (קֵץ)',[31] whereby the metaphorically founded doom message of an 'end' for the people ('the end has come for my people, Israel') was, furthermore, extended by a direct proclamation: 'I will forgive them no longer (לֹא עוֹד)'. In this way, the prophetic preaching of an *eschaton* started as an actual doom message, as a radical 'end'-preaching, including also other elements among which the יום יהוה, 'the day of Yahweh' in Amos 5.18-20 became most effective. Substantially, this preaching meant a 'termination' of the people's present religious status and existence founded on the old sacral traditions; and in form and character it was indisputably *kerygmatic*. The case was similar, although each time different, in the preaching of Hosea, Isaiah and Micah.

If, further, this kind of original *kerygmatic eschatology* is compared with the terminologically similar and yet quite different units in Ezekiel 7 (A: 7.2-4, B: 7.5-27, with many signs of being reworked),[32] one will recognize that the prophetic tradition so far had developed in a way that is most interesting and significant in this connexion.[33] Whereas Amos 8 (and 5) were short and plain, Ezekiel 7 is characterized by a baroque repleteness of relatively synonymous words for 'end', 'day' and 'time'; it is obvious that Amos had set a standard and had had a most effective *Wirkungsgeschichte,* and that in later times the eschatological way of preaching became far more *learned* than before, although its direct actuality was not lost.[34] The prophetic eschatology had changed considerably from having an actual *kerygmatic* to having a more or less systematized *didactic* character. The eschatology was not only an actual preaching but a *received theological teaching* as well.

As also a positive preaching of renewed salvation for Israel developed, especially in Deutero-Isaiah who, inter alia, used the term אחרית

---

31. So J.L. Mays, *Amos* (OTL; London: SCM Press, 1969), p. 141.

32. See especially the scrutiny of this text by Zimmerli, *Ezechiel*, I, pp. 158-86.

33. On the prophetic tradition in general, cf. Mowinckel, *Prophecy and Tradition*; Knight, *Rediscovering the Traditions of Israel*.

34. Cf. Rudolph, *Joel–Amos–Obadja–Jona*, p. 239 n. 6: 'Dieses aus der Vision herausgewachsene בא הקץ hat Schule gemacht: Ez 7,2.6; Gn 6,13 P (vgl. Hab 2,3). In der Apokalyptik wird קץ(ה) geradezu der Terminus technicus für die Endkatastrophe…'; see also Zimmerli, *Ezechiel*, I, pp. 169-70.

of a new future for the people (Isa. 41.22; 46.10; also Jer. 29.11; 31.17, cf. *BHS*), and by Zechariah who changed the old 'no longer' (לֹא עוֹד) of Amos 8.2 into a positive 'again' (עוֹד; Zech. 1.17, cf. 2.16), and thereby revived some older traditions, another aspect of prophetic eschatology grew stronger: A more advanced *systematization* of the eschatological themes and metaphors, attested in later texts like, first of all, Isaiah 24–27, Ezekiel 38–39 as well as in the book of Joel, generated also a trend of *dramatization* of the 'end time' crises and struggles that in various forms is exhibited in Zechariah 12–14.[35] Closely connected with the conception of a dramatic 'end' of history was further the concept of a *periodization* of history; and here as well Deutero-Isaiah was productive, as when he contrasted the 'former things' to the coming 'new things' (e.g. Isa. 41.21-29; 42.9; 43.18-19).[36]

The long and complex growth of a prophetic eschatology of this character may mainly have developed within the prophetic movement and tradition itself as well as on the Prophecy's own terms; and, as a result, the *learned* character of eschatology became considerably enhanced. To a great extent, then, eschatology developed as a *didactic—and also intellectual—tradition*. The transmitting of it did not, however, preclude an actual preaching or an existential–personal engagement.

Second, this inner-prophetic development of eschatology in the direction of a greater *learnedness*, including an increasing systematizing and theorizing tendency—in direction of a sort 'scholasticism', may have attracted themes and subjects that otherwise were typical of the Wisdom tradition; in this way, then, the learned trend of the younger eschatology may have been directly fostered by this tradition. Here, special attention may be paid to the important role that *creation* motives played in the preaching of Deutero-Isaiah, focusing not only on the God of

---

35. Cf., i.a., B. Otzen, *Studien über Deuterosacharja* (AThD, 6; Copenhagen: Munksgaard, 1964), pp. 199-212; H.-M. Lutz, *Jahwe, Jerusalem und die Völker: Zur Vorgeschichte von Sach 12,1-8 und 14,1-5* (WMANT, 27; Neukirchen–Vluyn: Neukirchener Verlag, 1968); Sæbø, *Sacharja 9–14*, esp. pp. 252-317; see, further, studies by Plöger, Hanson, North, Gese and Willi-Plein, listed in n. 5 above.

36. Cf. von Rad, *Theologie des Alten Testaments*, II, pp. 254-60; also C.R. North, 'The "Former Things" and the "New Things" in Deutero-Isaiah', in H.H. Rowley (ed.), *Studies in Old Testament Prophecy* (Festschrift T.H. Robinson; Edinburgh: T. & T. Clark, 1950), pp. 111-26.

Israel as their Saviour, praised for his mighty deeds in the salvation history, but also as the omnipotent Creator (cf., e.g., Isa. 40.12-31; 42.5; 43.1; 44.24; 45.11-25; 48.12-15; 51.9-10; 54.5); so, he is also the Lord of the history (cf., i.a., Isa. 43.9-10; 55.10-11).[37]

Third, there was also a beginning of a *transcendentalizing* construct in later eschatology, as when Zechariah in the first of his 'night visions', 1.8-17, received insights into the heavenly world, mediated through an *angelus interpres*; thereby, it is revealed to him what God will do and bring to pass—although, for the present, 'the whole earth is tranquil and at rest' (v. 11).[38] In this and similar traits there is an idea of divine determination of time that is really near to the apocalyptic understanding of history; and, further, the distance from Daniel as the 'wise' receiver of divine revelation of 'secret' (Aram. *rāz*[39]) in a 'night vision' (Dan. 2.19) is in fact not far. Even an esoteric tendency may here be near at hand.

In conclusion, it may be asserted that in the prophetic eschatology of the Old Testament, especially in its later stages, there was a progressively stronger tendency of *learnedness* that represented a specific tradition of *sapientializing*, like the 'intellectual tradition' of Wisdom,[40] and that the new phenomenon of Danielic Apocalyptic was created and developed in the matrix of this learned or *didactic eschatology*.

37. Cf Rendtorff, 'Die theologische Stellung des Schöpfungsglaubens bei Deuterojesaja'; von Rad, *Theologie des Alten Testaments*, II, pp. 250-53, in his treatment of Deutero-Isaiah; O.H. Steck, 'Deuterojesaja als theologischer Denker', *KD* 15 (1969), pp. 280-93, now in *idem*, *Wahrnehmungen Gottes*, pp. 204-20; von der Osten-Sacken, *Apokalyptik*, pp. 53-54.

38. See further the theologically significant description by von Rad, *Theologie des Alten Testaments*, II, pp. 296-98.

39. Cf. M. Sæbø, 'סוֹד *sōd* Geheimnis', *THAT*, II, cols. 144-48.

40. Cf. R.N. Whybray, *The Intellectual Tradition in the Old Testament* (BZAW, 135; Berlin: Alfred Töpelmann, 1974); G.T. Sheppard, *Wisdom as a Hermeneutical Construct: A Study in the Sapientializing of the Old Testament* (BZAW, 151; Berlin: Alfred Töpelmann, 1980).

Part IV
FROM PLURIFORM TRADITION HISTORY TO THEOLOGICAL UNITY

Chapter 15

FROM COLLECTIONS TO BOOK: A NEW APPROACH TO THE HISTORY
OF TRADITION AND REDACTION OF THE BOOK OF PROVERBS

In modern biblical research—particularly in the past 30 years—there
has been a strongly growing interest in the wisdom literature of the Old
Testament and of its literary context in the ancient Near East. Much of
the study in this field has been concentrated on the book of Proverbs—
both its text and various literary forms, its social background and its
theological characteristics, and also its composite character of being a
collection of collections.[1] The last issue, however, seems to be paid less
attention and consideration than the others mentioned, although
recently some scholars have focused more on the questions of composition and final shape of the book than was usual earlier. In view of the
future scrutiny of the book these questions should be given higher priority; in this brief essay attention can only be focused on some of
them—primarily some basic methodological ones.

1. The Main Collections of the Book

That the book of Proverbs is a collection that embodies separate and
different literary units is generally agreed upon and needs no discussion. The problems—and the lack of agreement—start when one asks
for an accurate description of the literary character of the individual
unit, and, first of all, examines the question how the different units

---

1. Among numerous contributions in the recent study of the book cf. von Rad,
Weisheit in Israel; H.-J. Hermisson, *Studien zur israelitischen Spruchweisheit*
(WMANT, 28; Neukirchen–Vluyn: Neukirchener Verlag, 1968); J.L. Crenshaw
(ed.), *Studies in Ancient Israelite Wisdom* (New York: Ktav, 1976). See
C. Westermann, *Forschungsgeschichte zur Weisheitsliteratur 1950–1990* (Stutt-
gart, 1991); R.N. Whybray, *The Book of Proverbs: A Survey of Modern Study*
(Leiden: E.J. Brill, 1995).

which make up the final shape of the book, are related to each other. This question seems to be the most neglected one and has hardly had any substantial impact on the exposition of the book; generally, the units are treated separately, as disintegrated parts.

The separation of the main units starts usually with the superscriptions of the book (1.1; 10.1; 24.23; 25.1; 30.1; 31.1). They are different in kind; and there are parts—like the concluding acrostic composition 31.10-31—which have no superscription at all; 22.17 is a special case where a reconstruction is needed. But also with limitations like these the superscriptions have proven to be most useful for the discerning of the main units, and even more so as their indications match with decisive shifts in style of differing literary forms. That being the case, the first main unit, chs. 1–9, is dominated by instructions and admonitions (using the verb mainly in the imperative) and also by longer speeches, partly by a personified wisdom. The second unit, chs. 10–22.16, which forms the central bulk of the book, is gnomic in character; here the single, short sentence, the 'proverb', which simply states a matter (sometimes without using a verb) represents the basic element. The third unit, 22.17–24.22, also known as an Israelite parallel to the Wisdom book of Amenemope (particularly in 22.17–23.11), has again the admonitory instruction style; while the short fourth unit, 24.23-34, is composite in form, showing both sentence, instruction and also narrative style. The second bulk of gnomic character makes up the fifth unit, chs. 25–29. The division of the two last chapters (30–31) is a matter of discussion; they may be divided into four parts: (6) 30.1-6, with 'The words of Agur'; (7) 30.7-33, which is a collection of numerical sayings; (8) 31.1-9 with 'The instruction received by Lemuel'; and (9) 31.10-31, a 'poem' of a good wife. In the LXX the units following the third one have a different order (see §4 below). All units, then, are collections of minor units, compositions or elements; the exact subdivision may be discussed; most notable is the division of the second unit into two: (a) chs. 10–15; and (b) chs. 16–22.16, which may be argued for with some reason.[2]

This state of affairs does not only display the complexity of the book, but challenges an explanation of its possible unity. It may be methodologically exposing, in this connexion, to observe and compare various ways in which scholars have made references to the collections and

2. See esp. U. Skladny, *Die ältesten Spruchsammlungen in Israel* (Göttingen: Vandenhoeck & Ruprecht, 1962).

thus to the composite character of the book of Proverbs; from the recent literature three different approaches may quite briefly illustrate the case. First, recently, Otto Plöger has divided and arranged his commentary, according to the three Solomon-superscriptions in 1.1; 10.1 and 25.1, into three parts; he regards the units, 1, 2 and 5 to be the basic ones, to which the others have been attached as later addenda.[3] In this way—that perhaps may be classified as a literary-critical one—the gnomic 'Solomon' parts have been focused, but not the whole complexity of the book, nor the interrelations of the two main literary forms in the book. Second, W. McKane has, quite in another way, focused on the form-historical diversity of the book, and he too has divided his commentary into three parts, in accordance with the book's main literary forms across the collections: the 'instruction genre'; the 'sentence literature'; and finally, the 'poems and numerical sayings' of the two last chapters. He maintains that there exists 'no context in the sentence literature', and he adopts a classification of this material of the book into three different classes of content (from 'secular' to 'religious' sayings) and examines them separately.[4] With his rather 'atomistic' methodical procedure McKane breaks up the existing order of the proverbs and disregards the factual composition of the book and its collections; and this is done although he admits that in the sentence literature 'there are editorial principles of different kinds according to which sentences are grouped'.[5] Third, B.S. Childs has—contrary to McKane—urged hard on 'a more profound understanding of the present text'. Critical to research that only focuses on the 'pre-history' of the text, he calls for a greater attention to the 'final text' as 'the canonical shape of Proverbs', and he detects an intentional editorial work in the superscriptions, in the chs. 1–9 as a 'framework' and a 'hermeneutical guide' for the rest of the book, and also in 30.5-6. Along with McKane, on the other hand, Childs counterposes chs. 1–9 and chs. 10–29, which he discusses quite briefly; and he states in this latter part: 'There is no significant ordering of the individual proverbs into larger groups'.[6] Likewise, G. von Rad asserts that there is a 'great gap' (*grosse Kluft*) between these two blocks of the book.[7]

3. Plöger, *Sprüche Salomos*.
4. McKane, *Proverbs: A New Approach*.
5. McKane, *Proverbs: A New Approach*, p. 10.
6. Childs, *Introduction to the Old Testament*, pp. 545-59, esp. p. 555.
7. Von Rad, *Theologie des Alten Testaments*, I, p. 455.

2. *Some Minor Compositions*

Quite in contrast to this it may be contended that in the present situation of study the fundamental issue at stake is to determine whether a bridging of the formal and theological gap between the different parts of the book, especially between the units 1 and 2, might be possible, at least to some extent. It will be most challenging to start with the proverbs of unit 2.

By a comparison of the units 1 and 2, chs. 1–9 and chs. 10–22.16, it is truly the differences between them that at first arouse one's interest. For a long period of time one has observed the formal contrasts between the mainly longer compositions of the first unit and the apparently arbitrary sequence of independent and 'autonomous' sentences in the second. And when von Rad stressed 'the great gap' between chs. 1–9 and chs. 10–29, it was to him not only a 'gap' in a formal sense, but also at the same time a 'gap' between two different types of wisdom, namely, the empirical wisdom of chs. 10–29 and the wisdom dominated by theological reflection in chs. 1–9 (he opposed, however, a distinction between so-called 'secular' and 'religious' wisdom). But a greater differentiation is desirable.

There are, to a certain extent, in the sequences of proverbs in chs. 10–22.16 clear signs of a creative and systematizing work that has generated small compositions which may be called *miniature collections* of proverbs.

In ch. 10 the introductory verse presents the addressee and object for the teaching and education of wise men: the 'wise son', contrasted to his negative counterpart, the 'foolish son'; the same pair of persons are also in v. 8. The verses in between, vv. 2-7, show a remarkable structure: the middle verses, 4-5, have poverty and richness as their theme.

> Careless work makes a man poor,
> whereas diligent effort brings wealth.
> A son who gathers (fruit) in summer shows intelligence,
> but a son who sleeps at harvest is a disgrace.[8]

It is the challenge of this double sentence that it lies in a man's hand to become rich or poor; but becoming rich requires prudence and foresight—in one word, practical wisdom—contrary to laziness that causes poverty. The verses around these core sentences, vv. 2-3 and 6-7,

---

8. Scott, *Proverbs: Ecclesiastes*, pp. 81 (vv. 4-5) and p. 82 (v. 22).

however, have quite another character and 'message'; they are stamped by ordinary Israelite piety and theology, stating first that 'the Lord does not let the righteous go hungry' (v. 3a), and then that his 'blessings are on the head of the righteous' (v. 6a). The kernel saying on poverty and richness in vv. 4-5 is in line with similar sayings in, for instance, 12.24 and 13.4—but without the same framing as in 10.4-5. At this point it is significant to note that the frame of the enclosing verses in 10.2-3, 6-7, wrapped around a piece of traditional wisdom (vv. 4-5), attributes to the traditional saying *a new context* that effects its original meaning. The meaning of the frame is explicitly expressed in a later statement of the chapter (v. 22a):

> It is the blessing of Yahweh that makes a man rich,
> and painful toil can add no more.

This meaning runs contrary to the meaning of the kernel. The frame, then, does not only function as a 'hermeneutical guide', but represents a *reinterpretation* of an element of old wisdom tradition.

This small composition, to which also vv. 1 and 8 may belong as the last, outer part of the frame, is a real masterpiece of traditio-historical work which displays the live and creative process of tradition: *around a nucleus of an element of wisdom teaching a cyclic composition is skilfully woven that gives the older element a new setting, and thereby, to some extent, even a new meaning*. The traditors of the wisdom teaching were not neutral bearers of the tradition, but creatively they gave a new shape to it—which eventually could also become its final one. In their activity they combined empirical insight, and knowledge of a general character with religious and ethical tenets they shared with the people they belonged to.

The position of the *mini-composition* 10.1-8 is a special one, since it may be regarded to be the introduction to the most prominent 'Solomon-collection' (chs. 10–22.16). But its evidence for intentional traditio-historical or editorial work in the book of Proverbs is not exceptional. There are particular sequences and minor collections of a different kind in the following chapters, often connected with special themes or motifs like the frequent polarization of the reputable 'righteous' and the 'wicked' (e.g. 10.27-32; 11.3-11, 30-31; a parallel to the polarity between 'wise' and 'foolish') or the importance of proper (wise) speaking and listening—and silence (e.g. 10.11-14, 18-21 or 15.1-4), to mention but two examples.

The theological character of 10.1-8, then, may be explained by its introductory function. However, as the theological impact is considerable upon the rest of the chapter as well, it seems fair to regard the whole of ch. 10 as a theological 'entrance hall' to the following collection of proverbs. Also the assumed 'great gap' to unit 1 is reduced substantially by this; and it may be reduced even more. For, if one takes the theological character of the entire unit 2 (10–22.16) into consideration, one gets the impression that the theological aspects—although they are variously extant—in their main points form a specific pattern which deserves serious attention, and which, additionally, may support the above-mentioned division of unit 2 in (a) chs. 10–15, and (b) chs. 16–22.16. In sub-unit (a) where all chapters have theological elements, and which, on the whole, seems to be more theologically influenced than the sub-unit (b), the second theological main point—besides ch. 10—is in the 'concluding' ch. 15 (partly also in chs. 11 and 14), while in the chapters in between, especially in chs. 12–13, the independent proverbs of empirical character are prevailing. That means that also in this greater sub-unit a technique of cyclic composition seems to have been operative. Similarly, the beginning of sub-unit (b) in ch. 16 (esp. vv. 1-9 and v. 33) and its end in ch. 21 (esp. vv. 1-4 and 27-31) and 22 (esp. vv. 2, 6, 9, 11-12 and 14) have a clear cast of theological reflection and tradition. Again, the theological impression of the empirical wisdom tradition is accomplished by a procedure of framing. Through this the pious men of the transmission of wisdom have achieved two matters: first, an inconsistent bulk of proverbial wisdom has, to some degree, attained unity; and second, the distance to the collections of the instruction form of wisdom, especially to the theological teaching of the first unit (chs. 1–9), has been somewhat reduced.

3. *The Context of the First Solomonic Collection*

The recognition of the traditio-historical procedure of framing older material forming a cyclic composition may be pursued further, by comparing unit 2, the first Solomonic collection, with its literary context.

Among several differences between the sub-units (a) chs. 10–15 and (b) chs. 16–22.16 of unit 2[9] there is also a difference in the use of the

---

9. Cf. Skladny, *Die ältesten Spruchsammlungen*; see further J. Conrad, 'Die innere Gliederung der Proverbien: Zur Frage nach der Systematisierung des Spruchgutes in den älteren Teilsammlungen', *ZAW* 79 (1967), pp. 67-76; also R.N. Whybray, 'Yahweh-sayings and their Contexts in Proverbs, 10.1–22.16', in

other main form of wisdom talk and teaching, namely, the instruction style (with direct address and use of the imperative or a similar verb form). In (a) there is nearly no example of this style (cf. only 14.7), but in (b), especially in its latter part there are some occurrences (cf. 16.3; 19.18, 20, 27; 20.16, 18, 22; 22.6, 10); and this may be considered as a link to unit 3 in 22.17–24.22, where the instruction style is predominant (but where there are also some instances of proverbial style: 23.17; 24.3-5, 7-9, 16, and in 23.29-35 a mini-composition). Through this bridging as well as by other features[10] the interrelations between the units 2 and 3 are underscored. The same style of instruction, moreover, also prevails in the chs. 1–9, on the other side of unit 2, so that this central unit of proverbial wisdom has become 'wrapped' in a framework of instruction wisdom, which has its purpose and function in teaching and guidance, especially in the education of young people. This has an obvious hermeneutical effect for the great sentence collection. Besides, it raises important questions of the milieu and social background of the wisdom tradition as well as of the existence of a specific wisdom school which, probably, may have been connected with the royal court.[11]

As regards the composition of the first unit, which has been much scrutinized in recent research,[12] it seems to be the best specimen of a cyclic composition technique in the whole book. Within chs. 1–9 there are, most likely, two core blocks of tradition which are different in content. First, there is in chs. 2–4 an admonitory wisdom teaching that mainly refers to the personal acquiring of wisdom and its incomparable gifts as the highest benefit for men. Second, the next three chapters, 5–7, constitute a section of ethical, mostly sexual-ethical, advices. Around this double kernel of practical teaching and guidance there is laid a

M. Gilbert (ed.), *La Sagesse de l'Ancien Testament* (BETL, 51; Leuven: Leuven University Press, 1979), pp. 153-65; regrettably this article came to my sight after the text above first was written—it is most important.

10. Cf., i.a., instances mentioning the *king*, 16.9-17, 19.12, 20.2, 8.26; 21.1 and 24.21, as well as the importance of correct behaviour among rulers, 23.1ff.

11. See esp. Lemaire, *Les écoles et la formation de la Bible*, with reference to older literature; further Hermisson, *Studien*, pp. 97-136; B. Lang, 'Schule und Unterricht im alten Israel', in Gilbert (ed.), *La Sagesse*, pp. 186-201.

12. Cf., i.a., R.N. Whybray, *Wisdom in Proverbs* (SBT, 45; London: SCM Press, 1965); C. Kayatz, *Studien zu Proverbien 1–9* (WMANT, 22; Neukirchen–Vluyn: Neukirchener Verlag, 1966); B. Lang, *Die weisheitliche Lehrrede: Eine Untersuchung von Sprüche 1–7* (SBS, 54; Stuttgart: KBW, 1972).

most remarkable speech in the first person by the personified Wisdom, which is unparalleled in the entire Bible; the Wisdom speaks with divine authority, first in 1.20-33, and then, on the other side of the enclosed blocks, in 8.1-36; here its relation to God as Creator is unique. Finally, one may hold the rest of unit 1 to be its last, framing 'ring', beginning with the so-called 'prologue' in 1.2-7,[13] and an introductory admonition, 1.8-19, and ending with the contrasting allegory of Wisdom, in the figure of a woman, contrary to 'the foolish woman', 9.1-6 and 13-18, separated by a series of admonitions, 9.7-12, which, to some degree, stands counter to the 'prologue' (cf. 9.10 with 1.7). As a whole, then, unit 1, chs. 1–9, leaves the impression of being an intentionally formed cyclic composition.

Finally, through the framing composition technique also, the redaction of the greater part of the book of Proverbs, chs. 1–24 (units 1–3, expanded with 4), was accomplished. And this main part has, by the same method, been granted a higher degree of coherence than is usually assumed.

4. *Some Concluding Remarks*

Behind the final editorial work, however, the independence of the collections is recognizable, not at least through the different version of the LXX. It displays both extensions in comparison with the Hebrew text (at the end of ch. 9 there are three extra verses after v. 12 and four after v. 18, and after the end of the third unit in 24.22 it has five verses in addition) as well as a differing order of the collections: it places 30.1-14 after unit 3 and after the end of 4 in 24.34 it has 30.15-33 and 31.1-9 before it proceeds with chs. 25–29; the last sub-unit, however, is also in the LXX version the acrostical song in 31.10-31: perhaps it is meant to connect with the various speakings of woman in the first unit.

Further, the cyclic composition technique which could be discerned in chs. 1–24 is lacking in chs. 25–31 where the forming procedure may more accurately be characterized as *additive*. In chs. 25–29 a differentiation may be made between chs. 25–27 to be more empirical and general, and chs. 28–29 to be more theological in character.[14] In other words, the theological reflection is here following after, not preceding a

---

13. Cf. C. Bauer-Kayatz, *Einführung in die alttestamentliche Weisheit* (BSTh, 55; Neukirchen–Vluyn: Neukirchener Verlag, 1969), pp. 39-42.

14. Cf. Skladny, *Die ältesten Spruchsammlungen*, pp. 46-57, 57-67.

more traditional sentence collection. Additionally, one may also call attention to a conspicuous form in ch. 29, which may be called a *plait pattern*; it is a kind of systematizing of proverbs that consists in combining a proverb with a similar one in the next-but-one verse (cf. vv. 1 and 3, 2 and 4, 7 and 9, 12 and 14, 15 and 17, 19 and 21, 20 and 22).[15]

In conclusion it may be asserted that as for the process of tradition and redaction in the book of Proverbs it should be differentiated between chs. 1–24 and chs. 25–31, because of differences in the formation procedure. While the former and greater part is marked by a framing procedure and cyclic composition, at different stages, the latter has an additive way of formation. On the whole, the long and complex history of tradition and redaction that lies behind the final shape of the book, to a great extent was *a history of creative reinterpretation, for theological reasons mainly*. In later Jewish tradition a similar cyclic composition technique is to be found both in the form of the Talmud and in rabbinic Bibles.

15. For further documentation see my commentary on the Proverbs (*Fortolkning til Salomos ordspråk: Forkynneren, Høysangen, Klagesangene* [Oslo: Luther Forlag, 1986]).

Chapter 16

FROM THE INDIVIDUAL TO THE COLLECTIVE:
A PATTERN OF INNER-BIBLICAL INTERPRETATION

1. *Introductory Remarks*

During a visit to Professor I.L. Seeligmann in Jerusalem in 1951 he told
me that his students had raised a spontaneous protest against him when
he lectured on an individual interpretation of the Servant Songs. That is
natural, for it greatly opposes the traditional Jewish interpretation of
עבד יהוה which has seen the people of Israel in the figure of the
'servant'.

Over and above the traditional Jewish and Christian interpretation, in
modern research the question of individual or collective interpretation
together with a host of other aspects of the Songs has been a long,
much-debated and difficult problem.[1] Naturally, there is not space here
to consider in detail this almost unsurveyable research with its vastly
varying opinions. Yet on the question of the relationship between individual and collective in the Old Testament we may quickly observe that
the question can be considered also in a wider context, as shown for
example in the debate on the use of 'I' in the Psalms.[2] Also, scholars
have often sought to discover a psychological explanation, particularly
through the assumed occurrence in ancient Israel of the adoption of a

1. For example, see the reviews of research by C.R. North, *The Suffering Servant in Dentero-Isaiah* (London: Oxford University Press, 1956), pp. 6-119;
H. Haag, *Der Gottesknecht bei Deuterojesaja* (EdF, 233; Darmstadt: Wissenschaftliche Buchgesellschaft, 1985); D. Michel, 'Deuterojesaja', *TRE*, VIII,
pp. 510-30; and for older research see E. Ruprecht, 'Die Auslegungsgeschichte zu
den sog. Gottesknechtliedern...bis zu Bernhard Duhm' (Theol. Dissertation, University of Heidelberg, 1972).
2. Cf., e.g., Gunkel and Begrich, *Einleitung in die Psalmen*, pp. 173-75;
S. Mowinckel, *The Psalms in Israel's Worship* (2 vols.; New York: Abingdon
Press, 1962), *passim*.

'corporate personality'.[3] And, finally, the question has been cleared up, to a certain extent, by means of a form-historical analysis of the phenomenon of the collective 'thou' as a form of address in the Old Testament.[4] All in all, however, scholars have proceeded rather timelessly and have happily been inclined to diminish, or even to build a bridge over, an all too obvious disparity by using the individual-collective alternative.

On the other hand, a specific *traditio-historical* as well as an interpretative *redaction-historical* perspective may well be especially desirable for future research, for thus one might succeed in taking the debate a further step forward. An explanation of this kind is now to be attempted by means of a very limited amount of material.

For reasons of space, two presuppositions must be made here: first, the existence of four so-called Servant Songs (Isa. 42.1-4; 49.1-6; 50.4-9; 52.13–53.12), as singled out for the first time by Duhm as a special layer within Deutero-Isaiah;[5] and second—with Westermann[6] and many others—a further individual interpretation of the character of

3. Cf. H.W. Robinson, *Hebrew Conception of Corporate Personality: Corporate Personality in Ancient Israel* (Philadelphia: Fortress Press, rev. edn, 1980), pp. 49-62; J.W. Rogerson, 'The Hebrew Conception of Corporate Personality: A Reexamination', *JTS* 21 (1970), pp. 1-16; and O. Eissfeldt, *Der Gottesknecht bei Denterojesaja (Jes 40–55) im Lichte der israelitischen Anschauung von Gemeinschaft und Individuum* (BRGA, 2; Halle, 1933).

4. I undertook an examination of this kind in the 1960s, but for various reasons did not finish it; but cf. my study *Sacharja 9–14*, pp. 176-79; cf. also O. Kaiser, *Der königliche Knecht* (FRLANT, 70; Göttingen: Vandenhoeck & Ruprecht, 1959), pp. 45-52 ('Exkurs: Die traditionsgeschichtlichen Wurzeln der Anrede der Gemeinde als einer Einzelperson in den Heilsorakeln Deuterojesajas').

5. Duhm, *Das Buch Jesaia*, pp. 284-87. The dispute concerning the existence of a level of this kind, as has been established recently by T.N.D. Mettinger, *A Farewell to the Servant Songs* (SMHVL, 1982–83.3; Lund: C.W.K. Gleerup, 1982–83), is not convincing; here only what emerges from the following remarks can be regarded indirectly for the time being as a tentative response.

6. Cf. C. Westermann, 'Sprache und Struktur der Prophetie Deuterojesaja', in *idem*, *Forschung am Alten Testament* (TBü, 24; Munich: Chr. Kaiser Verlag, 1964), pp. 92-170, especially p. 163, and *idem*, *Das Buch Jesaja: Kapitel 40–66* (ATD, 19; Göttingen: Vandenhoeck & Ruprecht, 5th edn, 1986; ET *Jesaja* [Philadelphia: Westminster Press, 1969; London: SCM Press, 1969]), and *idem*, *Theologie des Alten Testaments in Grundzügen* (ATDSup, 6; Göttingen: Vandenhoeck & Ruprecht, 1978), pp. 70-71, and 'עֶבֶד '*æbæd* Knecht', *THAT*, II, cols. 182-200, esp. cols. 193-95.

these texts, which actually are not 'songs'. No further rationale can be given for this supposition than that which emerges from the following discussion.

2. *The Servant Songs—Some Aspects of Theological Interpretation*

To facilitate an understanding of the four 'songs', it will be expedient first to explain them thoroughly in their own right and also with regard to their current editorial context. Their peculiarities should not be smoothed over hastily or harmonized with the remaining parts of Deutero-Isaiah, but should be explained in their relationship to them both historically and theologically.

In the first Song, Isa. 42.1-4, the addressee is first called 'my servant' (עבדי) and 'my elect' (בחירי) and is subsequently clearly portrayed as an individual.

The word עבד ('servant') has had many uses in its history.[7] At this point it is particularly worth mentioning that the word can be used as a theological 'name of honour' which was used for renowned individuals such as Moses, Abraham and David as well as the prophets and which, apart from one's relationship to God, above all expressed his appointing of a person for special service.[8] In addition, the word can be used to describe the saints, especially in the Psalms (Pss. 86.2; 116.16; 123.2-3, etc.). From this comes a use 'which must have had its roots in Deutero-Isaiah',[9] in which 'Israel is described singularly as עבד יהוה. This surprising development of the term עבד is made possible in Deutero-Isaiah by means of the form of the salvation oracle which appears in the language of the lament of the individual and thus addresses Israel as a single person'.[10] In this point, Isa. 41.8-10 is especially interesting because here the text in its introductory addressing of the people ('but you, Israel, my servant, Jacob, whom I have chosen') comes phraseologically close to the start of the first 'song' (cf. also 44.1-2, 21, 26; 45.4; 48.20), which recently for Mettinger has become an important

---

7. Cf., e.g., C. Lindhagen, 'The Servant Motif in the Old Testament' (Theol. Dissertation, University of Uppsala, 1950); R. Riesener, *Der Stamm* עבד *im Alten Testament* (BZAW, 1949; Berlin: W. de Gruyter, 1978); Westermann, 'עֶבֶד *'œbœd* Knecht', *THAT*, II, cols. 182-200; and W. Zimmerli, 'παῖς θεοῦ (A-B)', *TWNT*, V, pp. 655-76.

8. Cf. Westermann, 'עֶבֶד *'œbœd* Knecht', *THAT*, II, col. 193.

9. Thus Zimmerli, 'παῖς θεοῦ', p. 660.

10. Thus Westermann, 'עֶבֶד *'œbœd* Knecht', col. 193.

argument for the contesting of all talk of an individual עבד figure.[11]

As for this several points should be noted: first, through a comparison with the section 41.8-13 undertaken by Mettinger and others, 42.5-9 and 42.1-4 are included in one section, which will be considered shortly; second, 41.8-10 (13) and 42.1-4 are completely different in genre;[12] and third, Zimmerli has correctly pointed out that Israel is portrayed passively where it is called עבד in Deutero-Isaiah, that primarily here it is the object of Yahweh's comforting address and help, while the servant of the Servant Songs is active and has a particular task and function.[13] Thus עבד in Deutero-Isaiah has clearly separate meanings, despite the phraseological proximity of single texts, especially as, in general, the forms of the sections quickly change.

Thus the section 42.1-4, designated as a 'word of presentation', and the very difficult section 42.5-9 should be kept as far apart as possible.[14] Different from the first section, as well as the other Songs, 42.5-9 is introduced with the messenger formulation כה אמר יהוה, which is expanded with hymnic creation statements (v. 5), and it is concluded by an address in second-person plural (v. 9), which stands out remarkably from the singular address (in vv. 6-7); finally, v. 8 is introduced by means of the formula of divine self-presentation and in a number of ways this verse corresponds to the introductory v. 5.[15] For these and other relatively good reasons one should be able to assume that vv. 5 and 8-9 surround the kernal section of vv. 6-7 like a framework. This kernal, which has on occasion been interpreted as a quotation,[16] has

---

11. Mettinger, *A Farewell*, pp. 30-32.

12. Cf., e.g., J. Begrich, *Studien zu Deuterojesaja* (TBü, 20; Munich: Chr. Kaiser Verlag, 1963), pp. 14ff.; K. Elliger, *Jesaja*, II (BKAT, 11; Neukirchen–Vluyn: Neukirchener Verlag, 1963), pp. 132ff.; repr. in *idem, Kleine Schriften*, pp. 174-98; Westermann, *Jesaja*, pp. 57ff.

13. Zimmerli, 'παῖς θεοῦ', pp. 661-71.

14. Westermann believes that '42.5-9 belongs to the pericopes of the book of Deutero-Isaiah which have as yet not been really explained' (*Jesaja*, p. 81). Cf. also Elliger, *Jesaja*, II, pp. 198-221, 222-40; and more recently R.F. Melugin, *The Formation of Isaiah 40–55* (BZAW, 141; Giessen: Alfred Töpelmann, 1976), pp. 64-69.

15. Cf. also F. Crüsemann, *Studien zur Formgeschichte von Hymnus und Danklied in Israel* (WMANT, 32; Neukirchen–Vluyn: Neukirchener Verlag, 1969), pp. 86ff.

16. Elliger, *Jesaja*, II, pp. 224, 228.

been seen by Begrich as a prophetic call oracle,[17] while Elliger has interpreted it as a call oracle to Cyrus.[18] Moreover, there is a proximity to the salvation promise to Israel in 41.8-10, inasmuch as the verbs קרא ('call/summon') and חזק ('seize/grasp') appear both in 41.9 and 42.6a, with the result that 42.6-7 has often been regarded as a salvation oracle to the people.[19] Whatever the original sense of the kernel section 42.6-7 may have been, as the nucleus of its current wider framework (vv. 5 and 8-9) it may best be interpreted as a salvation oracle to the people, whereby its comforting character is enhanced by the encompassing amplification which praises God in a hymn.

The kernel utterance of 42.6-7 contains, however, within its framework context, not only a possible new meaning in its own right, but its location immediately after the section of the first Song may be determined by the fact that it is meant to add to the understanding of the preceding section (42.1-4). For inasmuch as the kernel part is very close to the first section because of its 'thou' address and partly also in its very content, and the use of 'thou' in vv. 6-7 now in the collective sense refers to the people, this collective understanding becomes all the more consequential for 42.1-4 in that the collective reference to the people in the second section should possibly suggest a collective interpretation of עבד in 42.1. Thus the complex section 42.5-9 may redaction-historically be meant as *an expansion of, or commentary on, the first Servant Song which is interpretative in a collectivizing sense.*

Now it is certainly obvious that a commentary of this kind represents a very moderate and carefully tentative interpretation which will still be subject to a certain amount of uncertainty. On the other hand, the LXX translation gives here a more unequivocal commentary which moves in the same collectivizing direction, when it translates 42.1a with Ιακωβ ὁ παῖς μου, ἀντιλήμψομαι αὐτοῦ· Ισραηλ ὁ ἐκλεκτός μου, προσεδέ-ξατο αὐτὸν ἡ ψυχή μου. Thus the LXX has clearly understood עבד as *the people of Israel.*[20]

What appears particularly informative from these findings is, first,

17. Begrich, *Studien*, p. 61.
18. Elliger, *Jesaja*, II, pp. 228-29.
19. A. Eitz, 'Studien zum Verhältnis von Priesterschrift und Deuterojesaja' (PhD Dissertation, University of Heidelberg, 1969), pp. 46-47, has described the whole unit 42.5-9 as a salvation oracle to Israel; however, cf. Elliger, *Jesaja*, II, p. 226.
20. Cf., e.g., Westermann, *Jesaja*.

the fact that in Deutero-Isaiah there exist both an individual and a collective use of עבד, both of which must be taken into account and considered; and second, that we observe *a tendency gradually to replace the first use with the second*. This point must now be pursued more closely.

In this regard, as far as the second Song in Isa. 49.1-6 and the third Song in Isa. 50.4-9 are concerned, it may be noticed first of all that both Songs are followed by sections which deal with the nation of Israel, namely, 49.7 and—with a new introduction—49.8-12 and 50.10-11. In both cases the sections refer to the previous Song.[21]

As far as 50.10-11 is concerned, it is different from the 'I'-address of the third Song because of its use of the plural (vv. 10a, 11), where, although the people themselves are not addressed directly, representative groups within the people are. In the section preceding the Song, 50.1-3, which likewise uses the plural form of address, the reference to the people is more direct still. Indeed, the most important point here is that in these sections which encompass the Song and which are aimed at the people, there exists a direct reference to the 'servant' when we read in v. 10a: 'Who among you fears the Lord and obeys the voice of *his servant*?'[22] Thus here there exists no collectivizing new interpretation of the figure of the servant of Yahweh, but rather a clear difference between servant and people or groups within the people.

However, this may be different in the sections which follow the second Song, namely, 49.7 and 49.8-12. They seem to be linked with the sections preceding the Song, namely, 48.17-19, 20-21.[23] It is noticeable in 49.7 that in v. 7a the word עבד is used of the people and that v. 7b is to a certain extent phraseologically linked with the beginning of the fourth Song in 52.13-15. Here it is possible that the word עבד not only forms a bridge between the word in v. 7 which refers to the people and the Song in 49.1-6, but significantly the two uses of עבד may possibly have been mutually transparent with the result that the collective sense of the word in v. 7 will have coloured the sense of the עבד description of the Song. Additionally, 49.8 is close to the nucleus of 42.5-9, that is, vv. 6-7, which can be understood as a commentary on the first Song. This proximity is complex, to be sure, for the expressions in 42.6b which are difficult to interpret, namely, לברית עם ('to a covenant for

21. Cf. Westermann, *Jesaja*, pp. 189-90.
22. Thus Westermann, *Jesaja*, p. 188.
23. Cf. Duhm, *Das Buch Jesaia*, pp. 337-38; 343.

the people') and לאור גוים ('to a light for the Gentiles') are divided in Isaiah 49 in such a way that לאור גוים appears in the assumed individual Song (49.6b) and לברית עם appears in the collective word of the people (49.8b).[24] Seen as a whole, however, 49.7-8 seems to be linked with the second Song in the same way as 42.5-9 is with the first.[25]

If thereby a possible interpretation of the figure of the Song in the collective sense could be proposed from the current context of the second Song, such an interpretation is expressed clearly in the 'Israel' which is introduced in 49.3. The question of the origin of this element has been debated at length. It has recently been carefully discussed and substantiated by Lohfink in particular.[26] But even in his extremely thorough study it is difficult to avoid an impression of the matter which may be expressed as follows: 'This text 49.1-6 is one of those cases where clinging to the text as it has been handed down actually forces one to alter the text as a whole much more than if one admits that the "Israel" in v. 3 is an addition.'[27] Now one will need to argue against this element certainly less from the point of view of the text history—although it is not totally insignificant even here[28]—or from the point of

24. On the latter, cf. J.J. Stamm, '*Berît 'am* bei Deuterojesaja', in Wolff (ed.), *Probleme biblischer Theologie*, pp. 510-24.

25. Cf. Westermann, *Jesaja*, pp. 172-73.

26. N. Lohfink, ' "Israel" in. Jes 49, 3', in *Wort, Lied und Gottespruch* (Festschrift J. Ziegler; Würzburg: Echter Verlag, 1972), II, pp. 217-29; cf. also Haag, *Gottesknecht*, p. 170.

27. Westermann, *Jesaja*, p. 169.

28. 'Israel' is missing in a Hebrew MS, namely, in Kenn. 96. Lohfink draws attention to J.A. Bewer's criticism of this manuscript ('Two Notes on Isaiah 49.1-6', in *Jewish Studies in Memory of George A Kohnt* [1935], pp. 86-90). Also worthy of mention here are H. Gese, 'Die hebräischen Bibelhandschriften zum Dodekapropheton nach der Variantensammlung der Kennicott', *ZAW* 69 (1957), pp. 55-69, and M.H. Goshen-Gottstein, 'Die Jesaia-Rolle und das Problem der hebräischen Bibelhandschriften', in *idem, Text and Language in Bible and Qumran* (Jerusalem; Tel Aviv: Orient Publishing House, 1960), pp. 51-64, both of which stress the very variable value of the hundreds of MSS used by Kennicott, but which at the same time designate MSS 96 and 150 as especially valuable. Particularly since 'Israel' must have entered the Hebrew text very early, such a 'non-Massoretic' testimony gains in significance. Furthermore, the fact that 'Israel' appears in the Isaiah MSS from Qumran should come as no surprise, for the word is of course already a firm element of the text of the LXX (even if there it may occasionally be exchanged for 'Jacob').

view of the versification[29] than from the point of view of the style and contents of the Song. For the formal details of the 'I'-address of the Song, which cannot be considered in further detail on this occasion, appear primarily to refer to a single person, given that its phraseology is very close to the presentation of the calling and the lamentations of Jeremiah. Yet because, to a certain extent, the Song also has a prophetically exemplary nature, it may be conceivable that an 'Israel' could be inserted here. Nevertheless, one needs to keep to the divided use of עבד in Deutero-Isaiah and thus also the original individual understanding of the figure of the second Song concerning the servant of God, whereas the 'Israel' in v. 3 which was added at an early date results in 'the earliest proof of the collective meaning of the servant of God'.[30]

Finally, as far as the fourth Servant Song in Isa. 52.13–53.12 is concerned, its context does not appear to be of the same significance for its interpretation as may have been the case for the first three Songs. Yet even in the context of the fourth Song, in a different way it has to do with the people of Israel, whether in the form of a summons to flee (52.11-12), in the 'thou'-address to Zion/Jerusalem as the central point and embodiment of the people of God (51.1ff.), or even as a metaphorical address of Zion/Israel as a woman (54.1ff.). But in the midst of these surrounding sections, the fourth Song both in form and content stands as a very independent unit, like a steep cliff rising from the sea.

Thus, given this situation, the later Jewish interpretation of the fourth Song, in a collective sense, may become perspectivally more interesting and informative. Thereby the circle of these deliberations may be regarded as complete, given the link with the beginning of this paper.

Yet again the picture is divided. On the one hand, the figure of the Song is understood both individually and messianically, and on the other hand, it refers to the people.[31] This duality is, first of all,

---

29. Cf., e.g., Mowinckel, *He That Cometh*, pp. 462-64 (additional note XI), who among others comments: 'It is plain that *yisrael* here makes any metrical reading of the half line impossible. The Hebrew form of 42.1 presupposed by G clearly reveals the same defect', p. 463.

30. Thus Westermann, *Jesaja*, p. 169; cf. von Rad, *Theologie des Alten Testaments*, II, pp. 271-72.

31. See in particular S.R. Driver and A. Neubauer, *The Fifty-Third Chapter of Isaiah According to the Jewish Interpreters* (2 vols.; New York: Hermann Press, 1969 [1877]); also H.W. Wolff, *Jesaja 53 im Urchristentum* (Theol. Dissertation, University of Halle-Wittenberg, Bethel, 2nd edn, 1942; Berlin, 1950), pp. 38-54. Generally on the Songs, see among others J. Jeremias, 'παῖς θεοῦ in Spätjudentum

expressed in a unique way in the very paraphrased translation of the Targum.[32] In the Targum three of the nineteen עבד references are interpreted messianically, namely, 42.1; 43.10 and 52.13, where in addition to the use of the term עבד the title of 'Messiah' is also introduced;[33] the figure of the fourth Song is indeed portrayed throughout as the Messiah, yet now without all the statements about the suffering of the servant of God. Since in addition reference is made to the people through various kinds of paraphrase, one is faced with the following noteworthy final result, as has been formulated, for example, by Jeremias: 'Step by step Targ. Isa. 52.13–53.12 portrays the splendid setting up of the messianinc dominion over Israel'.[34] Later on, the collective interpretation of עבד that the people of Israel is the servant of Yahweh is to become the standard and traditional Jewish reading.[35]

Thus with an understanding of the servant of God in Deutero-Isaiah there clearly emerges *an interpretative tendency which moves from the individual to the collective* and which may be recognized already in the subsequent editing of the Massoretic text as well as in the oldest textual history of the Servant Songs.

In the attempt above to prove this tendency, for good reasons the many explanations and theories about the person and identity or the function and role of the Servant of God have not been discussed. Neither could a literary or even chronological orientation or categorization of this tendency be undertaken with regard to the framework of the preaching of Deutero-Isaiah or as regards the possible additions to the work in the way as, for example, Begrich has attempted 'to classify the

in der Zeit nach der Entstehung der LXX(C)', *TWNT*, V, pp. 676-98; North, *Suffering Servant*, pp. 6-22; and Haag, *Gottesknecht*, pp. 34-66.

32. On the text see Sperber, *The Bible in Aramaic*, III, pp. 107-109; also Stenning, *The Targum of Isaiah*, pp. 178-81; Driver and Neubauer, *The Fifty-Third Chapter*, II, pp. 5-6; Jeremias, 'παῖς θεοῦ', pp. 691-92; Mowinckel, *He That Cometh*, pp. 330-32; cf. S.H. Levey, *The Messiah: An Aramaic Interpretation. The Messianic Exegesis of the Targum* (Cincinnati: Hebrew Union College–Jewish Institute of Religion, 1974).

33. Cf. Jeremias, 'παῖς θεοῦ', p. 691, inc. n. 29; also Levey, *The Messiah*, pp. 59-67.

34. Jeremias, 'παῖς θεοῦ', p. 693; cf. H.S. Nyberg, 'Smärtornas man: En studie till Jes, 52,13–53,12', *SEÅ* 7 (1942), pp. 35-36; and Mowinckel, *He That Cometh*, pp. 330-33.

35. Cf., e.g., North, *Suffering Servant*, p. 18: 'Since the twelfth century the collective interpretation has been usual.'

עבד יהוה texts within the overall understanding of Deutero-Isaiah'.[36] Of importance here has merely been the attempt to show the tradition and redaction history of the tendency which has been discussed.

3. Further Tendencies

In conclusion, two more texts should be discussed briefly which to a certain extent are able to expand on the picture which has been established of the tendency mentioned above.

Within the setting of the section in Isa. 55.1-5 or especially 55.3b-5, which contains an address to the people, there is in v. 3b a unique reference to the special promise concerning David: 'I will make with you an everlasting covenant, the manifestations of my love for David'.[37] On the basis of the promise to David in 2 Sam. 7.8-16, an independent David tradition had been established which not only played a legitimate role for the Davidic kings in Jerusalem but was of fundamental importance for the messianic proclamation of several pre-exilic prophets.[38] In Deutero-Isaiah, however, this David tradition, especially in a phraseological form which is close to Psalm 89,[39] is not extended in an individually messianic sense, but is transferred in a productively new interpretative manner to the *people* in the usual collective sense of the word. This process, which corresponds to the tendency demonstrated above, is generally characterized by means of the term 'democratization', though this designation is not accurate enough and may be misleading, and should therefore rather be avoided.

In this connexion, also the vision of the 'Son of Man' (בר אנש) in Dan. 7.13-14 may be used for comparison. Now this vision within its context, particularly its mysterious figure within the framework of Jewish apocalyptic, has attracted many theories,[40] which can be pursued

36. Begrich, *Studien*, pp. 135ff.

37. Thus in Westermann, *Jesaja*, p. 225; also von Rad, *Theologie des Alten Testaments*, II, p. 254; H.G.M. Williamson, '"The Sure Mercies of David": Subjective or Objective Genetive?', *JSS* 23 (1978), pp. 31-49.

38. Cf., e.g., Rohland, 'Die Bedeutung', pp. 179-85.

39. Cf. O. Eissfeldt, 'Die Gnadenverheissungen an David in Jes 55,1-5', in *idem, Kleine Schriften* (Tübingen: J.C.B. Mohr, 1968), IV, pp. 44-52; Seybold, *Das davidische Königtum im Zeugnis der Propheten*, pp. 152-62; Veijola, *Verheissung in der Krise*, pp. 166-67, 170-73.

40. See Ch. 14 above, and cf., among others, Mowinckel, *He That Cometh*, pp. 346-450; von Rad, *Theologie des Alten Testaments*, II, pp. 315-37; J.J. Collins, 'The Son of Man and the Saints of the Most High in the Book of Daniel', *JBL* 93

here no more than has been possible with the Servant Songs.

In this case too the relationship of individual and collective has been a topic of debate inasmuch as some scholars have interpreted the 'Son of Man' in a collective sense.[41] However, such problematization is hardly suitable for the figure of the בר אנשׁ because in all probability he is portrayed as a single figure.[42] The problem of individual and collective may lie rather in another section of Daniel 7, namely, in the editorial relationship between the vision (7.13-14, linked with that in 7.9-10) and its subsequent interpretation (7.15-28), where in fact there exists a notable shift which to a certain degree may correspond to the interpretative process expounded above.

For it is immediately striking that the figure of the בר אנשׁ, who cannot be correctly understood without reference to the four large beasts from the sea which are named in the preceding passage,[43] conspicuously does not appear in the complex interpretation which follows (7.[15-16], 17-27). On the contrary, there is here a number of references to 'the holy ones of the Most High' (vv. 18, 22, 25, 27) or 'the holy ones' (vv. 21, 22, 25) as well as in v. 27 also to 'the people of the holy ones of the Most High'. Thus on the one side of the polarity of beasts and 'Son of Man' in the first part (vv. 2-14) it is characteristic that the beasts have their power removed (v. 12), while the 'Son of man' receives 'dominion and glory and kingship'; and 'his dominion is an everlasting dominion that shall not pass away' (v. 14). On the other hand, however, in the interpretation of the dominion 'the kingdom' or 'the government' is now given to 'the holy ones of the Most High' (v. 18) or 'the holy ones' (v. 22). And finally, the following summarizing proclamation is made in v. 27: 'The power and dominion and greatness of the kingdoms under the whole heaven shall be given to the

(1974), pp. 50-66; Russell, *Method and Message*, pp. 324-52; Kvanvig, *Roots of Apocalyptic*, pp. 442ff. For general reading on apocalyptic and its research, see, e.g., Schmidt, *Die jüdische Apokalyptik*.

41. Cf., e.g., A. Bentzen, *Daniel* (HAT, 1.19; Tübingen: J.C.B. Mohr, 1952), p. 63: 'In Daniel 7 "Son of Man" is in no way a designation of the Messiah, but rather a symbol for the chosen people.' See also Plöger, *Das Buch Daniel*, pp. 112-13.

42. Von Rad, *Theologie des Alten Testaments*, II, p. 334; and more recently Kvanvig, *Roots of Apocalyptic*, pp. 491-502.

43. Cf. H.S. Kvanvig, 'Struktur und Geschichte in Dan. 7,1-14', *ST* 32 (1978), pp. 95-117, esp. pp. 112-14.

people of the holy ones of the Most High. His kingdom is an ever-lasting kingdom...'[44]

Thus for Daniel 7 it is characteristic that whereas in the first part (vv. 2-14) the 'beasts' and the 'Son of Man' form the polarity, this polarity is valid in the following interpretative section (vv. 17-27) for the contrast between the 'beasts' and the 'holy ones of the Most High', with the result that the 'holy ones of the Most High' have totally usurped the role and political power of the 'Son of Man'. The 'holy ones of the Most High' are not to be understood as 'heavenly beings', as Noth has it, but they may be linked with 'the holy ones' (vv. 21, 22, 25) and with the 'people' (v. 27), and thus with the people of Israel.[45] This means, then, that *the interpretation replaces an individual figure with a collective entity*, namely, *the people of Israel*, or at least that it has interpreted the figure of the 'Son of Man' in a collective way. This interpretative tendency is intrinsically the same as that which was observed above with reference to the Servant Songs.

In conclusion, I would like to draw attention to a brief remark which Sara Japhet once made concerning Ezra–Nehemiah and the early post-exilic period, because it may quickly point out a more comprehensive historico-sociological outlook for a theological interpretation: 'A close look at the narrative of the Restoration shows how the author transfers the emphasis from the leader to the public or its representatives—a tendency which is to be discerned from the very start.'[46]

Here, however, it has been my primary purpose to draw attention to an interpretative tendency which leads from the individual to the collective. This tendency is already discernible in theologically important texts in the Old Testament, but later on it gradually increases in intensity.[47]

---

44. Trans. after Plöger, *Das Buch Daniel*, pp. 102-103.

45. M. Noth, 'Die Heiligen des Höchsten', in *idem*, *Gesammelte Studien zum AT* (TBü, 6; Munich: Chr. Kaiser Verlag, 3rd edn, 1966 [1957]), pp. 274-90; his interpretation cannot be examined here in further detail, however.

46. S. Japhet, 'Sheshbazzar and Zerubbabel', *ZAW* 94 (1982), pp. 66-98 (83).

47. Cf., among others, I. Abrahams, 'Jewish Interpretation of the Old Testament', in A.S. Peake (ed.), *The People and the Book* (Oxford, 1925), pp. 403-31; and J. Bonsirven, *Exégèse rabbinique et exégèse paulinienne* (Paris: Beauchesne, 1939), pp. 11-265.

Chapter 17

ON THE CANONICITY OF THE SONG OF SONGS

1. *Aspects of the Book's Interpretation History*

The old dictum *libelli sua fata* seems to be particularly appropriate to the biblical book of שִׁיר הַשִּׁירִים, *the Song of Songs, Canticum canticorum* [Cant]. The interpretations of it through the ages, as well as modern critical discussion of its problems, have differed more widely than for nearly any other book of the Hebrew Bible. This state of affairs is, first of all, related to the very variegated *Wirkungsgeschichte* and *Rezeptionsgeschichte* of the Song of Songs; through the centuries, scholars tended to be especially attracted to these later (or postbiblical) stages of the history of the book.[1] During the last two centuries, on the other hand, questions of the book's pre-literary and literary character have been frequently and differently focused upon by modern critical scholarship. As for these *earlier* stages of the history of the book, scholars often discussed the background and origin of its individual songs and units, their specific genres and composition; further, they debated issues such as the possible opposition of popular versus art poetry, and the secular versus sacred character of the songs.[2]

---

1. Cf. C.D. Ginsburg, *The Song of Songs* (London: Longman, 1857; repr. New York: Ktav, 1970); H.H. Rowley, 'The Interpretation of the Song of Songs', in *idem, The Servant of the Lord and Other Essays on the Old Testament* (Oxford: Basil Blackwell, 2nd rev. edn, 1965); U. Köpf, 'Hoheliedauslegung als Quelle einer Theologie der Mystik', in M. Schmidt (ed.), *Grundfragen christlicher Mystik* (Stuttgart–Bad–Carnstatt: frommann-holzboog, 1987), pp. 50-72; D. Lerch, 'Zur Geschichte der Auslegung des Hohenliedes', *ZTK* 54 (1957), pp. 257-77; F. Ohly, *Hohelied-Studien: Grundzüge einer Geschichte der Hoheliedauslegung des Abendlands bis zum 1200* (Wiesbaden: Steiner, 1958); M.H. Pope, *Song of Songs* (AB, 7c; New York: Doubleday, 1977), pp. 89-229.

2. Cf. recently R.E. Murphy, *The Song of Songs* (Hermeneia, 1990), pp. 57-91 and the reviews by C. Kuhl, 'Das Hohelied und seine Deutung', *TRev* NF 9 (1937),

In contrast to these historical perspectives on the Song of Songs, the specific problems of the process of its *canonization*—being actually in between what might be called the *Vorgeschichte* and the *Nachgeschichte* of the book—seem not to have received as much attention.[3] And when the issue of canonization was brought up it was often related to the later interpretations of the book, especially the allegorical one. Nevertheless, I would maintain, *the foundation was laid for the book's canonization in different ways in the final stages of redaction.* It may enhance our understanding of the book to locate the question of its canonization particularly in the final traditio-historical and redactional process of the book. After all, current scholarship tends to view the canonization of the Hebrew Bible as less localized, rejecting the older connexion with the so-called 'council' of Jamnia, at the end of the first century CE. Rather, it is viewed as a longer formative and traditio-historical process.[4]

As already stated, the canonicity of the Song of Songs has often been

pp. 137-67; E. Würthwein, 'Zum Verständnis des Hohenliedes', *TRev* 32 (1967), pp. 177-212; also Pope, *Song of Songs*, pp. 21-85; H. Graf Reventlow, 'Hoheslied. I. Altes Testament', *TRE*, XV, pp. 499-502.

3. E.g. is Pope giving little more than one page to the questions of canonicity in the very long Introduction of his Commentary (*Song of Songs*, pp. 15-288) that otherwise has a broad discussion of many aspects of the book, especially of its religio-historical context.

4. See first W.M. Christie, 'The Jamnia Period in Jewish History', *JTS* 26 (1925), pp. 347-67 (352-56, esp. p. 356): 'There never seems to have been a formal canonizing of any portion of the Old Testament... by any judicial authority. The books gradually made their way to universal acceptance ... and in these disputes on the part of individuals or schools we see the process in operation'; and then P. Katz, 'The Old Testament Canon in Palestine and Alexandrina', *ZNW* 47 (1956), pp. 191-217; J.P. Lewis, 'What Do We Mean by Jabne?', *JAAR* 32 (1964), pp. 125-32; J.C.H. Lebram, 'Aspekte der alttestamentlichen Kanonbildung', *VT* 18 (1968), pp. 173-89; D. Barthélemy, 'L'état de la Bible juive depuis le début de notre ère jusqu'à la deuxième révolte contre Rome (131–135)', in J.-D. Kaestli and D. Wermelinger (eds.), *Le canon de l'Ancien Testament: Sa formation et son histoire* (Geneva: Labor et Fides, 1984), pp. 9-45 (25-36). Cf. also S. Zeitlin, *An Historical Study of the Canonization of the Hebrew Scriptures* (Philadelphia, 1933), pp. 9-21.37; M. Haran, 'מבעיות הקנוניזציה של המקרא [Problems of the Canonization of Scripture]', *Tarbiz* 25 (1956), pp. 254-71 (259-62); A. Jepsen, 'Zur Kanongeschichte des Alten Testaments', *ZAW* 71 (1959), pp. 114-36 (131-32); S.Z. Leiman (ed.), *The Canon and Masorah of the Hebrew Bible: An Introductory Reader* (New York: Ktav, 1974), pp. 113-282; see further Ch. 18 below.

assumed to require a prior allegorical reading and interpretation of the book, and occasionally this even may seem to have been made a *conditio sine qua non* for its canonization.[5] But the contrary is apparently to be the case.

After having critically reviewed the Jewish and the Christian allegorical view, as well as different forms of a dramatic theory[6] and the modern wedding-cycle theory,[7] and also the cultic theory of an Adonis–Tammuz liturgy,[8] Rowley asserts that he 'finds in it nothing but what it appears to be: lovers' songs, expressing their delight in one another and the warm emotions of their hearts'; and he adds: 'All of the other views find in the Song what they bring to it.'[9] Be that as it may, Rowley has regrettably not confronted his view with the problem of canonization.[10] This problem represents an even harder challenge when one assumes— as Rowley does—that the songs have an exclusively 'secular' character and background.[11]

5. See, i.a., Gordis, *The Song of Songs*, pp. 2, 43; A. Bentzen, 'Remarks on the Canonization of the Song of Solomon', in *Studia orientalia Ioanni Pedersen... dicata* (Copenhagen: Hauniae, 1953), pp. 41-47; A. Lacoque, 'L'insertion du Cantique des Cantiques dans le canon', *RHPR* 42 (1962), pp. 38-44; cf. the critical remarks by Rowley, 'The Interpretation of the Song of Songs', pp. 198-215; Childs, *Introduction to the Old Testament*, p. 578; Murphy, *The Song of Songs*, pp. 5-7, and especially G. Gerleman, *Ruth–Das Hohelied* (BKAT, 18; Neukirchen–Vluyn: Neukirchener Verlag, 1965), p. 51: 'Als Voraussetzung seiner [i.e. Cant's] Aufnahme in den Kanon pflegt man ziemlich unreflektiert die allegorische Auslegung anzugeben. Die Deutung der Lieder auf Jahwe und Israel habe dem Büchlein die erforderte religiöse Legitimierung gegeben und es für den Kanon fähig gemacht.'

6. See recently R.J. Tournay, *Quant Dieu parle aux hommes le langage de l'amour: Etudes sur le Cantique des Cantiques* (CRB, 21; Paris: J. Gabalda, 1982); M.V. Fox, *The Song of Songs and the Ancient Egyptian Love Songs* (Madison, WI: University of Wisconsin Press, 1985), pp. 253-66; for recent criticism cf. O. Keel, *Das Hohelied* (ZBK.AT, 18; Zürich: Theologischer Verlag, 1982), pp. 24-27.

7. Cf., i.a., Gordis, *The Song of Songs*, pp. 17-18; Rudolph, *Das Buch Ruth*, pp. 101-106, 140-42; Würthwein, 'Zum Verständnis', pp. 202-206, 209-12; 1969, pp. 31-33; Fox, *The Song of Songs*, pp. 330-32.

8. Subsequently broadly expanded by Pope, *Song of Songs*; cf. a critical review by Würthwein, 'Zum Verständnis', pp. 196-201.

9. Rowley, 'The Interpretation of the Song of Songs', p. 243.

10. Cf. Childs, *Introduction to the Old Testament*, p. 571, who holds that 'the simple recounting' of the history of different views, as by Ginsburg and Rowley, 'has failed to make clear the exact nature of the hermeneutical problems at stake'.

11. Cf. the scrutiny of Rudolph, *Das Buch Ruth*, pp. 82-109.

274   *On the Way to Canon*

The history of interpretation of the Song of Songs shows that a proper point of departure and direction of argumentation is crucial to the general understanding of the book. In this respect it will be appropriate not to start with some interpretation within the book's further 'history' (its *Nachgeschichte*) and move 'backward' to the book itself, nor to start with its alleged religio-historical or cultic 'pre-history' (its *Vorgeschichte*), but to take as the point of departure the book's own literary character and composition, a procedure that has become increasingly customary.[12] Childs is surely right when, in his search for 'the canonical shape' of the book, he seeks 'the particular stamp which the collectors of Israel's Scripture left as a key for its interpretation',[13] and also when he focuses on the role of Solomon in the book. But when he also relates, rather one-sidedly, the mention of Solomon to the realm of 'wisdom' and states that 'the Song is to be understood as wisdom literature',[14] he is making a dubious claim, although the book seems to have some contact with wisdom. Besides, 'the particular stamp' of the 'collectors' was related not only to King Solomon. Nevertheless, there are good reasons for starting with the role of Solomon in the Song.

2. *The Role of King Solomon in the Song*

It has long been registered that the figure of King Solomon seems to have special significance in the Song of Songs.[15] But it should not be overlooked that the various references to Solomon (1.1, 5; 3.7, 9, 11; 8.11-12), as well as the anonymous mention of a 'king' (1.4, 12; 7.6[5]; cf. 4.4), differ in character and function. This fact may have a bearing on various issues, including the question of 'royal travesty' in some of the songs, and on the Song as a whole.

In the superscription of the book in Cant. 1.1 (שיר השירים אשר לשלמה) the mention of Solomon seems to indicate his *authorship* of the Song. Traditionally it was understood in this way, but the majority of

12. Recently also structural aspects have been focused upon; cf. J.C. Exum, 'A Literary and Structural Analysis of the Song of Songs', *ZAW* 85 (1973), pp. 47-79; R. Alter, *The Art of Biblical Poetry* (New York: Basic Books, 1985); F. Landy, 'The Song of Songs', in R. Alter and F. Kermode, *The Literary Guide to the Bible* (Cambridge, MA: Harvard University Press, 1987), pp. 305-19.

13. Childs, *Introduction to the Old Testament*, p. 573.

14. Childs, *Introduction to the Old Testament*, p. 574; cf. J.-P. Audet, 'Le sens du Cantique des Cantiques', *RB* 62 (1955), pp. 197-221 (203-207).

15. See esp. Gordis, *The Song of Songs*, pp. 18-22.

modern scholars do not so regard it (nor does Childs, *Introduction to the Old Testament*, pp. 573-78).[16] It is, by the way, most remarkable that the Vulgate leaves out the name of Solomon, starting the book—after the title—with v. 2 (as v. 1; cf. 8.11). Modern scholars have challenged actual Solomonic authorship, arguing on the basis of a historical perspective as well as reasons internal to the book. At the same time, some have sought to explain the role of Solomon in the Song in other ways than that of authorship. In all this, the question of canonicity of the Song has been made more complicated.

We should also raise the critical question as to whether the mention of Solomon in Cant. 1.1 is intended to be not as much an expression of authorship as one of *authority*.[17] For in this way the Song of Songs seems to have been 'laid under' or 'covered by' the authority of King Solomon. Hermeneutically and traditio-historically a 'borrowed' authority of this kind may be understood as a typical *pre-*(or: *proto-*) *canonical phenomenon*. For it may be argued that before a biblical book had reached the canonical status of being a holy and authoritative entity it was provided with the authority of some past personage of undisputable authority, like the Law with Moses and the Psalms with David.[18]

It was surely not mere chance that Solomon, of all important persons of the past, became the 'front figure' of the Song—its tutelary genius. There may have been various reasons for this. First, there are references elsewhere in the book both to Solomon and to 'the king'. These references, recurring predominantly at the beginning and the end (perhaps the younger sections) of the collections of the Song, may have been effective links.[19] Second, commentators usually connect Cant. 1.1 with 1 Kgs 5.9-14, where Solomon is portrayed as the wisest king. Indeed, v. 12 [4.32] says (in a partly uncertain Hebrew text [see *BHS*]) that he had 'composed [וַיְדַבֵּר] three thousand proverbs [מָשָׁל], and *his songs* [שִׁירוֹ] numbered one thousand and five'.[20] In the following verse,

16. Cf. Childs, *Introduction to the Old Testament*, pp. 573-78.

17. The syntactical and translational problems of the formulation cannot be discussed here; but cf. M.H. Segal, 'The Song of Songs', *VT* 12 (1962), pp. 470-90 (481); Gerleman, *Ruth*, p. 93; Keel, *Das Hohelied*, p. 47; Murphy, *The Song of Songs*, pp. 119-22; H.-P. Müller, *Das Hohelied* (ATD, 16.2; Göttingen: Vandenhoeck & Ruprecht, 1992), p. 11.

18. See, further, the next chapter.

19. Cf. Rudolph, *Das Buch Ruth*, p. 121.

20. So the modern Jewish translation, *The Prophets* (Philadelphia: The Jewish Publication Society of America, 1978), p. 234.

however, there are many references to nature, as in the wisdom literature, but not to human love and marriage, the specific content of the Song. Third, Solomon is also elsewhere associated with wisdom, first of all at the beginning of Proverbs (and in Prov. 10.1 and 25.1), as well as, somewhat cryptically, at the beginning of Ecclesiastes (1.1, קהלת בן־דוד מלך בירושלם, cf. also the 'royal travesty' in 1.12, 16). This state of affairs has important consequences for a canonical perspective; but in evaluating these circumstances one has to be very cautious.

It is noteworthy that the Song of Songs is regularly located together with Proverbs and Ecclesiastes in some canon lists, especially in the supposedly oldest 'Hebrew-Aramaic list', that might have originated in a Jewish milieu at the end of the first century CE.[21] This triad of 'Solomonic' books, with the Song of Songs at the third place,[22] may not, however, be regarded as much in terms of a Solomonic authorship as in the perspective of a securing of the books' authority with the help of the name of a person of authority. Nor should this order be taken in favour of the assumption of a basically wisdom character of the Song of Songs. It is not because of an allegedly wisdom character that it has been attributed to Solomon, but the other way round.

In the remaining instances of the Song where Solomon is mentioned, Solomon never speaks. There are only references to him, directly by his name, and indirectly if also 'the king' (see p. 280 below) may be referred to him. But how this speaking of him is to be understood has all the time been a matter of discussion.

21. J.-P. Audet, 'A Hebrew–Aramaic List of Books of the Old Testament in Greek Transcription', *JTS* NS 1 (1950), pp. 135-54; Audet, 'Le sens du Cantique', p. 202; see, however, the critical remarks by Katz, 'The Old Testament Canon', pp. 204-208, and Jepsen, 'Zur Kanongeschichte', pp. 114-32; see further Zeitlin, *An Historical Study*, pp. 9-15, 15-21; H.B. Swete *et al.*, *An Introduction to the Old Testament in Greek* (Cambridge: Cambridge University Press, 1914 [1902]; repr.; New York: Ktav, 1968), pp. 197-219, 226-29; also Barthélemy, 'L'état de la Bible', pp. 20, 22-30; E. Junod, 'La formation et la composition de l'Ancien Testament dans l'église grecque des quatre premiers siècles', in Kaestli and Wermelinger (eds.), *Le canon de l'Ancien Testament*, pp. 9-45, pp. 114, 118-20, 135-38, 144-51.

22. As for the books' present order in the Hebrew Bible, Pope (*Song of Songs*, p. 18) says: 'This order may be a secondary development since the Talmud (Baba Bathra 14b, 15a), some Spanish MSS, and the Massora indicate that the older order was Proverbs, Ecclesiastes, Song of Songs, putting the putative Solomonic compositions together.'

With regard to 'Solomon' in Cant. 1.5b the Hebrew text may not be in order. Because of the parallelism between 'like the tents [כְּאָהֳלֵי] of Kedar' and 'like the curtains [כִּירִיעוֹת] of Solomon' (so the NRSV) some scholars, starting with Winckler and Wellhausen, have found 'Solomon' to be an inadequate parallel to 'Kedar', a tribe of northern Arabia (cf., i.a., Gen. 25.13), and have proposed to read שַׁלְמָה Shalma (see *BHS*), a south Arabian tribe,[23] instead of שְׁלֹמֹה,[24] but without any support from the ancient versions. The Massoretic is preferable. The form might be understood as a reference by the girl—competing with 'the daughters of Jerusalem'—to some fine, royal 'curtains', in parallel to 'exotic' ones from the distant Kedar.[25] Alternatively, 'Solomon' might be a redactional rereading intended to strengthen the Solomonic element in the songs. So, when Murphy finds 'a certain "historicizing" interest' in the mention of Solomon in Cant. 1.1, the same may be the case in 1.5b as well.[26]

Something similar may be said of Cant. 8.11-12. In v. 11 there is a narrative style and what might be called a 'historical' reference to Solomon: 'Solomon had a vineyard in Baal-hamon. He gave...' (the place remains unidentified). The Vulgate in this instance does not quite omit the royal name (as it does in 1.1), but translates the alleged sense of the noun as '*Vinea fuit Pacifico*' (v. 11a) and '*tui Pacifici*' (v. 12). In this it may be influenced by the postcanonical allegorical understanding of the Song as a whole; and that may have weakened the role of the 'historical' Solomon in the Song. The allegorical approach of Targum, referring the Song to the history of Israel, has been discussed by Rudolph and Pope.[27] However, in Hebrew the reference to Solomon here is surprisingly ambiguous. The male lover (possibly the groom),

23. So, among recent commentators, Rudolph (*Das Buch Ruth*, p. 123), Gerleman (*Ruth*, p. 99), Würthwein ('Zum Verständnis', pp. 39-40), Pope (*Song of Songs*, pp. 319-20), Müller (*Das Hohelied*, p. 14), also NEB and REB.

24. 'Solomon' is kept by Gordis (*The Song of Songs*, p. 46): 'Solomonic hangings'; H.L. Ginsberg (ed.), *The Five Megilloth and Jonah: A New Translation* (Philadelphia: Jewish Publication Society of America, 1975), p. 5; and Murphy (*The Song of Songs*, pp. 124-26): 'the pavilions of Solomon'; G. Krinetzki (*Hoheslied* [Die Neue Echter Bibel; Würzburg: Echter, 1980], p. 9): 'wie Salomos Decken'.

25. Murphy, *The Song of Songs*, p. 128.

26. Murphy, *The Song of Songs*, p. 120.

27. Rudolph, *Das Buch Ruth*, p. 184; Pope, *Song of Songs*, pp. 21, 689, 692.

who may be the speaker in this small unit,[28] at first introduces Solomon and his great and unsurpassed richness (cf. 1 Kgs 10.14-29) in a positive and literal way. Then, however, he employs the immense richness of Solomon as a discrediting contrast by making use of the *double entendre* of the word 'vineyard', both in a literal sense (v. 11), and as a metaphor for his beloved (v. 12; cf. 1.6).[29] The effect of this shift, its 'ironische Wirkung', as Müller says (*Das Hohelied*, p. 88), expresses the unique preciousness of his own girl; and the comparison of his 'own vineyard' with that of the incomparable king gives expression to the incomparability of his beloved and—possible—bride. This subtle way of using the wealth of Solomon, has, to some extent, made the king a type-figure, a *typos,* in the framework of the literary composition. In this and other respects the song may be understood as a multi-levelled literary composition.[30]

The composition of Cant. 3.6-11, which has a threefold mention of Solomon (vv. 7, 9 and 11) that is different and more positive than Cant. 8.11-12, may be considered to be the most important unit with respect to the Solomonic aspect of the Song. Gordis even regards it as the oldest part of the book, deriving it from the time of Solomon, and 'as the nucleus for the tradition attributing the entire book to Solomon'.[31] Be that as it may, the Solomonic element is definitely stronger here than in other parts of the Song, and there might well be a historical Solomonic kernel in it. However, the unit's complexity, being more conspicuous than its unity, refers not only to the many lexical, text-historical and syntactical problems of the verses, but also to the complex relation between 'her' (doubtless present in v. 6, because of the verbal forms, possibly also in vv. 7-8) and 'him' (possibly in v. 7 and certainly in vv. 9-11) and 'them', the 'daughters of Jerusalem' paralleled by the

28. Rudolph, *Das Buch Ruth*, 1962: 185; Sæbø, *Fortolkning til Salomos ordspråk*, pp. 313; Müller, *Das Hohelied*, p. 88.

29. See Fox, *The Song of Songs*, pp. 211, 288; Müller, *Das Hohelied*, p. 88.

30. See esp. H.-P. Müller, *Vergleich und Metaphor im Hohenlied* (OBO, 56; Freiburg: Universitätsverlag; Göttingen: Vandenhoeck & Ruprecht, 1984); *idem*, *Das Hohelied*, pp. 88-89.

31. R. Gordis ('A Wedding Song for Solomon', *JBL* 63 [1944], pp. 263-70 [266-70]; *The Song of Songs*, pp. 18-23), says: 'It is at present the oldest datable unit in the book. By contributing to the growth of the tradition of Solomonic authorship, it helped to win inclusion for the entire Song of Songs in the canon of Scripture' (*The Song of Songs*, p. 23).

'daughters of Zion' (only in v. 11).[32] But, first of all, it may be referred to *the problematic relation of vv. 9-10 to the rest of the unit.*

It is, surely, hard to pronounce with certainty upon the prehistory of the complex unity 3.6-11, but there seems to be some literary incoherence regarding the place and function of vv. 9-10 in the present context. In v. 11b, the only instance in the Song where there is a *direct* reference to a wedding situation,[33] it is said of King Solomon: 'the day of his marriage' (יוֹם חֲתֻנָּתוֹ); further, he is 'crowned' by 'his mother', which is also unique to this verse. It is likely that v. 11 should be combined with vv. 6 and 7-8 where too the marriage setting is the most probable one, regardless how the individual elements of vv. 6-8 are to be explained. In these verses the colourful description of a wedding situation is marked by a participial and nominal style. It gives an impression of something present, that is currently happening, so also in v. 11, in spite of one verb form in the suffix conjugation (עִטְּרָה). Verses 9-10, however, present a remarkable shift of attention. By a narrative style and verbs in the past tense in v. 9, the attention is abruptly directed to the past and, moreover, to one single object, rather than to the whole festive situation. This single object is a 'palanquin (אַפִּרְיוֹן) that King Solomon made for himself (עָשָׂה לוֹ) from Lebanon wood' (v. 9); attention is first of all drawn to the way in which it had been made (v. 10). The point of departure for this puzzling digression was in all probability the word מִטָּה 'bed'/'litter' (cf. 1 Sam. 19.13ff.; 2 Sam. 3.31) which belongs to opening phrase of v. 7: 'Look, it is the litter of Solomon!' (NRSV). Some commentators, however, delete v. 7aα as a gloss occasioned by v. 9.[34] But this proposal has 'no valid cause'.[35] On the contrary, the first line of v. 7a is most likely related to the preceding verse and has in this context 'an articular and emphatic function'.[36] Since vv. 9-10, on the other hand, hark back to v. 7aα, with its older and more common word מִטָּה, by means of the late (probably Greek) loan word

32. One should not be deluded by the late verse division or by any alleged metrical rule to delete the first vocative in v. 10bβ (cf. *BHK*), but let the chiastic parallelism in vv. 10bβ-11aα remain (cf. *BHS*; and recently Murphy, *The Song of Songs*, pp. 148, 150).

33. But see also 4.8-11, 12; 5.1 and 8.8-10; cf. Fox, *The Song of Songs*, pp. 230-32, 314, and n. 7 above.

34. The argument of Rudolph is *metri causa*, 1962, pp. 138-39; cf. Müller, *Das Hohelied*, p. 36; *BHS*.

35. Pope, *Song of Songs*, p. 432.

36. Murphy, *The Song of Songs*, p. 149.

אַפִּרְיוֹן 'palanquin',[37] this reference to Solomon differs from those else-where in the unit. In v. 11, as well as v. 7, Solomon is referred to as a bridegroom. There is some ambiguity as to whether this is the historical King Solomon or a literary fiction, a 'royal travesty', representing any groom as 'king' in Israel. Because of the link of v. 9a to v. 7a, King Solomon might be regarded as a groom even in vv. 9-10, likewise with the same ambiguity between reality and fiction.

However, it may be more significant hermeneutically that the narra-tive style and the detailed 'technical' description in vv. 9-10, primarily related to the past, seem to point in another direction. Just the 'technical' character of the two verses, besides leaving the impression of being an insert,[38] makes it more probable that the intent of the verses is to focus upon the *historical* Solomon, the rich and illustrious *roi du soleil* of ancient Israel. The final aim of Cant. 3.9-10, therefore, may be the same as was revealed in 1.1, and possibly also in 1.5b: in what might be called a 'historicizing interest' it will focus upon the picture of King Solomon as *the exalted figure of authority* in the book.[39]

The mention of Solomon, then, is relatively distinct; but the mention of a 'king' (Cant. 1.4, 12 and 7.6[5]) seems to be indefinite. Possibly also 'the king' might refer to Solomon, at least in the present shape of the book. Whether a relation to him was intended originally is doubtful; but at the same time, this is less relevant to the final form of the book.

Still, if these three instances are treated separately and seen in their respective contexts they certainly turn out to be very different, yet they have in common that 'the king' in all of them is described as the lover/beloved of the young girl—in 1.4, 12 by the girl herself, in 7.6 by others. This description, however, may easily be understood as a 'literary fiction',[40] being the girl's effusive praise, in a festive style, of her lover/beloved (or groom); and in this way he is depicted under the guise of a 'king', by a 'royal travesty'.[41] Müller calls it a royal lyric

---

37. Cf., i.a., F. Rundgren, 'אַפִּרְיוֹן "Tragsessel, Sänfte"', *ZAW* 74 (1962), pp. 70-72; M. Görg, 'Die "Sänfte Salomos" nach HL 3,9f', *Biblische Notizen* 18 (1982), pp. 15-25; Pope, *Song of Songs*, pp. 412, 441-42 ('litter'); Murphy, *The Song of Songs*, pp. 148-50 ('carriage').

38. Also the present problematic transition from v. 10 to 11 (cf. *BHS*) confirms the impression that vv. 9-10 were inserted in an existing composition; cf. n. 19 above.

39. Murphy, *The Song of Songs*, p. 120.

40. Cf., Murphy, *The Song of Songs*, pp. 47, 83, 127.

41. Rudolph (*Das Buch Ruth*, p. 123) sees in Cant. 1.4 an 'Anspielung an die

'upwards Travesty' (*Travestie-nach-oben*).[42] Also Fox who is critical of some current uses of the term 'travesty' rightly grants that 'there is a "royal disguise" in Canticles, namely in 1.4, 12 and 3.7-11, where the girl speaks of her lover as if he were a king. This disguise is not an attempt on the characters' part to escape their social situation, but a way of expressing their emotional exaltation, their joy in their current state' (p. 293).[43]

When, finally, these references to 'the king' are compared with the references to '(King) Solomon', it seems—somewhat unexpectedly— that the differences between them are more prominent than their common ambiguity. On the one hand, contributing to this ambiguity, there is a link between the 'royal disguise' of the 'king' references and the possible aspect of a similar disguise in some of the Solomon references, namely, Cant. 8.11-12 and 3.6-8, 11, perhaps also 1.5. On the other hand, the most conspicuous trait in the Solomon references is the 'historicizing interest', primarily in Cant. 1.1 and 3.9-10, possibly also in 1.5, focusing on the historical King Solomon as the wisest and richest man of old, whereas the use of the 'king' phrase should be assessed as an integral part of the 'love language' of the songs. So, the 'king' references and the Solomon references are not as similar as one might have expected them to be; therefore, they should be kept properly apart and not be mixed up uncritically.

As for the important *Solomonic element* in the Song, then, it seems to have a dual character: there are two tendencies extant that apparently run contrary to each other. Both of them may have been significant to the canonization and later understanding of the book, but in different ways.

In one line Solomon as a *king* is part of the sophisticated 'literary fiction' that is found as 'royal travesty' in some songs, partly in the framework of a wedding situation; and this element may have 'prepared' for a later allegorical understanding and interpretation of the book.

In the other line Solomon as the unique King *Solomon*, a man of

Hochzeit', and Gerleman (*Ruth*, p. 98) the 'Verkleidung eines Königs'; cf. also Pope (*Song of Songs*, pp. 303, 347, 630).

42. And Müller goes on to say: 'weil für eine vordemokratische Gesellschaft im Königtum die klassische Wunschrolle liegt' (*Das Hohelied*, p. 13; cf. 89 on Cant. 8.11).

43. Fox, *The Song of Songs*, pp. 292-94; quotation from p. 293.

indisputable authority in ancient Israel,[44] is focused upon, in a most specific 'historicizing interest'. His honour, status and authority seem to have contributed decisively to the status and authority of the collection of songs, now constituting the Song, and may have been a primary cause for the upcoming process of 'sacralization' and canonization of the book; and in due time it was like a shield against attack on it. 'The Song must have been regarded as in some way part of the national religious literature *before* it was read allegorically'.[45]

3. *On the Canonical Aspect*

It may be beyond any dispute that it was the complex Solomonic element in the Song, as discussed above, that had the primary significance for the process of 'sacralization' and canonization, as part of the final stages in the tradition and redaction history of the book, when the collection of old love and marriage songs became the Song of Songs. But, as results of this process, there are also other 'particular stamps' that 'the collectors of Israel's Scripture left as a key for its interpretation'.[46] In the end, some of them may be briefly commented on. Partly they look like fragments and belong to what Müller has called 'versprengte Fragmente' (1.12, 13-14; 2.6-7, 15; 4.8; 7.11, 14) and 'redaktionelle Rahmenverse' (5.9, 16b; 6.1), without fully recognizing, however, their function in the concluding redactional process that has a bearing on the later canonization of the book.[47]

There has been much discussion about the character and function of the utterance in Cant. 2.7 that returns in nearly the same form also in 3.5 and 8.4. It is, in particular, hard to explain their respective locations. They are thought either to be out of place,[48] or to express a request not to disturb the lovers. But these explanations may be regarded as missing the aim of these most particular words. Nor are they some sort of 'refrain'.

---

44. This may have its validity in spite of the Deuteronomistic criticism of his 'love affairs' in 1 Kgs 11.1-8 (9-13).

45. Fox, *The Song of Songs*, p. 250.

46. Childs, *Introduction to the Old Testament*, p. 573.

47. Müller, *Das Hohelied*, p. 7.

48. Cf. Rudolph, *Das Buch Ruth*, p. 131; E. Würthwein, 'Ruth, Das Hohelied, Esther', in *Die fünf Megilloth* [HAT, 1.18; Tübingen: J.C.B. Mohr, 1969], p. 44; Gerleman, *Ruth*, p. 120; cf. also Müller, *Das Hohelied*, p. 26.

Nevertheless, the observation of being out of place that some commentators have made of these words, may well be correct even though their explanation turns out to be faulty. For the words' respective places are not accidental. On the contrary, it is most noteworthy that in all three instances the call, 'I adjure you, O Daughters of Jerusalem… Do not arouse, do not stir up love, until it be ready!',[49] follows upon the most intimate description of sexual intercourse that is to be found in the songs, especially 2.6 and 8.3, but also 3.4b indirectly. Therefore, the point may be made with good reasons that the three words are to be understood as moral *admonitions*, that on purpose are set in sharp contrast to the direct preceding description; otherwise this may have been felt to be on the edge of what was morally tolerable. In this way, these three words of contrast to the preceding are to be understood positively as some sort of theological 'safeguarding' of the understanding of a 'daring' love description. Thus, the admonitions of Cant. 2.7, 3.5 and 8.4 may have fostered the coming canonization of the Song.

In the light of the explanation of Cant. 2.7; 3.5; 8.4, as given above, some other instances may be better understood in an ethical or theological perspective that otherwise is not distinctive in the Song. First of all, the word in 2.15 that seems to be unrelated to its context and has been characterized as 'enigmatic' and 'obscure',[50] may best be taken as a *moral reminder*, placed between the strongly hortative descriptions in 2.8-14 and 2.16-17. Perhaps also Cant. 8.8-9, with its 'rather solemn air about the announcement of the brothers concerning their little sister',[51] might be reckoned to the efforts of 'safeguarding' the text of the Song (cf. also Gen. 24.29ff.; Judg. 21.22). For obvious reasons, little can be said with certainty in this respect; nevertheless, a certain pattern of redactional procedure seems to have been operative in these instances.

Finally, a most difficult item may be brought up, namely, the divided text tradition in Cant. 8.6b. Here the Ben Asher text reads: שַׁלְהֶבֶתְיָה, whereas the Ben Naphtali tradition as well as many manuscripts and editors (*BHK*) have: שַׁלְהֶבֶת־יָה, with the short form of the holy name of God of Israel.[52] Is this divided text tradition a witness of a deep theological disagreement regarding the theological 'safeguarding' of the Song? As is well known, there is no mention of any name of God in the

---

49. Murphy, *The Song of Songs*, pp. 130, 144, 180.
50. Murphy, *The Song of Songs*, p. 141.
51. Murphy, *The Song of Songs*, p. 198.
52. See, i.a., Fox, *The Song of Songs*, p. 170; and the major commentaries.

Song. However, it might well be that among some Jewish sages there was a wish to set the stamp of the Name of God on the Song—but this was rejected by other sages, confirmed by the most authoritative text tradition: the Ben Asher text.

And with this echo of disagreement one may be at the boundary of the ancient discussion of the canonicity of the Song of Songs.

In conclusion, the problem of the canonicity of the Song of Songs is much more complex and the process of its canonization may have started much earlier than is usually stated in the text books. There may be good reasons to maintain that the early stages of the canonization of the book, starting with some sort of 'sacralization', were interwoven with the late stages of the tradition and redaction history of the Song. In this centre point between the 'pre-history' (*Vorgeschichte*) and the 'post-history' (*Nachgeschichte*) of the book the collection of old love and marriage songs in Israel became the Song of Songs.

Chapter 18

FROM 'UNIFYING REFLECTIONS' TO THE CANON:
ASPECTS OF THE TRADITIO-HISTORICAL FINAL STAGES
IN THE DEVELOPMENT OF THE OLD TESTAMENT

1. *Introductory Remarks on the Theological Problem*

From the works of two most creative scholars of our time, who have
provoked much debate, it is possible to illustrate to a certain extent the
current state of Old Testament scholarship as a historical and theological science.

First, we might mention Gerhard von Rad's two-volume *Theologie
des Alten Testaments* (1957–60), which in a number of ways resulted in
a watershed in recent Old Testament scholarship. His work has proved
to be particularly influential not only in the narrower area of theology;[1]
in a noteworthy way it has contributed to the fact that individual disciplines of Old Testament studies have been related to each other more
closely than was previously the case, especially since von Rad has
brought the 'Theology' of the Old Testament considerably closer to the
discipline of 'Introduction'—and thus to the results of historical-critical
exegesis. In this way, and also by means of his traditio-historical
research, he has made extremely topical the important question of
methodical unity in Old Testament (or biblical) studies.

Twenty years later, Brevard S. Childs turned to this attractive inter-
disciplinary interest—and the theological question of unity—from the

1.   On the influence of von Rad's *Theologie des Alten Testaments*, I–II, see esp.
Schmidt, '"Theologie des Alten Testaments" vor und nach Gerhard von Rad',
pp. 1-25; Spriggs, *Two Old Testament Theologies*. Especially significant was the
debate about the relationship between plurality and 'middle' (or centre) in Old Testament theology which resulted from his presentation. Cf., e.g., Smend, *Die Mitte
des Alten Testaments*; and H. Graf Reventlow, *Hauptprobleme der alttestamentlichen Theologie im 20. Jahrhundert* (EdF, 173; Darmstadt: Wissenschaftliche
Buchgesellschaft, 1982). See also Ch. 14 above.

other side, as it were, by expressly placing the discipline of 'Introduction' to the Old Testament within the area of theology through his completely newly structured *Introduction to the Old Testament as Scripture*.[2] Childs tried to attain this by means of a particularly profiled use of the term 'canon', and thus he speaks of both a 'canonical shaping' of the Old Testament books and of their 'canonical history'.[3]

It may be obvious that the very concept of the 'canon' must have been very suited to the theological aims of Childs, especially as 'Introduction' and 'Theology' overlap in this concept and because here there is the closest link between history (the forming of the canon) and the theologically normative (the canonical collection of holy books as norm). Moreover, it must be generally characteristic of recent theological study that such great attention has been shown towards the concept of canon, and towards the Old Testament canon in particular.[4] The

2.   Cf. Childs, *Introduction to the Old Testament,* esp. pp. 39-41 on the criticism of traditional Introductions.

3.   It is true that Childs's basic conception can be found in earlier works (*Biblical Theology in Crisis* [Philadelphia: Westminster Press, 1970], esp. pp. 97-122; 'The Old Testament as Scripture of the Church', *CTM* 43 [1972], pp. 709-22; 'The Exegetical Significance of Canon for the Study of the Old Testament', in *Congress Volume: Göttingen 1977* [VTSup, 29; Leiden: E.J. Brill, 1978], pp. 66-80); but the debate concerning his particular method, which took place especially in Anglo-American territory, only began after the appearance of his *Introduction to the Old Testament.* See the contributions by B. Kittel, J. Barr, J. Blenkinsopp, H. Cazelles, G.M. Landes, R.E. Murphy, and R. Smend in *JSOT* 16 (1980), pp. 2-51 ('Brevard Childs' Development of the Canonical Approach'; 'Childs' *Introduction to the Old Testament as Scripture*'; 'A New Kind of Introduction: Professor Childs' *Introduction to the Old Testament as Scripture*'; 'The Canonical Approach to Torah and Prophets'; 'The Canonical Approach to Introducing the Old Testament: Prodigy and Problems'; 'The Old Testament as Scripture'; and 'Questions about the Importance of the Canon in the Old Testament Introduction', respectively), as well as by B.C. Birch, D.A. Knight, J.L. Mays, D.P. Polk and J.A. Sanders in *HBT* 2 (1980), pp. 113-97. In both places Childs gives responses to his critics: see 'A Response to Reviewers of *Introduction to the Old Testament as Scripture*', *JSOT* 16 (1980), pp. 52-60, and 'A Response', *HBT* 2 (1980), pp. 199-211. Cf. the detailed discussion of his book by W. Zimmerli, *VT* 31 (1981), pp. 235-44; J. Barr, *Holy Scripture: Canon, Authority, Criticism* (Philadelphia: Westminster Press, 1983), pp. 75ff. and 130ff; and H.M. Barstad, 'Le canon comme principe exégétique', *ST* 38 (1984), pp. 77-91; and esp. Brett, *Biblical Criticism in Crisis?*.

4.   Apart from Childs, the following—from among many scholars—may be mentioned: Sanders, *Torah and Canon*; *idem, Canon and Community: A Guide to*

'canon' could even be described as a key word of the recent theological thought of many exegetes, where the accent is placed on the significance of the final form of the Old Testament. In his time von Rad was very interested in this final form, and, to a greater extent than others, Childs has discussed it and given it theological prominence.

The question emerges as to whether the multifaceted recent use of the concept of canon is sufficiently clear or essentially suitable. The question should certainly be pursued more closely and broadly, which of course can only occur to a limited extent. It should be taken special note of one particular point, because it may be regarded as an especially complicating one, namely the *transition* or shift from the (forward-looking) *tradition history* to the (basically backward-looking) *canon history*, where 'canon history' is meant in the narrower sense of the word. How and when this transition or the change in position of those who dealt with the tradition material took effect, should now be given more careful consideration. In looking at this point, a few pertinent, current questions may be discussed.

2. Comments on the Current Use of the Concept of Canon

In recent biblical scholarship the assessment of the biblical canon in relationship to the traditional view has become more colourful, not only from a theological point of view, but also from a historical perspective. Moreover, as a historical phenomenon the canon of the Hebrew Bible is not understood today to the same extent from its final stage—or even from a 'resolution' of the so-called synod of Jamnia around 90–100 CE—but it is rather assessed as the end of a longer and complex development and not regarded so dogmatically as in a 'tradition historical' perspective.[5] At first glance one might be inclined to link this longer

---

Canonical Criticism (Philadelphia: Fortress Press, 1984); *idem*, 'Text and Canon: Concepts and Method', *JBL* 88 (1979), pp. 5-29; S.Z. Leiman, *The Canonization of Hebrew Scripture: The Talmudic and Midrashic Evidence* (Hamden, CT: Archon Books, 1976); Leiman (ed.), *The Canon and Masorah of the Hebrew Bible*, pp. 5-282; J.-D. Kaestli and O. Wermelinger (eds.), *Le canon de l'Ancien Testament: Sa formation et son histoire* (Geneva: Labor et Fides, 1984). See also the informative article by H. Graf Reventlow in his *Hauptprobleme der biblischen Theologie im 20. Jahrhundert* (EdF, 203; Darmstadt: Wissenschaftliche Buchgesellschaft, 1983), pp. 125-37.

5. Cf., e.g., the comments by E. Sellin and G. Fohrer, *Einleitung in das Alte Testament* (Heidelberg: Quelle & Meyer, 1965), p. 535; or G.W. Anderson,

perspective of the history of the canon with the canon-theological position of Childs, for he places the beginnings of the development of the
canon relatively early in the pre-exilic era. The question now, however,
is how Childs and other scholars of similar opinion describe the beginnings and subsequent development of the formation of the canon. An
understanding of this development is made more difficult to a certain
extent when Childs expresses the view that he does not understand the
concept of 'canon' in the traditional sense of the word, but rather in a
broader sense, in which he is concerned more with a theological concept than with a literary and historical one, for in the 'canon' he primarily sees a normative whole which has sprung from a supporting and
moulding interaction between tradition/text and a believing community.[6]

The fact should not be overlooked that Childs is here on middle
ground which has not always been regarded appropriately by his critics
as proper. On the one hand, he is watching closely the historical questions and stresses the necessity of differentiating clearly between the
literary origins of the biblical books and the development of the

'Canonical and Non-Canonical', *CHB* 1 (1970), pp. 113-59, with the literature
referred to above in nn. 3 and 4. See also Lebram, 'Aspekte der alttestamentlichen
Kanonbildung', pp. 173-83; J. Barton, 'The Significance of a Fixed Canon of the
Hebrew Bible', in M. Sæbø (ed.), *Hebrew Bible/Old Testament: The History of its
Interpretation*. I.1. *Antiquity* (Göttingen: Vandenhoeck & Ruprecht, 1996), pp. 67-
83; the relevant literature is otherwise almost countless. On the recent
problematization of the so-called synod of Jamnia, cf. Lewis, 'What Do We Mean
by Jabne?', pp. 125-32; R.C. Newman, 'The Council of Jamnia and the Old Testa-
ment Canon', *WTJ* 38 (1975), pp. 319-50; P. Schäfer, 'Die sogenannte Synode von
Jabne', *Judaica* 31 (1975), pp. 54-64, 116-24; G. Stemberger, 'Die sogenannte
Synode von Jabne und das frühe Christentum', *Kairos* NS 19 (1977), pp. 14-21.
Additionally, there are the canon problems of the LXX (and other ancient versions)
as well as the special problems of the Apocrypha: see, e.g., Sundberg, *The Old Testament and the Early Church*; R. Beckwith, *The Old Testament Canon of the New
Testament Church and its Background in Early Judaism* (Grand Rapids: Eerdmans,
1985); E.E. Ellis, 'The Old Testament Canon in the Early Church', in M.J. Mulder
(ed.), *Mikra* (CRINT, 2.1; Assen: Van Gorcum, 1988), pp. 653-90. Also, the Qumran findings have repeatedly placed the canon questions in a different light: see,
e.g., Sanders, *Torah and Canon*, pp. 12-15; Reventlow, *Hauptprobleme der biblischen Theologie*, pp. 126-27.
    6.   See, e.g., Childs, *Introduction to the Old Testament*, pp. 46ff.; and Childs,
'A Response to Reviewers', pp. 53-55.

canon[7]—thus disagreeing with scholars like Leiman or Kline, who have tried 'to establish an unbroken canonical continuity from the Mosaic period', and who thus appear to uphold an identity of the development of Scripture and the canon.[8] On the other hand, it is obviously even more important to him that the development of Scripture and canon should not be split away from each other as has often been the case, as then the development of the canon is regarded and presented merely as a separate act after the completion of the formation of Scripture.[9]

There are however, certain differences of opinion among scholars who generally share the view of a longer development of the canon. Thus, for example, Childs disagrees with Sanders since, among other things, the latter has described his own method as 'canonical criticism', whereas Childs prefers to see his method not as *one* critical method next to other modern methods such as literary criticism or form criticism, but rather prefers to regard it as a comprehensive view under which various critical methods may be used. Because Sanders extends his 'canonical criticism' existentially into the present, Childs rather emphasizes the 'objectivity' of the text in its final form, und thus its unique and still valid normativity.[10] Just as Laurin does, among others, Childs also calls the concluding phase in the development of the canon 'canonization'; yet he marks his own point of view by adding immediately: 'The earlier decisions were not qualitatively different from the later ones'.[11]

7. Cf. Childs, *Introduction to the Old Testament*, pp. 58-62, 71; and Childs, 'A Response', pp. 201, 204, and 209-10.

8. Childs, *Introduction to the Old Testament*, pp. 55-56, 60-62, 128; cf. Childs, 'A Response', pp. 209-10.

9. Childs, *Introduction to the Old Testament*, pp. 51-55. In his lecture at the Göttingen Congress in 1977, Childs forewards a 'classic' view of Gunkel which characterizes well the opinion which the development of Scripture plays off against the subsequent canonization; see Childs, 'Exegetical Significance', p. 66.

10. Childs, *Introduction to the Old Testament*, pp. 56-57, 82-83. Sanders also disagrees with Childs; see, e.g., Sanders, 'Canonical Context and Canonical Criticism', *HBT* 2 (1980), pp. 173-97; *idem, Canon and Community*, pp. 17-19, 37-38; *idem, Torah and Canon*, pp. xi-xv. Cf. Barr, *Holy Scripture*, pp. 156-57. See also n. 49 below.

11. Childs, 'Exegetical Significance', p. 67; cf. *Introduction to the Old Testament*, p. 66; 'A Response', p. 209. When Laurin, who is close to the existential view of Sanders, makes 'a distinction between "canonizing" (the dynamic process of tradition growth) and "canonization" (the static event of tradition closure)', he assesses this differentiation differently from Childs by adding: 'Canonization has

Thus it is important for Childs—as well as for others like Sanders and Sheppard—not to understand the development of the canon as a separate final event, but as a process of a special kind which has been integrated into the development of Scripture.[12] How this is to be judged in every way should be left undecided. Yet in comparison with current interpretation, as a starting point this should be regarded as something well worth considering and positive. If, however, one thereby arrives at a concrete description of the relationship between the development of Scripture and canon, much is left to be desired as far as a detailed profiled clarification of this relationship is concerned.[13] Finally, in this context one has also spoken of a 'holistic reading of the Hebrew Bible';[14] but even so one cannot avoid having to consider as precise differentiations as possible in the material, both historically and theologically.[15]

For the relationship between the development of Scripture and canon must first be explained analytically and critically by means of historical and theological differences and distinctions. When that which separates has been thoroughly brought out can the homogeneous lines of the whole emerge more clearly. It will certainly also be useful for the theological question of unity not to throw methodically too much into the one pot.

been untrue to the canonizing process of tradition history' (R.B. Laurin, 'Tradition and Canon', in Knight [ed.], *Tradition and Theology*, pp. 261-74 [261]). Cf. G.T. Sheppard, 'Canonization: Hearing the Voice of the Same God through Historically Dissimilar Traditions', *Int* 36 (1982), pp. 21-33.

12. Cf. Childs, *Introduction to the Old Testament*, pp. 77-78, as well as his comment in 'A Response', p. 209: 'The canonical history is not a history which is separated from the larger literary history, but one aspect of the whole. It never replaced the literary history, but increased in importance and intensity in the post-exilic period.'

13. Childs, *Introduction to the Old Testament*, pp. 50-62. Cf. his discussion of single books. The same may be said, however, of the pertinent deliberations of other scholars who hold the same position.

14. Thus Sheppard, 'Canonization', p. 21; cf. Childs, *Introduction to the Old Testament*, pp. 252-53; Sanders, *Torah and Canon*, p. ix; and Sanders, *Canon and Community*, pp. 36-37.

15. It may be significant that Childs does not find it of 'great exegetical importance to be able always to distinguish sharply between the literary and canonical aspects of this history. Particularly in the early period, it is often impossible to know why stories were included in a cycle, or why various sources were joined' ('A Response', p. 210).

Now, one may take this opportunity of aiming at a particular marking of the boundary which was envisaged above at the end of the first section. In order to get a better handle on its definition, two different sets of facts ought now to be considered in somewhat greater detail.

3. *'Unifying Reflections' and 'Midrash'*

As far as further clarification of the relationship between the development of Scripture and canon is concerned, may the starting point be taken from a fundamental statement of Childs's. He expressed his canon-theological point of view as follows: 'What is important to recognize is how a particular religious perspective, governed by a process of fixing the tradition into authoritive writings, more and more shaped the tradition toward a particular canonical goal.'[16] It may be informative to compare this statement with another, which Walter Baumgartner formulated in a letter to Karl Barth dated 16 July 1942, on the occasion of the publication of Volume 2.2 of the *Kirchliche Dogmatik*:

> Certainly the sense of a piece of text can change when it is drawn into a wider context. But to what extent have the editors of the whole books and particularly the final editing of the whole canon woven in a specific interpretation *in detail*, and, if this is the case, is not then the point of departure a Jewish one, with the result that a further giant leap is required to reach Christian ground?[17]

Although both the Old Testament scholars quoted above each define their views with care, there appears to be a gaping difference of opinion between their different statements as to how the development of the canon relates to the alleged development of Scripture, or to put it more specifically, how the mutual correlation of the two processes is to be understood and described in concrete terms.

At the same time the distance between the two positions should not be overestimated, since Childs's 'broader concept of canon' mentioned above—like that of Sanders and others—in the final analysis is in fact not so unorthodox or radical as may appear to be the case at first. For if one compares the views of Childs[18] or Sanders[19] with those of literary

16. Childs, 'A Response', p. 210.
17. R. Smend (ed.), 'Karl Barth und Walter Baumgartner: Ein Briefwechsel über das Alte Testament', in E. Jüngel (ed.) *Zur Theologie Karl Barths* (ZTK.B, 6; Tübingen: J.C.B. Mohr, 1986), pp. 240-71 (254).
18. Childs, *Introduction to the Old Testament*, pp. 62-67, and esp. pp. 127-35

critics such as Eissfeldt[20] or even Hölscher,[21] one can see clearly the proximity and similarity of their opinions. Common to all of them is the historical-critical picture of the gradual rise of traditions, collections and writings in biblical Israel. However, while the literary critics—as well as the form critics—have stressed the *development of the literature*, and in the Pentateuch, for example, the especial importance of D and P, in order thus to discover 'the conditions necessary for the development of a collection which enjoys canonical validity' above all in the 'law and the prophets',[22] Childs and Sanders have taken as their premise the final form of the canon and have aimed chiefly at those religious 'forces' which left their mark in this way or that on the literary evolution of this canonical final form—where even the particular significance of D and P has been considered.

One may not be far off asserting that in this point there are merely different aspects of the same story; however, there is more to it than that. Because the literary-historical and form-historical descriptions of the development of the literature very often have not progressed beyond the half-way stage and, therefore, have not explained adequately the reality and nature of the final form of the text historically and theologically, it is most understandable that in recent years attention has been directed so emphatically towards the final form of the Scriptures and towards the canon, especially since the canon did not of course suddenly appear without any previous background. Nevertheless, the danger exists of interpreting the pre-canonical stages and 'pre-conditions' or particular themes in Old Testament theology prematurely and thus inappropriately as canonical. For example, when Sanders explains more closely what he regards as his 'canonical hermeneutics' in five points, he is dealing with very general—although central—theological themes

(on the Pentateuch), p. 224 (on Deuteronomy), pp. 236-38, 306-310 (on the 'early' and 'later' Prophets), and pp. 501-503 (on the 'Writings').

19. Sanders, *Torah and Canon*, pp. 1-53, 54-116; cf. also his *Canon and Community*, pp. 21-45, and 46-68, where 'canonical process', on the one hand, and 'canonical hermeneutics', on the other hand, are discussed separately.

20. O. Eissfeldt, *Einleitung in das Alte Testament* (Tübingen: J.C.B. Mohr, 3rd edn, 1964), pp. 765-70.

21. G. Hölscher, *Kanonisch und Apokryph* (Naumburg/S., 1905), pp. 7-18, 19-24, 25-35.

22. Eissfeldt, *Einleitung*, p. 761.

in the Old Testament, whereas at the same time any points of interest in the 'law and the prophets' are missing.[23]

In these circumstances it now appears very necessary to investigate more accurately the boundary points between the development of Scripture and of the canon. First, mention should be made of a phenomenon which may be termed 'unifying reflections'. The phrase 'unifying reflections' (*Zusammen-Denken*) was used theologically by Walther Zimmerli when, in a discussion of Gerhard von Rad's *Theologie des Alten Testaments*, he asked for a greater 'risk of unifying reflections'.[24] Here it was a question of the current structuring and presentation of a theology of the Old Testament. However, the term can also be used in the historical sense of an important process in Old Testament tradition history itself, as may become apparent from several examples. In his work on the Deuteronomistic History Martin Noth discussed the attitude of the Deuteronomistic compiler '*vis-à-vis* the traditions which had come down to him'.[25] Here he ascertains that the compiler 'did not only collect and select his material but also, since he wanted to create a united work which was complete in itself, linked with each other the various traditions at his disposal and tried to balance the discrepancies between them'.[26] 'On the whole' the compiler 'gave his historical account the character of a work of tradition whose intention was the collecting and explaining of the traditions of the history of his people which were still extant'.[27] Noth has likewise pointed out that this historical account was also heavily theological in content, although he could have dealt even more fully with this aspect.[28]

The phenomenon of collecting and selecting traditions and above all of the creative formation of historical works, which in his *Studien*—as

---

23. Sanders, *Canon and Community*, pp. 50-57. On p. 51 he lists the five points as follows: 'One, the Bible is a monotheizing literature. Two, it bears a broad theocentric hermeneutic. Three, much of it celebrates the theologem *errore hominum providentia divina* (God's grace works in and through human sinfulness). Four, in it God betrays a divine bias for the weak and dispossessed. Five, there is a fourfold hermeneutic process by which it adapted international wisdom.'

24. Zimmerli, review of *Theologie des Alten Testaments*, p. 105.

25. Noth, *Überlieferungsgeschichtliche Studien*, pp. 95-100.

26. Noth, *Überlieferungsgeschichtliche Studien*, p. 98.

27. Noth, *Überlieferungsgeschichtliche Studien*, p. 100.

28. Noth, *Überlieferungsgeschichtliche Studien*, pp. 100-10, §13 ('Die theologischen Leitgedanken'). It may well be said, however, that in this regard his work is well supplemented by von Rad's *Theologie des Alten Testaments*.

well as in his examination of the Pentateuch[29]—Noth has shown as an important characteristic of Old Testament tradition and redaction history, may be comprehended as immense an 'unifying reflection' of the very many extant individual traditions. *A gradual unification of the historical multiplicity ensued which was theologically motivated and influenced.* This was true not only of the historical traditions but also of other tradition areas of the Old Testament such as the prophetic and wisdom literature traditions and their collections.

The book of Jeremiah admittedly has a particularly complicated tradition and redaction history, from which only a few points can be considered here.[30] Among the frequently treated traditions one may note particularly the interlinked statements about the 'word of Yahweh' which are often exemplified in the book of Jeremiah, and in an especially profiled way in the account of his calling which legitimizes his prophetic office (1.4ff.) as well as in the section with the editorial superscription 'concerning the prophets' (לנבאים, 23.9-32), where Jeremiah quarrels with other prophets. In these and many other sections the unique function and significance of the 'word of Yahweh' is firmly expressed. Here scholars have spoken of a particular 'word theology', which cannot be further examined here.[31]

When we consider the unusually broad heading in 1.1-3 in this light, a double meaning in the superscription becomes especially worthy of note, since first, 'the words of Jeremiah' (1.1) and then the 'word of Yahweh' (1.2) are noted, whereas the LXX has moved the formulation 'the word of God, which went forth to Jeremiah' to the top of the first verse.[32] Here three points concerning the current complex form of the superscription may be noted. First, by means of the introductory

---

29. Cf. Noth, *Überlieferungsgeschichte des Pentateuch*, where he also discusses the 'literary formation' and the 'account of the Pentateuch as a whole' (pp. 247-71).

30. From the vast amount of literature on this topic one can take this opportunity of referring especially to Mowinckel, *Zur Komposition des Buches Jeremia*; Nielsen, *Oral Tradition*, pp. 64-79; W. Thiel, *Die deuteronomistische Redaktion von Jeremia 1–25* (WMANT, 41; Neukirchen–Vluyn: Neukirchener Verlag, 1973); and *idem*, *Die deuteronomistische Redaktion von Jeremia 26–45* (WMANT, 52; Neukirchen–Vluyn: Neukirchener Verlag, 1981). Cf. Kaiser, *Einleitung in das Alte Testament*, pp. 246-59, and more recently S. Herrmann's article 'Jeremia/Jeremiabuch', *TRE*, XVI, pp. 568-86.

31. Cf. von Rad, *Theologie des Alten Testaments*, II, pp. 93-111, esp. p. 107.

32 Cf. Rudolph, *Jeremia*, pp. 2-3; Thiel, *Die deuteronomistische Redaktion von Jeremia 1–25*, pp. 49-61.

information—'the words of Jeremiah'—in the first verse, which presumably forms 'the oldest component' of the superscription,[33] there are summarized in the single concept of 'word' (in the plural) not only the multi-faceted proclamation and the lamentations of Jeremiah, but also his use of symbolism and deeds as well as various reports about him.[34] Second, this 'summarizing' is brought to a head by means of the singular form 'word of Yahweh' in the relative clause which introduces the next verse and the interest is removed from the person of the prophet to God, his caller and Lord, and his powerful and effective word. Third, this 'development' is moved a considerable step forward by means of the form of the LXX, where the emphasis is laid even more strongly on the function of the 'word of God'. Here one may observe, therefore, a tradition proceeding in a state of flux.[35] And in the course of this prophetic tradition there has resulted an unmistakable theological 'systematization' and significance of the tradition materials.[36]

The duality of the 'words of Jeremiah' and the 'word of Yahweh' is noticeable also in Jeremiah 36. Moreover, this chapter also permits to a certain extent an insight into the scriptural development of the prophetic proclamation, which thus turns out to be valid not only for the present generation but also for the future generations of the nation.[37] In addition, this account exhibits that the prophetic tradition was not fixed forever with a first manuscript, but that it was still part of the formation process and that an oral tradition also continued to develop.[38]

33. Thiel, *Die deuteronomistische Redaktion von Jeremia 1–25*, p. 49.

34. Cf. Mowinckel, *Zur Komposition des Buches Jeremia*, p. 25. When Rudolph, *Jeremia*, p. 2, translates the opening words as 'the story of Jeremiah', it is clear that he has misunderstood the fundamental meaning of the word-concept.

35. Cf. Thiel, *Die deuteronomistische Redaktion von Jeremia 1–25*, pp. 49ff.

36. Even B.S. Childs, 'The Canonical Shape of the Prophetical Literature', *Int* 32 (1978), pp. 46-55, speaks (on p. 53) of 'the creative dimension involved in the collecting process', except that he calls this process 'canonical shaping of the prophetic literature', which raises the question of terminological and factual classification.

37. Cf. Isa. 8.16-18. See also Nielsen, *Oral Tradition*, pp. 64-79, esp. pp. 68-69, 73.

38. Cf. Mowinckel, *Prophecy and Tradition*, pp. 21-23, 61-65. On p. 21 he says: 'It is indeed a fact that some of the longer, strongly deuteronomizing prose speeches by Jeremiah...are actual parallels to (variants of) metrically formed sayings which obviously have been contained in Baruch's book roll... Jeremiah's sayings have *also* continued to live as oral tradition *beside* Baruch's book and, in a way, independently of it.'

For, as is mentioned in the conclusion, to the new scroll dictated by Jeremiah 'were still added many words of a similar nature' (36.32).

From these few texts one receives a picture of the tradition and the scriptural development of the prophetic proclamation, which other texts and prophetic writings can confirm, namely, that the prophetic tradition was an exceedingly alive and variable process which was distinguished in its *continual movement by productive formation and reinterpretation*. The *final form*, however, did not come into being by chance, but *may be regarded as intentional 'unifying reflections'* which from a theological point of view above all bore the stamp of the knowledge of the powerful and effective word of God.

Fundamentally the traditio- and redaction-historical process is the same also in the area of wisdom literature, although with somewhat different stresses, as may be seen from the form of the book of Proverbs. Generally a 'large chasm' is assumed between the first main section, Proverbs 1–9, which is distinguished by lengthy sections of speech and a decidedly theological content, and the next section, Prov. 10.1–22.16, which forms the first 'Solomonic collection' of proverbs of the wisdom of experience.[39] Certainly there are considerable differences here. Yet several things could be said against such a great contrast. Here two facts ought to be mentioned which otherwise have remained unconsidered.[40]

In the 'Solomonic collection' in chs. 10ff. there is in general no specific composition as such, but almost only a more or less coincidental joining together of the individual thoughts.[41] At the beginning of ch. 10 a mini-composition is observable, however, which may be regarded as informative for an understanding of the process of the final development. Between vv. 1 and 8(-10), which are linked by means of the contrast between 'wise' and 'foolish', vv. 2-7 provide us with an interesting structure which contrasts 'rich' and 'poor'. Whereas the theme is

---

39. Thus, with many others, von Rad, *Theologie des Alten Testaments*, I, p. 455; cf. also his *Weisheit in Israel*, p. 224.

40. See the more detailed discussion above in Chapter 15, and see also my commentary *Fortolkning til Salomos ordspråk*, pp. 29ff., 167ff.

41. Cf., e.g., McKane, *Proverbs: A New Approach*, pp. 10ff.; Childs, *Introduction to the Old Testament*, p. 555 ('There is no significant ordering of the individual proverbs into larger groups. Occasionally single proverbs are linked in a loosely connected group either by word association or by general similarity of content'); and more recently Plöger, *Sprüche Salomos*, pp. 118-19.

developed according to the wisdom of experience in vv. 4-5, the nucleus of the section in question, inasmuch as a 'slack hand' results in poverty but a 'diligent hand' and intelligence bring riches (poverty is here regarded as self-imposed); the theme is then explained further and differently in vv. 2-3 and 6-7 by means of a framework which surrounds this nucleus, and this in such a manner that the relationship between poverty and riches is explained by means of the terms 'wantonness' and 'malefactor', and 'righteousness' and 'righteous', as well as by means of the deeds and blessings of Yahweh, with the stress on the actual deeds of a person being ascribed to the influence of God and thus placed on a clearer religious—or theological—plane. Later in the chapter, moreover, this is expressed directly as a maxim in v. 22:

> It is the blessing of Yahweh which makes rich,
> And as far as he is concerned one's own labours add nothing.[42]

Thus through its contextualization (10.2-3, 6-7) a statement about the wisdom of experience (10.4-5) has received a new ethico-religious and theological meaning which stands in unmistakeable contrast with the 'original' statement, especially since the framework has been fleshed out by a further framework (10.1, 8-10) and the tension which results has been intensified (10.22). When Childs believes that the first main section 'chs. 1–9 serve as a hermeneutical guide for reading what follows' and that 'the older collection of chs. 10ff. has been left largely in an unedited stage',[43] one can cling to the view that the mini-composition of 10.1-10 may be regarded as 'a hermeneutical guide' to the first 'Solomonic collection'.

Second, the proposition of the theological character of 10.1-10 can be substantiated by the observation that the theological 'revision' of this collection extends even further. Within the generally accepted two parts of the first 'Solomonic collection', chs. 10–15 and 16.1–22.16, we find the chapters which are most heavily ethico-religious or theological in nature both at the beginning and at the end of these collections, which gives rise to the assumption that even in this wider context we are faced with a specific framework. The traditional proverb material was collected theologically in this framework manner, and to a certain extent it was systematized and thereby interpreted.

Given that the 'Solomonic collection' with its aphoristic style is

---

42. Cf. Plöger, *Sprüche Salomos*, p. 120. Cf. also Deut. 8.12-14, 17-18; 9.4-5.
43. Childs, *Introduction to the Old Testament*, p. 555.

surrounded by compositions of an admonishing didactic style (22.17ff., and particularly the long theological 'introduction' in chs. 1–9 with its quite unique partial compositions), one may be inclined to place a considerably higher emphasis on the theological factor in the final development of the book of Proverbs than is usually the case.[44] Thus there can be seen, even in the area of Israelite wisdom literature, theologically very significant 'unifying reflections' of the rich tradition material which is rooted in belief in Yahweh.

Whether with Childs one should call this process 'the canonical shaping' of Old Testament works of literature is just the critical question in current debate. In order to answer this question satisfactorily, which tentatively will be done in the next section, it may be useful to make a few short remarks concerning recent usage of the term 'midrash'.

The frequent use of 'midrash' nowadays—and the same is true of the term 'canon'—has resulted not only in a true renaissance of the term, but also in an amplification of it, with a multiplicity of meanings. After Robert Gordis endeavoured in 1930 to bridge the traditional gap between the Bible and later rabbinic exegesis by attempting to establish the existence of 'midrashim' within the Bible itself (especially in Chronicles, Hos. 12.4-5 and Isa. 30.26),[45] later on particularly Seeligmann[46] and Bloch,[47] but also several other biblical scholars, attempted to expand this area of research considerably.[48] To put it mildly, there

44. When McKane (*Proverbs: A New Approach*, pp. 10–22) divides the individual proverbs into three groups and later (pp. 413ff.) traces these groups in chs 10ff. under the supposition that there is 'no context in the sentence literature', he has ruined right from the start any possibility of fully understanding this final editorial phase. It seems that we are in great need of a new commentary on Proverbs which will trace the final development of the book and its theological components right to the end.

45. R. Gordis, 'Midrash in the Prophets', *JBL* 49 (1930), pp. 417-22.

46. Seeligmann, 'Voraussetzungen der Midraschexegese', pp. 150-81; cf. also his 'Indications of Editorial Alteration and Adaptation in the Massoretic Text and the Septuagint', *VT* 11 (1961), pp. 201-21.

47. R. Bloch, 'Midrash', *DBSup*, V (1957), pp. 1263-81.

48. For various views on the phenomenon see, e.g., P.R. Ackroyd, 'Some Interpretative Glosses in the Book of Haggai', *JJS* 7 (1966), pp. 163-67; J. Weingreen, 'Rabbinic-Type Glosses in the Old Testament', *JSS* 2 (1967), pp. 149-62; S. Sandmel, 'The Haggada within Scripture', *JBL* 80 (1961), pp. 105-22; G. Vermes, 'Bible and Midrash: Early Old Testament Exegesis', *CHB* 1 (1970), pp. 199-231; B.S. Childs, 'Psalm Titles and Midrashic Exegesis', *JSS* 16 (1971), pp. 137-50;

now exists considerable terminological uncertainty. In recent years this has been fuelled by work which in one way or another has attempted to consider the close relationship between 'midrash' and 'canon' in the area of biblical studies, as is the case with Sanders, for example, who speaks not only of 'canonical criticism' but also of a biblical 'comparative midrash' as 'a new sub-discipline' (next to textual criticism).[49] On the other hand, attempts to use 'midrash' in a narrower and stricter way do not appear to have had the desired effect.[50]

It is significant that in his important work *Biblical Interpretation in Ancient Israel*, in which in a variety of ways he takes up and explains more broadly the threads of various attempts to demonstrate a midrash within the Bible itself, Michael Fishbane completely avoids the term 'midrash' as far as the Bible is concerned and instead speaks of inner-biblical 'comments' and 'revisions', 'interpretation' and 'exegesis'.[51]

M. Fishbane, 'Torah and Tradition', in Knight (ed.), *Tradition and Theology*, pp. 275-300; E. Tov, 'Midrash-Type Exegesis in the LXX of Joshua', *RB* 85 (1978), pp. 50-61; A. Pietersma, 'David in the Greek Psalms', *VT* 30 (1980), pp. 213-26. See also the following notes.

49. Sanders, 'Text and Canon', pp. 5-29, esp. pp. 6-7; see also Sanders, *Canon and Community*, pp. 25-26. See also n. 10 above. Cf. Sheppard, *Canonization*, pp. 21-23.

50. See, e.g., A.G. Wright, *The Literary Genre Midrash* (Staten Island, NY, 1967), with whom R. le Deaut has disagreed in 'A propos d'une definition du midrash', *Bib* 50 (1969), pp. 395-413. His article has been translated into English and has appeared with a preface by J.A. Sanders in *Int* 25 (1971), pp. 259-82. Later on D. Patte attempted an explanation of the terminology of the midrash in *Early Jewish Hermeneutic in Palestine* (SBLDS, 22; Missoula, MT: Scholars Press, 1975), esp. pp. 315-24 ('Postscript: A Proposal for the Normalization of Terminology'), where he approaches the position of Vermes, 'Bible and Midrash', pp. 199-231. He proposes 'to keep the term "midrash" to designate a literary genre... A *midrashic hermeneutic* can be characterized as an interpretation which assumes that Scripture is the final and complete revelation of the election and vocation of the community...it is furthermore characterized by an interpretation of Scripture by Scripture' (p. 319).

51. Fishbane, *Biblical Interpretation in Ancient Israel*, pp. 274-75, 287-91, 429, 431-33. He also differentiates between 'legal' (pp. 91ff.), 'aggadic' (pp. 281ff.) and 'mantological' (pp. 443ff.) exegesis in the Hebrew Bible. Cf. among his earlier works especially 'The Qumran Pesher and Traits of Ancient Hermeneutics', in *Proceedings of the Sixth World Congress of Jewish Studies*, I (Jerusalem, 1977), pp. 97-114; and 'Revelation and Tradition: Aspects of Inner-Biblical Exegesis', *JBL* 99 (1980), pp. 343-61; as well as 'Inner-Biblical Exegesis', in Sæbø (ed.), *Hebrew Bible/Old Testament*, I.1, pp. 33-48.

He is at pains, as he says, 'to distinguish between the received text, the *traditum*, and the scribal annotations addressed to it, the *traditio*'.[52] By means of the dual terminology *traditum/traditio* he is able to criticize the 'anthological' establishment of biblical '*écrits midrashiques*' by Roberts and his school[53] as well as agree with Mowinckel's view of prophetic tradition.[54] He also sees the relationship between parallel texts in the light of these terms, noting with reference to Chronicles, for example, in relationship to Samuel and Kings, that it has its own *bias*—which, however, should not be confused with exegesis.[55]

The main thrust of Fishbane's argument, as has become clear from the above examples, is that the long and complex tradition history to which the Hebrew Bible bears such manifold witness, was a living and variable process which resulted in the final form of the Bible only by means of a collection and interpretation which in many different ways acted as a unifying factor. Throughout this collection and interpretation comprehensive theological 'unifying reflections' run like a scarlet thread. *The 'motor' was thus no 'canonical goal' which lay in the distant future*—to refer to a phrase in the quotation from Childs with which I began this section—*but, 'from behind', the driving force was the moulding power of the monotheistic Yahweh theology of ancient Israel.*

4. *Tradition History and the Development of the Canon*

From the above discussion it may be evident, among other things, that there is certainly inner-biblical interpretation and reinterpretation, but that at the same time the question arises as to how far it is appropriate to describe this interpretation already as 'midrash'. We may ascertain,

52. Fishbane, *Biblical Interpretation in Ancient Israel*, pp. 42-43.

53. Fishbane, *Biblical Interpretation in Ancient Israel*, pp. 286-88. Page 287 reads: 'Indeed, the textual references which are supposed to derive from earlier sources are generally so vague and disconnected, with virtually no clusters of parallel terms or analogous contexts, that little is gained by calling them exegetical or "midrashic".'

54. Fishbane, *Biblical Interpretation in Ancient Israel*, p. 289: 'Rather, a learned vocabulary may simply have been reapplied by later prophetic tradents... Thus, one may, in principle, agree with S. Mowinckel that, since the words of a prophet were living words, "they were again and again reactualized in new, analogous situations by men who showed themselves to be authorized, inspired transmitters and perpetuators of the heritage".'

55. Fishbane, *Biblical Interpretation in Ancient Israel*, pp. 290-91, 380ff.

of course, that a number of articles which have been written on the matter have concealed rather than exposed the relationship between biblical tradition history and the development of the canon which followed on from that. However, scholarship has benefitted indirectly, inasmuch as this problem has come more clearly into view.

In 1953 Seeligmann spoke cautiously only of 'the pre-history of the midrash' and 'the change of biblical thinking into that of the midrash'. But, on the other hand, he also stressed 'that the oldest midrashic exegesis developed organically from the individuality of biblical literature'.[56] Thus, while some discontinuity throughout the canon may be noted, it is possible to speak of the continuity of Jewish midrash with the biblical writings.[57] From his point of view Childs attempted to realize his valuable interest in demonstrating and portraying the continuity of the final form of the canon with the preceding development of the literature. Beyond that some scholars have also spoken of a 'canonical consciousness' in the development of the literature.[58]

What exactly does this new view have to say to us, or more precisely, how and when did this canonization finally occur? And in conclusion, what significance did the canon acquire when it finally came into being? Just a few comments can be made here on the historical-theological and hermeneutical 'triangle' of *tradition*, *canon* and *midrash*, with the explanation of which scholarship now ought to become more intensively engaged.

In all discussion of continuity of different kinds, which there certainly has been, one must cling to and rightly pay attention to the fact of the canon as a final phase and conclusion, despite sporadic later discussion. For after all, the development of the Scriptures reached a

56. Seeligmann, 'Voraussetzungen der Midraschexegese', pp. 150-51. Fishbane, 'Revelation and Tradition', p. 343, notes concerning the exegetical tradition of the Jewish midrash 'that its roots lie in the biblical period—both pre- and post-exilic'.

57. Cf. Seeligmann, 'Voraussetzungen der Midraschexegese', p. 150: 'In the old midrashim... we have the feeling that they face the biblical text with creative freedom. Sometimes it seems as if they do not really interpret a fixed text but rather that they continue one which is still in a state of flux and inconclusive, and play around with various thoughts.'

58. See, e.g., Childs, *Introduction to the Old Testament*, p. 50; Fishbane, 'Revelation and Tradition', pp. 349, 361; Sheppard, 'Canonization', pp. 23ff. Cf. also Seeligmann, 'Voraussetzungen der Midraschexegese', p. 152 (see immediately below).

significant end stage. When Vermes says in this context that 'post-biblical midrash is to be distinguished from the biblical only by an external factor, canonisation', and then goes on to say that 'by common though mysterious consent, and using criteria which largely elude us, the Palestinian religious authorities decided, probably at about the end of the third century BCE, to arrest the growth of sacred writings and establish a canon',[59] then he seems to have interpreted the developmental process too 'mysteriously' and the significance of the canon too superficially. The continuity cannot be appropriately understood and described by means of a kind of evaporization of canonical discontinuity, but rather through a real contrast to it.

In profiling this fundamental duality, particularly as far as the comments about 'canonical shaping' and 'canonical consciousness' are concerned, first, reference should again be made to the traditio-historical peculiarity of the development of Israelite literature which was discussed in the previous section. For when Childs—like others—begins his delineation of the 'development of the Hebrew canon' with Deuteronomy,[60] or explains clearly in his Göttingen lecture his intention 'to describe the influence of canon on the formation of the Hebrew Bible',[61] the impression can scarcely be avoided that his statements are coincidental rather than sufficiently general. With this may be contrasted the other picture of the development of biblical literature which has been identified above. As a result, the final form of the biblical writings can be understood not as something which had already been given, but generally as something which had *become* both historically and theologically, and which had come into being after prior conditions by means of *a creative and productive process*. Its unity in the multiplicity of traditions was obtained by means of theological 'unifying reflections' which were based on a belief in Yahweh and the effect of which was felt in various circles in Israel. Thus were created the necessary conditions and preparation for the canon, without which the canon would never be canon.

Authority is often linked with the canon, a point which is appropriate to a certain extent, for canon signifies authority. However, on the other

59. Vermes, 'Bible and Midrash', p. 199.

60. Childs, *Introduction to the Old Testament*, pp. 62ff. See also §3 above.

61. Childs, 'Exegetical Significance', pp. 66ff. The comments in his *Introduction to the Old Testament* to the individual writings in the Old Testament may also be added.

hand, authority does not need to signify canon;[62] yet—like unity—it is a necessary condition for the formation of the canon. It is of considerable importance here that these points (unity, authority, canon) be clearly differentiated, although they are indeed related.

The superscriptions of individual books, which have attracted attention not least from the point of view of canon-historical interest, unite the aspects of unity and authority, as was noted above in connexion with the superscription of Jer. 1.1-3. Particularly the superscriptions of prophetic writings and Psalms have been considered in this regard.[63] In this context, among the many Psalms which are ascribed to David, particularly those which give details of a specific situation are especially informative (Psalms 7, 18, 34, 51, 54, 56, 57, 59, 60, and even more Psalms in the LXX).[64] For thereby first, an integration of original cult psalms, and particular history traditions, was undertaken, and thus an important unifying step taken in the direction of a Scripture consisting of Scriptures. Second, through the heavy concentration on the person of David many different psalms were handed down under his great and indisputable authority, especially later on, as is clear from Chronicles.[65] It is a question here of a 'borrowed' personal authority which has lent these psalms a new status, at least in part. This is comprehensible, however, only from a pre-canonical situation.

This set of circumstances is further substantiated when we refer to the similar role played by Solomon with regard to the status and authority of wisdom writings such as Proverbs, Ecclesiastes and the Canticles, as well as *Wisdom of Solomon* and *Psalms of Solomon* in the post-biblical era. The most striking point in these cases is not so much the superscription in Prov. 1.1 (next to the older superscriptions in 10.1 and 25.1) as the circumstances in Ecclesiastes 1 and Canticles 1 and 3.6-11. For in Ecclesiastes 1 the superscription in v. 1 is supported in vv. 12-18 by means of the description of the wise king of Jerusalem— without, however, mentioning the name of Solomon. And in Canticles

62. See, e.g., Anderson, 'Canonical and Non-Canonical', pp. 117-18.

63 Cf. Childs, 'Psalm Titles and Midrashic Exegesis', pp. 137-50, and his *Introduction to the Old Testament*, pp. 520-21. See also G.M. Tucker, 'Prophetic Superscriptions and the Growth of a Canon', in G.W. Coates and B.O. Long (eds.), *Canon and Authority* (Philadelphia: Fortress Press, 1977), pp. 56-70.

64. Cf., e.g., Kaiser, *Einleitung in das Alte Testament*, pp. 351-52.

65. Cf., e.g., Sæbø, 'Chronistische Theologie/Chronistisches Geschichtswerk', *TRE*, VIII, pp. 74-87.

1 there is the term 'king', presumably to expand the superscription of v. 1 in vv. 4 and 12. Even more interesting, however, is the historicizing interpolation of 3.9-10 in Cant. 3.6–8, 11, where suddenly Solomon is described in the past tense to portray his splendid bed. With reference to the bed of Solomon in v. 7, the theme of Solomon, which is important for authority, is enlarged in this way in vv. 9-10.[66]

The decisive point from Ecclesiastes and the Canticles is that *the Solomonic authority aspect may belong to the developing tradition history, the composition and development of Scripture*, although in their *final stage, without the name of Solomon having been all-decisive*; for his name did not manage to 'aid' the later *Wisdom of Solomon* and *Psalms of Solomon* to become 'canonical'. Yet it may be valid to say that together with the Davidic superscriptions of a number of psalms this Solomonic authority demonstrates above all that this phenomenon was peculiar to the pre-canonical final stage of tradition history. *It prepared the canon*, but may hardly be described as 'canonical' in its own right.

On the other hand, the matter may be completely different as far as Eccl. 12.12-14 (and especially vv. 13 and 14), the 'second epilogue' of Ecclesiastes, is concerned. For, if one compares these last few verses, which have been described as 'a dogmatic revision' of the preceding passage,[67] with Eccl. 11.9, which has been interpreted as a verse which contradicts Num. 15.39, or even with alleged contradictions within the book itself which have not been 'revised',[68] this exibits something very fundamental for the canon question: these 'revisions' have not been made in the body of the book, but have only been appended at the end of the book. This means, then, that here we have to deal with a tradition material differently from that in the earlier developing tradition history. Here one is dealing with *a book which has attained its final form* or is at least regarded as being complete, and which one is not 'entitled' to make any alteration of the written text. Furthermore, it is a question of classifying this book into a greater literary whole, into a collection of

66. For further substantiation, see Ch. 17 above, esp. pp. 290-97.

67. Thus A. Lauha, *Kohelet* (BKAT, 19; Neukirchen–Vluyn: Neukirchener Verlag, 1978), p. 7; cf. pp. 20-21.

68. Cf. H.W. Hertzberg, *Der Prediger* (KAT, 17.4; Gütersloh: Gütersloher Verlagshaus, 1963), pp. 23-25. See also S. Holm-Nielsen, 'The Book of Ecclesiastes and the Interpretation of It in Jewish and Christian Theology', *ASTI* 10 (1976), pp. 55-96.

authoritative writings, and harmonizing it—with this as far as possible—if necessary by an 'addition'.

It is not until this late stage that one can observe 'the transition from literary growth to the beginnings of interpretation'. Only at this point one can rightly accept 'the rise of a canon consciousness', to refer again to Seeligmann.[69] Thus there exists a far-reaching change in attitude towards and view of that which had been handed down, the *traditum*, such as it had never been known before; one is looking back to something complete. That is especially true for a part of the extant literature which has been singled out as a collection of 'holy books'. In this way, then, the *traditum* has essentially been determined and defined. As 'holy Scripture' it bears an authority of its own which supersedes the personally based authority of single writings (like the books of Samuel, Psalms of David, or, the three Solomonic Writings).

The fact that a transition of this kind, which testifies to an unmistakable 'canon consciousness', took place at all, remains the decisive point. On the other hand, it is not so important to determine the exact time frame of this transition, since it had been prepared and occurred at different times and in a variety of ways, as has been pointed out in recent research.[70] The observation of the mentioned transition should enable us to recognize a general characteristic of the development of the canon, just as for example it also thus emerges that the comments above on Ecclesiastes 12 find their equivalent in a statement from the late period of canon history around 95 CE, namely, in the well-known statement of Josephus in *Apion* 1.38: 'For we do not have an endless number of books which differ from each other and which mutually contradict each other, but just twenty-two which depict all of the past and which are rightly regarded as divine.'[71] Moreover, in Josephus a common view is represented that attributes to the prophets a fundamental role in the development of the canon. If only the Pentateuch was at first able to enjoy a special position and canonical authority, this fact should not be played off against the prophetic books, for the development of the canon—including the wisdom and other 'writings'—does

69. Cf. Seeligmann, 'Voraussetzungen der Midraschexegese', p. 152. Even Childs ('Exegetical Significance', p. 67) admits that 'the term "canonization" should be reserved for the final fixing of the limits of Scripture'.

70. See nn. 4 and 5 above, as well as n. 72 below.

71. Cf. Lebram, 'Aspekte der alttestamentlichen Kanonbildung', p. 173; also Hölscher, *Kanonisch und Apokryph*, pp. 2-3.

not exhibit a straight-lined history. The variety displayed within the canon should be preserved in interpretation and validity.[72]

Furthermore, one can still recognize the transition both in the 'parallel' phenomenon of the unifying text history, which resulted in the 'standardized' Massoretic Text,[73] as well as in the change in the method of producing scrolls in ancient Israel.[74]

Even in the wider context of tradition and intellectual history there have been transitions and changes which may be informative for an understanding of the development of the canon. In the second 'epilogue' to Ecclesiastes (12.13-14), for example, there may rightly be recognized a law-oriented tendency. This is also precisely true for the final stage of the very complex formation history of the Psalter, inasmuch as it is divided into five sections and is introduced by means of a 'law-psalm'.[75] Yet because Psalm 1 is also regarded as a wisdom psalm, this particular introduction to the Psalter may also be taken as an example of a *sapientializing tendency* which brought its influence to bear more and more in the later period.[76] At this time there were, of course, various theological off-shoots and new groups which read and interpreted the 'holy Scriptures' differently.[77]

72. Cf., e.g., Lebram, 'Aspekte der alttestamentlichen Kanonbildung', and also the relevant criticism of Sanders, particularly of his study *Torah and Canon*, by R.E. Clements, 'Covenant and Canon in the Old Testament', in R.W.A. McKinney (ed.), *Creation, Christ and Culture* (Edinburgh: T. & T. Clark, 1976), pp. 1-12, esp. pp. 9-11, and Sheppard, 'Canonization', pp. 25ff. Among the very rich recent literature on the subject, see Barthélemy, 'L'état de la Bible juive', pp. 9-45.

73. Cf., e.g., S. Talmon, 'The Old Testament Text', *CHB* 1 (1970), pp. 159-99, as well as several articles in Cross and Talmon (eds.), *Qumran and the History*; D. Barthélemy, *Etudes d'histoire du texte de l'Ancien Testament* (OBO, 21; Freibourg: Editions Universitaires; Göttingen: Vandenhoeck & Ruprecht, 1978), esp. pp. 341-64; Sanders, 'Text and Canon', pp. 6ff. See also Chapter 2 above.

74. Cf. M. Haran, 'Book-Scrolls at the Beginning of the Second Temple Period: The Transition from Papyrus to Skins', *HUCA* 54 (1983), pp. 111-22.

75. Cf., e.g., C. Westermann, 'Zur Sammlung des Psalters', in his *Forschung am Alten Testament: Gesammelte Studien* (TBü, 24; Munich: Chr. Kaiser Verlag, 1964), pp. 336-43; H. Gese, 'Zur Geschichte der Kultsänger am zweiten Tempel', in *idem, Vom Sinai zum Zion*, pp. 147-58.

76. Cf., e.g., Sheppard, *Wisdom as a Hermeneutical Construct*, esp. pp. 120-50, where the following texts in the Old Testament are discussed: 2 Sam. 23.1-7; Pss. 1-2; Eccl. 12.12-14; Hos. 14.10. Several others could also be mentioned.

77. Cf., e.g., Talmon, 'Typen der Messiaserwartung um die Zeitwende', pp. 571-88.

With the existence of 'holy Scriptures', in limited numbers and with its own authority, not only did a new kind of *traditum* appear, but also a new *traditio* came into being which, fundamentally tied to the binding standards of the canon, was particularly realized in the form of the interpretation of the holy texts, both in the Midrash and in the New Testament.

5. *Conclusion*

A very complicated and controversial problem area of the pre-history and the formation of the canon of the Hebrew Bible has been discussed.

The introduction included thoughts on the theological position vis-à-vis the canon of Brevard Childs, who particularly stressed and demonstrated the continuity of the canon with the preceding process of the development of Scripture. This position is certainly to be welcomed and to be taken seriously. Nevertheless, the discussion above has shown that *with the canon—despite all continuity—there resulted a significant and effective transition and turning point.* And after the canon 'intervened', the relationship between *traditum* and *traditio* changed. The attempt has been made to explain in a new way the relationship between the alleged tradition history, the canon of the Hebrew Bible or the Old Testament, and the post-canonical exegesis.

Part V
WRITING THE HISTORY OF TRADITIONS:
SCHOLARS OF THREE CENTURIES

Chapter 19

JOHANN PHILIPP GABLER AT THE END OF THE
EIGHTEENTH CENTURY: HISTORY AND THEOLOGY

On 30 March 1787 the 33-year-old theologian Johann Philipp Gabler
gave his inaugural address as professor at the former University of Altdorf. Rarely, if ever, has greater significance been accorded to the inaugural address of a young theologian. However, whether Gabler can thus
be rightly regarded as the 'father' of 'biblical theology'—as is generally the case—is open to debate.

Gabler was very important for the theological and ecclesiastical life
of his day. Yet gradually his work has been reduced to the significance
of his inaugural address which, moreover, appears to be better known
for its title than its content. However, in the last few decades interest in
Gabler and his influence has once again been awakened.[1] Otto Merk in
particular has succeeded in discovering material about him which has
been hard to find.[2]

---

1. Cf. R. Smend, 'Universalismus und Partikularismus in der alttestamentlichen Theologie des 19. Jahrhunderts', *EvT* 22 (1962), pp. 169-79; *idem*, 'Johann
Philipp Gablers Begründung der biblischen Theologie', pp. 345-57 both articles
repr. in *idem*, *Epochen des Bibelkritik*, pp. 117-27 and 104-16; K. Leder, *Universität Altdorf: Zur Theologie der Aufklärung in Franken. Die theologische Fakultät
in Altdorf, 1750–1809* (Nürnberg: Lorenz Spindler Verlag, 1965) (on Gabler, see
particularly pp. 273-312).

2. O. Merk, *Biblische Theologie des Neuen Testaments in ihrer Anfangszeit:
Ihre methodischen Probleme bei Johann Philipp Gabler und Georg Lorenz Bauer
und deren Nachwirkungen* (MTS, NS 9; Marburg, 1972); *idem*, 'Biblische Theo-
logie II', *TRE*, VI, pp. 457f.; *idem*, 'Gabler, Johann Philipp (1753–1826)', *TRE*,
XII, pp. 1-3. Cf. H.-J. Dohmeier, 'Die Grundzüge der Theologie Johann Philipp
Gablers' (PhD Dissertation, University of Münster, 1976); J. Sandys-Wunsch and
L. Eldredge, 'J.P. Gabler and the Distinction between Biblical and Dogmatic
Theology: Translation, Commentary, and Discussion of his Originality', *SJT* 33
(1980), pp. 133-58. On Gabler's biography, see his autobiographical sketch in

1. *Biographical Material*

Johann Philipp Gabler was born on 4 June 1753 in Frankfurt am Main as the son of a lawyer. From childhood on he received a thorough, humanistic education, first with private teachers. After studying philosophy and history as well as other subjects—especially theology, which he began in Jena in 1772 and completed there in 1778 with a dissertation on Heb. 3.3-6 and his Master's examination—he took the ministerial examination in his native town. He practised as a preacher there and was ordained before moving to Altdorf. At the same time he worked as a teacher of Hebrew in Frankfurt. From 1780 he worked as a theological private tutor in Göttingen, and was employed in 1783 as Professor of Philosophy and Pro-Rector at the Archigymnasium in Dortmund. Two years later he was called as Professor of Theology to the University of Altdorf, east of Erlangen, as well as town deacon. The thematic breadth of his scholarship and interests, and his combination of church duties and academic theology, which became apparent at this time, were not only significant for the first part of his life, but remained so throughout it. His theological research and his publications were extensive and comprehensive, as will be shown. In all his activities and thoughts Gabler was a cautious, circumspect bridge-builder, but he was also a conscious reformer.

Gabler stayed in Altdorf for 18 years, and he would have liked to remain there—having turned down very favourable calls to Giessen in 1793 and to Dorpat at the beginning of 1804—if the town officials and the Nuremberg Council had not to a certain extent forced him, due to their 'financial-political shortsightedness', to accept a call to Jena, the university where he had studied. In May 1804 Gabler left the University of Altdorf, which in any event was closed down five years later.[3]

In Jena his academic career came full circle. Here the theological

---

Schattenrisse der jetzt lebenden Altdorfischen Professoren (Altdorf, 1790), pp. 17-34; W. Schröter, *Erinnerungen an Johann Philipp Gabler* (Jena, 1827); G.E. Steitz, 'Gabler, Joh. Philipp', *ADB* 8 (1878), pp. 294-96 (cf. Merk, *Biblische Theologie*, pp. 45ff.; and Dohmeier, 'Die Grundzüge', pp. 34ff.).

3.   Leder, *Universität Altdorf*, p. 310: 'After Semler and Döderlein, the financial-political shortsightedness of the Nuremberg Council had now sacrificed the last great Altdorf theologian to Jena, the university which was in a better position to pay'. For further information on the closure of the University of Altdorf (to the benefit of the University of Erlangen), see Leder, *Universität Altdorf*, pp. 351-63.

views of the young student had been formed permanently in a neological direction, especially by teachers almost contemporary in age such as
Johann Gottfried Eichhorn (1752–1827)[4] and Johann Jakob Griesbach
(1745–1812).[5] Johann Salomo Semler (1725–91)[6] and Johann August
Ernesti (1707–81) also contributed considerably to his neological
views. Moreover, in his Göttingen period, the philologian Christian
Gottlob Heyne (1729–1812) had a considerable influence on him.[7] In
Jena, Gabler became a colleague of his teacher Griesbach, and after the
latter's death in 1812 he became his successor and the head of the faculty. In his research Griesbach had been chiefly a New Testament
scholar, and the same was true of Gabler.[8]

His literary activity consisted above all of his works on the New
Testament, particularly in his younger years, but thematically it was
more far reaching. Actually, it is worthy of note in many ways, especially when one considers Gabler's enormous influence, for Gabler
never published a completed work of any great length, if one ignores
his comprehensive new edition of Eichhorn's *Urgeschichte*, which was
in itself a very unusual undertaking.[9] Apart from his Master's thesis and

4. Cf. H.-J. Zobel, 'Eichhorn, Johann Gottfried (1752–1827)', *TRE*, IX,
pp. 369-71; and O. Kaiser, 'Eichhorn und Kant: Ein Beitrag zur Geschichte der
Hermeneutik', now in *idem, Von der Gegenwartsbedeutung des Alten Testaments:
Gesammelte Studien* (Göttingen: Vandenhoeck & Ruprecht, 1984), pp. 61-70.

5. Cf. B.M. Metzger, 'Griesbach, Johann Jakob (1745–1812)', *TRE*, XIV,
pp. 253-56.

6. Cf. G. Hornig, *Die Anfänge der hist.-krit. Theologie: J.S. Semlers
Schriftverständnis und seine Stellung zu Luther* (FSThR, 8; Göttingen: Vanden-
hoeck & Ruprecht, 1961); L. Zscharnack, *Lessing und Semler: Ein Beitrag zur
Entstehungsgeschichte des Rationalismus und der kritischen Theologie* (1905);
O. Kaiser, 'Johann Salomo Semler als Bahnbrecher der modernen Bibelwissen-
schaft', now in *idem, Von der Gegenwartsbedeutung*, pp. 79-94.

7. Cf. C. Hartlich and W. Sachs, *Der Ursprung des Mythosbegriffes in der
modernen Bibelwissenschaft* (Tübingen: J.C.B. Mohr, 1952), pp. 20-38; and Merk,
Biblische Theologie, pp. 46, 52ff.

8. In Göttingen in 1782, Gabler had written in a letter: 'Since my third year at
the university in 1775, when I went to Griesbach's classes, the exegesis and criticism of the New Testament were always my favourite occupation.' Cf. Leder, *Universität Altdorf*, p. 274, and p. 281 n. 38.

9. *Johann Gottfried Eichhorns Urgeschichte: Herausgegeben mit Einleitung
und Anmerkungen von J.P. Gabler* (Altdorf; Nürnberg: Monath & Kussler, 1790–
93); hereafter referred to as Gabler, *Urgeschichte*. In the first part (1790), Gabler's
foreword (pp. iii-xxviii) and introduction (pp. 1-136) take up more than half the

a work from his Göttingen period on 2 Corinthians 9–13, he published almost only occasional writings, particularly in the journals which he edited.[10] As an example, his much-revered work 'Über den Unterschied zwischen Auslegung und Erklärung' appeared in fact as 'Ein Nachtrag des Herausgebers zu vorstehender Recension', consisting of almost 20 pages.[11]

Gabler's strength lay in his many smaller works as well as his lectures, which he always prepared thoroughly.[12] Still busy with his work, Gabler died at his desk, shortly after a lecture, on the morning of 17 February 1826, a man honoured widely. Five years later two of his sons edited a few of his *Kleinere theologische Schriften*, including his inaugural address at Altdorf in 1787, which must be regarded as the true heart of his research and theological thinking.[13]

book. The first volume of the second part (1792) consists only of his foreword (pp. iii-xxxii) and introduction (pp. 1-670); and in the second volume (1793) his foreword is equally comprehensive (pp. iii-cxxviii).

10. *Neuestes theologisches Journal* 1–6 (1798–1800); *Journal für theologische Literatur* 1–6 (1801–1803); *Journal für auserlesene theologische Literatur* 1–6 (1805–11). A detailed Gabler bibliography is available in Dohmeier, 'Die Grundzüge', pp. 201-206; cf. Merk, *Biblische Theologie*, p. 289, and Merk, 'Gabler, Johann Philipp', *TRE*, XII, p. 3.

11. *Neuestes theologisches Journal* 6 (1800), pp. 224-42; cf. Merk, *Biblische Theologie*, p. 75 nn. 188-89.

12. Cf. Steitz, 'Gabler, Joh. Philipp', p. 295; see also the overview of his other work in Merk, 'Gabler, Johann Philipp', *TRE*, XII, p. 2 (points 2.5–2.6).

13. *D. Johann Philipp Gabler's kleinere theologische Schriften: Herausgegeben von seinen Söhnen, Theodor August Gabler und Johann Gottfried Gabler*, I–II (Ulm: Stettinische Buchhandlung, 1831; hereafter referred to as Gabler, *Kleinere theologische Schriften*). In the second volume, which includes his *Opuscula Academica*, the inaugural address is in fourth place: *De iusto discrimine theologiae biblicae et dogmaticae regundisque recte utriusque finibus. Oratio, qua recitata...*, pp. 179-98. Today only this text is available, but the address was actually published as early as 1787. Cf. Diestel, *Geschichte des Alten Testaments*, p. 711 n. 11. The address has been translated in extract form in W.G. Kümmel, *Das Neue Testament: Geschichte der Erforschung seiner Probleme* (Freiburg; Munich: Verlag Karl Alber, 1970 [1958]), pp. 115-18; in an almost complete English translation in Sandys-Wunsch and Eldredge, 'J.P. Gabler', pp. 134-44; and in a complete translation in Merk, *Biblische Theologie*, pp. 273-84 ('Anlage I'). In one place Sandys-Wunsch and Eldredge disagree with Merk's translation (p. 144 n. 1); these translations also differ in other ways, which in itself is very informative. As for translations here cf. Sandys-Wunsch and Eldredge, pp. 134-44.

2. *Gabler's Inaugural Address in the Context of his Work*

Gabler's academic lecture *De iusto discrimine theologiae biblicae et dogmaticae regundisque recte utriusque finibus* of 30 March 1787 certainly cannot be understood or fairly evaluated without consideration of its theological and spiritual background. It cannot be my task to go into detail on this point here, especially as this has been dealt with thoroughly in the last two decades, particularly by Leder, Merk and Dohmeier. Nevertheless, it is not out of place to take a second look and to stress that Gabler was a renowned representative of the end of the neological tradition—a point which has been particularly emphasized by Leder—and to remind ourselves that the general political and cultural horizon of the age was extremely dark, two years before the French Revolution.[14] In many ways it was an age of ferment, a time of disintegration of traditional positions and norms; and the theological and ecclesiastical position had become unclear and more diverse. The ambitious young Gabler wanted to make a fundamental contribution to this critical situation.

Gabler took as his point of departure the obvious discrepancy which exists between the Holy Scriptures as a source of religious knowledge and the numerous differences of religious opinion and the 'many splinter groups' which all refer to the same Scriptures. In Reformation language, as far as Gabler was concerned it was a question of the validity of the *sola scriptura*. To put it in more modern terms, it was a question of the disturbing theological pluralism of the age. In general, however, the problems stemmed from an inadequate system of hermeneutics and thus were the expression of an as-yet-unresolved question of theological method.

First of all Gabler gives four hermeneutical reasons by way of explanation for the critically and methodologically unsatisfactory situation: 'Given this agreement of all these religious opinions, why then do these points of contention arise?' First, he mentions 'the occasional obscurity of the sacred Scriptures themselves', second, the 'depraved custom of reading one's own opinions and judgments into the Bible', third, that

---

14. Thus, e.g., his teacher and friend Eichhorn published a two-volume work about the French Revolution in 1797, and in 1806 Gabler himself had a 'meeting and discussion with Napoleon about the protection of the town and university of Jena' (see Merk, 'Gabler, Johann Philipp' *TRE*, XII, p. 1; cf. Sandys-Wunsch and Eldredge, 'J.P. Gabler', pp. 144-45).

'the dissension also arises from the neglected distinction (*a neglecto discrimine*) between religion and theology', and finally, 'it arises from an inappropriate combination [*a male mixta*] of the simplicity and ease of biblical theology with subtlety and difficulty of dogmatic theology'. In the following discussion of these points, he reaches relatively quickly the third, and above all the fourth point which clearly makes his heart beat more quickly.

The *neglecto discrimine* is here the equivalent of the *male mixta* and finds its counterpart in the *iusto discrimine* and the *regundis recte finibus* of the title. In addition to the concepts of 'biblical' and 'dogmatic' theology which, for good reason, have always been at the fore of any discussion, the other parts of the title deserve to be considered more than is usually the case. For the 'separation'/ 'differentiation' and 'boundary marking' are like a red thread throughout his ideas. Both in this address and in later writings he uses a lot of terms in pairs which are important not only for his analyses but also for his syntheses. In different ways it is a question of terms and ideas which must be kept apart—as it were, according to the old maxim 'to each his own'.[15] Through this bipartition he not only permits fundamental differences to come to light, but just as much the parts that belong together, because at the same time they are facing each other. Through the duality, a unity is obvious which in the final analysis exists, but which should not be attained too easily so as not to explain it wrongly. Gabler's aim is clearly to establish here a methodologically appropriate procedure, or, as he has it towards the end of his address, 'to point to a better way and more carefully to describe the most appropriate way of dealing with these matters'.[16]

As far as the difference between religion and theology is concerned,

15. Thus the translation 'right' or 'proper' for *iusto* is scarcely adequate, for it represents more than simply a synonym for the following *recte*, having rather the meaning of 'just' or 'righteous'. Cf. Gabler, *Kleinere theologische Schriften*, II, p. 190 (Merk, *Biblische Theologie*, pp. 279-80), and n. 31 below. To be noted is Gabler's later comment, reproduced by Schröter: 'If not earlier, then at least in this address on biblical theology I have helped to put reason *in its rightful place*' (quoted from Dohmeier, 'Die Grundzüge', p. 71).

16. Gabler, *Kleinere theologische Schriften*, II, p. 194 (Merk, *Biblische Theologie*, p. 281). Dohmeier ('Die Grundzüge', pp. 38ff.) has described Gabler's demand here as 'a new structuring of theological discussion in general'. Indeed, the question may be asked whether he expressed himself too formally here, but one can agree with his intention to call attention to the basic question of methodology.

this had already been expressed by others, among whom he first of all points to Ernesti and Semler.[17] 'Religion' was regarded as a 'divine teaching' which had been handed down historically and in written form (*doctrina diuina in scripturis tradita*) and was thus an 'every-day transparently clear knowledge (*scientia popularis et perspicua*)', while, on the other hand, 'theology is subtle, learned knowledge, surrounded by a retinue of many disciplines.[18]

Now, however, the gap between (biblical) 'religion' and (dogmatic) 'theology' had grown too large for this differentiation alone to suffice, because of the historico-critical exegesis of Scripture which generally held sway.[19] Moving to the fourth point, the discussion of which was to form the kernel of his address, Gabler complains about 'that readiness to mix completely different matters (*miscendi res plane diuersas*), for example, the simplicity (*simplicitas*) of so-called biblical theology with the subtlety (*subtilitas*) of dogmatic theology, although, it seems to me that one thing must be more sharply distiguished from the other than has been the common practice up to now'.[20] When Gabler here picks up the notion of a 'biblical theology' which had long been in vogue,[21] yet now refers to it as 'the so-called biblical theology', after he has just spoken about a disastrous 'mixing' of 'completely different matters', in order subsequently to talk about the necessity of a differentiation between biblical and dogmatic theology, then it is clear first that he fundamentally distances himself from the term 'biblical theology' as used up to that time, because compared with dogmatic theology it had not been seen as an independent discipline, but rather as an auxiliary area which enabled the application to dogmatic theology of the necessary biblical 'proof texts' (*dicta probantia*). In so doing, Gabler laid his

17. Cf. Zscharnack, *Lessing und Semler*, pp. 280ff; Kaiser, 'Johann Salomo Semler', pp. 79ff.

18. Cf. Gabler, *Kleinere theologische Schriften*, II, p. 182 (Merk, *Biblische Theologie*, p. 275; Sandys-Wunsch and Eldredge, 'J.P. Gabler', p. 136).

19. Cf. Smend, 'Universalismus', p. 170; Leder (*Universität Altdorf*, pp. 287-88) says that here 'the gulf between neologico-rationalistic exegesis and Protestant dogmatic is too large'.

20. Gabler, *Kleinere theologische Schriften*, II, p. 183 (Merk, *Biblische Theologie*, p. 275; Sandys-Wunsch and Eldredge, 'J.P. Gabler', p. 137).

21. On the history of the term, cf. G. Ebeling, 'Was heisst "Biblische Theologie"?', in *idem*, *Wort und Glaube* (Tübingen: J.C.B. Morh, 1967), pp. 71ff.; Kümmel, *Das Neue Testament*, pp. 115ff.; and Merk, *Biblische Theologie*, pp. 13-20, 21-28.

finger on the wound of the critical theologico-ecclesiastical situation. Furthermore, it is clear that Gabler believed that he gave direction to a new, beneficial solution for the problems of fundamental methodology by prising biblical theology loose from dogmatic theology, as well as by his redefining their role in current theological thinking.[22]

Vis-à-vis the earlier differentiation between religion and theology, just mentioned above, Gabler now takes the idea of 'theology' into the realms of 'religion' by establishing 'biblical theology' as a 'historical science'. In so doing he not only makes a new differentiation between biblical and dogmatic theology, but he introduces a further, new differentiation between 'historical' (traditional) and 'didactic' (philosophical) by designating their relationship as follows:

> There is truly a biblical theology, of historical origin, conveying what the holy writers felt about divine matters (*Est vero theologia biblica e genere historico tradens*); on the other hand, there is a dogmatic theology of didactic origin, teaching (*theologia contra dogmatica e genere didactico docens*) what every theologian philosophises rationally about divine matters, according to the measure of his ability or of the times, age, place, sect, school, and other similar factors.[23]

Thus Gabler took the first step. The next was certainly more important for him, although it may appear difficult to understand for the modern reader when he states concerning the nature of biblical theology that although it 'argues historically', it is 'always essentially similar'.[24] Gabler's task here was to separate things which are locally and temporally determined from those which are universally valid, 'from

22. In his work *Biblische Theologie, oder Untersuchung des biblischen Grundes der vornehmsten theologischen Lehren*, I–IV (1771–72), G.T. Zachariä (1729–77) had attempted to bring independence to biblical theology compared with dogmatic theology, yet in his statement he had been completely traditional. The work, which was completed with a fifth volume in 1786 by J.C. Volborth, was particularly referred to by Gabler in his address (*Kleinere theologische Schriften*, II, p. 185 [Merk, *Biblische Theologie*, pp. 276-77]), in which he praised its progressive ideas when compared with other similar works, but in which he also pointed out its limitations; cf. Merk, *Biblische Theologie*, pp. 24-26, 35.

23. Gabler, *Kleinere theologische Schriften*, II, pp. 183-84 (Merk, *Biblische Theologie*, pp. 275-76; Sandys-Wunsch and Eldredge, 'J.P. Gabler', p. 137).

24. *Illa, cum historici sit argumenti, per se spectata semper sibi constat* (Gabler, *Kleinere theologische Schriften*, II, p. 184; cf. Merk, *Biblische Theologie*, p. 276, and Sandys-Wunsch and Eldredge, 'J.P. Gabler', p. 137); *cum* here is the equivalent of *quom* with a conjunction.

those pure notions (*notiones puras*) which divine providence wished to be characteristic of all times and places', so 'that we distinguish carefully (*diligenter dignoscamus*) the divine from the human'.[25] In order to achieve this, there was no other method than the historical, with which one has to 'separate the individual periods of old and new religion [i.e the Old Testament and the New Testament], the individual authors, and finally the individual forms of speech which each used according to time and place', as well as 'carefully collect and classify each of the ideas of each patriarch'.[26]

This historically differentiating methodology can be divided into two further parts or stages which could arguably be described as analytical and synthetic stages, first, that of the 'correct (*legitima*) interpretation' of individual passages, which primarily occurs on a philologico-exegetical plane with special regard to the changing use of vocabulary and sentence meaning, and then the other which consists of 'the careful comparison of the ideas of all the sacred writers among themselves'.[27] What, then, concerns particularly the second, comparative—and synthetic—method are the historical differentiations which in this case too are an indispensable 'condition' or 'rule' (*lege*). At the same time, however, a further, decisive step is taken here, when it is stated—allowing for the preservation of the historical differences—that one has to 'submit individual views [of the Scriptures] to universal notions' (*subiiciendae sunt... singulae sententiae notionibus universis*). The 'universal notions' (*notiones universae*), also translated by Merk as 'general concepts (*Allgemein begriffe*)',[28] presumably equate here to the earlier

25. Gabler, *Kleinere theologische Schriften*, II, pp. 184-85 (Merk, *Biblische Theologie*, p. 276; cf. p. 41; Sandys-Wunsch and Eldredge, 'J.P. Gabler', p. 139). Smend, 'Universalismus', pursues this point of view in the nineteenth century, especially with reference to the renowned de Wette (1780–1849) who was a pupil of Gabler's; see also R. Smend, *W.M.L. de Wettes Arbeit am Alten und am Neuen Testament* (Basel, 1958), pp. 77ff.

26. Gabler, *Kleinere theologische Schriften*, II, pp. 186-87 (Merk, *Biblische Theologie*, p. 277; Sandys-Wunsch and Eldredge, 'J.P. Gabler', p. 140). Immediately before this Gabler discusses briefly the relationship between the different biblical writers and the *theopneustia* which has not destroyed 'a holy man's own native intelligence and his natural way of knowing things' (*Kleinere theologische Schriften*, II, p. 186).

27. Gabler, *Kleinere theologische Schriften*, II, pp. 187-88 (Merk, *Biblische Theologie*, p. 278; Sandys-Wunsch and Eldredge, 'J.P. Gabler', p. 140).

28. Gabler, *Kleinere theologische Schriften*, II, p. 190; Merk, *Biblische*

stated 'always alike' (*semper sibi constat*) and represent therefore the notional *constancy* of the Scriptures—presumably particularly of the New Testament—whereby for biblical theology not only has a balance been brought about between its constancy and its historical variability of different kinds (corresponding to the 'argues historically' mentoned above), but an *a priori* aim has been set up as far as the remaining *unity* of the Scriptures is concerned, despite all historical differences.

With this Gabler reached a point where he was able to formulate comprehensively a methodically fundamental, though not yet definitive, conclusion (*Kleinere theologische Schriften*, II, p. 190):

> But if this comparison with the help of the universal notions (*comparatio ope notionum universarum*) is established in such a way that for each author his own work remains inviolate, and it is apparent wherein the separate authors agree in a friendly fashion, or differ among themselves, then finally there will be the happy appearance of biblical theology, pure and unmixed with foreign things (*purae nec alienis mixtae theologiae biblicae facies*).

Thus he showed how it is possible to obtain a historically conceived 'system of biblical theology', 'established with the help of universal notions', which is just as descriptive as it can be a presentation of stoic philosophy.[29] Gabler calls this 'system' a 'pure' biblical theology to which there clings no pernicious 'commingling' of ideas, which moreover is 'pure' in the sense that here an obviously observable and effective way of reduction of the biblical material from its generally accepted historical variability to its theological general concepts has been carved out, whereby the main thrust is concerned with the latter.[30]

From this historically secure 'archimedian' point Gabler then takes one last important step towards the dogmatic theology which of course was his point of departure. For when, in the methodically accepted

Theologie, p. 280; Sandys-Wunsch and Eldredge, 'J.P. Gabler', p. 142 has: 'universal ideas'.

29. Gabler, *Kleinere theologische Schriften*, II, p. 190 (Merk, *Biblische Theologie*, p. 279; Sandys-Wunsch and Eldredge, 'J.P. Gabler', p. 142); cf. Smend, 'Johann Philipp Gablers Begründung der biblischen Theologie', p. 348.

30. Cf. Gabler, *Kleinere theologische Schriften*, II, p. 185 (Merk, *Biblische Theologie*, p. 276) with Merk, *Biblische Theologie*, pp. 40-41. Inasmuch as it may be informative 'to filter out' Gabler's procedure on this point as 'the theological concentrate which is normative for all time' (thus Leder, *Universität Altdorf*, p. 288), or to label it the 'filtration of a biblical theology', is open to question.

way, the variable biblical 'opinions' are 'carefully collected from Holy Scripture and suitably digested, carefully referred to the universal notions, and compared exactly with each other, then the question of their dogmatic use may profitably be established, and the boundaries of both biblical and dogmatic theology correctly assigned'.[31]

In 'crossing the boundary' between biblical and dogmatic theology, also a procedure of fundamental considerations now occurs, and now, considerations of a factually critical nature in which reason plays a not unimportant role. For not everything in the Scriptures is theologically transferrable into 'the permanent form of Christian teaching' or into our present time. Rather, some things must be omitted, because they were intended 'only for people of a specific era', such as the Mosaic ritual law in the Old Testament or, in the New Testament, 'the directive of Paul that women should cover their heads in church'. When 'ultimately those passages of the Holy Scriptures' have become 'singled out and transparent (*selecta atque perspicua*)', then one has the *dicta classica* of the Scriptures, 'truly then the result is "biblical theology in the stricter sense of the word" (*tum vero resultat theologia biblica, ex significatione quidem vocis pressiori*)', by means of their 'appropriate interpretation'. Summing up, he states: 'And finally, unless we want to follow uncertain arguments, we must so build only upon these firmly established foundations of biblical theology, again taken in the stricter sense as above, a dogmatic theology adapted to our own times'.[32]

The dogmatic theology constructed upon this methodical and biblical basis will, however, need to be multifaceted just like the original biblical theology, as well as 'heterogeneous', according to the various needs of the time, 'since it is after all actually a *philosophia christiana*'. On the other hand, 'biblical theology itself remains the same, namely in that it deals only with those things which holy men perceived about matters pertinent to religion, and is not made to accommodate our point of view'.[33]

---

31. Gabler, *Kleinere theologische Schriften,* II, pp. 190-91, with the same expressions as in the second part of the title of the address (see n. 15 above; cf. Merk, *Biblische Theologie,* p. 280; Sandys-Wunsch and Eldredge, 'J.P. Gabler', p. 142, where *finibus* is rendered 'goals').

32. Gabler, *Kleinere theologische Schriften,* II, p. 191-93; cf. Sandys-Wunsch and Eldredge, 'J.P. Gabler', p. 142-44, and p. 144 n. 1; Merk, *Biblische Theologie,* p. 280-81.

33. Gabler, *Kleinere theologische Schriften,* II, p. 193; translation by Sandys-

Right up to the conclusion of Gabler's methodical argument it is easy to observe how anxious he was not only to divide and separate 'correctly', but also to link and bridge in order to produce a wider theological unity. By means of his distinctions as far as biblical theology was concerned, however, he did not just quietly sit on both sides of the great divide between 'religion' and 'theology', between historical-critical exegesis and normative dogmatics,[34] but he also really tried to build a bridge over the abyss. And the bridge is the biblical theology 'in the stricter sense' which was based on the *dicta classica*, and which was given up by the 'pure biblical theology' and received by the dogmatic theology as its 'foundation'; thereby is the hermeneutic and objectively normative role which is here ascribed to the biblical *dicta classica* a completely different one from that conferred upon the *dicta probantia* of orthodox theology. In other words, Gabler announced in his address a very broad path which led from a maximum of historical variability and change in the Scriptures through interpretation and comparative reflection to a reduction which resulted in a theologically safe minimum and which then led on from this minimum to an extensive and adaptable maximum of accommodating dogmatic theology. In this way he attempted to render the possibility of a historico-theological and ecclesiastical unity and completeness. One can hardly justice to Gabler's hermeneutic and theological interest if one does not consider this all-encompassing aspect of his thinking sufficiently.

Gabler finished his inaugural address with the single word *Dixi*, 'I have spoken'. However, in the following almost 40 years of his research he never finished with the methodical interest of his address, but returned to it often and in different ways. In so doing, he partly further justified his statements in the address, partly defended them and partly developed them in the direction of a delineation of biblical theology without ever completing or publishing a book of this kind. In order to expand on what has gone before, one may now concentrate on this context of his address.[35]

Thus first, he further justified—and in some points somewhat modified—his hermeneutical method as well as its significance not only

---

Wunsch and Eldredge, 'J.P. Gabler', p. 144.

34. Cf. Smend, 'Universalismus', p. 170; Dohmeier, 'Die Grundzüge', p. 42.

35. Cf. the detailed comments in Leder, *Universität Altdorf*, pp. 290-305; and esp. Merk, *Biblische Theologie*, pp. 47-140; also Dohmeier, 'Die Grundzüge', pp. 43-71.

for (historical) exegesis but also for theology in general. Among others, just two of the works referred to above should be particularly considered, namely, the introductions and commentaries of his three-volume edition of Eichhorn's *Urgeschichte* and his fundamental observations 'Über den Unterschied zwischen Auslegung und Erklärung'.[36]

In his inaugural address Gabler naturally had to make his remarks in a fundamental and concentrated form. In his edition of the *Urgeschichte* three years later he expresses himself in far more detail, including comments on how he came to do this edition. While in his address it was important for him to provide dogmatics with a solid exegetical basis, the work of his teacher now gave him the occasion not only to expand on the primacy of exegesis with the remark that has become classic, namely, 'dogmatics must depend on exegesis and not vice versa',[37] but also to explain more fully how best to proceed in concrete terms with a responsible, historical exegesis. For this purpose he makes use of 'the Mosaic cosmogony', because the true character of 'history' can be investigated well in this theologically important material. Just as he speaks up elsewhere in New Testament works for a necessary 'separation of *factum* and *interpretatio facti*', where 'the recognition of the temporally conditioned both formally and materially' is a prerequisite for this separation, in connexion with Eichhorn and their common teacher C.G. Heyne he concludes that 'the use of the mythical form of imagination and expression among ancient peoples in general and the biblical writers in particular' belongs to such temporally determined elements.[38] This is not a question of history in the actual sense of the word, in that both a 'natural' and allegorical interpretation become superfluous—one is here rather closer to the scriptural understanding of the Reformation, because the approach is according to 'the more recent, amended hermeneutical principles, according to which no *sensus duplex* is accepted, but only *unicus, isque literalis s. grammaticus*'.[39]

---

36. See the discussion above in this section as well as nn. 9 and 11. Cf. also Smend, 'Johann Philipp Gablers Begründung der biblischen Theologie', pp. 353-56; Leder, *Universität Altdorf*, pp. 290-95; Merk, *Biblische Theologie*, pp. 52-54, 69-81; and Dohmeier, 'Die Grundzüge', pp. 43-45.

37. Gabler, *Urgeschichte*, I, p. xv.

38. Thus Leder, *Universität Altdorf*, p. 293, with reference to Gabler, *Kleinere theologische Schriften*, I, pp. 331, 699-700; cf. Merk, *Biblische Theologie*, pp. 52ff.

39. Gabler, *Urgeschichte*, II.1, pp. 399-400 n. 167; cf. Merk, *Biblische*

Some ten years later, in 1800, Gabler felt compelled, on the occasion of a review in his journal, 'to add a few hermeneutical observations on the correct way of explaining the story of the temptation of Jesus...in order to make clear from this example the not insignificant difference between "exegesis" and "explanation"'.[40] The difference relates, on the one hand, to the philological 'word explanation' and, on the other hand, to the 'subject explanation', which must be linked with the former, for as Gabler has it, 'both together complete the task of the biblical interpreter'. Thus he expresses the view that proper exegesis comprises methically different steps which, although separated in the execution, still need to complement one another.[41] As far as this comprehensive task of scriptural explanation is concerned, he closes his little treatise as follows: 'Above all in exegesis the different interest of the philologian and the theologian should not be overlooked: the philologian is interested only in the exegesis; on the other hand, the theologian is primarily interested in the explanation of the Bible. The genuine exegete links both, taking exegesis as his starting point with explanation as his goal.'[42]

Second, Gabler had to defend his methical or hermeneutical position, which means that his 'defence' often took the form of sharp polemics. At about the same time as Gabler edited the volumes of the *Urgeschichte*, in 1792 C.F. von Ammon brought out a new biblical theology volume with the title *Entwurf einer reinen biblischen Theologie*. From the title it is obvious to conclude that it is a question here of a

Theologie, pp. 53-54. On the mythological research of the age, see especially Hartlich and Sachs, *Der Ursprung des Mythosbegriffes*, pp. 20-47; and Merk, *Biblische Theologie*, pp. 54-58.

40. *Neuestes theologisches Journal* 6 (1800), p. 225, as well as n. 11 above, and Merk, *Biblische Theologie*, pp. 75-77. The full title is 'Über den Unterschied zwischen "Auslegung" und "Erklärung", erläutert durch die verschiedene Behandlungsart "der Versuchungsgeschichte Jesu"'.

41. *Neuestes theologisches Journal* 6 (1800), pp. 227-28. Referring to 'Abgenöthigter Nachtrag' (*Journal für theologische Literatur* 1 [1801], pp. 309-41), Merk notes appropriately: 'How can the exegete understand a text from the past in terms of its own day and yet at the same time render it comprehensible for his own time, without sacrificing thought and reason? The exegete can only be successful here by completing the step from exegesis to explanation, and when he makes it clear that both steps relate to each other and cannot be separated' (Merk, *Biblische Theologie*, p. 76).

42. *Journal für theologische Literatur* 6 (1803), p. 242.

realization of the methodical views of Gabler;[43] yet this was not the case at all. Gabler subjected it immediately to a fundamental critical review,[44] although at first indirectly by means of a sharp attack on the von Ammon-based hermeneutics of Immanuel Kant, which he compares with an outmoded allegorization of the Church Fathers.[45] The reason for such a designation lay particularly in Kant's own evaporation of the historical, as well as of biblical revelation, as when he was able to characterize it as 'something irrelevant'.[46] In his address of 1787 Gabler particularly had attacked such a view—then in the guise of traditional dogmatics—and now it was a matter of fighting against it in the guise of a morally delivered (and celebrated) philosophy, for in this case he was also concerned with a historically and theologically relevant exegesis of the Bible as a foundation for the rest of theological thinking.[47]

Third, since his inaugural address it had been Gabler's burden to draft a biblical theology which was relevant and appropriate in a variety of ways, not only methodically and programmatically, but also to be able to shape it in concrete terms. In his address he excused himself by saying that this was 'not the task of the beginner, but of the experienced thinker (*non tironum est, sed veteranorum*)'.[48] Even in the final volume of the *Urgeschichte* he declares that he sees himself 'compelled to set [his] own hand to the task'.[49] Yet he never totally realized his plans.

43. Cf. Kraus, *Geschichte der historisch-kritischen Erforschung* (1956), p. 140, whose incorrect information has been corrected by Smend, 'Johann Philipp Gablers Begründung der Biblischen Theologie', p. 349 (and others), yet has been maintained by Kraus in the 3rd revised edition (1982) of his *Geschichte der historisch-kritischen Erforschung*, p. 151.

44. Cf. Merk, *Biblische Theologie*, p. 59 n. 106; pp. 60-61, and esp. p. 85 nn. 221-22.

45. Gabler, *Urgeschichte*, II.2, pp. xiv-xv; cf. particularly Merk, *Biblische Theologie*, pp. 58-69, 82-90; also Smend, 'Johann Philipp Gablers Begründung der Biblischen Theologie', pp. 349-53; Leder, *Universität Altdorf*, pp. 303-305; and Dohmeier, 'Die Grundzüge', pp. 56ff.

46. I. Kant, *Die Religion innerhalb der Grenzen der blossen Vernunft* (1793), p. 161; cf. p. 158. Cf. also Smend, 'Johann Philipp Gablers Begründung der Biblischer Theologie', p. 350, and Merk, *Biblische Theologie*, pp. 62-63.

47. Cf. Merk, *Biblische Theologie*, p. 63.

48. Gabler, *Kleinere theologische Schriften*, II, p. 194 (Merk, *Biblische Theologie*, p. 282).

49. Gabler, *Urgeschichte*, II.2, pp. xv-xvi.

Here, however, one should not primarily see any expression of methodical weakness, as might be obvious, but one should rather try to explain this state of affairs from his own way of working and from his particular circumstances. Besides, as particularly Merk has shown, Gabler did important spadework for a biblical theology such as the study referred to above on 'exegesis' and 'explanation', which has been described by Merk as the methodical climax of Gabler's preparatory exegetical studies for a biblical theology; additionally, Gabler gave lectures on the topic, with his *prolegomena* on biblical theology from the year 1816 being particularly worthy of mention and consideration.[50]

From the background of the literary context of Gabler's inaugural address, which has been touched on here only sketchily, it will have become clear that in Gabler's methodical and hermeneutical thinking and writing the main thrust and the thesis of his address of 1787 have always maintained their central meaning, although he slightly modified his original views on a few points.[51]

3. *Concluding Thoughts on the Influence and Significance of his Work*

As may well have become clear from the remarks above, Gabler's inaugural address and his following statements on the topic were 'not immediately particularly influential', as Smend carefully put it, but the effect of his work only gradually became apparent in the nineteenth century, first in the work of his pupil W.M.L. de Wette.[52] Yet his academic reputation has grown considerably in the course of time.

Up until now Gabler—like most of the great theologians—has been assessed in a variety of ways. For example, whereas Heussi has described the thought process of his address as that of a 'shrewd methodological treatise',[53] Leder says in general that 'Gabler was not a systematic theologian', and points to his lack of large, complete

---

50. Merk, *Biblische Theologie*, pp. 77, 81-140, esp. pp. 113ff., where E.F.C.A.H. Netto's work on Gabler's lecture on biblical theology has been commented upon and partially reproduced.

51. Cf. Merk, *Biblische Theologie*, pp. 98ff.

52. Cf. Smend, 'Universalismus', pp. 169ff., and also see n. 25 above.

53. K. Heussi, *Geschichte der theologischen Fakultät zu Jena* (Weimar: Hermann Böhlaus Nachfolger, 1954), p. 216, where he also uses the designation 'a noteworthy milestone'; cf. further Leder, *Universität Altdorf*, p. 287.

works,[54] which represents a very superficial evaluation. His 'systematics' and the strength of his thinking in general lay particularly in the clarity and consistency of his methodical and hermeneutical reflections—despite temporally conditioned limitations within the neological tradition—as well as in his clear view of the wholeness and the unity of theology.

As far as Gabler's significance for biblical theology in particular is concerned, one may agree with Merk's general judgment when he says: 'It may today be regarded as certain that only since Gabler's inaugural address in 1787 have we been able to speak of biblical theology as a discipline in its own right.'[55] And with regard to the contents of his work, one of Merk's pertinent summarizing statements may be repeated:

> If for Gabler it has to be decided from 'pure biblical theology' whether we remain theologians, he thereby proved the theological necessity of *this* biblical theology for his time, and at the same time by implication—though unintentionally—revealed the temporal conditioning of his views. Only by bearing this in mind one can discover what remains most important: it is *the call to theological reflection about biblical statements*, it is the demand for theological exegesis which attempts to provide validity across the ages to reformatory scriptural interpretation. However construed, questionable and above all temporally conditioned this 'immutable', 'pure biblical theology' may be, Gabler's interest remains worthy of note: namely, to give a biblical-reformatory basis to dogmatics which are constantly in a state of flux and which always attract into any dogmatic discussion the problems of the times.[56]

In conclusion, however, one can answer the question which was posed at the beginning of this chapter by claiming with confidence that despite certain predecessors one may regard Johann Philipp Gabler as the 'father' of modern biblical theology, and also honour him as such. His significance for current biblico-theological discussion may be greater than one may be inclined to believe.

---

54. Leder, *Universität Altdorf*, p. 279.
55. Merk, *Biblische Theologie*, p. 3.
56. Merk, *Biblische Theologie*, p. 106.

Chapter 20

WILLIAM ROBERTSON SMITH AT THE END
OF THE NINETEENTH CENTURY: THEOLOGY AND
HISTORY AND SOCIOLOGY OF RELIGION

1. *Introduction*

In modern study of the Old Testament the last half and especially the last quarter of the nineteenth century turned out to be more turbulent than any earlier period; for in these years Old Testament research went through a paradigm shift that was more radical than any before. The main area of new insights and theories as well as of disagreement and dispute was in particular represented by the Pentateuch (or Hexateuch), partly also by the historical and prophetical books. The leading country in the new scholarly debate was Germany; and the key figure was Julius Wellhausen of Göttingen. He had brilliantly managed to combine earlier ideas into a new comprehensive concept with regard to the growth and composition of the Hexateuch and to the development of the religion of ancient Israel. Before long his theories were received by many scholars worldwide. All of this is well known and may be read in every handbook.

Less well known in this period, however, at least on an international scale, seems to be the work of William Robertson Smith.[1] But his remarkable life and work undoubtedly deserve far greater historiographical attention than has been the case hitherto, and even more so since he was a real 'storm centre' of his time in Scottish academic and church life, also called 'the period of the fiercest fighting'.[2] He has been characterized as a 'pioneer and martyr'; and his brilliant intellectual

---

1. It is surprising that Kraus, in his *Geschichte der historisch-kritischen Erforschung* (1982), only has some short references to Robertson Smith (pp. 275, 373, 379).

2. R.A. Riesen, *Criticism and Faith in Late Victorian Scotland* (Lanham: University Press of America, 1985), p. xix.

capacity as well as 'the breadth of his competence' have been recognized as 'amazing' by many.[3] Further, the scholarly work of Robertson Smith was, in a most specific way, interwoven with the dramatic course of his life; and this fact is, above all, manifest in his first two important books.[4] Both in the turbulence of his life and in the literary legacy of his extensive and variegated research on the Old Testament in its historical environment, there were elements that will, also on an international scale, remain significant for the historiographic description of Old Testament studies in the last quarter of the nineteenth century.

On this occasion one general and two specific historiographical problems may be discussed briefly; then also how they are mirrored in the life and work of William Robertson Smith.

2. *The Individualization of Biblical Studies*

Generally speaking, there will always be personal factors and aspects involved in scholarly work. The history of Christian theology on the whole, as well as that of Bible studies in particular, shows abundantly that it is just the work of individual scholars that have most decisively promoted the progress of study. But, at the same time, scholars are dependent on their institutional context and pursue their investigation under specific social conditions that may be more or less influential on their work. So, by necessity, there will always exist a reciprocity and

---

3. Riesen, *Criticism and Faith*, pp. 94, 111; 108-15. Besides the fuller biographies by J.S. Black and G. Chrystal (eds.), *Lectures and Essays of William Robertson Smith* (Edinburgh: A. & C. Black, 1912), and T.O. Beidelman, *W. Robertson Smith and the Sociological Study of Religion* (Chicago: University of Chicago Press, 1974), pp. 3-28; see also G.W. Anderson, 'Two Scottish Semitists', in *Congress Volume: Edinburgh 1974* (VTSup, 28; Leiden: E.J. Brill, 1975), pp. ix-xix (x-xv); E. Ball, 'Smith, W. Robertson', in *A Dictionary of Biblical Interpretation* (London: SCM Press, 1990), pp. 633-35; and J. Rogerson, *Old Testament Criticism in the Nineteenth Century: England and Germany* (London: SPCK, 1984), pp. 275-80.

4. Some of his articles in *Encyclopaedia Britannica,* especially the article on 'Bible' in 1875, had given rise to the serious charges against him (cf. Black and Chrystal (eds.), *Lectures and Essays*, pp. 179ff.; Beidelman, *W. Robertson Smith*, pp. 15-22, 85-92), and his first two books were some lectures he delivered in his defence: *The Old Testament in the Jewish Church* (Edinburgh: A. & C. Black, 1881; 2nd edn, 1892), and *The Prophets of Israel and their Place in History* (Edinburgh: A. & C. Black, 1882; 2nd edn [ed. T.K. Cheyne], 1895)—cf. their respective prefaces.

sometimes even a tension or a conflict between these two sides of personal versus 'extra-personal', or what might be called 'suprapersonal' factors in the process of studies; and that has to be reflected in any analysis and writing of the history of research. In this respect, however, some histories of research display a tendency that generates serious historiographic problems, in that they relate the presentation overall to *persons*. It is, of course, impossible and quite undesirable to neglect biographical and other person-related factors; but, on the other hand, if one exaggerates the person-related side of the historical presentation, there may be a risk that a research history becomes an aggregate of personal histories.[5]

In cases of this kind it remains historiographically problematic, first, that in analysis and description there may be a possible neglect of the longer lines and of the dynamics of scholarly streams of tradition as well as of specific ideas and movements,[6] second, that there may be less awareness of the significance of social institutions—in the broadest sense—or, putting it the other way round, that there may be less sensitivity to the power of authority that institutions, including both University and Church, may have over the individual scholar.

This general phenomenon became acute in the history of Old Testament studies in the latter part of the nineteenth century. The description of this period has rightly focused on Julius Wellhausen and German critical scholarship; but when Kraus in his *Geschichte der historisch-kritischen Erforschung* maintains that no other Old Testament scholar was so vehemently combatted as Wellhausen,[7] he might have compared him with the no less dramatic case of Robertson Smith.

5.   Cf., e.g., most of R.P.C. Hanson, 'The Biblical Exegesis in the Early Church', in *CHB*, I, pp. 412-563, is taken up with portraits of Origen, Theodore of Mopsuestia, Jerome and Augustine as 'biblical scholars'. To some extent, Kraus, *Geschichte der historisch-kritischen Erforschung* (1982), also has this bias.

6.   When Eissfeldt, 'Julius Wellhausen', was to characterize Wellhausen as 'historian', he says of him: 'Geschichte ist ihm nicht ein Nebeneinander und Nacheinander von Ereignissen und Personen, Geschichte ist ihm ein Miteinander und Gegeneinander von Kräften und Ideen' (p. 69). This goes for a research history as well: cf. Smend, *Epochen der Bibelkritik*, pp. 11-32; also H. Graf Reventlow, *The Authority of the Bible and the Rise of the Modern World* (ET London, 1984); and Rogerson, *Old Testament Criticism*, pp. 1-11, 138-40, 291-93.

7.   Kraus, *Geschichte der historisch-kritischen Erforschung* (1982), pp. 225-26.

On the Way to Canon

Both Wellhausen and Smith were, indeed, brilliant scholars and strong personalities;[8] but, at the same time, both of them were bound by a double dependence. On the one hand, they were determined by specific traditions of historical and critical research. These relations and perspectives have often been described, especially with regard to Wellhausen,[9] but also as for Smith.[10] On the other hand, their work was influenced by the mighty institutions of University and Church. Also these relations have been paid some historiographical attention, more regarding Smith than Wellhausen.

In this connexion two most interesting testimonies, namely, two letters from the early 1880s, one from Wellhausen and another from Smith, may be illustrative, not only in a personal respect but even for the period in general. The letter of Wellhausen is rather well known and has often been commented upon; the letter of Smith seems to be far less known. The letters are different in form but rather similar in their subject matter; and they may be regarded as typical for their authors and their respective situations.

In his letter of 5 April 1882, addressed to the Prussian Minister for Church Affairs, Wellhausen asked to be transferred from the Theological Faculty to the Faculty of Arts because he regarded his teaching as insufficient or, rather, destructive for educating theological students for their future service.[11] Less than a year later Smith sent a longer public letter to the Editor of *The Scotsman*; it was published on the 30 March

---

8. The relationship of Wellhausen and Smith has been further elaborated by R. Smend, 'William Robertson Smith and Julius Wellhausen', in W. Johnstone (ed.), *William Robertson Smith: Essays in Reassessement* (JSOTSup, 189; Sheffield: Sheffield Academic Press, 1995), pp. 226-42.

9. Cf., e.g., Kraus, *Geschichte der historisch-kritischen Erforschung* (1982), pp. 242-74; Smend, *Deutsche Alttestamentler*, pp. 99-113; Smend, *Epochen der Bibelkritik*, pp. 168-215; also his 'Kuenen und Wellhausen', in P.B. Dirksen and A. van der Kooij (eds.), *Abraham Kuenen (1828–1891): His Major Contributions to the Study of the Old Testament* (OTS, 29; Leiden: E.J. Brill, 1993), pp. 113-27.

10. Cf. Reventlow, *Authority of the Bible*; Riesen, *Criticism and Faith*, pp. 115-29; Rogerson, *Old Testament Criticism*, pp. 147ff. (Part Two); also R.C. Fuller, *Alexander Geddes, 1737–1802: Pioneer of Biblical Criticism* (Sheffield: Almond Press, 1984) and W. McKane, *Selected Christian Hebraists* (Cambridge: Cambridge University Press, 1989), pp. 151-90.

11. See Kraus, *Geschichte der historisch-kritischen Erforschung* (1982), p. 256; cf. Smend, *Deutsche Alttestamentler*, p. 108.

1883, under the headline 'The Theological Chairs'.[12]

The issue raised by Smith was 'the subject of the Divinity Chairs in the Scottish universities'; and his opening question was whether 'the Divinity Halls of the Established Church [ought] to have the privileges of University faculties'. His first prompt answer to this 'must be negative', he says; and then follows a longer consideration.

On the one hand, he finds a contradiction between the function of the universities that is 'national', and the denominational instruction of the Divinity Halls that is exclusive 'with the view to the ministry of one Church, and consisting of teachers who are all in a certain position of legal dependence on the Presbytery of their bounds'; this he maintains to be 'plainly an anomaly'.

On the other hand, he argues for the place and function of theology in the universities and their Faculties of Arts, since religion—'in spite of our friends the Secularists'—'will always continue to occupy a large part in human life and thought', and 'even as a mere phenomenon in human life it will always claim and receive scientific study'. That theology should be studied only by candidates for the ministry he contends to be 'quite a modern idea'. He therefore maintains 'that there is a demand for scientific theology... as there is for metaphysics, or the higher philology, or any other study that is not directly a bread-study'. He also states that 'the theological controversies of the Churches are the very strongest reason for the encouragement of a theology independent of the Churches.' By 'the elevation of theology into a faculty of pure and unfettered science', as he says, he will still keep the four traditional Chairs of Divinity, including the Chair of Dogmatic, since 'Dogmatic is essentially a combination of history and metaphysics, and both of these are recognised as fit subjects for a University'.

When Smith in this way argued for a radical separation of the Divinity Halls from the universities it had nothing to do with a loss of his personal faith or anything of that kind; on the contrary.[13] When he became a Professor of Divinity he was also ordained as a minister; as long as he stayed in Scotland, he preached and held services. In spite of

12. A copy of the letter has kindly been put at my disposal by Professor William Johnstone, for which I owe him best thanks. The letter is registered by Black and Chrystal (eds.), *Lectures and Essays*, p. 622; Beidelman, *W. Robertson Smith*, p. 80; and Riesen, *Criticism and Faith*, p. 456.

13. Cf. Riesen, *Criticism and Faith*, pp. 129-38; 186-215; also Anderson, 'Two Scottish Semitists', p. xiv.

all the fierce controversies with his Church, on the whole he remained faithful to her; and, theologically, it was a lifelong concern of his to bridge religious faith and critical scrutiny.[14]

The affair in his letter was of quite another kind, it was about academic freedom or 'unfettered science'. Thereby, he also made a reference to the 'German Universities, where the Professors are practically tied by no test', as he—somewhat questionably—contends. Whereas he focused on the connectedness of revelation and history, bridging faith and science, he contrasted decisively the institutions of Church and University.

Here, harking back to the beginning of this section, one may in fact see another side of the increasing phenomenon of individualization of research; and for him the University was obviously expected to provide the individual scholar, in the best way, with the necessary conditions and freedom. When it comes to the institution of the University, however, it would be proper to look at it in a broader framework and draw lines in a very long perspective, even back to the situation in the Middle Ages when biblical interpretation and scrutiny 'moved' from the Monastic to the Cathedral Schools and to the first new universities.[15] Then and later, when in the time of the Renaissance there were founded universities also north of the Alps and east of the Rhine, a distinct development of growing academic independence was fostered. But with regard to existing research histories in theology and biblical studies it may be fair to say that the function and influence of academic institutions in general, and the universities in particular, have scarcely been estimated properly.

When Rogerson, reviewing the situation of Old Testament studies in the nineteenth century asks 'why, in comparison with England, German Old Testament scholarship continued to be far more innovative',[16] a reason, not mentioned by him, may be considered as significant, namely, the influential axis of Church and University and, especially, the importance of the latter in providing better conditions for individual

14. Remarkable in this respect, differently in relation to Wellhausen, is his sharp criticism of the theological views of A. Kuenen (cf. Riesen, *Criticism and Faith*, pp. 115-19).

15. See M. Sæbø (ed.), *Hebrew Bible/Old Testament: The History of its Interpretation. I.2. The Middle Ages* (Göttingen: Vandenhoeck & Ruprecht; forthcoming).

16. Rogerson, *Old Testament Criticism*, p. 292.

biblical studies—that might have been larger in Germany than in Britain.

When Smith is viewed in these longer perspectives, first, the importance of his case, research and writings may surely be more adequately understood; but, second, his achievement will also contribute considerably to a better understanding of biblical research in his own time—even outside his own country.

Finally, it remains most remarkable that it was just in the matrix of the Free Church of Scotland, having been split off from the Established Church in 1843, for most conservative reasons, that a scholar like William Robertson Smith, together with his teacher A.B. Davidson and his temporary replacement George Adam Smith, pursued his way of critical research on the Old Testament. That may be a most impressive witness for the new and stronger personal and individualistic trend that rose against the 'collective' powers in academic and Church life of the latter part of the nineteenth century.

3. *The Internationalization of Biblical Studies*

Along with the described trend—and historiographical problem—of individualization, a second growing trend that may be called internationalization of biblical research is recognizable as well.

Prima facie, the tendency of internationalization might seem to be contrary to the first, but in fact this trend was just another side of the same modern situation in Old Testament studies of the late nineteenth century. For there were not only social and 'suprapersonal', but now also increasing 'supranational', factors in its complex structure; a new western world of Old Testament scholarship was about to gain strength. But, as regards modern descriptions, these factors—like those of the first trend—seem not to have been paid sufficient attention as a phenomenon of general character nor as a historiographical problem.

As has been demonstrated above, modern scholarship first of all has been promoted by individuals of genius. It has, however, been of great importance for the progress of study that the new theories and views of leading scholars could be spread and thus cross national and regional borders as well as confessional ones. In the last part of the nineteenth century this seemed to happen more easily and faster than ever before; and the national, local and confessional traditions of learning were proportionally weakened. Prerequisites for a stronger development of this kind were, besides the general improvement of communication, first of all the existence of other congenial scholars who functioned as mediators—like, for instance, Smith; in addition, he transmitted the new ideas in a most independent way. It was typical of him that he frequently visited German Universities.

Another aspect of the stronger internationalizing tendency may, lastly, be seen in the relatively new phenomenon of exchange of scholars between the larger centres of learning. Again, Smith may serve as an example; for after being deposed from his Chair in Aberdeen, he was offered a Chair of Hebrew and Other Oriental Languages at Harvard University—which he declined.[17]

4. *The Specialization of Biblical Studies*

Finally, there existed a third growing area in late nineteenth-century investigation of the Old Testament; it may be seen in the tendency of specialization of biblical studies. Also this tendency represents a historiographical problem that deserves due attention, and even more so as it has only escalated in the course of the past 100 years.

The phenomenon of specialization in Old Testament studies that was strongly increasing in the second half of the last century is of a different kind. On this occasion it is not so much the specialization within traditional disciplines that may be brought into focus, as the specialization of studies in the sense of emancipation of some specific disciplines from the realm of theologians. By this process, which may even be called secularization, various traditionally theological disciplines and other near-related ones—such as Semitic Philology, with new branches such as Assyriology, Palestinian Archaeology, History of Religion as well as General History of the ancient Near East, to mention but some of them—were taken over by scholars who did not start as theologians but as linguists or archaeologists or general historians.[18]

In this respect, Smith, especially 'in his Cambridge exile',[19] developed as a pioneer and innovator of a sociological study of religion, first

17. Black and Chrystal (eds.), *Lectures and Essays*, pp. 340-43; Riesen, *Criticism and Faith*, p. 111.

18. Kraus has in his *Geschichte der historisch-kritischen Erforschung* (1982) described some of the new disciplines (cf., e.g., pp. 295ff.; 315ff.), but not so much as a common phenomenon, characteristic for the latter part of the nineteenth century.

19. Rogerson, *Old Testament Criticism*, p. 282.

of all of Social Anthropology, as may be seen from his two outstanding last books (from 1885 and 1889) as well as from the posthumously edited *Lectures and Essays* (of 1912). Standing in between the Scottish anthropologist J.F. McLennan and the well-known James Frazer, not least Smith himself has had a well-recognized great impact on international Sociology, and then especially—mainly through E. Durkheim and M. Mauss—on French sociology.[20]

In this case, Smith was not an independent mediator but a creative innovator. Here, the lines were not leading from abroad into Britain, but were going out from Britain to the scholarly new world. Through his specialization of the Old Testament studies he made a unique contribution to the internationalizing of these studies.

5. *Conclusion*

In conclusion, the task of writing a research history of Old Testament studies in the nineteenth century, especially for its last part, involves many intricate problems since the complexity of this history is probably more broad and its paradigm shift more radical than ever before.

In view of the specific tendencies that have now been discussed most briefly, a new research history of Old Testament studies in the nineteenth century should, first, be international in character and outlook because Old Testament scholarship has developed into a world phenomenon; a German-centred way of history writing, such as that undertaken by Kraus, may be regarded as anachronistic.

Second, as for the complexity of the variegated factors of this history, the reciprocity of personal/individual and institutional elements should be paid due attention—and greater than has been usual until now.

20. Beidelman, *W. Robertson Smith,* p. xi, and esp. pp. 28-68.

Chapter 21

SIGMUND MOWINCKEL IN THE FIRST HALF
OF THE TWENTIETH CENTURY:
LITERARY CRITICISM AND TRADITION HISTORY

1. *Introduction*

The hundredth anniversary of Sigmund Mowinckel (1884–1965) has
recently passed. In 1974—in an article on Mowinckel's last works[1]—I
expressed the hope, as an urgent desideratum, that someone should
publish a book on him at this jubilee of his. But no such book has
appeared. It is understandable, however, that this work has not been
undertaken as yet. In view of Mowinckel's vast and wide-ranging
authorship and of the fact that he was occupied with nearly all parts of
Old Testament study,[2] it may fairly be said that a book on him will
undoubtedly be a great enterprise which will entail much hard work and
will take some time to complete. This will even more be the case as one
considers that owing to Mowinckel's central place and position in Old
Testament studies for more than half a century, a book on him, to some
extent, will be a book of Old Testament research in general, for the
period of 1910–65.

A book on Sigmund Mowinckel, then, will for different reasons be a
rather painstaking and complicated piece of work. In the time of wait-
ing for it—and I do hope that someone will take up the gauntlet—it

---

1. M. Sæbø, 'Sigmund Mowinckels siste arbeider', *TTK* 45 (1974), pp. 161-
73.
2. Dagfinn Kvale and Dagfinn Rian (eds.), *Sigmund Mowinckel's Life and
Works: A Bibliography. With an Introduction on Sigmund Mowinckel and Old
Testament Study by Arvid S. Kapelrud* (Småskrifter utgitt av Institutt for
Bibelvitenskap, Universitetets i Oslo, 2; Oslo, 1984 [originally edited by Religionsvitenskapelig Institutt of the University of Trondheim; Trondheim, 1980]).
This bibliographical work also lists reviews of (and other references to) the works
of Mowinckel.

may be most useful if scholars, from different angles, discuss more limited issues in the works of Mowinckel—as will be done here. The significance of smaller contributions, as well as of more comprehensive ones, should be obvious at any rate for the history of our discipline.

In these perspectives I have chosen to discuss Mowinckel's relation to the literary-critical school. And I have done it deliberately for two reasons: first, more attention should be paid to this point in Mowinckel's work because it usually tends to lie in the shadow of his favourite concern—the Israelite cult, especially as seen in the light of the Psalms;[3] and second, the position of Mowinckel may be of some importance for the current debate on the use of the literary-critical method in the study of the Pentateuch—in particular as the questions have recently been posed by R. Rendtorff and H.H. Schmid.[4]

Now, for the sake of proper balance, on this occasion, it may be wise not to rush into the specific topic of this chapter but let the point of departure be Mowinckel's main interest and approach.

2. Mowinckel's Approach: The Cultic Aspect as a Principle of Exegetical Method

The very heart of the writings of Sigmund Mowinckel is his interest in the cultic aspect which he traced and meant to find in so many Old Testament texts. His greatest scholarly achievement—for which he will be remembered in the history of Old Testament studies—was his success in getting this aspect accepted as a point of vital importance for the exegetical work on the Old Testament in general and especially for the understanding of the ancient Israelite religion.[5]

The working out of this aspect was not part of his work from the beginning (1909), but it originated in his studies on the Psalms, which

3.   Cf., i.a., H. Birkeland, *Mowinckel, Sigmund Olaf Plytt, 1884–* (Norsk Biografisk Leksikon, 9; Oslo: H. Aschehoug, 1940), pp. 397-401; J. de Fraine in *DBSup*, V, pp. 1387-90; see also D.R. Ap-Thomas, 'An Appreciation of Sigmund Mowinckel's Contribution to Biblical Studies', *JBL* 85 (1966), pp. 315-25; A.S. Kapelrud, 'Sigmund Mowinckel and Old Testament Study', *ASTI* 5 (1967), pp. 4-29 (see also n. 2 above); recently Sæbø, 'Mowinkel, Sigmund (1884–1965)', *TRE*, XXIII, pp. 384-88; see also Ch. 13 above, esp. pp. 203-209.

4.   Rendtorff, *Das überlieferungsgeschichtliche Problem des Pentateuch*; Schmid, *Der sogenannte Jahwist*.

5.   Cf. J. Lindblom, 'Sigmund Mowinckel in memoriam', *STK* 41 (1965), pp. 191-92.

started with his book on the Royal Psalms (1916),[6] and which very soon became centred on his interpretation of the New Year Festival in the autumn as an Enthronement Festival of YHWH. After having presented this new interpretation in one of his doctoral lectures in 1916 and also shortly stating it in his book on the Royal Psalms,[7] Mowinckel argued his case in an article published in 1917 and, first of all, in his famous *Psalmenstudien*, I–VI (1921–24), where he examined the texts in a most broad and basic way.[8] He also discussed some methodological questions of this aspect in a paper of fundamental character which he read in Lund in 1923; its title was 'The Cultic Viewpoint as a Research Principle in Old Testament Studies'.[9] Here Mowinckel—without making the 'cultic viewpoint' dependent on his theory of the Enthronement Festival—passed distinct criticism on J. Wellhausen and other representatives of the literary-critical school for their extremely negative estimate of the Israelite cult, treating it as a phenomenon of inferior value in relation to personal and ethical religion and to the religion of the prophets.[10] Also H. Gunkel and religio-historical scholars like him came under Mowinckel's criticism for having failed to take appropriate consequences of their new methodological approach. In particular, they stressed too heavily—as the older criticism—the religious conceptions and ideas, instead of—like Mowinckel now focused it—the different forms of the religious life as it was exercised and experienced by the people in the cult. Therefore, Gunkel's 'sociological'

6.   Mowinckel, *Kongesalmerne i det gamle testamente*.
7.   See Mowinckel's most interesting autobiographical sketch 'Fragmenter', in *Norsk litteraturvitenskap i det 20. århundre* (Festschrift Francis Bull; Oslo: Gyldendal Norsk Forlag, 1957), pp. 117-30, esp. p. 127, with reference to his doctoral lecture; see also *Kongesalmerne i det gamle testamente*, pp. 75f.
8.   S. Mowinckel, 'Tronstigningssalmerne og Jahves tronstigningsfest', *NTT* 18 (1917), pp. 13-79. As well known as his *Psalmenstudien*, I–VI, are, it should not be necessary here to indicate the title of each volume; they were photomechanically reprinted as *Psalmenstudien*, I–VI (2 vols.; Amsterdam: P. Schippers, 1961; 2nd edn, 1966), and now are provided with a new Preface (unpaginated) by Mowinckel.
9.   S. Mowinckel, 'Det kultiske synspunkt som forskningsprincipp i den gammeltestamentlige videnskap', *NTT* 25 (1924), pp. 1-23.
10.   Mowinckel, 'Det kultische synspunkt', p. 3: 'kulten synes de [i.e. Wellhausen and Duhm] vesentlig å ha opfattet som det negativt insiterende moment i Israels religiøse utvikling...Så sterkt som denne eldre kritikerskolen har fremhevet at Israels religion før profetene var en kultreligion, så litet har den gjort alvor av å påvise kultens betydning i utviklingen'. Cf. also his article on J. Wellhausen (obituary), 'Julius Wellhausen', *For Kirke og Kultur* 25 (1918), pp. 277-88.

quest for the *Sitz im Leben* of the various forms (*Gattungen*) of the texts appeared to be most significant to Mowinckel. Along these lines he wanted to correct Gunkel with Gunkel—or as he put it in the preface to his *Psalmenstudien*, I: 'One has to play off Gunkel against Gunkel'.[11]

When the cult, then, happened to be of such paramount importance to Mowinckel, the motive was—as he has said in some autobiographical remarks from 1927—his 'search for the very "place" of the religious notion of life'; and this 'place' is just represented by the cult because it has the capacity of leading one to 'the real religious of the religion'.[12] Similarly, he characterized the cult by saying in his lecture of 1923: 'In the cult the religion as act finds its proper expression, long before the recognition that religion as act is moral, wins; experiences which in a true sense are religious, are associated with the cult'.[13] Mowinckel has also described his new approach as a 'cult-historical' and a 'cult-functional' one;[14] and he regarded it as a further development of the 'form-historical' method of his teacher Gunkel.[15]

Mowinckel did have his teachers. In one-and-a-half years from autumn 1911 onwards, he visited universities abroad and met scholars who made a lasting impression on him and who were conducive to the direction and the profile of his further studies and of his rich authorship. In Copenhagen and in Giessen he came to know the outstanding religio-historical scholars Vilhelm Grønbech and Hermann Gunkel, and in

11. Mowinckel, 'Det kultische synspunkt', pp. 4-5; *Psalmenstudien*, I, p. v: 'Man muss Gunkel gegen Gunkel ausspielen'.

12. S. Mowinckel, *Studentene fra 1902: Biografiske oplysninger* (Oslo: Grøndahl & Søn, 1927), p. 254: '…alltid vært mig mest om å gjøre å finne inn til det egentlige religiøse i religionen, til selve fromhetslivet og de virkelighetsoplevelser det bygger på. Dette i bevisst motsetning både til litterærkritiske og såkalt "religionshistoriske", i virkeligheten myte—og motivhistoriske ensidigheter. Det nye jeg mener å ha tilført gammel-testamentlig videnskap, er derfor en bevisst metode for opsporingen av det egentlige "sted" for de religiøse livsopfatninger og et bevisst forsøk på å forstå de religiøse tekster og finne det religiøse livs—og forestillingsinnhold ut ifra et slikt synspunkt; derav min sterke betoning av kultus'ens betydning.'

13. 'I kulten finner religionen som handling sitt egentlige uttrykk, lenge før den erkjennelse vinner frem at religionen i handling er moral; til kulten knytter de oplevelser sig som i særlig forstann er religiøse', 'Det kultische synspunkt', p. 1.

14. Cf. 'Det kultische synspunkt', p. 7; and 'Fragmenter', p. 126.

15. So in the Preface to his *Offersang og sangoffer* (Oslo: H. Aschehoug, 1951; 2nd edn, Oslo: Universitetsforlaget, 1971), p. v.

Marburg—where he stayed for the longest time—he met the literary critic Gustav Hölscher, with whom he seemed to have formed a life-long friendship.[16] Mowinckel never forgot to acknowledge his debt to his teachers, especially to Grønbech and Gunkel; but at the same time he was a very independent personality who could be sharp in his criticism, even of his own teachers. He had his roots in the Literary-critical and in the Form-historical School; but he was also in opposition to them, although scarcely not in discontinuity with them.

There are scholars—like, for instance, Wellhausen—whose work represents decisive turning points in Old Testament studies and who have the rare gift of combining different concerns and ideas of research of their time into a new, coherent, scholarly view which is more than the sum of its given presuppositions. Sigmund Mowinckel was also a scholar of this kind and character. And his organizing idea was—as has been indicated—that of the cult as the concrete expression of a living and active religion.[17]

From what now—rather briefly—has been said about Mowinckel's 'cult principle' approach, it has become apparent that it involved decisive criticism of the Literary-critical School—as also of form-historical scholars—for their neglecting the cultic aspect of many Old Testament texts, especially the Psalms. Here Mowinckel pointed to a weak trait or tendency in their studies; and to some degree it caused tension in his relation to the literary-critical school. His main interest was not congruent with theirs.

As has also been pointed out, however, Mowinckel was deeply rooted in the literary-critical school; and the question may now be raised how he—standing on the shoulder of the elder representatives of this school—made his own position in other parts of Old Testament studies than the Psalms and the New Year Festival question. How did he find his own way in matters where he might have common concerns with the literary critics, including the practice of the literary-critical method of which he made use all his life as a scholar? Did he also here act rather independently?

16. Cf. G. Hölscher's instructive article: 'Sigmund Mowinckel som gammel-testamentlig forsker [S.M. as an Old Testament Scholar]', *NTT* 24 (1923), pp. 73-138; and Mowinckel's obituary on Hölscher, 'Prof. D. Dr. Gustav Hölscher', *NTT* 56 (1955), pp. 296-98.

17. Cf. also his book *Religion og kultus* (Oslo: Landog Kirke, 1950; 2nd edn, 1971).

In this connexion it may be convenient to differentiate between two periods in his authorship, making a break with the early post-war time, because of some differences in his attitude and expressions which are noteworthy from 1946 onwards. Yet this break should not be over-stated, since the periods partly overlap each other, and Mowinckel's basic position was very much the same all the time.

3. *First Period: Aspects of Mowinckel's Literary-critical Work until 1944*

In Mowinckel's first three books—on the one hand, his study on the composition of the book of Jeremiah (1914),[18] and on the other hand, his double study on the books of Ezra and Nehemiah (1916)[19]—one will easily find the usual literary-critical way of working with text-critical conjectural readings, philological notes, literary-critical differentiation of sources, etc., as well as many fresh insights and new standpoints which actually did involve revision of points of view which were more or less generally accepted by scholars of the Wellhausen school.[20] Most typical in this respect are his studies on Nehemiah the Governor—his doctoral thesis—and on Ezra the Scribe; and it may be suitable to our purpose to focus on them for a while.

In an autobiographical retrospective of his works, Mowinckel has given a short comment on these studies, explaining why he started with these historical books.[21] After having described Gunkel's new approach, partly as a form- and literary-historical one, and partly as a religio-historical approach—whereby, in criticism of the last he calls for a keener recognition of structural changes of ideas when they have

18. Mowinckel, *Zur Komposition des Buches Jeremia.*

19. S. Mowinckel, *Studier til den jødiske menighets historie og litteratur.* I. *Statholderen Nehemia*; and *idem, Studier til den jødiske menighets historie og litteratur.* II. *Ezra den skriftlærde* (Kristiania [Oslo]: Olaf Norlis Forlag, 1916); cf. also his article, 'Om den jødiske menighets og provinsen Judæas organisation ca. 400 f.Kr.', *NTT* 16 (1915), pp. 123-48, 226-80.

20. Cf. Hölscher's both laudatory and critical assessment in 'Sigmund Mowinckel'; and A. Bentzen, 'Om Sigmund Mowinckels indsats i den gammel-testamentlige forskning [On S.M.'s achievement in Old Testament studies]', *NTT* 45 (1944), pp. 163-75 (also in a separate edition, *Acta Mowinckeliana*, 1884.4 August 1944 [Oslo: Grøndahl & Søn, 1944], pp. 3-15).

21. Mowinckel, 'Fragmenter', p. 122. Cf. also the Preface in *Studier til den jødiske*, I, pp. xi-xiv.

changed use in new contexts—he then says with reference to his Ezra and Nehemiah studies: 'It was from these points of view I started with an issue from the *historical literature* of the OT'.[22] In view of the decline of influence which the literary-critical way of working—especially its search for sources—to some extent suffered with the relatively favourable outcome of Gunkel's new approach, Mowinckel somehow—it seems—had the fear that the historical aspects of the Old Testament, and of the development of its religion, might now be at stake. Be that as it may, he chose to focus again on the historical problems— as had J. Wellhausen done in his way before. In this connexion it may be of some interest to quote what Mowinckel in a memorial article on Wellhausen, in the year 1918, regarded to be the lasting merit of the work of the great maestro; he says—to quote only this: 'First of all he has laid the foundation of a *historical* understanding of the Old Testament'.[23] This article is, by the way, rather illustrative with regard to Mowinckel's own relation to the literary-critical school. He obviously—like Wellhausen—wanted to be primarily an exegete of the Old Testament, and as such to be a historian. In carrying out his historical research, however, he very much used the form-historical method of Gunkel, although he—to some degree—was critical to his religio-historical approach; later on he stated that he 'has never considered himself as belonging to the "school of history of religion" in the proper sense'.[24] On the whole, then, the aim of Mowinckel was apparently to combine the literary-critical and the form-historical methods. How he managed this may be demonstrated by his Ezra and Nehemiah studies, in three points.

In the first place, it is scarcely at random that Mowinckel started with postexilic historical books. Similarly, Wellhausen—as Wilhelm de Wette had done earlier—took his point of departure in postexilic books, namely Chronicles (as well as Ezra and Nehemiah), when he was to establish the age and character of the Priestly Code which he regarded as the youngest of the alleged four main sources of the Pentateuch (and Joshua), and—in consequence of this—to substantiate a postexilic appearance and promulgation of the Mosaic Law, expressed in his

22. Mowinckel, 'Fragmenter', p. 122: 'Det var ut fra disse synspunkter jeg gav meg ikast med et emne fra den *historiske litteratur* i G.T.'.

23. 'Julius Wellhausen', p. 288; 'Først og fremst har han da lagt grunnvollen for en *historisk* forstaaelse av G.T.' [= Det gamle testamente].

24. Mowinckel, *Prophecy and Tradition*, p. 14; see §4 of this chapter.

famous *lex post prophetas*, 'the law after the prophets'.[25]

In principle, Mowinckel did not oppose this. But nonetheless, in his scrutiny of the texts he found evidence for taking a different view on many points, and not least with regard to the assessment and to the definite dating of the Priestly Code. Mowinckel not only regarded it necessary to differentiate between its final literary form and the antiquity of its various material—its antiquity might have been higher than usually assumed by the literary critics, but he even dated the final form earlier than according to the current literary-critical view. Contrary to Wellhausen's picture of a 'too straight and schematic development of Israel's spiritual history', as Mowinckel put it in his memorial article on him,[26] Mowinckel himself, particularly in a longer chapter in his Ezra study, presented a far more complex and variegated description—which may be called a tradition history—of the emergence of Israelite laws, ending up in the Priestly Code.[27] And again, in opposition to the Wellhausen school, Mowinckel did not combine the finalization of the Mosaic Law with Ezra, as its 'promulgator'; that process had taken place before his time. Furthermore, in relation to Nehemiah the figure of Ezra was, according to Mowinckel, not only later in time but also of minor historical significance.[28]

Along these lines—not to mention others—Mowinckel's studies on Nehemiah and Ezra were meant to contribute to a better 'historical understanding' of an important part of the postexilic Old Testament; and they did it in both a fresh, stimulating and a provocative way.[29] Although they were carried out on the ground of Wellhausen's historical work, they differed greatly from it; but they served the same purpose as his, the 'historical understanding', and so far they represented a creative continuation of it.[30] With some minor revisions Mowinckel

25. See T. Willi, *Die Chronik als Auslegung* (FRLANT, 106; Göttingen: Vandenhoeck & Ruprecht, 1972), pp. 44f.; and Chapter 10 above.

26. '...den Wellhausenske utvikling av Israels aandshistorie er for rettlinjet, for skematisk', 'Julius Wellhausen', p. 287.

27. Mowinckel, *Studier til den jødiske*, II, pp. 72-138.

28. Mowinckel, *Studier til den jødiske*, II, pp. 138ff.

29. Cf., i.a., Hölscher, 'Sigmund Mowinckel', pp. 80ff.; Bentzen, 'Om Sigmund Mowinckel's indsats', pp. 164-65; Lindblom, 'Sigmund Mowinckel in memoriam', pp. 191-92.

30. Cf. *Studier til den jødiske*, II, p. 91; 'Fragmenter', pp. 120ff.

maintained his position on these questions also in his later years.[31]

As for the Nehemiah material, in the second place, Mowinckel brought new insights by using a *comparative form-historical* method in examining the so-called Nehemiah source, where Nehemiah speaks of himself in the first person. Rejecting the traditional understanding of these passages as 'memoirs' or 'autobiography', because he regarded these terms to be misleading modern ones, Mowinckel recognized that their form is unique in the Old Testament but had equivalents in royal inscriptions in the ancient Near East, especially in Assyria–Babylonia.[32] And in a similar way he also explained the passages where Ezra speaks in the first person, but now by comparison with Egyptian material as well as with Jewish.[33] In this way too, Mowinckel acted as a historian; by interpreting an Old Testament text in its broader setting, which was proper for the new situation of research, he continued intentionally— one might say—the historical programme of Wellhausen, although differing from him.

In the third place, it may briefly be mentioned that Mowinckel in his Nehemiah study even had an eye for the *oral tradition* as a basic form of transmission of the prophetic preaching. He says:

> The prophetic books now existing are works of collections after an oral tradition, like the Gospels. The individual, mostly very brief, oracles of various kind at first, for some time, circulated in the oral tradition, and were then, little by little, written down and collected...[34]

Somewhat similarly, Mowinckel also expressed himself in his first book, a couple of years earlier, on the composition of the book of

31. S. Mowinckel, *Studien zu dem Buche Ezra–Nehemia*. I. *Die nachchroni-[sti]sche Redaktion des Buches: Die Listen* (Oslo: Universitetsforlaget, 1964); II. *Die Nehemia–Denkschrift* (1964); III. *Die Ezrageschichte und das Gesetz Moses* (1965).

32. *Studier til den jødiske*, I, pp. 124ff.; cf. the German version of this in his article: 'Die vorderasiatischen Königs—und Fürsteninschriften: Eine stilistische Studie', in *Eucharisterion*, I (Festschrift H. Gunkel; FRLANT, 36; Göttingen: Vandenhoeck & Ruprecht, 1923), pp. 278-322.

33. *Studier til den jødiske*, II, pp. 49ff.; cf. also his article: ' "Ich" und "Er" in der Ezrageschichte', in *Verbannung und Heimkehr* (Festschrift W. Rudolph; Tübingen: J.C.B. Mohr, 1961), pp. 211-33.

34. *Studier til den jødiske*, I, pp. 116-17: 'De nu foreliggende profetbøker er samleværker efter en mundtlig tradition, likesom evangelierne et det. De forskjellige enkelte, for det meste meget korte, orakler har først en tidlang løpet rundt i mundtlig tradition, er saa efterhaanden blit opskrevet og samlet...'

Jeremiah. In both cases he was speaking of 'redactors' who did the work of 'collecting'.[35]

With this, then, another area of Mowinckel's work has been reached: his studies on the Old Testament *prophets*. In this field he started with his first article in 1909, and here he published numerous contributions over the years, especially with regard to literary and form-historical problems as well as to the structure and composition of the books of Isaiah 1–39, Deutero-Isaiah, Jeremiah and of other prophets.[36] He further focused on the character and development of Old Testament prophecy and of the emergence of the prophetic literature.[37] In the course of time he apparently took an increasing interest in traditio-historical viewpoints. In his valuable study from 1926 on the prophets between Isaiah and Jeremiah, called *The Disciples of Isaiah* (Micah, Zephaniah, Nahum and Habakkuk) he did not speak as much of 'redactors' any more as of 'circles of disciples' or 'school' of the great prophets, although he was also aware of the literary and redaction history of their books.[38] In his autobiographical 'Fragments' Mowinckel, in a comment to the Prophet-volume (1944) of the scholarly translation of the Old Testament into Norwegian, with introductions, literary-critical notes and annotations, made the remark that his 'manner of treatment really is more a traditio-historical than a literary-critical one'.[39]

---

35. *Studier til den jødiske*, I, p. 117; *Zur Komposition des Buches Jeremia*, *passim*, esp. pp. 3-4, in a criticism of some of the tendencies of the traditional literary-critical treatment of the prophetic books.

36. Cf., i.a., S. Mowinckel, *Profeten Jesaja: En bibelstudiebok* (Oslo: H. Aschehoug, 1925); *Jesaja-disiplene*; 'Motiver og stilformer i profeten Jeremias diktning', *Edda* 26 (1926), pp. 233-320; 'Die Komposition des deuterojesajanischen Buches', *ZAW* 49 (1931), pp. 87-112, 242-60; 'Die Komposition des Jesaja-Buches Kap. 1–39', *AcOr* 11 (1933), pp. 267-92; 'Opkomsten av profetlitteraturen', pp. 65-111.

37. In addition to the last article mentioned in n. 36 cf. also the general introduction and the introductions to the individual books in Mowinckel and Messel, *De senere profeter*, where most (834 pages) was from Mowinckel's hand, except for Ezekiel. Cf. also his 'The "Spirit" and the "Word" in the Pre-Exilic Reforming Prophets', *JBL* 53 (1934), pp. 199-227; 'Ecstatic Experience and Rational Elaboration in Old Testament Prophecy', *AcOr* 13 (1935), pp. 264-91, cf. *AcOr* 14 (1936), p. 319.

38. *Jesaja-disiplene*, pp. 10-13; see also 137ff. (literary-critical analysis).

39. 'Fragmenter', p. 125: 'Når disse forskjellige overleveringslag i oversettelsen er antydet med slike randbokstaver som T (tillegg), Gl (glose), så er det bare en

Also, in view of the two previous volumes of this translation (on the Pentateuch, 1929, and the former Prophets, 1935) Mowinckel now directly diminished the strong literary-critical character of their introductions and notes for the benefit of new traditio-historical viewpoints.

4. *Second Period: Methodological Clarifications from 1946 Onwards*

The second period, about 20 years in length, beginning from 1946, did not really bring much that was new into Mowinckel's relation to the literary-critical school; his position remained—as said before—basically the same. However, in parts of his rich authorship—which flowed as abundantly as ever before—there now came a somewhat sharper tone of polemical defence of the literary-critical method, combined with a clarification of the conception of 'tradition history' which had come into fashion. Besides, he also clarified—and partly revised—his view of the classical theory of the Pentateuchal sources. It may be convenient to discuss these matters in three points, and necessarily as briefly as possible.

First, beginning with Mowinckel's treatment of the prophets with which the preceding section ended, special attention has to be paid to his—methodologically most important—study *Prophecy and Tradition*.[40] As mentioned above, Mowinckel had increasingly focused on a traditio-historical approach, especially as far as prophecy was concerned. However, much had happened at this point in the last decade before Mowinckel's book appeared: H.S. Nyberg had, in a very effective way, drawn attention to the basic importance of oral tradition in 1935; and in 1938 H. Birkeland worked out his idea with regard to all the prophetic books of the Old Testament;[41] in 1943, M. Noth described in detail the tradition history of the so-called Deuteronomistic History.[42] Contrary to these scholars who with their traditio-historical approach did not abandon the literary-critical way of working, I. Engnell (of Uppsala), however, opposed very strongly the literary-critical

terminologi som er en arv fra den litterækritiske arbeidsmåte, som jeg kansje ikke lenger ville bruke; behandlingsmåten er i virkeligheden mer tradisjonshistorisk enn litterærkritisk'.

40. See n. 24.

41. Birkeland, *Zum hebräischen Traditionswesen*; cf. Mowinckel's review, 'Om tilblivelsen av profetbøkene', *NTT* 39 (1938), pp. 318-20.

42. Noth, *Überlieferungsgeschichtliche Studien*.

school and made his traditio-historical method an exclusive alternative to the literary-critical one—and attacked other scholars, not least Mowinckel, who did not take the same extreme position.[43] In view of the confusing variegated understanding and use of the new keyword 'tradition history', Mowinckel felt a need for clarification, especially when used exclusively to refer to older historical and critical work on the Old Testament, or used phenomenologically in a religio-historical context. The crucial point to Mowinckel, now as it was before, is the true '*historical* understanding of the OT' and he points out:[44]

> In Engnell's terminology the term 'traditio-historical' seems to have lost much of its original relation to the history, i.e. the study and explanation of the origin, growth and development of the different traditions and the tradition mass; it refers above all to the mere stressing of the fact that the composition of the original units (separate traditions) and the compilation and elaboration of the present books have been the oral, not literary work, of the transmitting circles … no real attempt is made to distinguish between older and younger traditions or between older and younger 'strata' in the traditions. The interest is above all directed antithetically against the literary point of view and method … And his sketch of the religious and inner historical development of Israel often appears to represent a giving-up of the attempt to create clarity by a penetrating historical criticism of tradition; 'tradition' sometimes appears to be understood as something static rather than as a dynamic process, as a real *history*.

Second, the same concern with the real historical aspects of the Old Testament texts which Mowinckel expressed so clearly here, he also put into words in the case of an article by his old friend Johs. Pedersen on Exodus 1–15, where Pedersen—abandoning the literary-critical approach—regarded these chapters to be an entity, having the character of being a 'cult legend' for the Paschal Festival.[45] The article was written as early as 1934 and Mowinckel might have argued about it earlier, but he did not before 1951, following up the methodological concern of his *Prophecy and Tradition*.[46] To Mowinckel, Exodus 1–15 in its present context will be understood as a historical account, consisting of two different literary sources. As for historical as well as for prophetic

43. Engnell, *Gamla testamentet*; vol. 2 never appeared, but cf. several relevant articles by Engnell in SBU, I–II.

44. *Prophecy and Tradition*, pp. 18f.

45. Pedersen, 'Passahfest und Passahlegende', pp. 161-75.

46. S. Mowinckel, 'Die vermeintliche "Passahlegene" Ex. 1–15 in Bezug auf die Frage: Literarkritik und Traditionskritik', *ST* 5 (1951), pp. 66-88.

texts, he regarded it to be the task of a traditio-historical approach to give a critical presentation of the *history* of tradition.[47]

Third, Mowinckel made an attempt in this respect—simultaneously correcting some of his earlier standpoints[48]—when, at the age of 80, he published different studies where he tried to solve the old problem of the character of the Elohist source of the Pentateuch. As he interpreted the relevant texts now, he considered the process of tradition history not to have come to an end with the completion of the J source, but to have continued in oral form; the alleged E source then being the continued oral tradition of the material which was already literarily fixed in J. Mowinckel, therefore, preferred to call the traditional E material *Jahvista variatus*.[49]

5. *Summary and Conclusion*

To the very last Mowinckel continued to discuss and correct scholarly points of view and theories, others as well as his own.[50] *In his relation to the literary-critical school there are stages of different attitudes, especially due to his recognition of the tradition history as a 'dynamic process'. His relation may, therefore, be described as a continuity with creative renewal. He did not abandon the literary-critical approach but combined it with form-historical as well as traditio-historical methods.* He always, then, kept to the literary-critical way of scrutiny, although differently at different times; and the motive for it was first of all his search for a '*historical* understanding of the Old Testament'. In many ways he managed to achieve this.

47. Cf. *Prophecy and Tradition*, pp. 12, 24-25, 30, 33, 35-36 and 84-88.

48. In 'Fragmenter', p. 121, Mowinckel retracts with few but clear words his opinion of finding E in the Primaeval History, as he had done 20 years earlier in his *The Two Sources of the Predeuteronomic Primeval History (JE) in Gen. 1–11* (ANVAO.HF, 1937.2; Oslo: Jacob Dybwad, 1937).

49. Mowinckel, *Tetrateuch–Pentateuch–Hexateuch*; *idem*, *Erwägungen zur Pentateuchquellenfrage*.

50. The most interesting of his self-corrections may refer to his *Psalmenstudien*; cf. the Preface to *Offersang og sangoffer*, p. vf., where he pays tribute to what he has learnt from Harris Birkeland, as well as his 'Preface' to the new edition of *Psalmenstudien* (1961), where further references may be found.

BIBLIOGRAPHY

Abba, R., 'The Divine Name of Yahweh', *JBL* 80 (1961), pp. 320-28.

Abel, F.M., *Géographie de la Palestine*, I–II (Paris: J. Gabalda, 1967).

Abrahams, I., 'Jewish Interpretation of the Old Testament', in A.S. Peake (ed.), *The People and the Book* (Oxford: 1925), pp. 403-31.

Ackroyd, P.R., 'Some Interpretative Glosses in the Book of Haggai', *JJS* 7 (1966), pp. 163-67.

—*Exile and Restoration: A Study of Hebrew Thought of the Sixth Century BC* (London: SCM Press, 1968).

Aharoni, Y., *The Land of the Bible* (London: Burns & Oates, 1968).

Ahlström, G.W., *Psalm 89: Eine Liturgie aus dem Ritual des leidenden Königs* (Lund: C.W.K. Gleerup, 1959).

Albertz, R., *Persönliche Frömmigkeit und offizielle Religion* (Stuttgart: Calwer Verlag, 1978).

Albrektson, B., *Studies in the Text and Theology of the Book of Lamentations* (Studia Theol. Lundensia, 21; Lund: C.W.K. Gleerup, 1963).

—*History and the Gods: An Essay on the Idea of Historical Events as Divine Manifestations in the Ancient Near East and in Israel* (ConBOT, 1; Lund: C.W.K Gleerup, 1967).

—'The Syntax of אהיה אשר אהיה in Exodus 3:14', in *Words and Meaning: Festschrift D.W. Thomas* (London: Cambridge University Press, 1968), pp. 15-28.

—'Recension eller tradition? Några synpunkter på den gammaltestamentliga konsonanttextens standardisering', *SEÅ* 40 (1975), pp. 18-35.

Albright, W.F., 'Further Observations on the Name Yahweh and its Modifications in Proper Names', *JBL* 44 (1925), pp. 158-62.

—'The Name Yahweh', *JBL* 43 (1924), pp. 370-78.

—'New Light on Early Recensions of the Hebrew Bible', *BASOR* 140 (1955), pp. 27-33.

—*Yahweh and the Gods of Canaan: A Historical Analysis of Two Contrasting Faiths* (London: Athlone Press, 1968).

Alfrink, B., 'La prononciation "Jehova" du Tétragramme', *OTS* 5 (1948), pp. 43-63.

Alt, A., 'Ein ägyptisches Gegenstück zu Ex 3[14]', *ZAW* 58 (1940), pp. 159-60.

—'Zum "Gott der Väter" ', *Palästinajahrbuch* 36 (1940), pp. 53-104.

—*Kleine Schriften zur Geschichtes des Volkes Israel*, I–II (Munich: Chr. Kaiser Verlag, 1953).

—'Das Grossreich Davids', in *idem, Kleine Schriften*, II, pp. 66-75.

—'Die Ursprünge des iraelitischen Rechts', in *idem, Kleine Schriften*, I, pp. 278-332.

—'Das Königtum in den Reichen Israel und Juda', in *idem, Kleine Schriften*, II, pp. 116-34.

—'Die Staatenbildung der Israeliten in Palästina', in *idem, Kleine Schriften*, II, pp. 1-65.

—'Der Gott der Väter', in *idem*, *Kleine Schriften*, I, pp. 1-78.

Alter, R., *The Art of Biblical Poetry* (Edinburgh: T. & T. Clark, 1990).

—*The Art of Biblical Narrative* (London: Allen & Unwin, 1981).

—*The Art of Biblical Poetry* (New York: Basic Books, 1985).

Ammon, C.F. von, *Entwurf einer reinen biblischen Theologie* (Erlangen, 1792).

Andersen, K.T., 'Der Gott meines Vaters', *ST* 16 (1962), pp. 170-88.

Anderson, G.W., 'Canonical and Non-Canonical', *CHB* 1 (1970), pp. 113-59.

—'Two Scottish Semitists', in *Congress Volume: Edinburgh 1974* (VTSup, 28; Leiden: E.J. Brill, 1975), pp. ix-xix.

Anderson, G.W. (ed.), *Tradition and Interpretation: Essays by Members of the Society for Old Testament Study* (Oxford: Clarendon Press, 1979).

Ap-Thomas, D.R., 'An Appreciation of Sigmund Mowinckel's Contribution to Biblical Studies', *JBL* 85 (1966), pp. 315-25.

Aptowitzer, V., *Das Schriftwort in der rabbinischen Literatur* (5 vols.; New York: Ktav, repr. 1970).

Arnold, W.R., 'The Divine Name in Exodus iii.14', *JBL* 24 (1905), pp. 107-65.

Audet, J.-P., 'A Hebrew–Aramaic List of Books of the Old Testament in Greek Transcription', *JTS* NS 1 (1950), pp. 135-54.

—'Le sens du Cantique des Cantiques', *RB* 62 (1955), pp. 197-221.

Bach, R., *Die Aufforderungen zur Flucht und zum Kampf im alttestamentlichen Prophetenspruch* (WMANT, 9; Neukirchen Kreis Moers: Neukirchener Verlag, 1962).

Bainton, R.H. *et al.*, *The Idea of History in the Ancient Near East* (New Haven; London, 1966).

Ball, E., 'Smith, W. Robertson', in *A Dictionary of Biblical Interpretation* (London: SCM Press, 1990), pp. 633-35.

Barr, J., 'Revelation through History in the Old Testament and in Modern Theology', *Int* 17 (1963), pp. 193-205.

—*Old and New in Interpretation* (London: SCM Press, 1966).

—'Jewish Apocalyptic in Recent Scholarly Study', *BJRL* 58 (1975), pp. 9-35.

—'Childs' *Introduction to the Old Testament as Scripture*', *JSOT* 16 (1980), pp. 12-23.

—*Holy Scripture: Canon, Authority, Criticism* (Philadelphia: Westminster Press, 1983).

Barstad, H.M., 'Le canon comme principe exégétique', *ST* 38 (1984), pp. 77-91.

Barth, H., 'Jes. 8, 23b–9, 6', in Struppe (ed.), *Messiasbild*, pp. 199-299.

Barthélemy, D., *Etudes d'histoire du texte de l'Ancien Testament* (OBO, 21; Freibourg: Editions Universitaires; Göttingen: Vandenhoeck & Ruprecht, 1978).

—'L'état de la Bible juive depuis le début de notre ère jusqu'à la deuxième révolte contre Rome (131–135)', in Kaestli and Wermelinger (eds.), *Le canon de l'Ancien Testament*, pp. 9-45.

Barton, J., 'Understanding Old Testament Ethics', *JSOT* 9 (1978), pp. 44-64.

—*Reading the Old Testament: Method in Biblical Study* (repr.; London: Darton, Longman & Todd, 1989).

—'The Significance of a Fixed Canon of the Hebrew Bible', in Sæbø (ed.), *Hebrew Bible/Old Testament*, I.1, pp. 67-83.

Bauer, H., and P. Leander, *Historische Grammatik der hebräischen Sprache*, I (Halle: M. Niemeyer, 1922).

Bauer-Kayatz, C., *Einführung in die alttestamentliche Weisheit* (BSTh, 55; Neukirchen–Vluyn: Neukirchener Verlag, 1969).

Baumgarten, W., 'Ein Vierteljahrhundert Danielforschung', *ThR* NF 11 (1939), pp. 59-83, 125-44, 201-28.

—'Ein Kapitel vom hebräischen Erzählungstil', in *Eucharisterion für H. Gunkel* (FRLANT, NF, 19; Göttingen: Vandenhoeck & Ruprecht, 1923), pp. 145-57.

Becker, J., *Messiaserwartung im Alten Testament* (SBS, 83; Stuttgart: KBW, 1977).

Beckwith, R., *The Old Testament Canon of the New Testament Church and its Background in Early Judaism* (Grand Rapids: Eerdmans, 1985).

Begrich, J., *Studien zu Deuterojesaja* (TBü, 20; Munich: Chr. Kaiser Verlag, 1963).

Beidelman, T.O., *W. Robertson Smith and the Sociological Study of Religion* (Chicago: University of Chicago Press, 1974).

Bendix, R., *Nation-Building and Citizenship* (New York: Anchor Books, 1969).

Ben-Hayyim, Z., 'On the Pronunciation of the Tetragrammaton by the Samaritans', *ErIs* 3 (1954), pp. 147-54.

Bentzen, A., 'Quelques remarques sur le mouvement messianique parmi les juifs aux environs de l'an 520 avant J.-C.', *RHPR* 10 (1930), pp. 493-503.

—*Fortolkning til de gammeltestamentlige Salmer* (Copenhagen: G.E.C. Gad, 1939).

—'Om Sigmund Mowinckels indsats i den gammeltestamentlige forskning', *NTT* 45 (1944), pp. 163-75; also in a separate edition, *Acta Mowinckeliana*: 1884.4, August 1944 (Oslo: Grøndahl & Søn, 1944), pp. 3-15.

—*Jesaja*, I (Copenhagen: G.E.C. Gad, 1944).

—*Daniel* (HAT, 1.19; Tübingen: J.C.B. Mohr, 1952).

—'Remarks on the Canonization of the Song of Solomon', in *Studia orientalia Ioanni Pedersen . . . dicata* (Copenhagen: Hauniae, 1953), pp. 41-47.

—*Introduction to the Old Testament*, I (Copenhagen: G.E.C. Gad, 1961).

Bergson, H., *Les deux sources de la morale et de la religion* (Paris: Librairie Felix Alcan, 1932).

Bernhardt, K.-H., *Das Problem der altorientalischen Königsideologie im Alten Testament* (VTSup, 8; Leiden: E.J. Brill, 1961).

Beuken, W.A.M., *Haggai-Sacharja 1–8: Studien zur Überlieferungsgeschichte der frühnachexilischen Propetie* (Studia Semitica Neerlandica, 10; Assen: Van Gorcum, 1967).

Betz, H.D., 'Das Verständnis der Apokalyptik in der Theologie der Pannenberg-Gruppe', *ZTK* 65 (1968), pp. 257-70.

Bewer, J.A., 'Two Notes on Isaiah 49.1-6', in *Jewish Studies in Memory of George A. Kohnt* (1935), pp. 86-90.

—*The Book of Isaiah*, I (Harper's Annotated Bible Series; New York: Harper & Row, 1950).

Beyerlin, W., 'Das Königscharisma bei Saul', *ZAW* 73 (1961), pp. 186-201.

Birkeland, H., *Zum hebräischen Traditionswesen: Die Komposition der prophetischen Bücher des Alten Testaments* (ANVAO.HF, 1938.1; Oslo: Jacob Dybwad, 1938).

—*Mowinckel, Sigmund Olaf Plytt, 1884–* (Norsk Biografisk Leksikon, 9; Oslo: H. Aschehoug, 1940).

—*Akzent und Vokalismus im Althebräischen* (SNVAO.HF, 1940–43; Oslo: Jacob Dybwad, 1941).

Birnbaum, S.A., 'The Leviticus Fragments from the Cave', *BASOR* 118 (1950), pp. 20-27.

Black, J.S., and G. Chrystal (eds.), *Lectures and Essays of William Robertson Smith* (Edinburgh: A. & C. Black, 1912).

Blau, J., 'Zum angeblichen Gebrauch von את vor dem Nominativ', *VT* 4 (1954), pp. 7-19.

— 'Gibt is ein emphatisches '*eṯ* im Bibelhebraeisch', *VT* 6 (1956), pp. 211-12.

Blenkinsopp, J., 'A New Kind of Introduction: Professor Childs' *Introduction to the Old Testament as Scripture*', *JSOT* 16 (1980), pp. 24-27.

—*Wisdom and Law in the Old Testament: The Ordering of Life in Israel and Early Judaism* (Oxford: Oxford University Press, 1983).

Bloch, R., 'Midrash', *DBSup*, V, pp. 1263-81.

Boecker, H.J., *Die Beurteilung der Anfänge des Königtums in den deuteronomistischen Abschnitten des I. Samuelbuches* (WMANT, 31; Neukirchen–Vluyn: Neukirchener Verlag, 1969).

Boer, P.A.H. de, 'The Counsellor', in *Wisdom in Israel and the Ancient Near East* (Festschrift H.H. Rowley; VTSup, 3; Leiden: E.J. Brill, 1955), pp. 42-71.

Bonsirven, J., *Exégèse rabbinique et exégèse paulinienne* (Paris: Beauchesne, 1939).

Bowman, R.A., 'Yahweh the Speaker', *JNES* 3 (1944), pp. 1-8.

Brandscheit, R., *Gotteszorn und Menschenleid: Die Gerichtsklage des leidenden Gerechten in Klgl 3* (Trierer Theol. Studien, 41; Trier: Paulinus Verlag, 1983).

Brekelmans, C.H.W., 'Exodus XVIII and the Origins of Yahwism in Israel', *OTS* 10 (1954), pp. 215-24.

Brett, M.G., *Biblical Criticism in Crisis? The Impact of the Canonical Approach on Old Testament Studies* (Cambridge: Cambridge University Press, 1991).

Brockelmann, C., *Hebräische Syntax* (Neukirchen Kreis Moers: Neukirchener Verlag, 1956).

Brock, S.P. (ed.), *The Old Testament in Syriac*, III.1 (Leiden: E.J. Brill, 1987).

Brueggemann, W., 'The Kerygma of the Priestly Writers', *ZAW* 84 (1972), pp. 397-414.

Brunet, G., *Les lamentations contre Jérémie: Réinterpretation des quatre premières Lamentations* (Bibliothèque de l'école des hautes études: Sciences religieuses, 75; Paris, 1968).

Buber, M., *Der Glaube der Propheten* (Zürich, 1950).

Budde, K., *Der Kanon des Alten Testaments* (Giessen, 1900).

—*Jesaja's Erleben: Eine gemeinverständliche Auslegung der Denkschrift des Propheten* (Gotha, 1928).

Buhl, F., *Psalmerne, oversatte og fortolkede* (Copenhagen, 1900).

—*Jesaja* (Copenhagen: Gyldendalske Boghandel, 2nd edn, 1912).

Burkitt, F.C., 'On the Name Yahweh', *JBL* 44 (1925), pp. 353-56.

Burrows, E., 'The Meaning of El Šaddai', *JTS* 41 (1940), pp. 152-61.

Burrows, M., *The Dead Sea Scrolls* (New York: Viking Press, 1956).

Burrows, M. (ed.), *The Dead Sea Scrolls of St. Mark's Monastery*, I (New Haven: The American Schools of Oriental Research, 1950).

Carmignac, J., 'La notion d'eschatologie dans la Bible et à Qumran', *RevQ* 7 (1969), pp. 17-31.

Cazelles, H. *Le Messie de la Bible* (Paris: Desclée, 1978).

—'The Canonical Approach to Torah and Prophets', *JSOT* 16 (1980), pp. 28-31.

Cheyne, T.K., *Founders of Old Testament Criticism* (London: Methuen, 1893).

Childs, B.S., *Biblical Theology in Crisis* (Philadelphia: Westminster Press, 1970).

—'Psalm Titles and Midrashic Exegesis', *JSS* 16 (1971), pp. 137-50.

—'The Old Testament as Scripture of the Church', *CTM* 43 (1972), pp. 709-22.

—*Exodus: A Commentary* (OTL; London: SCM Press, 1974).

—'The Exegetical Significance of Canon for the Study of the Old Testament', in *Congress Volume: Göttingen 1977* (VTSup, 29; Leiden: E.J. Brill, 1978), pp. 66-80.

—'The Canonical Shape of the Prophetical Literature', *Int* 32 (1978), pp. 46-55.

—*Introduction to the Old Testament as Scripture* (London: SCM Press, 1979).

—'A Response to Reviewers of *Introduction to the Old Testament as Scripture*', *JSOT* 16 (1980), pp. 52-60.

—'A Response', *HRT* 2 (1980), pp. 199-211.

Christie, W.M., 'The Jamnia Period in Jewish History', *JTS* 6 (1925), pp. 347-67.

Clements, R.E., 'The Deuteronomistic Interpretation of the Founding of the Monarchy in I. Sam. VIII', *VT* 24 (1974), pp. 398-410.

—*A Century of Old Testament Study* (London: Lutterworth Press, 1976).

—'Covenant and Canon in the Old Testament', in R.W.A. McKinney (ed.), *Creation, Christ and Culture* (Edinburgh: T. & T. Clark, 1976), pp. 1-12.

—'*Das Überlierferungsgeschichtliche Problem des Pentateuch* by R. Rendtorff', *JSOT* 3 (1977), pp. 45-56.

—'Pentateuchal Problems', in Anderson (ed.), *Tradition and Interpretation*, pp. 96-124.

—*Loving One's Neighbour: OT Ethics in Context* (London, 1992).

Clines, D.J.A., *Interested Parties: The Ideology of Writers and Readers of the Hebrew Bible* (JSOTSup, 205; Sheffield: Sheffield Academic Press, 1995).

Coats, G.E., 'The Yahwist as Theologian? A Critical Response', *JSOT* 3 (1977), pp. 28-32.

Cohon, S.S., 'The Name of God', *HUCA* 23 (1951), pp. 579-604.

Collins, J.J., 'The Son of Man and the Saints of the Most High in the Book of Daniel', *JBL* 93 (1974), pp. 50-66.

Collins, J.J. (ed.), *Apocalypse: The Morphology of a Genre* (Semeia, 14; Missoula, MT: Scholars Press, 1979).

Conrad, J., 'Die innere Gliederung der Proverbien: Zur Frage nach der Systematisierung des Spruchgutes in den älteren Teilsammlungen', *ZAW* 79 (1967), pp. 67-76.

Cooper, A., and M.H. Pope, 'Divine Names and Epithets in the Ugaritic Texts', in *Ras Shamra Parallels*, III (Rome: Pontificium Institutum biblicum, 1981).

Coppens, J., 'La bénédiction de Jacob: Son cadre historique à la lumière des parallèles ougaritiques', in *Congress Volume: Strasbourg 1956* (VTSup, 4: Leiden: E.J. Brill, 1957), pp. 97-115.

Cortese, E., 'La teologia del Documento Sacerdotale', *RevistB* 26 (1978), pp. 113-37.

Crenshaw, J.L., *Gerhard von Rad* (Waco, TX: Word Books, 1979).

Crenshaw, J.L. (ed.), *Studies in Ancient Israelite Wisdom* (New York: Ktav, 1976).

Crenshaw, J.L., and J.T. Willis (eds.), *Essays in Old Testament Ethics: J. Philip Hyatt in Memoriam* (New York: Ktav, 1974).

Cross, F.M., 'Yahweh and the God of the Patriarchs', *HTR* 55 (1962), pp. 225-59.

—'The History of the Biblical Text in the Light of Discoveries in the Judean Desert', *HTR* 57 (1964), pp. 281-99.

—'The Contribution of the Qumran Discoveries to the Study of the Biblical Text', *IEJ* 16 (1966), pp. 81-95.

—'The Evolution of a Theory of Local Texts', in Cross and Talmon (eds.), *Qumran and the History*, pp. 306-20.

—*Canaanite Myth and Hebrew Epic: Essays in the History of the Religion of Israel* (Cambridge, MA: Harvard University Press, 1973).

—'אל', *ThWAT*, I, col. 273.

Cross, F.M., and D.M. Freedman, *Studies in Ancient Yahwistic Poetry* (Missoula, MT: Scholars Press, 1975).

Cross, F.M., and S. Talmon (eds.), *Qumran and the History of the Biblical Text* (Cambridge, MA: Harvard University Press, 1975).

Crüsemann, F., *Studien zur Formgeschichte von Hymnus und Danklied in Israel* (WMANT, 32; Neukirchen–Vluyn: Neukirchener Verlag, 1969).

—*Der Widerstand gegen das Königtum* (WMANT, 49; Neukirchen–Vluyn: Neukirchener Verlag, 1978).

—*Die Tora: Theologie und Sozialgeschichte des alttestamentlichen Gesetzes* (Munich: Chr. Kaiser Verlag, 1992; ET *The Torah: Theology and Social History of Old Testament Law* [Edinburgh: T. & T. Clark, 1996]).

Culley, R.C., *Studies in the Structure of Hebrew Narrative* (Philadelphia, 1976).

Dahood, M., 'Is "Eben Yiśrā'ēl a Divine Title? (Gen. 49,24)', *Bib* 40 (1959), pp. 1002-1007.

—*Psalms*. II. *50–100* (AB; Garden City, NY: Doubleday, 1968).

Davis, M.C., *Hebrew Bible Manuscripts in the Cambridge Genizah Collections*. I. *Taylor-Schechter Old Series and Other Genizah Collections in the Cambridge University Library* (Cambridge: Cambridge University Press, 1978).

Day, J., R.P. Gordon and H.G.M. Williamson (eds.), *Wisdom in Ancient Israel: Essays in Honour of J.A. Emerton* (Cambridge: Cambridge University Press, 1995).

Deaut, R. le, 'Lévitique XXII 26–XXIII 44 dans le Targum palestinien: De l'importance des gloses du codex Neofiti 1', *VT* 18 (1968), pp. 458-71.

—'A propos d'une définition du midrash', *Bib* 50 (1969), pp. 395-413 (ET with preface by J.A. Sanders in *Int* 25 [1971], pp. 259-82]).

Delcor, M., *Le livre de Daniel* (Paris, 1971).

Delekat, L., 'Yáho-Yahwáe und die alttestamentlichen Gottesnamenkorrekturen', in *Tradition und Glaube: Festschrift K.G. Kuhn* (Göttingen: Vandenhoeck & Ruprecht, 1971), pp. 23-75.

Delitzsch, F., *Commentar über das Buch Jesaia* (BCAT, 3.1; Leipzig, 4th edn, 1889).

—*Messianische Weissagungen in geschichtlicher Folge* (Leipzig [1890]: A. Edelmann, 2nd edn, 1899).

Delkurt, H., *Ethische Einsichten in der alttestamentlichen Spruchweisheit* (BTSt, 21; Neukirchen–Vluyn: Neukirchener Verlag, 1993).

Dhorme, E., 'Le nom du Dieu d'Israel', *RHR* 141 (1952), pp. 5-18.

Diestel, L., *Geschichte des Alten Testaments in der christlichen Kirche* (Jena: Mauke's Verlag, 1869; repr. Leipzig, 1981).

Dietrich, W., *Jesaja und die Politik* (BEvT, 74; Munich: Chr. Kaiser Verlag, 1976).

Díez Macho, A., *The Recently Discovered Palestinian Targum: Its Antiquity and Relationship with Other Targums* (VTSup, 7; Leiden: E.J. Brill, 1960).

—*Neophyti 1: Targum palestinense MS de la Biblioteca Vaticana*. III. *Levitico* (Madrid and Barcelona: Consejo Superior de Investigaciones Científicas, 1971).

Dillmann, A., *Der Prophet Jesaia* (KEHAT, 5; Leipzig, 1890).

Dohmeier, H.-J., 'Die Grundzüge der Theologie Johann Philipp Gablers' (PhD Dissertation, University of Münster, 1976).

Driver, G.R., 'The Interpretation of *Yhwh* as a Participial Form', *JBL* 73 (1954), pp. 125-31.

—'The Original Form of the Name "Yahweh": Evidence and Conclusions', *ZAW* 46 (1928), pp. 7-25.

Driver, S.R., and A. Neubauer, *The Fifty-Third Chapter of Isaiah According to the Jewish Interpreters* (2 vols.; New York: Herman Press, 1969 [1877]).

Drummond, A.L., and J. Bulloch, *The Church in Late Victorian Scotland, 1874–1900* (Edinburgh: The Saint Andrew Press, 1978).

Dubarle, A.-M., 'La signification du nom de Iahweh', *RSPT* 35 (1951), pp. 3-21.

Duhm, B., *Das Buch Jesaia: Übersetzt und erklärt* (HKAT, 3.1; Göttingen: Vandenhoeck & Ruprecht, 5th edn, 1968 [1892]).

Dumermuth, F., 'Zur deuteronomischen Kulttheologie und ihren Voraussetzungen', *ZAW* 70 (1958), pp. 59-98.

Dürr, L., *Ursprung und Ausbau der israelitisch-jüdischen Heilandserwartung* (Berlin, 1925).

Ebeling, G., 'Was heisst "Biblische Theologie"?', in *idem*, *Wort und Glaube* (Tübingen: J.C.B. Mohr, 1967).

Eerdmans, B.D., 'The Name Jahu', *OTS* 5 (1948), pp. 1-29.

Eichrodt, W., *Der Heilige in Israel: Jesaja 1–12* (Die Botschaft des Alten Testaments, 17.1; Stuttgart: Calwer Verlag, 1960).

—*Theologie des Alten Testaments*, I–III (Göttingen: Vandenhoeck & Ruprecht, 1933–39; ET *Theology of the Old Testament*, I–II [London: SCM Press, 1961–67]).

Eissfeldt, O., *Hexateuch-Synopse: Die Erzählung der fünf Bücher Mose und des Buches Josua mit dem Anfange des Richterbuches* (Darmstadt: Wissenschaftliche Buchgesellschaft, 2nd edn, 1962 [1922]).

—'Jahwe als König', *ZAW* 46 (1928), pp. 81-105; repr. in *idem*, *Kleine Schriften*, I, pp. 172-93.

—*Der Gottesknecht bei Deuterojesaja (Jes 40–55) im Lichte der israelitischen Anschauung von Gemeinschaft und Individuum* (BRGA, 2; Halle, 1933).

—'Neue Zeugnisse für die Aussprache des Tetragramms als Jahwe', *ZAW* 53 (1935), pp. 59-76; repr. in *idem*, *Kleine Schriften*, II, pp. 81-96.

—'Israelitisch-jüdische Religionsgeschichte und alttestamentliche Theologie', in *idem*, *Kleine Schriften*, I, pp. 105-14.

—*Kleine Schriften* (6 vols.; Tübingen: J.C.B. Mohr [Paul Siebeck], 1962–79).

—*The Old Testament: An Introduction* (Oxford: Oxford University Press, 1965).

—'*'äh°yäh* '*°šär* '*äh°yäh* und '*Ēl* '*ôlām*' (1965), in *idem*, *Kleine Schriften*, IV, pp. 193-98.

—'Julius Wellhausen', in *idem*, *Kleine Schriften*, I, pp. 56-71.

—*Einleitung in das Alte Testament* (Tübingen: J.C.B. Mohr, 3rd edn, 1964).

—'Die Gnadenverheissungen an David in Jes 55,1-5', in *idem*, *Kleine Schriften*, IV, pp. 44-52.

Eitz, A., 'Studien zum Verhältnis von Priesterschrift und Deuterojesaja' (PhD Dissertation, University of Heidelberg, 1969).

Elliger, K., 'Zur Frage nach dem Alter des Jahweglaubens bei den Israeliten', *TBl* 9 (1930), cols. 97-103.

—'Sinn und Ursprung der priesterlichen Geschichtserzählung', *ZTK* 49 (1952), pp. 121-43; repr. in *idem*, *Kleine Schriften*, pp. 174-98.

—*Jesaja*, II (BKAT, 11; Neukirchen–Vluyn: Neukirchener Verlag, 1963).

—*Kleine Schriften zum Alten Testament* (TBü, 32; Munich: Chr. Kaiser Verlag, 1966).

—*Leviticus* (HAT, 1.4; Tübingen: J.C.B. Mohr, 1966).

Ellis, E.E., *The Old Testament in Early Christianity: Canon and Interpretation in the Light of Modern Research* (WUNT, 54; Tübingen: J.C.B. Mohr, 1991).

—'The Old Testament Canon in the Early Church', in M.J. Mulder (ed.), *Mikra* (CRINT, 2.1; Assen: Van Gorcum, 1988), pp. 653-90.

Emerton, J.A., 'New Light on Israelite Religion: The Implications of the Inscriptions from Kuntillet 'Ajrud', *ZAW* 94 (1982), pp. 2-20.

Engnell, I., 'Studies in Divine Kingship in Ancient Near East' (Dissertation, Uppsala, 1943).

—*Gamla Testamentet: En traditionshistorisk inledning*, I (Stockholm: Svenska Kyrkans Diakonistyrelses Bokförlag, 1945).

—'Profetia och tradition', *SEÅ* 12 (1947; Festschrift J. Lindblom), pp. 94-123.

—*The Call of Isaiah: An Exegetical and Comparative Study* (UUÅ, 1949.4; Uppsala: Lundeqvistka Bokhandeln, 1949).

—'Methodological Aspects of Old Testament Study', in *Congress Volume: Oxford 1959* (VTSup, 7; Leiden: E.J. Brill, 1960).

—*Critical Essays on the Old Testament: A Rigid Scrutiny* (trans. J.T. Willis, with the collaboration of H. Ringgren; London: SPCK, 1970).

Ernst, A.B., *Weisheitliche Kurtkritik: Zu Theologie und Ethik des Sprüchebuchs und der Propetie des Jahrhunderts* (BTSt, 23; Neukirchen–Vluyn: Neukirchener Verlag, 1994).

Exum, J.C., 'A Literary and Structural Analysis of the Song of Songs', *ZAW* 85 (1973), pp. 47-79.

Exum, J. Cheryl, and D.J.A. Clines (eds.), *The New Literary Criticism and the Hebrew Bible* (JSOTSup, 143; Sheffield: Sheffield Academic Press, 1993).

Fabry, H.-J., 'עוּר', *ThWAT*, VI, cols. 968-83.

Feldmann, F., *Das Buch Isaias* (EHAT, 14.1; Münster, 1925).

Fell, W., 'Der Bibelkanon des Flavius Josephus', *TZ* 9 (1909), pp. 1-16, 113-22, 235-44.

Fichtner, J., 'Zu Jesaja 7,5-9', *ZAW* 56 NF 15 (1938), p. 176.

—'Jahves Plan in der Botschaft des Jesaja', *ZAW* 63 (1951), pp. 16-33.

Fischer, J., *Das Buch Isaias* (HSAT, 7.1.1; Bonn, 1937).

Fishbane, M., 'Torah and Tradition', in Knight (ed.), *Tradition and Theology*, pp. 275-300.

—'The Qumran Pesher and Traits of Ancient Hermeneutics', in *Proceedings of the Sixth World Congress of Jewish Studies*, I (Jerusalem, 1977), pp. 97-114.

—'Revelation and Tradition: Aspects of Inner-Biblical Exegesis', *JBL* 99 (1980), pp. 343-61.

—*Biblical Interpretation in Ancient Israel* (Oxford: Clarendon Press, 1985).

—'Inner-Biblical Exegesis', in Sæbø (ed.), *Hebrew Bible/Old Testament*, I.1, pp. 33-48.

Fisher, L.R. (ed.), *Ras Shamra Parallels*, I (AnOr, 49; Rome: Pontificium institutum Biblicum, 1972).

Fohrer, G., *Messiasfrage und Bibelverständnis* (Tübingen: J.C.B. Mohr, 1957).

—'Der Vertrag zwischen König und Volk in Israel', *ZAW* 71 (1959), pp. 1-22.

—*Das Buch Jesaja*, I (Zürcher Bibelkommentare; Zürich: Zwingli-Verlag, 1960).

—*Das Buch Jesaja*, II (Zürcher Bibelkommentare; Zürich: Zwingli-Verlag, 1962).

—'Die Strukter der alttestamentlichen Eschatologie', *TLZ* 85 (1960), pp. 401-20.

—'Tradition und Interpretation', *ZAW* 73 (1961), pp. 1-30.

—'Zehn Jahre Literatur zur alttestamentlichen Prophetie (1951–1960)', *TRev* 28 (1962), pp. 1-75, 235-97, 301-74.

—*Überlieferung und Geschichte des Exodus: Eine Analyse von Ex 1–15* (BZAW, 91; Berlin: W. de Gruyter, 1964).

—*Studien zur alttestamentlichen Prophetie* (BZAW, 99; Berlin: Alfred Töpelmann, 1967).

—*Geschichte der israelitischen Religion* (Berlin: W. de Gruyter, 1969).

—'Das Alte Testament und das Thema "Christologie" ', *EvT* 30 (1970), pp. 281-98.

—*Theologische Grundstrukturen des Alten Testaments* (Berlin: W. de Gruyter, 1972).

Fox, M.V., 'Scholia to Canticles', *VT* 33 (1983), pp. 199-206.

—*The Song of Songs and the Ancient Egyptian Love Songs* (Madison, WI: University of Wisconsin Press, 1985).

Freedman, D.N., 'The Name of the God of Moses', *JBL* 79 (1960), pp. 151-56.

—'Divine Names and Titles in Early Hebrew Poetry', in F.M. Cross *et al.* (eds.), *Magnalia Dei: The Mighty Acts of God. Essays on the Bible and Archaeology in Memory of G. Ernest Wright* (Garden City, NY: Doubleday, 1976), pp. 55-107.

Freedman, D.N., and K.A. Matthews, *The Paleo-Hebrew Leviticus Scroll (11QpaleoLev)* (Winona Lake, IN: Eisenbrauns, 1985).

Freedman, D.N., and P. O'Connor, 'יהוה JHWH', *ThWAT*, III, cols. 533-54.

Fritz, V., 'Die Deutungen des Königtums Sauls in den Überlieferungen von seiner Entstehung I Sam 9–11', *ZAW* 88 (1976), pp. 346-62.

Frye, N., *The Great Code: The Bible and Literature* (New York and London, 1982).

Fuerst, W.J., *The Books of Ruth, Esther, Ecclesiastes, the Song of Songs, Lamentations* (Cambridge Bible Commentary; Cambridge: Cambridge University Press, 1975).

Fuller, R.C., *Alexander Geddes, 1737–1802: Pioneer of Biblical Criticism* (Sheffield: Almond Press, 1984).

Gabel, J.B., C.B. Wheeler and A.D. York, *The Bible as Literature: An Introduction* (Oxford: Oxford University Press, 3rd edn, 1996).

Gabler, J.P., *Schattenrisse der jetzt lebenden Altdorfischen Professoren* (Altdorf, 1790).

—'Abgenöthigter Nachtrag', *Journal für theologische Literatur* 1 (1801), pp. 309-41.

—*Johann Gottfried Eichhorns Urgeschichte: Herausgegeben mit Einleitung und Anmerkungen von J.P. Gabler* (Altdorf; Nürnberg: Monath & Kussler, 1792–93).

—*D. Johann Philipp Gabler's kleinere theologische Schriften: Herausgegeben von seinen Söhnen, Theodor August Gabler und Johann Gottfried Gabler*, I–II (Ulm: Stettinische Buchhandlung, 1831).

Gadamer, H.-G., *Wahrheit und Methode* (Tübingen: J.C.B. Mohr, 1960; 5th edn, 1986; ET *Truth and Method* [New York: Crossroad, 1982]).

Gamberoni, J., 'סֵעֵבָה', *ThWAT*, IV, cols. 1064-74.

Gardiner, P. (ed.), *Theories of History* (London: Macmillan, 1959).

Geiger, L. (ed.), *Abraham Geigers Nachgelassene Schriften*, IV (Berlin, 1876).

Gerleman, G., *Ruth–Das Hohelied* (BKAT, 18; Neukirchen–Vluyn: Neukirchener Verlag, 1965).

Gese, H., 'Die hebräischen Bibelhandschriften zum Dodekapropheton nach der Variantensammlung des Kennicott', *ZAW* 69 (1957), pp. 55-69.

—'Geschichtliches Denken im Alten Orient und im Alten Testament', *ZTK* 55 (1958), pp. 127-45.

—*Lehre und Wirklichkeit in der alten Weisheit* (Tübingen: J.C.B. Mohr, 1968).

—'Anfang und Ende der Apokalyptik, dargestellt am Sacharjabuch', *ZTK* 70 (1973), pp. 20-49.

—'Zur Geschichte der Kultsänger am zweiten Tempel', in *idem*, *Vom Sinai zum Zion* (BEvT, 64; Munich: Chr. Kaiser Verlag, 1974), pp. 147-58.

—*Vom Sinai zum Zion* (BEvT, 64; Munich: Chr. Kaiser Verlag, 1974).

—'Der Davidsbund und die Zionserwählung', in *idem*, *Vom Sinai zum Zion*, pp. 113-29.

—'Das Problem von Amos 9,7', in *idem*, *Alttestamentliche Studien* (Tübingen: J.C.B. Mohr, 1991), pp. 116-21.

Gese, H. *et al.*, *Tradition und Theologie im Alten Testament* (Neukirchen–Vluyn: Neu-kirchener Verlag, 1978; ET *Tradition and Theology in the Old Testament* [ed. D.A. Knight; Philadelphia: Westminster Press, 1977]).

Geus, C.H.J. de, *The Tribes of Israel* (Assen: Van Gorcum, 1976).

Gilbert, M. (ed.), *La Sagesse de l'Ancien Testament* (BETL, 51; Leuven: Leuven University Press, 1979).

Ginsburg, C.D., *The Old Testament. I. The Pentateuch* (London: British and Foreign Bible Society, 1926 [1911]).

—*Introduction to the Massoretico-Critical Edition of the Hebrew Bible* (New York: Ktav, 1966).

—*The Song of Songs* (London: Longman, 1857; repr. New York: Ktav, 1970).

Ginsberg, H.L. (ed.), *The Five Megilloth and Jonah: A New Translation* (Philadelphia: Jewish Publication Society of America, 1975).

Gloege, G., *Offenbarung und Überlieferung: Ein dogmatischer Entwurf* (Theologische Forschung, 6; Hamburg-Volksdorf: Reich, 1954).

Goitein, S.D., '*YHWH* the Passionate: The Monotheistic Meaning and Origin of the Name of *YHWH*', *VT* 6 (1956), pp. 1-9.

—*A Mediterranean Society: The Jewish Communities in the Arab World as Portrayed in the Documents of the Cairo Geniza* (3 vols.; Berkeley: University of California Press, 1967–78).

Golka, F.W., 'Die israelitische Weisheitsschule oder "der Kaisers neue Kleider" ', *VT* 33 (1983), pp. 257-70.

Gordis, R., 'Midrash in the Prophets', *JBL* 49 (1930), pp. 417-22.

—'A Wedding Song for Solomon', *JBL* 63 (1944), pp. 263-70.

—*The Song of Songs and Lamentations: A Study, Modern Translation and Commentary* (New York: Ktav, rev. and augmented edn, 1974).

Görg, M., 'Die "Sänfte Salomos" nach HL 3,9f', *Biblische Notizen* 18 (1982), pp. 15-25.

Goshen-Gottstein, M.H., 'Die Jesaia-Rolle und das Problem der hebräischen Bibelhand-schriften', in *idem*, *Text and Language in Bible and Qumran* (Jerusalem; Tel Aviv: Orient Publishing House, 1960), pp. 51-64.

—'The Rise of the Tiberian Bible Text', in A. Altmann (ed.), *Biblical and Other Studies* (Cambridge, MA: Harvard University Press, 1963).

—'The Textual Criticism of the Old Testament: Rise, Decline, Rebirth', *JBL* 102 (1983), pp. 365-99.

Gottlieb, H., *A Study on the Text of Lamentations* (Acta Jutlandica, 48.12; Århus: Det lærde Selskab, 1978).

Gottwald, N.K., *Studies in the Book of Lamentations* (SBT, 1.14; London: SCM Press, 1954).

Gowan, D.E., 'The Use of *ya'an* in Biblical Hebrew', *VT* 21 (1971), pp. 168-85.

—*Eschatology in the Old Testament* (Edinburgh, 1987).

Gray, G.B., *The Book of Isaiah. I. 1–27* (ICC; Edinburgh: T. & T. Clark, 1912).

—*Sacrifice in the Old Testament: Its Theory and Practice* (New York: Ktav, 2nd edn, 1971 [1925]).

Gray, J., 'The God *YW* in the Religion of Canaan', *JNES* 12 (1953), pp. 278-83.

—*The Legacy of Canaan* (VTSup, 5; Leiden: E.J. Brill, 1965).

Greenberg, M., 'The Stabilization of the Text of the Hebrew Bible, Reviewed in the Light of the Biblical Materials from the Judean Desert', *JAOS* 76 (1956), pp. 157-67.

—'The Thematic Unity of Exodus III–XI', in *idem*, *Fourth World Congress of Jewish Studies: Papers*, I (Jerusalem, 1967), pp. 151-54.

Gressmann, H., *Der Ursprung der israelitisch-jüdischen Eschatologie* (FRLANT, 6; Göttingen: Vandenhoeck & Ruprecht, 1905).

—*Altorientalische Texte zum Alten Testament* (Berlin, 1926).

—*Der Messias* (FRLANT, 43; Göttingen: Vandenhoeck & Ruprecht, 1929).

Grether, O., *Name und Wort Gottes im Alten Testament* (BZAW, 64; Giessen: Alfred Töpelmann, 1934).

Grimme, H., 'Sind Jaho und Jahwe zwei verschiedene Namen und Begriffe?', *BZ* 17 (1926), pp. 29-42.

Grønbaek, J.H., 'Zur Frage der Eschatologie in der Verkündigung der Gerichtspropheten', *SEÅ* 24 (1959), pp. 5-21; repr. in Preuss (ed.), *Eschatologie*, pp. 129-46.

—*Die Geschichte vom Aufstieg Davids (1. Sam. 15–2. Sam. 5): Tradition und Komposition* (AThD, 10; Copenhagen: Munksgaard, 1971).

Gunkel, H., *Schöpfung und Chaos in Urzeit und Endzeit* (Göttingen: Vandenhoeck & Ruprecht, 2nd edn, 1921 [1895]).

—*Die israelitische Literatur* (1906; repr. Darmstadt: Wissenschaftliche Buchgesellschaft, 1963).

—*Genesis* (HKAT, 1.1; Göttingen: Vandenhoeck & Ruprecht, 8th edn, 1969 [1901]).

—*Reden und Aufsätze* (Göttingen: Vandenhoeck & Ruprecht, 1913).

Gunkel, H., and J. Begrich, *Einleitung in die Psalmen: Die Gattungen der religiösen Lyrik Israels* (HKAT, Ergänzungsband; Göttingen: Vandenhoeck & Ruprecht, 1933).

Gunneweg, A.H.J., *Mündliche und schriftliche Tradition der vorexilischen Prophetenbücher als Problem der neueren Prophetenforschung* (FRLANT, 73; Göttingen: Vandenhoeck & Ruprecht, 1959).

—'Über den Sitz im Leben der sog. Stammessprüche (Gen 49 Dtn 33 Jdc 5)', *ZAW* 76 (1964), pp. 245-55.

Haag, H., *Der Gottesknecht bei Deuterojesaja* (EdF, 233; Darmstadt: Wissenschaftliche Buchgesellschaft, 1985).

Habets, G., 'Eschatologie—Eschatologisches', in J.G. Botterweck, *Bausteine Biblischer Theologie: Festschrift für G. Johannes Botterweck* (BBB, 50; Bonn: Hanstein, 1977), pp. 351-69.

Hammershaimb, E., 'Om lignelser og billedtaler i de gammeltestamentlige Pseudepigrafer', *SEÅ* 40 (1975), pp. 36-65.

Hanson, P.D., *The Dawn of Apocalyptic: The Historical and Sociological Roots of Jewish Apocalyptic Eschatology* (Philadelphia: Fortress Press, rev. edn, 1979).

Hanson, R.P.C., 'The Biblical Exegesis in the Early Church', *CHB* I, pp. 412-563.

Haran, M., 'מבעיות הקנוניזציה של המקרא [Problems of the Canonization of Scripture]', *Tarbiz* 25 (1956), pp. 245-71.

—'The Religion of the Patriachs: An Attempt at a Synthesis', *ASTI* 4 (1965), pp. 30-55.

—*Biblical Research in Hebrew: A Discussion of its Character and Trends* (Jerusalem: Magnes Press, 1970).

—*Temples and Temple-Service in Ancient Israel: An Inquiry into the Character of Cult Phenomena and the Historical Setting of the Priestly School* (Oxford: Clarendon Press, 1978).

—'Book-Scrolls at the Beginning of the Second Temple Period: The Transition from Papyrus to Skins', *HUCA* 54 (1983), pp. 111-22.

Harrison, R.K., *Introduction to the Old Testament* (London: Tyndale Press, 1970).

Hartlich, C., and W. Sachs, *Der Ursprung des Mythosbegriffes in der modernen Bibelwissenschaft* (Tübingen: J.C.B. Mohr, 1952).

Hartman, L.F., and A.A. Di Lella, *Daniel* (AB; New York: Doubleday, 1978).

Harvey, V.A., *The Historian and the Believer* (London, 1967).

Hasel, G.F., *Old Testament Theology: Basic Issues in the Current Debate* (Grand Rapids: Eerdmans, rev. edn, 1975).

—'בְּגִיד *nāgîd*', *ThWAT*, V, pp. 203-19.

Hatch, E., H.A. Redpath *et al.*, *A Concordance to the Septuagint and the Other Greek Versions of the Old Testament* (3 vols.; Oxford: Clarendon Press, 1987; repr. Grand Rapids: Baker Book House, 1983).

Haupt, P., 'Der Name Jahwe', *OLZ* 5 (1909), pp. 211-12.

Hausmann, J., 'קַיִץ *qajiṣ*', *ThWAT*, VII, pp. 26-29.

Hayes, J.H., and J.M. Miller (eds.), *Israelite and Judaean History* (London: SCM Press, 1957).

Hayes, J.H., and F.C. Prussner, *Old Testament Theology: Its History and Development* (London: SCM Press, 1985).

Heck, J.D., 'A History of Interpretation of Genesis 49 and Deuteronomy 33', *BSac* 147.585 (1990), pp. 16-31.

Heinisch, P., *Christus, der Erlöser im Alten Testament* (Graz: Verlag Styria, 1955).

Hempel, J., *Hebräisches Wörterbuch zu Jesaja* (1936).

—*Das Ethos des Alten Testaments* (BZAW, 67; Berlin: Alfred Töpelmann, 2nd edn, 1964 [1938]).

Hengel, M., *Judaism and Hellenism* (London, 1974).

Herrmann, S., *Die prophetischen Heilserwartungen im Alten Testament* (BWANT, 85; Stuttgart: W. Kohlhammer, 1965).

—'Der alttestamentliche Gottesname', *EvT* 26 (1966), pp. 281-93.

—'Jeremia/Jeremiabuch', *TRE*, XVI, pp. 568-86.

Hermisson, H.-J., *Studien zur israelitischen Spruchweisheit* (WMANT, 28; Neukirchen–Vluyn: Neukirchener Verlag, 1968).

Herntrich, V., *Der Prophet Jesaja: Kapitel 1–12* (ATD, 17; Göttingen: Vandenhoeck & Ruprecht, 2nd edn, 1954).

Hertzberg, H.W., *Die Samuelbücher* (ATD, 10; Göttingen: Vandenhoeck & Ruprecht, 1956).

—*Der Prediger* (KAT, 17.4; Gütersloh: Gütersloher Verlagshaus, 1963).

—*I and II Samuel: A Commentary* (OTL; London: SCM Press, 1964).

Hesse, F., 'Kerygma oder geschichtliche Wirklichkeit?', *ZTK* 57 (1960), pp. 17-26.

—'Bewährt sich eine "Theologie der Heilstatsachen" am AT? Zum Verhältnis von Faktum und Deutung', *ZTK* 81 (1969), pp. 1-17.

—'Die Erforschung der Geschichte Israels als theologische Aufgabe', *KD* 4 (1958), pp. 1-19.

—*Abschied von der Heilsgeschichte* (ThSt, 108; Zürich: Theologischer Verlag, 1971).

—'III. מָשִׁיחַ im Alten Testament', *TWNT*, IX, pp. 491-500.

Heussi, K., *Geschichte der theologischen Fakultät zu Jena* (Weimar: Hermann Böhlaus Nachfolger, 1954).

Hillers, D.R., *Lamentations* (AB, 7A; Garden City, NY: Doubleday, 1984 [1972]).

Hoftijzer, J., *Die Verheissungen an die drei Erzväter* (Leiden: E.J. Brill, 1956).

Holm-Nielsen, S., *Hodayot: Psalms from Qumran* (AThD, 2; Aarhus: Universitetsforlaget, 1960).

—'The Book of Ecclesiastes and the Interpretation of It in Jewish and Christian Theology', *ASTI* 10 (1976), pp. 55-96.

Hölscher, G., *Kanonisch und Apokryph* (Naumburg/S., 1905).

—'Die Entstehung des Buches Daniel', *TSK* 92 (1919), pp. 136ff.

—'Sigmund Mowinckel som gammeltestamentlig forsker', *NTT* 24 (1923), pp. 73-138.

—*Die Ursprünge der jüdischen Eschatologie* (Giessen, 1925).

—review of *Der Messias* (FRLANT, 43; Göttingen: Vandenhoeck & Ruprecht, 1929), by H. Gressmann, in *DLZ* 3rd ser. 1.37 (1930), pp. 1729-44.

Hooke, S.H. (ed.), *Myth and Ritual* (Oxford, 1933).

Hopkins, S., *A Miscellany of Literary Pieces from the Cambridge Genizah Collections: A Catalogue and Selection of Texts in the Taylor-Schechter Collection, Old Series, Box a45* (Cambridge: Cambridge University Press, 1978).

Hornig, G., *Die Anfänge der hist.-krit. Theologie: J.S. Semlers Schriftverständnis und seine Stellung zu Luther* (FSThR, 8; Göttingen: Vandenhoeck & Ruprecht, 1961).

Horst, F., and T.H. Robinson, *Die Zwölf Kleinen Propheten* (HAT, 1.14; Tübingen: J.C.B. Mohr, 2nd edn, 1954).

House, P.R. (ed.), *Beyond Form Criticism: Essays in Old Testament Literary Criticism* (Sources for Biblical and Theological Study, 2; Winona Lake, IN: Eisenbrauns, 1992).

Huffmon, H.B., *Amorite Personal Names in the Mari Texts* (Baltimore, 1965).

Humbert, P., *La 'Terou'a': Analyse d'un rite biblique* (Receuil de travaux publié par la Faculté des Lettres, Université de Neuchâtel, 23; Neuchâtel, 1946).

Hyatt, J.P., 'Yahweh as the "God of my Father"', *VT* 5 (1955), pp. 130-36.

—'Was Yahweh Originally a Creator Deity?', *JBL* 86 (1967), pp. 359-77.

Illman, K.-J., 'Modern judisk bibelforskning', *Nordisk Judaistik/Scandinavian Jewish Studies* 1 (1975), pp. 3-14.

Irsigler, H., 'Zeichen und Bezeichnetes in Jes. 7, 1-17', in Struppe (ed.), *Messiasbild*, pp. 155-97.

Jacob, E., *Grundfragen alttestamentlicher Theologie* (Franz Delitzsch-Vorlesungen 1965; Stuttgart: W. Kohlhammer, 1970).

Jahnow, H., *Das hebräische Leichenlied im Rahmen der Völkerdichtung* (BZAW, 36; Giessen: W. de Gruyter, 1923).

Jamieson-Drake, D.W., *Scribes and Schools in Monarchic Judah: A Socio-Archaeological Approach* (Sheffield: Almond Press, 1991).

Janssen, E., *Das Gottesvolk und seine Geschichte* (Neukirchen–Vluyn: Neukirchener Verlag, 1971).

Janzen, J.G., 'What's in a Name? "Yahweh" in Exodus 3 and the Wider Biblical Context', *Int* 33 (1979), pp. 227-39.

Japhet, S., 'Sheshbazzar and Zerubbabel', *ZAW* 94 (1982), pp. 66-98.

Jenni, E., יהוה *Jhwh* Jahwe', *THAT*, I, cols. 701-707.

—'אָב *'āb* Vater', *THAT*, I, cols. 9-11.

—'Die Rolle des Kyros bei Deuter.jesaja', *TZ* 10 (1954), pp. 241-56.

—*Die politischen Voraussagen der Propheten* (ATANT, 29; Zürich: Zwingli-Verlag, 1956).

—'אחר *'ḥr* danach', *THAT*, I, cols. 110-18.

Jepsen, A., 'Zur Kanongeschichte des Alten Testaments', *ZAW* 71 (1959), pp. 114-36.

Jeremias, J., 'παῖς θεοῦ im Spätjudentum in der Zeit nach der Entstehung der LXX(C)', in *TWNT*, V, pp. 676-98.

—'Gott und Geschichte im Alten Testament: Überlegungen zum Geschichtsverständnis im Nord- und Südreich Israels', *EvT* 40 (1980), pp. 381-96.

—'Lade und Zion: Zur Entstehung der Ziontradition', in Wolff (ed.), *Probleme biblischer Theologie*, pp. 183-98.

Jirku, A., *Kannaanäische Mythen und Epen aus Ras Shamra-Ugarit* (Gütersloh, 1962).

Johnson, A.R., *Sacral Kingship in Ancient Israel* (Cardiff: University of Wales Press, 1955).

Johnson, B., 'Form and Message in Lamentations', *ZAW* 97 (1985), pp. 58-73.

Johnstone, W., 'Solomon's Prayer: Is Intentionalism Such a Fallacy?', *ST* 47 (1993), pp. 119-33.

—'Reactivating the Chronicles Analogy in Pentateuchal Studies, with Special Reference to the Sinai Pericope in Exodus', *ZAW* 99 (1987), pp. 16-37.

Jones, G.H., *The Nathan Narratives* (JSOTSup, 80; Sheffield: JSOT Press, 1990).

Jowett, B., 'On the Interpretation of Scripture', in *Essays and Reviews* (London: Longman, Green, Longman, and Roberts, 9th edn, 1861), pp. 330-433.

Junod, E., 'La formation et la composition de l'Ancien Testament dans l'église grecque des quatre premiers siècles', in Kaestli and Wermelinger (eds.), *Le canon de l'Ancien Testament*.

Junker, H., *Ursprung und Grundzüge des Messiasbildes bei Isajas* (VTSup, 4; Leiden: E.J. Brill, 1957).

Kaestli, J.-D., and O. Wermelinger (eds.), *Le canon de l'Ancien Testament: Sa formation et son histoire* (Geneva: Labor et Fides, 1984).

Kahle, P., *The Cairo Geniza* (Oxford: Basil Blackwell, 2nd edn, 1959).

Kaiser, O., *Der königliche Knecht* (FRLANT, 70; Göttingen: Vandenhoeck & Ruprecht, 1959).

—'Jesaja/Jesajabuch', *TRE*, XVI, pp. 636-58.

—'Geschichtliche Erfahrung und eschatologische Erwartung: Ein Beitrag zur Geschichte der alttestamentlichen Eschatologie im Jesajabuch', *NZSTh* 15 (1973), pp. 272-85.

—*Das Buch des Propheten Jesaja: Kap. 1–12* (ATD, 17; Göttingen: Vandenhoeck & Ruprecht, 5th edn, 1981).

—*Einleitung in das Alte Testament* (Gütersloh: Gütersloher Verlagshaus, 5th rev. edn, 1984).

—'Eichhorn und Kant: Ein Beitrag zur Geschichte der Hermeneutik', in *idem*, *Von der Gegenwartsbedeutung des Alten Testaments: Gesammelte Studien* (Göttingen: Vandenhoeck & Ruprecht, 1984), pp. 61-70.

—'Johann Salomo Semler als Bahnbrecher der modernen Bibelwissenschaft', in *idem*, *Von der Gegenwartsbedeutung*, pp. 79-94.

—*Klagelieder* (ATD, 16.2; Göttingen: Vandenhoeck & Ruprecht, 4th edn, 1992).

Kallai, Z., *Historical Geography of the Bible: The Tribal Territories of Israel* (Jerusalem: Magnes Press; Leiden: E.J. Brill, 1986).

Kannengiesser, C., (ed.), *Bible de tous les temps*, I–VIII (Paris: Beauchesne, 1984–89).

Kant, I., *Die Religion innerhalb der Grenzen der blossen Vernunft* (1793).

Kapelrud, A.S., *Joel Studies* (UUÅ, 1984.4; Uppsala: A.-B. Lundeqvistka Bokhandeln, 1948).

—'Sigmund Mowinckel and Old Testament Study', *ASTI* 5 (1967), pp. 4-29.

—'אֲבִיר אָבִיר', *ThWAT*, I, cols. 43-46.

—'אָבֵן', *ThWAT*, I, cols. 50-53.

—*Central Ideas in Amos* (Oslo: Universitetsforlaget, 2nd edn, 1971).

Katz, P., 'The Old Testament Canon in Palestine and Alexandria', *ZNW* 47 (1956), pp. 191-217.

Kayatz, C., *Studien zu Proverbien 1–9* (WMANT, 22; Neukirchen–Vluyn: Neukirchener Verlag, 1966).

Keel, O., *Das Hohelied* (ZBK.AT, 18; Zurich: Theologischer Verlag, 1982).

Kennicott, B. (ed.), *Vetus Testamentum Hebraicum, cum variis lectionibus*, I–II (Oxford, 1776–80).

Kermode, F., 'The Argument about Canons', in F. McConnell (ed.), *The Bible and the Narrative Tradition* (Oxford: Oxford University Press, 1986), pp. 78-96.

Kilian, R., 'Die Hoffnung auf Heimkehr in der Priesterschrift', *BibLeb* 7 (1966), pp. 39-51.

—*Die Verheissung Immanuels Jes. 7,14* (SBS, 35; Stuttgart: KBW, 1968).

—*Jesaja 1–39* (EdF, 200; Darmstadt: Wissenschaftliche Buchgesellschaft, 1983).

Kinyongo, J., *Origine et signification du nom divin Yahvé à la lumière de récents travaux et de traditions sémitico-bibliques (Ex 3,13-15 et 6,2-8)* (BBB, 35; Bonn: Peter Hanstein, 1970).

Kissane, E.J., *The Book of Isaiah*, I (Dublin, 1941).

Kittel, B., 'Brevard Childs' Development of the Canonical Approach', *JSOT* 16 (1980), pp. 2-11.

Kittel, H.-J., 'Die Stammessprüche Israels: Genesis 49 und Deuteronomium 33 traditionsgeschichtlich untersucht' (Theol. Dissertation, Kirchliche Hochschule, Berlin, 1959).

Kittel, R., *Geschichte des Volkes Israel*, II (Stuttgart, 1925).

Klatt, W., *Hermann Gunkel* (FRLANT, 100; Göttingen: Vandenhoeck & Ruprecht, 1969).

Klausner, J., *The Messianic Idea in Israel: From its Beginning to the Completion of the Mishnah* (trans. W.F. Stinespring; New York: Macmillan, 1955 [1927/1949]).

Knight, D.A., *Rediscovering the Traditions of Israel: The Development of the Traditio-Historical Research of the Old Testament, with Special Consideration of Scandinavian Contributors* (SBLDS, 9; Missoula, MT: SBL, 1973; rev. edn, 1976).

Knight, D.A. (ed.), *Tradition and Theology in the Old Testament* (Philadelphia: Westminster Press, 1977).

—'Revelation through Tradition', in *idem* (ed.), *Tradition and Theology*, pp. 143-80.

Knowles, M.P., '"The Rock, his work is perfect": Unusual Imagery for God in Deut. xxxii', *VT* 39 (1989), pp. 307-22.

Koch, K., *Ratlos vor der Apokalyptik: Eine Streitschrift über ein vernachlässigtes Gebiet der Bibelwissenschaft* (Gütersloh: Gütersloher Verlagshaus, 1970).

—*Die Priesterschrift von Exodus 25 bis Leviticus 16* (FRLANT, 71; Göttingen: Vandenhoeck & Ruprecht, 1959).

—*Was ist Formgeschichte?* (Neukirchen–Vluyn: Neukirchener Verlag, 2nd edn, 1967; ET *The Growth of the Biblical Tradition: The Form-Critical Method* [London: A. & C. Black, 1969]).

—'Die Götter, denen die Väter dienten', in *idem, Studien zur alttestamentlichen und altorientalischen Religionsgeschichte* (Göttingen: Vandenhoeck & Ruprecht, 1988), pp. 9-31.

—'Šaddaj', in *idem, Studien zur alttestamentlichen*, pp. 118-52 (= *VT* 26 [1976], pp. 229-332).

—*Spuren des hebräischen Denkens: Beiträge zur alttestamentlichen Theologie* (Gesammelte Aufsätze, 1; Neukirchen–Vluyn: Neukirchener Verlag, 1991).

Koch, K., and J.M. Schmidt (eds.), *Apokalyptik* (WdF, 365; Darmstadt: Wissenschaftliche Buchgesellschaft, 1982).

Köckert, M., *Vätergott und Väterverheissungen: Eine Auseinandersetzung mit Albrecht Alt und seinen Erben* (Göttingen: Vandenhoeck & Ruprecht, 1988).

Koenig, J., 'Le livre d'Isaïe', in E. Dhorme (ed.), *La Bible: L'Ancien Testament*, II (Paris: Bibliothèque de la Pleiade, 1959).

Köhler, L., 'Jod als hebräisches Nominalpräfix', *WO* 1.5 (1950), pp. 25-42.

Köhler, W. 'Prophetie und Eschatologie in der neueren alttestamentlichen Forschung', *BibLeb* 9 (1968), pp. 57-81; repr. in Preuss (ed.), *Eschatologie*, pp. 259-92.

König, E., 'Die formell-genetische Wechselbeziehung der beiden Wörter Jahweh und Jahu', *ZAW* 17 (1897), pp. 172-79.

—*Historisch-kritisches Lehrgebäude der hebräischen Sprache. II.2. Historisch-comparative Syntax der hebräischen Sprache* (Leipzig, 1897)

—*Hebräisches und aramäisches Wörterbuch zum AT* (Wiesbaden: M. Sändig, 1910).

—*Die messianischen Weissagungen des Alten Testaments vergleichend, geschichtlich und exegetisch behandelt* (Stuttgart, 2nd and 3rd edn, 1925 [1922]).

—*Das Buch Jesaja* (Gütersloh, 1926).

Köpf, U., 'Hoheliedauslegung als Quelle einer Theologie der Mystik', in M. Schmidt (ed.), *Grundfragen christlicher Mystik* (Stuttgart–Bad Cannstatt: frommann-holzboog, 1987), pp. 50-72.

Koster, M.D., 'Which Came First: The Chicken or the Egg? The Development of the Text of the Peshitta of Genesis and Exodus in the Light of Recent Studies', in P.B. Dirksen and M.J. Mulder, *The Peshitta: Its Early Text and History* (Leiden: E.J. Brill, 1988), pp. 99-126.

Kraeling, E.G., *The Old Testament Since the Reformation* (New York: Schocken Books, 1969 [1955]).

Kraus, H.-J., *Prophetie und Politik* (ThExh, NF, 36; Munich: Chr. Kaiser Verlag, 1952).

—*Geschichte der historisch-kritischen Erforschung des Alten Testaments* (Neukirchen–Vluyn: Neukirchener Verlag, 3rd rev. edn, 1982 [1956]).

—*Die prophetische Verkündigung des Rechts in Israelischer* (ThSt, 51; Zollikon: Evangelischer Verlag, 1957).

—*Klagelieder (Threni)* (BKAT, 20; Neukirchen–Vluyn: Neukirchener Verlag, 2nd edn, 1960 [4th edn, 1983]).

—*Psalmen*, I–II (BKAT, 15; Neukirchen–Vluyn: Neukirchener Verlag, 5th rev. edn, 1978 [1960]).

—*Gottesdienst in Israel* (Munich, 2nd edn, 1962).

—'Die ausgebliebene Endtheophanie: Eine Studie zu Jes 56–66', *ZAW* 78 (1966), pp. 317-22.

—*Die biblische Theologie* (Neukirchen–Vluyn: Neukirchener Verlag, 1970).

—'Zur Geschichte des Überlieferungsbegriffs in der alttestamentlichen Wissenschaft', in *idem*, *Biblisch-theologische Aufsätze* (Neukirchen–Vluyn: Neukirchener Verlag, 1972), pp. 278-95.

Krauss, S., *Talmudische Archaeologie* (repr.; 3 vols.; New York: Arno Press, 1979 [1910–12]).

Kreuzer, S., *Die Frühgeschichte Israels in Bekenntnis und Verkündigung des Alten Testaments* (Berlin: W. de Gruyter, 1989).

Krinetzki, G., *Hoheslied* (Die Neue Echter Bibel; Würzburg: Echter, 1980).

Kuhl, C., 'Das Hohelied und seine Deutung', *TRev* NF 9 (1937), pp. 137-67.

Kuhn, K.G., 'יו, יהו, יהוה: Über die Entstehung des Namens Jahwe', in *Orientalistische Studien: Festschrift E. Littmann* (Leiden: E.J. Brill, 1935), pp. 25-42.

Kuhn, T.S., *The Structure of Scientific Revolution* (International Encyclopedia of Unified Science, 2.2; Chicago, 1962).

Kümmel, W.G., *Das Neue Testament: Geschichte der Erforschung seiner Probleme* (Freiburg; Munich: Verlag Karl Alber, 1970 [1958]).

Kutsch, E., 'Die Dynastie von Gottes Gnaden: Probleme der Nathanweissagung in 2. Sam. 7', *ZTK* 58 (1961), pp. 137-53.

—*Salbung als Rechtsakt im Alten Testament und im Alten Orient* (BZAW, 87; Berlin: Alfred Töpelmann, 1963).

Kvale, D., and D. Rian (eds.), *Sigmund Mowinckel's Life and Works: A Bibliography. With an Introduction on Sigmund Mowinckel and Old Testament Study by Arvid S. Kapelrud* (Småskrifter utgitt av Institutt for Bibelvitenskap, Universtitets i Oslo, 2; Oslo, 1984 [originally edited by Religionsvitenskapelig Institutt of the University of Trondheim; Trondheim, 1980]).

Kvanvig, H.S., *Roots of Apocalyptic: The Mesopotamian Background of the Enoch Figure and of the Son of Man* (WMANT, 61; Neukirchen–Vluyn: Neukirchener Verlag, 1988).

—'Struktur und Geschichte in Dan. 7,1-14', *ST* 32 (1978), pp. 95-117.

Laato, A., *Who is Immanuel? The Rise and the Foundering of Isaiah's Messianic Expectations* (Åbo: Åbo Academy Press, 1988).

Lacoque, A., 'L'insertion du Cantique des Cantiques dans le canon', *RHPR* 42 (1962), pp. 38-44.

Lagarde, P. de, *Anmerkungen zur griechischen Übersetzung der Proverbien* (Leipzig, 1863).

Lambert, G., 'Que signifie le nom divin YHWH?', *NRT* 74 (1952), pp. 897-915.

Lambert, W.G., 'The Historical Development of the Mesopotamian Pantheon: A Study in Sophisticated Polytheism', in H. Goedicke and J.J.M. Roberts (eds.), *Unity and Diversity: Essays in the History, Literature, and Religion of the Ancient Near East* (Baltimore: Johns Hopkins University Press, 1975), pp. 191-200.

—'Babylonien und Israel', *TRE*, V, pp. 67-79.

Lanahan, W.F., 'The Speaking Voice in the Book of Lamentations', *JBL* 93 (1974), pp. 41-49.

Landes, G.M., 'The Canonical Approach to Introducing the Old Testament: Prodigy and Problems', *JSOT* 16 (1980), pp. 32-39.

Landy, F., 'The Song of Songs', in R. Alter and F. Kermode, *The Literary Guide to the Bible* (Cambridge, MA: Havard University Press, 1987), pp. 305-19.

Lang, B., 'Schule und Unterricht im alten Israel', in Gilbert (ed.), *La Sagesse*, pp. 186-201.

—*Die weisheitliche Lehrrede: Eine Untersuchung von Sprüche 1–7* (SBS, 54; Stuttgart: KBW, 1972).

Lauha, A., *Kohelet* (BKAT, 19; Neukirchen–Vluyn: Neukirchener Verlag, 1978).

Laurin, R.B., 'Tradition and Canon', in Knight (ed.), *Tradition and Theology*, pp. 261-74.

Lebram, J.C.H., 'Apokalyptik/Apokalypsen, II. Altes Testament', *TRE*, III, pp. 192-202.

—'Perspektiven der gegenwärtigen Danielforschung', *JSJ* 5 (1975), pp. 1-33.

—'Daniel/Danielbuch und Zusätze', *TRE*, VIII, pp. 325-49.

—'Aspekte der alttestamentlichen Kanonbildung', *VT* 18 (1968), pp. 173-83.

Leder, K., *Universität Altdorf: Zur Theologie der Aufklärung in Franken. Die theologische Fakultät in Altdorf, 1750–1809* (Nürnberg: Lorenz Spindler Verlag, 1965).

Leiman, S.Z., *The Canonization of Hebrew Scripture: The Talmudic and Midrashic Evidence* (Hamden, CT: Archon Books, 1976).

Leiman, S.Z. (ed.), *The Canon and Masorah of the Hebrew Bible: An Introductory Reader* (New York: Ktav, 1974).

Lemaire, A., *Les écoles et la formation de la Bible dans l'ancien Israël* (OBO, 39; Fribourg: Editions universitaires; Göttingen: Vandenhoeck & Ruprecht, 1981).

Lemche, N.P., *Early Israel: Anthropological and Historical Studies on the Israelite Society before the Monarchy* (Leiden: E.J. Brill, 1985).

Lerch, D., 'Zur Geschichte der Auslegung des Hohenliedes', *ZTK* 54 (1957), pp. 257-77.

Levey, S.H., *The Messiah: An Aramaic Interpretation. The Messianic Exegesis of the Targum* (Cincinnati: Hebrew Union College–Jewish Institute of Religion, 1974).

Lewis, J.P., 'What Do We Mean by Jabne?', *JBR* 32 (1964), pp. 125-32.

Liedke, G., *Gestalt und Bezeichnung alttestamentlicher Rechtsätze* (WMANT, 39; Neukirchen–Vluyn: Neukirchener Verlag, 1971).

Liagre Böhl, F.M.T. de, 'Die fünfzig Namen des Marduk', *AfO* 11 (1936), pp. 191-218; repr. in *idem*, *Opera Minora*, pp. 282-312, 504-508.

—*Opera Minora* (Groningen/Djakarta, 1953).

Lindblom, J., 'Gibt es eine Eschatologie bei den alttestamentlichen Propheten?', *ST* 6 (1952), pp. 79-114; repr. in Preuss (ed.), *Eschatologie*, pp. 31-72.

—*A Study on the Immanuel Section in Isaiah, Isa. vii,1–ix,6* (SMHVL, 4; Lund: C.W.K. Gleerup, 1958).

—*Prophecy in Ancient Israel* (Oxford: Basil Blackwell, 1962).

—'Noch einmal die Deutung des Jahwe-Namens in Ex 3,14', *ASTI* 3 (1964), pp. 4-15.

—'Sigmund Mowinckel in memoriam', *STK* 41 (1965), pp. 191-92.

Lindhagen, C., 'The Servant Motif in the Old Testament' (Theol. Dissertation, University of Uppsala, 1950).

Lisowsky, G., *Konkordanz zum hebräischen Alten Testament* (Stuttgart: Privileg. Württ. Bibelanstalt, 1958).

Lohfink, N., 'Die priesterschriftliche Abwertung der Tradition von der Offenbarung des Jahwenamens an Mose', *Bib* 49 (1968), pp. 1-18.

—'Die Priesterschrift und die Geschichte', in *Congress Volume: Göttingen 1977* (VTSup, 29; Leiden: E.J. Brill, 1978), pp. 189-225.

—'Zur Geschichte der Diskussion über den Monotheismus im Alten Israel', in E. Haag (ed.), *Gott, der einzige: Zur Entstehung des Monotheismus in Israel* (Freiburg: Herder, 1985), pp. 9-25.

—' "Israel" in Jes 49,3', in *Wort, Lied und Gottespruch* (Festschrift J. Ziegler; Würzburg: Echter Verlag, 1972), II, pp. 217-29.

Loretz, O., 'Die theologische Bedeutung des Hohenliedes', *BZ* NF 10 (1966), pp. 29-43.

Luck, U., 'Das Weltverständnis in der jüdischen Apokalyptik dargestellt am äthiopischen Henoch und am 4. Esra', *ZTK* 73 (1976), pp. 283-305.

Luckenbill, D.D., 'The Pronunciation of the Name of the God of Israel', *AJSL* 40 (1924), 277-83.

Lutz, H.-M., *Jahwe, Jerusalem und die Völker: Zur Vorgeschichte von Sach 12,1-8 und 14, 1-5* (WMANT, 27; Neukirchen–Vluyn: Neukirchener Verlag, 1968).

Maag, V., 'Der Hirte Israels', in *idem*, *Kultur, Kulturkontakt und Religion* (Göttingen: Vandenhoeck & Ruprecht, 1980), pp. 111-44.

MacIntyre, J., *The Christian Doctrine of History* (Grand Rapids: Eerdmans, 1957).

MacLaurin, E.C.B., 'YHWH: The Origin of the Tetragrammaton', *VT* 12 (1962), pp. 439-63.

Marron, H.-I., *Über die historische Erkenntnis* (Munich, 1973).

Marti, K., *Das Buch Jesaja* (KHAT, 10; Tübingen: J.C.B. Mohr, 1900).

Martínez, F.G., *Qumran and Apocalyptic* (STDJ, 9; Leiden: E.J. Brill, 1992).

Mayer, R., 'Der Gottesname Jahwe im Lichte der neuesten Forschung', *BZ* NF 2 (1958), pp. 26-53.

Mays, J.L., *Amos* (OTL; London: SCM Press, 1969).

Mathys, H.-P., *Liebe deinen Nächsten wie dich selbst: Untersuchungen zum alttestamentlichen Gebotr der Nächstenliebe* (OBO, 71; Freiburg: Universitätsverlag; Göttingen: Vandenhoeck & Ruprecht, 1987).

McCarthy, D.J., 'Exod 3:14: History, Philology and Theology', *CBQ* 40 (1978), pp. 311-22.

McConnell, F. (ed.), *The Bible and the Narrative Tradition* (Oxford: Oxford University Press, 1986).

McEvenue, S.E., *The Narrative Style of the Priestly Writer* (AnBib, 50; Rome: Biblical Institute Press, 1971).

McKane, W., *Proverbs: A New Approach* (London: SCM Press, 1970).

—review of *Das überlieferungsgeschichtliche Problem des Pentateuch* (BZAW, 147; Berlin: W. de Gruyter, 1977), by R. Rendtorff, in *VT* 28 (1978), pp. 371-82.

—*Selected Christian Hebraists* (Cambridge: Cambridge University Press, 1989).

Meissner, B., *Babylonien und Assyrien*, II (Heidelberg: Carl Winter, 1925).

Melugin, R.F., *The Formation of Isaiah 40–55* (BZAW, 141; Giessen: Alfred Töpelmann, 1976).

Merk, O., *Biblische Theologie des Neuen Testaments in ihrer Anfangszeit: Ihre methodischen Probleme bei Johann Philipp Gabler und Georg Lorenz Bauer und deren Nachwirkungen* (MTS, NS 9; Marburg, 1972).

—'Biblische Theologie II', *TRE*, VI, pp. 457f.

—'Gabler, Johann Philipp (1753–1826)', *TRE*, XII, pp. 1-3.

Meshel, Z., and C. Meyers, 'The Name of God in the Wilderness of Zin', *BA* 39 (1976), pp. 6-10.

Mettinger, T.N.D., *King and Messiah: The Civil and the Sacral Legitimation of the Israelite Kings* (ConBOT, 8: Lund: C.W.K. Gleerup, 1976).

—'The Last Words of David: A Study of Structure and Meaning in II Samuel 23.1-7', *SEÅ* 41.42 (1976–77), pp. 147-56.

—*A Farewell to the Servant Songs* (SMHVL, 1982–83.3; Lund: C.W.K. Gleerup, 1982–83).

Metzger, B.M., 'Griesbach, Johann Jakob (1745–1812)', *TRE*, XIV, pp. 253-56.

Meyer, R., *Hebrew Grammar* (London: SPCK, 1973).

Michel, D., 'Studien zu den sogenannten Thronbesteigungspsalmen', *VT* 6 (1956), pp. 40-68.

—'Deuterojesaja', *TRE*, VIII, pp. 510-30.

Millard, A.R., '*YW* and *YHW* Names', *VT* 30 (1980), pp. 208-12.

Montgomery, J.A., 'The Hebrew Divine Name and the Personal Pronoun Hu', *JBL* 63 (1944), pp. 161-63.

Moore, G.F., 'Notes on the Name Yhwh', *AJSL* 25 (1909), pp. 312-18.

Moor, J.C. de, *The Rise of Yahwism: The Roots of Israelite Monotheism* (Leuven: Leuven University Press, 1990).

Morgan, R., with J. Barton, *Biblical Interpretation* (Oxford: Oxford University Press, 1988).

Morgenstern, J., 'The Elohist Narrative in Exodus 3:1-15', *AJSL* 37 (1920/21), pp. 242-62.

Mowinckel, S., *Zur Komposition des Buches Jeremia* (SVSK.HF, 1913.5, Kristiania [Oslo]: Jacob Dybwad, 1913).

—'Om den jødiske menighets og provinsen Judeas organisation ca. 400 f.Kr.', *NTT* 16 (1915), pp. 123-48, 226-80.

—*Kongesalmerne i det gamle testamente* (Kristiania [Oslo]: H. Aschehoug, 1916).

—*Studier til den jødiske menighets historie og litteratur. I. Statholderen Nehemia* (Kristiania [Oslo]: Olaf Norlis Forlag, 1916).

—*Studier til den jødiske menighets historie og litteratur. II. Ezra den skriftlærde:* (Kristiania [Oslo]: Olaf Norlis Forlag, 1916).

—'Tronstigningssalmerne og Jahves trongstigningsfest', *NTT* 18 (1917), pp. 13-79.

—'Julius Wellhausen', *For kirke og kultur* 25 (1918), pp. 277-88.

—*Psalmenstudien. II. Das Thronbesteigungsfest Jahwäs und der Ursprung der Eschatologie* (Kristiana [Oslo]: Jacob Dybwad, 1922).

—'Die vorderasiatischen Königs—und Fürsteninschriften: Eine stilistische Studie', in *Eucharisterion*, I (Festschrift H. Gunkel; FRLANT, 36; Göttingen: Vandenhoeck & Ruprecht, 1923), pp. 278-322.

—'Det kultiske synspunkt som forskningsprincipp i den gammeltestamentlige videnskap', *NTT* 25 (1924), pp. 1-23.

—*Profeten Jesaja: En bibelstudiebok* (Oslo: H. Aschehoug, 1925).

—*Jesaja-disiplene: Profetien fra Jesaja til Jeremia* (Oslo: H. Aschehoug, 1926).

—'Motiver og stilformer i profeten Jeremias diktning', *Edda* 26 (1926), pp. 233-320.

—*Studentene fra 1902: Biografiske oplysninger* (Oslo: Grøndahl & Søn, 1927).

—'Die Komposition des deuterojesajanischen Buches', *ZAW* 49 (1931), pp. 87-112, 242-60.

—'Die Komposition des Jesaja-Buches Kap. 1–39', *AcOr* 11 (1933), pp. 267-92.

—'The "Spirit" and the "Word" in the Pre-Exilic Reforming Prophets', *JBL* 53 (1934), pp. 199-227.

—'Ecstatic Experience and Rational Elaboration in Old Testament Prophecy', *AcOr* 13 (1935), pp. 264-91.

—*The Two Sources of the Predeuteronomic Primeval History (JE) in Gen. 1–11* (ANVAO.HF, 1937.2; Oslo: Jacob Dybwad, 1937).

—*Det gamle testament som Guds ord* (Oslo: Gyldendal Norsk Forlag, 1938; ET *The Old Testament as Word of God* [Oxford, 1960]).

—'Om tilblivelsen av profetbøkene', *NTT* 39 (1938), pp. 318-20.

—'Opkomsten av profetlitteraturen', *NTT* 43 (1942), pp. 65-111.

—*Prophecy and Tradition: The Prophetic Books in the Light of the Study of the Growth and History of the Tradition* (ANVAO.HF, 1946.3; Oslo: Jacob Dybwad, 1946).

—*Religion og kultus* (Oslo: Landog Kirke, 1950; 2nd edn, 1971).

—'Die vermeintliche "Passahlegene" Ex. 1–15 in Bezug auf die Frage: Literarkritik und Traditionskritik', *ST* 5 (1951), pp. 66-88.

—*Han som kommer: Messiasforventningen i Det gamle testament og på Jesu tid* (Copenhagen: G.E.C. Gad, 1951; ET *He That Cometh* [trans. G.W. Anderson; Oxford: Basil Blackwell, 1956]).

—*Offersang og sangoffer* (Oslo: H. Aschehoug, 1951; Oslo: Universitetsforlaget, 2nd edn, 1971; ET *The Psalms in Israel's Worship* [2 vols.; New York: Abingdon Press, 1962]).

—'Prof. D. Dr. Gustav Hölscher', *NTT* 56 (1955), pp. 296-98.

—'Fragmenter', in *Norsk litteraturvitenskap i det 20. århundre* (Festschrift Francis Bull; Oslo: Gyldendal Norsk Forlag, 1957), pp. 117-30.

—'Jahwes dag', *NTT* 59 (1958), pp. 1-56, 209-29.

—' "Ich" and "Er" in der Ezrageschichte', in *Verbannung und Heimkehr* (Festschrift W. Rudolph; Tübingen: J.C.B. Mohr, 1961), pp. 211-33.

—'The Name of the God of Moses', *HUCA* 32 (1961), pp. 121-33.

—*Psalmenstudien*, I–VI (2 vols.; Amsterdam: P. Schippers, 1961).

—*Erwägungen zur Pentateuchquellenfrage* (Oslo: Universitetsforlaget, 1964; sep. edn of *NTT* 65 [1964], pp. 1-138).

—*Tetrateuch–Pentateuch–Hexateuch: Die Berichte über die Landnahme in den drei altisraelitischen Geschichtswerken* (BZAW, 90; Berlin: Alfred Töpelmann, 1964).

—*Studien zu dem Buche Ezra–Nehemia*. I. *Die nachchroni[sti]sche Redaktion des Buches: Die Listen* (Oslo: Universitetsforlaget, 1964); II. *Die Nehemia–Denkschrift* (1964); III. *Die Ezrageschichte und das Gesetz Moses* (1965).

Mowinckel, S., and N. Messel, *Det gamle testamente*. III. *De senere profeter* (Oslo: H. Aschehoug, 1944).

Mühlenberg, E., 'Gott in der Geschichte: Erwägung zur Geschichtstheologie von W. Pannenberg', *KD* 24 (1978), pp. 244-61.

Müller-Lauter, W., 'Konsequenzen des Historismus in der Philosophie der Gegenwart', *ZTK* 59 (1962), pp. 226ff.

Müller, D., 'Der gute Hirte', *ZÄS* 86 (1961), pp. 126-44.

Müller, H.-P., *Ursprünge und Strukturen alttestamentlicher Weisheit* (BZAW, 109; Berlin: Alfred Töpelmann, 1969).

—'Mantische Weisheit und Apokalyptik', in *Congress Volume: Uppsala 1971* (VTSup, 22; Leiden: E.J. Brill, 1972).

—*Vergleich und Metaphor im Hohenlied* (OBO, 56; Freiburg: Universitätsverlag; Göttingen: Vandenhoeck & Ruprecht, 1984).

—*Das Hohelied* (ATD, 16.2; Göttingen: Vandenhoeck & Ruprecht, 1992).

Murphy, R.E., 'The Unity of the Song of Songs', *VT* 29 (1979), pp. 436-43.

—'The Old Testament as Scripture', *JSOT* 16 (1980), pp. 40-44.

—*Wisdom Literature* (FOTL, 13; Grand Rapids: Eerdmans, 1981).

—*The Song of Songs* (Hermeneia, 1990).

Murtonen, A., *A Philological and Literary Treatise on the Old Testament Divine Names* (StudOr, 18.1; Helsinki, 1952).

Neusner, J. *et al.* (eds.), *Judaisms and their Messiahs at the Turn of the Christian Era* (Cambridge: Cambridge University Press, 1987).

Newman, R.C., 'The Council of Jamnia and the Old Testament Canon', *WTJ* 38 (1975), pp. 319-50.

Nielsen, E., *Oral Tradition: A Modern Problem in Old Testament Introduction* (SBT, 11; London: SCM Press, 1954).

Nielsen, K., *There is Hope for a Tree: The Tree as Metaphor in Isaiah* (JSOTSup, 65; Sheffield: JSOT Press, 1989).

—'Intertextuality and Biblical Scholarship', *SJOT* 2 (1990), pp. 89-95.

Nissen, A., 'Tora und Geschichte im Spätjudentum', *NovT* 9 (1967), pp. 241-77.

Noble, P.R., *The Canonical Approach: A Critical Reconstruction of the Hermeneutics of Brevard S. Childs* (Biblical Interpretation Series, 16; Leiden: E.J. Brill, 1995).

Nöldeke, T., *Untersuchungen zur Kritik des Alten Testaments* (Kiel, 1869).

Norin, S., 'Jô-Namen und Jᵉhô-Namen', *VT* 29 (1979), pp. 87-97.

North, C.R., *The Old Testament Interpretation of History* (London, 1946).

—'The "Former Things" and the "New Things" in Deutero-Isaiah', in H.H. Rowley (ed.), *Studies in Old Testament Prophecy* (Festschrift T.H. Robinson; Edinburgh: T. & T. Clark, 1950), pp. 111-26.

—*The Suffering Servant in Deutero-Isaiah* (London: Oxford University Press, 1956).

North, R., 'Prophecy to Apocalyptic via Zechariah', in *Congress Volume: Uppsala 1971* (VTSup, 22; Leiden: E.J. Brill, 1972), pp. 47-71.

Norton, D., *A History of the Bible as Literature*, I–II (Cambridge: Cambridge University Press, 1993).

Noth, M., *Die israelitischen Personennamen* (BWANT, 3.10; Stuttgart: W. Kohlhammer, 1928).

—'Die Heiligen des Höchsten', in *idem*, *Gesammelte Studien zum AT* (TBü, 6; Munich: Chr. Kaiser Verlag, 3rd edn, 1966 [1957]), pp. 274-90.

—*Überlieferungsgeschichtliche Studien* (Tübingen: M. Niemeyer, 1943; Darmstadt: Wissenschaftliche Buchgesellschaft, 2nd edn, 1957; ET *The Deuteronomistic History* [JSOTSup, 15; Sheffield: JSOT Press, 1981]).

—*Das zweite Buch Mose: Exodus* (ATD, 5; Göttingen: Vandenhoeck & Ruprecht, 1959).

—*Überlieferungsgeschichte des Pentateuch* (Stuttgart: W. Kohlhammer, 1948; 3rd edn, 1966).

—'David und Israel in 2. Samuel 7', in *idem*, *Gesammelte Studien zum AT* (TBü, 6; Munich: Chr. Kaiser Verlag, 3rd edn, 1966), pp. 334-45.

—'Die Gesetze im Pentateuch', in *idem*, *Gesammelte Studien zum AT* (TBü, 6; Munich: Chr. Kaiser Verlag, 3rd edn, 1966), pp. 9-141.

Nyberg, H.S., *Studien zum Hoseabuche* (UUÅ, 1935.6; Uppsala: A.-B. Lundeqvistka, 1935).

—'Smärtornas man: En studie till Jes. 52,13–53,12', *SEÅ* 7 (1942), pp. 35-36.

—*Hebreisk grammatik* (Uppsala: Almqvist & Wiksell, 1952).

Obermann, J., 'The Divine Name *Yhwh* in the Light of Recent Discoveries', *JBL* 68 (1949), pp. 301-23.

Ohly, F., *Hohelied-Studien: Grundzüge einer Geschichte der Hoheliedauslegung des Abendlands bis zum 1200* (Wiesbaden: Steiner, 1958).

Olofsson, S., *God Is my Rock: A Study of Translation Technique and Theological Exegesis in the Septuagint* (ConBOT, 31; Stockholm: Almqvist & Wiksell, 1990).

Olyan, S.M., *Asherah and the Cult of Yahweh in Israel* (SBLMS, 34; Atlanta, GA: Scholars Press, 1988).

Osswald, E., 'Geschehene und geglaubte Geschichte in der alttestamentlichen Theologie', *Wissenschaftliche Zeitschrift der Universität Jena* 14 (1965), pp. 705-15.

Osten-Sacken, P. von der, *Die Apokalyptik in ihrem Verhältnis zu Prophetie und Weisheit* (ThExh, 157; Munich: Chr. Kaiser Verlag, 1969).

Otto, E., 'Stehen wir vor einem Umbruch in der Pentateuchkritik?', *VF* 22 (1977), pp. 82-97.

—'Kultus und Ethos in Jerusalemer Theologie: Ein Beitrag zur theologischen Begründung der Ethik im Alten Testament', *ZAW* 98 (1986), pp. 161-79.

—*Wandeln der Rechtsbegrundungen in der Gesellschaftsgeschichte des antiken Israel* (Leiden: E.J. Brill, 1988).

—'Israels Wurzeln in Kanaan: Auf dem Wege zu einer neuen Kultur- und Sozialgeschichte des antiken Israels', *TRev* 85 (1989), pp. 3-10.

—'Forschungsgeschichte der Entwürfe einer Ethik im Alten Testament', *VF* 36 (1991), pp. 3-37.

—'Die Geburt des moralischen Bewusstseins', in E. Otto and S. Uhlig, *Bibel und Christentum im Orient* (Glückstadt: J.J. Agustin, 1991), pp. 63-97.

—review of *Die Tora: Theologie und Sozialgeschichte des alttestamentlichen Gesetzes* (Munich: Chr. Kaiser Verlag, 1992), by F. Crüsemann, in *TLZ* 118 (1993), cols. 903-10.

—*Theologische Ethik des Alten Testaments* (Theologische Wissenschaft, 3.2; Stuttgart: W. Kohlhammer, 1994).

Otzen, B., *Studien über Deuterosacharja* (AThD, 6; Copenhagen: Munksgaard, 1964).

—'Old Testament Wisdom Literature and Dualistic Thinking in Late Judaism', in *Congress Volume: Edinburgh 1974* (VTSup, 28: Leiden: E.J. Brill, 1975), pp. 146-57.

Oyen, H. van, *Ethik des Alten Testaments* (Gütersloh: Gütersloher Verlagshaus, 1967).

Pannenberg, W., 'Heilsgeschehen und Geschichte', *KD* 5 (1959), pp. 218-37.

—'Kerygma und Geschichte', in R. Rendtorff and K. Koch (eds.), *Studien zur Theologie der alttestamentlichen Überlieferungen* (Festschrift G. von Rad; Neukirchen–Vluyn: Neukirchener Verlag, 1961), pp. 129-40.

Pannenberg, W. *et al.* (eds.), *Offenbarung als Geschichte* (Göttingen: Vandenhoeck & Ruprecht, 1963 [1961]).

Parke-Taylor, G.H., *YAHWEH: The Divine Name in the Bible* (Waterloo/Ontario, 1975).

Patte, D., *Early Jewish Hermeneutic in Palestine* (SBLDS, 22; Missoula, MT: Scholars Press, 1975).

Peake, A.S. (ed.), *The People and the Book* (Oxford, 1925).

Pedersen, J., 'Die Auffassung vom Alten Testament', *ZAW* 49 (1931), pp. 161-81.

—*Hebræisk Grammatik* (Copenhagen: P. Brammer, 2nd edn, 1933).

—'Passahfest und Passahlegende', *ZAW* 52 (1934), pp. 161-75.

Perlitt, L., *Vatke und Wellhausen: Geschichtsphilosophische Voraussetzungen und historiographische Motive für die Darstellung der Religion und Geschichte Israels durch Wilhelm Vatke und Julius Wellhausen* (BZAW, 94; Berlin: Alfred Töpelmann, 1965).

—*Bundestheologie im Alten Testament* (WMANT, 36; Neukirchen–Vluyn: Neukirchener Verlag, 1969).

[Peshitta] *The Old Testament in Syriac According to the Peshiṭta Version*, I.1 (Leiden: E.J. Brill, 1977).

Pettinato, G., 'The Royal Archives of Tell-Mardikh-Ebla', *BA* 39 (1976), p. 50.

Pfeiffer, R.H., 'Facts and Faith in Biblical History', *JBL* 70 (1951), pp. 1-14.

Pietersma, A., 'David in the Greek Psalms', *VT* 30 (1980), pp. 213-26.

Ploeg, J.P.M. van der, 'Lev. IX,23–X,2, dans un texte de Qumran', in Siegfried Wagner (ed.), *Bibel und Qumran* (Festschrift H. Bardtke; Berlin: Evangelische Haupt-Bibelgesellschaft, 1968), pp. 153-55.

—'Eschatology in the Old Testament', *OTS* 17 (1972), pp. 89-99.

Plöger, O., *Theokratie und Eschatologie* (WMANT, 2; Neurkirchen–Vluyn: Neukirchener Verlag, 2nd edn, 1963 [1959]).

—*Das Buch Daniel* (KAT, 18; Gütersloh: Gütersloher Verlagshaus, 1965).

—*Die Klagelieder* (HAT, 1.18; Tübingen: J.C.B. Mohr, 2nd edn, 1969).

—*Sprüche Salomos (Proverbia)* (BKAT, 17; Neukirchen–Vluyn: Neukirchener Verlag, 1984).

Pope, M.H., *Song of Songs* (AB, 7c; New York: Doubleday, 1977).

Porteous, N.W., 'Jerusalem—Zion: The Growth of a Symbol', in *Verbannung und Heimkehr: Festschrift W. Rudolph* (Tübingen: J.C.B. Mohr, 1961), pp. 235-52.

—*Daniel* (OTL; London: SCM Press, 2nd edn, 1979).

Preuss, H.D., *Jahweglaube und Zukunftserwartung* (BWANT, 5.7; Stuttgart: W. Kohlhammer, 1968).

—*Theologie des Alten Testaments*, II (Stuttgart: W. Kohlhammer, 1992; ET *Old Testament Theology*, II [Edinburgh: T. & T. Clark, 1995]).

Preuss, H.D. (ed.), *Eschatologie im Alten Testament* (WdF, 480; Darmstadt: Wissenschaftliche Buchgesellschaft, 1978),

Procksch, O., *Jesaja*, I (KAT, 9; Leipzig: A. Deichert, 1930).

—*Theologie des Alten Testaments* (Gütersloh: C. Bertelsmann, 1950).

Provan, I.W., 'Past, Present and Future in Lamentations III 52–66: The Case for a Precative Perfect Re-examined', *VT* 41 (1991), pp. 164-75.

Quell, G., 'Κύριος, C. Der alttestamentliche Gottesname', *TWNT*, III, pp. 1056-80.

Rad, G. von, *Das Geschichtsbild des chronistischen Werkes* (BWANT, 55; Stuttgart: W. Kohlhammer, 1930).

—*Die Priesterschrift im Hexateuch* (BWANT, 65; Stuttgart: W. Kohlhammer, 1934).

—*Das formgeschichtliche Problem des Hexateuch* (BWANT, 4.26; Stuttgart: W. Kohlhammer, 1938; repr. in *idem, Gesammelte Studien zum Alten Testament* [TBü, 8; Munich: Chr. Kaiser Verlag; 4th edn, 1971], pp. 9-86).

—*Der heilige Krieg im Alten Israel* (Göttingen: Vandenhoeck & Ruprecht, 3rd edn, 1958).

—'Das Alte Testament ist ein Geschichtsbuch', *EvT* 12 (1952/53), pp. 17-33, in C. Westermann (ed.), *Probleme alttestamentlicher Hermeneutik* (TBü, 11; Munich: Chr. Kaiser Verlag, 1960), pp. 11-17.

—*Theologie des Alten Testaments. I. Die Theologie der geschichtlichen Überlieferungen Israels*; II. *Die Theologie der prophetischen Überlieferungen Israels* (Munich: Chr. Kaiser Verlag, 1957–60; 9th edn, 1987; ET *Old Testament Theology* [2 vols.; London: SCM Press, 1975]).

—*Weisheit in Israel* (Neukirchen–Vluyn: Neukirchener Verlag, 1970; ET *Wisdom in Israel* [London: SCM Press, 1972]).

—'Beobachtungen an der Moseerzählung Exodus 1–14', *EvT* 31 (1971), pp. 579-88.

—*Gesammelte Studien zum Alten Testament*, II (TBü, 48; Munich: Chr. Kaiser Verlag, 1973).

Rast, W.E., *Tradition History and the Old Testament* (Philadelphia: Fortress Press, 1972).

Ratschow, C.H., *Werden und Wirken* (BZAW, 70; Berlin: Alfred Töpelmann, 1941).

Rehm, M., *Der königliche Messias im Licht der Immanuel-Weissagungen des Buches Jesaja* (Kevelaer: Butzon & Bercker, 1968).

Reider, J., 'Etymological Studies: ירע or ידע and רעע', *JBL* 66 (1947), pp. 315-17.

Reif, S.C., *A Guide to the Taylor-Schechter Genizah Collection* (Cambridge: Cambridge University Press, 1973).

Rendtorff, R., 'Die theologische Stellung des Schöpfungsglaubens bei Deuterojesaja', *ZTK* 51 (1954), pp. 3-13; repr. in *idem, Gesammelte Studien zum AT* (TBü, 57; Munich: Chr. Kaiser Verlag, 1975), pp. 209-19.

—'Geschichte und Überlieferung', in R. Rendtorff and K. Koch (eds.), *Studien zur Theologie der alttestamentlichen Überlieferungen* (Festschrift G. von Rad; Neukirchen Kreis Moers: Neukirchener Verlag, 1961), pp. 81-94.

—*Die Gesetze in der Priesterschrift* (FRLANT, 62; Göttingen: Vandenhoeck & Ruprecht, 1954; 2nd edn, 1963).

—*Studien zur Geschichte des Opfers im Alten Testament* (WMANT, 24; Neukirchen–Vluyn: Neukirchener Verlag, 1967).

—'Die Offenbarungsvorstellungen im Alten Isrel', in Pannenberg *et al.* (eds.), *Offenbarung als Geschichte*, pp. 21-41.

—'Der "Jahwist" als Theologe? Zum Dilemma der Pentateuchkritik', in *Congress Volume: Edinburgh 1974* (VTSup, 28; Leiden: E.J. Brill, 1975), pp. 158-66.

—*Das überlieferungsgeschichtliche Problem des Pentateuch* (BZAW, 147; Berlin: W. de Gruyter, 1977).

—'Pentateuchal Studies on the Move', *JSOT* 3 (1977), pp. 43-45.

—*Leviticus* (BKAT, 3.1; Neukirchen–Vluyn: Neukirchener Verlag, 1985).

Renkema, J., 'The Literary Structure of Lamentations (I–IV)', in W. van der Meer and J.C. de Moor (eds.), *The Structural Analysis of Biblical and Canaanite Poetry* (JSOTSup, 74; Sheffield: JSOT Press, 1988), pp. 294-396.

Reventlow, H. Graf, 'Die Völker als Jahwes Zeugen bei Ezechiel', *ZAW* 71 (1959), pp. 33-43.

—*Hauptprobleme der alttestamentlichen Theologie im 20. Jahrhundert* (EdF, 173; Darmstadt: Wissenschaftliche Buchgesellschaft, 1982)

—*Hauptprobleme der biblischen Theologie im 20. Jahrhundert* (EdF, 203; Darmstadt: Wissenschaftliche Buchgesellschaft, 1983).

—*The Authority of the Bible and the Rise of the Modern World* (ET London, 1984).

—'Hoheslied. I. Altes Testament', *TRE*, XV, pp. 499-502.

—'Das Ende der sog. "Denkschrift" Jesajas', *BN* 38/39 (1987), pp. 62-67.

Richter, W., 'Die *nagid*-Formel', *BZ* 9 (1965), pp. 71-84.

—*Traditionsgeschichtliche Untersuchungen zum Richterbuch* (BBB, 18; Bonn: Peter Hanstein, 1966).

—*Die sogenannten vorprophetischen Berufungsberichte* (FRLANT, 101; Göttingen: Vandenhoeck & Ruprecht, 1970).

Riesen, R.A., *Criticism and Faith in Late Victorian Scotland* (Lanham: University Press of America, 1985).

Riesener, R., *Der Stamm* עבד *im Alten Testament* (BZAW, 149; Berlin: W. de Gruyter, 1978).

Rignell, L., 'Das Orakel "Maher-salal Has-bas" Jesaja 8', *ST* 10 (1956), pp. 40-52.

—'Das Immanuelzeichen: Einige Gesichtspunkte zu Jes. 7', *ST* 11 (1957), pp. 99-119.

Ringgren, H., 'אב', *ThWAT*, I , cols. 2-19.

—*The Messiah in the Old Testament* (SBT, 18; London: SCM Press, 1956).

—'Literarkritik, Formgeschichte, Überlieferungsgeschichte: Erwägungen zur Methodenfrage der alttestamentlichen Exegese', *TLZ* 91 (1966), cols. 641-50.

Robert, A. and A. Feuillet (eds.), *Introduction à la Bible*, I (Paris: Desclée, 2nd rev. edn, 1959).

Robert, P. de, *Le berger d'Israël* (Neuchâtel, 1968).

Robertson Smith, W., *The Old Testament in the Jewish Church* (Edinburgh: A. & C. Black, 1881; 2nd edn, 1892).

—*The Prophets and Israel and their Place in History* (Edinburgh: A. & C. Black, 1882; 2nd edn [ed. T.K. Cheyne], 1895).

Robinson, J.M., and J.B. Cobb (eds.), *Theology as History* (New Frontiers in Theology, 3; New York: Harper & Row, 1967).

Robinson, H. Wheeler, *The Old Testament: Its Making and Meaning* (repr.; London, 1961 [1937]).

—*The History of Israel* (London, 1957 [1938]).

—*Hebrew Conception of Corporate Personality: Corporate Personality in Ancient Israel* (Philadelphia: Fortress Press, rev. edn, 1980).

Robinson, T.H., and F. Horst, *Die zwölf kleinen Propheten* (HAT, 1.14; Tübingen: J.C.B. Mohr, 2nd edn, 1954).

Rogerson, J., *Old Testament Criticism in the Nineteenth Century: England and Germany* (London: SPCK, 1984).

—'The Old Testament', in J. Rogerson *et al.*, *The Study and Use of the Bible* (The History of Christian Theology, 2; Grand Rapids: Pickering, 1988), pp. 1-150.

—'The Hebrew Conception of Corporate Personality: A Reexamination', *JTS* 21 (1970), pp. 1-16.

Rohland, E., 'Die Bedeutung der Erwählungstraditionen Israels für die Eschatologie der alttestamentlichen Propheten' (PhD Dissertation, University of Heidelberg, 1956).

Rose, M., *Jahwe: Zum Streit um den alttestamentlichen Gottesnamen* (ThSt, 122; Zürich: Theologischer Verlag, 1978).

Rosenmüller, E.F.K., *Handbuch der biblischen Kritik und Exegese*, I (Göttingen: Vandenhoeck & Ruprecht, 1797).

Rossi, J.B. de, *Variae lectiones Veteris Testamenti...examinatae opera et studio*, I–IV (Parma, 1784–88).

Rössler, D., *Gesetz und Geschichte* (WMANT, 3; Neukirchen–Vluyn: Neukirchener Verlag, 2nd edn, 1962 [1960]).

Rowley, H.H., 'The Interpretation of the Song of Songs', in *idem*, *The Servant of the Lord and Other Essays on the Old Testament* (Oxford: Basil Blackwell, 2nd rev. edn, 1965).

Rowley, H.H. (ed.), *The Old Testament and Modern Study: A Generation of Discovery and Research* (Oxford: Clarendon Press, 1951).

Rudolph, W., 'Das Hohe Lied im Kanon', *ZAW* NF 18 (1942/43), pp. 189-99.

—*Das Buch Ruth–Das hohe Lied–Die Klagelieder* (KAT, 17.1–3; Gütersloh: Gütersloher Verlagshaus, rev. edn, 1962 [1939]).

—*Joel–Amos–Obadja–Jona* (KAT, 13.2; Gütersloh: Gütersloher Verlagshaus, 1971).

—*Jeremia* (HAT, 1.12; Tübingen: J.C.B. Mohr, 2nd edn, 1958).

Rundgren, F., 'אפריון "Tragsessel, Sänfte" ', *ZAW* 74 (1962), pp. 70-72.

Ruprecht, E., 'Die Auslegungsgeschichte zu den sog. Gottesknechtliedern . . . bis zu Bernhard Duhm' (Theol. Dissertation, University of Heidelberg, 1972).

Russell, D.S., *The Method and Message of Jewish Apocalyptic* (London: SCM Press, 1971 [1964]).

Sæbø, M., *Sacharja 9–14: Untersuchungen von Text und Form* (WMANT, 34; Neukirchen–Vluyn: Neukirchener Verlag, 1969).

—'Sigmund Mowinckels siste arbeider', *TTK* 45 (1974), pp. 161-73.

—'Grenzbeschreibung und Landideal im Alten Testament: Mit besonderer Berücksichtigung der *min-'ad*-Formel', *ZDPV* 90 (1974), pp. 14-37.

—'Hvem var Israels teologer? Om struktureringen an "den gammeltestamentlige teologi" ', *SEÅ* 41–42 (1976–77; Festschrift H. Ringgren), pp. 189-205; repr. in *OoO*, pp. 25-41.

—'Messianism in Chronicles? Some Remarks to the Old Testament Background of the New Testament Christology', *HBT* 2 (1980), pp. 85-109.

—'Chronistische Theologie/Chronistisches Geschichtswerk', *TRE*, VIII, pp. 74-87.

—*Fortolkning til Salomos ordspråk: Forkynneren, Høysangen, Klagesangene* (Oslo: Luther Forlag, 1986).

—'סוֹד *sōd* Geheimnis', *THAT*, II, cols. 144-48.

—'יוֹם *jôm*', *ThWAT*, III, cols. 559-86.

—'The Relation of Sheshbazzar and Zerubbabel Reconsidered', *SEÅ* 54 (1989), pp. 168-77.

—'Mowinckel, Sigmund (1884–1965)', *TRE*, XXIII, pp. 384-88.

—'Eschaton und Eschatologia im Alten Testament—in traditionsgeschichtlicher Sicht', in J. Hausmann and H.-J. Zobel (eds.), *Alttestamentlicher Glaube und biblische Theologie* (Festschrift H.D. Preuss; Stuttgart: W. Kohlhammer, 1992), pp. 321-30.

Sæbø, M. (ed.), *Hebrew Bible/Old Testament: The History of its Interpretation*. I.1. *Antiquity* (Göttingen: Vandenhoeck & Ruprecht, 1996).

—*Hebrew Bible/Old Testament: The History of its Interpretation*. I.2. *The Middle Ages* (Göttingen: Vandenhoeck & Ruprecht, forthcoming).

Sanders, J.A., *Torah and Canon* (Philadelphia: Fortress Press, 1972).

—'Text and Canon: Concepts and Method', *JBL* 88 (1979), pp. 5-29.

—'Canonical Context and Classical Criticism', *HBT* 2 (1980), pp. 173-97.

—*Canon and Community: A Guide to Canonical Criticism* (Philadelphia: Fortress Press, 1984).

Sandmel, S., 'The Haggada within Scripture', *JBL* 80 (1961), pp. 105-22.

Sandys-Wunsch, J., and L. Eldredge, 'J.P. Gabler and the Distinction between Biblical and Dogmatic Theology: Translation, Commentary, and Discussion of his Originality', *SJT* 33 (1980), pp. 133-58.

Schechter, S., *Studies in Judaism* (2 vols.; Freeport, NY: Books for Libraries Press, 1976 [1896]).

—'The Child in Jewish Literature', in *Studies in Judaism*, I, pp. 343-80.

Schäfer, P., 'Die sogenannte Synode von Jabne', *Judaica* 31 (1975), pp. 54-64, 116-24.

Schenker, A., review of *Theologische Ethik des Alten Testaments* (Theologische Wissenschaft, 3.2; Stuttgart: W. Kohlhammer, 1994), by E. Otto, in *Bib* 77 (1996), pp. 560-62.

Schild, E., 'On Exodus iii 14 —" I am that I am"', *VT* 4 (1954), pp. 296-302.

Schleiff, A., 'Der Gottesname Jahwe', *ZDMG* 90 (1936), pp. 679-702.

Schmid, H.H., *Wesen und Geschichte der Weisheit* (BZAW, 101; Berlin: Alfred Töpelmann, 1966).

—*Gerechtigkeit als Weltordnung* (BHT, 40; Tübingen: J.C.B. Mohr, 1968).

—*Der sogenannte Jahwist: Beobachtungen und Fragen zur Pentateuchforschung* (Zürich: Theologischer Verlag, 1976).

—'In Search of New Approaches in Pentateuchal Research', *JSOT* 3 (1977), pp. 33-42.

—'אַבִּיר *'abbîr* stark', *THAT*, I, cols. 25-27.

Schmidt, H., 'Jesaja 8, 9 und 10', in G. Bertram (ed.), *Stromata* (Giessen, 1930), pp. 3-10.

—*Der Mythos vom wiederkehrenden König im Alten Testament* (Giessen: Alfred Töpelmann, 2nd edn, 1933 [1925]).

Schmidt, J.M., *Die jüdische Apokalyptik* (Neukirchen–Vluyn: Neukirchener Verlag, 1969).

—'Forschung zur jüdischen Apokalyptik', *VF* 14 (1969), pp. 44-69.

Schmidt, L., *Menschlicher Erfolg und Jahwes Initiative* (WMANT, 38; Neukirchen–Vluyn: Neukirchener Verlag, 1970).

—'Überlegungen zum Jahwisten', *EvT* 37 (1977), pp. 230-47.

Schmidt, W.H., *Das erste Gebot: Seine Bedeutung für das Alte Testament* (ThExh, 165; Munich: Chr. Kaiser Verlag, 1970).

—'Die Ohnmacht des Messias: Zur Überlieferungsgeschichte der messianischen Weissagungen im Alten Testament', *KD* 15 (1969), pp. 18-34.

—'Kritik am Königtum', in Wolff (ed.), *Probleme biblischer Theologie*, pp. 440-61.

—'"Theologie des Alten Testaments" vor und nach Gerhard von Rad', *VF* 17 (1972), pp. 1-25.

—*Alttestamentlicher Glaube und seine Umwelt* (Neukirchen–Vluyn: Neukirchener Verlag, 4th rev. edn, 1982 [1968]).

—'Der Jahwename und Ex 3,14', in *Textgemäss: Festschrift E. Würthwein* (Göttingen: Vandenhoeck & Ruprecht, 1979), pp. 123-38.

—*Old Testament Introduction* (trans. M.J. O'Connell; New York: Crossroad, 1984).

—'אֵל *'ēl* Gott', *THAT*, I, cols. 142-49.

—*Exodus* (BKAT, 2.1; Neukirchen–Vluyn: Neukirchener Verlag, 1988).

—*Die zehn Gebote im Rahmen alttestamentlicher Ethik* (EdF, 281; Darmstadt: Wissenschaftliche Buchgesellschaft, 1993).

Scholem, G., *The Messianic Idea in Judaism* (London: Schocken Books, 1971).

Schröter, W., *Erinnerungen an Johann Philipp Gabler* (Jena, 1827).

Schwally, F., *Semitische Kriegsaltertümer*. I. *Der heilige Krieg im alten Israel* (Leipzig, 1901).

Scott, R.B.Y., *Proverbs: Ecclesiastes* (AB, 18; Garden City, NY: Doubleday, 1965).

—*The Way of Wisdom in the Old Testament* (New York: Macmillan, 1971).

Seebass, H., 'Die Stämmeliste von Dtn. XXXIII', *VT* 27 (1977), pp. 158-69.

—'Erwägungen zum altisraelitischen System der zwölf Stämme', *ZAW* 90 (1978), pp. 196-220.

—'Die Stämmesprüche Gen 49,3-27', *ZAW* 96 (1984), pp. 333-50.

—'אָמַרְיָה', *ThWAT*, I, cols. 224-28.

—*Herrscherverheissungen im Alten Testament* (BTSt, 19; Neukirchen–Vluyn: Neukirchener Verlag, 1992).

Seeligmann, I.L., *The Septuagint Version of Isaiah: A Discussion of its Problems* (Mededelingen en Verhandelingen, 9; Leiden: E.J. Brill, 1948).

—'Voraussetzungen der Midraschexegese', in *Congress Volume: Copenhagen 1953* (VTSup, 1; Leiden: E.J. Brill, 1953), pp. 150-81.

—'Indications of Editorial Alteration and Adaptation in the Massoretic Text and the Septuagint', *VT* 11 (1961), pp. 201-21.

Segal, M.H., 'The Promulgation of the Authoritative Text of the Hebrew Bible', *JBL* 72 (1953), pp. 35-47.

—'El, Elohim and YHWH in the Bible', *JQR* 46 (1955), pp. 89-115.

—'The Song of Songs', *VT* 12 (1962), pp. 470-90.

Seibert, I., *Hirt, Herde, König: Zur Herausbildung des Königtums in Mesopotamien* (Berlin: Akademie Verlag, 1969).

Seierstad, I.P., 'Det gamle testament som Guds ord', *TTK* 10 (1939), pp. 95-116, 154-64.

—*Budskapet: Et utvalg av gammeltestamentlige artikler* (Oslo: Universitetsforlaget, 1971).

Sellin, E., 'Wesen und Ursprung der alttestamentlichen Eschatologie', in *idem*, *Der alttestamentliche Prophetismus* (Leipzig: A. Deichert, 1912).

Sellin, E., and G. Fohrer, *Einleitung in das Alte Testament* (Heidelberg: Quelle & Meyer, 1965).

Seybold, K., *Das davidische Königtum im Zeugnis der Propheten* (FRLANT, 107; Göttingen: Vandenhoeck & Rupecht, 1972).

—'מָשַׁח I *māšaḥ*', *ThWAT*, V, pp. 46-59.

Sheppard, G.T., *Wisdom as a Hermeneutical Construct: A Study in the Sapientializing of the Old Testament* (BZAW, 151; Berlin: Alfred Töpelmann, 1980).

—'Canonization: Hearing the Voice of the Same God through Historically Dissimilar Traditions', *Int* 36 (1982), pp. 21-33.

Simons, J., *The Geographical and Topographical Texts of the Old Testament* (Leiden: E.J. Brill, 1959).

Skehan, P.W., 'The Qumran Manuscripts and Textual Criticism', in *Congress Volume: Strasbourg 1956* (VTSup, 4; Leiden: E.J. Brill, 1957), pp. 148-60.

Skladny, U., *Die ältesten Spruchsammlungen in Israel* (Göttingen: Vandenhoeck & Ruprecht, 1962).

Smend, R., *W.M.L. de Wettes Arbeit am Alten und am Neuen Testament* (Basel, 1958).

—'Johann Philipp Gablers Begründung der biblischen Theologie', *EvT* 22 (1962), pp. 345-57; repr. in *idem*, *Epochen der Bibelkritik*, pp. 104-16.

—'Universalismus und Partikularismus in der alttestamentlichen Theologie des 19. Jahrhunderts', *EvT* 22 (1962), pp. 169-79; repr. in *idem*, *Epochen der Bibelkritik*, pp. 117-27.

—'Das Nein des Amos', *EvT* 23 (1963), p. 404-23; repr. in *idem*, *Die Mitte des Alten Testaments*, pp. 85-103.

—'Zur Geschichte von הֶאֱמִין', in *Hebräische Wortforschung* (Festschrift W. Baumgarten; VTSup, 16; Leiden: E.J. Brill, 1967), pp. 284-90; repr. in *idem*, *Die Mitte des Alten Testaments*, pp. 118-23.

—*Elemente alttestamentlichen Geschichtsdenkens* (ThSt, 95; Zürich: EVZ-Verlag, 1968); repr. in *idem*, *Die Mitte des Alten Testaments*, pp. 160-85.

—*Die Mitte des Alten Testaments: Gesammelte Studien*, I (BEvT, 99; Munich: Chr. Kaiser Verlag, 1986).

—*Die Entstehung des Alten Testaments* (Theol. Wissenschaft, 1; Stuttgart: W. Kohlhammer, 1978).

—'Questions about the Importance of the Canon in the Old Testament Introduction', *JSOT* 16 (1980), pp. 45-51.

—'"Das Ende ist gekommen": Ein Amoswort in der Priesterschrift', in J. Jeremias and L. Perlitt (eds.), *Die Botschaft und die Boten* (Festschrift H.W. Wolff; Neukirchen–Vluyn: Neukirchener Verlag, 1981), pp. 67-72; repr., in *idem*, *Die Mitte des Alten Testaments*, pp. 154-59.

—'Das Nein des Amos', in *Die Mitte des Alten Testaments*, pp. 85-103.

—*Deutsche Alttestamentler in drei Jahrhunderten* (Göttingen: Vandenhoeck & Ruprecht, 1989).

—'Ethik, III: Altes Testament', *TRE*, X, pp. 423-35.

—'Eschatologie, II (AT)', *TRE*, X, pp. 256-64.

—*Epochen der Bibelkritik: Gesammelte Studien*, III (BEvT, 109: Munich: Chr. Kaiser Verlag, 1991).

—'Kuenen und Wellhausen', in P.B. Dirksen and A. van der Kooij (eds.), *Abraham Keunen (1828–1891): His Major Contributions to the Study of the Old Testament* (OTS, 29; Leiden: E.J. Brill, 1993), pp. 113-27.

—'William Robertson Smith and Julius Wellhausen', in W. Johnstone (ed.), *William Robertson Smith: Essays in Reassessment* (JSOTSup, 189; Sheffield: Sheffield Academic Press, 1995), pp. 226-42.

Smend, R. (ed.), 'Karl Barth und Walter Baumgartner: Ein Briefwechsel über das Alte Testament', in E. Jüngel (ed.), *Zur Theologie Karl Barths* (ZTK.B, 6; Tübingen: J.C.B. Mohr, 1986), pp. 240-71.

Smith, M.S., *The Early History of God: Yahweh and the Other Deities in Ancient Israel* (San Francisco: Harper & Row, 1990).

Soden, W. von, 'Jahwe "Er ist, Er erweist sich" ', *WO* 3 (1966), pp. 177-87.

Soete, A., *Ethos der Rettung—Ethos der Gerechtigkeit: Studien zur Struktur von Normbegründung und Urteilsfindung im Alten Testament und ihrer Relevanz für die ethische Diskussion der Gegenwart* (Würzburg: Echter, 1987).

Soggin, J.A., 'Der prophetische Gedanke über den heiligen Krieg, als Gericht gegen Israel', *VT* 10 (1960), pp. 79-83.

—*Das Königtum in Israel* (BZAW, 104; Berlin: Alfred Töpelmann, 1967).

—'מֶלֶךְ *maleek* könig', *THAT*, I, cols. 908-20.

—'וְעָה *r'b* weiden', *THAT*, II, col. 793.

—'Charisma und Institution im Königtum Sauls', *ZAW* 75 (1963), pp. 53-65.

—'Zum zweiten Psalm', in H.F. Stoebe (ed.), *Wort–Gebot–Glaube: Festschrift für W. Eichrodt* (ATANT, 59; Zürich: Zwingli-Verlag, 1970), pp. 191-207.

Sperber, A., *The Bible in Aramaic* (5 vols.; Leiden: E.J. Brill, 1959–73).

Spoer, H.H., 'The Origin and Interpretation of the Tetragrammaton', *AJSL* 18 (1901), pp. 9-35.

Spriggs, D.G., *Two Old Testament Theologies: A Comparative Evaluation of the Contributions of Eichrodt and von Rad to our Understanding of the Nature of Old Testament Theology* (SBT, 2.30; London: SCM Press, 1974).

Staerk, W., 'Warum steht das hohe Lied im Kanon?', *ThBl* 16 (1937), pp. 289-91.

Stamm, J.J., 'Neuere Arbeiten zum Immanuel-Problem', *ZAW* 68 (1956), pp. 46-53.

—'*Berît 'am* bei Deuterojesaja', in Wolff (ed.), *Probleme biblischer Theologie*, pp. 510-24.

Steck, K.G., *Die Idee der Heilsgeschichte* (ThSt, 56; Zollikon: Evangelische Verlag, 1959).

Steck, O.H., 'Das Problem theologischer Strömungen in nachexilischer Zeit', *EvT* 28 (1968), pp. 445-68.

—'Deuterojesaja als theologischer Denker', *KD* 15 (1969), pp. 280-93; repr. in *idem*, *Wahrnehmungen Gottes*, pp. 204-20.

—'Strömungen theologischer Tradition im Alten Israel', in *idem*, *Wahrnehmungen Gottes*, pp. 291-317.

—*Wahrnehmungen Gottes im Alten Testament: Gesammelte Studien* (TBü, 70; Munich: Chr. Kaiser Verlag, 1982).

—*Der Abschluss der Prophetie im Alten Testament: Ein Versuch zur Frage der Vorgeschichte des Kanons* (BTSt, 17; Neukirchen–Vluyn: Neukirchener Verlag, 1991).

Steitz, G.E., 'Gabler, Joh. Philipp', *ADB* 8 (1878), pp. 294-96.

Stemberger, G., 'Die sogenannte Synode von Jabne und das frühe Christentum', *Kairos* NS 19 (1977), pp. 14-21.

—*Messias/Messianische Bewegungen, II (Judentum)*', *TRE*, XXII, pp. 622-30.

Stenning, J.F., *The Targum of Isaiah* (Oxford, 1949).

Steuernagel, C., *Lehrbuch der Einleitung in das Alte Testament* (Tübingen: J.C.B. Mohr, 1912).

—'Die Strukturlinien der Entwicklung der jüdischen Eschatologie', in *Festschrift A. Bertholet* (Tübingen: J.C.B Mohr, 1950), pp. 479-87.

Stolz, F., *Jahwes und Israels Kriege* (ATANT, 60; Zürich: Zwingli-Verlag, 1972).

Strack, H.L., 'Kanon des Alten Testaments', *RE* 9 (1901), pp. 741-68.

Strauss, H., 'Messias/Messianische Bewegungen, I. Altes Testament', *TRE*, XXII, pp. 617-21.

—*Messianisch ohne Messias* (EHS, 23.232; Frankfurt am Main: Peter Lang, 1984).

Struppe, U. (ed.), *Studien zum Messiasbild im Alten Testament* (SBA, 6; Stuttgart: W. Kohlhammer, 1989).

Sundberg, A.C., Jr, 'The Old Testament of the Early Church (A Study in Canon)', *HTR* 51 (1958), pp. 205-26.

—*The Old Testament and the Early Church* (HThS, 20; Cambridge, MA: Harvard University Press, 1964).

Swete, H.B. *et al.*, *An Introduction to the Old Testament in Greek* (Cambridge: Cambridge University Press, 1914 [1902]; repr.; New York: Ktav, 1968).

Tallqvist, K., *Akkadische Götterepitheta* (Helsingfors: Finska orientsällskapet, 1938).

Talmon, S., 'DSIa as a Witness to Ancient Exegesis of the Book of Isaiah', *ASTI* 1 (1962), pp. 62-72.

—'Aspects of the Textual Transmission of the Bible in the Light of Qumran Manuscripts', *Textus* 4 (1964), pp. 95-132.

—'Typen der Messiaserwartung um die Zeitwende', in Wolff (ed.), *Probleme biblischer Theologie*, pp. 571-88; repr. in *idem*, *Gesellschaft und Literatur*, pp. 209-24.

—'Königtum und Staatsidee im biblischen Israel', in *idem*, *Gesellschaft und Literatur*, pp. 11-43.

—''In jenen Tagen gab es keinen מלך in Israel" (Ri. 18–21', in *idem*, *Gesellschaft und Literatur*, pp. 44-55.

—'The Old Testament Text', *CHB* 1 (1970), pp. 159-99.

—*Gesellschaft und Literatur in der hebräischen Bibel: Gesammelte Aufsätze*, I (Information Judentum, 8; Neukirchen–Vluyn: Neukirchener Verlag, 1988).

—'קץ qeṣ', *ThWAT*, VII, cols. 84-92.

Thiel, W., *Die deuteronomistische Redaktion von Jeremia 1–25* (WMANT, 41; Neukirchen–Vluyn: Neukirchener Verlag, 1973).

—*Die deuteronomistische Redaktion von Jeremia 26–45* (WMANT, 52; Neukirchen–Vluyn: Neukirchener Verlag, 1981).

—'Vom revolutionären zum evolutionären Israel? Zu einem neuen Modell der Entstehung Israels', *TLZ* 113 (1988), cols. 401-410.

Thierry, G.J., 'The Pronunciation of the Tetragrammaton', *OTS* 5 (1948), pp. 30-42.

Tigay, J.H., *You Shall Have No Other Gods: Israelite Religion in the Light of Hebrew Inscriptions* (HSS, 31; Atlanta, GA: Scholars Press, 1986).

Tournay, R.J., *Quand Dieu parle aux hommes le langage de l'amour: Etudes sur le Cantique des Cantiques* (CRB, 21; Paris: J. Gabalda, 1982).

Tov, E., 'L'incidence de la critique textuelle sur la critique littéraire dans le livre de Jérémie', *RB* 79 (1972), pp. 189-99.

—'Midrash-Type Exegesis in the LXX of Joshua', *RB* 85 (1978), pp. 50-61.

—*The Text-Critical Use of the Septuagint in Biblical Research* (Jerusalem, 1981).

—*Textual Criticism of the Hebrew Bible* (Minneapolis: Fortress Press, Assen: Van Gorcum, 1992).

Tucker, G.M., 'Prophetic Superscriptions and the Growth of a Canon', in G.W. Coates and B.O. Long (eds.), *Canon and Authority* (Philadelphia: Fortress Press, 1977), pp. 56-70.

Tur-Sinai, N.H., *Die heilige Schrift*, III (Jerusalem, 1954).

Uffenheimer, B., 'Eschatologie, III. Judentum', *TRE*, X, pp. 264-70.

Van Seters, J., 'The Yahwist as Theologian? A Response', *JSOT* 3 (1977), pp. 15-17.

—'The Religion of the Patriarchs in Genesis', *Bib* 61 (1980), pp. 220-33.

Vaux, R. de, *Les institutions de l'Ancien Testament*, II (Paris, 1960; New York: McGraw–Hill, trans. J. McHugh, 1961; ET *Ancient Israel: Its Life and Institutions* [trans. J. McHugh; London: Darton, Longman & Todd, 1961]).

—'El et Baal, le Dieu des pères et Yahweh', in *Ugaritica*, VI (Paris, 1969).

—'The Revelation of the Divine Name YHWH', in *Proclamation and Presence: Festschrift G.H. Davies* (London, 1970), pp. 48-75.

—*The Early History of Israel* (2 vols.; London: Darton, Longman & Todd, 1978).

Vawter, B., 'The Canaanite Background of Genesis 49', *CBQ* 17 (1955), pp. 1-18.

Veijola, T., *Die ewige Dynastie: David und die Entstehung seiner Dynastie nach der deuteronomistischen Darstellung* (AASF.B, 193; Helsinki: Suomalainen Tiede-akatemia, 1975).

—*Das Königtum in der Beurteilung der deuteronomistischen Historiographie: Eine redaktionsgeschichtliche Untersuchung* (AASF.B, 198; Helsinki: Suomalainen Tiede-akatemia, 1977).

—*Verheissung in der Krise: Studien zur Literatur und Theologie der Exilszeit anhand des 89. Psalms* (AASF.B, 220; Helsinki: Suomalainen Tiedeakatemia, 1982).

Vermes, G., 'Bible and Midrash: Early Old Testament Exegesis', *CHB* 1 (1970), pp. 199-231.

Vermeylen, J. (ed.), *The Book of Isaiah* (BETL, 81; Leuven: Leuven University Press, 1989).

Vigano, L., *Nomi e titoli di YHWH alla luce del semitico del nord-ovest* (Rome: Biblical Institute Press, 1976).

Vischer, W., *Die Immanuel-Botschaft im Rahmen des königlichen Zionsfestes* (ThSt, 45; Zürich: Theologischer Verlag, 1955).

Vollmer, J., 'Zur Sprache von Jesaja 9, 1-6', *ZAW* 80 (1968), pp. 343-50.

Volz, P. and W. Rudolph, *Der Elohist als Erzähler: Ein Irrweg der Pentateuchkritik?* (BZAW, 63; Giessen: Alfred Töpelmann, 1933).

Vorländer, H., *Mein Gott* (Neukirchen–Vluyn: Neukirchener Verlag, 1975).

Vriezen, T.C., *"ehje 'ašer 'ehje'*, in *Festschrift Alfred Bertholet zum 80. Geburtstag* (Tübingen: J.C.B. Mohr, 1950), pp. 498-512.

—'Prophecie und Eschatologie', in *Congress Volume: Copenhagen 1953* (VTSup, 1; Leiden: E.J. Brill, 1953), pp. 199-299.

—*Theologie des Alten Testaments in Grundzügen* (Neukirchen–Vluyn: Neukirchener Verlag, 1957; ET *An Outline of Old Testament Theology* [Oxford: Basil Blackwell, 2nd edn, 1970]).

—'Einige Notizen zur Übersetzung des Bindewortes *ki*', in J. Hempel and L. Rost (eds.), *Von Ugarit bis Qumran* (Festschrift O. Eissfeldt; BZAW, 77; Berlin: Alfred Töpelmann, 1958), pp. 266-75.

Vriezens C., *Theologie des Alten Testaments in Grundzügen* (Neukirchen–Vluyn: Neukirchener Verlag, 1956).

Wagner, N.E., 'A Response to Professor Rolf Rendtorff', *JSOT* 3 (1977), pp. 20-27.

—'קֵץ *qēṣ* Ende', *THAT*, II, cols. 659-63.

Walker, N., 'Concerning the Function of *'ēth*', *VT* 5 (1955), pp. 314-15.

Wallis, G., 'רָעָה *rāʿāh*', *ThWAT*, VII, cols. 566-76.

Wambacq, B.N., "*ehᵉyeh ʾᵃšer 'ehᵉyeh*', *Bib* 59 (1978), pp. 317-38.

Wanke, G., 'Zu Grundlagen und Absicht prophetischer Sozialkritk', *KD* 18 (1972), pp. 2-17.

Waschke, E.-J., 'Die Frage nach dem Messias im Alten Testament als Problem alttestamentlicher Theologie und biblischer Hermeneutik', *TLZ* 113 (1988), pp. 321-32, 330.

Waterman, L., 'Method in the Study of the Tetragrammaton', *AJSL* 43 (1926), pp. 1-7.

Weber, R. (ed.), *Biblia Sacra iuxta Vulgatam Versionem*, I (Stuttgart: Württembergische Bibelanstalt, 1969).

Weidmann, H., *Die Patriarchen und ihre Religion* (Göttingen: Vandenhoeck & Ruprecht, 1968).

Weinfeld, M., *Deuteronomy and the Deuteronomic School* (Oxford: Clarendon Press, 1972).

—*Getting at the Roots of Wellhausen's Understanding of the Law of Israel: On the 100th Anniversary of the Prolegomena* (Jerusalem: The Institute for Advanced Studies, The Hebrew University of Jerusalem, Report No. 14/79, 1979).

Weingreen, J., 'Rabbinic-Type Glosses in the Old Testament', *JSS* 2 (1967), pp. 149-62.

Weippert, M., 'שַׁדַּי *Šaddaj* (Gottesname)', *THAT*, II, cols. 873-81.

Weiser, A., *Die Psalmen*, II (ATD, 15; Göttingen: Vandenhoeck & Ruprecht, 10th edn, 1987 [1963]).

—*Einleitung in das Alte Testament* (Göttingen: Vandenhoeck & Ruprecht, 5th edn, 1963).

Wellhausen, J., 'De gentibus et familiis Judaeis quae I Chr. 2.4. enumerantur' (Theological Dissertation, Göttingen, University of Göttingen, 1870).

—*Der Text der Bücher Samuelis untersucht* (Göttingen: Vandenhoeck & Ruprecht, 1871).

—*Prolegomena zur Geschichte Israels* (Berlin: W. de Gruyter, rev. edn, 1981 [3rd edn, 1886]).

—*Die Composition des Hexateuchs und der historischen Bücher des Alten Testaments* (Berlin: W. de Gruyter, 4th edn, 1963 [2nd edn, 1889]).

—*Israelitische und jüdische Geschichte* (Berlin: W. de Gruyter, 1958).

—*Grundrisse zum Alten Testament* (TBü, 27; Munich: Chr. Kaiser Verlag, 1965).

—*Die Chronik als Auslegung: Untersuchungen zur literarischen Gestaltung der historischen Überlieferung Israels* (FRLANT, 106; Göttingen: Vandenhoeck & Ruprecht, 1972).

Wenham, G.F., '*Der sogennante Jahwist* by H.H. Schmidt', *JSOT* 3 (1977), pp. 57-60.

Wernberg-Møller, P., 'An Inquiry into the Validity of the Text-critical Argument for an Early Dating of the Recently Discovered Palestinian Targum', *VT* 12 (1962), pp. 312-30.

Westermann, C., 'עֶבֶד *ʿœbœd* Knecht', *THAT*, II, cols. 182-200.

—'Zur Sammlung des Psalters', in *idem*, *Forschung am Alten Testament: Gesammelte Studien* (TBü, 24; Munich: Chr. Kaiser Verlag, 1964), pp. 336-43.

—'Die Herrlichkeit Gottes in der Priesterschrift', in *Wort–Gebot–Glaube: Beiträge zur Theologie des Alten Testaments* (Festschrift W. Eichrodt; ATANT, 59; Zürich: Zwingli-Verlag, 1971), pp. 227-49.

—*Genesis. I. Genesis 1–11* (BKAT, 1.1; Neukirchen–Vluyn: Neukirchener Verlag, 3rd edn, 1983 [1974]).

—*Forschung am Alten Testament: Gesammelte Studien*, II (TBü, 55; Munich: Chr. Kaiser Verlag, 1974).

—*Genesis*. II. *Genesis 12–36* (BKAT, 1.2; Neukirchen–Vluyn: Neukirchener Verlag, 1981).

—*Genesis*. III. *Genesis 37–50* (BKAT, 1.3; Neukirchen–Vluyn: Neukirchener Verlag, 1982).

—'Zur Frage einer biblischen Theologie', *JBTh* 1 (1986), pp. 13-30.

—*Die Klagelieder: Forschungsgeschichte und Auslegung* (Neukirchen–Vluyn: Neukirchener Verlag, 1990).

—'Sprache und Struktur der Prophetie Deuterojesaja', in *idem*, *Forschung am Alten Testament: Gesammelte Studien* (TBü, 24; Munich: Chr. Kaiser Verlag, 1964), pp. 92-170.

—*Das Buch Jesaja: Kapitel 40–66* (ATD, 19; Göttingen: Vandenhoeck & Ruprecht, 5th edn, 1986; ET *Jesaja* [Philadelphia: Westminster Press, 1969; London: SCM Press, 1969]).

—*Theologie des Alten Testaments in Grundzügen* (ATDSup, 6; Göttingen: Vandenhoeck & Ruprecht, 1978).

—*Forschungsgeschichte zur Weisheitliteratur 1950–1990* (Stuttgart, 1991).

Westermann, C. (ed.), *Probleme alttestamentliche Hermenutik* (TBü, 11; Munich: Chr. Kaiser Verlag, 1960; ET *Essays on Old Testament Interpretation* [London: SCM Press, 1963]).

Wette, W.M.L. de, *Beiträge zur Einleitung in das Alte Testament* (2 vols.; Halle: M/. Niemeyer, 1806–1807).

Wevers, J.W., *Genesis* (Septuaginta, 1; Göttingen: Vandenhoeck & Ruprecht, 1974).

Whybray, R.N., *Wisdom in Proverbs* (SBT, 45; London: SCM Press, 1965).

—*The Intellectual Tradition in the Old Testament* (BZAW, 135; Berlin: Alfred Töpelmann, 1974).

—'Response to Professor Rendtorff', *JSOT* 3 (1977), pp. 11-14.

—'Yahweh-sayings and their Contexts in Proverbs, 10.1–22.16', in Gilbert (ed.), *La Sagesse de l'Ancien Testament*, pp. 153-65.

—*The Book of Proverbs: A Survey of Modern Study* (Leiden: E.J. Brill, 1995).

Wiesmann, H., 'Das 3. Kap. der Klagelieder', *ZKT* 50 (1926), p. 147.

—'Der Verfasser des Büchleins der Klagelieder—Ein Augenzeuge der behandelten Ereignisse?', *Bib* 17 (1936).

Wildberger, H., 'Jesajas Geschichtsverständnis', in *Congress Volume: Bonn 1962* (VTSup, 9; Leiden: E.J. Brill, 1963), pp. 83-117.

—*Jesaja*. I. *Jesaja 1–12* (BKAT, 10.1: Neukirchen–Vluyn: Neukirchener Verlag, 2nd edn, 1980 [1972]).

Willi, T., *Die Chronik als Auslegung* (FRLANT, 106; Göttingen: Vandenhoeck & Ruprecht, 1972).

Williams, A.L., 'The Tetragrammaton—Jahweh, Name or Surrogate?', *ZAW* 54 (1936), pp. 262-69.

Williamson, H.G.M., ' "The Sure Mercies of David": Subjective or Objective Genitive?', *JSS* 23 (1978), pp. 31-49.

Willi-Plein, I., *Prophetie am Ende: Untersuchungen zu Sach. 9–14* (BBB, 42; Bonn: P. Hanstein, 1975).

—'Das Geheimnis der Apokalyptik', *VT* 27 (1977), pp. 62-81.

—'Spuren der Unterscheidung von mündlichem und schriftlichem Wort im Alten Testament', in G. Sellin and F. Vouga (eds.), *Logos und Buchstabe: Mündlichkeit und Schriftlichkeit im Judentum und Christentum der Antike* (Tübingen: Francke Verlag, 1996), pp. 77-89.

Wolff, H.W., 'Herrschaft Jahwes und Messiasgestalt im Alten Testament', *ZAW* 54 (1936), pp. 168-202.

—*Das Zitat im Prophetenspruch: Eine Studie zur prophetischen Verkündigungsweise* (BEvT, 4; Munich: Chr. Kaiser Verlag, 1939).

—*Jesaja 53 im Urchristentum* (Theol. Dissertation, University of Halle-Wittenberg, Bethel, 2nd edn, 1942; Berlin, 1950).

—*Immanuel: Das Zeichen, dem widersprochen wird* (Bibl. Stud., 23; Neukirchen Kreis Moers: Neukirchener Verlag, 1956).

—*Frieden ohne Ende: Eine Auslegung von Jesaja 7, 1-17 and 9, 1-6* (Bibl. Stud., 35; Neukirchen–Vluyn: Neukirchener Verlag, 1962).

—*Amos' geistige Heimat* (WMANT, 18; Neukirchen–Vluyn: Neukirchener Verlag, 1964).

—*Dodekapropheton. I. Hosea* (BKAT, 14.1; Neukirchen–Vluyn, Neukirchener Verlag, 4th edn, 1990).

—'Zur Thematik der elohistischen Fragmente im Pentateuch', *EvT* 29 (1969), pp. 59-72.

—*Dodekapropheten. II. Joel und Amos* (BKAT, 14.2: Neukirchen–Vluyn: Neukirchener Verlag, 3rd edn, 1985 [1969]).

—*Gesammelte Studien zum AT* (TBü, 22; Munich: Chr. Kaiser Verlag, rev. edn, 1973).

—'Das Kerygma des Jahwisten', in *idem*, *Gesammelte Studien zum AT*, pp. 345-73.

—'Das Kerygma des deuteronomistischen Geschichtswerks', in *idem*, *Gesammelte Studien zum AT*, pp. 308-24.

Wolff, H.W. (ed.), *Probleme biblischer Theologie* (Festschrift Gerhard von Rad; Munich: Chr. Kaiser Verlag, 1971).

Woude, A.S. van der, *Micha* (De Prediking van het OT; Nijkerk: G.F. Callenbach, 1985).

—'צור *ṣūr* Fels', *THAT*, II, cols. 538-43.

Wright, A.G., *The Literary Genre Midrash* (Staten Island, NY, 1967).

Wright, C.J.H., *The Use of the Bible in Social Ethics* (Bramcote: Grove Books, 1983).

Wright, G. Ernest, *God Who Acts: Biblical Theology as Recital* (repr.; SBT, 8; London: SCM Press, 1956 [1952]).

Würthwein, E., 'Jesaja 7,1-9. Ein Beitrag zu dem Thema: Prophetie und Politik', in *Theologie als Glaubenswagnis* (Festschrift K. Heim; Hamburg: Furche Verlag, 1954), pp. 47-63; repr. in *idem*, *Wort und Existenz*, pp. 127-43.

—'Zum Verständnis des Hohenliedes', *TRev* 32 (1967), pp. 177-212.

—'Ruth, Das Hohelied, Esther', in *Die fünf Megilloth* (HAT, 1.18; Tübingen: J.C.B. Mohr, 1969).

—*Wort und Existenz: Studien zum Alten Testament* (Göttingen: Vandenhoeck & Ruprecht, 1970).

Wyatt, N., 'The Problem of the "God of the Fathers" ', *ZAW* 90 (1978), pp. 101-104.

Zachariä, G.T., *Biblische Theologie, oder Untersuchung des biblischen Grundes der vornehmsten theologischen Lehren*, I–IV (Göttingen, 1771–75).

Zeitlin, S., *An Historical Study of the Canonization of the Hebrew Scriptures* (Philadelphia, 1933).

Ziegler, J., *Isaias* (Septuaginta Vetus Testamentum Graecum, 14; Göttingen: Vandenhoeck & Ruprecht, 1939).

Zimmerli, W., 'Das Wort des göttlichen Selbsterweises (Erweisort), eine prophetische
    Gattung', in *Mélanges bibliques: Rédigés en l'honneur de André Robert* (Travaux de
    l'Inst. Cath. de Paris, 4; Paris: Bloud & Gay, 1957), pp. 154-64; repr. in *idem, Gottes
    Offenbarung*, pp. 120-32.
—'παῖς θεος (A-B)', *TWNT*, V, pp. 655-76.
—'Sinaibund und Abrahambund: Ein Beitrag zum Verständnis der Priesterschrift', *EvT* 16
    (1960), pp. 268-80; repr. in *idem, Gottes Offenbarung*, pp. 205-16.
—review of *Theologie des Alten Testaments*, I–II (Munich: Chr. Kaiser Verlag, 1957–60),
    by G. von Rad, in *VT* 13 (1963), pp. 100-11.
—*Das Gesetz und die Propheten: Zum Verständnis des Alten Testaments* (Göttingen: Van-
    denhoeck & Ruprecht, 1963).
—*Gottes Offenbarung: Gesammelte Aufsätze* (TBü, 19; Munich: Chr. Kaiser Verlag,
    1969).
—'Prophetic Proclamation and Reinterpretation', in Knight (ed.), *Tradition and Theology*,
    pp. 69-100.
—' "Offenbarung" im Alten Testament', *EvT* 22 (1962), pp. 15-31.
—'Ich bin Jahwe', in *idem, Gottes Offenbarung*, pp. 11-40.
—*Grundriss der alttestamentlichen Theologie* (Theologische Wissenschaft, 3; Stuttgart:
    W. Kohlhammer, 1972).
—*Ezechiel*, I (BKAT, 13.1; Neukirchen–Vluyn: Neukirchener Verlag, 2nd edn, 1979
    [1969]).
—*Ezechiel*, II (BKAT, 13.2; Neukirchen–Vluyn: Neukirchener Verlag, 2nd edn, 1979).
—review of *Introduction to the Old Testament as Scripture* (London: SCM Press, 1979),
    by B.S. Childs, in *VT* 31 (1981), pp. 25-44.
Zobel, H.-J., 'Eichhorn, Johann Gottfried (1752–1827)', *TRE*, IX, pp. 369-71.
—*Stammesspruch und Geschichte* (BZAW, 95; Berlin: Alfred Töpelmann, 1965).
Zscharnack, L., *Lessing und Semler: Ein Beitrag zur Entstehungsgeschichte des Rational-
    ismus und der kritischen Theologie* (1905).

INDEXES

INDEX OF REFERENCES

OLD TESTAMENT

Genesis		49.23-24	65, 66	3.15	81-84,
1.1–2.4	84	49.24	59-66, 69-		89-91
1.28	154		70, 74	3.16-17	81
2.4	84	49.24 LXX	61	6.2-3	76
3.14	54	49.24-25	58-60, 62-	6.2	91
3.15	199		69, 73-76	14	105
17.2	73	49.25-26	73, 74, 76	14.13-14	106
24.29	283	49.25	60, 61, 63-	14.31	106
25.13	277		66, 72, 74,	15	112
28.3	73		76	15.2	88
28.11	71	49.26	60, 65, 66	15.14-16	112
28.17-19	71			20–23	150
28.18-19	73	Exodus		20	181
32.30	91	1–15	347	20.1	170
35.11-15	73	1–14	80	20.2-17	170
35.11	73	3	77, 79, 81,	20.22–23.19	170
35.14-15	72		84, 91	20.22-26	170
43.14	73	3.1	81	21.1	170
46.3	71	3.2-4	81	21.2-11	173
48.3	73	3.4	81	22.20	173
48.15	68, 70, 71,	3.5	81	22.21-22	173
	75	3.6	81, 91	23	157-58
49	66-68, 75-	3.7-8	80, 81, 91	23.4-5	173
	76	3.9-15	81, 91	23.6	170
49.3-27	59, 65, 66	3.9-12	80, 81	23.14-17	156, 157
49.5-7	67	3.9-10	91	23.14	157
49.7	67	3.10	81	23.15	157
49.8-12	66	3.11	81, 91	23.16	157
49.13-17	67	3.12	81, 84, 91	23.17	157
49.13	68	3.13-15	78, 80-82,	23.22	157
49.18	67, 68		84, 90	23.31	128
49.22-26	60, 66	3.13	81-83, 91	25–40	148
49.22-24	66	3.14-15	82, 83	32–34	148
49.22-23	62	3.14	78, 81-86,	34	150, 157
49.22	62, 66		89-91	34.6	92

Exodus (cont.)				*Numbers*	
34.14	92	11.42-43	49	1–10	148
34.18	156	11.42	54	11.19-20	97
34.19-21	157	12.8	53	15–19	148
34.22-23	156	13	55	15.39	304
		13.3-4	55	25–36	148
		13.20	55	28–29	157, 158
Leviticus		13.25	55	34	127
1–7	84	13.28	53	34.3-12	127
1.3	53	13.30-32	55	34.3	128
1.5	49	13.34	55		
1.11–4.35	53	14.27	49	*Deuteronomy*	
2.4	49	14.40	54	1.21	111
2.15	53	16.2	49, 55	4.28	72
4.3	219	16.11	55	5	181
4.5	219	16.19	49	5.7-21	170
4.6	53	16.21	55	8.12-14	297
4.7	55	16.27	49, 55	8.17-18	297
4.8	53	16.31	53	9.4-5	297
4.16	219	17–26	171	10.18-19	173
4.22	53	17.4	49	10.19	173
4.25	49, 54	17.6	53	12–26	171
5.5	49	17.10-12	50	16	157-58
5.9	53	17.14	53	16.1-17	156
5.11	53	18.30	53	16.16-17	158
6.8	53	19.1	179	16.22	72
6.10	53	19.3-4	181	17.14-20	222
6.15	219	19.11-13	181	28	135
7.34	53	19.18	172	31.7-8	112
7.35	84	20.21	47	31.8	111
7.36	84	23	157-58	33	66-68, 76
7.37	84	23.4-44	156	33.2-5	67
7.38	53, 84	23.19	55	33.2	67
8–9	84	24.4	49	33.7	67
8.15	49	24.9	53	33.8-11	67
9.7	49, 53	24.18	54	33.13-17	67
10.8	55	25.10	53	33.13-16	76
10.10	53	25.11	53	33.13	59, 67, 77
10.12	55	25.12	53	33.21	67
11.2	53	25.14-15	49	33.23	67
11.4-5	49	25.18-19	49	33.26-29	67
11.6	49	25.18	55	33.26-27	67
11.15	49, 53	26.1	72	33.29	67
11.21	54	26.4-22	55	34.1	152
11.25	54	26.13	49, 55	34.7-9	152
11.27	54	26.16	55		
11.28	54	26.20	55	*Joshua*	
11.39	53	27.33	49	1.2-9	111
11.40	54				

1.9	111, 112	24.21	100	10.14-29	278
1.29	112	25.30	221	11.1-8	282
8.1	111	26	222	11.9-13	282
10.25	111	26.9	222	12.25-33	69
15.2-4	127	26.11	222	13.21	97
		26.16	222	19.15	219
		26.23	222	19.16	219
Judges				21.29	97
6.34	221				
7.3	112	*2 Samuel*		*2 Kings*	
8.15	109	1.14	222	1.8	113
9.8-15	219	1.16	222	9.3	219
13.17	91	1.21	219	9.6	219
19.30	111	2.4	219	9.12	219
21.22	283	2.7	219	11.12	219
		3.31	279	15.37	95
Ruth		5.2	221	23.30	219
4.1	170	5.3	219	25	141
		5.17	219	25.1-21	140
1 Samuel		6.21	221	25.1-7	140, 141
2.10	111	7	100, 103,	25.7	141
7.15-17	171		125, 142,	25.27-30	141
8–12	220		222, 223		
8.10-18	222	7.1-17	222	*1 Chronicles*	
9.16	219, 221	7.8-16	267	1.1-9	149
10.1	219, 221	7.8	221, 222	1.10–2.36	149
10.6	221	7.12	100	2	149
10.10	221	7.13-16	223	4	149
11.15 LXX	219	7.13	100	11.3	219
12.3	222	7.14	103-105,	16.22	219
12.5	222		142, 223	17.13	104
12.12-15	222	7.16	101, 105	19.22	219
13	100	12.7	219	22	104
13.13	100	19.22	222	22.10	104
13.14	100, 221	22.40	113	22.11-13	104
13.16	100	22.51	222	22.13	111
15.17	219	23.1-7	306	28.4-10	104
16.3	219	23.1	219, 222,	28.5	225
16.6	222		223	28.6	104
16.12	219	23.2	223	28.10	104
16.13-14	221	23.5	103	28.20	111
16.13	219	23.27	223	29.23	225
16.14–					
2 Sam. 5	222	*1 Kings*		*2 Chronicles*	
17.11	111, 112	1.34	219	6.42	219, 230
19.13	279	1.39	219	9.8	225
24	222	1.45	219	20.15-17	111
24.7	222	5.15	219	20.15	111
24.11	222	9.26	128		

2 Chronicles (cont.)

20.17	111
22.7	219
23.11	219
28.5	95
32.7	111
35.25	132

Ezra

6.3	73

Job

12.7-10	176, 195
21.19	109
30.18	113
38.3	113
40.7	113

Psalms

1-2	306
1	84, 178, 306
2	101, 114, 120, 123, 202, 224
2.2	225
2.8-10	225
7	303
8	176
15	172, 181
15.1	172
18	123, 303
18.33	113
18.40	113
18.44-45	123
19	176, 178
23.1	70
24.2	124
24.3-6	172
30.12	113
34	303
45	224
46	114
46.5	124
48	114
50	68
51	303
54	303
56	303
57	303
59	303
60	303
67.7	113
67.14	63
68.5	67
68.6	173
68.15	63
72	124, 202, 224
72.8-11	225
72.8	122-24, 126-28
76	114
78	185
80	68
80.2	70
80.9	127
80.10	128
80.12	127, 128
86.2	261
89	128, 142, 185, 223, 224, 267
89.4-5	223
89.19-38	142
89.20	125
89.21	219, 220
89.26	122, 124, 125, 127, 128, 225
89.27-30	224
89.28	224
89.31-34	104
89.31-33	142
89.31-32	104
89.31	104
89.33	104
89.34	142
89.35	223
89.39-52	104, 223
89.39-46	142
89.39	125
89.50-52	224
89.51-52	142
90.1	63
91.1	63
93.1	113
93.3	124
104	176
105	185
105.15	219
106	185
110	123, 202, 224
110.1-2	225
110.1	225
110.6	225
116.16	261
117	216
123.2-3	261
132	185, 223
132.1-5	224
132.2	62, 69
132.5	62, 69
132.10-17	223
132.10	223, 224
132.12	103
135	185
135.13	83
138.6	109
146.9	173

Proverbs

1-24	257, 258
1-9	84, 251-53, 255, 256, 296-98
1.1	251, 252, 303
1.3	177
1.7	178
1.8	178
1.20-33	178
2-4	256
6.23	178
8.22-31	178
8.26	256
9	257
9.10	178
9.12	257
9.18	257
10-31	178
10-29	252, 253
10-22.16	178, 251, 253-55

10–15	251, 255, 297	19.21	99	29.12	258
10	255, 296, 297	19.27	256	29.14	258
		20.2	256	29.15	258
10.1–22.16	296	20.16	256	29.17	258
10.1-10	297	20.18	256	29.19	258
10.1-8	254	20.22	256	29.20	258
10.1	251, 252, 254, 276, 296, 297, 303	21	255	29.21	258
		21.1-4	255	29.22	258
		21.1	256	30–31	251
		21.27-31	255	30.1-14	257
		22	255	30.1-6	251
10.2-7	178, 253, 296	22.2	255	30.1	251
		22.6	255, 256	30.5-6	252
10.2-3	178, 254, 297	22.9	255	30.7-33	251
		22.10	256	30.15-33	257
10.3	254	22.11-12	255	31.1-9	251, 257
10.4-5	178, 253, 254, 297	22.14	255	31.1	251
		22.17–24.22	251, 256	31.10-31	
10.6-7	178, 253, 254, 297	22.17–23.11	251	LXX	257
		22.17	251, 298	31.10-31	251
10.8-10	296, 297	22.24	110		
10.8-9	178	23.1	256	*Ecclesiastes*	
10.8	253, 254, 296	23.17	256	1	303
		23.29-35	256	1.1	276, 303
10.9	109	24.3-5	256	11.9	304
10.11-14	254	24.7-9	256	12	305
10.18-21	254	24.16	256	12.12-14	304, 306
10.22	254, 297	24.21	256	12.13-14	306
10.27-32	254	24.22	257	12.13	304
11	255	24.23-34	251	12.14	304
11.3-11	254	24.23	251		
11.30-31	254	24.34	257	*Song of Songs*	
12.24	254	25–31	257, 258	1	303, 304
13.4	254	25–29	251, 257	1.1	274, 275, 277, 280, 281, 304
13.14	178	25–27	257		
14	255	25.1	251, 252, 276, 303	1.2	275
14.7	256			1.4	274, 280, 281, 304
15.1-4	254	28–29	257		
16–22.16	251, 255	28.4	178	1.5	274, 277, 280, 281
16	255	28.7	178		
16.1–22.16	297	28.9	178	1.6	278
16.1-9	255	29	258	1.12	274, 276, 280-82, 304
16.3	256	29.1	258		
16.9-17	256	29.2	258	1.13-14	282
16.33	255	29.3	258	1.16	276
19.12	256	29.4	258	2.6-7	282
19.18	256	29.7	258	2.6	283
19.20	256	29.9	258		

Song of Songs (cont.)

2.7	282, 283
2.8-14	283
2.15	282, 283
2.16-17	283
3.4	283
3.5	282, 283
3.6-11	278, 279, 303
3.6-8	281, 304
3.7-11	281
3.7	274, 278, 304
3.9-10	280, 281, 304
3.9	274, 278
3.11	274, 278, 281, 304
4.4	274
4.8-11	279
4.8	282
4.12	279
5.1	279
5.9	282
5.12	275
5.16	282
6.1	282
7.6	280
7.6[5]	274, 280
7.11	282
7.14	282
8.3	283
8.4	282, 283
8.6-8	279
8.6	278, 279, 283
8.7-8	278, 279
8.7	278-80
8.8-10	279
8.8-9	283
8.9-11	278
8.9-10	279, 280
8.9	279, 280
8.10-11	279
8.10	279
8.11-12	274, 277, 278, 281
8.11	275, 278-80
8.12	277, 278

Isaiah

1–39	345
1–12	118
1.24	62, 69
3.16	97
5.8-24	172
5.19	114
5.20	172
6	96
6.1–9.6	93, 228
6.1-5	228
7	105, 208
7.1-17	98, 226
7.1-2	118
7.1	95, 96, 103, 114, 118, 119
7.3-9	93, 96, 98
7.3-6	96-98, 107, 114, 227
7.4-9	114
7.4-6	98
7.4-5	97
7.4	95, 97, 104, 107, 118
7.5-7	95, 97
7.5	93-95, 97-99, 102, 114
7.6–7.9	227
7.6	93, 96
7.7-9	94, 97-99, 106, 107
7.7	94-96, 99, 101, 102
7.8-9	102
7.8	95, 102, 103
7.9	102, 103, 106, 107
7.10–14.15-17	227
7.10-16	226
7.10-14	228
7.10	98
7.11	100
7.14	199, 226
8.2	227
8.6-7	97
8.8	119
8.9-10	108-10, 115-19
8.9	108-10, 116, 117, 119-21
8.10	99, 113, 114, 116, 117, 119
8.14	71
8.16-18	228, 295
8.18	119
9.1-6	208, 228
9.5-6	228
10.1-14	172
10.3	121
10.33-34	228
11.1-5	228
11.1	229
11.2	228
11.7	110
13–23	173
14.4-21	118
14.24-27	101
14.24	99, 101
17.13	121
21.11–23.4	229
22.11	105
24–27	246
28.16	105
28.29	114
29.9-10	115
29.21	170
30.1	114
30.2	114
30.15	105
30.26	298
30.27	121
37.19	72
37.22-29	118
37.47	118
38.11	89
40.8	99
40.12-31	247
41.8-13	262
41.8-10	261, 262
41.9	262

41.21-29	246	51.1	265	46.9-10	117
41.22	217, 246	51.9-10	247	46.9	117
42–53	174	52.11-12	265	51.13	217
42.1-4	260-62	52.13–53.12	260, 265	51.29-30	99
42.1	262, 264,	52.13-15	263	51.29	99, 101
	266	52.13	266	52.4-11	141
42.4	174	53.11-12	174	52.11	141
42.5-9	262-64	53.11	174		
42.5	247, 262	54.1	265	*Lamentations*	
42.6-7	262, 263	54.5	247	1–4	132
42.6	262, 263	55.1-5	267	1–2	132, 135
42.8-9	262	55.3-5	267	1	140
42.8	262	55.3	267	1.7	132
42.9	246, 262	55.10-11	247	1.21	132
43.1	247	60.16	62, 69	2–4	142
43.9-10	247			2–3	140, 142
43.10	266	*Jeremiah*		2	140
43.18-19	246	1.1-3	294, 303	2.4	139
44.1-2	261	1.1	294	2.6	141
44.21	261	1.2	294	2.9	141
44.24	247	1.4	294	2.19	132
44.26	261	1.17-19	112	3–4	140, 142
45.1	113, 230	2.27	72	3	132-42
45.4	261	3.9	72	3.1	131, 136-
45.5	113	6.4	117		38, 140-42
45.11-25	247	9.9	132	3.2	141
46.10	99, 101,	11.18-23	136	3.5-6	141
	217, 246	12.1-5	136	3.7-9	141
46.11	101	15.10-12	136	3.7	141
48.12-15	247	18.18	176	3.10-15	141
48.17-19	263	20.7-18	136	3.14-15	142
48.20-21	263	22–23.8	142	3.14	138, 139
48.20	261	23.2–23.4	229	3.15-16	141
49	264	23.5-6	142, 226,	3.17-18	142
49.1-6	260, 263,		229	3.21-29	139
	264	23.9-32	294	3.27	139
49.3	264	25.11-12	240	3.31-33	142
49.6	174, 264	29.10	240	3.40-47	138
49.7-8	264	29.11	217, 246	3.52-54	141
49.7	263	31.17	217, 246	3.59-61	142
49.8-12	263	34	229	4–5	135
49.8	263, 264	34.23	229	4	132, 140
49.26	62, 69	36	295	4.20	141, 142,
50.1-3	263	36.32	296		219
50.4-9	260, 263	44.28-29	99, 101	5	132, 133
50.10-11	263	44.28	99	5.1-21	133
50.10	263	46–51	173	5.2-18	133
50.11	263	46.3-6	117		

Ezekiel		9.25-26	219, 240	*Nahum*	
2.5	112	9.26	217	1.2-10	101
3.9	112	10.14	218, 244	1.6	100, 101
7	216, 244,	11	240		
	245	11.27	218	*Habakkuk*	
17.22-24	229	11.35-40	244	2.1-5	217
19.7	109	11.35	218	3.3	67
20.32	72	11.40	218	3.13	219
21	217	12.4-9	244		
25–32	173	12.4	218	*Zephaniah*	
30	217	12.7	240	2.4-15	173
33.5	217	12.9	218		
34	217	12.13	218, 244	*Haggai*	
34.23	230			2.20-23	230
37.15-28	229	*Hosea*			
38–39	246	1.9	92	*Zechariah*	
45	158	10.3	114	1.7	217
45.18-25	156	10.4	114	1.8-17	247
47	124, 127	12.4-5	298	1.11	247
47.1	124	14.10	306	1.17	246
47.15-20	127			2.14	230
47.18	128	*Joel*		2.16	246
48.1-2	127	2.20	128	3.8	230
		4.9	117	4.6-10	230
Daniel		4.18	124	6.11-13	230
1.3-5	237			7.9-10	172
2	240	*Amos*		9–14	44, 230
2.19	247	1.3–2.3-16	173	9.1-8	173
2.28	218, 244	1.3–2.3	173	9.9	70, 230
2.48	237	2.1-3	174	9.10	122, 126-28
7	231, 240,	3.1-2	216	12–14	217, 246
	269	3.1	174		
7.2-14	268, 269	4.1-3	216	*Tobit*	
7.9-10	268	5.1	132	13–14	236
7.12	268	5.18-20	216, 245		
7.13-14	267, 268	7.2	100, 101	*Wisdom of Solomon*	
7.14	268	8.2	215, 217,	1–9	257
7.15-28	268		227, 244,	1.2-7	257
7.15-16	268		246	1.7	257
7.17-27	268, 269	8.10	132	1.8-19	257
7.18	268	8.12	129	1.20-33	257
7.21	268, 269	9.7	174	4.1	178
7.22	268, 269	9.9	174	8.1-36	257
7.25	268, 269			9.1-6	257
7.27	268, 269	*Micah*		9.7-12	257
8–12	244	5.1-5	229	9.10	257
8.17	217, 244	6.6-8	172	9.13-18	257
9.24	240				

Ecclesiasticus
24   178

New Testament
Matthew
5.44   181

Luke
2.4   231

1 Corinthians
3.15   103

2 Corinthians
9–13   313

Galatians
4.4   231

Hebrews
3.3-6   311

Pseudepigrapha
1 Enoch
37–71   237

Psalms of Solomon
17   236

Ass. Mos.
12.4-5   237

Targums
Targ. Isa.
52.13–53.12 266

Mishnah
B. Bat.
14b-15a   131

Josephus
Apion
1.38   305

INDEX OF AUTHORS

Abba, R. 78
Abel, F.M. 123
Abrahams, I. 270
Ackroyd, P.R. 298
Aharoni, Y. 123
Ahlström, G.W. 124, 125
Albertz, R. 15, 69
Albrektson, B. 45, 78, 90, 134, 135, 139, 140, 194, 195
Albright, W.F. 40, 58, 78
Alfrink, B. 78, 89
Alt, A. 69, 72, 78, 100, 106, 127, 129, 170, 171, 223, 224
Alter, R. 23, 274
Althaus, P. 184
Ammon, C.F. von 323
Andersen, K.T. 72
Anderson, G.W. 11, 24, 159, 204, 288, 303, 328, 331
Ap-Thomas, D.R. 337
Aptowitzer, V. 39
Arnold, W.R. 78, 83
Audet, J.-P. 274, 276
Auld, A.G. 14

Bach, R. 116-18, 120
Ball, E. 328
Barr, J. 184, 186, 194, 233, 286, 289
Barstad, H.M. 286
Barth, H. 227, 291
Barthélemy, D. 272, 276, 306
Barton, J. 22, 23, 165, 167, 288
Bauer, H. 120
Bauer-Kayatz, C. 257
Baumgarten, W. 98, 233
Beck, J.T. 186
Becker, J. 213, 226

Beckwith, R. 288
Begrich, J. 133, 259, 263, 268
Beidelman, T.O. 328, 331, 335
Beinton, R.H. 186
Bendix, R. 170
Bentzen, A. 38, 93, 98, 109, 110, 114, 123, 230, 269, 273, 341
Bergson, H. 168
Bernhardt, K.-H. 224
Bertam, G. 120
Betz, H.D. 234
Beuken, W.A.M. 230, 231
Bewer, J.A. 93, 265
Beyerlin, W. 221
Birch, B.C. 286
Birkeland, H. 29, 88, 337, 346, 348
Birnbaum, S.A. 47
Black, J.S. 328, 331, 334
Blau, J. 65
Blenkinsopp, J. 178, 179, 286
Bloch, R. 298
Bloom, H. 23
Blum, E. 13
Boecker, H.J. 220
Boer, P.A.H. de 113
Böhl, F.M.T.L. de 75
Bonsirven, J. 270
Bowman, R.A. 78
Brandscheidt, R. 131, 133, 135, 137-39
Brett, M.G. 22, 286
Brockelmann, C. 71, 102
Broek, S.P. 110
Bruegemann, W. 154
Buber, M. 217, 226
Budde, K. 93-95, 110, 115, 119
Buhl, F. 109, 126

Burrows, E. 72
Burrows, M. 39, 110

Cassuto, U. 145
Cazelles, H. 197, 286
Childs, B.S. 21, 22, 33, 81, 133-35,
     137, 171, 252, 273-75, 282, 285-
     92, 295-98, 300-303, 305, 307
Christie, W.M. 272
Chrystal, G. 328, 331, 334
Clements, R.E. 146, 159, 165, 220, 306
Clines, D.J.A. 12, 23
Coates, G.W. 303
Coats, G.E. 146
Cobb, J.B. 184
Cohon, S.S. 78
Collins, J.J. 233, 268
Conrad, J. 255
Cooper, A. 67, 71
Coppens, J. 59, 69
Cortese, E. 160
Crenshaw, J.L. 28, 165, 250
Cross, F.M. 38-45, 58, 59, 72, 73, 75,
     78, 306
Crüsemann, F. 145, 167, 169-72, 178,
     180, 220, 222, 223, 262
Culley, R.C. 23

Dahood, M. 60, 71, 128
Davidson, A.B. 333
Davis, M.C. 48, 50-54
Day, J. 175
Deaut, R. le 47, 299
Delekat, L. 78, 85-89
Delitzsch, F. 93, 198, 199
Delkurt, H. 164, 177
Dhorme, E. 94
Diestel, L. 22, 314
Dietrich, M. 49, 120, 227
Dietrich, W. 118
Dillmann, A. 93
Dirksen, P.B. 63, 330
Dohmeier, H.-J. 310, 315, 321, 322
Driver, G.R. 78, 267
Driver, S.R. 266
Dubarle, A.-M. 78, 90
Duhm, B. 93, 109, 111, 114, 115, 121,
     260, 264

Dumermuth, F. 69
Durkheim, E. 335

Ebeling, G. 316
Eerdmans, B.D. 78
Eichorn, J.G. 313
Eichrodt, W. 108, 109, 118, 163, 165,
     166, 190, 315, 322
Eissfeldt, O. 73, 118, 144, 147, 152,
     161, 187, 188, 206, 260, 268,
     292, 329
Eitz, A. 263
Eldredge, L. 310, 314, 315, 317-21
Elliger, K. 53, 54, 78, 83, 152-54, 262,
     263
Ellis, E.E. 288
Emerton, J.A. 58
Engnell, I. 29-31, 96, 109, 159, 208,
     209, 347
Ernesti, J.A. 313, 316
Ernst, A.B. 177
Exum, J.C. 23, 274

Fabry, H.-J. 71
Feldmann, F. 93, 109
Fichtner, J. 113
Fischer, J. 94
Fishbane, M. 31, 32, 299-301
Fisher, L.R. 122
Fohrer, G. 31, 80, 86, 108, 109, 114,
     115, 195, 200, 206, 210, 214, 287
Fox, M.V. 15, 273, 278, 279, 281-83
Fraine, J. de 337
Frazer, J. 335
Freedman, D.N. 47, 58, 59, 71, 75, 78,
     84, 88
Frei, H.W. 23
Fritz, V. 221
Frye, N. 23
Fuller, R.C. 330

Gabel, J.B. 23
Gabler, J.P. 166, 187, 190, 200, 310,
     311, 314-26
Gadamer, H.-G. 24, 25
Gamberoni, J. 71
Gardiner, P. 186
Geiger, A. 39, 46

Geiger, L. 39
Gerleman, G. 273, 275, 277, 281, 282
Gese, H. 174, 176, 194, 222, 233, 246, 265, 306
Geus, C.H.J. de 59
Gilbert, M. 256
Ginsberg, H.L. 277
Ginsburg, C.D. 42, 46, 64, 271
Gloege, G. 33
Goedick, H. 76
Goitein, S.D. 48, 51, 52
Golka, F.W. 15
Gordis, R. 137, 273, 274, 277, 278, 298
Gordon, R.P. 175
Görg, M. 280
Goshen-Gottstein, M.H. 42, 50, 265
Gottwald, N.K. 134
Gowan, D.E. 97
Graf, K.H. 148
Graussner, A. 164
Gray, G.B. 93, 108, 156
Gray, J. 78, 123, 124
Greenberg, M. 39, 43
Gressman, H. 198
Gressmann, H. 93, 126, 144, 199-205, 207-11, 214
Griesbach, J.J. 313
Gronbaek, J.H. 216, 222
Gronbech, V. 339, 340
Gunkel, H. 25-26, 28, 30, 68, 75, 133, 144, 203, 204, 211, 241, 259, 289, 338, 339, 342
Gunneweg, A.H.J. 28-30, 59

Haag, E. 77
Haag, H. 259, 265, 267
Hammershaimb, E. 237
Hanson, P.D. 233, 246
Haran, M. 73, 145, 159, 160, 272, 306
Harrison, R.K. 37
Hartlich, C. 313, 323
Hartman, L.F. 239
Harvey, V.A. 186
Hasel, G.F. 192, 221
Hatch, E. 61, 62, 215
Hausmann, J. 214, 216
Hayes, J.H. 166, 185

Heck, J.D. 59
Heinisch, P. 198, 199
Hempel, J. 102, 120, 159, 163, 165
Hengel, M. 233
Hermisson, H.-J. 250, 256
Herntrich, V. 94
Herrmann, S. 78, 224, 294
Hertzberg, H.W. 100, 101, 103, 113, 304
Hesse, F. 192, 218
Heussi, K. 325
Heyne, C.G. 313, 322
Hidal, S. 13
Hillers, D.R. 134, 137, 140
Hoffmann, D. 145
Hoftijzer, J. 69
Holm-Nielsen, S. 111, 304
Hölscher, G. 203, 207, 238, 292, 340, 341, 343
Holzinger, 82
Hooke, S.H. 208
Hopkins, S. 48
Hornig, G. 313
Horst, F. 101
House, P.R. 23
Humbert, P. 120
Hyatt, J.P. 79

Illman, K.-J. 145

Jacob, B. 145
Jacob, E. 184
Jahnow, H. 132
Jamieson-Drake, D.W. 51
Janssen, E. 243
Janzen, J.G. 79
Japhet, S. 270
Jenni, E. 72, 93, 215, 230
Jeppesen, K. 14
Jepsen, A. 272, 276
Jeremias, J. 13, 185, 224, 266, 267
Jirku, A. 124
Johnson, A.R. 124
Johnson, B. 13, 134
Johnstone, W. 15, 23, 149, 330
Jones, G.H. 222
Jowett, B. 21
Junker, H. 227

Junod, E. 276

Kaestli, J.-D. 272, 276, 287, 306
Kahle, P. 38-41, 46, 48
Kaiser, O. 108, 109, 114, 115, 119,
    120, 134-38, 140, 227, 228, 260,
    294, 303, 313, 316
Kallai, Z. 127
Kannengiesser, C. 22
Kant, I. 324
Kapelrud, A.S. 69-71, 129, 173, 337
Katz, P. 272, 276
Kaufmann, Y. 145
Kayatz, C. 256
Keel, O. 273, 275
Kegler, J. 15
Kennicott, B. 37, 38, 64, 265
Kermode, F. 23, 274
Kilian, R. 154, 227
Kinyongo, J. 79, 86
Kissane, E.J. 93, 109
Kittel, H.-J. 47, 59, 226, 286
Klatt, W. 25
Klausner, J. 210
Knight, D.A. 11, 24, 25, 27-33, 182,
    185, 245, 286, 290, 299
Knowles, M.P. 71
Koch, K. 25, 58, 69, 73, 75, 158, 177,
    184, 233, 234
Köckert, M. 58, 69
Koenig, J. 94
Köhler, L. 87
Köhler, W. 212
König, E. 89, 94, 109, 198-201
Kooij, A. van der 330
Köpf, U. 271
Koster, M.D. 63
Kraus, H.-J. 25, 103, 104, 107, 113,
    122, 123, 128, 129, 133, 136,
    144, 146, 156, 171, 187, 224,
    225, 324, 327, 329, 330, 334
Krauss, S. 51, 52
Kreuzer, S. 169
Krinetzki, G. 277
Kuenen, A. 332
Kuhl, C. 271
Kuhn, K.G. 79
Kuhn, T.S. 26, 86, 88

Kümmel, W.G. 314, 316
Kutsch, E. 218, 219, 222
Kvale, D. 336
Kvanvig, H.S. 233, 269

Laato, A. 227
Lacoque, A. 273
Lagarde, P. de 37, 38, 41
Lambert, G. 79
Lambert, W.G. 76
Lanahan, W.F. 133
Landes, G.M. 286
Landy, F. 274
Lang, B. 256
Lauha, A. 304
Laurin, R.B. 289
Leander, P. 120
Lebram, J.C.H. 233, 239, 240, 272,
    288, 305, 306
Leder, K. 310, 311, 315, 316, 319,
    321, 322, 324-26
Leiman, S.Z. 272, 287, 289
Lella, A.A. Di 239
Lemaire, A. 13, 51, 256
Lerch, D. 271
Levey, S.H. 267
Lewis, J.P. 272, 288
Liedke, G. 170
Lindblom, J. 93, 98, 119, 212, 213,
    215, 337, 343
Lindhagen, C. 261
Lisowsky, G. 113
Lohfink, N. 77, 154, 265
Löhr, M. 136
Long, B.O. 303
Luck, U. 233
Luther, M. 99
Lutz, H.-M. 246

Maag, V. 60, 70
MacIntyre, J. 186
MacLaurin, E.C.B. 79
Macho, A.D. 47, 48, 55, 62
Macholz, C. 13
Mandelkern, S. 110
Marron, H.-I. 186
Marti, K. 93, 120
Martínez, F.G. 233

Mathys, H.-P. 172
Matthews, K.A. 47
Mauss, M. 335
Mayer, R. 79, 80, 84, 86, 90, 91
Mays, J.L. 245, 286
McCarthy, D.J. 79, 82, 84
McConnell, F. 23
McEvenue, E. 154
McKane, W. 146, 175, 252, 296, 298, 330
McKinney, R.W.A. 306
McLennan, J.F. 335
Meissner, B. 125, 129
Melugin, R.F. 262
Merk, O. 310, 311, 313-26
Messel, N. 99, 109, 345
Mettinger, T.N.D. 13, 218, 221, 223, 260-62
Metzger, B.M. 313
Meyer, R. 89
Michel, D. 206, 259
Millard, A.R. 79
Miller, J.M. 185
Miskotte, K.H. 184
Mogstad, S.D. 14
Moor, J.C. de 58, 72
Mowinckel, S. 26, 29-31, 79, 99, 109, 126, 145, 152, 153, 188, 189, 192, 193, 198, 201, 203-11, 215, 216, 225, 226, 241, 245, 259, 266, 267, 268, 294, 295, 300, 336, 337-48
Mühlenberg, E. 193
Mulder, M.J. 63
Müller, D. 70
Müller, H.-P. 65, 232, 242, 275, 277-79, 281, 282
Müller-Lauter, W. 187
Murphy, R.H. 271, 275, 277, 279, 280, 283, 286
Murtonen, A. 79

Netto, E.F.C.A.H. 325
Neubauer, A. 266, 267
Neusner, J. 210
Newman, R.C. 288
Nielsen, E. 25
Nielsen, K. 14, 23, 228, 295

Nissen, A. 234
Noble, P.R. 22
Nöldeke, T. 151
Norin, S. 13, 79
North, C.R. 186, 233, 234, 246, 259, 267
Norton, D. 23
Noth, M. 27, 28, 81, 84, 112, 144, 146, 151-53, 171, 222, 270, 293, 294, 346
Nyberg, H.S. 29, 60, 102, 120, 267, 346

O'Connor, P. 84, 88
Obermann, J. 79
Ohly, F. 271
Olofsson, S. 61, 70-73
Orlinsky, H.M. 42
Osswald, E. 184
Osten-Sacken, P. von der 233, 238, 239, 244, 247
Ostnor, L. 14
Otto, E. 58, 73, 146, 164, 165, 167, 169, 170, 172, 173, 175, 178, 180
Otzen, B. 13, 232, 246
Oyen, H. van 164, 179

Pannenberg, W. 184, 192, 193
Parke-Taylor, G.H. 79
Patte, D. 299
Peake, A.S. 270
Pedersen, J. 159, 347
Perlitt, J. 13, 144, 145, 147
Pettinato, G. 84
Pfeiffer, R.H. 183, 185, 188
Pietersma, A. 299
Ploeg, J.P.M. van der 47
Plöger, O. 51, 133, 136, 233, 235, 239, 242, 246, 252, 270, 296, 297
Polk, D.P. 286
Pope, M.H. 67, 71, 271-73, 276, 277, 279-81
Porteous, N.W. 140, 239
Preuss, H.D. 165, 211-16, 227
Procksch, O. 93, 105, 109, 114, 120, 121, 226
Prussner, F.C. 166

Rad, G. von 11, 27, 28, 31-33, 81, 90,
    92, 94, 98-100, 103-107, 112,
    114, 119, 120, 144-46, 155, 166,
    175-78, 183, 184, 189-91, 193,
    194, 216, 221, 222, 224, 225,
    232-44, 246, 247, 250, 252, 253,
    266, 268, 269, 285, 293, 294, 296
Rahlf, A. 95
Rast, W.E. 25
Redpath, H.A. 61, 62, 215
Rehm, M. 227
Reif, S.C. 48, 49
Rendtorff, R. 47, 146, 152, 158, 159,
    174, 184, 189, 192, 193, 234,
    247, 337
Reuss, E. 148
Reventlow, H.G. 93, 119, 121, 285,
    287, 288, 329, 330
Rian, D. 336
Richter, W. 81, 221
Riesen, R.A. 327, 328, 332
Riesener, R. 261, 331
Rignell, L.G. 95, 98, 99, 102, 103, 109,
    120
Ringgren, H. 25, 30, 31, 72, 224
Robert, P. de 70
Roberts, J.J.M. 76, 300
Robinson, H.W. 137, 182, 183, 260
Robinson, J.M. 184
Robinson, T.H. 101
Rogerson, J.W. 260, 328, 330, 332,
    334
Rohland, E. 104, 119, 216, 228-30,
    268
Rose, M. 79
Rosendal, B. 14, 85, 89
Rosenmüller, E.F.K. 37
Rossi, J.B. de 37, 64
Rössler, D. 234
Rost, L. 102
Rowley, H.H. 24, 246, 271, 273
Rudolph, W. 128, 133, 136, 140, 145,
    216, 229, 245, 273, 275, 277-80,
    282, 294, 295
Rundgren, F. 280
Ruprecht, E. 259
Russell, D.S. 233, 237, 269

Sachs, W. 313, 323
Sæbø, M. 29, 31, 33, 44, 50, 60, 70,
    123, 127-29, 149, 160, 184, 204,
    205, 214, 215, 217, 230, 244,
    246, 247, 278, 288, 303, 332,
    336, 337, 343
Sanders, J.A. 45, 286, 288, 289, 291-
    93, 299, 306
Sandmel, S. 298
Sandys-Wunsch, J. 310, 314, 315, 317-
    21
Schäfer, P. 288
Schechter, S. 48, 52
Schild, E. 90, 91
Schmid, H.H. 69, 146, 176, 337
Schmidt, H. 202
Schmidt, J.M. 233
Schmidt, L. 146, 219, 220
Schmidt, M. 271
Schmidt, W.H. 69, 72, 79-83, 86, 90,
    91, 120, 164, 166, 190, 195, 201,
    220, 223, 230, 269, 285
Scholem, G. 210
Schröter, W. 311
Scott, O. 253
Scott, R.B.Y. 175, 177, 178
Seebass, H. 59, 69, 72, 215, 228-30
Seeligmann, I.L. 96, 240, 259, 298,
    301, 305
Segal, M.H. 43, 79, 275
Seibert, I. 70
Seierstad, I.P. 189
Sellin, E. 203, 287
Sellin, G. 28, 204
Semler, J.S. 313, 316
Seybold, K. 218, 219, 227, 268
Sheppard, G.T. 247, 290, 299, 301,
    306
Simons, J. 122
Skehan, P.W. 42, 43, 47
Skladny, U. 251, 255, 257
Smend, R. 105, 136, 144, 155, 167,
    174, 186, 187, 198, 200, 201,
    216, 285, 286, 291, 310, 316,
    318, 319, 321, 322, 324, 325, 330
Smith, G.A. 333
Smith, M.S. 58, 69, 76
Smith, W.R. 327-31, 333-35

Soden, W. von 79, 84, 85, 87, 205
Soete, A. 162, 179
Soggin, J.A. 70, 100, 106, 123, 218,
    221
Sperber, A. 62, 267
Spriggs, D.G. 28, 285
Stamm, J.J. 227, 265
Steck, K.G. 186, 187
Steck, O.H. 242, 247
Stegemann, E.W. 13
Steitz, G.E. 311, 314
Stemberger, G. 288
Stenning, J.F. 96, 267
Sternberger, G. 198
Steuernagel, C. 37, 214
Stoebe, H.F. 123
Stolz, F. 120
Strauss, H. 198, 210, 226
Struppe, U. 212, 227, 230
Sundberg, A.C. Jr 45, 288
Swete, H.B. 276

Tallqvist, K. 75
Talmon, S. 38-45, 54, 215, 217, 220,
    221, 231, 306
Thiel, W. 169, 294, 295
Thierry, G.J. 79
Tigay, J.H. 58
Torm, F. 21
Tournay, R.J. 273
Tov, E. 43, 44, 61, 299
Tucker, G.M. 303
Tur-Sinai, N.H. 94

Uffenheimer, B. 198
Uhlig, S. 165

Van Seters, J. 69, 76, 146
Vaux, R. de 72, 79-82, 87, 91, 112
Vawter, B. 71
Veijola, T. 221-23
Vermes, G. 298, 299, 302
Vermeylen, J. 93
Vielhauer, P. 239
Vischer, W. 94
Volborth, J.C. 317
Vollmer, J. 228
Volz, P. 145

Vorländer, H. 69, 72
Vouga, F. 28
Vriezen, T.C. 79, 90, 102, 103, 163,
    166, 210, 212
Vriezens, C. 90

Wagner, M. 215
Wagner, N.E. 146
Wagner, S. 47
Walker, N. 65
Wallis, G. 70
Wambacq, B.N. 79
Wanke, G. 164
Waschke, E.-J. 218, 231
Weber, R. 64
Weidmann, H. 69
Weinfeld, M. 145, 147, 159
Weingreen, J. 298
Weippert, M. 61, 69, 73
Weiser, A. 159
Wellhausen, J. 25, 43-46, 82, 144-51,
    153, 158, 161, 164, 277, 327,
    329, 330, 338, 342, 343
Wenham, G.F. 146
Wermelinger, D. 272, 276, 287, 306
Wernberg-Moller, P. 47
Westermann, C. 59, 60, 65, 66, 68, 131,
    133, 135, 136, 138, 160, 190,
    193, 199, 250, 260-66, 268, 306
Wette, W.M.L. de 148, 149, 318, 325,
    342
Wevers, J.W. 61
Wheeler, C.B. 23
Whybray, R.N. 146, 247, 250, 255,
    256
Wiesmann, H. 134, 136
Wildberger, H. 93, 108, 110, 172, 226,
    228
Willi, T. 149, 343
Willi-Plein, I. 28, 233, 246
Williamson, H.G.M. 175, 268
Willis, J.T. 30, 165
Winckler, 277
Wolff, H.W. 80, 84, 93, 94, 96, 98, 99,
    102, 107, 114, 145, 173, 174,
    185, 206, 216, 217, 266
Woude, A.S. van der 71, 229
Wright, A.G. 299

Wright, C.J.H. 164
Wright, G.E. 188, 189, 191, 194
Würthwein, E. 94, 99, 106, 272, 273,
    277, 282
Wyatt, N. 72

York, A.D. 23

Zachariä, G.T. 317

Zeitlin, S. 272, 276
Ziegler, J. 96, 109
Zimmerli, W. 32, 90, 92, 106, 112, 160,
    173, 185, 189, 192, 217, 229,
    245, 261, 262, 286, 293
Zobel, H.-J. 59, 69, 214, 313
Zscharnack, L. 313, 316

JOURNAL FOR THE STUDY OF THE OLD TESTAMENT
SUPPLEMENT SERIES

86   Alviero Niccacci, *The Syntax of the Verb in Classical Hebrew Prose*

87   David J.A. Clines, Stephen E. Fowl & Stanley E. Porter (eds.), *The Bible in Three Dimensions: Essays in Celebration of Forty Years of Biblical Studies in the University of Sheffield*

88   Rodney K. Duke, *The Persuasive Appeal of the Chronicler: A Rhetorical Analysis*

89   Rolf Rendtorff, *The Problem of the Process of Transmission in the Pentateuch*

90   Mark F. Rooker, *Biblical Hebrew in Transition: The Language of the Book of Ezekiel*

91   Frank H. Gorman Jr, *The Ideology of Ritual: Space, Time and Status in the Priestly Theology*

92   Yehuda T. Radday & Athalya Brenner (eds.), *On Humour and the Comic in the Hebrew Bible*

93   William T. Koopmans, *Joshua 24 as Poetic Narrative*

94   David J.A. Clines, *What Does Eve Do To Help? And Other Readerly Questions to the Old Testament*

95   Rick Dale Moore, *God Saves: Lessons from the Elisha Stories*

96   Laurence A. Turner, *Announcements of Plot in Genesis*

97   Paul R. House, *The Unity of the Twelve*

98   K. Lawson Younger Jr, *Ancient Conquest Accounts: A Study in Ancient Near Eastern and Biblical History Writing*

99   R.N. Whybray, *Wealth and Poverty in the Book of Proverbs*

100   Philip R. Davies & Richard T. White (eds.), *A Tribute to Geza Vermes: Essays on Jewish and Christian Literature and History*

101   Peter R. Ackroyd, *The Chronicler in his Age*

102   Michael D. Goulder, *The Prayers of David (Psalms 51–72): Studies in the Psalter, II*

103   Bryant G. Wood, *The Sociology of Pottery in Ancient Palestine: The Ceramic Industry and the Diffusion of Ceramic Style in the Bronze and Iron Ages*

104   Paul R. Raabe, *Psalm Structures: A Study of Psalms with Refrains*

105   Pietro Bovati, *Re-Establishing Justice: Legal Terms, Concepts and Procedures in the Hebrew Bible*

106   Philip Peter Jenson, *Graded Holiness: A Key to the Priestly Conception of the World*

107   Christiana van Houten, *The Alien in Israelite Law*

108   Paula M. McNutt, *The Forging of Israel: Iron Technology, Symbolism, and Tradition in Ancient Society*

109   David W. Jamieson-Drake, *Scribes and Schools in Monarchic Judah: A Socio-Archeological Approach*

110   Niels Peter Lemche, *The Canaanites and their Land: The Tradition of the Canaanites*

111   J. Glen Taylor, *Yahweh and the Sun: The Biblical and Archaeological Evidence for Sun Worship in Ancient Israel*

112   Leo G. Perdue, *Wisdom in Revolt: Metaphorical Theology in the Book of Job*

113   Raymond Westbrook, *Property and the Family in Biblical Law*

114   Dan Cohn-Sherbok (ed.), *A Traditional Quest: Essays in Honour of Louis Jacobs*

115   Victor Hurowitz, *I Have Built You an Exalted House: Temple Building in the Bible in Light of Mesopotamian and Northwest Semitic Writings*

116   David M. Gunn (ed.), *Narrative and Novella in Samuel: Studies by Hugo Gressmann and Other Scholars, 1906–1923* (trans. David E. Orton)

117   Philip R. Davies (ed.), *Second Temple Studies. I. Persian Period*

118   Raymond Jacques Tournay, *Seeing and Hearing God with the Psalms: The Prophetic Liturgy of the Second Temple in Jerusalem*

119   David J.A. Clines & Tamara C. Eskenazi (eds.), *Telling Queen Michal's Story: An Experiment in Comparative Interpretation*

120   R.H. Lowery, *The Reforming Kings: Cult and Society in First Temple Judah*

121   Diana Vikander Edelman, *King Saul in the Historiography of Judah*

122   Loveday Alexander (ed.), *Images of Empire*

123   Elizabeth Bloch-Smith, *Judahite Burial Practices and Beliefs about the Dead*

124   Baruch Halpern & Deborah W. Hobson (eds.), *Law and Ideology in Monarchic Israel*

125   Gary A. Anderson & Saul M. Olyan (eds.), *Priesthood and Cult in Ancient Israel*

126   John W. Rogerson, *W.M.L. de Wette, Founder of Modern Biblical Criticism: An Intellectual Biography*

127   Diana Vikander Edelman (ed.), *The Fabric of History: Text, Artifact and Israel's Past*

128   Thomas P. McCreesh, OP, *Biblical Sound and Sense: Poetic Sound Patterns in Proverbs 10–29*

129   Zdravko Stefanovic, *The Aramaic of Daniel in the Light of Old Aramaic*

130   Mike Butterworth, *Structure and the Book of Zechariah*

131   Lynn Holden, *Forms of Deformity*

132   Mark Daniel Carroll R., *Contexts for Amos: Prophetic Poetics in Latin American Perspective*

133   Roger Syrén, *The Forsaken Firstborn: A Study of a Recurrent Motif in the Patriarchal Narratives*

134   Gordon Mitchell, *Together in the Land: A Reading of the Book of Joshua*

135   Gordon F. Davies, *Israel in Egypt: Reading Exodus 1–2*

136   Paul Morris & Deborah Sawyer (eds.), *A Walk in the Garden: Biblical, Iconographical and Literary Images of Eden*

137   Henning Graf Reventlow & Yair Hoffman (eds.), *Justice and Righteousness: Biblical Themes and their Influence*

138   R.P. Carroll (ed.), *Text as Pretext: Essays in Honour of Robert Davidson*

139   James W. Watts, *Psalm and Story: Inset Hymns in Hebrew Narrative*

140   Walter Houston, *Purity and Monotheism: Clean and Unclean Animals in Biblical Law*

141   Gregory C. Chirichigno, *Debt-Slavery in Israel and the Ancient Near East*

142   Frederick H. Cryer, *Divination in Ancient Israel and its Near Eastern Environment: A Socio-Historical Investigation*

143   J. Cheryl Exum & David J.A. Clines (eds.), *The New Literary Criticism and the Hebrew Bible*

144   Philip R. Davies & David J.A. Clines (eds.), *Among the Prophets: Language, Imagery and Structure in the Prophetic Writings*

145   Charles S. Shaw, *The Speeches of Micah: A Rhetorical-Historical Analysis*

146   Gösta W. Ahlström, *The History of Ancient Palestine from the Palaeolithic Period to Alexander's Conquest* (ed. D. Edelman, with a contribution by G.O. Rollefson)

147   Tony W. Cartledge, *Vows in the Hebrew Bible and the Ancient Near East*

148   Philip R. Davies, *In Search of 'Ancient Israel'*

149   Eugene Ulrich, John W. Wright, Robert P. Carroll & Philip R. Davies (eds.), *Priests, Prophets and Scribes: Essays on the Formation and Heritage of Second Temple Judaism in Honour of Joseph Blenkinsopp*

150   Janet E. Tollington, *Tradition and Innovation in Haggai and Zechariah 1–8*

151   Joel Weinberg, *The Citizen–Temple Community* (trans. Daniel L. Smith Christopher)

152   A. Graeme Auld (ed.), *Understanding Poets and Prophets: Essays in Honour of George Wishart Anderson*

153   Donald K. Berry, *The Psalms and their Readers: Interpretive Strategies for Psalm 18*

154   Marc Brettler & Michael Fishbane (eds.), *Min'ah le-Na'um: Biblical and Other Studies Presented to Nahum M. Sarna in Honour of his 70th Birthday*

155   Jeffrey A. Fager, *Land Tenure and the Biblical Jubilee: Uncovering Hebrew Ethics through the Sociology of Knowledge*

156   John W. Kleinig, *The Lord's Song: The Basis, Function and Significance of Choral Music in Chronicles*

157   Gordon R. Clark, *The Word Óesed in the Hebrew Bible*

158   Mary Douglas, *In the Wilderness: The Doctrine of Defilement in the Book of Numbers*

159   J. Clinton McCann (ed.), *The Shape and Shaping of the Psalter*

160   William Riley, *King and Cultus in Chronicles: Worship and the Reinterpretation of History*

161   George W. Coats, *The Moses Tradition*

162 Heather A. McKay & David J.A. Clines (eds.), *Of Prophets' Visions and the Wisdom of Sages: Essays in Honour of R. Norman Whybray on his Seventieth Birthday*

163 J. Cheryl Exum, *Fragmented Women: Feminist (Sub)versions of Biblical Narratives*

164 Lyle Eslinger, *House of God or House of David: The Rhetoric of 2 Samuel 7*

166 D.R.G. Beattie & M.J. McNamara (eds.), *The Aramaic Bible: Targums in their Historical Context*

167 Raymond F. Person, *Second Zechariah and the Deuteronomic School*

168 R.N. Whybray, *The Composition of the Book of Proverbs*

169 Bert Dicou, *Edom, Israel's Brother and Antagonist: The Role of Edom in Biblical Prophecy and Story*

170 Wilfred G.E. Watson, *Traditional Techniques in Classical Hebrew Verse*

171 Henning Graf Reventlow, Yair Hoffman & Benjamin Uffenheimer (eds.), *Politics and Theopolitics in the Bible and Postbiblical Literature*

172 Volkmar Fritz, *An Introduction to Biblical Archaeology*

173 M. Patrick Graham, William P. Brown & Jeffrey K. Kuan (eds.), *History and Interpretation: Essays in Honour of John H. Hayes*

174 Joe M. Sprinkle, *'The Book of the Covenant': A Literary Approach*

175 Tamara C. Eskenazi & Kent H. Richards (eds.), *Second Temple Studies. II. Temple and Community in the Persian Period*

176 Gershon Brin, *Studies in Biblical Law: From the Hebrew Bible to the Dead Sea Scrolls*

177 David Allan Dawson, *Text-Linguistics and Biblical Hebrew*

178 Martin Ravndal Hauge, *Between Sheol and Temple: Motif Structure and Function in the I-Psalms*

179 J.G. McConville & J.G. Millar, *Time and Place in Deuteronomy*

180 Richard L. Schultz, *The Search for Quotation: Verbal Parallels in the Prophets*

181 Bernard M. Levinson (ed.), *Theory and Method in Biblical and Cuneiform Law: Revision, Interpolation and Development*

182 Steven L. McKenzie & M. Patrick Graham (eds.), *The History of Israel's Traditions: The Heritage of Martin Noth*

183 John Day (ed.), *Lectures on the Religion of the Semites (Second and Third Series) by William Robertson Smith*

184 John C. Reeves & John Kampen (eds.), *Pursuing the Text: Studies in Honor of Ben Zion Wacholder on the Occasion of his Seventieth Birthday*

185 Seth Daniel Kunin, *The Logic of Incest: A Structuralist Analysis of Hebrew Mythology*

186 Linda Day, *Three Faces of a Queen: Characterization in the Books of Esther*

187 Charles V. Dorothy, *The Books of Esther: Structure, Genre and Textual Integrity*

188 Robert H. O'Connell, *Concentricity and Continuity: The Literary Structure of Isaiah*

189 William Johnstone (ed.), *William Robertson Smith: Essays in Reassessment*

190   Steven W. Holloway & Lowell K. Handy (eds.), *The Pitcher is Broken:*
       Memorial Essays for Gösta W. Ahlström
191   Magne Sæbø, *On the Way to Canon: Creative Tradition History in the Old*
       Testament
192   Henning Graf Reventlow & William Farmer (eds.), *Biblical Studies and the*
       Shifting of Paradigms, 1850–1914
193   Brooks Schramm, *The Opponents of Third Isaiah: Reconstructing the Cultic*
       History of the Restoration
194   Else Kragelund Holt, *Prophesying the Past: The Use of Israel's History in*
       the Book of Hosea
195   Jon Davies, Graham Harvey & Wilfred G.E. Watson (eds.), *Words Remem-*
       bered, Texts Renewed: Essays in Honour of John F.A. Sawyer
196   Joel S. Kaminsky, *Corporate Responsibility in the Hebrew Bible*
197   William M. Schniedewind, *The Word of God in Transition: From Prophet to*
       Exegete in the Second Temple Period
198   T.J. Meadowcroft, *Aramaic Daniel and Greek Daniel: A Literary Comparison*
199   J.H. Eaton, *Psalms of the Way and the Kingdom: A Conference with the*
       Commentators
200   Mark Daniel Carroll R., David J.A. Clines & Philip R. Davies (eds.), *The*
       Bible in Human Society: Essays in Honour of John Rogerson
201   John W. Rogerson, *The Bible and Criticism in Victorian Britain: Profiles of*
       F.D. Maurice and William Robertson Smith
202   Nanette Stahl, *Law and Liminality in the Bible*
203   Jill M. Munro, *Spikenard and Saffron: The Imagery of the Song of Songs*
204   Philip R. Davies, *Whose Bible Is It Anyway?*
205   David J.A. Clines, *Interested Parties: The Ideology of Writers and Readers of*
       the Hebrew Bible
206   Møgens Müller, *The First Bible of the Church: A Plea for the Septuagint*
207   John W. Rogerson, Margaret Davies & Mark Daniel Carroll R. (eds.), *The*
       Bible in Ethics: The Second Sheffield Colloquium
208   Beverly J. Stratton, *Out of Eden: Reading, Rhetoric, and Ideology in Genesis*
       2–3
209   Patricia Dutcher-Walls, *Narrative Art, Political Rhetoric: The Case of*
       Athaliah and Joash
210   Jacques Berlinerblau, *The Vow and the 'Popular Religious Groups' of*
       Ancient Israel: A Philological and Sociological Inquiry
211   Brian E. Kelly, *Retribution and Eschatology in Chronicles*
212   Yvonne Sherwood, *The Prostitute and the Prophet: Hosea's Marriage in*
       Literary-Theoretical Perspective
213   Yair Hoffman, *A Blemished Perfection: The Book of Job in Context*
214   Roy F. Melugin & Marvin A. Sweeney (eds.), *New Visions of Isaiah*
215   J. Cheryl Exum, *Plotted, Shot and Painted: Cultural Representations of*
       Biblical Women
216   Judith E. McKinlay, *Gendering Wisdom the Host: Biblical Invitations to Eat*
       and Drink

217 Jerome F.D. Creach, *Yahweh as Refuge and the Editing of the Hebrew Psalter*

218 Gregory Glazov, *The Bridling of the Tongue and the Opening of the Mouth in Biblical Prophecy*

219 Gerald Morris, *Prophecy, Poetry and Hosea*

220 Raymond F. Person, Jr, *In Conversation with Jonah: Conversation Analysis, Literary Criticism, and the Book of Jonah*

221 Gillian Keys, *The Wages of Sin: A Reappraisal of the 'Succession Narrative'*

222 R.N. Whybray, *Reading the Psalms as a Book*

223 Scott B. Noegel, *Janus Parallelism in the Book of Job*

224 Paul J. Kissling, *Reliable Characters in the Primary History: Profiles of Moses, Joshua, Elijah and Elisha*

225 Richard D. Weis & David M. Carr (eds.), *A Gift of God in Due Season: Essays on Scripture and Community in Honor of James A. Sanders*

226 Lori L. Rowlett, *Joshua and the Rhetoric of Violence: A New Historicist Analysis*

227 John F.A. Sawyer (ed.), *Reading Leviticus: Responses to Mary Douglas*

228 Volkmar Fritz and Philip R. Davies (eds.), *The Origins of the Ancient Israelite States*

229 Stephen Breck Reid (ed.), *Prophets and Paradigms: Essays in Honor of Gene M. Tucker*

230 Kevin J. Cathcart and Michael Maher (eds.), *Targumic and Cognate Studies: Essays in Honour of Martin McNamara*

231 Weston W. Fields, *Sodom and Gomorrah: History and Motif in Biblical Narrative*

232 Tilde Binger, *Asherah: Goddesses in Ugarit, Israel and the Old Testament*

233 Michael D. Goulder, *The Psalms of Asaph and the Pentateuch: Studies in the Psalter, III*

234 Ken Stone, *Sex, Honor, and Power in the Deuteronomistic History*

235 James W. Watts and Paul House (eds.), *Forming Prophetic Literature: Essays on Isaiah and the Twelve in Honor of John D.W. Watts*

236 Thomas M. Bolin, *Freedom beyond Forgiveness: The Book of Jonah Re-Examined*

237 Neil Asher Silberman and David B. Small (eds.), *The Archaeology of Israel: Constructing the Past, Interpreting the Present*

238 M. Patrick Graham, Kenneth G. Hoglund and Steven L. McKenzie (eds.), *The Chronicler as Historian*

239 Mark S. Smith, *The Pilgrimage Pattern in Exodus* (with contributions by Elizabeth M. Bloch-Smith)

240 Eugene E. Carpenter (ed.), *A Biblical Itinerary: In Search of Method, Form and Content. Essays in Honor of George W. Coats*

241 Robert Karl Gnuse, *No Other Gods: Emergent Monotheism in Israel*

242 K.L. Noll, *The Faces of David*

243 Henning Graf Reventlow, *Eschatology in the Bible and in Jewish and Christian Tradition*

244   Walter E. Aufrecht, Neil A. Mirau and Steven W. Gauley (eds.), *Aspects of Urbanism in Antiquity: From Mesopotamia to Crete*

245   Lester L. Grabbe, *Can a 'History of Israel' Be Written?*

246   Gillian M. Bediako, *Primal Religion and the Bible: William Robertson Smith and his Heritage*

248   Etienne Nodet, *A Search for the Origins of Judaism: From Joshua to the Mishnah*

249   William Paul Griffin, *The God of the Prophets: An Analysis of Divine Action*

250   Josette Elayi and Jean Sapin (eds.), *Beyond the River: New Perspectives on Transeuphratene*

251   Flemming A.J. Nielsen, *The Tragedy in History: Herodotus and the Deuteronomistic History*

252   David C. Mitchell, *The Message of the Psalter: An Eschatological Programme in the Book of Psalms*

253   William Johnstone, *1 and 2 Chronicles, Vol. 1: 1 Chronicles 1–2 Chronicles 9: Israel's Place among the Nations*

254   William Johnstone, *1 and 2 Chronicles, Vol. 2: 2 Chronicles 10–36: Guilt and Atonement*

255   Larry L. Lyke, *King David with the Wise Woman of Tekoa: The Resonance of Tradition in Parabolic Narrative*

256   Roland Meynet, *Rhetorical Analysis: An Introduction to Biblical Rhetoric* translated by Luc Racaut

257   Philip R. Davies and David J.A. Clines (eds.), *The World of Genesis: Persons, Places, Perspectives*

258   Michael D. Goulder, *The Psalms of the Return (Book V, Psalms 107–150): Studies in the Psalter, IV*

259   Allen Rosengren Petersen, *The Royal God: Enthronement Festivals in Ancient Israel and Ugarit?*

262   Victor H. Matthews, Bernard M. Levinson and Tikva Frymer-Kensky (eds.), *Gender and Law in the Hebrew Bible and the Ancient Near East*

269   David J.A. Clines and Stephen D. Moore (eds.), *Auguries: The Jubilee Volume of the Sheffield Department of Biblical Studies*

272   James Richard Linville, *Israel in the Book of Kings: The Past as a Project of Social Identity*